HILLBILLIES
TO
HEROES

HILLBILLIES
TO
HEROES

Journey from the Back Hills of Tennessee
to the Battlefields of World War II

A TRUE STORY

**The Memoir of JAMES QUINTON KELLEY
As Told to S. L. KELLEY**

Outstanding
Literature
Publishers

OUTSTANDING LITERATURE PUBLISHERS LLC

Copyright © 2017 by S. L. KELLEY

It should be understood that the home remedies and wild plant descriptions mentioned in this book are for information purposes only, and should not be used to gather plants in the field, nor to prepare or ingest them for any purpose. The author and publisher disclaim any liability whatsoever with respect to any damage, injury or loss resulting from the imitation of any actions contained within this book.

Published by Outstanding Literature Publishers LLC, Farmingdale, New York

All inquiries, please visit OutstandingLit.com

OutstandingLit and OutstandingLit.com are trademarks of Outstanding Literature Publishers LLC.

Cover design by Michael Mancusi

Book design by Kevin Callahan

Printed in the United States of America

Hillbillies to Heroes/ S. L. Kelley. —
FIRST EDITION
ISBN 978-1-64077-122-2 (hardcover)
ISBN 978-1-64077-222-9 (ebook)

Library of Congress Control Number: 2017911157
1 2 3 4 5 6 7 8 9 10 11 12

Dedicated to Daddy

"Moral courage is the most valuable and usually the most absent characteristic in men."
— **General George S. Patton, Commander of the Third Army, World War II**

"If you do the right thing, sometimes it'll actually rub off on other people."
— **James Quinton Kelley, March 4, 2008**

Contents

Preface

S. L. Kelley

This was the kind of phone call I always dreaded: Mom in tears, her voice breaking.

"I think you'd better get here as quick as you can," she said. "The nurse was just here checking on your daddy and she told me, 'Call your daughter who lives out of state.'"

Then mom went silent.

My knees actually buckled—that really does happen—and I struggled to comprehend.

"Is Daddy still with us?"

"Yes," she said. "But they say he's had a bad stroke and it won't be long . . ."

It was January 2015. My elderly dad was in Tennessee and I was in Florida, and a widespread snowstorm up north had socked in major airports, causing a cascade of delays and canceled flights.

Thankfully, my partner, Michael, drove the interstate like a long-distance bomber pilot on a mission.

He wondered aloud as we headed north, "Do you think your dad will get to be with you before he passes, or will we drive fourteen hours and get there too late? I guess we'll get to see what kind of an end God has planned for a man like Quinton Kelley."

"I guess we will," I agreed.

We drove into the night.

Like many in his generation—those born of the Great Depression and part of the "Greatest Generation"—my father, James Quinton

Kelley, never really talked much about the past, if at all. None of us in the family knew anything about his service in World War II.

That was until one day, some years back, when Michael struck up a conversation with him and stumbled onto a flood of astounding true stories that had never been told. He suggested that I interview Dad about the heart-wrenching battle action he'd lived through in Nazi Germany, but even more fascinating, his boyhood experiences growing up around moonshiners in a lawless and gold-bearing region of Tennessee. It was a place where murder went without consequences, and children, like my dad, saw some of that early on.

I'd interviewed many people in my career as an award-winning video writer/producer, but I'd never seriously turned a microphone toward anyone in my own family. I started off thinking it was an opportunity to cover two aspects of history: a tanker's eyewitness account of what it was like to fight under General Patton, and a rare glimpse of a mysterious community hidden away in the Unicoi Mountains about which very little is known to this day, a place once notoriously closed to outsiders. And yes, life was *unusual* up there.

I traveled with my father back into those mountains where he grew up, and on the way, we stopped at a restaurant. Our waiter widened his eyes when he heard where we were going, and he said, "I don't know if I'd go up there if I were you. Be careful. That's a really strange place."

Well, we weren't worried. But the forbidding local reputation of this secluded community lingers.

What I unwittingly discovered through a series of in-depth interviews was a rare glimpse into yesteryear on that mountain, the way it really was. These are the last remaining echoes of that gritty and peculiar way of life.

While this story is American history, and Southern history, and world history with regard to World War II, I was surprised to discover that it is a story relevant to life today because of a very real thread that runs throughout the life experience revealed in the interviews. By careful listening as my father talked, I began to realize that there was a powerful influence that enabled him and his family to thrive despite being surrounded by danger and hardship. And that is something worth knowing because it is universally true, then, now, and always.

My father was in his early eighties when I began interviewing him, at a point when he was still able and eager to dredge up every memory of his younger years. My initial interviews in 2003 stretched out over a three-month visit and yielded fifty-eight hours of video and audio tape, which was only the beginning of the story-finding process. Intrigued, I continued questioning him, recording and transcribing verbatim many hours of recollections during extended visits back home. I questioned him everywhere—washing the car, in his workshop, at breakfast, and if I wasn't recording, I'd often run to scribble some phrase he said on a scrap of paper. Dad's stories poured forth like gold flakes and nuggets, like the ones he looked for in the streams he used to pan, little glimmers of a kind of life that has passed into American lore.

On many stories, I asked him to tell me again, each time gleaning more details. Even several years apart, they were all remarkably consistent.

"Some things stick with you," he told me.

For a few years, I was able to go back to the well for more details, until one day Dad said, "I believe you've got about everything I can remember. Or want to."

I found it interesting to note what kind of memories stay with a person well into the later years of life, and what kind are maybe best forgotten.

I was able to interview two of Dad's army buddies as well. I am grateful to Lonnie Edward Johnson and Herbert Atlas Davis for sharing their memories with me, and also to Richard Knode for his father's World War II photos.

In Part Two, the quotes chosen are limited to material that my dad knew, to keep the story pure; they are voices from his contemporaries who shared in the events of the war, to give perspective to his telling of a simple life that intersected with a momentous time in history.

In compiling this book, I edited my father's words for clarity and a comfortable read, but I kept true to his voice, to what he told me in countless interviews. This story is *his* life, as he experienced it. As he remembered it.

S. L. Kelley interviews her father at his home in Tennessee

I was able to read drafts of my father's memoirs back to him twice, and both times, his attention was palpable and his eyes burned with engagement. He said to me, "I don't remember telling you all those details, but I must have. It's like you were right there with me."

"Well, you know I wasn't, Daddy. Is everything the way it should be? Is it like it was?" I asked him.

I could see from the tears filling his fading blue eyes that, in working together on telling this story, his story, he felt we had hit the mark.

He nodded. "Yes, I believe it is."

Captured at the proverbial eleventh hour, this is the faithfully told story of a personal journey through extraordinary times in American history, snatched from oblivion to be preserved and shared with younger generations. Much more than an old man's recollections of hair-raising action on the battlefield of World War II and the remarkable boyhood that prepared him for it, this is the story of an authentic life that has much wisdom to teach us.

PART 1

1922–1942

CHAPTER 1

Frontiers

People today don't have any idea what it was like growin' up the way I did. We lived like pioneers. When I was a boy, some winter mornings I'd wake up to find snowdrifts on my bed. I'd just brush that snow off the quilt, jump up out of my nest of featherbeds and run barefoot through a little snow to get to our kitchen. It'd be way before dawn, but I'd always get up to eat biscuits with my daddy before he left our log cabin and went off a walkin' down the road. He'd walk sometimes as far as eight miles away to get a day's wages.

I remember the last of America's simple ways. In the 1920s and '30s, our little community in the back hills of Tennessee was a place where people lived off the land. We survived by what we grew and made and traded with our own hands. It was a peaceful place—but plenty dangerous, too—and progress did find us eventually.

I remember seeing horses and wagons left in the dust of the first T-Model Fords that came bouncin' over our one-lane dirt roads. I remember when the pistol-wavin' moonshiners and their lawless violence started fadin' away out there. 'Course, change happened slow back in "them hills," as we called 'em. I was grown by the time electricity lit up the homes of our neighbors for the first time, snuffing out the kerosene lamps that everybody'd used for generations, even though my family's three-room log cabin never did get electrified.

Naturally, we had no plumbing. No one in them hills did back then.

I've taken many a bath in a No. 2 washtub, barely big enough to stand in. I'd go down the hill to our little spring and carry up two buckets of water for my bath. Then my mother'd heat it on the woodstove in the kitchen and pour it in the washtub. When the weather was real cold, you didn't shiver as much if you put the tub behind that cast iron cookstove, 'cause it gave off heat, 'bout the only heat we had.

My family and I lived a rough life back in the Unicoi Mountains of Tennessee, no question about that. We lived by our sweat and the food that we raised, but we never were short on laughter and joy. It was a good life. We worked hard and long, went to church on Sundays, respected our fellow man, and loved our family so much that if one was sick, it made us all sick. We worried about each other in times of trouble.

I still try to live by those same values today and now, as I'm tellin' you this, I'm an old man.

Not everyone out there lived a clean life, though. When I was a growin' up, our community was a treacherous place, filled with hot-tempered moonshiners and violent bigots. In one cemetery that I know of, about fifty men are buried up there who died in local gun battles. You know those stories you mighta heard about the Hatfields and McCoys, the deadly fights that raged back in the hills of Kentucky? Well, true moonshiner and outlaw goin's-on around the Unicoi Mountains in Southeast Tennessee make some of that look pretty tame. But, out there, we kept it to ourselves.

The only local store we had for years, the owner had a loaded pistol right by the cash register—with the hammer cocked back—ready to go. And he used it, too. That store had big bullet holes all over it, from different shoot-outs. A lot of roughnecks lived in the community I grew up in. They always carried a gun. They made moonshine, got to drinkin' and it made 'em crazy, and they got into trouble, big trouble. But I'll get around to tellin' more about that, later on.

My father taught me all about guns and how to steer clear of the kind of men who were known to use them for evil. Our guns were primarily for game. We'd go rabbit or squirrel hunting starting when I was about six years old. By the time I was eleven, when my daddy bought

Little Quinton Kelley holds a bugle at his grandmother's house, around 1924

me my first rifle, I already had a lot of experience behind a sight out in the deep woods.

I was a good shot, like my dad. My dog'd tree a squirrel and I'd squeeze the trigger and that squirrel'd fall to the ground. Sometimes that'd be the only meat we had.

I liked shootin'. But I never did want to aim my gun at a human being, or have to shoot a man, even to defend myself. 'Course, I could if I had to.

Between stayin' clear of dangerous people and stayin' off starvation — unlike a lot of families I knew — my rugged upbringing turned out to be a great help to me. It toughened me up for the greatest test of a young man's life: going off to war.

World War II had been raging in Europe and I remember how the newspapers called Hitler "a madman." But that's about all I knew. I was drafted into the army at the age of twenty, one of the "plowboys" as some of 'em called us, one of many young men from rural farms who proudly went off to serve our country. We weren't exactly fighter pilot material, but we had grit. A lot of our skills had been honed on the farm.

The men in my Sherman tank crew were all from country backgrounds, and maybe that's why we got along better than most, even in what had to be the worst time of our lives. We fought with great U.S. Armies — Patton's Third Army and Hodges' First Army — in Nazi Germany. We saw, up close, the end of Hitler's evil hold on Europe. Of course, we were just a small part of the Allied forces that went over there, but it took all our personal sacrifices to go from war to peace.

I can remember it like it was yesterday, bein' shut up in a tank that was belching fire, fighting through enemy countryside with shells hittin' all around us.

Our tank commander would be calling to the loader and the gunner, "Armor-piercing at two o'clock — behind that barn!" And that tank would recoil and jar us all down in there. We knew that any second, we could be gone. That's somethin' you don't forget.

World War II was a war that happened in much simpler times. Now the ways of warfare have changed, like everything else, but the human

Quinton Kelley, age eleven, with his new .22 rifle and his hunting dog,
at his old homeplace, Coker Creek, Tennessee

cost of war is one of those things that will never change. Over sixty years later, I still choke back tears when I remember some of those boys that I knew well, who never made it home—never saw the farm they loved again, nor the women who waited for them.

CHAPTER 2

Ol' Tennessee Homeplace

Long before the war, things were relatively peaceful in the winter of 1922 in a little Tennessee community called Coker Creek. I was born by a midwife in the middle of the night in my parents' log cabin. It was February second—making my birth date 2/2/22. I've always felt those numbers, double twos, were favorable to me and they've come back around a few times in my life.

My daddy had built our cabin out of rough logs that he'd split himself and it made a good home for our family of five. I had two older sisters, Edth—she was five years older than I was—and Thelma, the middle child—she was two years older—and both of 'em were pretty plump. I was the little'un, the only son, James Quinton.

We were descended from pioneers and settlers. My mother, Mary Virginia—everyone called her Verdie—she was just a little slip of a woman and there wasn't no foolishness about her. She was of German descent on her mother's side. Her mother's family, the Land family, had filtered down south through Virginia way, and my mother had kin up there.

Mother was Scotch-Irish on her father's side. Her maiden name was Davis and that family, the Davis family, had come to Coker Creek from a place called Hanging Dog, a summit up on one of those blue ridges over in North Carolina.

My father, William Marion Kelley, his parents were both old Scotch-Irish. His mother's people, the Brannons, they'd lived somewhere in North Carolina a hundred years earlier and had moved to Coker Creek, but that's about all anybody knew about the Brannons.

As for the Kelleys, as far as my dad knew, that side of the family had once lived in South Carolina in the 1700s, but for as long as anyone could remember, my father said, "the Kelleys had been a livin' right here, out on Coker Creek, in the green state of Tennessee."

I guess you could say the place was "countrified." And really, it was. The little community of Coker Creek was, and is, nestled in the hills and hollows—"hollers," we said—of an elevated valley set among the western foothills of the Great Smoky Mountains. We were about two miles, as the crow flies, to the North Carolina state line, but that was just someplace out there in the wilderness.

Coker Creek was always cut off from the outside world to a certain degree because it sprang up back in there where it was surrounded by rugged terrain. Like the side of a big basket, the Unicoi Mountain rose up all along the southeast side to hem us in. To the north, Tellico Mountain had to be crossed just to get to the nearest little ol' village for trading. Cataska Mountain, Black Mountain, Ducket Ridge, they circled us, too, and out from that, rows of ridges and peaks overlapped to the horizon. Coker Creek sits about 1,600 feet above sea level, but some of those peaks around it go on up over 5,000 feet. We could climb up and see those knobs and balds and summits peeking through the clouds at the lookout tower on top of the mountain.

Where there was a dip in the mountains lower than the rest, they'd call that a "gap" and that's where they'd try to put in a road. 'Course, all they had for miles and miles back then were bad dirt roads that cut through gaps best they could. A man took his life in his hands if he drove through there. If he didn't meet a skittish mule team comin' 'round a steep curve and get run off the road and down a mountainside, then he had to look out for those blind-drunk drivers a haulin' timber or moonshine as fast as they could go. You could hear their souped-up vehicles just a revvin' and a poppin' a long ways off.

Back when all they had were zigzag dirt roads to cut across them mountains, Coker Creek wasn't an easy place to get in or out of. So, naturally, Coker Creek stayed isolated—a pocket of pioneer life well into the twentieth century.

Oh, was it a beautiful place to call home. Coker Creek's landscape was densely wooded, with severe slopes and steep peaks, though they were misty and hidden by low clouds a lot of times. Rushing creeks and bubbling springs made the scenery lush and green all summer long. The woods were thick with rhododendron, mountain laurel, ferns, sassafras and wild huckleberry bushes. Treetops twittered at first light with songbirds, and at dusk those hills buzzed with the rhythms of crickets and katydids.

It was good land, too. There were places where the land flattened out and along some dirt roads stretched open pastures where the countryside was cleared and tamed. Old homesteads and farms broke up the wilderness with well-tended fields of crops. Cows'd be wandering along the meadows, or the roads, too.

Out on Coker Creek, people didn't fence their livestock. They just let it run loose, but they fenced their crops and their yards. Occasionally, there'd be what we called a "rogue cow" that'd break down a fence and get into somebody's garden.

Livin' back in there, we had to travel about thirty-five miles to the nearest town, which was Madisonville, the Monroe County seat. It had the courthouse, a real grocery store, a small local college and a few places for trading, but we rarely ever went.

The closest village where we did our trading was ten miles away, as the old road snaked, down to a fertile valley where the Cherokee Indians had once lived. Since the railroads went in, though, it'd been a trading place—Tellico Plains—but we just said "Tellico." When we went there, we called that "goin' to town."

Even ten miles the way we traveled made goin' to town pretty much an all-day event. We had to go by mule and wagon or horse and buggy. Unless, of course, you ran the back trails on foot, which was a little bit closer, mileage-wise. Mostly we took the old, steep dirt roads with our horse and buggy, and crossed the switchbacks where only one could pass. If you met somebody, you'd have to find a wide place. A lot of times one of you would have to back up before the other could pass.

Once a year, I guess, is about as much as I ever went to town. Boy, I thought that was something great, to go to town, buy cheese and crackers at the general store and watch the trains. They had a train come in there once a day to haul away lumber and logs. And they had passenger coaches, one train a day. A few times my mother and I rode the passenger coach to visit my grandmaw over the state line in Bristol, Virginia, which is the other half of Bristol, Tennessee, around two hundred miles from home. That's the only place I ever went when I was growin' up. Most people were like that.

Not many people had radio on Coker Creek either. For years we only knew one neighbor who had a radio. It wasn't until about 1936 that I saved up enough money to buy one for our family.

The only man who had a telephone for years and years was the U.S. Forest Service ranger, up on top of the mountain. People would go up there to call if there was an emergency, but phone calls were not part of our life.

Pretty much the only way we'd know what was happening in the rest of the world was through the man who owned the only store we had on Coker Creek back then. I don't know what the sign on it said, but we called it "Dave's Store." Dave Lenderman got the Knoxville paper and he would read it and tell everyone what was going on when they went in to buy their cornmeal and such. Of course, he got it a day or two late. But he kept us informed, and probably added a little of his own reckoning. He was a big feller and he'd lean on the counter and peer over his spectacles at you and say, "Well, saw a big sandstorm's out in Texas. It'll be a blowin' some dust in here in a day or two. Better get you one of these here neckerchiefs 'fore the dust gets here."

Not many travelers came through Coker Creek, except for the Southern preachers who would come visiting to hold revivals. I think most people were a little bit afraid. It was generally known that black men were not safe in those mountains. Sometimes strange gold prospectors from up north would stake a claim and set up mining operations. And, occasionally, wild game hunters from big cities would come through, too, and hire a local guide to spend a few days shooting wild boar and bears — they were plentiful in those woods. But there wasn't much else to travel out there for.

Coker Creek, as we referred to it, was actually made up of five little communities. We'd say, "Oh, them young'uns live down at Sandy Lane." Or "They got kin up at Eperson and Ironsburg." Smithfield was the name of the community where I went to school in a one-room schoolhouse. And next to it, the community we also called Coker Creek, 'cause it was down along the creek, that was the area my father's people had settled in. A lot of the roads back then weren't named, so that's how we indicated what part of the mountain a family was from. Those five communities of cabins and farms on Coker Creek were about all we knew when I was growin' up.

There were lots of good families, big families, living out on Coker Creek when I was a boy. The Witts and the Daltons were the oldest families, having been in those hills since just after the Revolutionary War. A few of the other common names were West, Ellis, Davis, Rose, Radford, Payne, Murphy, and Kelley (we were "-*EY*" but some other families spelled it with "just a *Y*"). Most of the families up there were of Scotch-Irish or German descent.

One thing that a lot of the old families had in common was bright blue eyes, just as clear. Every one of us had 'em.

One time two visitors stopped in Coker Creek, they had to pass through there for some reason, and I heard one of the men down at Dave's Store talking about them. He said, "Them two fellers was a walkin' off and one of 'em said to the other 'un, said, 'People up here, their eyes is just as blue as the sky. I'm afraid of them blue-eyed people — they's all crazy!'" and he laughed about that.

Well, I don't know, but maybe that visitor'd had some dealings with those ol' blue-eyed moonshiners. They'd get crazy on that corn liquor, likely to do about anything, including gunnin' a man down for sayin' a wrong word.

Of course, most of the people on Coker Creek were just good, hardworking people. They stayed busy farming. They had a saying out there, "If you didn't farm, you didn't eat." Pretty much, what each family raised, they survived on. Some of the men worked in gold mines, or on government road projects, but work opportunities were few and far between. Some worked in logging. They would cut, haul and sell the big timber that grew on those hills. And they'd man the sawmills that processed the timber. That was about all the industry we had on Coker Creek, except if you count all the moonshinin' that went on back in the hollers.

There were wet hollers and dry hollers — those with sources of water and those without. All the moonshiners would have their stills hidden back in those wet hollers, under cover of the mountain laurel that grew thick along little creeks, so they could stay hidden from the law. They needed that fresh water to distill their corn mash into alcohol, stuff some people call "white lightnin'" because it's clear as water and as powerful as a thunderbolt. The Tennessee mountain country's always been noted for moonshine, because people didn't have a way to make a livin' much, and they'd make moonshine and sell it. And they drank a good bit of it, too.

There was one wet holler on Coker Creek that was definitely *not* a place known for moonshinin'. My parents were dead again' it and I don't believe any of us ever touched the stuff, even once. Our family lived in a quiet, fertile valley, just past a bend and a dip in the road, in an area known locally as Kelley Holler, after my father.

Everybody in the community thought a lot of my dad. Some people called him Bill and some called him Will, but pretty much he was known as Will Kelley. He was a tall man with dark hair, but he was losin' his hair, so he had a pretty high forehead. He wore bib overalls and a blue shirt to work in every day of his life.

We lived just a little ways back from the road in a clearing, and everybody that would pass by our house, they'd stop and visit if they saw him. If they couldn't stop, they'd holler. They'd call out, "Hello there, Will, how's everything today!"

He'd holler back to them and wave. I don't believe he had an enemy in that whole community.

My daddy had strong arms because he was good at building things and he knew how to handle tools. He had a lot of skills necessary to survive in the wilderness, could work different jobs, and he always managed to provide for his family. We didn't have much by today's standards, but this is what we did have and we were thankful for it:

We had eighty acres that my daddy bought back before I was born and he'd built us a good, workable farm with his own hands. We had a chicken house where we kept our chickens for eggs. There was a place up on the hill behind our log cabin where my daddy kept his bee boxes—we used to sell the honey and save a few jars for ourselves. There was a corncrib down the hill below the house where we put our corn, and a barn down there, too, where we kept the livestock. We usually had about two cows that we milked and occasionally we had a hog that we'd fatten up for the kill. We had a horse, or sometimes a mule, to do work—plow fields and pull wagons. We had a buggy shed near the road for our buggy that we used to go to town and our wagon that we used to haul our crops to market. Connected to the buggy shed, my daddy had a little building that he used as a blacksmith shop, for shoeing horses and sharpening saws. And, of course, we had an outhouse, too, a little ways from the house.

Our farm had big, cleared fields where we raised cane to make molasses and we raised corn and beans and different vegetables in there. I've worked a lot of days in those fields.

Naturally, the lifeblood of our homeplace was our water source. We had one spring that was closer to the house, but the water wasn't very cold. My mother used to do some of her washing out there. We had a second spring on further down the slope and the water was real cold that came out of it.

Our cold spring was one of the headsprings of that rushing brook they called Coker Creek that runs along the entire community. It came right out of the mountain, where the land turns up. My daddy'd dug down into the earth and fixed our spring up good. It gushed sweet, clean water and it never did go dry back then, even in a drought year. We always had plenty of cold water.

We had a springhouse downstream from the cold spring, where we put our milk, and supplies that we wanted to keep cold. It was built so the water ponded up in the springhouse, and we could sit big crocks down in there with the food, 'cause we didn't have an icebox, nothin' like that. We had to keep everything cooled in the spring water. Our butter and milk, we'd put it in there in the summer and it would get cool enough. We weren't used to it being any colder, so it was fine with us.

We had to carry all the water we used up to the house, drinking water, and what we used for dishwater, cooking or boiling clothes. Had to walk quite a little distance. As kids, it was our duty, me and my two sisters, to take turns about carrying the water buckets to the house.

We had a big, long shelf on our back porch and that's where we kept our water, in a whole bunch of wooden water buckets, all lined up. We'd have to go back and forth up the slope from the spring to the back porch, filling those buckets two at a time, tryin' not to spill any water and by the end of the next day, we'd need more. It took several trips down to that spring every evening, no matter what kind of weather we's havin'.

When it was my turn to go and get the water, I knew it, and if I didn't, Thelma or Edth would say, "Quinton, are you a fixin' to get the water? 'Cause it's your turn." So everybody had to share alike.

It might be hard for people in America today to imagine living under such rugged conditions, but if you're not used to havin' things, you don't miss 'em, 'cause you don't know what they're like. Rough as it was, to us, our homeplace was a paradise.

CHAPTER 3

The Warm Hearth

Two tall, straight oak trees grew up on the crest of a knoll and our three-room log cabin sat right up between them where the hill flattened out. Our cabin was a typical home for the Coker Creek area, a little better than most of 'em, in fact. Some of those little ol' houses were about like a barn. But like all of 'em, our house was made from what was available to us from the land around us.

First, the foundation was built on rocks that my dad had collected. They were all flat rocks, stacked up one on top of the other and leveled. On one side of the house, though, where the hill sloped off, my dad used locust posts to support the house, so that side looked like it was up on stilts.

The sills that the house sat on were made out of logs and they sat up on the rocks and locust posts. The floor went on top of that. All of the cabin, except the flooring, was made out of rounded logs. My dad felled the trees—he used pine because it was softer and easier to work with—and he peeled the bark off them, hauled them in, and made every cut himself. He used an ax to flatten the logs—the inside was flattened and the outside, too, but the top and bottom he left rounded. He notched the logs where they interlocked on the corners and kept building up as high as he wanted the roof to be. Then he put the rafters on and covered that with some wood that he and my uncle split. They call it shakes now; we called it a board roof.

My dad covered all the cracks in the logs with split boards that he'd split out himself, and he nailed them over the cracks on the outside of the house. He did the same thing on the inside. I don't know why he didn't use mud or mortar in between. He could've done that. A lot of people did.

They'd find a vein of red clay in a bank somewhere to collect—there was a lot of clay on Coker Creek—and it was good mud to use for building. You can't just use any kind of dirt for mud. You've got to have some dirt that will bond and stick together. My dad could have put the boards on the inside of the house to catch the mud and filled the cracks full of mud and it would have been a much warmer house had he done that, but he didn't do that. I imagine he was in a hurry when he built it, with his family on the way.

It seems strange, too, but my mother, she had us in the spring of the year to scrape away all the grass and weeds around the house, as soon as it started coming up. We'd take a sharp hoe and we'd scrape the yard down to the dirt. Then we'd take a broom and sweep the yard, so we didn't have no grass in the yard. We could have had grass, but that was just my mother's idea. And, of course, when it rained, it got muddy. We had to have stepping-stones to get in the house to keep from carryin' the mud in. The dirt yard circled the house and was surrounded by a rough paling fence with a gate, our version of a picket fence to keep the chickens from flyin' into our yard.

Our cabin was crude, no doubt about it. It wasn't painted or nothin', just the color of dead wood. 'Course, we did brighten the place up with lots of flowers in the spring, summer, and fall. My oldest sister, Edth, took care of the yard more than anybody. She made the house look nice and cheerful, for what we had.

Edth was always working around the homeplace in one of her printed feed-sack dresses, with her hair braided up, pruning her roses, or plucking weeds out of her dahlias. She'd save seeds year after year and do the planting. She'd stretch cords all along the front porch in different directions and she had flowering vines climbing that trellis all summer long, what she called "wild honeysuckle." They were funnel-shaped flowers and bloomed in lots of colors—pink, dark red, light red, white, and yellow—covering the side of the house and shading the porch like a big, colorful crazy quilt.

The porch sheltered the front entrance to our house, which was just an open hallway, or breezeway, as we called it, between the living room and the one bedroom. You didn't see a front door when you came up to the house. It was about a five-foot-wide breezeway that you walked down before you came to our front door on the right and that went into the living room.

There was just one window in the front of the house for many years, where the living room looked out onto the front porch and from there, you could look out over the whole farm. Beyond the dirt yard and the paling fence, the land was cleared, and you could see down to the corn and cane fields, all the way to the edge of the woods. We never did have stuff piled up on our property, no junk of any kind. Not everybody lived that way, but we did.

At the back of the house, we had an L-shaped porch and it wrapped around the side of the kitchen in the back. You could walk from the front porch to the back porch through that breezeway. We sat out on the back porch sometimes to do kitchen chores, or even sat in the breezeway if rain was a blowin'. Mostly, though, we used our front porch, especially when we relaxed at the end of the day. We spent every summer evenin' a sittin' out there together. The ol' front porch was as central to our family as the hearth.

My dad used to sit out there and play with my little black dog. He was black as coal all over. That dog—I'll tell you his name later 'cause it needs explainin'—he used to lie down on the porch when we'd sit out after a hard day's work. He'd lift his head off the floorboards and his short ears'd perk up. He expected my dad to call him and he'd keep lookin' up at my dad. My dad would see that dog a lookin' and he'd say, "Come on up here!" and slap his knee.

That dog would just make a dive and jump up in his lap. My dad had him pretty well trained for that. My dad thought more of my dog, I guess, than I did. He'd fool with that dog for hours and I'd get a kick out of that. He'd pinch the dog's toes and that dog would jerk his feet back. My dad'd scratch his short ears and laugh.

When we used to sit out on the front porch in the summertime, a lot of whip-poor-wills would fly in close to the house. They holler pretty loud. One was sitting on the fence one evening, making a lot of noise. I was just a young boy, playing around the yard, and my dad said, "Quinton, knock that whipperwhil offa there."

I picked up a rock and threw it, and I killed it.

My dad said, "Well, I didn't aim for you to kill it."

I said, "Well, I didn't know I was a gonna hit it." That shocked me. I killed that whip-poor-will, I guess, because I naturally had pretty good aim. My dad kind of hated that he told me to do that. He just wanted me to scare it off.

My dad was a kind, gentle man and he respected animals. I think animals could sense that. He knew how to get along with all of God's creatures, from a stubborn mule to a roughneck neighbor. And with his family, he was always jolly because of his natural affection for us.

I used to pull pranks on my dad all the time and he wouldn't get peeved at me. A couple of times, I took some real fine wire out of a T-Model coil, so fine you couldn't see it unless you were right up close to it, and I'd see my dad coming to the house and I'd stretch some of that wire from one post of the porch to the other where he had to come up the steps. It was like a spiderweb. He'd run into that slack wire and he'd go to fightin' and throwin' up his hands, gettin' tangled up, and then he'd discover what it was.

I'd be in the house, watching him through the window to see what he'd do. That would really tickle me and he'd just laugh, too, when he found out I'd pulled a joke on him. Some parents would have gotten mad, I guess, but he didn't. He was what you'd call good-natured and he loved a joke as well as anybody.

He'd just say, "Aw, Quinton, you pulled a good'un on me." Then we'd sit out on the porch and we'd laugh together.

It was the family time together on the front porch that let us share our biggest laughter in our loudest voices. Sometimes we'd laugh till we doubled over. We had a big time talking and telling little jokes. We'd tell stories from work or school or church, news from the community. Sometimes we had music from my dad's banjo, or my harmonica. Other evenings we'd sit and listen to the long, drawn-out, high-pitched call of the katydids up in the trees. If there was still a glimmer of daylight out, up until the time of year when we couldn't stand the chill, we were out there on that front porch.

If we had to prepare food for the next day, like green beans, we'd sit out there and string them, break them up. My mother's strong bony hands were always faster than us kids. She'd have a dishpan of beans ready in no time. We'd all share the chore, snapping off the ends: snap-snap, snap-snap. 'Course, later in the harvest season, the hulls would get tough, so we'd have to shell the beans, what we called "shellies." I always liked those. My mother would tell us kids, "Now, keep on shellin'. You'll be glad at dinnertime."

We'd stay out there till it got dark and then we had to go to bed, 'cause we didn't have lights except the kerosene lamp. Kerosene was cheap back then, but we didn't have money to buy it, even if it was cheap. We had to save all the kerosene we could 'cause we had to use the lamp for the kitchen to prepare meals and then to eat the meal. We were used to "goin' without" and we didn't think nothin' about it.

Our log cabin was dim inside. Even in the daytime, big shadows fell across the living room, and the corners never were bright. Our kitchen was a little brighter. It had been added onto the living room in the back, and for a window in the kitchen, we had a windshield out of a T-Model car. The T-Model had a two-piece windshield and my dad had made a frame for it and built it into the wall. The kitchen also had another sliding window that we'd open when the weather was warm. Most of the time that's the way my mother fed the dogs and cats—right out the slide window. She didn't have to go out of the kitchen to throw the scraps into the backyard for the domestic animals.

My mother, Verdie Kelley, was a real small woman and she always dressed neatly. She got about quick, kind of like a cricket. We'd refer to her like that, a little cricket, her movements were so fast and full of energy. She got her work done in a hurry. She kept that house clean as a pin all the time.

The house had a wooden floor made out of rough, sawed lumber, boards about six inches wide, with cracks in between them. My mother would scrub those floors, keep them real clean and all those years when we were kids, we helped her. We'd go along the creek and get a big bucketful of sand and we'd just cover the floor with sand, mix water with it and then we'd take a broom and scrub. It was just sort of like sanding the floor with sandpaper. We'd worn that floor down pretty smooth. We'd wash all that sand away and it would go through the cracks under the floor.

We had to be careful about dropping anything that could go through a crack in the floor, coins—which we didn't have very many of—or a needle, something like that. If it fell under the house, I could crawl up under there and get it. Of course, in the wintertime when the wind was a blowin', we got a lot of cold air up through those cracks. On one side of the house, it was close to four feet off the ground. That's where we had an underground cellar, where we kept our canned food that my mother put up.

About all the time, my mother was busy at canning, cleaning, mending, or stitching one of her beautiful quilts. She made a lot of quilts to keep us warm. She saved all the little scraps of old clothes and colorful feed sacks and flour sacks, and she sewed them together into different patterns. Then we took cotton—she showed us kids how to do it—and we carded the cotton between the fine teeth of hand carders and we shaped it in pads and put it between the quilt lining and the top. Then my mother put that quilt in a frame and she quilted it.

We had quilting frames that swung from the ceiling in the living room. When my mother got ready to work on a quilt, she'd unroll it. She'd quilt in a chair by the fire and she could roll the quilt frame up another notch and move her chair in, and just keep on quilting. It took a lot of sewing, and she could sew her stitches just all the same. She'd work a long time on one quilt. When she needed to finish up, she'd roll the quilt up and tie it up overhead.

When my mother wasn't busy doing something to make our home cozy, she was doing something that would help feed us. We had to work pretty hard at keeping our food supplied. We each did our part, working in the fields, tending animals, hunting. But my mother, she was a wonder in the kitchen, and for our country community, she was one of the smartest homemakers around.

We were able to turn everything that we got hold of into food or something that we could use. We wasted nothing. Now, all families weren't like that. Some of them were pretty wasteful, and they suffered for it. We called it being "on starvation." Those kind never did have much to eat, 'cause they wasted what little they got. But we kept what we got and preserved it. If she didn't need something today and could use it a week from now, or later, my mother figured out a way to keep it, so she'd have it when she needed it.

We raised plenty of cabbage and never let our cabbage go to waste. We had a lot of big twelve-gallon crocks and my mother always made sauerkraut and put it in those speckled crocks. She had a board she put down in the crocks on top of the sauerkraut, and she had some big white flint rocks that she kept washed clean to lay on the boards. That mashed down on the sauerkraut so the water would come to the top, and it'd cover the kraut. That's the way she stored it. My mother knew when to make the kraut—when the moon was waxing, just after the new moon—and then the water would always stay above the kraut and that kept it from spoiling.

Most everyone liked "Verd Kelley's sauerkraut," as people called it, because she knew how to fix it. Her mother's people were from Germany and I imagine her mother had passed old family secrets down the line, little tricks to making it taste good. Because of that, I reckon, I always liked kraut. And my sister Thelma—she was a big, husky girl, with a hearty appetite—oh, she was a kraut eater, and she really liked Mother's sauerkraut. Thelma really liked Mother's pickled beans, too. I never was so fond of them. Every summer, Momma would make big crocks of pickled beans and she'd fill up her crocks with preserved food that we could eat all through the wintertime.

We ate only what you grow on a farm. In the summertime, we had peas and okra and corn and carrots and a variety of foods out of the garden. We ate mostly vegetables, but our favorite snack after school or after work in the fields was cornbread and buttermilk.

We had cows for milk. My mother churned her own butter and made buttermilk and sweet milk. We never did kill beef. Some of the neighbors would kill beef, and we'd buy a cut from them, once a year or less, maybe. We did raise our own hogs for pork meat, though we didn't always have it.

We all had a sweet tooth. Occasionally, we'd take molasses and make something we called "syrup candy." You can boil molasses down and get it to the right consistency, and you can twist it up into a stick and when it gets hard, you can break it up, sort of like stick candy. We used to make that 'cause we didn't have money to buy candy from the store. So we made our candy the only way we could.

We had honey from my dad's bees and wild blackberry jam. My sisters would go out into the woods and bring back big buckets of blackberries. My mother made the jam on the cookstove in a big kettle. It would bubble up in that kettle, all thick and syrupy, and the steam would rise and fill the house with smells that'd make your stomach growl. You'd get hungry just smelling Momma's kitchen.

My mother baked a lot of cakes, that was her specialty. Just at Christmastime, she'd be able to get some coconut down at the store and she'd bake her famous coconut cake, a cake as white as snow. The rest of the year, though, she baked what we called a "fruitcake," usually made from dried apples. She made it like she made biscuits, in her big wooden dough bowl, but the dough was real dark—I know she used allspice and sweetened it with molasses. She'd roll it out thin and cut it with a scalloped pie pan. She baked about seven layers, then she put cooked apples between the layers. It made a tall cake. After the cake sat for a day or two, the sticky juice from the apples soaked through the layers and made it all soft and sweet, and, boy, we thought it was the tastiest cake in the world. I'd sure look forward to occasions for cake.

Other than mother's fruitcakes, we didn't have the little luxuries, just the basics. My mother always tried to save her eggs to sell, to trade for things at the store, but on my birthday she'd say, "Now, Quinton, I'm gonna give you a fried egg for your birthday." She'd fry me an egg for dinner, on my birthday, once a year. Boy, I thought that was a treat to get something that none of the others got. That's about all any of us ever got on our birthday, a fried egg, but we were happy enough.

From my earliest years, I was rail-thin and I usually wore a blue shirt and overalls and they'd just hang on me, so my mother always wanted me to eat bread with everything to put a little meat on my bones. I didn't want to eat bread sometimes, but she'd just insist that I eat it. One time, my grandmother spent the night with us and the next morning my mother was in the kitchen kneading dough in her dough bowl.

I couldn't have been more than five or six years old at the time. My mother pulled me aside and whispered, "Well, Quinton, I don't have enough dough to make as much bread as I wanted to. You're always wantin' to eat without bread, so you can eat without bread this mornin', and that'll give a little more bread for the rest of us."

Of course, I didn't know it then but my mother was very concerned about being a good hostess for her mother-in-law.

When I got to the table, I just got up there and said, "Momma said I could eat my cereal without bread this mornin'. She's a runnin' short on bread!" Naturally, that was the first thing I told.

Boy, that really embarrassed my mother, but she laughed about it for years.

My mother did most of her cooking on the potbellied woodstove in the kitchen, but when she used the fireplace in the living room to make bread, it made the best bread you ever melted country butter on. She had one of those cast iron Dutch ovens. She'd put it in the fireplace and have coals under it, around it, on top of it. The lid was made with a rim around it, so she could put fire coals up on the lid. She'd bake bread a lot of times in that Dutch oven and use cornmeal for yellow cornbread. Boy, was it good. It made a real thick crust on the bread, cooked that way. She'd cook our bread in the fireplace when it was real cold out and we had a pretty good fire going in the living room. We didn't have heat in the kitchen, except the cookstove and, of course, it didn't heat the kitchen too well, 'cause the house wasn't insulated much with just logs, split boards and homemade wallpaper between us and the weather.

The fireplace in the living room was built up out of rocks, maybe eight feet high. It had a mantel, a big wooden board that my dad had planed and sanded, and he'd laid it in there when he built the fireplace.

Outside, he had two black metal smokestacks, side by side, twin smokestacks that carried the smoke up above the roof. A lot of people referred to it as "Will's double-barrel chimley."

"*Chimley*," we all called it, that was the old Scotch-Irish way.

My dad had those two metal smokestacks—just some old pipe from somewhere—suspended away from the house with a cross-cut saw. He'd taken a rusty cross-cut saw blade, bowed it around in a semicircle and fastened each end to the house and fastened the pipes to that saw, to hold the hot pipes away from the house.

Those pipes did a good job of getting the smoke out of there, but occasionally, soot would build up in those pipes and they'd catch afire and, boy, we had a time keepin' it from settin' the house afire. Fire would be shootin' up out of those two pipes, flames just a roarin'. Those pipes would get so hot, they'd start scorching the split boards and we'd all have to carry water up from the spring just as hard as we could go and we'd throw that water on the side of the house, to wet it down, then run back for more.

Some of my earliest memories were around Christmastime when we were just little, and my parents told us that Santa Claus came down the chimney. They were always saying, "If Santa Claus gets one leg down one of them chimley pipes and one leg down the other, he may not get in here."

Then, on Christmas Eve, they played Santa Claus. They'd usually buy a box of stick candy. I think it came in a two-pound box. They'd divide up so many pieces of that candy. They'd have us hang our stockings on the mantel beneath my daddy's chiming clock. He had a fancy wooden clock on that mantel that he thought a lot of. We'd hang our stockings up there and after we went to bed, they'd put the candy in a paper bag and put it down in our stockings. They'd be able to get oranges just at Christmastime, and they'd put an orange and a few different pieces of store-bought fruit in there, too. Those were our only presents and they seemed wonderful.

We had nothing but one kerosene lamp for light and we didn't want to burn too much oil, so most of the year, quick as it would go to gettin' dark, we'd go to bed. In the wintertime, though, we'd sit around the fireplace for a little while until we'd go to gettin' sleepy. Up on the mantel, Daddy's wooden clock would chime out as we passed the time together.

About every two weeks my dad would say, "Well, I reckon it's 'bout time to wind that ol' clock." We could always tell when that clock was winding down, the chimes didn't strike as strong. He'd open up the glass in the center—I believe it had some forest scenery painted on it—and it had two keys in there that he turned to wind it. One was for the power to run the clock, the other was to power the chimes. My dad always kept that clock wound himself—he wouldn't let us kids or even my mother touch it—and he took real good care of it down through the years.

When it was colder than whiz out, my dad would get the fire beneath the mantel real hot, really pile on the wood. The flames would be blazin' up behind the hearth, filling the living room with light as we tried to get ourselves as warm as we could before bedtime.

We each had our place to sit around the fire. My father sat on the far left to tend the fire, then my mother sat next to him. I sat next to my mother, in the middle. My sister, Thelma, sat next to me, and then my oldest sister, Edth, sat on the far right close to the light. All the years we were together, we always sat in that order.

Everyone sat on one of our ladder-backed chairs, except for me. I had a block that my dad had cut out of a maple tree when he was sawing it up. He'd cut me off a short stump and he'd peeled the bark off of it and knocked the rough edges off. That maple block made a good seat for a kid to sit on, and oh, I liked that little stool. I didn't want anybody fooling with my seat. I used to crack walnuts on it and we'd eat them as we sat around together.

My sister Edth was a good reader and she read stories and history books aloud to us pretty often when we sat by the fire. She had a gentle voice and she was really a bookworm. What my father liked best was to hear a book on the history of Kit Carson. I guess he liked Kit Carson because he was a frontiersman, lived kind of like we did, only he traveled around and had adventures back in the 1800s. He was a skilled trapper and a guide who helped open the territory of California to settlers from the Eastern United States and he'd fought in the Civil War. Edth would read that book—no tellin' how many times she read that book to my dad—and, of course, to all of us. We didn't have a lot of books, so we heard them all over and over, but we loved every one.

My mother would read the Bible to us pretty often. Sometimes my father would get the Bible out and he'd sit down and he'd try to read the Bible, but it was hard for him. My father never got an education, very little, he just went through the third grade. He had to walk four miles to get to a school back in the mountains where he grew up. He just barely could sign his name.

My mother had gotten a pretty good grade school education. She could read and write and she helped him all the time with any forms and papers that had to be filled out; she took care of it. My dad could read, though he was a painfully slow reader. He had to spell each word. The only book I ever saw him try to read was the Bible. He lived by all of its principles. One thing he told me was to always tell the truth.

He said to me, "Quinton, no matter how bad it hurts you, tell the truth. Be honest with people, no matter what you do. If you sell them something for a price, well, you stick to it. Be honest in every dealing. You'll get along in life, if you'll do that."

My daddy lived that way all his life and I followed his advice from the start, since he showed me by his actions what kind of man to be. I think my daddy considered me a good son. But, of course, as a kid, I'd still get into trouble.

For some reason, little boys are more *mischeevious* than little girls, seems like. I had to do something to amuse myself, I reckon. Oh, when I was pretty small, I'd pick at one of my sisters when they were busy at housework; maybe I'd pull Edth's braids when she was sitting by the fire trying to sew. She'd get pretty mad and that would delight me. I'd pretend to stop, but I'd have me a broom straw and I'd start ticklin' her on the back of the neck when she wasn't lookin', get her all upset and she'd holler and carry on. I'd keep on till my mother would threaten to get after me with a switch. She's the one who kept us in line.

My mother didn't have a whole lot to say when we were around the fireplace, because the children did most of the talking, but she got a kick out of listening to us. She'd sit there in her second chair and listen to each one of us, smile and nod, or maybe she'd add a few words. On many nights, the five of us would pop popcorn on the open fire, warm our feet on the hearth, and have a big time, talking and laughing together until it was time to go to bed. We'd stay there till the flames flickered blue and the embers glowed, and if it was a Saturday night, we might wait for my mother's long hair to dry by the warmth of the hearth.

My mother never cut her hair in her life, I don't reckon. It was way past her waist when it was down, about the color of chestnut, without a speck of gray. She never did get gray hairs hardly at all, even when she got to be a real old woman. When she was young, and all her life, she wore her hair curled up tight into a bun in the daytime. Only in the evening, at home, did she take down her thick straight hair and brush it out. She'd usually stand in front of the mirror that hung over the hand-me-down oak dresser, take the hairpins out of the knot and then her long hair would ripple down, as shiny as a creek in sunlight.

She would embrace us at bedtime—my mother was a loving woman—but other than that, we didn't hug and kiss very much as a family, even though we thought the world of each other. We were just a real close-knit family. We treated each other in such a manner that we knew we loved each other. I don't believe there was any family that loved each other more than we did. Maybe everybody thinks that.

The last thing my father did every night before he went to bed was to tend to the fireplace and put the "backlog" in there. He always had a big log that he'd put in the back of the fireplace after the fire died down and he'd rake the coals and ashes up against that log and it would smolder and stay warm. That backlog was ready to burn the next morning and made starting the next fire easy.

My mother and father slept in the living room, by the fireplace, where they had a beautiful carved, darkly varnished bed with a rolled footboard and a tall headboard. It was the nicest thing we had, and my parents had gotten it new when they got married. My daddy's shotgun hung over that bed. It was loaded and my dad told us kids never to go near that.

The children slept in the bedroom, which was separated from the living room by the open breezeway. That breezeway had a roof and rough wood floor, but was exposed to the elements on either end. The three of us children had to leave the comfort of the warm living room to get to our beds, and in the winter, a lot of times it would come a big snow and it would blow snow through that breezeway. We'd have to wade through the snow to go to bed, or to come into the living room when we got out of bed in the morning. We liked wading through the snow barefooted. I don't know why we liked it so, but Thelma and I'd slip outside and run around barefooted in the snow a little bit anyway, even though my mother didn't like that.

It seems like, back then, the winters were a lot colder. We'd have as much as a foot of snow on the ground at least two months solid in the winter. Sometimes those snowdrifts'd get as tall as a man, nearly, that wind'd blow back in them mountains so.

We had weather vanes and all kinds of windmills around the yard so we could see what direction the wind was a comin' from. I made most of 'em when I got old enough, put 'em up on a pole so they'd catch the wind. Some of those whirligigs looked like ducks with wings that'd spin, or an airplane with propellers that turned, and that wind could blow till you couldn't hardly see those blades a spinnin'.

We had no heat in the bedroom at all. None of the house was heated through the night. Since that house wasn't insulated, any heat you had would dissipate pretty quick if you didn't have a fire going all the time, and, of course, we couldn't keep a woodstove or a fireplace a goin' all night long. So we slept in the cold. That's just how people lived and slept back then, back in them hills. But even when the wind would howl in the dead of a February freeze, I'd sleep warm. Even in the coldest winter.

In the early years, we bedded down on homemade mattresses, sacks filled with corn shucks that we'd shredded with table forks. They'd rustle like dead leaves every time one of us would move. In later years, we got us some real mattresses. We had enough layers to keep us warm when we slept, Mother's quilts and featherbeds. We'd always sleep on top of and under featherbeds and, boy, that's really a warm bed, an old-fashioned featherbed is.

My sisters shared a simple oak bed. I slept in my rusty iron bed. When I got to be around ten years old, I'd take my bed apart and move it upstairs to the open loft in the summertime, just put it in the middle of the attic under the roof peak. I could just lay up there and look at the rafters angling up from the floor. I couldn't sleep up there when it was cold, though, 'cause the loft was open on one end over that breezeway. Just had a couple of logs at the bottom to keep me from falling over the edge. Of course, I was about like a cat.

How I'd get up there was to climb the wall. A log cabin, it's made so a kid can just climb up the corner of the wall on the rough logs. It was years before my dad put stairs in there and they were in my sisters' room, so even when I was older, I used to climb the wall when I wanted to go to bed in the loft. In the winter, though, all three of us kids had to share the one bedroom downstairs that could shelter us from the weather, and that wasn't really what you'd call shelter today.

At the top log of that room, just below the ceiling, we left a crack open for the cats to go in and out and that's how the snow blew in on my bed. The cats'd climb up the wall and come through that crack and jump down on my bed and stay in the house when it was real cold. Sometimes they'd wake me up if I was asleep. When they wanted to go out, they'd hop up on the bed and climb the wall to the top log. We always had from two to three cats, sometimes more. They were good to keep mice under control. We didn't overfeed them and they earned their keep, but they never really caught up with the pests.

The cats would go after the mice, but there were other pests around there that cats wouldn't touch, nor most dogs, neither—snakes. We killed snakes that got in the house a few times. They were black snakes.

There were plenty of 'em around there. They wouldn't bite you at all.

A house built like that, mice could get in the walls and den up, and snakes had a way of gettin' in, too. They could go in those cracks and crawl around in between the walls, and sometimes, we had snakes to get inside the walls after the mice.

Throughout the house, my mother had papered over the rough split board walls and she used magazines that people had given her. She'd take the magazines, pull out the pages and plaster them all over the walls with a paste of flour and water. When the wind blew, that paper—Momma had so many layers, it was thick—it would just go in and out, swell in and out with the rhythm of the wind.

I remember layin' in my bed on a real still night and hearin' something rattling the paper on the wall, and that paper got to goin' and a comin', movin' in and out, and I figured it was a snake a travelin' in there. I just hauled off and hit the wall. That'd scare 'em out of there.

The wallpaper was so thick it wouldn't break, it was just like heavy cardboard with all those layers on there—color advertisements, pictures and words overlapped in rows. I learned to spell by reading the ads on those walls. I'd just lie there in bed when I was school-age, and I'd memorize every ad that was in those magazines, all those big block letters. I had just about the whole bedroom memorized. My mother would try to paper the walls pretty often, and she'd change the scene. So I'd start reading again and learning all the ads. There were a lot of ads for Lucky Strike and Prince Albert, there were a lot of tobacco ads, that's what I remember most. But I never did take up smokin' or chewin'—mainly 'cause my daddy cautioned me against it.

I'd be in bed and I could hear the sound of Daddy's chiming clock from the living room. A bell, just as clear and true, rang from the fireplace mantel and chimed the hour, and it also chimed once on the half hour. That was the only way we knew the time at night. Now, certain hours, you couldn't tell. When it was twelve-thirty, that clock would chime once, then at one o'clock, chime once, then at one-thirty, chime once again.

Sometimes I'd wake up and wonder what time it was and I'd listen for Daddy's clock. If I just heard it chime once, I might have to wait an hour to know the time, and I'd listen for that double chime. I could hardly go to sleep anyways, I was so eager to be up doin' somethin'. I'd listen and wonder how much longer till I could go a huntin', or get my homemade wagon fixed up, and eventually I'd drift off again. I ended each day looking forward to the next, and I always fell into the soundest sleep that a country boy ever slept.

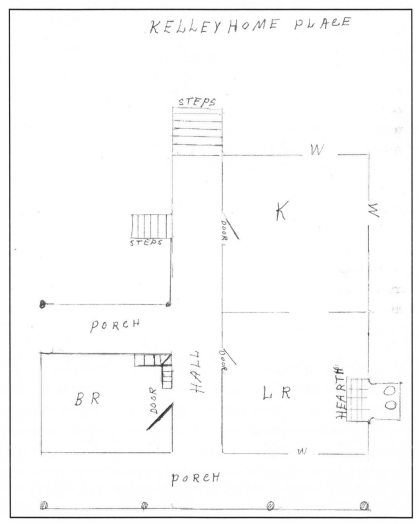

When he was eighty-four, Quinton Kelley drew this floor plan of his childhood home, the log cabin built by Will Kelley.

CHAPTER 4

My Father's Hands

The first sound I'd hear every morning was my father grinding coffee in his little hand-crank coffee grinder. My mother and father would get up real early in the morning to get breakfast ready. My father would start a fire in the living room and start a fire in the kitchen—burn wood in the cookstove. It kept the kitchen warm once my mother started cooking.

My mother would try to get us kids to stay in bed. She'd say to us, "Now, there's no use you gettin' up this early." But we never stayed in bed. My father left the house around four o'clock, to walk to work, and by then we'd all had our breakfast together. Of course, most likely, we'd all gone to bed about dark.

We kids were always up a long time before we had to go to school. I don't know why we did that; we could have slept a couple more hours. It's just a testament to how we all wanted to be together as much as we could, 'cause we didn't always get to see our daddy, he had to work so hard to keep us all fed and clothed.

My daddy used his arms, his hands, his back and his sweat to keep us a goin'. He worked pretty much from sunup to sundown every day. When he had a job he could do, he'd come in a lot of times well after dark.

While he worked as hard as any man could, even he'd get down on his luck sometimes.

When times were hard, he'd go places and do work for people in the community. He was a pretty good carpenter; he just trained himself. He knew how to figure the lumber and how to cut everything to fit. He swung an ax and he could fell the trees and chop them out to use for lumber and he was good at building log cabins. He mastered that on his own. He built houses for people all over the Coker Creek community. Built a lot of barns, too. He was busy a lot, but, out there, people didn't ever pay him much.

My dad didn't ever have a negative attitude, didn't seem like, he was always positive about whatever he said and did. But there were some things that would get to him. One of the things was not having the means to buy what he needed. Sometimes he needed money and he just didn't have it. One day when I was about nine or ten years old, he took out his pocketbook and I remember him unfolding the leather, unsnapping the top and showing it to me and he said, "Well, son, right here is a dime. That's all the money I've got."

I could tell by his face that it was really a hurtin' him.

But he said to me, "Now, Quinton, everything's gonna be all right. Don't let it bother you none. There'll be better days ahead."

He just had an optimistic look at life, no matter what the circumstances. He'd get down-and-out like a lot of people in those lean years, during the Great Depression, but he'd find a way to make enough money to keep us a goin'. Maybe he'd build bee boxes for a neighbor and they'd pay him in corn and we'd trade that to get flour so we could make biscuits. That kind of thing.

Locally, there wasn't much in the way of steady jobs, so my daddy had to create some of his own opportunities. He'd sell some of the white oak that we had—that eighty acres had a lot of timber on it. They used to call timber a "poor man's crop." How he sold it, my daddy used to hew crossties, the kind they used for railroads. He said the hand-hewn crossties lasted longer out in the weather than the ones from a sawmill and they were more in demand. They'd be just-cut trees and my dad would chop them out. When he'd get six crossties hewn, he'd sell 'em down in Tellico 'cause that's about all one mule could haul through those steep roads—six green crossties. For years and years, I'd be on these railroads and see a lot of hand-hewn ties under the rails. A lot of 'em were my dad's ties. And there may be some out there today, somewhere, I don't know.

I don't know what they paid him for it. Crossties didn't bring much. I venture to say about maybe a dollar each, but I'm not sure whether they even brought that much. Six dollars would have bought us a lot of clothes from the Sears, Roebuck and Company catalog. That would be a pretty good payday. It took my dad a long time, though, to chop out that many ties. He had a lot of hours of work in it, probably didn't make ten cents an hour.

My daddy also ran a blacksmith shop on our property, a little shack up by the road—and he served the community as they needed it. He was a good blacksmith. He had a big block of wood with an iron anvil fastened on it, and a row of different hammers hanging nearby, tongs to handle the hot iron, and a pair of heavy, leather-palmed gloves. He'd shoe horses, sharpen saws and knives, and he made wagon wheels. He repaired wagon and buggy wheels, too, and I helped him, when I got old enough to handle a bellows.

People used a lot of mattocks back then for all kinds of digging, and my dad would draw them out in his forge and sharpen them. First, he'd put all the iron tools that needed to be sharpened in the furnace and my job was to pump the bellows and keep the fire hot. I was just a skinny little kid, but he'd have me a pumpin' with all my might, blowin' air at those flames to get the fire a blazin' up. Then he'd take the tongs and pull out a mattock or plow point, almost ready to melt. Metal will almost turn white when it's that hot. He'd hit that glowing metal with a hammer against his anvil and it splattered liquid metal as he pounded it.

Ping!-ping! Ping!-ping!

At first, his hammer would make a dull thud, but as the metal cooled, the sound got sharper. He worked in a fast rhythm, his hands a swingin' that hammer, beatin' the anvil like an iron drum.

PING!-Ping! PING!-Ping!

Neighbors could hear the loud ringin' and pingin' of metal hittin' metal for miles and miles, I reckon, from Will Kelley's blacksmith shop.

My daddy had rhythm in his hands. It seemed to make the work go smoother when he worked in a rhythm.

He'd hammer the metal out thin on the edge, then grind the metal while it was still hot to sharpen it, and put it back in the fire to temper it. It had to be tempered just right. If it was too soft, it would wear down too quick; too hard, it would shatter if you hit a rock while digging or plowing. If you got it just right, it would really hold an edge. My dad knew exactly what color the metal had to be — "cherry red," he said — to get it to the right temperature before he took it out of the fire. He'd put it in the water to cool it down and it would just hiss like a den of stirred-up snakes. He'd have a lot of tools in the fire when he worked. While he was hammering one, he'd be heating another.

In those days, they used cross-cut saws to cut timber. They needed to be sharpened pretty often and my dad was good at it. It'd take him over an hour to sharpen a cross-cut saw and he would just charge people a quarter. He would do his work for nothing, nearly, because he did it more or less for accommodation to his neighbors, since none of us out there had any money.

We'd work the homeplace and sell some of our crops when we could. We sold fresh corn, a dozen ears at a time, for about a nickel to neighbors. If people really needed the food, of course, we wouldn't charge them, we'd just give it to them. That's the way it was in that community; most people helped each other. In the fall, if we had a bumper crop, we'd sell pumpkins and squash. Most of the time, we had to keep about everything else we grew to feed us, though.

We raised fryer chickens to eat occasionally and we sold some of them. If our hens got too old to lay eggs, we'd sell them, too. We'd catch those hens and tie their legs together so we could handle 'em. We'd have a bunch of chickens tied at either end of a rope and my dad'd carry the whole bunch across one shoulder, some in front and some behind. The old chickens would be hanging there, wings a floppin', and sometimes they'd squawk out. It was a common thing around Coker Creek to see someone with a shoulder-load of chickens walking down the road to Dave Lenderman's store.

We also sold chickens to the "rolling store" that came by once a week. Two men had 'em a truck fixed up with sideboards that raised up, and underneath they had shelves stocked with canned goods. They had a chicken coop on top of the truck, and they'd go driving around with those chickens a cacklin' up there, feathers flyin', and they'd stop for you if you came up to the road and waved to them.

It was a lot more convenient than walking to the store. The rolling store traveled all the roads, and we knew what day and time they'd come by, usually late in the day. They carried feed that we bought for the cows — cottonseed meal. It was pretty rich, couldn't feed 'em much of that. We'd always sell whatever we could sell when the rolling store came by. Oh, you could get about eight to ten cents a dozen for eggs. And beans were almost a giveaway price, but we counted our pennies.

When times began to pick up a little bit, my daddy got a job building a road, working on Steer Creek Road at the foot of Tellico Mountain. He swung a mattock for the Works Progress Administration (WPA) government program and helped dig out and grade better roads through those mountains. They paid him so much a day, not much, and he had to walk about eight miles to where he worked. Of course, he had to walk that eight miles back home. So he was gone all day and a little bit of the night, gettin' back.

They used to build country roads by hand — wheelbarrows and mattocks and shovels and men — they didn't have machinery. His foreman said my daddy was the best man he had, that he could dig out an entire ditch line by hand and it would just fit their template to a T. 'Cause he was good at it, my daddy got the job of digging out the ditch line all along that road and after a while, it hurt one of his feet, 'cause he had to stand on an angle down in that ditch all day long. He'd complain about it when he'd get home, and my mother'd heat up a dishpan of water and Epsom salts for a foot soak.

He always favored that foot a little when he walked, after he dug that ditch line. Of course, he had to keep that job. They usually gave my daddy a hard job, 'cause he was good at whatever he did.

He'd tell me, "Son, I hope you never have to go out on public works, where you work with a bunch of roughneck people, 'cause you hear all kinds of talk that's not good. 'Bout all you hear is a lot of dirty jokes and drunken tales. I wish we just had a big farm where you could be at home and work with family, away from that kind of exposure. But," he said, "someday, you'll be out there, so you'll just have to take care of yourself, and not participate in the rough stuff that goes on."

★ ★ ★

Now, I liked to hunt so well, when my dad came in from his job at night, I'd ask him if he'd go hunting with me. He'd say, "Well, Quinton, I'm awful tired, but I'll go a huntin' with you for a little while."

My dad had been a hunter all his life. He could bring in meat from the woods. It was second nature to him and he passed it on to me. Back when he first taught me, I was pretty young, just old enough to be in the first grade. He took me out in the field one day, lifted his Winchester rifle in his big square hands, put it up to his shoulder, and showed me how to steady a shot.

He said, "You line that bead up on the end of the barrel with the sight notch. When you aim for somethin', as soon as you get that bead on your target, just as soon as it lines up, now, you've got to squeeze that trigger. Don't you pull on it—if you pull it fast, you'll jerk your gun off the target."

He'd eye up a shot, and as that gun was still a movin' up towards the target, he'd fire. He'd usually hit right on whatever he wanted to shoot.

"Never point your gun at anythin' you don't want to kill," he told me. "'Cause it'll kill whatever you're aimin' at."

A rifle bullet travels a long distance and I had to know what direction people's houses were located back in the woods. My dad really cautioned me not to point a gun in any direction that could reach a neighbor's house.

I was eleven years old when I got my first gun, a .22 Ranger rifle that we'd ordered from Sears. It arrived down at the post office in the little ol' store we had then. We walked down there to get it and, boy, was I excited about it! It was bolt action, single shot. My dad really gave me instructions on how to be safe with it before he'd allow me to take it out on my own.

My dad taught me to be careful, but he didn't just say, "Now, son, you be careful," without teaching me what he meant. He took the time to show me and point out where the danger was as we hunted down through the years.

"Now, Quinton, you see right here," my dad pointed with a stick, "that's where a big ol' snake'd like to be. They like to hide along the edge of a big log. When you come to a pole across a pathway, don't ever step *over* it, step up on it first and see that there's nothing on the other side. If you don't, snakes can bite you on the leg before you know they're around."

So I'd always just jump across things I couldn't see over, get out of the way of anything that might be hiding on the other side. I kept that in mind when I was out.

My dad showed me how to climb a tree and how to be careful to test the limbs so I wouldn't break a limb, fall out and maybe get crippled up. He'd tell me to always be alert to dead timber, that even on a perfectly still day, a big limb or a tree can fall without warning. Sometimes we'd hear a big tree falling in the woods, and it'd shake the ground.

If we went hunting on a creek, my dad would tell me how to know where the deep water was and be sure I didn't get over where it was too deep for me to wade, or too swift. Sometimes we'd be knee-deep or higher in that creek at a crossing place from one hunting spot to another. We had areas picked out where we knew the hunting ground was more plentiful.

I was a good shot with my rifle 'cause I did it a lot. I could hit the bull's-eye of one of my homemade targets just about every time. 'Course, I didn't get to practice as much as I'd like because it cost quite a bit to fire a rifle. But I hunted a lot and I was able to bring in a little bit of game.

Now, today, I don't care nothin' about killing a squirrel or animals like them, but that's what we had for food when I was growin' up. We'd eat rabbits and squirrel. My mother used to fry that squirrel in a skillet and it was good. My dad used to turkey hunt, too, and he'd get some meaty wild turkeys. He'd get out in the woods and wait for the turkeys to start gobblin' and when they gobbled he knew they couldn't hear him and he'd slip up on 'em. My dad never did hunt boar, but some of the neighbors would track wild boars and they'd give us meat from what they got. That was all a part of the daily life in the Coker Creek community.

A lot of times I'd go hunting after my dad left for work, before I went to school. I knew what time I had to be back to the house in order to get my chores done and get to school. It was dark, of course, so I'd take an old kerosene lantern, light it, and I'd go deep into the woods with my dog and rabbit hunt.

I wouldn't go out at that time of day to try to shoot a rabbit. I just liked to hear my dog run 'em. Now, to hunt in the dark, of course, you have to have a dog. Going out there without a dog, that would be useless. You have to hunt by listening for your dog. The dog will get on a track and they'll trail an animal.

Once you have a good dog, you can tell whether it's a hot track, where the animal is nearby, or a cold track, where the animal has been gone a long time. The dog barked differently; if it was a cold track, he didn't bark very fast. But if he was on a hot track, he'd bark a lot faster — rapid-fire — and you knew he's about ready to tree something, put it up a tree, or down in a hole. A lot of places there were holes in the ground, and the animals would go in the ground and the dog would dig and try to get them out. When that happened, I'd have to just catch my dog, I couldn't get him to leave with me, hardly; he'd be determined to get what was down in there, but I didn't bother to dig animals out of the ground.

Sometimes my dog would run a rabbit into a hollow log and keep it trapped there. Then I'd bring in the game. I'd take a long twig, push it back in the hollow log, and twist it up on the rabbit's fur. You have to pull real slow — they'll really hold on — pull a little more, wait, and twist that stick into their fur, and keep pullin' till you can grab 'em. It seems cruel to think about now, but that's how we got some of our food. Wild rabbits were real good to eat.

In the daytime, I'd squirrel hunt and use a rifle, shoot squirrels out of the trees. Sometimes my dog'd tree a 'possum and I'd climb up in the tree, shake that 'possum out. My dog'd circle 'round waiting for it and he'd catch it.

We sold the 'possum fur, but didn't eat them, though some people did. I'd skin those 'possums, nail the pelts on a board and dry them—they had to be good and dry or you couldn't sell them—and I'd sell them to the rolling store or to Dave Lenderman's store for money at Christmastime. That's about the only way I had a gettin' money when I was a kid. Now, racoon pelts sold a lot higher, they were in more demand, but there were no racoons much around us, because too many people had dogs.

At night, I'd go hunting if I could get anybody to go with me. Usually, it would be my dad, sometimes my sister Thelma, or occasionally one of my cousins. Sometimes I'd go by myself. I'd take that lantern and go way back in the woods and wander around. I never was afraid of nothin' much around there. I grew up there. Some people are afraid to get out at night back in the mountains, but I never did think nothin' about it. I'd be a little bit more scared to go out in a thickly populated town and wander around at night than I would to go back in the mountains. It was safer.

Sure, you'd run into some people, some hunters. I remember one night, I met up with three hunters and they stopped and were talking to me and one of them had a little puppy dog in his hunting coat pocket. He got that little puppy out, showed it to me, and he put that little feller back in his pocket and went on hunting. I enjoyed knowing that he was taking care of that puppy like that, getting it used to hunting.

My hunting dog was a little black dog that one of my uncles gave me and I thought the world of that dog. He was a good little dog to tree squirrels and 'possums and different small game. I hunted a lot with him, had a wonderful time.

My hunting dog was named something that you wouldn't want to say now. But back then in the 1930s, in Tennessee and in nearby areas, things were a lot different. My Uncle Ernest—he'd married one of Mother's sisters—he'd named the dog Nigger because he was solid black. When I first met that little dog, he was already well-trained and he came runnin' when you called his name. No one thought anything about it.

That was the year we rode the passenger train to Bristol, Virginia, to visit my mother's kin for Christmas—it was shortly before I got my .22 rifle. We stayed at their home and Uncle Ernest had that black dog and every time I'd start out in the yard, here that dog would come. He made a run right for me and I was sure he was going to nip me on the leg. He wasn't a big dog, just about knee-high, but sometimes it's the smaller dogs that are more apt to bite you. He was a mix, part cocker spaniel, part bulldog. He looked like a mean dog to me. And, boy, I was afraid of him and I'd run back in the house. I wouldn't get out of the house the whole visit, 'cause if I did, here'd come that dog, just a runnin' and a barkin' at me.

But then one morning, I overheard Uncle Ernest tell my mother, "Well, I's aimin' to give Quinton that little black dawg to take home with 'im. But I don't believe he'd take 'em, 'cause he's afraid of that dawg, so I don't guess I'll give 'em to 'im."

When I heard that, boy, I made friends with that little dog. I went right outside and started calling him. I talked to him, got to pettin' him, foolin' with him, and he just took up with me and I took up with him. I found out the dog was just wantin' to play with me. He never did scare me anymore. We took him back home with us; hid him in a cardboard box on the train and he kept quiet the whole trip!

That little black dog's short hair was just as slick—boy, did his coat shine like just-polished Sunday shoes. He liked when I scratched behind his ears. He had short ears and speckled brown eyes. That dog turned out to be the best little dog.

He'd come a runnin' from the house when I was comin' in from school, or if I'd been somewhere and didn't have him with me. Of course, I took my dog with me nearly every time I went anywhere unless I was going to somebody's house. And that dog knew just as well when he could go, and when he couldn't.

He'd never, never try to follow me when I went down a dirt road. If I started to the post office, I went up and got in the road and stood there, and when he saw me, he wouldn't follow me. But if I started back in the fields, or through the woods, he'd go with me. If he didn't go with me right away, he'd come over there when he found out where I was. He always wanted to stay around pretty close to where I was at.

If I started back through the fields to go to a neighbor's house and didn't want him to go with me, I'd get on him, say, "Git out of here! Go on! Git!" and make him go back, but he'd slip around and come on anyhow. He wouldn't let me see him, he'd stay back in the woods out of sight, but he'd usually get after a rabbit before long and start his barking. Then I knew he'd come along.

That little ol' dog was tough. He'd tackle the biggest dog that came on our land. He'd go after 'em all and he'd run every one of 'em off, too, even some twice his size.

Momma would come to the door of our cabin and call out for my dog in her big, booming voice that came from such a little quiet person. If he didn't come right away, she'd say to me, "Now, where's Nigger at? I'm wantin' to feed him and I can't get him to come!"

Then I'd holler for him and he'd come a runnin'.

When we'd go hunting, I'd be deep in the woods, calling out my dog's name as it echoed through the hills. I didn't think nothin' about it. None of us did for years and years. Now I wouldn't use that name because I respect the black people just like I do white people. They're just human beings like I am. But back then, and especially back in those hills, people didn't think of it like that.

When I's a growin' up in the back hills of Tennessee, black men didn't have a "Chinaman's chance"—that's the kind of thing people said. People out there was down on 'em, talked bad about 'em. Some people were really mean if a black man happened to come through Coker Creek. They'd run him off or worse. Well, my family never thought that was the way to be.

Sometimes we'd hear stories that traveled through the community about the Ku Klux Klan and their activities, but my daddy steered me away from that kind of thinking. I'm glad I see the light and I don't hold anything against black people just because of the color of their skin. That there's ridiculous for people to be like that. But it wasn't that way out there around Coker Creek and the surrounding areas before the war.

Blacks never were allowed out there until after World War II. They had a big sign at the entrance to Tellico Plains, on the highway going from Madisonville to Tellico Plains, a big sign that said, *Black Man — Don't Let the Sun Go Down on You Here.*

It wasn't a fancy sign or anything, but it was painted on a big, flat board and somebody'd posted it along the roadway. It hung there all the years I lived on Coker Creek. So it was known that if a black man went up into those hills during the day, it wasn't safe for him to spend the night. They always called black people "darkies," and they'd call out to a black man if they saw him walking along the road, "Hey there, darkie, where you a goin'? Don't you know, no darkies allowed 'round here!"

Even after World War II, black people wouldn't go out there unless they had an escort, got the law to accompany them, because they were afraid that there were still some of that kind of people out there. There were when I was growing up, because I knew of a shooting that happened with one of my neighbors, a boy I went to school with. He stayed back in the mountains around Coker Creek hunting a lot of the time, just a mountaineer, you might say.

There were a lot of wild boar, bear, deer and different game to hunt in those mountains. People would come from New York and Chicago and other cities, somehow they knew about the place. They'd come to Coker Creek to hunt wild boar, mainly; they were interested in them because there weren't too many places you could hunt wild boar. When those city hunters came down there, they'd bring their chef with them — usually a black man — to do their cooking. They'd set up a camp somewhere along a little creek. That was before they allowed white people to mix with black people very much.

Well, this neighbor of mine, he was back in there hunting and he ran up on this black man in the woods, a cook for some hunters preparing the evening meal. And my neighbor shot him. Just shot him on sight. He didn't happen to kill the black man, but he wounded him.

When the group of hunters came in and found their cook shot, well, of course, they loaded him in the car and they had to take him to the hospital, I think all the way to Knoxville. As far as I know, the black man recovered. And the neighbor who shot him, well, he never did have to serve any time over it.

It was just like that out there, and people accepted it. I don't know why some of 'em out there hated the black man so. They're just good people, a lot of 'em. 'Course, a lot of 'em's like white people, they'll do most anything, too. I never did say anything out of the way to a black man. I always treated them with respect just like I did anybody else.

My father always said, "If you want to be treated right, that's the way you have to treat others." He always lived up to what he said. That was our pattern to follow, and it just came naturally. My father was considerate of the feelings of others, all of 'em—black and white, men and women, family and strangers, even the domestic animals.

When my dad and I were hunting one night, my dog treed a 'possum and he said to me, "Reckon you can go up in there and shake that 'possum out?"

I said, "Yeah, I can get up in there."

I climbed up in that tree and I shook that 'possum out. When it hit the ground, my dad had the lantern down low and that lantern blinded my dog so the dog couldn't see the 'possum. That 'possum ran up another tree.

My dad was watching it and he went over to the next tree, trying to show my dog where it went. He held that lantern up and he put his hand up on the tree and he called the dog, said, "Here he is! Look over here!"

That dog couldn't see for the light of the lantern and, of course, he thought it was that 'possum when he jumped up there and grabbed my daddy's hand between his teeth and really nailed him. And, boy, he really bit my daddy bad. He had to keep that hand bandaged up for a long time and it hurt his ability to work for a while. But it didn't seem to worry him when it happened. He took it in stride.

Me bein' a kid, I was laughing about it as we were walking through the woods a headin' home, it was just ticklin' me to death how it'd happened. My dad was such a good-natured fellow—or "feller," as we all said—he wouldn't get mad at you for laughing at him, no matter what happened. He was always one of the best-natured persons you've ever seen.

Now, that dog realized what he'd done, and he was really afraid we were gonna get on him, so he'd go off and lie down by himself. He wouldn't get close to us—he knew he'd done something wrong. But my dad didn't get mad at the little dog because it wasn't the dog's fault. Some people might have been mad, but my dad couldn't stand to see that dog so downhearted. He kept calling the dog, real gentle-like. He talked to him, coaxed him and, finally, he got the dog to come to him and he petted that dog with his good hand until he was a waggin' his tail again. My dad was a kindhearted man all the way through.

A lot of times he'd come in after working all day at manual labor, some backbreaking job, and he'd go hunting with me into the night. Anytime I asked him nearly, he'd go. I don't know how he got enough rest to work as hard as he did. He was just that kind of a person, he wouldn't hardly turn you down if there was any way he could do what you wanted him to do, as long as it was something reasonable.

But my mother would discourage me from asking him. She'd say, "Now, your daddy's worked hard all day. Don't ask him to go a huntin' with you."

So, later on, I quit doing that. After I got older, I realized that it was really asking too much of him after he'd worked all day.

Many a day, I've seen him come home sore and spent, his tall brow smudged with dirt, his clothes as wet with sweat as if he'd been in the creek. Sometimes his hands were scraped up, the skin around his fingernails rough and ragged. I'd watch him take out his pocket knife and he'd clean under his nails with the tip of the blade. My daddy's hands were calloused hands, hands that supported us, and they told of a hard life.

It didn't matter what job he did, my father got in there and got the job done. Then he found a way to spend time with his family, each one of us, because first and foremost, he was a family man. He always said to me, "Son, if somethin's worth doin', it's worth doin' *right*."

CHAPTER 5

Livin' Off the Land

From our earliest years, we had our chores—I had mine and Edth and Thelma had theirs. Just one time was the only time I ever tried to get out of doin' a chore and that was back when my sisters were in school, but I was still too young to go.

Out in the chicken house, we'd always set an old hen on the eggs when we wanted to have more chickens. One hen could hatch about fifteen eggs. She'd sit on those eggs for two or three days until she needed to get some water. Then she'd come off the nest and start cackling and my mother would hear it. This day, Momma was washing clothes down at the little spring below our house and I was playing in the backyard, and she said, "Son, feed that ol' hen. She's off the nest."

It was my place to pitch in with that chore. And I knew it. But I was playing around there, havin' a big time, and I told Momma, "If you want her fed, you feed her yourself!"

I never had talked to her like that before. I don't know what got into me, but I just sassed her. And she said nothin'. Not a thing.

I saw her leave her washin' down at the spring. There was a little patch of woods by the creek where the willow trees grew, and I saw her go down there and cut a switch. A willow switch is really flexible.

I started hollering, "I'm a gonna feed her, Momma! I'm a gonna feed her!"

She said, "Yeah, I know you are, but I got somethin' else for you first!"

She came up there and she gave me a good whippin' and, boy, a willow switch will sting! I was *glad* to feed that ol' hen.

Of course, after it was over, my mother would joke with me and laugh about the trouble I got myself into. I'm glad she didn't let me get away with it, 'cause if she had, I'd a been pullin' it again. She was a kind woman, but also the disciplinarian. Whatever she said, she meant it. It was that way, or you'd get a whippin'. We kids realized that, but sometimes we'd go a little too far.

Edth and Thelma would get into a fight every now and again. They'd get into an argument and start yelling, then one of them would shove the other and she'd shove back. Then they'd get to hittin' each other and they'd tear into each other just like two tomcats. It was a sight when they did, two big angry girls in overalls pulling at each other's braids and scuffling around on the floor. They'd get into it pretty heavy, and if my mother was where she happened to see it, she'd stop them, but they could put up a pretty good fight before she'd get 'em stopped.

There was one thing I remember they got into a fight about. It was nothing to be fighting about. Thelma had a ball of twine thread and Edth thought it belonged to her and Edth said, "I want my twine. I want that ball of twine."

Thelma said, "You're not a gettin' it."

They got into it and Thelma put that ball of twine into her mouth so Edth couldn't take it away from her. They wound up a rasslin' on the floor. When my mother saw that, she told them to stop right then. Well, they didn't. And she gave them both a good whippin'.

When momma said she was gonna give you a whippin' you just as well to stand there and take it, 'cause you were gonna get it. She didn't back down. I got a few of 'em myself. And I needed the ones that I got, I realize that now. 'Course, I didn't think I did then. My mother was a nice, wonderful person, but she made you do what she knew was right.

★ ★ ★

Since my dad worked away from home and didn't get home till after dark, I had to feed the stock. I'd go down to the barn after I did my schoolwork and feed the cows and the horse or the mule, feed the pig and the chickens, too.

The chickens could make it on their own most of the year, until frost, then we'd have to start feeding them. If we wanted the hens to lay well, though, we'd feed them some corn through the laying season. Corn made the eggs taste a lot better.

Some people built a pen with chicken wire, but we'd usually let our chickens run loose in the day around the homeplace. They'd wander around, go down to the stream, get water, find some worms along the bank. Then we'd put them up in the chicken house at night to roost.

At first, you had to make your chickens go in the chicken house. I liked to do that chore myself—it's just the nature of little boys to like to chase those chickens, run 'em down and catch 'em. Some of 'em were pretty hard to catch. They'd be beatin' their wings, a cacklin' and a runnin' around in crazy circles in front of our house. My sister Thelma, she'd get out there in her patched overalls to help me and we'd kick up clouds of dust, trying to corner those chickens. We'd catch 'em, one by one—oh, they flapped and squawked—but we put 'em in the chicken house and fastened 'em up. I could always pick out which chickens were the lead chickens that the others would follow. If I put them in the chicken house first, the others would come on in. Every time we got some new hens, we'd have to train 'em to go in there every day for the first few days.

My uncle gave me some duck eggs and I set them under a hen, and I raised a whole bunch of ducks for their eggs; that was my project. Duck eggs had a stronger taste, not as good as chicken eggs, because ducks live off of insects and crawfish they find along the water.

The funny thing is, the mother hen would treat those ducklings just like her baby chicks, and they'd follow her around, but when they'd start to get in the creek, that momma hen would throw a fit, like she was just about to die. That hen would run back and forth along the bank, a cacklin' and a flappin' her wings. She must have been surprised when her "baby chicks" started swimming right off. They never had any trouble—those ducklings'd just take to that water—go up one stream, down another.

They'd go several miles away, following a stream, so I'd have to go find them, drive them back in sometimes. I'd look for a stream that was a little bit muddy. They'd take their bill and stir up the muck along the bank, foraging for food, and that's how I tracked them. Then I'd herd them back to the chicken house for the night.

After we'd train them good, both the ducks and the chickens would come in about dark and go to the chicken house on their own and we'd lock them up and let them out in the morning. If you let 'em out too early, they'd go down by the stream and lay their eggs along the water and you couldn't find the eggs.

Sometimes, Thelma gathered the eggs and sometimes I did. We'd share that chore. We'd go into the chicken house in the morning, pick up all the eggs and turn the chickens and ducks out.

My oldest sister, Edth, she never did those kinds of chores. She always worked around the house. She'd keep things clean around the yard and she worked in the kitchen with my mother.

My two sisters were pretty husky girls, especially when they were younger. In fact, a lot of people referred to them as "the big Kelley girls," and they never did like that. They were strong girls 'cause they were hard workers.

During canning season, when our food was ripe from the orchard or garden, we used a lot more water than usual puttin' up that food. While my mother was filling her glass Ball jars in the kitchen, all through the day Edth would carry a lot of that water herself so Thelma and I could do other chores.

Edth couldn't pull a cross-cut saw or anything like that, but Thelma and I did physical things, men's work. In the summertime, we'd cut a lot of firewood to use through the winter. My dad would fell the trees. He'd swing that ax, chop a V in the trunk, and it'd fall to the ground with a big thud. We'd cut down green trees and split 'em up, so they'd dry out good. We'd usually pick out just ol' scrubby trees and we thinned out the forest. We wouldn't cut down good trees. We had a lot of forest on those eighty acres—most of the land was in timber.

Thelma and I would get out in the woods and do our part. Outside work suited her. Even when she was just a girl, Thelma could work like a man. She'd take one end of a cross-cut saw and I'd take the other and we'd push and pull in rhythm—you had to get it right—and that saw would just carve up shavings, as we cut logs into short pieces. Then my dad would finish up with his ax and split the wood into firewood. We'd stack that in the woodshed, clear up to the top. Then we'd rick some up by the house.

Every day, it was my chore to carry in all the wood we'd use. I'd carry it in at night, have it ready, so we'd have plenty of wood for the next day. I'd try to get rich pine, 'cause rich pine will really burn good. Rich pine knots are full of rosin and you split them up into little splinters for kindling. My dad always wanted that pine kindling there so he had something to start the fire with first thing in the morning. I never missed a day, havin' it ready for him.

I'd always take care of my dad's bees when I was a boy. He'd tell me to watch out for a swarm of bees. They swarm in the spring of the year and that's the way they divide—you increase your number of hives. Usually, they'd light on the apple trees and there'd be a big ball of bees hangin' on a limb. When they come out and swarm, you've got to run and put them in a new box right away. I never was afraid of bees. I had a veil and heavy clothes that I put on to keep them from stinging me and I had a smoker. I put rags in that smoker and set them afire and pumped air through those burning rags and it would puff out smoke. I could handle those bees fine, they couldn't take that smoke.

I'd cut the twig off they were hangin' on, lay it down in front of a new box, and take the smoker and start smokin' 'em, and evidently, they know what to do. Those bees will go into that box. I'd leave the bees trapped in there for a day, then take the box up to where we kept our bees and they'd just start working, making honey. That hive of bees lived in that box from then on.

In the springtime, the hill behind our cabin bloomed with the sweet smells of apple blossom, peach blossom, plum blossom — and it all went into that honey. The apple and peach trees had pink petals, the plums had white, and when they were in full bloom, the blue sky up on the hill was a buzzin' all the time with our busy honeybees.

When it came time to rob the bees — that's what we called it when we harvested the honey — if the bees didn't want to give up the honey, I could puff a little smoke in the box and they'd move off that honeycomb. I didn't want to bring out a lot of bees with the honeycomb. I'd put the honeycomb in a pan and that comb would be drippin' clear, golden, fruit-blossom honey. We had several hives of bees and we always had plenty of honey to sell and just enough to last us year 'round. We never wanted to do without honey, 'cause a sticky spoonful of that was one of the few sweet treats we had.

We couldn't get by without milk, either. Sweet milk, buttermilk and fresh churned butter. If the cows didn't come back on their own in the evening, I'd go to the pasture and I'd bring them to the barn for my mother to milk. Then I'd always fasten the cows up for the night.

My mother milked them the next morning, too, and I'd let them out and they'd go back to the pasture. That was in the summertime. In the wintertime, we kept them up in the barn — wasn't much point in letting the cows out. Then I had to feed them hay or corn stalk fodder.

Of course, we all learned how to milk, but my mother didn't like for us to do the milking. She said, "You'll turn my cow dry."

If you don't milk a cow, they'll soon quit giving milk. You have to know how to milk them and get all the milk every time and they'll give milk for several months after they have a new calf. Then they'll go dry before the next calf comes along. To keep giving milk, the cow had to keep having calves. We'd usually sell the calves after they got to be a pretty good size.

There were people who would travel through the country buying cattle and they'd drive by and ask us if we had any calves to sell. If we did, we'd sell 'em. We couldn't raise them for beef because there wasn't a slaughterhouse till you got to Knoxville, around seventy-five miles away — too far for us to transport livestock.

★ ★ ★

It seemed like whatever I wanted to do, as long as it was good, my mother would back me in it. She was always with me on everything. One time, my uncle had some piglets and I wanted to buy a pig from him and raise it, and he said, "I'll tell you what I'll do. I'll give you one of them little pigs for twenty gallons of huckleberries."

So my mother got all five of us together and we went as a family and picked twenty gallons of huckleberries and we all earned that pig. It took us two whole mornings, talking and laughing with each other out in the sunshine.

In the summer, we picked a lot of huckleberries in our woods and every one of us went. They'd give me a bucket and my mother would say, "Now, when you get that bucket full, you can eat all you want from the bushes, but I don't want you eatin' none till you get your bucket full." She knew if we started eatin' 'em, we never would fill our bucket. That was one of the rules we had. And we stuck to it.

Back then the huckleberries, oh, you could just rake them off, almost. In the woods, there was just timber, mostly, no underbrush much, except huckleberries—they're about like a small blueberry—and you could just get them by the handfuls.

Used to, people would burn the woods off, burn the leaves off and the underbrush. They'd do that about every two years. The flames would go fast through the forest and they'd just smoke the bark a little bit on the trees—it didn't hurt the big timber, it just burnt the briars and weeds up, sort of like a grass fire. That kept the underbrush from getting too big and it let the huckleberries grow up.

Back then, you could just walk anywhere, nearly, through the woods. But today, if you get a fire with all that underbrush that's grown up in there, it'll just burn the trees and kill them. It'll just kill the forest now. I heard that after I was a grown man, the government stopped the people on Coker Creek from burning off the woods and it just all grew up in underbrush and briars and crowded the huckleberries out. Where we used to pick huckleberries when I was a boy, I doubt if there's even one today. So I don't know if the government had a good idea or not, doin' that. Those new ways just got rid of some of the best plants in the woods.

The one plant that I remember more than any of them from back then was what we called "spicewood," though, now, I don't think there's any of it out there. Boy, spicewood made the best tea you've ever tasted!

You could break off a limb and smell it and know it was sweet. We used to gather it along a little creek. There was only one place in the community where it grew and that's the only place I know where you could find it, close to a tributary of Coker Creek. Spicewood's a small tree, more of a bush, and it's got a slick bark on it. The leaves look a little like the leaves on a pear tree.

We'd break up the twigs and some of the leaves, put them in a pot, boil it down, strain it, and we sweetened it with a little honey. It was meant for enjoyment, it was not considered medicinal. In our kitchen, we'd drink that spicewood tea with our meals instead of drinking milk, and it was a real delight.

A lot of people used to make sassafras tea. I never did particularly like the flavor of sassafras, but it was popular in that community. People on Coker Creek had a little singsong tune they'd chant sometimes: "Cornbread, molasses and sassafras tea . . . cornbread, molasses and sassafras tea . . ." That was an old sayin' from way on back, when people didn't have much and that's all they had for dinner a lot of times.

Every year, a lot of people that I knew would drink that sassafras tea in the spring for a tonic. Said it "purified the blood" after the winter. My grandmother would always send us kids out to harvest that sassafras for her.

There were plenty of sassafras bushes growing around there, they grew like weeds. They grow in the field and you can tell them easily because that one plant has three different-shaped leaves. One of them is shaped like a mitten. You can make tea out of the leaves or out of the roots. If you dig the roots up, the roots make a little better tea, I think. The roots were always a little older and stronger.

Sometimes we'd use herbs and bark out of the woods for medicines, too. We used to make some tonic that they called "herb tea," even though it probably should've been called "bark tea." When it came time to do it, my dad'd say, "Well, it's time to make us a run of that herb tea. I'll get out and get the bark and stuff."

He'd go through the woods and he'd take a little bark off of, oh, I guess, about every type of tree that grew in the woods, except pine. We didn't use pine, I don't know why. He'd take his pocketknife and slice a narrow cut of bark from white oak, sweet gum and maples. He'd add a little dogwood bark, cherry tree bark, red oak bark, birch bark and some sassafras and put it all in a big pot and boil it down, strain it, and make a tea out of it. That tea would be a real dark color, the color of waterlogged wood. I believe we used molasses to sweeten it, but it didn't help much. That tonic would be so bitter, you had to force yourself to drink it. You sure didn't have a desire to want to drink it. Yeah, you didn't want much of it at a time, neither.

We'd take a swig of it every morning for a while in the spring of the year, when people were having a lot of problems with colds and flu. We took it as a medication, for a preventative. We thought it would keep us from getting sick and it might have helped. We hardly ever had the flu. A lot of people would come down with the flu and it would just go raging in the community. But in our family, we'd always make that spring tonic and we never had much problem.

We took a little better care of ourselves than a lot of people did. We were careful about getting out in bad weather and runnin' around with wet clothes on for half a day. A lot of people would do that, and they'd come down with a terrible cold.

But, I'll tell you, in our family, when one of us got sick, seems like we were worried to death about the one that was sick. We'd do everything we could to help. We just really had a great love for each other.

I wasn't sick very much and Edth wasn't, but Thelma had tonsilitis problems and she'd get sick a lot with that. And we'd worry about her, take care of her and try to help her. We'd just hover over her. It worried my mother and father real bad. 'Cause back then the doctors that they had weren't much—they were just first-aid people, that was about all. And we lived so far away from a hospital, it was just out of the question to think about going to the hospital. So, of course, some strange-seeming solutions for a lot of ailments sprang up back in those hills. And they worked.

For sore throats, we used to go into the woods and get some peach tree bark and several other herbs — I'm not even sure what they were — and we'd put it together and boil it down and Thelma would gargle it, warm. I don't know how many generations back they'd been doin' that — my parents learned it from someone — but for a sore throat, peach tree bark was the thing. It really helped. I reckon it was a whole lot safer than the home remedy I heard about one afternoon down at Dave's Store when I was just a boy.

There were always men sitting around Dave's Store, playing checkers, and this feller I knew came down there, Henry Burnett, he was a bachelor. He was staying with somebody and they'd sent him to the store with a gallon can to get kerosene. They used to have those cans with a spout on them so you could pour the kerosene into a lamp.

Henry was coughin' up a storm, tryin' to buy some kerosene from ol' Dave and Dave wasn't likin' that much. "You oughta get you some of this stuff here, or else get on outta here!" Dave pointed to a bottle of some medicine, but Henry didn't have money to buy it, I don't reckon.

As he left, Henry told some fellers who were standing around the door, "I've had the awfulest cold that I can't get rid of. I'm just a coughin' myself to death."

One of them said, "Take you a big swaller a that kerosene and it'll cut that outta there."

Henry didn't take it there. He went on up the road a ways. It was hot and that kerosene was warm. He turned that can up and he got strangled on that kerosene.

"Oh, law, it come in a hair a killin' me!" he told me about it later on. "It took my breath and I couldn't breathe or nothin'. I must a poured too much down my throat. That kerosene liked to killed me — but it did get rid of my cough."

It's a wonder it didn't kill him, I reckon. I don't know whether those fellers were just having fun with him or not, but people out there would take all kinds of remedies, things they heard about. Everybody had their own theories.

A lot of times you'd hear about somebody who had stomach problems, and people'd always say about it, "Nothin' that a mess of poke sallet won't cure." Poke greens used to grow wild around there, they were real bitter, and people said that if you cooked 'em just right, it was true that they could take care of stomach complaints. And if you didn't cook 'em right, they could make you sick.

Most people on Coker Creek said that strong tobacco on a rag made a good poultice for a sore. They thought tobacco helped it heal faster, and it may have, I don't know.

Some remedies were downright mysterious, but they worked. I remember one time when I was a kid, I stepped on an old, rusty nail—my foot got so sore I couldn't walk on it. I was hobblin' around on my heel, a sufferin'.

An old feller I knew said, "What's ailin' you there, Quinton?"

I told him and he said, "I tell you what you do. When you get home, get you a bucket and put you some hot coals in it, and take you an old felt hat, cut it up into pieces and put them pieces on them hot coals. Hold your foot over it till the coals burn up all them little felt pieces. It'll draw that poison out and 'fore long, your foot'll be fine as fuzz on a frog."

So I tried that. My dad always wore a black felt hat and he'd wear it till he wore it out, and we didn't throw a thing away. I cut up one of his old felt hats with my pocketknife, burned it and held my foot over the smoke like the feller said, and the next day, I could walk on that foot. Most of the soreness went out of it that night, over the smoking coals. I could have gotten lockjaw, I guess, but there was no one to give such a thing as a tetanus shot. So people in the community had their own remedies. I don't know how they came about, or how many of 'em really worked, or if people just thought they did. But I've seen some pretty amazing cures myself.

I personally knew a man who could remove warts. Just by talking with you, he could make your warts disappear in a little while. He was known for that. His name was Pony Payne and there's a mountain up there named after his family, Payne Mountain. When I was about fourteen, I had a lot of warts come up on my hand and I went to Pony Payne, who was a deacon in our church.

He said, "I can't tell you how I do it, and I can't tell you what I'm a gonna say. I'll just whisper it, so you can't hear it. But I can remove them warts—ever one of 'em—if you'll believe what I say."

I agreed to believe it, even though I wouldn't be able to hear it.

Pony Payne bent over my hand and his lips moved for a while. He just mumbled. Then he announced, "Them warts'll go away quicker than they came."

And do you know, in a few days, *every one of those warts disappeared and they never came back.*

All I can think is, it must have been a special gift from God. Of course, someone must have told ol' Pony how to do those things, or how could he have known what the secret was? And when he got old, he passed the secret on to someone in the family. Pony Payne told me that the secret, that knowledge, had to be passed to a woman next. A man could only pass the secret to a woman and she could only pass the knowledge along to a man—at least that's what ol' Pony Payne said.

There were people on Coker Creek who used bags of different herbs and knew just what each herb would do and sick people in the community came to them for cures. We called 'em "herb doctors." The Cherokee Indians, whose language was the source for both the names Tennessee and Coker Creek, they'd taught the white settlers way on back about the local herbs they used for medicine and that knowledge had been handed down to us, too.

Those herb doctors had herbs that were good for kidney trouble, croup, rheumatism, about any ailment. They'd gather roots and leaves in bunches, put them in a paper bag tied with a string, and hang them up to dry in their cabins. When somebody came to their home that needed medicine, they'd take down those bags, select some herbs and make up a tea. Everybody said those herb doctors could cure you in a day or two.

Nobody does that anymore today. And nobody would believe it, but back in the Tennessee hills, in those days, we knew a lot of things that maybe sound ridiculous, but we got along fine with 'em.

We depended on our surroundings for just about everything: shelter, food, medicine, and livelihood. We really lived off the land and we tried to improve on nature every way we could.

We had a big orchard on the slope up behind our house. My Grandmaw Kelley tended it and she had some trees up there that could grow three or four different apple varieties on one tree.

My Grandmaw Kelley, whose name was Cynthia Irene, she was known to everybody as Serene. It suited her well because she was a calm, good-natured woman. There was something about her, kind and gentle, you couldn't keep from lovin' her. But she had her own ideas. She didn't believe a woman's hair should ever be cut; she kept hers balled up on the back of her head. Serene Kelley was a widow and she lived in her son Edd Lee's house, a little ways from our house, but she was the one who kept our orchard up. She had the greenest thumb of anyone I ever knew.

Grandmaw Kelley was tall and graceful like the trees she tended and she was an expert at grafting fruit trees. She showed me how to do it. She'd cut a little slit in the trunk of an apple tree and take a young limb from another variety of apple tree and cut the end into a V. Then she'd place that limb in a crosswise fashion into that slit on the tree, bandage it up with cloth and tie it. The limb would usually start growing right away, and in a season or two, it would bear fruit.

When I was a kid I'd go up in that orchard and she'd reach out and pluck a red apple and hand it to me. I'd look up, and on other limbs of the same tree, other kinds of apples would still be green. The Sweet June Sweet would get ripe first, then on another branch, some Yellow Delicious would start comin' in. Grandmaw would have an established trunk supporting kinds of apples that were harder to grow if you didn't graft them onto a heartier trunk. It improved the fruit, it would grow bigger. She'd usually graft on a limb of tart apples, too — they were good for fruitcakes. The Thompson Sour or the Limber Twigs were her favorites.

I loved them all. I'd go up that hill pretty regular all through my years at the homeplace. Grandmaw's orchard was almost magical to me. Every summer we had plums and sweet cherries and one whole hill in peaches, nearly. We picked bushels and bushels of peaches some years. You could walk under those trees and grab you a peach and bite into it and the juices would just drip, sweet and warm from the sunshine.

Just about everything we ate grew right out of the earth, eaten with hardly any delay — fruits and vegetables at their peak. I loved the growing and harvesting seasons because food was abundant. Of course, it required hard work six days a week, three seasons a year, but we grew healthy and strong because of it.

In the spring, just as soon as it got out of danger of frost, we'd plant our crops and spread that barnyard manure. If we planted too early, it'd come a big frost and kill the tender shoots and then we'd have to do it over.

We'd try to wait till the signs of the moon were favorable, then plant our corn and beans and potatoes, all the things you can plant early. We used the moon to go by, whether it was a full moon or a new moon. Most crops have a tendency to get taller if you plant them in the new of the moon, as the moon begins to wax, then your corn will grow tall before it puts on the ears. But if you plant corn just after the full of the moon, as it begins to wane, it doesn't get so tall, and then the plant is stockier, the stalk is thicker and the plants look healthier. The ears of corn are more firm and have more grains of corn on them. We liked to plant our corn so it didn't grow too tall, so we'd wait for the full moon. We tried to do that, if the weather didn't interfere with our planting days.

Most people in the community planted like that, following the phases of the moon and the signs, generally what's found in a Farmer's Almanac today. People thought it worked good. I know one feller on Coker Creek who didn't, though. He said, "I don't plant my crops in the moon, I plant 'em in the ground!" And he did pretty well, too. You can plant about anytime and get a yield, but it just does better at certain times.

If it come time that we needed to plant and the moon wasn't right, we'd just go ahead and plant and we always did all right. But we could tell a difference when we planted by the signs. Tomatoes, okra, butter beans, greasy back beans, yellow squash, pumpkins, cabbage, peas, and mustard greens were some of the foods we raised and we always got a good yield.

We raised a lot of onions and we dug them up according to the phases of the moon, so they would keep longer through the winter. If you dig onions at the full of the moon or after, they won't rot in the cellar, but if you dig them in the new of the moon, they won't last through the winter, they'll just start turning mushy within a few weeks. We usually raised sweet potatoes and Irish potatoes, too, and we'd dig them according to the moon, so they wouldn't sprout right away.

We had a shed by the side of our corncrib and we'd put the potatoes in there and we'd cover them. My mother would save all her frayed quilts that were 'bout wore out and we'd cover the potatoes with those quilts. Sometimes we'd put some straw on 'em if we didn't have enough quilts to keep the potatoes from freezing. That way we'd eat off of 'em all winter long.

Some of our crops were more like treats. We raised peanuts, which we roasted in the shell, and sorghum cane for the sweet syrup that came from it. People where I grew up called it "sawgum," now a lot of people call it molasses. We ate it like you would maple syrup, put it on pancakes, ate it with butter and biscuits. My mother used that sorghum molasses instead of sugar when she baked. That's about all we'd use for sweetener most of the time. That molasses was thick and gooey and as sweet as it was dark. It was almost black.

We raised cane every year to get our molasses. There was a lot of work to that sorghum cane. We put out cane seed. Cane has a fine seed and you sow it in rows. It's not in hills the way you plant corn, so many feet apart. We'd make furrows in the ground and sprinkle the seed real close together. It comes up real thick. Then you've got to thin it out, if you want it to grow tall and big. When it gets ready, it'll "head out"—have big heads on it, full of seeds.

My dad would go through the field when the cane got about ripe and break the heads down. If you turn them upside down, the seeds won't shatter out so much. Then, when the seed goes to turnin' brown, it's time to cut that cane down.

All five of us'd go through the fields and cut the cane down and strip all the fodder off of it. Cut the heads off and pile them up—we kept that to feed the chickens. They really liked that cane seed; you didn't have to shell it, just throw the cane heads out and the chickens would pick the seed out of the bunch.

Then we'd cut the cane into pieces to make molasses and we'd load up our wagon and mule and take that cane to a molasses mill. Some of our neighbors had a place to make molasses. They'd run that cane through some rollers and just squeeze the juice out. They'd boil it down and turn it into molasses. There was an art to that, to make it come out sweet and not bitter. We'd usually get a yield of maybe thirty-five or forty gallons at one time and we'd have to give a certain percent of that to the man who made it, usually it was a third of the yield, for processing it. And we'd have enough to do us till the next season.

We saved our own seed, potatoes, and corn kernels to start the garden with each season. We tried to pick out the biggest and the best of the crop for seed. We figured we'd grow better crops if we picked out the best ones for seed and, of course, it worked.

We always had the prettiest, plumpest ears of corn you ever saw. We only grew white corn to eat on. Yellow corn was what we used for animal feed. We'd grow enough corn for us to eat on in the summer, to feed the animals, to save for seed, and to have enough ground cornmeal to make cornbread till the next year. That was a lot of corn. We raised several acres of corn, and we spent a lot of time working in it. We didn't waste a bit of it, neither.

We'd strip the fodder off of the stalks, leave the stalks bare and cut that fodder up, put it in the barn to feed the livestock. All we'd have out in the field when we went to gather our corn would be the ears of corn up on the stalk. The corn would dry out a lot faster after it matured when you strip all that off—the air and sun got to it better.

You could gather the corn a little earlier by doing it that way.

When we harvested, we did what we called "slipshuckin'." When you pull the ears of corn off the stalk, you leave most of the outside shuck on the stalk. We'd just keep a little thin layer of shuck around the ears, the grains of corn, but we didn't want to carry all of those thick shucks in and have to put them in the corncrib. We had more room in the crib if we slipshucked the corn.

What was left in the field, the shucks and stalks, we'd grind that up and we used it for feeding the cattle. And the roots we left in the field—we'd go through there and chop them up and they would rot and fertilize the soil. So we did use every bit of our corn plants to our advantage.

After harvest, we had to get the corn ground up into meal. We loaded that corn in big meal sacks made of white canvas material, and we'd take our corn to the mill in that sack and when they ground it, they'd put the cornmeal back in the same sack.

When the grist mill was open, my dad was usually working away from home and my mother didn't have a way of taking it, so it was always up to me to take the corn to mill. I was a young boy when I started doin' that chore, just maybe six years old, something like that. I wasn't even big enough to put a sack of corn on a mule. Corn is heavy, if you've got a bag of it. It took my two strong sisters and my mother to load it on the mule at home.

The first time I went to mill, I took off down the road and I was a ridin' that mule, had a saddle on there. I had the sack of corn on the mule, it was a layin' up behind me. Before I got to the mill, though, that sack of corn slid off the mule right in the middle of the road.

It happened on a road where there was high bank on one side. I saw that bank and said to myself, "Now, reckon I can drag that corn up there and use that to help me?" The mule's back was about as high as that bank.

I was scared, 'cause I didn't know what I was gonna do. That put a little more pep in me. I dragged that sack of corn down the road and up on that bank. I led that mule over to the side of the road and he just stayed where I put him. He was a good mule.

I was able to push that corn off the bank, right onto the mule's back and then I went on to the mill. If I hadn't got that corn on the mule in a few tries, I'd have gone on to the mill and found somebody to help me, but I was just determined to do it myself.

A few years later when I got a little older, I had a yoke of oxen and a two-wheeled cart for that job. I'd hook those oxen to that cart and take 'em to the grist mill to get the corn ground into the meal we'd use to make our cornbread. We just about lived on cornbread. Cornbread and beans. Cornbread and buttermilk. Cornbread and butter 'n' honey. Cornbread, molasses and sassafras tea.

"I don't believe you can handle that plow, yet, son," my dad would say when I asked him if I could plow the field, to help him out. That was when I was probably about nine or ten. He kept putting me off and I kept wanting to plow the field and finally, a year or two later, he decided that he'd let me try it. It was a single foot plow, just had a big shovel blade.

I picked it right up, didn't have any trouble. So, from then on, I got to do all the plowing. Our mule was so well trained, when you went through the field, if you wanted him to turn to the right or left at the end of the row, you'd turn him that direction the first time, and from then on, you could plow all day long and when you got to the end of each row, he'd turn the way you wanted him to, every time, on his own. He never would turn the wrong way. His name was Joe. I remember my dad always calling him Joe-Boy. He was a red mule. When red mules get older, they turn gray, and we kept ol' Joe-Boy till he became an ol' gray mule.

The feller who sold that mule to my dad told him, "Now, you'll have to put a muzzle on 'im when the corn gets big enough and you go to plowin' your corn, he'll be a eatin' your corn, nippin' off them tops."

The first time our corn got big enough that he could get it, sure enough, that mule reached down and jerked off a stalk and my dad just stopped him right there in the middle of the field. He went around and pried that mule's mouth open and packed it full of big, crumbly clods of dirt.

He never had to do that again and he never had to put a muzzle on that mule. It didn't hurt the mule. Joe-Boy never did bother the corn after that. That mule understood what he'd done wrong. He was real smart.

Now, the thing about that mule — the man who sold him to us raised him from a colt and he'd kept that poor mule shut up in a barn all his young life. When my dad first got Joe-Boy, he let him run out free in the pasture to graze. Well, that mule was so happy he was free, he'd see my dad a comin' and he'd start his brayin' and he'd take off a runnin' towards him so fast, I's afraid he wouldn't stop, just run my dad over. But he'd always come to a halt and let my dad pat his neck. Ol' Joe-Boy turned out to be the best mule we ever had. My dad should've never traded him off.

For years and years, when my dad was gone to work I'd plow all the fields with Joe-Boy and get them ready to plant seed. I'd plow one furrow and move over, and plow the next one till the dirt would break over in the first furrow, just like my dad told me to. I kept his rows straight, and he noticed that.

"You did a fine job on that, Quinton," he'd say.

If some of our crops were already coming up and my dad wanted us to plow between the rows to take out weeds, I couldn't use Joe-Boy.

"That mule's big feet'll trample all over those young plants," my dad'd say.

So, then, my two sisters would harness up — they were strong enough to pull that big plow — and I'd get behind the plow to guide it, and the three of us would plow between the rows of corn. That was just about like play for us. Then we'd take a hoe and go through the garden a choppin' out the rest of the weeds so they wouldn't take the substance out of the soil, and we raked a little dirt around each stalk of corn. We always plowed three times a season and worked the garden by hand. That kept the soil loose and the crops grew better.

My dad worked in the fields right beside us when he could. Back when I was growin' up, families hoed their cornfields together, tended them regularly all through the growing season. Some people would call it the simple life. About everyone would call it a hard life. We never were idle. But we were, by and large, always happy. We thought life was wonderful. I wouldn't have traded it off for what life is like today, I don't guess.

Everybody, it seemed like, was in a good mood—talkin' and laughin' and pickin' at each other. That's all I knew and I enjoyed it. I don't regret that I had to live that way. I think it did something to me that made me a survivor, more of a survivor than if I'd had it easy. I had a pretty tough time, but it didn't bother me, why, I thought nothin' about it. In fact, it gave me somethin' inside. I know you can survive without having everything that you want. And enjoy yourself. 'Cause I done that.

I was a happy young boy when I grew up at the homeplace. Nothin' didn't ever seem to bother me at all. I went about "a whistlin' and a sin-gin'," as my sisters said. They were always talking about how they could tell where I was at, just by listenin'.

I'd whistle a little tune as I went to the spring, swingin' the empty buckets in rhythm, or maybe I'd sing an old spiritual on my way to the cornfields with my hoe on my shoulder.

★ ★ ★

Popcorn was my project. I'd sow my own popcorn with the seed I'd saved from the year before. After all our eating corn was harvested, I'd let the popcorn stay on the stalk till it dried out some. Then I'd go through the garden, put the ears in a burlap bag, and hang it to dry. Took about two weeks to dry out good. I could hardly wait to start a poppin'. By then, I'd already popped all of what I'd grown the year before, I liked popcorn so good.

To see if that corn would pop, I'd take an ear—it had to be a deep, golden yellow—and I'd pick the kernels off the cob and cook them in a cast iron skillet with a lid. I could eat a skilletful in the blink of an eye. Pretty soon I made myself a popcorn popper out of a five-gallon bucket.

My dad had his personal project, too—he always raised a crop of tobacco. He raised it just for his own use and he wouldn't let any of us work in it, we couldn't even touch it. We had a brush pile, where we'd clean up around fences and buildings, and we'd put all our trash in that brush pile and burn it. The fire would kill all the weeds and it made a good place to have a seed bed. That's where my dad raised his tobacco, in that seed bed. He didn't raise much, but sometimes he'd take a spell where he'd smoke that tobacco for two or three weeks, then he'd quit smokin' it. But he'd always chew. Chew and spit. He was lost without his tobacco. One thing was for sure, though. He didn't want me to touch it.

What would my dad have done if he'd seen me tryin' to smoke or chew his tobacco? He'd have given me a whippin'—you better believe it. 'Cause I'd really have violated one of his strict rules.

Sometimes, he'd mention the difference between what he did and what he wanted me to do. He'd say, "Now, Quinton, I've got the habit. And it's hard for me to quit. I'm not gonna allow you to do it, 'cause I don't want you to get them bad habits. Law, me—it's an awful thing to let that ol' tobacco get ahold of you." He'd always tell us why he was strict about something. He said to me, "Once you get that habit, you can't hardly quit. You're miserable without it."

My daddy wasn't a perfect example, of course. But he made up for it by admitting his shortcomings, talking with us about it, and tellin' us how to avoid his mistakes. I always respected him enough to listen to him when he had something to say to me, even though I was just a typical kid who liked to try things out for myself.

Oh, like any boy, I tasted of his tobacco a time or two, when nobody was lookin', but I never could stand it. I'd say to myself, "I don't see how in the world anybody can chew that stuff! It tastes awful."

I remember smoking part of a cigarette I found once, too, and when I went to eat my dinner, I could hardly taste a thing. I said, "Anything with a taste that stays in your mouth like that, well, that ain't for me. I like to enjoy tastin' my food."

It's good I got broke from tobacco when I was a boy. I never did want to try it again. But my daddy, he had that habit the rest of his life, and I'm satisfied he wished he didn't.

★ ★ ★

From where we lived, we could hear the whistle blow from Stokley's canning factory down in Tellico Plains, ten miles away. Stokley's was a company that canned local produce—green beans, corn, and so forth. They also had a big farming operation down in that valley, row after row of crops. They grew enough food for an army and they employed a lot of people to work out in those fields.

You could hear the whistle blow through those mountains for twelve o'clock, to signal to the pickers that it was dinnertime. Then they'd blow it for quittin' time. And, of course, in the morning, they'd blow it when it was time to start work. We kept up with the time of day like that. My dad was always checking his chiming clock by that whistle and that was the only way he had of knowing if his clock was set right, by Stokley's blowin' that whistle down in Tellico. If the wind was right, you could hear the train whistle from down there, too. It would echo through the hills, a long wail that faded away.

"*Waaaaahhh . . . WAAAA-aaaahhh . . .*"

The train wasn't hardly on time like Stokley's sharp, one-note whistles.

We'd all look forward to hearing that noontime whistle blow, 'cause we knew what that meant. It was time for my mother to go to the house, clean up and prepare a meal. It was what we all worked for. We ate three meals a day. A certain time would come, we had a meal.

When she got the meal just about prepared, she'd holler from the porch and we could hear her for a long ways. She had a real loud voice for a little woman, for any woman.

"Dinner! Dinner! Come and get it!"

We'd rush to the house to eat our dinner—which was our main meal, in the middle of the day. We didn't have "lunch." Lunch was only when we went on a picnic or took food out to work. Dinner was what everybody called the midday meal—the big meal—and "supper" was the evening meal. Supper usually wasn't much, just cornbread and buttermilk a lot of times. We'd crumble it up in the milk and eat it with a spoon.

When we worked in the field, we'd work barefooted most of the time, so when we'd come in, we'd all have to take a foot bath and wash our legs. I'd usually have my overall legs turned up two or three turns to keep from getting them dirty in the field. We'd wash our feet and hands on the back porch with some of the water buckets. Then we'd come in and sit down around the kitchen table.

It was a simple pine table with straight legs, a long rectangle made out of boards that weren't matched together, but they fit tight. My dad had built it, planed it by hand, smoothed it down. My mother kept the table covered with an oilcloth in different colors from time to time. We had room for the five of us to eat around the table and a little extra room for company. We sat in slatted-backed chairs on cushions that my mother sewed from scraps of cloth.

If dinner wasn't ready by the time we got washed up and we had to wait for it, my dad would drum his fingers on the table and he'd tap out a little tune. A lot of times, though, my mother would sit on my dad's lap until dinner was ready, and she'd put her arms around his neck, and they'd talk until the cornbread had a good golden crust. My parents really enjoyed each other's company. If they ever had a cross word, I never did know it. We all enjoyed bein' together, especially at dinnertime and every one of us loved my mother's good country cookin'.

My mother had some good white porcelain dishes to set the table and she served simple food: potatoes, beans, cornbread, maybe some greens, right from the kettles and skillets on the woodstove. We all drank milk. If we wanted something sweet, we'd eat honey. That was usually about all we had for dinner on a regular day. It wasn't always that we had meat or game. Didn't matter what we ate, though, we'd clean our plates, just about lick them clean.

About every afternoon, everybody in the family would go to bed and take a little nap before they went back to the field to work. Usually, I didn't want to lie down, I wanted to do something else.

Now, sometimes I was a little bit *mischeevious*. I started sneaking into my dad's blacksmith shop when I thought everybody was asleep. He kept a lot of tools in there and he kept it locked.

One day, he asked my sister Thelma, "Do you know anything 'bout somebody a goin' in my shop? Somebody's been movin' my tools around."

She told him, "Quinton's been a goin' in there. He goes in through the buggy shed and he crawls in the shop between the logs."

Thelma told me that my dad said, "Well, if that boy wants to work with tools that bad, I'll take the lock off, and let him at it." And he did.

After that, most afternoons while everyone slept a little nap I'd usually be around my daddy's blacksmith shop, working on a wagon or bicycle. I'd just work on it a little at a time when I didn't have to do chores. I was always comin' up with an idea for some two-, three-, or four-wheeled design, especially anything that went fast. I'd get it built, tinker with it, and *look out*! For a long time, I was the fastest kid on Coker Creek.

CHAPTER 6

How to Make an American Wagon Wheel

I was raised to be truthful and I nearly got in trouble one time when I told what everybody thought was a tall tale. I was pretty young, not old enough to go to school, and my cousins were out at our homeplace a playin' with June bugs—big, green beetles that buzz around during the hot summer days. They were catchin' those June bugs and they'd tie a string to one of the bug's legs, hold on to that string, and those bugs would fly around and around in a big circle. That was something boys did a lot on Coker Creek. We'd all get a kick out of that.

I said to my cousins, "Aw, that's nothin'. I caught me some June bugs and I tied them to a wagon and I had them pullin' a wagon."

My daddy heard that and he really got on me. He said, "Now, Quinton! You shouldn't tell no such a story as that."

"But it's true, Daddy," I said. And really, it was.

I had made a little wagon, fashioned it out of corn stalks. I took the husks that you strip off the stalks, used little sticks like toothpicks and pinned the husks together to make a four-sided "wagon." I made the wheels out of slices of the hard cornstalks that I cut with my pocket-knife. Then I took a twig off a tree and made a front and rear axle and slipped the wheels on the ends. I took some thread and I tied a team of June bugs to that little cornstalk wagon. The June bugs tried to fly away, of course, but they were weighted down by my wagon. Then the wheels moved and the little wagon scooted over the floorboards of the porch. That team of June bugs pulled it across the floor! Oh, that just tickled me.

As a kid, I was always making vehicles to play with, especially ones that I could ride. I started out with wagons that I could use to coast downhill. My dad made my first wagon for me. He repaired wagons and he made wagon wheels for people in the community. So, of course, I got the pattern from there.

Will Kelley was known in the community for his well-made wagon wheels. I remember watching him make wheels at his blacksmith shop and I helped him when I got old enough.

To make a wagon wheel, first, he had to make the wooden spokes to fit in the hub of the wheel. He'd cut and plane the spokes out of oak that he'd split out. Oak is strong and the grain runs straight. He'd find wood like that when we were out hunting. My dad could look at a tree and tell if it would suit the job he had in mind.

He'd see a tree and say, "That'll make me some good wheel spokes."

We'd cut the tree down, saw it up. Then he'd split that oak out with an ax and he'd let it dry out. He'd have it layin' up, ready, in his black-smith shop.

To make the spokes for the wagon wheels, he'd take the oak strips, put one in his vice and take what he called a "drawin' knife, 'cause you draw it towards you," he said, and he'd shape up the spoke like he wanted it. The spokes would be about two feet long, and they were tapered from the hub out to the rim.

The hub of the wheel is drilled out for spokes with a row of rectangu-lar holes. My dad would drive the spokes down in the holes all the way around that hub and then he'd put the rim on the outside.

Like the rest of the wheel, the rim is made of wood. The rim, or wooden tire, came in four or more curved sections. It depended on how big the wheel was, might have six on a big wheel. My dad would fit the spokes into the holes on the rim sections, then to keep it all together, he'd put a metal band on the outside of that wheel. The metal band was the tricky part.

My dad would buy metal bands and he'd curve them in the black-smith shop and measure them to fit the wheel when he was done. He had a way of measuring them, but he didn't have a tape measure, nothin' like that. Livin' like we did, we had to figure things out for ourselves, how to do something, make it from scratch, 'cause we didn't have nothin' much that was ready-made. My dad made a lot of his own tools.

He'd made a little disk about an eight inch diameter out of a thin piece of wood. It had a handle and a pin that went through it so the disk would turn. To measure, he'd make a mark on that round disk and he'd make a mark on the rim of the wagon wheel. He'd start rolling that disk around the wagon wheel and he'd count how many times his disk rotated. When he got back to his mark, it might not come out exactly on the mark, but he knew how to make the adjustments.

Then he'd lay the metal band out and roll the measuring wheel over it, to measure how much to cut. He had a formula and he made the band a little smaller than the wagon wheel. When he heated the band, it expanded and he knew just how much smaller to make it so it would fit that wheel when he got done.

He took the metal band, cut it with a notch in one end and a point on the other, and he put the ends together. He'd heat that in the forge till it started melting, then he'd jerk it out of the fire, hammer it, and the metal would just run together. Made a loop. Then he'd heat that loop and it would expand so he could slip it on the wagon wheel. You have to have that wagon wheel a layin' flat.

He'd take tongs—me and him together—we'd take tongs and we'd pick up that glowing-hot band and lay it down around the wagon wheel and he'd pick that wheel up right away. If we didn't get it in the water pretty quick, it would set the wooden rim afire. It'd burn it a little bit black anyway, but that made it shrink up good.

My dad had a shallow depression in the ground that held water. As soon as he put the band around the wheel, he'd stand the wheel up and roll it in that water and it would just steam and sizzle. As the water cooled, that metal band would go to shrinkin'. It would draw down, pop and crack, and it would just pull those spokes down tight into the hub and into the rim, too.

My dad knew just how much smaller to make that band, so it would draw tight, really tight. Then you've got a really good wheel. If you don't get that band tight enough, you don't have a good wheel. It will come off when you get to using it. And, just as important, you had to have a certain amount of "dish."

A wagon wheel needs to be dished so when the pressure goes on it, the spokes won't shoot through the hub. Where that comes from, if you take a dinner plate, the center of it sits lower than the edges when it's laying flat and that's where they get the term "dish." The wheel is not straight up and down, it leans out a little bit from the axle, all the way around. If it wasn't like that, when you get on a hillside, the pressure would make that wheel buckle the wrong way and just come apart. That pressure, it's got to go somewhere. When a wheel is dished, it puts the pressure so that the wheel tightens up, and it'll tighten the band. You have to know a lot about making wagon wheels to get the right amount of dish. If you get that band too tight, it'll dish the wheel too much. My dad made sure he had that right, so when somebody was using their wagon on a slope, or going around the side of a hill, his wheel wouldn't buckle through itself. He'd lay the wheel down and press it in the right direction. If he got it turned wrong, he couldn't use it then. He'd have to take that band off and start over.

There were not a lot of people who could make wagon wheels anymore, even back then. There were only two people in the community who made wagon wheels. I really don't know what my dad charged people for a job like that. It was a pretty good job to make a wagon wheel, but my dad made them quicker and cheaper than you could buy them from the factory. And a lot better because he handpicked his wood. He made wagon wheels for that whole community, and he made buggy wheels the same way.

I was always right there to do my part of the job when I was a boy.

"Quinton, now, keep focused on the task at hand," my dad'd say if my attention wandered. I'd pump my bellows and keep his fire going, help my dad get the wheel in the water and all of that, so, naturally, I learned all about making wheels and wagons, too.

I must have built at least a half dozen wagons or more when I was a kid. I had one all the time, and I rode 'em pretty hard. I couldn't have been more than seven or eight when I made my first wagon. I had to use scrap wood, whatever I could find. I got a lot of wooden boards from an old moonshine operation that the law busted up and I made my wagons from that. I cut out the wooden parts in my dad's blacksmith shop and I made the metal parts in the forge from my dad's scraps. The first wagon I started out with, about all that I had was a board and four wheels. I guided the front axle with my feet. I'd take my wagon up the hill and coast down.

One wagon had a little bed on the back of it, made to haul stuff, and I'd go up the hill behind our house and get wood for Momma when it was washin' day. She'd fill a cast iron kettle full of water, put a big fire under there and boil those clothes. Mother always boiled our clothes. It would really get them clean.

I'd load the firewood on my wagon and come a flyin' down to the little spring where she did her washin' and I'd ride that wagon right through the creek with a splash. Then I'd deliver Momma's firewood and tow that wagon back up the hill for another load. Yeah, washin' day was a lot of fun.

As I got a few years older, I got to making the wagons a little better. I wanted one with wheels that turned like they did on a car, with a steering wheel.

My dad didn't want me wastin' my time, so he said, "Why, son, you know you can't do that. You just don't have the means to do it."

That just made me more determined. I found some chain somewhere and I fixed the wheels so they turned independent of the axle, and I could control them with that chain. I put in a steering wheel and made me some foot brakes. I'd ride that wagon down the hill behind our house and I'd steer right through the buggy barn. It had double doors on each end, and I'd come down that hill just a flyin' and my dad was always saying to me, "Now, son, if you stray just a little, you'll miss that doorway and run into my plow, or hit the side of the barn and really hurt yourself."

But he didn't tell me not to do it, just to be careful. So I kept doin' it. I never did get hurt. Oh, I'd just zoom through that barn from one end to the other, a whoopin' and a hollerin', and I'd keep on a goin' and guide that wagon till I splashed right across the creek. Then I'd tow my wagon back up the hill and ride down again.

A group of my cousins would come over on Sundays after church, just farm boys in Sunday overalls, from both sides of the family. While the uncles and aunts sat on the front porch after dinner and talked up a storm, a bunch of us'd get out and ride.

We'd take turns riding one of my wagons, leaning forward, trying to be the one to go the fastest. Or we'd get out on those country lanes and we'd bounce over bumps and washouts. It'd 'bout jar your teeth out. Oh, we kicked up some dust with those little ol' wagons. I even made some with a hood on them. By that time, they were more like a go-cart.

I graduated to making bicycles. First, I made them with no brakes. I'd just slide my feet on the dirt when I wanted to stop. I kept doing a better job on the next one, putting brakes on them, handlebars and everything. I got to making them more like a bicycle should be. I did make one with pedals on it, but I didn't have the right kind of a sprocket or I could have pedaled that bicycle. I tried to use a chain that I had, but it wouldn't work, so I gave up on that idea. So I had to walk the bicycle up the hills and ride down. 'Course, out on Coker Creek, there were plenty of hills to keep me a goin'.

I made one bicycle with a big buggy wheel in the back. I guess it must have been four and a half feet tall. It had a regular small wheel in the front, and that bicycle would really pick up speed down a hill with that big buggy wheel a pushin' it.

Two of my cousins and I were riding it one day and one of my neighbors, an older feller, came along and said, "Would you boys care if I rode that thing? I'd like to ride that."

I said, "No, you can ride it if you want to."

We almost knew that he couldn't ride it. Out on Coker Creek, back then, it was as rare to have a bicycle as it was to have a car. I didn't tell him that he had to know how to balance himself on it, and he didn't know that. We were a little bit eager to see what kind of a show he might put on.

He climbed up on that big buggy-wheeled bicycle and he said, "Now, give me a little shove and get me started."

We gave him a pretty good shove and got that thing to goin' and he went down the hill and right away he saw he couldn't do a thing with it. He looked like he was scared to death. That's when he went right off the hill and landed in a big blackberry patch, a briar thicket.

He came out of the bushes all scratched up. Boy, he had a sad look on his face. Of course, my cousins and I were just howlin' with laughter. It tickled us to death.

That feller told that story on me everywhere he went, after that. He'd tell it differently than it happened, though. He'd say, "Them boys talked me into ridin' that contraption and they run me off down in a briar patch!" He never did come around and ask to ride anything again.

One day, I was riding one of my bicycles on a path that went down to the spring. My sister Edth started to go to the spring to get a bucket of water. I hollered at her, "You better get out of the trailway, I'm com-ing down through here!"

She said, "I'm not a movin'!" She just kept on walking down the trailway.

I guided the bicycle off the trailway to miss her, but she stepped over there, too—and I hit her. Boy, it knocked her for a loop. If Edth had stayed in the trailway, like she said, I wouldn't have hit her, but she stepped right in front of me. Oh, I hated that so bad. I knocked her down and that really made her mad. Didn't hurt her, though.

I yelled, "Well, I told you!" and I flew by, movin' on down that hill, pickin' up speed. I was just a kid and, oh, the faster I went, the happier I was. I'd let that bicycle go just as fast as it would go down whatever hill

I was on. I didn't put the brakes on for nothin'. It's a wonder I didn't get killed doin' that all the time.

I was going down a long hill one day, one of my neighbors was walking down the road—you can't hear a bicycle hardly, it just comes up on you—and, boy, I mean I zoomed by him in a fly. The wind behind me just ruffled up his clothes and he grabbed his hat. I looked back and laughed.

I loved wheels because they represented a little more freedom. I could get out, go down to Dave's Store and pick up our mail a lot quicker if I was coastin' down those hills half the time. That's about as far as I'd go on my homemade bicycles. But some wheels took me a lot further.

Wheels were the ticket to my favorite treats—those rare occasions when we would hitch up the buggy and go to town. I looked forward to getting a few things I didn't have at home.

We'd have to ride for about three hours to get to Tellico Plains. It was a hard ride, and usually it was just me and my dad.

We passed the time talking back and forth to each other. A lot of times we'd talk about what we saw along the road. He'd say, So and So lives over there in that house. And he'd tell me if he had a job, where he worked, what he did, who built his house and all that. We knew pretty much everybody's business in the community.

My dad, and I guess everybody, knew who was makin' moonshine. I remember one place he pointed out. Said, "Look over there, where that chimley's a standin' in the woods. A man was killed in that house."

The chimney was all that was left.

My dad said, "They killed that man and burnt his house down all for moonshine." He told me about the feller who'd been killed, he was a pretty decent kind of a feller. I don't remember whether he was a deputy sheriff, or what, but he reported some fellers for making moonshine. And these bunch of moonshiners, that's the reason they killed him. They burned the house down and burned his body up in there. Got rid of the evidence. But the people on Coker Creek knew who did it.

As far as I know, those moonshiners got clean away with the crime. I don't really know a whole lot about it, only what my dad told me. That chimney stood in the clearing alongside the old road to Tellico Plains for years. Every time I'd pass there, I'd think about that.

Back in that day, people were always afraid to go down a hill with a buggy or wagon, afraid their brakes would give way, afraid the buggy would run over their horse. My daddy worried about that whenever we were going anywhere in our buggy. He'd always talk about it. Our buggy didn't have brakes on it, but the horse had a rigid harness attached to it and that held the buggy back. My dad was always afraid that the harness might give way and, if it did, the buggy would bump into the horse, and the horse would run to get out of the way. It could run us off a steep embankment, right off into a ravine. It never did happen, but it could have happened. Those old roads were steep grades. They'd just go 'bout straight up a hill or straight down a hill. They didn't wind around the hills like they do today to get a good grade on the road.

A buggy rides pretty soft; it has springs so it bounces a little, but if we had crossties to sell, we'd take our wagon. A wagon doesn't have any springs and, boy, it's rough riding. You didn't relax on that ride. Of course, it was just an old dirt road we traveled, and it'd get ditched out. We'd jostle over washed-out gullies and keep close to the mountainside on the curves. The edges of the road, along the bank, they'd break off with you, if you got too close. And, of course, in a lot of places it was just straight down the mountain if you happened to get off the road.

I knew a feller who hauled his groceries in a wagon—he owned a little shack that sold a few items—and back then, you had to haul what you sold, you had to go to Tellico Plains to get it. This feller went down to Tellico and he got several bags of flour, meal, and sugar, all kinds of dry goods that he sold at a roadside stand. He had a full wagonload, and he was coming up the mountain. This feller was walking behind his team of mules to keep them from having to pull his weight up that hill.

The old mountain road had a turn so crooked, you came around a curve and you almost doubled back on yourself—a switchback. Somebody with a T-Model came along and that T-Model met the wagon coming around that switchback. It scared those mules and they started bucking and braying and they went so wild they ran that wagon off the mountain backwards.

That wagon tumbled way down in a deep holler, almost straight down. The feller climbed down in there to see about his mules and he found all his flour, meal, and sugar littered down the side of that mountain. At the bottom, the old mules were down there grazing around. They'd broken loose from the wagon and they still had part of their harness on and they were just standin' around, a nibblin' grass.

Somebody came along and they took that wagon apart and they carried it piece by piece up to the road and put it back together and the feller hooked up his team. Of course, he lost his groceries. It was a big loss to him. It probably just about shut him down. I heard about things like that happening from time to time.

A lot of people would have trouble pulling a load through there. One time I saw a man with a mule team hauling lumber and the old mules balked on him. They wouldn't pull the load up a steep hill. The old man, he got a switch and he whipped those mules. It was a sight how he whipped those mules. I was feeling so sorry for one of the mules especially. One mule was trying to pull the load and the other one wouldn't help it. That man just liked to beat those mules to death, but they finally pulled that load up over the hill.

Big trucks never went out to Coker Creek—they couldn't cross that mountain. To go through there, it was just a one-lane road and those roads were as crooked as a snake, 'cause they'd followed pig trails when they made 'em.

About all that could travel over that old mountain road was a buggy or wagon. Eventually, there got to being a few T-Models out there and a T-Model can go almost anywhere a wagon can go, the way they're made. They had big wheels on them and I guess they got the idea from the wagon to make the T-Model, I don't know. When I was a boy, there were two fellers in the community who had T-Models, and the mail carrier had a T-Model, and that's all the cars there were for a long time.

Sears and Roebuck used to send everybody a catalog and they'd usually come in around the same time and the mail carrier would get overloaded. That T-Model couldn't cross those mountains with all of those Sears catalogs. I was told that when the mail carrier came to Coker Creek, a lot of times he'd take the catalogs out and just throw them away, 'cause he couldn't haul 'em. Of course, people didn't know why they didn't get their Sears catalog, but they were laying somewhere on the mountain in a culvert back under the road.

Even with those roads as bad as they were, I don't believe we ever had any trouble when my dad and I went to Tellico Plains. Usually, it was just a big thrill to get to go somewhere.

We approached the town of Tellico Plains by the dirt road until we got just a little ways outside of town. I remember when they paved that dirt road through the town, I was pretty young. My dad fussed about that. He said, "Oh, now, there they've put that blacktop. That'll wear them horses' shoes out. They can't stand up on that stuff." That was back when there weren't cars much, just wagons and horses and mules. He fussed about that every time we went to town.

The town of Tellico Plains was one short street with stores on one side. On the other side of the street was the train depot. The cargo train came in there once a day and it went right back behind the buildings and up along the river until they could get it switched and turn the train around in the switchyard.

We used to go to that switchyard when we sold our railroad crossties. There was a man there who would buy them and they'd ship them out to lay on the tracks. We'd get our money, then go to one of the stores.

Tellico Plains had a handful of stores—a couple of stores that sold groceries and a drugstore that sold all kinds of medications. The main place we went, and everybody went, was the general store.

Best I remember, it was a two-story weatherboarded building, with quarters above. Seems like it was Watson's General Store, but I won't say for sure. My dad knew the man who ran the store, and he'd go in there and talk with him for a while. They carried a lot of hardware, horseshoes and nails and all kinds of items for the house—clocks and kettles. They didn't carry a lot of ready-made clothes, but they had some women's dresses and men's work clothes. Back then, people had to make most of their clothes themselves unless they went to a bigger city or ordered them from Sears. It was just a country store.

I remember one time we were in that general store—this was way back when I wasn't old enough to go to school yet—I'd come along for the ride and I had my eye on a treat. My dad had sold some oak crossties that morning, ones he'd hewn out himself, but money was always tight. I never would ask him for anything. But I really wanted him to buy me some cheese and crackers.

Used to, if you bought so many ounces of cheese, they'd cut it off and they'd throw in so many crackers. That was included in it and they'd put the crackers in a paper bag for you to eat with your cheese. They didn't charge extra. They had a big round barrel of crackers sittin' right there in the general store.

At that time, they used to buy the crackers in wooden barrels, they didn't come in boxes like they do today. I remember when they started buying crackers in boxes, everybody was grumbling about that. They'd say, "Now you don't get nothin' hardly for your money, you have to buy them crackers in a box to go with them cheese. And there ain't many in them little ol' boxes."

People were concerned about every nickel and penny they had back then, because it was hard to come by. The man behind the counter used to be pretty generous with the loose crackers. He'd just reach into that cracker barrel and pull out a big handful. Yeah, when they had those cracker barrels, you got a lot for your money.

My dad shopped in the general store with the money from his crossties, and he bought a few things he needed. Then, we took our wagon and our mule and started back home.

I was real quiet on the ride, and we were already out of town when I started crying.

He said, "What's the matter with you?"

I said, "I's a wantin' me some cheese and crackers for dinner."

"Well, why didn't you tell me when we's down there in town?" He said. "I could've bought 'em a lot cheaper. Hush up now. We'll be a passin' one more little store on up the road, and I'll get you some up there—but I'll have to pay a lot for 'em."

My dad stopped and got me the cheese and crackers I wanted, without saying anything more about it. We went on up to the foot of the mountain, to what they called the "watering trough," where people watered their animals when they were hauling loads. There was a big spring up there and we stopped to eat our cheese and crackers together, sat on some rocks, and got a cold drink of water out of the spring. I was fine as fuzz on a frog then. Oh, I was happy, I'd gotten my cheese and crackers. Might not get them for another six months or a year.

Most store-bought food was a luxury. We savored it like Christmas presents. We knew about stuff like ice cream and Coca-Cola, but it was just above us. The first time I ever tasted a "Co-Cola," as we called them, I was around eleven and that carbonation belched back up through my nose and, boy, I didn't like it. It backfired on me and I said, "I can't drink this!" I gave it back to the man who sold it to me and he gave me my nickel back and drank it himself. It was years before I ever tried to drink another Co-Cola.

Now, ice cream I liked. The first scoop of ice cream I got was in the drugstore there in Tellico Plains when I was a boy. They had a little counter with seats where you could buy ice cream and drinks and when I first tasted ice cream, I thought it was out of this world! I didn't know there was any other flavor but vanilla till I was grown. I always thought that was the only flavor there was, 'cause that's all they ever had out there for years and years.

To us, it didn't matter that we didn't have all the extras that people in more populated areas had. We enjoyed what we were able to get, and besides, we had plenty of good things back home. After a day of goin' to town, gettin' back home was always sweeter than ice cream. Most of our joys were homespun and we loved them as well as—maybe better than—anything you could buy.

CHAPTER 7

Havin' a Big Time on the Mountain

In the little community of Coker Creek, we made our own entertainment. Pretty much had to. We never were bored. Everyone seemed to have a good time when they got together—they'd romp outdoors or make some old-time music. Some days and nights that mountain echoed with belly laughter and some cabin-shakin' foot stompin'.

In the day, we'd go on all kinds of picnics, go way up into the mountains. A group of us kin would get together, maybe ten or twelve of us, and we'd pack a basket of food for a lunch. My sisters usually made sandwiches. We'd invite cousins, aunts, and uncles to come along and they'd always just have a big time playin', talkin', laughin', and tellin' little jokes as we climbed the mountain on worn trails. I was usually about the youngest one that went—well, me 'n' Archie.

Yeah, "me 'n' Archie"—that's how I always said it—we did about everything together. In fact, Archie was with me just about all the time. He was my first cousin on my dad's side and pretty near my age. William Archie Kelley—he was named after my father, his Uncle Willie.

People that weren't kin to us or didn't know our family thought that Archie and I were brothers. And he was like a brother to me. People said we looked so much alike it was hard to tell us apart—some people even mistook us for twins. I never did see how. Archie did look like me in the face a little, and, of course, we both had blue eyes, like the rest of 'em. But my hair was lighter than Archie's. I never could do much with my hair and I never tried hardly when I's growin' up, I just let it run wild. My hair pretty much stood straight up all the time. Archie always kept his hair combed.

I was pretty thin and Archie was a little more husky-built—he had more muscles on him. He and I liked to compete athletically and I'd stay right with him—I'd keep up—but I couldn't outdo him. On those family picnics, Archie and I'd get up ahead of the rest of the group—we'd race each other to get to the top of the mountain. Hard as we'd try, we'd usually reach the top at pretty much the same time.

It'd be so quiet up there—just hawks floatin' overhead, and us catchin' our breath. The air was usually a little cooler than down in the valley. But the main thing about gettin' to the top of the mountain was how far you could see. Up there, we had some mighty big views of those Blue Ridge Mountains. Most of the time, the peaks off in the distance were just pale blue lines across the horizon, faded by mist hangin' in the air. Only on real clear days—when the sky was bluer than the mountains— then we could see the ridges' sharp outlines, row after row, like furrows of a cornfield.

The whole family would have a good time enjoying that lookout point. After a while we'd go down and eat our picnic lunch together by a little spring of cold water.

There were places up in those mountains where the hills met just so and you could yell across the valley and hear your own voice come back to you. Archie and I would go looking for places like that and we'd holler across to see if we'd hear an echo. We had good lungs and big voices 'cause we's used to hollerin' across hillsides. We used to do that a lot when we found an echo place. We had several places picked out where the mountain would bounce our voices back to us and, oh, we'd get a kick out of that. No tellin' what we boys were a hollerin'.

Archie was my closest friend and he lived near me. We played together 'bout all the time. We weren't allowed to go to each other's house unless we asked permission from our parents, but we could meet halfway in the woods anytime.

We'd signal to each other through the woods, by blowing into our hand. I could make a fist and blow into the end just a certain way and it would make a big sound, like a horn. If I twiddled my fingers in the air, it would make that sound wavy and I could signal like that. You could hear that call a long ways back in them hollers.

If Archie was where he could hear me, he'd signal back. I'd answer him. Then we'd head out to the woods, meet between his house and mine. We'd play for a few hours, climb trees, fish around little brooks or go in swimmin'.

We had us a swimmin' hole on a little creek off of Coker Creek. Archie and I built a pretty good dam across that little creek. We had the water ponded up about chin deep, and we put up a diving board. I'd go over to that swimmin' hole—on hot days that's where I'd get washed off after work in the fields—and then we'd go in swimmin'. Sometimes a bunch of my cousins, we'd get together and dive and splash around and try to dunk each other. It was all what you'd call good, clean fun.

Except one time, I remember, we were goin' in swimmin', and we just happened to discover that somebody had cut a long pole, sharpened one end of it into a spear and stuck it in the bottom into the soft mud, and they had it angled right towards our diving board. If we hadn't seen that spear, it would have ripped one of us open when we dived into the pond.

There was a boy who went to school with us who was capable of doing that. We always blamed him for it, but I never did really know who did it. Some of them were just mean back in that community. Why anybody would want to hurt any of us kids, I don't know, but it could have killed one of us. We were lucky that we saw the end of that pole through the water, and from then on, we were careful at the swimmin' hole.

Like a lot of boys, Archie and I were always making mischief ourselves—the harmless kind. We concocted little schemes to make ourselves laugh. We kept a little boat in that pond. I built that boat myself out of a big hollow log. I hewed it, dug it out, made ends for it, and then I had myself a boat. It was crude, of course, but it floated.

Archie and I used that boat to pull pranks on some of the other boys in the community who'd come over to the swimmin' hole. We'd see them coming and we'd take that boat— Archie would get at one end and I'd get at the other, and we'd turn it upside down in the water and it would catch enough air till it wouldn't sink. From the outside, it looked like a big floating log in the pond.

Whoever it was we wanted to trick, they'd be standing on the shore watching us dive and Archie and I would both make a big dive off in that pond. We'd disappear underwater and come up inside that boat with our head above the water. We had enough air to stay up in there a long time.

We could hardly contain ourselves, wantin' to bust out a laughin', knowing those boys were confounded by what we'd done. They didn't know what had happened to us and we could hear them outside the boat—wondering aloud to each other and calling out our names, suspecting us of a trick, but they couldn't figure out how we did it. We really had them puzzled.

Archie and I did all kinds of little things like that, seems simple now, of course, but you can't imagine how much we enjoyed those afternoons, playing like there was nothing else that mattered under the sun. We didn't realize it then, but we didn't have a care in the world.

As a boy, it seemed like time was just goin' by so slowly. If there was something I really wanted to do on the weekend, the week just seemed to drag along, and I thought Saturday would never come.

We'd gather up sometimes on Saturday nights in the fall of the year, way back in the woods, my uncles, cousins, and me, and we'd go fox huntin'. There were a bunch of us boys out there with the old-timers, and the group usually included Archie and older cousins, like Benton Davis and his younger brother, Herbert Atlas Davis—we all called him Atlas.

Atlas was my first cousin on my mother's side. He was a little older than me, but not much, and a good feller. Atlas was tall and he was always a person who really walked just like a soldier, even when he was a young boy.

My dad used to say to me, "Quinton, you ought to learn to walk like Atlas does. You bob up and down like a ball in a swimmin' hole when you're a walkin'. Atlas stands straight as an arrow. He carries himself with pride," he'd tell me.

Well, that wasn't my way of walking. My dad said I just bobbed up and down and I guess I did. I didn't much like for him to say that to me, compare me to my cousin.

Atlas liked to fox hunt so well, he never did miss a hunt, I don't reckon. He'd always bring one good dog with him. My other cousins, they'd bring their fox dogs—a few boys had two or three. We called it fox huntin', but we never did try to kill a fox. Really, the dogs did all the hunting and we sat around and got our entertainment from listening to them chase foxes out there in the dark. We'd build us a fire and I'd take that popcorn popper that I made out of an old five-gallon bucket and shake it back and forth over the flames. We'd gather around, eat that popcorn, and listen.

About the time it got dark, the dogs would be on a fox in fifteen minutes, and they'd run those foxes up in the hills. I got used to the way the dogs would bark—all the hunters did—and I could tell when a dog was just about to catch a fox. Each dog had a different voice. Some would yap in a high pitch and some would bellow like a drum as they got on the scent of those foxes.

The better dogs would quit barking. There was an old feller who had a real good fox dog, the dog's name was Ol' Buck. When all the other dogs were barking kind of slow, at some point you wouldn't hear Ol' Buck anymore.

That old feller said, "Now, you wait just a little, and that dog, he'll be half a mile ahead a the others."

Ol' Buck was experienced and he knew where that fox was going. He'd cut away from the pack to get ahead of the fox. He'd cut across a valley and head up a ridge to cut that fox off.

Sure enough, Ol' Buck was way up on that ridge when we heard him next. When that dog came out in sight of that fox, he'd go to barking real fast, excited like. They called it a "sight race" when a dog can see what he's running, and he'll really bark fast. Those foxes were fast, but sometimes Ol' Buck'd get one.

Most of the time, though, the fox would outfox the dogs. One trick the fox had, he would run far ahead, then turn around and double back towards the dogs. Then that fox'd make a big jump off to the side — just leap into the air and land several feet off the trail of his own scent. He did that to confuse the dogs. That's why they say "sly as a fox."

When the dogs got up there, they couldn't tell which way to go. They'd follow the trail to the end, then double back, back and forth, back and forth, barking like that for a while.

"Now, listen there, will you! They've lost that fox," those old hunters'd say when that happened. The old fox hunters knew just from listening what was a goin' on. They'd tell us about it and we could imagine those dogs and foxes, out there runnin' around in the moonlight.

We'd get into wrestling matches with each other. Archie and I would wrestle, or "rassle," as we said. We wouldn't get mad or anything. It was all good-natured roughhousing. He was a little bit younger than I was, but he had big arms. Everybody talked about him when he took his shirt off. They'd say, "Boy, look at the muscles on that boy!"

I had a lot of energy, but not too much meat on me. Archie was solid and strong as an ox. Most of the time, he could overpower me. I'd just rassle till I had to give up. I had a lot of determination, but between the two of us cousins, Archie was the stronger one.

Now, my cousin Atlas never did rassle. He'd tell stories with the best of 'em, though, and make us laugh about his practical jokes as we sat around the fire. Most of them were harmless. One time I remember, Atlas had a little fun with some boys who were the kind that we thought of as *real* mountaineers — they were from a lot deeper back in the mountains than we were. They lived up there near the top and some of 'em didn't know too much.

"You know them boys from up on top of the mountain that run that ol' peddlin' truck that come through here?" Atlas would get a glimmer in his blue eyes when he started a big tale.

"Aw, that one little ol' boy, the young'un, well, one day, he was a deliverin' groceries, and Benton and me, we's out there by the road a warmin' up at this big ol' fire we built up. It was real cold that mornin' and that little ol' boy come over there to the fire and I told him, said, "Git your finger good and warm here and you can stick it up in that hickory tree. It'll just go right through that wood." Atlas shook his head. "I didn't have no idea he'd do what he done.

"That little boy just held his finger up in front of that fire and got his hand good and hot, and he just jabbed his finger right into that tree as hard as he could! Oh, Lordamercy, that boy nearly broke his finger! He jus' fell over, a cryin' and a holdin' his hand 'tween his knees. Oh, law, Benton and me, we fell over a laughin' but we felt so bad. I didn't have no idea he'd really believe me when I told him to stick his finger in that tree."

We'd all laugh at the tellin', but I knew that boy didn't know any better, and it was kind of mean to do that to him, but Atlas was a little bit of a cutup. He never meant anybody harm, just tried to embarrass them and he told the stories afterwards.

For years and years, we'd come to those fox hunts to trade stories and listen to those dogs run foxes all evenin' long, a barkin' and a rustlin', back in them hollers. Why, the dogs'd go all night till dawn, if you let 'em. And we could have, too, Archie and Atlas and me, especially. We really had a lot of fun like that. But we usually stopped around midnight, especially if it was Saturday night. Our parents wouldn't let us hunt on Sunday and that started at midnight.

The most fun I ever had out on Coker Creek was on special Saturday nights when we listened to some of those musicians makin' music on the mountain. Coker Creek had a lot of talented musicians and I remember some of them as being top-notch. They didn't have nothin' else to do much, only practice. They'd sit around and play their instruments together and then they'd go in groups to different people's houses. They'd go all over the countryside, playin' their bluegrass and gospel music.

Some of those boys could make music that excited our spirits and touched our hearts. Most nights, the women even cried at some of those songs. A bunch of us'd gather together to hear the lively twang of a banjo meet up with the tender melody of a fiddle, and let me tell you, that was the kind of music you heard long after. Those banjos'd stay ringin' in my head. And the fiddle, well, the fiddle could get to me.

Uncle Edd Lee would always send somebody runnin' over to our cabin to tell me when he was having music at his house. He knew how I liked that music. Edd Lee was a real talented fiddle player, so these other musicians were always coming to his house — a rough cabin not much bigger than ours.

Usually there'd be four or five musicians together at one time. They played banjos and guitars and different kinds of instruments. They'd start just as it was gettin' dark, and a bunch of us would be sittin' around Edd Lee's cabin on about anything we could find to sit on. If it was winter-time, Edd Lee would have a big fire going and two lanterns flickering on his mantel. Of course, in a little while, we'd be so warm, we'd have to throw the windows open. If it was summertime, everybody'd just have the doors and windows wide open anyways, and anybody along the road could hear all that music a comin' from my uncle's house.

It would take those musicians a long time to get their instruments all in tune with each other. I'd watch the leader as he'd give them a note and they'd try to match it. As a kid, I'd get worried, listening to them tunin' up, all those sour notes.

Right when they got 'em all in tune, they'd take off and really play the music. Just one song right after another. They played a lot of songs that I knew and sometimes a few of those musicians would sing, or play the harmonica.

Some songs sounded like a distant locomotive — like the whine of a train whistle echoin' through the hills, hangin' in the air after a good rain. Some songs sounded like the clack, clack, clack of the tracks, or raced along with breakneck pickin', gettin' faster and faster as the song went on. And some of them songs would keep a goin' on for a good, long time.

Those musicians would swing and sway with the rhythm, all caught up in it. They'd have those bows a slippin' and a slidin' over those fiddle strings, carvin' out a tune. And those banjos would be a ringin' —it's a sight how loud they could play 'em.

Those musicians might play "Turkey in the Straw," and everybody at those shindigs, they'd raise some dust. They'd stomp their feet and clap their hands and holler and carry on. The floorboards of the house'd be vibratin' with all the foot tappin', people keepin' time. You could hear the knee slappin' and clappin', addin' to the beat of the music. Oh, yeah, people did that quite a bit during the lively tunes. They were just all good country people that liked to play and listen to music.

When I was a boy, I'd really watch those musicians, men like Rube Dalton and Jesse Holder, and my Uncle Edd Lee Kelley—they were the best in the community. Once they'd get warmed up, I think they just wanted to see how fast they could play some of those ol' tunes, and sometimes they'd challenge each other to keep up a pace. It's a wonder those instruments weren't smokin' a little.

Every face in the room was lit up with big smiles, except maybe one particular fiddle player and I'm a tellin' you, that one feller used to get down in the floor, he'd get so swept up in the music. Jesse Holder was a lanky feller and he'd get his limbs all every whichaway when he'd play that fiddle or guitar. What a show he'd put on! He put his whole body into it. He'd contort himself till he was almost a layin' down in the floor when he'd get to playin' a good tune, especially pickin' that guitar.

Everybody'd be laughin' at him carryin' on. And Jesse Holder didn't know why they were laughing, 'cause he didn't really know he was puttin' on such a show. It was just his nature to let the music get to him.

Jesse was from way back in the mountains—even more remote than we were—but he'd moved down to Coker Creek. He'd built a little store where he made rifles and he operated it alongside the road. He could handcraft one of the most beautiful rifles, stock and all, that you've ever seen. Jesse was an expert musician, too. He had the ability to play any kind of instrument that he touched, I reckon. He could play the mandolin, banjo, harmonica, dulcimer, and all the different instruments that they had to play. He had 'em all and he could play any of 'em. But he primarily played the violin and the guitar and I believe the guitar was his favorite.

A lot of tunes are adapted to certain types of instruments better than others and Jesse was good at picking out the tunes where he could show off each instrument. He didn't sing, but he'd play a lot of the old tunes that we'd all memorized from listening to other people, only Jesse Holder could play them better than anyone we knew. And, of course, everybody liked to watch him. That music just got ahold of him so, he'd really put on an act.

Back in that day on Coker Creek, only the men played instruments or sang at those shindigs. I don't know why, but people thought it was kind of a disgrace for a woman to participate in something like that. Of course, it was all right to be a spectator. They'd come and listen and enjoy the music when the musicians came visitin', but the women didn't want to perform. Women were expected to sing in the church—that was just the tradition. At the shindigs, the women would request some favorite religious songs, like "Church in the Wildwood," one I always liked. There were more religious songs than anything else, and the musicians back in there knew every one.

The music would go on till, oh, midnight. It was a clean show. There wasn't any drinking or anything like that because my uncle was strictly against alcohol, or "al-kee-haul," as he—and all of us—pronounced it. He wouldn't have let those musicians come to his home if they'd been the drinking type.

Edd Lee was my father's youngest brother. He didn't have any education to speak of, but he'd learned music. He used to teach music out at the church. Back in those days they used shaped notes, where the pitch was determined by the shape of the note, and when I was a boy, I went to some of my uncle's music classes where I learned to sing and read shaped-note music from him.

Edd Lee usually wore a pair of glasses with a dark-colored lens over one eye. Back when Edd Lee was just a young man, about eighteen or nineteen years old, he'd got cancer in that one eye. Back in that day, they didn't know how to treat cancer. Edd Lee went down to Ducktown and that's where they burnt that cancer out and they destroyed that one eye and, boy, it made a big scar, all around. So Edd Lee only had one eye, but it didn't seem to bother him, because he was young enough when it happened that he got used to it.

Edd Lee never let much bother him. He was an even-tempered man, like my father. But he wasn't as industrious. Edd Lee never did keep his garden up much. People said he was always out on his front porch, "a fiddlin' away."

Edd Lee Kelley was one of the best on the fiddle. People really enjoyed hearing him play. But he was a little bit peculiar about that. He didn't want people to think he was good at anything. I don't know why he felt that way. He was real humble, but he was an expert on that fiddle.

When it was his turn to play the music, Edd Lee would put that fiddle up to his chin, look over at me with his one eye, and say, "Now, Quinton, I guess I'd better try to play 'Mockingbird' for you, 'cause you'll be a askin' me to play it if I don't."

Yeah, that was my favorite tune that he'd play. He'd skip that bow over the strings and really make that fiddle sound like a mockingbird, which can imitate the other birds and insects in the forest. Oh, that fiddle would be a twitterin' and a chirpin' and a singin' all up and down the scale.

Edd Lee was creative and he wrote a lot of songs himself. He wrote a lot of religious songs, like "Babe of Bethlehem," "Climbing," and "Traveling on to Mansions." For some of 'em, he'd write the music to the songs in shaped notes and write the words, and he'd sing. He had a good voice, a smooth and steady tenor. He got his ideas for the songs from the stories that he'd heard or read somewhere.

One story I remember was about a little girl who got lost up in the mountains, about how they searched for her and how her momma cried. He put that story to music and it made a very sad ballad that people always requested. The title of it was "Lost on the Mountain Alone." His sister would just cry when she'd hear that. Boy, it'd get to her heart when he'd sing that song and she'd sit there and the tears would well up and spill down her face.

Edd Lee had a lot of sad songs. Another one was called "Put My Little Shoes Away," about a little girl who was dying of an illness and she told her parents that they could put her little shoes away, because she wouldn't need them. She was goin' on to walk with Jesus, walk on streets of gold where she didn't need her little shoes no more. I don't remember how the words went exactly, but the women cried at that song, too. Edd Lee'd make that fiddle just moan and weep, so pretty that it hurt, and his tender voice sang of sorrows that everyone could feel. Oh, my uncle could make you cry every time with some of the songs he wrote. Edd Lee had a few sorrows of his own, too, and you could feel it when the fiddle strings cried out a long, warbling note.

Edd Lee, and my daddy, once had another brother who was a banjo player, the middle brother of the three boys, Chester Kelley. I didn't get to know my Uncle Chester, though, 'cause he'd been killed by an old drunk just a couple of years before I was born. My Uncle Edd Lee and my dad related the story to me many a time.

Chester was walking home one day out on Coker Creek, and three old drunks came stumblin' around a curve on a deserted stretch of road and one of 'em was wavin' a pistol. The men were arguing about whiskey. One of 'em thought the others had stolen his whiskey and had it hid.

One drunk pointed to Chester, who was walking along the road about that time. He said, "*That's* the man took your whiskey! Right over there."

Chester had been to Tellico Plains that morning and was carrying a new .22 rifle that he'd just bought, probably had it slung over his shoulder. That didn't stop this ol' drunk with a cocked pistol from staggerin' over to Chester to demand that he give him his whiskey back. Chester Kelley didn't have any whiskey, of course.

As Chester turned to walk away, that ol' drunk shot him in the side.

Edd Lee and my daddy had been real close to their middle brother and I imagine it must've hurt them somethin' awful when he died. He was only twenty-two.

I heard that the drunk who killed Chester, well, about a year later, some other drunk shot and killed him. That's just the way it was out there, back then.

Chester had gotten a new banjo just before he died—they said he could play pretty well. My dad got that banjo and kept it. He could play a tune, but he didn't practice it enough to keep up with it. He just kept that banjo as a keepsake and I think the reason he didn't fool with it much was because it brought back sad memories of his brother Chester when he got that banjo down.

Quite a few of us in the Kelley family had some music in us. Several of my first cousins were real good fiddle players, too. My cousin Archie Kelley, the one who was like a brother to me, he was Edd Lee's son. Archie sure inherited his father's gift for music. But unlike his daddy, the banjo was Archie's instrument.

Archie Kelley was real young when he learned to play on a banjo that his daddy made for him. Everybody saw right away that Archie really had a talent for playin' that banjo. Since his father was one of the best fiddlers around, Archie and his daddy played together a lot.

Archie bought a good banjo later on when he got around twelve or thirteen and he started playing with different groups and he played solo, too. Edd Lee was real proud of his son's musical talent. He hoped maybe Archie'd get to be on the Grand Ole Opry in Nashville one day.

Archie Kelley wasn't like some of the musicians around there who put on a show with emotions and contortions. Archie had his own style. He wouldn't put much action in his body. When it was his turn to play, Archie'd put all his energy into his fingers moving over those banjo strings. Sometimes he'd do some real fancy pickin' and delight everybody who heard him.

He used to practice all the time. Edd Lee's house was a little ways through the woods, and I could listen to Archie from home. I could hear him playing that banjo, sittin' out on his front porch. Boy, he was good at it. Yeah, I could hear him a pickin' "Chicken Roost Blues" or "Goin' Down the Road Feelin' Bad." His banjo'd just be a ringin' through them hollers. Archie was back in the woods, so I couldn't see him, but the whole time we's growin' up on Coker Creek, I could hear him out there a playin' that banjo just as happy as you please for hours. It gave him a lot of enjoyment—all of us, really—but there would come a day when the war would hush Archie's fine pickin'.

I learned to pick out a few tunes on the banjo myself, but I wasn't gifted like some of the other boys. So I got me a harmonica—we all called it a French harp. I got to where I could play it a little bit. I never did master it, but I practiced. I'd go out there in the fields blowin' little ol' tunes, like "She'll Be Comin' Around the Mountain" or "Cripple Creek," my favorite tune to play. It was a fast, catchy tune and I always liked it:

Goin' up Cripple Creek,
goin' in a run.
Goin' up Cripple Creek
to have a little fun . . .

Yeah, that was me—goin' up *Coker* Creek, a bouncin' along.

In the springtime, I'd hear the woodpeckers a hammerin' away at the trunks of trees. *Tat-tat-tat-tat-tat-tat-tat-tat.* They'd pause for a beat, then they'd go at it again. *Tat-tat-tat-tat-tat-tat-tat-tat.* Over and over real fast, just as regular as some kind of machine.

I'd hear my dad, maybe, too, keepin' a rhythm out in his blacksmith shop. *PING!-ping! PING!-ping!* And the repeating *Crack!* of an ax as a neighbor in the next holler split wood. If I was walking to the fields with my hoe on my shoulder, I'd jump right in and play me a little tune on that French harp I kept in my pocket.

When I was out by myself, I was always doin' some kind of twittering along with the birds. People always said wherever I was, they could hear me playin' that French harp or singin' or whistlin' away. I'd only do that out where I thought nobody could hear me, but sometimes my neighbors would say, "I enjoyed hearin' you play that French harp by the road the other day," and that always embarrassed me a little.

One time Uncle Edd Lee, who sometimes led music at our church, told me, "Quinton, I heard you a singin' out in the cane field, I don't reckon you knew it. But you sounded real good. Why don't you come down to the church and we'll get us a little singin' group together?"

"Naw, I don't want to do that," I told him. "I just sing for myself." That's about how it was, and I stuck to that. I liked singin', but I was too shy to want to let people hear me. Of course, when I grew up a little bit, I did sing some in the choir at church.

Mostly, my singin' and whistlin' was just when I'd go around my chores, and I don't know why, it was just my habit. I'd always find myself a singin' some of them songs I'd hear at the Saturday night shindigs. Of course, a few songs I'd learned off of the radio—when we were lucky enough to hear one.

I remember when one of our neighbors bought a radio—the first one that was in the whole community for several years. It was back when I was about six years old and we went over to his house one evening to see what a radio looked like. It was an amazing thing to hear live people talkin' and singin' through a big wooden box.

You didn't need electricity to have a radio. They had a battery in them. But the radio at that time and in that location was unreliable. If there was any kind of interference in the air, it would pick up static. A lot of times, we'd go over to our neighbor's house to listen to the radio and we couldn't get a program—you couldn't hear a thing.

When Archie and I were growing up, we liked to listen to the Grand Ole Opry. We got to where we knew all the players, the old-timers who made the bluegrass music that everybody else followed. Roy Acuff was one of our favorites and Bill Monroe and the Blue Grass Boys were, too.

After the music on Saturday night, they'd have boxing matches. I didn't get to listen to it a whole lot, but boxing was one of the main things I liked to listen to. Of course, I just had to imagine the fighters, but I really listened in on all the details of the exciting fights that they announced from places like Madison Square Garden. It was almost unbelievable to me as a boy to hear an actual boxing match goin' on in New York City while I was a sittin' in a neighbor's cabin in the Tennessee hills.

All I'd ever had to listen to at home was the old Victrola that we had—we called it Ol' Hulda. I don't know why. My dad'd say, "Let's wind up Ol' Hulda and hear us some music." And I'd crank up that Victrola.

It'd go for a while, then I'd have to crank it again. That hand crank got pretty tiresome. We only had a few records, but we traded them around the community and I knew every record that everybody had.

When I got a little older, 'bout fourteen, I got a job at a sawmill and I said, "I'm a gonna buy me a radio!" I saved up my money and I ordered a radio from Sears. And, boy, I was really excited about that. You had to put an antenna up, run a wire about a hundred feet up in the air on a pole to pick up the signal. After that, some evenings our whole family would sit around that radio just like we'd sat around the hearth.

My mother and sisters, they liked the stories that were dramatized, with all kinds of actors' voices. I liked to hear the *Lone Ranger* and *The Shadow*, but mostly we listened to the Grand Ole Opry music shows with their funny soap and cereal commercials. That was the station we got better than any of them, the one out of Nashville, Tennessee.

My dad got a big kick out of listening to all that, but what he really liked best was to listen to the gospel music that they broadcast from Nashville on Sunday morning and the Sunday church services that they broadcast out of Knoxville, where they had old-time singin' and preachin'.

In our radio days, every Sunday morning my daddy listened to those preachers before we went to church. Of course, we attended church every week. We all liked to hear those old-time country preachers belt out a sermon about the Word of God. And, oh, boy, could they ever.

CHAPTER 8

Sunday Best

For our family, and many like them, church was the hub in the wheel of life on the mountain. I don't believe we hardly ever missed a Sunday morning church service. You might say it was the big event of the week, and we made sure we were all cleaned up and dressed up, at least as much as we were able.

They used to refer to the "Saturday bath," because Saturday was usually "bath day" for people. Everybody in the community lived about alike. If we worked in the field, we had to take a bath just about every day, 'cause it was hot and dusty. If we didn't work in the field, we didn't take a bath that often. We'd always take one, at least on Saturday afternoon, even if we weren't working where it was dirty, so for Sunday, we'd be all clean for church.

About everyone had a galvanized washtub; our size was called a No. 2, which I reckoned meant if you were older than two, you'd have a hard time taking a bath. When I was small, I could sit down in the No. 2 tub, but as I got bigger, I got to where I had to stand up. Of course, I just about had to take a sponge bath like that, but I managed.

On Saturday afternoon, my mother would say, "Now, I'm not gonna be in the kitchen for a little while. So go ahead and take your bath."

Anybody able to carry their own water carried it all the way up that long slope to the house when it was their turn to take a bath. The spring was far enough until you'd be out of breath when you got back, especially if you were runnin' up that hill to keep warm.

My mother'd start getting some of the water hot ahead of time in her biggest kettle on the cookstove, and we'd bring the cold water up from the spring and pour it in the washtub. She'd pour some hot water in that tub until she got the temperature like we wanted it, then she'd leave.

You'd just have to stand in the tub with your feet underwater and you'd bring the water up to wash the rest of you with a cupped hand and a washcloth. We scrubbed with soap that my mother cooked up in a big kettle twice a year, made out of lye — animal fat.

We ended up with some of that soap on our body after we dried off. We never thought anything about it. In the winter, we didn't go through two hot bath waters for one person, so we never had a lot of hot, clean water to rinse that soap off of us. Everybody did it that way, because you had to carry your water and heat it on the woodstove. The way we lived, you'd have to go through a whole lot to have two tubs of hot water.

After we finished our bath, we'd take the water and pour it outside. We lived on a sloping hill and it would just run off. That's the way we got rid of all our dirty water, dishwater and so forth, we'd just carry it out the back door.

It took a pretty good afternoon to get everybody all washed up, head to toe, and, of course, the women would wash their hair and wait for it to dry. We didn't have any toothbrushes, nothin' like that, so we'd cut a fresh twig from a sweet gum tree and dip the end in some salt and baking soda to brush our teeth.

Whatever we did on Saturday night, we wouldn't get too dirty so we'd be ready for church on Sunday. Most of times, Sunday mornings we'd get up a little later than usual. Just before dawn, we'd wake with the crowing of roosters, and we'd get up, eat biscuits, and get dressed in our "Sunday best." Everybody out there used the best they had to go to church in. Those were the clothes you didn't wear for anything else, only when goin' to church or goin' to visit somebody.

My dad would usually wear dress pants. He always had two pair of nice dark-colored pants. He favored navy blue. He wore suspenders and he'd wear a white shirt. When he dressed up, he was a real handsome person.

My dad once had a really nice head of hair, it was just as wavy and black. But over time, he lost most of it at the top, through the center. My father would dress in his small-brimmed, black felt hat. He had one black felt hat for Sunday and one for everyday. He favored black instead of brown.

My mother, she dressed pretty well. She always wore dark clothes and she favored white cuffs and a white collar for dress occasions. She always wore a hat to church. A lot of them would be colored straw hats in the summertime, and in the wintertime, felt hats. She'd always wear nylon stockings. My mother wore hers about midway between her knee and foot, and she held them in place with a band she put below her knee. At lot of women put the band up above their knees, but she wore her dresses down long so you wouldn't see the top of her hose. Back then in our community, women wore their dresses way down low on their legs, down to their ankles nearly.

Edth and Thelma dressed a lot like her until they got old enough to where she'd let them dress the way they wanted and they were almost grown by then. A lot of the younger girls got to wearing short dresses that came up to the knees. They'd started that fashion in the cities and people found it out in the little towns around there, so the styles drifted out there to the country. My mother never would allow my sisters to wear those kinds of dresses. They had to be well below the knees.

When they came out with those short dresses and the girls started wearing them, law me, you ought to have heard all the flap. Oh, those people on Coker Creek didn't like that. They said, "Why, that's a disgrace to the human race, to go 'round half naked!"

My mother's mother, Dosha Davis, she usually wore dark, long clothes, almost dragging the ground. She always had a sharp thing or two to say to any young girls who wore their dresses shorter than she approved of.

"Looks like you're runnin' a little short on cloth," she'd say.

Grandmaw Davis would sew some of our clothes to help us out. As a kid, I used to get a kick out of watching her laugh. Grandmaw Davis was big and round, and so fat that when she'd laugh, she'd just shake all over like jelly. But she was a serious woman and real particular about clothes. She'd sew my sisters some dresses that they didn't like, but they'd have to wear 'em to church anyhow. Of course, my sisters sewed, too, and they made themselves a lot of Sunday frocks.

Edth and Thelma would get all different kinds of material, they used calico some, and sometimes feed sacks that were printed in colorful patterns. Sometimes they'd dye cloth the color they wanted. They'd get a big hot kettle of water, they'd put dye in it and they'd put the cloth in there to color it. They'd hang it out on the line to dry. Then they'd sew a new dress for church the way they wanted it. They had some dresses with little puffed-up sleeves in the summer and they'd wear a lot of cheerful colors.

Most people would wear clothes that had stripes and flowers mainly for their dress wear. Their everyday clothes were plain. Later years, women got to wearing more bright, flowery stuff, with ruffles and all kinds of trim on it. When those clothes came out, people on Coker Creek called it "that new style," and they just fussed about it. Some of 'em didn't approve of it for a long, long time.

When my sisters got older, they'd work in the summer for different people and they'd buy a silk dress. Oh, they were proud of that. Very few people would wear silk at church. Silk was expensive back then. The poor people didn't have much of that kind of stuff to wear.

We dressed about as nice as anybody in the community, I guess. Men out there didn't usually have but one suit of clothes. I didn't have a suit of clothes until I was big enough to work and save money to buy my own pants and shirts. I guess because my dad wore suspenders, I got suspenders and I wore them for many years. But back when I was a kid, I'd just wear my good overalls to church.

In the wintertime, my dad would always buy me a jacket. They called it an overall jacket, made of the same material that overalls are made of. It was heavy and blanket-lined and it was warm. If I needed to, I could put on a sweater under the jacket. My Grandmaw Kelley knitted a lot of sweaters for us. She used wool and she could make some of the prettiest sweaters you've ever seen. She'd have stripes running up and down on the body of the sweater and in bands around the arms, all different colors mixed together. Grandmaw Kelley would sit in front of the fire and she could just knit away and she never had to watch what she was doing. She knitted all her grandchildren sweaters, scarves, and mittens.

I really liked both my grandmothers. They spent a lot of time sewing and knitting for the family. I didn't know my grandfathers, they died before I was born. But I really thought the world of my grandmothers, 'cause they were really good to help us out.

When they could, they'd walk to church with us. We went to church as one big family, sometimes my cousins, aunts, and uncles would walk with us, too. We'd all stroll down the dirt road. Like a lot of people, we'd go rain or shine, all year long.

One of the things we'd always wear on Sunday, at least for a few hours, was shoes. Now, my parents and grandmothers wore shoes a lot more than us young'uns. Most of the year, the only time we kids ever wore shoes was when we went to church, or to town. Even then, as quick as we'd get home, we'd pull 'em off. Sometimes, we'd pull our shoes off after church, and walk home barefooted.

Usually, wherever we went, we'd go barefooted. We went barefooted from the time it quit frosting in the spring till it came the first frost in the fall. We'd go to school barefooted. Down to Dave Lenderman's store barefooted. We worked around the homeplace barefooted, in the fields. Our feet got tough and it didn't hurt us to walk on gravel or stones. I'd go anywhere I'd want to like that. The bottoms of my feet would get about like leather, and I could go through briar patches.

As a kid, I was always glad to get rid of my shoes 'cause I could run faster. That's the first thing I'd do when I'd take my shoes off, coming home from church—I'd get going and see how fast I could run. I thought that was something great to have a little more speed.

In the fall of the year, we'd each get one new pair of shoes from the Sears catalog. It was always exciting when that catalog arrived; it was like the biggest general store I could imagine. Oh, yeah, boy, we all went through that catalog, page by page. People out there called it a "wish book." They called it that 'cause they wished they had this, and they wished they had that, but they didn't get none of it. That was what people said.

We ordered our shoes and all of the clothes that we didn't make ourselves from that catalog when we had money to get 'em. We'd save our money and we'd fill out an order blank in the catalog and send the bills, if we had any, and the coins, through the mail and wait. We'd really look forward to that package from Sears. From the time we mailed the order, it took three days to get our package. It came from Atlanta. That was pretty fast service, if you think about it, back in that day.

You could get everything a lot cheaper from the Sears catalog than anywhere else. A pair of shoes would cost you a little over a dollar. If you gave a dollar and a quarter, you got a really good pair of dress shoes, patent leather. But it was hard—you couldn't hardly find a dollar and a quarter to buy a pair with. Overalls were about seventy-nine cents a pair, something like that. And then they had a better grade that would be about a dollar. The cheaper grade was the kind I had to wear, the seventy-five- or seventy-nine-cent ones.

Now, I'll tell you, we didn't have hardly enough clothes to wear. I usually only had two pair of overalls when I was a young boy. I had one good pair that I wore to church and I had another pair that had been patched and patched and patched that I wore for everyday.

One Sunday when I was school-age, we went to visit my Uncle Edd Lee and I had my good overalls on. My cousin Archie and I got to playin' in the log barn and we were runnin' and crawlin' through a big crack in the barn, chasing each other, and there was a nail that caught my overalls and it tore a big three-cornered hole right in the seat.

When we started home, I told my mother, "I tore a hole in my overalls."

She said, "My goodness, now, you know that's all you've got to wear to church! I'll have to patch that and you'll have to wear patched overalls to church. You oughta had better sense." She put it on me pretty heavy.

Of course, she fixed the hole and I wore them to church, Sunday after Sunday, patch and all. It was no tellin' how long before I ever got another pair of overalls. I hated I'd done that, 'cause we worked so hard for everything we got.

My dad was always telling me not to get upset about the things that didn't mean a whole lot, though. He'd say, "Now, Quinton, don't let it worry you none. Right now, money's as tight as bark on a tree. But there'll be better days ahead. It won't seem like no time and you'll have you a new pair of

Will and Verdie Kelley

overalls. Look forward to gettin' 'em and you'll appreciate 'em."

My dad had good advice all the time. I don't remember him ever telling me anything that would have led me down the wrong pathway. He was an upright and righteous man. I guess the most memorable thing about my father and my mother is that they were Christian parents and they brought me up to go to church. And that's been a great blessing to me.

There were more than seven churches around the Coker Creek area back when I was a youngster, but none within easy walking distance of our neck of the woods. A bunch of people didn't have anywhere to go to church, so Altoona Baptist Church was organized but didn't have money, and they weren't in a hurry to build a church anyway. They asked the school board if they could use the community schoolhouse down in Smithfield, about a mile from our house. It was a little one-room clapboard building, painted white, with a sign that read, *Smithfield School* over the door, so even though it was actually Altoona Church, people all referred to it as Smithfield Church.

I was brought up in that church with my cousins and all of my friends—well, most of my friends were good people like that—so that gave me a moral start in life as a youngster.

Most of the time back then in the country churches, the men and women would gather in thirty or forty minutes before the church service started and they'd all stand around in the churchyard. My quiet little mother became real talkative when she got around a group of women from the community. They'd circle up and tell all about their farming experiences, whatever they'd heard in the community during the past week, women-talk, and so on. Of course, the men would gather in their groups, too, and the kids all played until the preacher got ready to start the service.

If the Christian people didn't come in and sit close to the front of the church, they were considered a "backslider," and people like that usually slumped into a pew towards the back of the church, if they came at all. Those country preachers were always talking about "them backsliders," people that used to live according to the Bible, but weren't living according to the Bible anymore. They'd get on to the backsliders in their sermons, if a number of people happened to be sitting in the back that Sunday, so most people that came to church tried to sit near the front. Our family sat about in the middle of the church.

The church services were conducted a whole lot like they are today, though they've grown much calmer now than they were back then. First, a group of people would do the singin' or someone would sing a solo.

When she got old enough, my sister Edth would sing solos in church. It was just her voice—we didn't have any instruments in the church, didn't even have a piano. Edth had a medium voice, not high, but not too deep either, for a young lady. She'd stand at the podium and her voice would ring, pretty as church bells. She didn't put on any physical motion, but she'd sing loud and clear where everybody could hear her, and we were always real proud of Edth's singin'. All through her teenage years, people liked to hear her and they'd ask her to sing often.

Thelma didn't sing. She was too much a tomboy to be interested in singin' and sewin' and flower gardenin' like her older sister, but she'd try her best to carry a tune when the congregation sang old-time spirituals together.

Over the years, a lot of times the church would go for months without having a choir and then they'd get somebody enthused about it, and they'd get a choir started and we'd have a choir for a while. Then the leader would move or drop out and we wouldn't have a choir, so then we'd just sing some hymns together as a congregation.

They always took up a collection for the preacher near the start of the service and that's how he got paid. Didn't get paid much. The deacons would take off their hats and take them from pew to pew to gather all the tithes and offerings, which usually didn't amount to a hill of beans, I don't reckon, 'cause nobody had hardly any money.

After the music and the offering and some prayers of thankfulness, the preacher would get up and he'd read his text from the pulpit and he'd preach from the Bible. They had some pretty good preachers back then, we thought so.

They were just country preachers, they didn't have much education, but they'd studied the Bible many, many hours on their own. They were good at quoting the Bible by heart, and preaching sermons from the different scriptures. Of course, they added their own stories to illustrate their points.

They were dramatic preachers. They'd really carry on. Those country preachers, they'd be preaching the Bible and they'd throw their arms up in the air and really holler out, pacing about until they had sweat on their brow. They'd wave that black Bible over the congregation and they'd thump on it and preach "fire and brimstone," and describe what would happen to the unrepentant sinners. Sometimes the preacher would grab himself across the chest in a big bear hug and just cry out.

Back when I was a small child, not even old enough to go to school, I remember how it really had me confused, the way the country preachers expressed themselves. There was one feller that visited our church — the first time he'd ever been there—he got to preachin' in a big way and he would just bend over and he'd put his hand across his stomach and holler out real loud.

Walking home, I said to my mother, "Boy, I sure was sorry for that preacher."

"Why is that?" she said.

"He must have had a terrible stomachache today, but he still had to preach," I said. I didn't know why he was bent over like he had a big bellyache, why he was shouting out like he was in pain, but she understood it. That just tickled my mother. She laughed and talked for years about what I'd said about that ol' preacher man.

When they got to preachin', most country preachers would holler, "Hallelujah!" and "Praise the Lord!" and they'd quote some Bible verses and tell us what it meant and they'd go on sometimes till they were out of breath, just go on without a pause. They'd get the congregation all worked up, all excited about their message, and they'd invoke the name of Jesus, just praise his name and all of that, and the preacher'd get in a rhythm, and he'd keep adding to the point he was a makin' till the congregation was a chimin' in with him.

"Preach it, brother, preach it!"

A lot of people would be hollering, "Amen! Amen!"

Some people would get really carried away with the Spirit of the Lord and get worked up, but some of them didn't like it when the congregation got all loud, some didn't go for that. They shifted around in their seats and just listened.

Back then, they held long, long, stretched-out church services. Sometimes the preacher'd preach two hours. You had to be prepared to stay in there for a good while. When I was a little boy, I had trouble sitting still for that long. I'd get sleepy and sometimes I'd go to sleep on the pew beside my mother. She wouldn't bother me. Better for me to be asleep than to be a squirmin' and a twistin' around.

I remember one time, there was such a commotion that I woke up in the middle of a sermon. Some of the congregation called out, "Amen, Brother! Preach it!" That wasn't unusual, I could sleep through that. But a different kind of commotion started up because the meanest dog in the neighborhood strolled right into the church.

The mean dog was my uncle's dog. I had an uncle who'd married into my mother's side, Napoleon Radford—everybody called him Pole—he'd gotten wounded as a doughboy in World War I. Uncle Pole had a big mean dog—Ol' Frank was his name—and that Sunday, Ol' Frank decided to go looking for his master, I reckon. But Uncle Pole wasn't there that Sunday for some reason. The door to the church was open—it was summertime and it was hot. This ol' dog just walked on down the aisle like he owned the place.

Now, Ol' Frank was a big, tough dog, walked bowlegged, and what a dog he was. That dog would go after snakes like you've never seen. All snakes, poisonous snakes, even diamondback rattlers. He'd grab 'em in his mouth and shake 'em till he killed 'em. A few times he got bit by a rattlesnake. When that happened, he'd go down to the creek for about three days, lie in the cold water with just his head a stickin' out. He always recovered and it made him meaner every time.

Oh, he was a mean dog. My cousins could put Ol' Frank up to mischief. They'd sic him on the cows and he'd jump up and sink his teeth into a cow's nose. That dog would hang on by his mouth, and that ol' cow'd be just a bawlin' and slingin' that dog around in the air, but he'd keep hangin' on till he was called off. That dog was a scrappy handful and there were only a few people who could handle him, 'cause he'd just as soon bite you as look at you.

When Ol' Frank came into the church that morning, he walked all the way down to the front, lookin' around. The preacher was shouting his sermon from the pulpit and people tried to pay attention, but you could hear the whispering and commotion because that dog was known in the community and people were a little bit afraid of Ol' Frank.

One man had the gumption to get up and grab the dog by the neck. He started pulling that dog down the aisle towards the door. Ol' Frank was resisting, putting his paws out to try to get a foothold as he was being pulled across the floor. But the floor of that church, that little schoolhouse, was rough sawed boards, with cracks in between, and that dog's toe got caught in between two boards. He let out a loud yelp, but the man kept tugging on Ol' Frank. Then that dog started howlin' and it took two men to get that dog's foot loose from the floorboards.

Ol' Frank never bit nobody through all that. He was a mean dog, but that day he behaved himself in the Lord's House and he went on out of there. It caused quite a disturbance, though, the dog yelpin' and the kids a laughin'. Even the preacher had to quit preachin' for a bit, and it was unusual that anything stopped a preacher when he was on a roll. I always looked forward to church as a child, long before I learned what it meant, because I never knew what might happen each Sunday.

A lot of times the preacher would preach against women wearing short hair. People out there back then thought it was a sin for a woman to cut her hair and wear it short. The preacher would describe those kind of women as being prostitutes. He'd go on about their wicked ways, talk about women he'd seen in the cities, how lewd they dressed and how shameful they acted, and he'd preach hellfire for the unrepentant. So the women in the congregation were very careful about keeping their hair long, though most of them kept it pinned up.

The country preachers we had preached from the Bible but they had a lot of their own interpretation and a lot of times maybe it wasn't correct. They'd get in a big way of preaching, holler and squall and carry on, and some of them hollered so loud, they'd make the windows rattle. Some of them would get to jumpin' around and they'd just put on a show. People didn't think of it as a show, but really it was. That was the country style.

When we got an educated preacher in later years, nobody would hardly go to church, they just about quit going. He'd gone to the seminary school and he was well educated on the Bible and was a good man. Everybody knew him and his whole family. But when he completed his college and they called him as pastor to our church, people didn't want to hear him. He'd learned a whole lot, how to use the Bible to teach lessons, but people didn't go for that because he didn't put on a dramatic show. People liked that show. They were used to that.

Now they don't practice that in the community. It's altogether different. That generation is already gone and the younger generation never fell in that line.

★ ★ ★

One of the big traditions we had was the old-time revival. A lot of times in the summer or fall we'd be "in revival." That was when the churches put on a big event with visiting preachers who preached every night of the week. Some of them traveled with singin' groups or maybe the preacher's wife would sing. Those traveling preachers drew a big crowd.

Revivals were exciting times. Backsliders got enthused about God's message all over again and nonbelievers were moved to change their ways and join the church. The churches really did that to try to win the lost people in the community and they usually had pretty good success. Sometimes eight or ten people would come forward at one time.

Three of the churches in the community were Baptist churches—Coker Creek, Long Ridge, and Altoona—and when they had a revival, we'd attend their revivals, and their congregations would attend ours. I heard some churches down around Tellico Plains held old-time tent revivals. But up at Coker Creek, we just held revivals in churches—and in Altoona's case, of course, it was in that Smithfield schoolhouse.

Those revivals were just about the only big gathering of people they ever had on Coker Creek. They would draw in a lot of ol' mountaineers, moonshiners, and the kind of women who didn't usually bother with church. They'd come into the church, 'cause they all wanted to see what was a goin' on.

Sometimes the gravediggers would come and stand around outside the church. They were the kind of men who always dug the graves at the cemeteries, and they wouldn't come inside a church, they didn't feel like they were good enough to do that, I don't reckon, but those gravediggers would come to revivals and they'd just stay outside the door and listen.

There'd be three or four preachers that would come to one church, besides the pastor of the church, and he'd let them alternate, a different preacher would preach each night. I think each one would try to out-preach the others. They all had their own way of preachin' and their own stories, too. Some of them had been pretty rough characters at one time, I understand, and they'd changed their ways. And some of 'em were just born preachers.

If it was a revival when they had a lot of people repenting, they figured they were doing a lot of good and they kept that revival going till there weren't any more people responding. The revivals would usually go on for about two weeks, but if it was going good, they'd keep it going for three weeks and sometimes a revival would go on for as much as a month.

They'd say, "Well, God's really blessin' us. We're gonna extend the revival another week. We can't leave here when believers are still a comin' forward every night."

"Amen, brother!" You'd hear men yell that a lot.

During those revivals, the congregation would shout and carry on, and a lot of times, it was women. Some of the women were what we called "shoutin' women." Some of them would get filled with emotions and they'd just throw their hands up in the air and holler, "Praise the Lord! Praise the Lord!" And they meant it with all their heart. They'd come up that way, learned to do that when they felt filled with the Holy Spirit—they felt so happy about how the Lord had blessed them or spared them or shown them a way, that they couldn't contain themselves.

When some of those women got happy, they'd just shout and wave their arms, run backwards, faint and fall down, and somebody'd have to lay 'em down on a pew and fan them to revive them. People might not believe that, but it actually happened. I've been to church many a time when they just about tore the house down, praisin' the Lord. People were just as happy as could be. Maybe one of their children had been saved or had come back into the fold and, boy, they'd just rejoice with everything they could muster. I thought that was the way worship services were supposed to be. It was kind of an exciting time, especially for anybody who'd never seen anything like that. I guess they'd escort you out of a church if you did that today.

My mother and dad never did take a part in that, though. They tended to be reserved. Most of our kin was like that. I don't think they really believed in doing all of that carryin' on.

Sometimes if we had a revival where we had services late into the night, we'd have some problems. A lot of the young boys in the community were mean and they would do things to cause calamity. They liked to do that for some reason.

During revival, more than usual, there was a mixed group in the church. The Christian people always sat up close to the front and the other people who hadn't made a profession of faith or joined the church, they sat in the back. Sometimes the people in the back would cause a disturbance. They'd get to talkin' out and they'd answer the preacher back. Some of the deacons would go back there and order them out of the church. They'd take them outside and try to talk to them.

Some of those people didn't know any better, just "growed up" that way, back in the hills. Didn't know how to behave in a church. They came to church just to have a big time, to get out with a group of people. They wouldn't come to Sunday services, but at the revivals, there'd be several of them and they'd carry on. A lot of 'em wobbled around, and the way they talked, you knew they were all liquored up.

We had to have the law to keep those drunks in line. Deputy Sheriff Will Taylor was pretty good to look after situations like that. He was a distant relative on my mother's side and I looked up to him as an upholder of the law, which was pretty rare in those parts. He didn't live on Coker Creek, but he passed through regularly. I knew him because occasionally he'd come by our house when he was on a mission, out lookin' for moonshine stills, and he'd stop and eat with us.

Deputy Taylor would come to revivals and when some of those roughnecks caused disturbances, he'd take 'em out of there. Those boys'd get to making a lot of noise and they tried to be as rude as they could, so then the preacher'd call 'em down and they'd get up to leave, making a big fuss as they went, upsetting the congregation. But when they saw that Deputy Taylor was there, they usually respected him. They settled down right away because they knew he'd take them into custody if they got to disturbing public worship. They protected public worship pretty well, the law did. But some of those drunks figured out how to disrupt the worship services, even get people hurt, and they got away with it for a little while, before anybody caught on.

There was one family out there from way back in the mountains, one girl in that family that was as mean as she could be and she'd come to revival and those same rowdy boys would put her up to doing theatrics. Her name was Josephine and they called her Josie.

Josie'd run around with those rough boys, go home with them after revivals and everything. She'd go out with ol' drunks, just anybody, and law, that girl, those drunks put her up to acting wild and they'd get a kick out of what she'd do.

When that preacher was preachin' and prayin' and sweatin' and shudderin' with all his might, hopin' that more nonbelievers would find the Lord, he'd really get the congregation all worked up. When they had the altar call, some of the women would get all happy and they'd get up and shout. They'd clap their hands and wave their arms like tree branches in a stiff wind. Those drunken boys would put Josie up to doin' that, too, and tell her to run backwards over some of those good women.

The boys would tell Josie, "Now, when all them Christians come up to the front of the church and get to shoutin', knock that'un down."

Josie'd look around and pick out who she was going to run over and she'd just go to hollerin' and throwin' up her hands, "Oh, Lord! Lift me up!" And she'd run backwards in circles, with her arms out of control like she was just overtaken by the Spirit.

She'd fall down backwards over the top of somebody and knock them down to the floor. She was a pretty good-size girl and she'd fall with all her weight on whoever she'd picked out. For a minute they'd be scuffling, like two chickens with ruffled feathers, flappin' about, tryin' to get up. She'd rough some of 'em up a little bit before the deacons could get Josie calmed down.

We figured out that Josie was just pretending that she got happy in the service. She'd get up there and really put on a show for those boys and they'd be in the back of the church laughing at all the commotion

Josie was causing, and they'd carry on to really encourage her to put on more of a show. She was doing all that just to knock people down. Now, the other women didn't do that. Some of 'em would take a few steps back or prance about and some might even faint, but they were sincere.

After a while, when everybody in the church started noticing what was a goin' on, Deputy Taylor came down to the altar one night to take Josie out of there.

Josie said, "Why, I ain't doin' nothin', Deputy. I'm just praisin' the Lord. Got the Holy Spirit in me."

He got up close to her and said, "Whew! Yeah, Josie, you've got some kind of spirit in you, all right, but there's nothin' holy about it. You'll have to get on out of here." Deputy Taylor took her out of the church and talked to her and that put a stop to her carryin' on at revivals, as far as I ever knew.

Now, I guess a lot of people might not believe that things like that went on. But I'm just tellin' it like it happened. That's what I try to do when I tell the stories from those days—just tell it like it was, best I remember.

Every three or four years, the churches would have a "foot washing," a ceremony to show that you were humble enough that you didn't care to wash your neighbors' feet. I can't tell you where they got that tradition exactly, but I know there are some verses in the Bible that mention washing feet. Back then, they'd have those foot-washin' services and I've been to a few.

They'd put water in washpans and two people would sit down and face each other. They'd alternate, one would wash the other's feet, dry them off, and then they'd switch. We'd go to church when they had a foot-washing service sometimes, but my family didn't participate in that. We just watched.

The ladies were pretty bad to go to jumping around barefooted in those services. They'd get up and holler and praise Jesus and jump around with their wet feet. That custom died out a long time ago. A lot of things changed through the years in those churches. Of course, some things stayed the same.

At the end of the preaching, back then, whether it was a Sunday church service or a revival service, the preacher would ask all of the Christian people to stand up and come up to the front of the church. They'd all file down there, leaving any non-Christians sitting in the pews. After that, they'd ask if any of the lost people wanted to come forward and be saved, to come into the fold, and once in a while somebody would, sometimes there'd be quite a few of them, and sometimes no one came forward. They went through that procedure every service.

In fact, I became a Christian during one of those revivals out there at Altoona Church, when I was fourteen years old. I was moved by a preacher on a cold November day to dedicate my life to the Lord. I don't know, I just felt like I needed to. My parents were good, Christian people and I liked the way they lived. I felt like I needed to go in the same direction and that's where I went. And I really got a lot out of that.

At the end of revivals, they'd have a baptismal service and it was usually at a creek. Most of the church members usually went to the baptismal service. I walked down to the creek with the congregation—it was a big group of us—and they crowded around the bank.

The church had built a dam across a little forceful fork of Coker Creek and had it ponded up into a pool, so it was still water and deep enough to baptize people.

It happened to be the first cold spell we had, it was along about Thanksgiving. And it was unusually cold that day. There were about five or six of us to be baptized in the creek at the same time, so they got us all together and we waded out in the water in our clothes and we each stood there in that water up to our chests while the preacher baptized one at a time, down the line, each time going through his ritual. Once he baptized us, we'd get out of the water right away and I was glad I was the second one to get baptized, 'cause that water was just about like ice. The last boy to get baptized must've been 'bout froze.

We had to walk a half a mile after we got out of the water to a house where we could put dry clothes on and, boy, we were a shiverin', but

I don't remember paying much attention to that, 'cause I was used to going through a lot of hardships and cold weather and I didn't think too much about it. Besides, I was warmed to the core with the conviction that I had a future in Heaven. Those country preachers may have put on a big show, but they got their message across and a lot of people became believers when we had a revival.

★ ★ ★

The visiting preachers had to eat somewhere when they were in Coker Creek, so, of course, they ate at people's homes. There were no restaurants out there when I was a boy, nothing like that. Sometimes preachers would come to our house and it was always a big event.

We were expecting a preacher man one Sunday, and he came around the back of the house and stepped up on the porch to come into the kitchen, and he stopped.

"Well, I didn't know I was making a stop at the penitentiary," he said.

One of my uncles was always giving me hard words to spell and daring me to learn them. When he gave me "penitentiary," I was determined to remember it and I just got out my pocketknife and carved it all in capitals right over our kitchen door: PENITENTIARY. It was the only word I'd ever carved on our house and I don't know why I did that, but no one seemed to mind. After that, our cabin was permanently labeled a house of punishment. The ol' preacher got a kick out of that.

Most of those preachers were old country fellers and they used a lot of language that would just tickle me to death to hear 'em, the way they'd talk. This one, every few words, he'd say, "big boy." Big boy, I done this and, big boy, I done that. It was just a habit, like saying "you know."

I remember one thing he told—he was helping his mother down at the washin' place and they had a big kettle for boiling clothes. The fire was dying down a little bit, and his mother told him, "Chunk that fire up."

The preacher man said, "I walked over to that fire—big boy—and I took my foot—big boy—and I kicked that big coal fire under there. And—big boy!—them coals rolled down there, got right under my foot—and BIG BOY!—it liked to burnt me up!"

The Kelleys: Will and Verdie in front of Thelma, Quinton, and Edth

He shook his head, said he couldn't walk for a week after it happened, but all I could think about was him saying "big boy!" so much.

I was holding my stomach, bent over a laughin', 'cause that was just his way of talkin'. The preacher man didn't know why I was so tickled, and I think it embarrassed my mother.

My mother was a little better cook than the average woman in the community and those country preachers liked to come to our house because they got a little better service.

In that area, everybody considered chicken more or less a fancy dish, and if you were lucky, you'd have it on a Sunday. My mother'd have chicken dinner on certain Sundays, especially if we had a visitor.

She'd cut up the chicken and fry it, crispy. We'd all sit down around the table, covered with mother's best oilcloth. We'd bow our heads and the visiting preacher would say grace over my mother's white dishes. We never said grace around the dinner table if it was just us. It wasn't our custom as a family.

One time an uppity woman who'd been visiting our church came for dinner. My mother was trying to ask her if she expected grace before dinner as we all sat down. She said, "Well, do you talk to your plate before you eat?" Of course, she didn't mean anything by it, but that woman sure talked back.

"No, I do *not* talk to my plate! And you better not be talking to your plate, either, when you pray. You better be talking to the Lord God Almighty! Whoever heard of talking to a plate! Well, I *never!*"

That really got my mother, her saying that. My parents were polite and quiet about their beliefs, and they never would have talked to anybody like that. Their prayers were silent. They never preached at us kids, either. We all just tried to live by the Ten Commandments, the Golden Rule, and the attitudes taught by the Bible, on Sunday and through the rest of the week.

Smithfield Schoolhouse as it looked in the early 1920s

CHAPTER 9

Public Education

*At Quinton Kelley's request, some real names introduced
in Chapter 9 have been changed to provide anonymity.*

Come Monday morning when I was a kid, much of the year, I'd return
to the same room where I'd seen so many preachers carry on and holler from the pulpit. Only now in the preacher's place, there'd be a strict
woman, or sometimes a man, standing in front of a chalkboard.

I went to school with my sisters and my cousin Archie and with
other kids who usually attended church with us in that little Smithfield
schoolhouse. Mixed in with us were now some roughneck boys from
families that maybe didn't go to church, families known for moonshinin'
and all kinds of bad behavior and we all had to learn to get along.

Smithfield School bein' a one-room schoolhouse, they taught first
grade through the eighth and, of course, we were all in there together.
It had six windows in it, three on one side, three on the other. The windows weren't the same on both sides. You could raise them up and down
on the west side and on the east side they tilted in. It had two cloak
rooms, one for the boys, one for the girls.

As pupils, we used the same pews they used for church. The first
several rows had desks on the back of the pews, and you leaned forward and used the back of the seat in front of you. The pews in the
back didn't have desks and if you were doin' real well in your studies,

you could sit in one of those to read or study while the teacher taught the other grades.

In the school I went to, I'd say thirty-five would have been the most students at one time, if everybody was in attendance—which didn't happen very often. I have gone to school when there weren't but six or seven kids there. Each Coker Creek community had its own school, Ironsburg, Eperson, and so forth, because all the kids walked to school. If it was bad weather, they wouldn't get out.

I was always anxious for school to start in the fall. It helped that my first year of school, the teacher made a positive impression on me. I was probably the littlest one in the classroom, dressed in my blue shirt and overalls, and it was close to the first day or two of school. The teacher said that she wanted the first grade to learn to write our numbers. She wrote all the single-digit numbers on a piece of paper. She wanted us to copy each number in a column under her handwriting.

I could make all of them except the 3, and the 3 really had me. Boy, that was the hardest thing for me to do. I worried and worried and finally I could scribble it out to where you could tell what it was.

The teacher had me to come up to the blackboard while the other children were doing their schoolwork, and she held my hand and helped me practice the 3 over and over. By her helping me, it wasn't long till I could do that without any trouble and from then on, I really liked numbers and arithmetic.

The teacher always arranged the classes so that each grade was seated together. She'd have the eighth grade in one section and the seventh grade next to them and so on around the room. I learned quite a bit from listening to her instruct the higher grades and I watched the other kids when they went to the blackboard.

One time, the teacher called me up to the blackboard because the eighth grade had an arithmetic problem and they couldn't work the problem. She said, "Quinton, come up here and show them how to work this problem."

Well, I was in the sixth grade and they were in the eighth grade and I knew how to work the math. I worked it the first time.

It made some of the children kind of ill at me. They made some sarcastic remarks. I reckon they felt like they were "showed up."

I was always pretty good in math and that's the reason the teacher asked me to do the example. She did that to impress on the older kids that they needed to get on the ball and learn a little more.

I always made good grades and I was proud of that. I did fairly well in our language classes, too, even though they were at odds with the way everybody talked on Coker Creek.

Now, most people think that all Southerners say "y'all" and some of them did on Coker Creek. But by and large, most people on Coker Creek said "you'uns." If a few neighbors were walking by, we might say, "Hey, where you'uns a goin' to?" Or when leaving church on Sunday afternoon we might tell a family, "You'uns come for dinner and bring them young'uns." Those were the kids.

Our parents' generation had pretty unpolished speech and we kids were a notch better, I reckon. Every generation got a little more education than the last. But the mountains still sheltered us and we were just mountain people, with our own special way a talkin', and we kept that a goin' in the community.

My name, everybody pronounced it "Kwint'n." If somebody accidentally spilled dye on clothes they were washing, we'd say, "You've gone and ruirned that warsh!" Whatever formal instruction we did get on speech, a lot of it just didn't catch on.

Besides our academic studies, the school board encouraged the teachers to give us experiences with the arts. The teacher would organize school plays, we'd learn our lines, and some of the musicians from the community would come in and take a part. The musician Jesse Holder came to Smithfield School many times with his guitars and banjos and we'd sing along if we were doing a musical.

I was in a play one time and I played the part of a little colored boy. That liked to tickle Jesse Holder to death, that part I played. We'd pull ladies' stockings over our heads for blackface. We'd cut three round holes for our eyes and lips and we must have looked a sight.

I wish I could remember now what the play was about. Whatever it was, I just leaned back with my thumbs under my suspenders and started drawling in an exaggerated Southern negro voice, as deep as I could make it.

It was the first time—the only time—I ever played the part of a little colored boy. I had practiced it a lot and I must have acted a whole lot like Jesse thought a colored boy acted, and he really got a kick out of that—he could hardly play his guitar, he was shakin' with laughter so. Oh, the students just fell over a laughin' as I'd imitate the way we thought the black people talked. Of course, not having any blacks around there on Coker Creek, we made up a lot of silly stuff on our own. Didn't know no better.

The school board back then was different. They'd allow things then that they wouldn't let you do now. They'd let them have Baptist revivals in the school not just at night but in the day, too. The teacher held up the classes and the children stayed in their seats like they had come to church and they listened to the visiting preacher. When the revival services were over, the children went back to their classwork. I remember that happened sometimes and we were used to it.

The teachers were sent to our community by the school board down in Madisonville. Smithfield School had several different teachers who would come and go within one school year. They'd just have to live with a family out on Coker Creek while school was being taught, so not many of them lasted too long like that.

One school year, one of the teachers stayed at our house. I think the school board furnished her with a bed and I moved my bed into the living room, while Edth and Thelma bunked with the teacher. All three of them slept in that one bedroom with no heat, all winter. That was just part of regular life. Everybody did their part to provide hospitality to outsiders if they were staying in the community to help us in some way. And we were glad that we had teachers who were willin' to come out there and teach us backwards kids a thing or two.

★ ★ ★

My cousin Archie and I were big buddies at recess and lunch period. When we got together, we'd come up with all sorts of games and dares. Sometimes, we'd get to bein' a little too adventurous.

The little schoolhouse was right in the edge of a big forest. Archie and I used to play all up in those woods and climb trees. We'd climb way up in the top of those trees, till the limbs were just bending over. If two trees were close together, we'd swing from one tree to the other, like monkeys. We did that a lot, howling with glee as we'd swing around through the forest, rustling the leaves and breaking a few tender branches. Archie would always take some chances that I wouldn't take and sometimes he'd come tumbling down and catch some branches to break his fall. I was a little more careful.

When the teacher found out what we were doing, she put a stop to that. Teachers used a birch switch to enforce their rules. So we had to quit that. And it was a good thing, because Archie and I would just try anything that you could think of. It's a wonder to goodness that we didn't get crippled up or killed.

I didn't give 'em much trouble in school. Give em a little bit, I guess, but that was part of growin' up. One of the things I learned on my own in the schoolyard was how to get along with some of the roughneck boys. One time, I chased a schoolyard bully home to teach him a lesson. I'll call him Eddie Trellis.

I'd play ball at recess with a few boys, some were my cousins and some were boys that I didn't associate with outside of school, like Eddie. But Eddie always wanted to play ball whenever me 'n' Archie started playin'.

We played ball a lot in the schoolyard and Archie was a good ball player, we both were. We could throw that ball further than any of 'em, because that's what we did when we were out playing, if we weren't climbing trees. We'd throw rocks and things, just to see how far we could throw. I think Archie had the edge on me. It was good-natured competition. But I think some of the other boys were a little bit peeved at us, 'cause we were better at playin' ball than they were.

We were probably around ten years old, playing ball with Eddie Trellis one day in the schoolyard and the teacher rang the five-minute bell for us to go to the outhouse if we needed to. The second bell, five minutes later, meant it was time to come in and get back to our studies.

Archie and I quit playing ball at the first bell and Eddie had the ball. Well, this boy was a little bit mean when he got a chance to be. In fact, we'd always suspected that it was Eddie who'd put that sharpened pole down in our swimmin' hole, lookin' to rip somebody open.

I started to the outhouse, and as quick as I turned my back, Eddie hit me in the back with the ball as hard as he could. It was a pretty hard ball and, boy, did that hurt. That made me mad, so I took after him and he started a runnin'.

I just picked up everything I could find—rocks and sticks and everything else—and I threw 'em at him. I pelted him good. And I ran him all the way home, about a half a mile.

They had a barn at the corner and they had a gate. I ran that boy to the gate and he disappeared into the barn, yellin' like he had a swarm of bees after him.

Class was already going on when I got back to school and the teacher said, "Quinton, where in the world have you been?"

"Well, Eddie hit me in the back with that ball and I run him home." I explained to her how it happened, catchin' my breath.

It wasn't a few minutes till Eddie's mother came in the door of the schoolhouse, with one hand on her hip, a baby on the other, and she was all puffed up and snortin' like an old horse.

Now, the Trellis family didn't associate with people like most of the families did. They always seemed like a peculiar bunch. Mrs. Trellis was a big woman and high-tempered. I don't know how many children she had, but she always had a young baby on her hip, carrying it around just about every time I'd ever see her. Must have had one about every year.

The teacher said, "Mrs. Trellis, can I help you with something?"

She said, "Yes. I come out here to see that you give Quinton and Archie a whuppin'."

"Why is that, Mrs. Trellis?"

"Quinton and Archie run Eddie home. They was a whizzin' rocks by his head. He said if they'd a hit him in the head, they'd a killed him."

She included Archie in it even though Archie didn't have anything to do with it, but Eddie told her he did, I reckon.

The teacher already knew what had happened from me. She said, "Did Eddie tell you what he did that caused Quinton to behave like that?"

Eddie's mother said, "No. He just said they's all a playin' ball and they just took after him and rocked him home."

The teacher told Mrs. Trellis the story, as I had related it. And she said, "Under the circumstances, I can't give Quinton a whipping, because a boy has a right to defend himself."

She went out of there, Eddie's mother did, mad, it was a sight how mad she was, all red-faced and fuming. She was a big fat woman and she marched out toting that baby on her hip.

Some of the kids started laughing and she wheeled around and said, "Snicker! If it's all the sense yer got!" She'd say that occasionally, if she heard people laughing around her, even when they weren't laughing at her. She was a little bit unusual.

I don't know why I chased that Trellis boy so hard. I shouldn't have done that. I was taking a chance; he could have turned and fought me and he was a mean'un. I just pelted him with everything I could get my hands on and didn't let up. That was a little bit mean of me. I needed to be punished for doing that, I guess. Of course, Eddie needed to be punished, too. If Mrs. Trellis had brought Eddie in there and told the teacher she wanted her to whip Eddie and me both, the teacher would have given us both a whippin'. But she didn't do that and I was glad.

Eddie laid out of school a couple of days and when he came back to school, pretty soon, we were just big friends, as big as ever. We played together, hit the ball around the schoolyard. Children forget stuff like that. We got along good as school friends. Of course, he knew right away that I wouldn't take nothin' off of him. And he never did try to act like a schoolyard bully again, at least not to me. Never did have any more problems at the swimmin' hole after that, neither.

My sister Thelma, she had a run-in with Eddie in school, too. I remember watching it on the playground. It happened so fast, he didn't know what hit him.

Eddie said to Thelma, "What'd you do with that box?"

"What box?" Thelma answered him.

"The one you stood on to kiss the elephant's ass!" Eddie told her.

Thelma hauled off and punched him square in the nose. Just a big roundhouse shot, and it knocked him down.

Eddie went to cryin'. Just a bawlin'.

The teacher heard the commotion and came out and Eddie told her, "Thelma punched me in the nose!"

Thelma told the teacher what Eddie'd said to her that made her so mad.

"Well, then, let him cry! That'll do him some good," the teacher said, and went back in the schoolhouse.

Thelma never did have any more trouble with that boy.

Eddie never did learn much in school. He was clean-lookin' and all, his momma kept him pretty neat. In fact, he was a pretty good-lookin' boy, and he looked like a nice feller when he grew up. But Eddie was always wantin' to do somethin' to somebody. I don't know why he was like that. His sisters were all nice girls. But this boy, as he grew up, he was bad to drink, drive around in old junk cars, out lookin' for trouble. Oh, he turned out to be a mean bird and a lot of people feared him.

Eddie was still just a boy, really, when he killed a game warden. Now, one of my first cousins was with Eddie when he killed that game warden—that's how I know about it. This cousin, Albert Davis, he was a first cousin to me and a first cousin to Atlas Davis. Atlas and Albert's fathers were my mother's brothers. Albert Davis was kind of a mean, rough bird for some reason, and I never did associate with him much.

Well, Eddie Trellis and Albert Davis were hunting way back in the mountains one day and they killed a bear out of season. The game warden was in that area and, of course, when he heard the guns a shootin', he located them and, sure enough, they had the dead bear.

The game warden told Eddie and Albert, "Well, boys, you've violated the law and what the law is, I'm gonna have to arrest you and take you in."

Eddie, somehow, he kind of walked around behind the game warden and he had his gun leaning up against a tree. He grabbed it and he warped that game warden over the head, probably with the butt of the gun. I don't know what part of his head Eddie hit, but he killed that warden right off. Killed the game warden while he was talkin' to 'em.

Albert, of course, was guilty as an accessory as well, because he was there, but he didn't hit the man himself. Albert told Eddie, "Oh, boy, when they find this out, me and you both'll serve time."

"Naw," Eddie said, "they won't nobody never pin this on me."

But Albert knew Eddie would be the man the law was going to look for, because everybody knew that Eddie hunted back in those mountains around there all the time.

Albert told him, "Look, now, they don't nobody know what's happened but me and you. If they git you up over this, if you don't tell 'em that I's with you, I won't have to serve no time over it."

Eddie said, "Well, I may have to serve time, but I'll never tell who was with me. You just keep quiet and you'll be all right."

It wasn't long until Eddie got up there hunting again, and they arrested him for killing the game warden and took him to jail down in Madisonville.

Eddie had a bunch of dogs with him out there hunting and he had those dogs trained, boy, those dogs really believed in him. The law took his dogs in with him and put them in a compound close to the jail — it was within hearin' of the jail. They said Eddie kept everybody in that jail awake all night, a hollerin' at his dogs. He'd holler for those dogs and when they'd hear his voice, they'd bark and howl and he kept those dogs all riled up, so nobody around there got any sleep.

Eddie went to trial. He was found guilty and had to serve time for that killin' and he had to serve, I believe, it was two years for that. That's not much time for takin' a man's life. They just had to try him on circumstantial evidence, because they didn't have any eyewitnesses. There weren't any, except Albert, and they never did know he was there. I don't know how they connected Eddie up with killing the game warden, but they did some way.

Eddie had said to Albert, "Don't you worry none, I'll never tell 'em nothin'." And he didn't. My cousin never did have to go to the pen. Eddie never did tell on him, but years later, Albert told some of us what had happened.

I ran into to Eddie after he got out of prison. By then, I was old enough to drive a car. He came out to the store at Coker Creek and I talked to him about what prison was like, and you'd think that he was one of the finest fellers you ever seen.

He was talking about his punishment and he said, "Boy, I'll tell you what, that penitentiary's a bad place. You don't never want to get in there." He went on and just talked like he was now a good feller and reformed and all.

Then right after that, some people claimed it was Eddie that killed another feller, an old man who had a cabin up in the mountains. This old man was standing at the open door of his cabin and Eddie — or somebody — was way back in the woods where he could see that old man standing on his front porch, and just shot him from the woods and killed him. The man fell over, slumped down in his doorway, and that's how they found him. I don't know much about that, but I know nobody never did serve time over it.

Eddie'd come walking around in the community, up and down those roads with his rifle, always had his rifle. He had a .30 caliber.

My Uncle Edd Lee told me, "Eddie come by here one day, he had that rifle and I could tell he was a drinkin'." Eddie was always bad to drink.

Edd Lee was out doing some work and Eddie had stopped along the road and started talking to him.

Edd Lee said, "I's afraid to say anything back to him. He was carryin' on somethin' awful about what somebody'd done to him. I didn't know what he might do."

Eddie told my uncle, "I carry this gun 'cause if somebody crosses me, they're gonna get it. But I'll never bother you."

So my uncle said he talked to him a little bit to calm him down.

Edd Lee told me, "Eddie said, 'I tell you one thing. I really like Archie and Quinton. We went to school together. Quinton's the one run me home from school when I hit him in the back with a ball.'"

He still remembered that and he said to Edd Lee, "Them two fellers, Quinton and Archie, I think more of them two fellers than anybody in the country. I never would harm 'em no way, no form, nor fashion."

But Eddie had other people that he didn't like — he was a little bit peculiar — and he was dangerous then. One time he started telling people around Coker Creek that he was going to kill a man named Frank Murphy because he was mad at Frank for some reason or other. May have had to do with moonshine or it may have not.

Eddie had stopped down at Dave's Store and he was telling Dave and some of them that he was gonna kill Frank Murphy. And that was gonna suit Dave just fine, because Dave had hated Frank Murphy for a long time.

But some feller got up, walked out of there, and he went down to see Frank and told him, "That Trellis boy is down there at Dave's Store and he's about drunk and he's got his gun and he said he's a comin' out here to kill you. I wanted you to be prepared for it."

Frank thanked him, got his brother and two other fellers — they each had a gun — and they hid out along the road in the bushes where they knew Eddie would pass. Frank stayed in sight, with his pistol hidden.

When Eddie came walking along, he saw Frank and sure enough he said, "Frank, I've come out here to kill you and I'm a gonna kill you." He raised up that rifle and aimed it at Frank.

Frank answered back, "I tell you what you better do. You better look around you a little bit before you pull that trigger."

When Eddie looked around, three men stepped out of the bushes with their guns drawn.

Frank told me that Eddie dropped his rifle, put his hands up, and went to cryin'. Just a bawlin'.

"Frank," he said, "now, you know I wouldn't harm you. You're the best friend I've got!"

He was drunk and he might have shot Frank Murphy. He said he was going to and the people out there usually did what they said, if they could.

Frank told him, "Go on, get out of here! And don't you cause no more trouble." Nothing ever did happen between him and Frank after that.

I ran into Eddie up on the mountain some time later when I was hunting, as a young man. Eddie was up there hunting with his dogs.

"I just lost the best bear dog I've got," he said to me. "I come up here to take another look at 'im. I got 'im a layin' behind a log out there." We walked out to where his dog was a layin', split open.

"Now, right out this trail here is where he cornered a bear and he's the only dog I had that'd really go after, really stop a bear. He'd take hold of a bear." Eddie was all broken up and he said, "That ol' bear wheeled around there and just split him open with his claws."

That was the last time I ever talked to Eddie. He was still out shooting and this time his best dog got killed. Boy, that feller was really a hunter; he could track and hunt down wild boars and bears. And people, too, they said.

He most likely killed two people that I know about and most people said he was the one who shot the black cook when those hunters from up north came down to Coker Creek. He never served but about two years in total. We didn't have much law out there on Coker Creek in those days and I sure know it.

Don't remember when or how Eddie Trellis died, but I do know that one of Eddie's brothers was killed in a gun battle by my second cousin. They said at the time that my cousin wasn't much better than that other Trellis boy, but I reckon he was the better shot.

Nobody served time over that crime, either. That was the usual story out there. They had a hard time getting evidence and pinning it on the killers. And people out on Coker Creek wouldn't tell a thing. They were afraid to.

All the years I lived there, Coker Creek had its fair share of dangerous people, maybe a good deal more than that. Back in those hills lived some independent mountain men who had hair-trigger tempers and usually some moonshine or whiskey not far from reach to fuel their violence. But those kind tended to leave good people alone, unless you just ran across an ol' drunk on a bad day, like my unlucky Uncle Chester.

The front door to our cabin had a metal lock that about everyone in the community had. I guess everyone had a key that would work that lock, so we never used it. In fact, we left the door wide open in summer at night while we slept. Everybody knew the roughnecks didn't usually bother the good people directly. But their deadly goin's-on happened all around us, and we just hoped to sidestep the dangers.

CHAPTER 10

Moonshiners and Outlaws

Now, first off, most of the people around Coker Creek were good people, not drunks and criminals. We were brought up to be honest, to respect our parents and respect other people. But back when I was a kid, once in a while, there'd be a family that'd have a member of the family that would steal, and, boy, everybody in the community found that out right quick. They really looked down on the whole family for that. So my parents really stressed to us, "Never take anything unless you paid for it, or it was give to you. Never steal."

People in that community used to be bad to steal chickens. There were a bunch of fellers who would get into people's chicken coops when nobody was home. They'd get about half-drunk, slip around and steal some chickens, build up a fire, and they'd dress those chickens, cook 'em and have themselves a big meal.

Back when my dad first built us a chicken house, he didn't make a door in it, so thieves would have a hard time getting his chickens out of there. The chicken house was made of logs and the chickens could go through the cracks and get in there. But years later, my dad decided we needed to clean that chicken house out better, so he cut a door in it. Soon after, we had a run-in with chicken thieves.

Grandmaw Davis was living in Virginia at that time and she came down to spend a few weeks with us. She was a heavy woman and she walked with a cane. We had a revival going at our church that summer, but she was tired. She'd traveled all day to get there and she didn't want to go with us that night.

So, while we were gone to church, somebody got into our chickens. Grandmaw heard those chickens a squallin'. That was back before I had my little black dog. Before that, we had a big 'ol hound dog around there that never did bark at anybody or do much of nothin', but that hound dog started barking.

Grandmaw sicced that dog on the intruders and she ran out on the porch and she hollered, "Victor, bring the shotgun!" Her youngest son was named Victor. He wasn't even there with her, he was back in Bristol, but she just went to hollering, "Victor, bring the shotgun! Somebody's stealin' our chickens!" And she scared those rogues off.

They were about to get away with it. They'd tied the bag and they'd started away from the house, but that hound dog was after them and Grandmaw was a hollerin', "Shoot, Victor, shoot them fellers!"

The next morning my dad went down there looking around and he found two hens in a burlap bag.

He told us, "Looks like your grandmaw got so hot on 'em, them fellers figured if them chickens made a noise, they'd get shot, so they throwed them chickens down and run!"

The bandits thought we'd all gone to church. I bet they were where they could see us leave the house and they didn't know my grandmaw had come to visit. That's the only time that anybody ever got our chickens in all those years and they didn't get away with it. But they would have if my grandmother hadn't been there. Why, they'd have filled that sack full of chickens, I guess. There used to be a lot of that on Coker Creek, we'd always hear about it. People stealing, because they were too drunk and lazy to earn their own food.

Public intoxication was another common occurrence around Coker Creek. Some of them out there were just as drunk as a skunk all the time. They called that moonshine "tangle-foot" 'cause when they'd get drunk, they'd get tangled up and fall down. They'd get all liquored up and they'd just be stumblin' all over the road and cause all kinds of commotion as they passed through the community. You steered clear of them, boy, you did. They were likely to be wavin' a loaded gun.

As kids, Archie and I were so used to seeing drunken men staggering down our country lanes, we liked to imitate them for fun. I remember one evening late when we were walking to church back when we were about nine or ten years old, we started pretending we were drunk. We just staggered around and hollered and threw up our hands. We thought it was funny to act drunk.

A car started coming down the road, so we hammed it up, toppled into each other and stumbled along. This car turned out to be the sheriff's. Well, he stopped the car and got out.

Archie was in front of me and the sheriff grabbed him by the arm and started putting him into the car. The sheriff had already picked up somebody that had violated the law and he had him in the back of his car. He was just pushing Archie into that open door and he was about to put him in there with a pretty bad feller.

I decided that I was taking off, myself. I said, "Boy, they'll have to run me down if they get *me*." I was movin' on down the road, lookin' back. It was a wooded area and I was a fixin' to take to the woods, I'd already made up my mind. If they started towards me, they were gonna have a hard time catchin' me. I was gonna run from the law and I hadn't done anything wrong, but children'll do things.

I was way down the road, looking back to see what they were doing with Archie and the sheriff was talking to him. I guess the sheriff saw right off that Archie was really okay, but he thought he'd put a scare into him, and he did. Then the sheriff let Archie go and drove away.

Archie came on down the road and caught up with me. He said the sheriff gave him a goin' over pretty hard. That really scared us and we didn't pretend like we were drunk anymore, a staggerin' around and a hollerin' at people. We'd picked it up from older people that were known drunks. It wasn't likely that children of that age would be staggering drunk along the road, even on Coker Creek. I think the sheriff just saw us and thought he'd have some fun out of it.

Coker Creek didn't have a sheriff, of course. He would come out from Tellico Plains or Madisonville and he'd pass through Coker Creek on a regular basis. All we had were a few deputy sheriffs who were deputized to arrest people if they got into trouble because there were a lot of rough characters up there. There were an awful lot of 'em.

The outlaws and the moonshiners always respected the people that went to church and did the right thing. That's the one thing about them—they just bothered each other. Our family lived in a safe community, or we thought so. But around us, the moonshiners fought among themselves with pistols and shotguns. There was always a bunch of them fightin' and killin' and a goin' on.

There's a cemetery on Coker Creek where I met two fellers one day who were walkin' around the graves like I was, just lookin' at tombstones, and they told me how many people they personally knew of that had been killed in gun battles and were buried in that cemetery. It was a big number for a little community. I forgot what the number was exactly—fifty-something. And that was just one cemetery that those fellers knew about. They told me stories about gun battles, where there'd been a shoot-out here, a shoot-out there. They were older people, and as we'd say, "they knowed."

It was always said about the people on Coker Creek, "They just had it in 'em not to take nothin' off of nobody."

Gun battles got started innocently a lot of times. Even if they didn't drink, a lot of those mountain men just had hair-trigger tempers. At the slightest insult, they could go off in a rage and get their gun. And they didn't cool down right away, no sir. If they got in an argument, one of them might take a notion to fight it out.

One man I knew of—Poly was his name, he was a pretty good family man, didn't fool with moonshine, but he had that well-known temper— he was working with some other fellers digging a ditch line and they were discussing the best way to dig it out.

Poly wasn't having anything to do with the discussion. He was just minding his business. Now, Poly was a lanky man and he had a long face with big jaws. One of the fellers turned to him and said, "Well, *Longjaws*, what do you think about this ditch here?"

Poly threw down his shovel and walked off. He came back with his shotgun, loaded and cocked, and pointed it at the man who'd called him Longjaws. Poly went to raisin' Cain.

That feller, he didn't know he'd done anything wrong. But Poly was mad. He wasn't going to stand for being called Longjaws.

He did have real long jaws.

The other fellers had to talk ol' Poly out of shootin' the man who'd called him the nickname, and they finally calmed Poly down and got him to go home.

Now, take that hotheaded attitude, add some moonshine, and, boy, the bullets will fly. Sometimes two or three of them would get killed at one time. Most of them out there used shotguns or rifles when they quarreled or feuded. That's what they had because they hunted. Only a few of 'em had pistols, and those were always the men most likely to be drunk and deadly.

I know a place in the woods where they had one shoot-out and they were using pistols, something like a .45 revolver. They just shot the bark off the trees. Two men were trying to get one feller. There were big old trees around there and the men got behind those trees, shooting at each other. I can remember seeing that myself as a kid, where they shot the bark off of the trees trying to kill each other. One of them got killed. And the other two, they just took off.

I always stayed clear of those kind of people. If I knew they'd been drinking, I stayed away from them. My dad always told me, "Don't go around people like that. You'll get in trouble; whether you're doing anything or not, they'll get you in trouble. Just steer clear of 'em."

Well, they were nice-seeming people when they weren't drinking. You'd see them down at the store or along the road. They were friendly. You'd think they were the finest people in the world, if you didn't know them. You wouldn't know that they ever fooled with moonshine. But when they'd "get on a drunk," as we said, they'd drink a lot of that ol' moonshine, and it would just make 'em go crazy.

I had distant relatives like that—some of my cousins that I never did even meet, I guess. A lot of them, I knew when I saw them that they were my relatives, but I didn't have much to do with them because they were the type of people that my dad didn't want me runnin' around with. They were bad to fool with moonshine, drink and carry on. He never would allow me to be around that type of people and I had a desire to stay away from them, too, 'cause I didn't participate in that and I didn't want any trouble. But I could have picked them all out.

We knew every moonshiner, I guess, in that whole community. Word gets around that so-and-so is making moonshine, even though most of 'em were pretty slick-type people. They knew how to do that in secret and get away with it.

They called it "moonshine" because they usually made it at night, by the light of a pretty full moon, so they could see to work and not get caught. The old moonshiners would set up back in the mountains along little creeks, where bushes grow thick, to hide their moonshine stills, and the law would always go up in those wet areas and follow a lot of little streams down into the hollers. The deputy sheriffs knew moonshiners had to have water, so that's where they'd look for them.

I went to one moonshine still, not far from our house, when I was just a young boy. The law had shut down this particular moonshine operation and my dad told me where they'd been making it. So I went over to where these old moonshiners had kept a still sittin' back behind their cabin to see what was left behind.

The sheriff had taken an ax and laid into that still. It was all broken up in pieces. The law had already taken the metal parts away, the coils. They'd busted up the wooden mash boxes, too, but left those behind.

I gathered up that lumber from the mash boxes and took it home because we didn't have any lumber to use at our house. Of course, that's what I used to make my wagons, what was left from that old moonshine operation.

Moonshiners had boxes for making their corn mash, big rough wooden pine boxes about as big as a woodstove, and those mash boxes were what the moonshiners put their corn mash in before they ran it through the still. They boiled that corn mash and they had a coiled-up tube that they called "the worm," that condensed the steam. When they turned that corn mash into steam, then they'd have to get it back to liquid form. That's when they used what they called a "thumpin' keg." The steam comes out of the coils and as it goes into the thumpin' keg, where they have water to cool it down, it turns back into liquid—it turns into the moonshine. They distilled the spirits—it was just the steam from what they were boiling, that was really the moonshine. They don't get a lot of moonshine. It takes a whole lot of ingredients to get a gallon, though I never did know exactly what the recipe was.

I've seen lots of moonshine stills—not in operation—but I've seen them where the law has brought them in. They all looked about alike, made of a big copper or aluminum drum, shaped kind of like a kettle. The law was always finding one still or another. They'd load 'em up in a wagon and get 'em out of there.

This one feller up in the mountains thought he could outwit the law by going to a dry holler to make his moonshine. It was government land.

One day when I was a boy, I went up there with a neighbor.

He said to me, "Do you know what these poplar bark things is here on the ground, curled up and put together? Do you know what that's for?"

I said, "No, what is that?"

"There's a feller had him a still back up in here and he piped his water that way over into this dry holler. 'Cause the sheriff don't usually search them dry hollers."

This ol' moonshiner had gone way up on the side of that mountain and he'd peeled bark off of poplar trees. Their bark will peel off easily. He'd split it down one side and when he peeled it off, that poplar bark would curl up and make like a hose. That ol' moonshiner ringed it into sections about ten feet long, put those pieces together, and he ran water from way up on the mountain across a ridge and over into that dry holler with that bark pipe to make his moonshine. He'd been pretty crafty and covered that pipe with leaves so the law wouldn't see it. But they found it out anyway and shut him down.

Those ol' moonshiners were a scruffy bunch, lived in kind of junky places. They stayed out of sight—mostly—and worked on their farms. Most moonshiners had little ol' farms. They raised quite a bit of corn. They liked to use that corn to make corn liquor. Some of them made moonshine from apples and peaches and they tended orchards in the summer, but mostly, they drank that corn alcohol. They'd drink that ol' moonshine, crude as it was, and it would cause 'em to act somethin' awful. When they got drunk, they were crazy and you didn't want to be around them then.

Some of the men out on Coker Creek wasted their lives like that, sometimes a whole family of them were given to drink and carouse and shoot off their mouths and their pistols. If there was an example of a family given over to drink, it was the Lenderman family. They ran the only general store Coker Creek had for many years.

In the 1920s and early '30s, Dave Lenderman's store was the local trading place where we bought dry goods, sold our eggs, and got our mail. My parents didn't allow me to go places alone until I got old enough to take care of myself, so I was about eight or nine when I started going to the store by myself. Had something like a mile and a half to go. I'd ride our mule sometimes. I'd have to bring back groceries and I could tie 'em on the saddle.

Dave's Store was a little rough board building along the main road, about what you'd call a shack now, but back then I thought it was something great. Ol' Dave Lenderman, he was the man of the Lenderman family and he ran the store. He was a short, fat feller, had a big gut on him, and he was always ready with a grumble or a complaint. Back then, he usually had him a bottle of liquor handy back there behind the counter.

Dave had a counter with a glass case and a walkthrough back to where he kept the cash register behind the counter. When he went to make change, he'd step back behind the counter and while he was back there he'd get whatever merchandise you wanted out of the show-case. He kept certain items behind the glass, like the tobacco.

When I was a kid, that store seemed like a big place. Dave kept everything in that store that people used—salt, soda, flour, lard, and all kinds of spices. All the dry goods like sugar and meal were sold loose in big barrels. Dave would scoop out the meal, however much somebody wanted, and he'd put it in a paper bag.

The aisles were filled with all kinds of tools you use on a farm—coils of rope, saws, rakes, shovels, and horseshoes. Nearly everybody had horses that they worked and you had to buy horseshoes. The horseshoes came in all different sizes and you had to know what size you needed for your horse or your mule. A mule has a different kind of a foot. You have to get a muleshoe for a mule and a horseshoe for a horse. Dave had his horseshoes hooked all around the top of a big "fifty keg" nail keg. Nails came in a wooden keg back then, and, of course, Dave also sold the nails to nail the horseshoes.

Decent people came in to the Lenderman store to trade—back when it was the only trading place there was—but most of the time, there were a bunch of roughnecks that loitered around there, it was a hangout for them. They sat around and smoked or chewed tobacco, spat, and played checkers part of the time and told big tales about all the time.

Dave didn't furnish chairs for them. He'd have a lot of empty nail kegs and they'd turn 'em upside down and sit on 'em. The men would come in there and stay two or three hours, or maybe some of them would stop in for a few minutes, exchange information, and be on their way. All day long, they'd come and go like that.

My dad never did let me hang around where men gathered up to tell big tales. Oh, I'd hear a little bit of it sometimes down at the store when I went to trade. They'd brag about the Ku Klux Klan activities, or go on about women, that's the kind of stuff they talked about. Never talked about moonshinin'.

My dad always cautioned me to buy what I had to and get out of that place, not be a listenin' to stuff that wasn't worthwhile. When I heard them a goin' on, I'd just walk away from it. For a long time, Dave's Store was the only gathering place in that community, except for the churches, and a lot of those fellers in there talked like they'd never set foot in any kind of a church.

Because Dave's Store was the only place we had to get our information about the outside world, my dad would come back home telling stuff that Dave'd told him, things he'd read in the Knoxville paper. Dave kept the community informed, especially before we had a radio.

He'd tell people what he'd read about business and if there was something new that was going to be built, Dave'd tell everybody who was building it and how much it would cost. Back then a lot of places were making improvements, towns were beginning to grow between Knoxville and Coker Creek and it was kind of exciting to hear of big building projects.

One of the towns nearby built a big aluminum plant when I was just a young boy. I can remember them talking about it down at the store. That manufacturing plant was later called ALCOA. Aluminum was just beginning to come on the market out there, and all kinds of kitchen items were coming out in the new light-colored metal. We thought it was good metal—lightweight, wouldn't rust.

"They got to usin' that aluminum to make aeroplanes 'cause it's light and pretty strong. Why, I bet they'll have them noisy planes a buzzin' overhead all the time 'fore long," Dave said to me.

As a storekeeper, he was pretty nice to children. He was decent to everybody that went in there unless they crossed him. Or shopped somewhere else.

Dave didn't want you buying your stuff anywhere else. He would get you about anything you wanted. If he didn't have it, he'd take an order. He'd say, "I'll be goin' out to Knoxville in a week and I'll bring whatever you want back fer ya."

Of course, you'd have to take a day trip to Tellico Plains or Madisonville, or order from Sears and Roebuck to get much of anything, unless you traded with Dave. If you ordered from Sears, ol' Dave, he knew about it. He used to have the post office back then and he was the postmaster, too. So, he saw all the packages.

He always wore his glasses a little bit down on his nose and he was mean-looking. If he wasn't agreeing with you, he'd look over the top of them at you.

"You ought to be buyin' your stuff at home instead of ordering it!" He talked short. Dave'd say something like that every time he'd hand out a package from Sears. He'd just have to say something hateful.

Of course, Dave didn't have the same quality or selection as that big catalog, but you didn't dare talk back to him. You didn't dare say nothin' back, 'cause then you were into a big argument with him and he was just crazy enough to shoot you if you pushed him too far.

My dad hated to go in there because Dave'd say something that would make my dad mad about every time. He'd go in the store to buy a little cottonseed meal, and sure enough, Dave'd say, "Where you been buyin' your feed? Ain't been a gettin' it out here, so I reckon you been givin' your money to them rollin' stores. Looks like you'd learn to buy your stuff where you oughta." He'd bring out whatever my dad bought and say, "Now, maybe you'll know where to find this the next time, instead of buying it off one of them rollin' stores." Ol' Dave sure was bitter against those rolling stores.

My dad was in Dave's Store and he knew what kind of people they were and if he'd given Dave any lip, why, he'd have shot my dad, I guess. You didn't know what he might do. Of course, Dave kept his pistol in the glass case right by his cash register, and the reason he kept it loaded with the hammer back was so he wouldn't have to do nothin' except pull the trigger if somebody gave him any trouble. He'd just grab that pistol and that was the end of the trouble. Dave was all the time gettin' into a "shootin' scrape" of one kind or another.

I must have been about eight or nine years old when Dave killed one old moonshiner's son, and I never will forget it, 'cause, boy, it made an impression on me.

There was an old man and his son and they lived way up on the mountain near the top, way back where nobody went, where rattlesnakes liked to hide out, and these men had 'em a moonshine still up there. They made off a run of liquor and the old man told his son, "Well, let's git us some of that liquor and go down in the valley and celebrate."

The old man's wife, who told the story later, said she told them, "Now, you'll go down there and git in trouble. You know what'll happen."

She tried to talk them out of going, but they didn't pay any attention to her. So the old man and his son came down off the mountain and wandered around Coker Creek one night on a big drunk.

It was along in the morning, about four o'clock, and they were out carousing around. They were drinkin' and shootin' their guns off. My Uncle Joe Davis lived not far from where they were stumblin' along the road. They fired into my uncle's house and knocked splinters all over his bed, hoping they'd kill somebody. He was in the bed. Uncle Joe said, "Them splinters was a flyin' all over the quilt when them bullets came through the wall!"

That scared the family somethin' fierce. They all jumped out of their beds and hit the floor. Of course, my uncle didn't know why anybody would be shooting at them, because he never got into any trouble at all.

Those drunken moonshiners shot a whole lot of holes in Uncle Joe's house, but they didn't happen to hurt anybody. The ol' moonshiner and his son, they were out there yellin' somebody's name and carryin' on. I reckon they thought they knew who lived in that house, but they didn't. They didn't have anything against my uncle, but they had something against the feller they thought lived there.

Right after that, the same morning, the ol' moonshiner and his son came on out to Dave's Store looking for trouble. And they found it.

My Grandmaw Davis was carrying a basket of eggs that morning, real early, making her way around the curve to the store—bein' a big old woman, she didn't move too fast. She was coming down there to sell the eggs and buy a few groceries.

As Grandmaw neared the store, she could hear men's voices raised and angry, but she couldn't hear what they were saying. Then she heard some guns a firin' and she saw a man run out the front door and he came runnin' around the side of the building where a fence was tied to the corner of the store, and he jumped that fence and ran around behind the store. Dave Lenderman was a runnin' after him and both men were a firin' guns at each other the whole time and splinters were a comin' off of that store.

Grandmaw was so upset, she didn't go on to the store right then. She went up to the house across the road from the store, where Mrs. Lenderman lived. Of course, she knew Mrs. Lenderman. So she sat a spell up there, until the dust settled.

Word spread and the whole community came down to the store all through the day to see what had happened. People said that the old moonshiner and his son had been out all night causing trouble up and down the community, before and after they shot into my uncle's house.

It was said that when they got to Dave's Store that morning, the boy went in there and started a fight with Dave in some way. The boy being drunk and mean, too, he didn't realize that Dave was just as tough as he was. He'd been a mean drunk all of his life himself, Dave had.

Now, nobody knows what the boy said to Dave Lenderman or what ol' Dave said back. No one will ever know what made Dave kill that boy, shoot him at point-blank range, right there in the store.

About that time, the boy's daddy, the old man, walked up and looked in the door and he saw his son just a layin' there in the floor and he knew what had happened. And he knew he was in trouble.

When Dave Lenderman saw the old man, he turned his pistol on him, made a dive for him and took off after him, 'cause he knew the old man was armed. All those moonshiners were.

Dave came out shootin' and the old man was runnin' and shootin' back, but Dave didn't hit him and he didn't hit Dave.

After the old man jumped that fence and ran around behind the store, then somebody from inside the store opened the back door and killed the old man from the back door. Shot him dead. They always thought it was Dave's brother—he was in there—but nobody would ever say for sure which one did it.

So, Dave killed one of them and somebody else killed the other one and that was the last drunken spree for the old man and his son.

It wasn't until late that afternoon before the law ever came out to pick up the bodies. The sheriff had to get word, get some deputies together and, oh, it took them most of the day before the law ever got up there. That body was just a layin' there in the middle of the store, and Dave kept his store a goin'. They never closed the store for a minute, just kept right on trading.

I can remember seein' that boy. His blood was puddled up in the floor. The ol' moonshiner's son had fallen right across where the two counters had a divided place, right in that opening. When somebody wanted to buy something and he needed to make change or get items from behind the counter, Dave'd step over that feller. He'd get a plug of tobacco, ring it up on the cash register with the toe of his boot touching that boy's body. Then he'd reach over and hand the tobacco to the customer. Did that all day. That brought a lot of business, people a comin' down to see, and they'd buy something.

When I was a kid, that was just how it was on Coker Creek. I saw some of that real early. I didn't think too much about it. It was a common thing to hear about shoot-outs in the community.

When the law finally arrived, no one got charged with murder. I think they excused them on self-defense. And really, part of that was probably self-defense, because those two fellers went in there all liquored up; they were gonna cause trouble and they went to the wrong place. That ol' feller, Dave, was just as tough as they were and it was his place of business. So that cleared him. Ol' Dave wasn't ever worried about the law much, anyway. He'd just always say they were threatenin' him and he was protecting his store when he shot somebody.

They'd had other gun battles in there, but that's the only one that I personally knew anything about. There were different places in that store where they'd covered up bullet holes, where they'd had a shoot-out. Dave would take a Prince Albert tobacco can and nail it up to the wall to hide the bullet holes. They'd shot holes in some of the counters, too, and Dave had nailed Prince Albert cans over those bullet holes. In the years when Dave Lenderman's store was the only trading place on Coker Creek, it was dangerous to go to the store. Yeah, it really was.

You took your life in your hands when you had to go in there.

Dave Lenderman didn't hesitate pointing his pistol at his own family, either. I have seen it when ol' Dave got drunk and he and his wife would get into an argument in the store.

Mrs. Lenderman, everybody called her Roshe. Roshe'd say something to Dave and he'd yell back at her, and she'd start walking away from him to go back to the house. Aw, he didn't like that.

One time I heard Dave call out, "I'm just a mind to shoot you!"

She said, "Shoot, then!" She was a rough woman—had to be to put up with Dave—and she was just as stubborn as he was.

Dave pointed that pistol at her and fired—fired several shots at the ground around her feet.

She never missed a step, didn't run, didn't dance, just kept on walking back to the house and those bullets were a kickin' up dust all around her. I reckon she knew Dave was a good shot.

Some years later, Dave got into a bad mess with some outlaws and that gun he kept in the store didn't do him any good. Everybody around there knew the story; in fact, it even made it into a detective magazine.

Now, as I remember it, Dave had closed his store and started home, was almost to the house and a car pulled up at his gas pumps. A man hollered at him from the driver's seat and said, "Are you closed?"

He said, "Yeah, I'm just closed. It's after closin' time."

The man said, "Well, we've got to have some gas. Would you come back down here and pump us some gas?"

Dave said, "Well, I guess I can do that." So he turned around and went back to the store. There were three men in the car and Dave was putting the gas in the car and one of them said, "I need to get a twist of tobacco when you go in there to make change."

Dave told us about it later. "I was thinkin', now, he's figurin' on me going in there to get that tobacco and drivin' off and not payin' for that gas. I thought that's what they's up to."

But the man volunteered and said, "I'll go with you in there to get the tobacco."

Dave knew they wouldn't drive off without paying then.

He went around behind the counter to get the tobacco—he kept it down where he had to bend over—and when he straightened up, that feller had a big pistol drawn on him.

The man said, "We're gonna take you for a ride." He hollered at his buddies, said, "Come on in here, boys, git you some rope. We're gonna take this'un for a ride."

They reeled off some new rope and they tied ol' Dave up, tied his feet together, tied his hands behind him. They tied a handkerchief around his mouth so he couldn't holler. Then they emptied the cash register.

Those men put Dave in their car and took off towards North Carolina, back over in the mountains. After they got over the mountain, a few miles away, they pulled that handkerchief down and asked Dave, "Do you know where you're at?"

"Naw, never been here before in my life," Dave said, but he knew where he was.

They took him out by the side of the road and dragged him up in the woods and they told him, "We're gonna leave you up here in the woods. And one of us is gonna stay down there and if you make a sound or even move, we'll drill you so full of holes, you'll look like a sieve."

Dave waited until the car left. He told us, "I knew that nobody was gonna stay down there a waitin' to see if I tried to get loose."

So he went to work. That new rope had some give in it, and he just kept twisting at it till it came untied. He got his legs loose. He never could get his hands loose, but he was able to run.

He knew where a ranger station was and the ranger had a telephone. He was within a quarter of a mile of the ranger station, so he took off.

He kicked on the forest ranger's door. Of course, the forest ranger knew Dave, and when he got him free, Dave told him, "I've been robbed and them robbers is headed for Murphy, North Carolina. If you get on that telephone, you might call the law and they might catch 'em as they come into Murphy."

So the forest ranger called over to Murphy, North Carolina, and the high sheriff gathered up his deputies and they set up a roadblock. To go over into Murphy there's a little river to cross and the law set up at the entrance to the bridge. The high sheriff had his car parked so the gang couldn't go across. He thought that would be a good place to stop them.

A car pulled up there and the high sheriff walked up to the window to make sure it was the people they were looking for, and when he walked up to the car, somebody just shot him down. Then his deputies started shooting at the car. They had a big shoot-out there at the bridge. The lawmen killed two of them—shot the one that killed the high sheriff and they killed another one. But the youngest one of the group, he jumped in the river and swam away. They never could find him that night.

Back then, about the only public transportation was by train. They said, "Now he'll go to Andrews and catch the train to get out of the country."

So one of the sheriffs went to the train station in Andrews, North Carolina, dressed as a civilian, and there was a man sitting in there, just one man, with his hat pulled down over his eyes.

The sheriff said about it later, "I figured that was the man, but I couldn't take no chance on him. If he had thought I was a sheriff, it would have been too bad for me."

He pretended not to notice the man slumped in his chair, and he walked up to the ticket agent and he said, "Give me a ticket to Knoxville." And he winked and the ticket agent understood that there was something wrong. The agent played along and pretended to be getting a ticket and the sheriff just jerked his gun out and wheeled around and aimed that gun on the bandit.

He didn't put up resistance when they got the drop on him. If he had resisted, they'd have probably killed him. They searched him and he had the thirty-five dollars that the gang had taken off of Dave. That's all the money they got off him. That boy had the thirty-five dollars in his shoe. He had to go to the penitentiary for a long time.

That particular event changed Dave Lenderman a lot. It's a wonder that gang didn't kill him back in those woods. He'd been bad to drink, but after that happened, he quit that alcohol. He quit that drinking and carousing around himself, it made a believer out of him, having that second chance.

It didn't change his boys, though. Those boys of his, they just continued to keep doing what they'd seen their father do all those years. Dave had about four sons and three daughters and all of them were bad to drink, every one of 'em, I reckon.

All Dave's children were nice-looking. They dressed pretty clean, they weren't like some drunks. Most of the time, they'd conduct themselves in a pretty nice manner. A stranger wouldn't know if they'd been drinking, but if you knew them, you could tell. I've seen them sober and I've seen them drunk, and I could always tell the difference.

Sometimes they'd sober up maybe in the first of the week, then along towards the last of the week, they'd get on another big'un. A big drunk. They'd cut up, have a big time tellin' all kinds of ol' dirty jokes, laugh and carry on. They were a bunch of happy drunks. But some of the Lenderman boys, if you crossed their path, you had to fight 'em. That's how come some of 'em got killed early on.

After I was old enough to drive, I've gone out to Dave's Store to get gas and Dave's oldest son, T.C., he'd drunk so much alcohol, he couldn't even tell how much gas he was selling. The pumps they had back then, you had to pump the gas up in a glass tank and the tank was marked off in gallons with big box car numbers. You pumped it up full to the top, and then you let out the number of gallons you wanted.

T. C. Lenderman was just a small feller. He said, "Now, you tell me when to stop. I can't read them figures. I can't see 'em." T.C. was practically blind, blind drunk.

But he'd drive. Oh, it's a sight how he'd drive. He'd get out there and he'd drive trucks on those hairpin turns. He and his brothers hauled wood, sometimes big timber, sometimes pulpwood.

Dave would buy his boys a new truck every couple of years, always bought a Chevrolet. He'd put those boys out there to haulin' that pulpwood—that's wood cut in five-foot lengths from trees too small to make lumber. They'd pile it up, haul it to Tellico Plains to pulverize for the paper industry. A lot of young trees on Coker Creek were cut down to make paper.

Of course, those Lenderman boys'd drink every time they'd get into town, they'd sell that load of wood, get 'em some beer or whiskey, drink till they were drunk, and just get back on those mountain roads.

The oldest boy, T.C., he always did the driving and he must have been an expert, because he'd cross those mountains with that Chevrolet truck all day long. Most of the people that hauled wood from out in there, they could make four loads a day and T. C. Lenderman always made five. The Lendermans gained a load on the competition every day.

Every time Dave'd buy them a new truck, they'd always soup up the engine and put a straight exhaust on it. You could hear it for miles. They'd come through there with that truck a poppin' and a crackin'. They hauled a lot of wood right past our house.

It was a sight how fast they'd drive. I've seen them cross one little bridge just a flyin'. That bridge was just a little higher than the road—you might not feel the bump in a car—but I've seen them load that truck so heavy with timber that two of the boys would be out riding on the big fenders that covered the wheels—they'd ride out there to hold the front end of that truck down. I've seen them hit the bridge at top speed and the front end of that truck just came up and skipped along till they hit the curve in the road, and the whole time, T.C. never did let off of the gas.

I could hear them goin' up the next slope, way on outta sight. I could hear when they shifted down and they never let that truck slow down before they'd throw it in another gear. They just always ran that thing at top speed and I don't know how in the world that boy ever managed that on those steep mountain roads, T.C. so near blind and everything. He was just blind from drinking that moonshine so much. T.C. was always the driver and the biggest drunk of the bunch, but that boy could drive. I never did know of him having a wreck. I don't know how he did it. It's a wonder he didn't get killed like that.

His brother told me once, "T.C. drinks a pint of liquor every mornin'. Quick as he gets up, he'll empty a whole pint to start off the day."

All Dave's boys were that way. They didn't drink as much as T.C. did, but the others were bad to drink, too.

The other brothers, now, they had a temper on 'em. If you crossed their path, you just as well get ready for a fight, 'cause they'd tear into you. They'd fight to whip you or to die—one way or the other. In fact, two of Dave Lenderman's boys got killed in drunken gun battles. Dee Lenderman and his uncle were about the same age, so they ran around together and one day they got into an argument. They had a T-Model car, and they were supposed to pick up Dave at a certain time. At that time, Dave was working out at a gold mine where they had a bunch of machinery set up and he was mining for gold. Dee and his uncle, they got to drinkin' and both of them wanted to drive the car to pick Dave up that evening. They got into a big argument about who was gonna drive.

One of them had a pistol, the other one had a shotgun, and they just bailed out of the car and went around the back, and when they came around the back of the car, they just opened fire on each other, didn't care who saw them. And they killed each other right there. That was the end for Dave's son, Dee, and for Dave's wife's little brother. They were drunk and they were mean. They didn't care what they did.

Dave Lenderman's other boy, Leonard, he was the worst one. He got married and he lived in a little house pretty close to where the store was. He was a clean-shaven man, real tough and manly, and always into some kind of trouble.

Leonard Lenderman and a bunch of those fellers got to drinkin', carousin' around, and they got into a fight out where the road turns up, right by our homeplace.

Leonard was with his buddy, Paul Morrow, and he told him, "Come on out here, Paul, I want to talk to you a minute."

They walked down the road a ways. Leonard Lenderman said to Paul, "Now, whatever happens here, I don't want you to get in on it. I ain't mad at you. I'm mad at Clarence and I'm gonna work on him." That was Clarence Murphy, another man in the bunch who was bad to drink.

So they walked back up there in the road, and Leonard Lenderman had a pistol and he just pulled it out on Clarence Murphy. Leonard told Clarence that he was going to kill him.

As soon as Paul Morrow saw that, he grabbed up a rock and threw it and hit Leonard Lenderman right in the mouth and knocked out two or three of his teeth. And that saved Clarence Murphy. Right quick, some of them took that pistol away from Leonard.

The next day, I went out to Dave's Store and Leonard Lenderman was sitting around there and, boy, his mouth was all swollen up where Paul Morrow had knocked those teeth out. He said, "I'll get even with him—one day."

So, sure enough, one night they ended up down there at Tellico Plains at a little ol' beer joint. Well, that Leonard Lenderman was in the beer joint, drinking beer, and Paul Morrow and his brother, they pulled up there, and that Lenderman boy, he saw them.

Of course, Leonard had a gun on him, but Leonard wasn't going to shoot Paul—he said—he told everybody he was just going to beat him up.

Leonard walked out into the street and he knocked Paul down in the road with his fist.

Paul had a pistol on him, and when he got on his feet, he jerked that pistol out and killed that Lenderman boy, right there in the street.

So that was two of Dave's boys that got killed in drunken fights. Plus, his wife's young brother. That's just the way they did. That was a family that was just wasted by alcohol. They're buried right there at Coker Creek in the same cemetery as my kin.

Victims of drunken violence are scattered around every cemetery out there, their graves hardly even marked, some of 'em. That's just the way a lot of 'em lived out there back then. It was something that went on from way back to the Civil War, maybe earlier, I don't know. Sometimes those fellers'd ambush from the woods, from a bend in the road, about anywhere but the churchyard. Some of the old-timers called it "bush-whacking." That was the first thing some of that kind thought of, if somebody crossed them, they wanted to get rid of 'em. So gun battles weren't anything shocking to me as a boy growin' up. It was just a common thing that happened around the community and we heard about it from time to time.

After the gun battles happened, the sheriff would investigate it and that's about as far as it ever went. It was dangerous for the lawmen. They were not too welcome way back in those hills and those drunks didn't think a thing about shootin' a lawman.

One of my distant cousins was a deputy sheriff out there at Sandy Lane. He got an important message to deliver to an old feller back in the mountains, an urgent message from the family, so he went out there to deliver it and that feller saw him coming. That feller had been into a lot of illegal activity and he thought the sheriff was coming out there to arrest him. So he grabbed his gun and went around behind his house.

When the deputy sheriff walked up to the front porch and hollered "Hello!" that feller just stuck that gun around the corner of the house and killed the deputy. Just shot him down. Best I remember, nobody got charged in that killing. I don't know why.

For most killings, the usual story was nobody paid for the crime. It seemed to be that everything was self-defense. And then, sometimes two men would kill each other and there was nobody to pay for the crime. They just ended it all, right there along a road.

Oh, there was a roughneck around every curve out there, nearly, who just wasted their lives on makin' moonshine, runnin' it, drinkin' it, and layin' about, when they weren't getting into scrapes and shootin' off their guns at each other. That lifestyle cut most of 'em down early, shortened their lives.

"Son, don't you get around that alcohol," my father told me when I was old enough—and back in those hills, that was pretty young.

"Back before I married your mother, I used to run with a crowd like that a little bit," he said. "But I quit that right quick when I found out that whiskey'll have you a pickin' a fight with your best friend."

From all I'd seen and heard already, I believed him.

My dad made sure I had an antidote to that kind of a life. It was called "work."

CHAPTER 11

Gainful Employment

Will Kelley was an upright man, a man a feller could respect, and that included his strong work ethic, which he passed on to me. Instead of drunken idleness or worse, we chose a clean, honest way to make a living—sweat. All the years I was growing up, my dad had me out there helping him with whatever task he was doing, even if he didn't need a helper, he had me out there learning to work. I loved my mother and father just the same, but I had opportunity to spend more time with my father. I depended on my dad for just about everything. And he depended on me. When I told him I was gonna do something, I always did it. In fact, a lot of times, I'd do a little extra just to please him.

My dad noticed that. He'd say, "You really give a hundred and ten percent when you do somethin', Quinton. A man gets along in life when he does his best at things."

When somebody gave me a job to do, I didn't want to fool around. I wanted to get it done. And, of course, it was ingrained in me: "Quinton, you're just wastin' your time if you do a poor job of somethin'. If you're gonna do a job, do it right."

Stokley's canning plant down at Tellico Plains rented out farms in the area to grow beans and my Uncle Fred raised beans for them. I started working for him when I was ten years old, picking beans in the summertime. He paid his pickers ten cents a bushel.

Uncle Fred had two boys that were pretty bad to play around and didn't want to work. One day he said to us, "You boys, now, I'm gonna give you an extra dime, the one that picks the most beans today."

So I really got in there and worked, from early in the morning till dark. I picked six bushels of beans that day—at least a bushel more than anyone else—and I got the ten cents. I was really proud of that bonus dime, but one of Fred's sons was awfully jealous over that. Some people caught that boy taking beans out of my boxes and putting them in his boxes, but he still didn't get the ten cents.

When I got a couple of years older, I started looking for a better job, but there were only two legitimate industries on Coker Creek that hired people: sawmilling and gold mining.

The industry that attracted me first was the one that involved gold. It was exciting to think that something so rare and valuable could be found right where I lived.

I've been told many a time that the area around Coker Creek is the only place in Tennessee where gold can be found. Coker Creek gold is some of the purest gold in the world, according to the old prospectors. Runs around 23 karat pure gold in its natural state. They've mined a lot of gold on Coker Creek and around the Unicoi Mountains.

We'd all learned about the special history of Coker Creek and Tellico Plains in that one-room schoolhouse, about how gold mining changed the fate of the Cherokee Indians who used to live there. I was always pretty good at history in school, because I liked to hear true stories.

The first place gold was found in the United States was in the western North Carolina mountains way back in 1799. The second place gold was found was along that same mountain range, but over in Coker Creek, Tennessee. Coker Creek's official discovery of gold was in 1827, well before the famous '49 California Gold Rush.

People said that gold had been discovered on Coker Creek when a U.S. soldier had met a Cherokee Indian maiden at a Saturday night shindig down in Georgia and the soldier noticed a gold nugget hanging around her neck. She told him it had been found up in *Tanasi*, the original Cherokee name for the Tennessee area, in a big creek at *Coqua*, the Cherokee name for the place the white settlers later came to call Coker

Creek. That soldier who talked to the Indian maiden probably followed her clues and went lookin' for some gold himself, and I reckon, word got out. That was how the story went.

After gold was discovered in those hills, the government relocated the Cherokee Indian tribes so the land could be used for mining on a bigger scale. That was why they had that famous Trail of Tears in the winter of 1838, when seventeen thousand Cherokees, many of them from Tellico Plains, were forced to march to Oklahoma and leave their Tennessee homeland forever.

Gold mining camps sprang up all over Coker Creek and a prospecting industry was booming until the Civil War interrupted the mining. Close to a thousand men worked in the Coker Creek mines back then and panned the streams. Several hundred thousand dollars' worth of gold came out of those mountains and was processed through Georgia.

The federal government had once offered the land for sale to the public at auction in forty-acre tracts called "gold lots." In fact, our homeplace consisted of two of those old gold lots, and it sat at the foot of Tunnel Ridge—a mountain known for gold mining where tunnels had been cut a long time ago.

All of our homeplace had been mined for years before we ever lived there. They'd dug shallow pits along our creek where they were looking for gold. One old man came along and told my dad that during the Civil War, he didn't have to go into the army, so he panned gold on what became our property and he made five dollars a day with the gold he found right in our creek. And during the Civil War, five dollars a day about made a man rich.

Other miners had dug big shafts straight down into the ground as much as thirty feet deep in areas near us. They left those pits and nobody filled 'em in. You couldn't get out a walkin' around at night, if you didn't know where you were.

One night, my little black dog that I loved so much didn't come home and I figured he was runnin' a rabbit and fell down a gold shaft. You heard about that a happenin' from time to time.

Me 'n' Archie, we got us some nails, a hammer, and a saw, and we went up behind Smithfield School. Of course, we knew every nook and cranny of that land.

When we got up there, sure enough, we heard my dog a barkin'. That little dog was way down at the bottom of one of those old gold mining pits. Boy, was he glad to see us!

We gathered some tree limbs, cut us some rungs, nailed them together, and had us a ladder in a few minutes. I climbed down and got my little dog out of there. I guess he thought he'd met his death when he fell down in that pit, but if it hurt him any, I never did know it.

The government used to let people come in there and prospect for gold and just leave those pits that they'd dug. Branches would fall over them and, especially at night, a dog or a man couldn't see them. I think the government finally stopped letting people dig for gold like that and they filled in most of those holes, but there might still be old gold pits back up in there.

Down in what they call Hotwater area, they used to find a whole lot of gold. My daddy sometimes worked down there as the prospector's blacksmith to keep the mining tools sharpened. Most of those gold miners found their gold along little creeks where it had washed in there during a storm, when the water gets up real high. I guess that's the reason it's just little flakes, mostly, the water wore it out, washin' it down from the mountain. There'd be sand pockets after the water went down and you could shovel up that sand, pan it, and get little particles of gold. Or pick up some quartz, break it in two, and find a little piece of gold in one or two places.

My dad would take a spell where he'd pan for gold, but he never did find much. He had his best luck on our property. He had some little bits of gold imbedded in white quartz that he'd found. He kept that laying up on what we called the wall plate of the porch, and when somebody would come by and get to talkin' about gold mining, he'd always get those rocks down and show them what he'd found.

Every once in a while, my dad would sign a lease on his property to somebody who wanted to come in there and prospect for gold. They'd set up machinery and work and work and work. They never found what they wanted, so then they'd leave. Nobody ever struck it rich that I knew, but we all heard stories about people finding gold.

People said a widow woman named Cindy Kelly—no relation—supported all her children with the gold she collected from a rich vein on her property, which was nearby. She carried the dirt home, panned it out at night, then she'd trade the gold she found for groceries.

I found gold around our homeplace myself. As a kid, I used to take an old tin washpan—it wasn't exactly like a gold pan, but I could get sand out of the creek, pan it down and find little flakes of gold in it. I used to put those flakes in glass bottles. So I know there's gold in those streams, because I found it. Of course, I didn't have much time to devote to panning. But I did get paid for helping commercial miners find gold.

In the mid-1930s, when I was of working age, quite a bit of mining was still conducted in the hills around Coker Creek. Some places, you'd hear the whirring and clanging of machines—the stamp mills and ball mills that crush the ore to free the gold, as prospectors tried their luck.

When I joined a commercial mining operation at twelve years old, I thought we might find the big vein of gold that everybody kept talkin' about, the "mother lode." But those gold veins are layered in white quartz belts that run zigzag through the Unicoi mountains, and they're buried pretty deep.

My first job at the gold mine was to dig with a pick and shovel down in tunnels. It wasn't a very good job, but it was close enough to my house so I could walk through the woods to work. I'd walk a long, long ways back over in the mountains, up a dirt trail near the old Whippoorwill Mine.

I worked for a man who had machinery set up to sift for gold: C. E. Clossman, from Ohio. Clossman came down to Coker Creek and he did gold mining in a big way. Clossman kept his hair cut close and he was a short man. He talked real fast and he'd swear about every other word. He was awful bad to use by-words. That's what we called profanity, "by-words." Most people on Coker Creek didn't use foul language. Clossman didn't fit in with the people out there at all.

He and his wife, when they went anywhere, they never rode in the same seat, never did sit side by side. If he drove the car, she rode in the backseat; if she drove, he rode in the back. They were into a fuss about half the time.

The thing I remember most about Clossman is what he said about women in front of his wife. He had a work truck and, one time, he left the window rolled down and he had a bunch of hens in the cab. One of the hens got loose, and it had roosted up on the door of the truck and it messed up his seat.

Clossman sat down in that mess before he knew it and, boy, that made him mad. He used a lot of cuss words and he said, "A chicken's just like a woman. If they can't tear up something, they'll mess it up." His wife was standing over there and she didn't say anything. I thought Clossman was a cranky person.

Clossman spent a lot of money trying to locate gold and he set up full-scale operations in different places. He had a tunnel at the Whippoorwill Mine, near a branch of Wildcat Creek, where a vein of gold had been discovered just after the Civil War. It had been mined since then and there were tunnels cut into the earth on that hillside. The Clossman tunnel was cut beneath those older tunnels up on Tunnel Ridge. He set up a ball mill—something like fifty steel balls, each weighing about ten pounds, and they broke up the quartz and crushed it into dust to separate out any nuggets of gold.

For a couple of years, I worked for Clossman's operation up there a half a mile away from the Whippoorwill Mine, where Clossman was cutting a new tunnel to see if there was a fresh vein of gold. My cousins Atlas and Archie used to work for him, too. There were about five of us young teenage boys digging side by side—we dug dirt and rock and we drilled that tunnel deeper into the mountain, a little at a time.

Back then, of course, we didn't have a jackhammer. It took two men to drive steel with a sledgehammer.

The steel bit that was made for driving had a four-pronged cross on the end of that drill, and the short steel claws could be sharpened when they got beat down to where they wouldn't cut a thing. The steel bit had a long shaft; you'd lay it across your shoulder and it stuck out behind you, if you were the feller who was gonna shake the steel. That's the one who would twist that bit, hold it steady, and shake off the chips of rock.

Another feller stood behind him and hit the shaft of that steel bit with a sledgehammer. The feller who did that had to be pretty good at drivin', 'cause if he missed and hit you in the back, you were in trouble. Most of the fellers had done so much of that work, they were good at it and you didn't have to worry about them a hittin' you. I've done both jobs, I've been the one shaking the steel and then I've driven it, too. I liked drivin' the steel the best. You get on a steady rhythm and those chips of rock and dust will fly.

Every time I'd hit it, with a loud, sharp *Clink!*, the man holdin' the drill bit, he turned that steel a little. I'd hit it, and he'd turn it, hit it and turn it. It just chipped the rock off fine. That's the only way we had of doin' it. It was a slow process. It would take us probably an hour to go a foot.

When we got that hole back far enough, about two feet, we'd put a load of dynamite in there to break loose a lot more rock. Or we'd put gun powder in the hole. The charges had a cap and a long fuse. We'd light that fuse and get out quick after we lit it, 'cause when the fuse hit that powder—*Kaboom!*—the ground would just shake.

When those charges went off, they'd blow a deep hole back in that rock. We'd wait for the dust to clear, then muck it out. That was the purpose of drilling that hole, so they could blast out another portion and look for gold in the new rock. We drilled holes and blasted, drilled holes and blasted.

We worked the dirt with mattocks and shovels and picks and after we mucked out all of that dirt and rock, we'd shovel it into wheelbarrows, take it up to Clossman's sifting machine, dump in it a hopper, and the machine sifted for the gold.

Clossman'd be there looking to see if he found any gold. I never did look for gold myself up there. I was too busy to even notice what we were putting in the wheelbarrows. So I never knew how well he did. If he didn't find anything much after a while, Clossman would close that mine up and he'd have us start somewhere else.

At one place, we were following a seam in the mountain where there was a vein of quartz way back under a bank. We dug into that bank at an angle and we had to get down on our knees to keep from having to dig such a big hole. Sometimes we had to lie down on our side to get back under there. We kept moving the earth, going further back under that big ledge of rock, to find the soft place where we could dig, between the rocks. It had a seam of sand and gravel and that's where we were finding gold.

There was a boy Clossman had hired who lived up on top of a high mountain. He was really a mountaineer. Clossman came over there, and we were working back under that ledge and this boy was digging with a pick. Ol' man Clossman was down under there scratching around, getting samples. He got too close and that boy never noticed it and his pick caught Clossman's hat, jerked it off his head. That pick went right through the brim of the hat, pinned it in the dirt.

Clossman, oh, he started getting onto that boy. "Watch where you put that pick! Now, look there, you've ruined my best hat. Boy, don't you know how to handle a pick?!" He used some curse words, too. Clossman didn't know what kind of a boy he was, from way back on top of the mountain.

That boy turned his head and spat in the dirt. He said, "Now, you listen here, ol' man. You crawled up under where I's a workin', and if you crawl up under me again, I'll stick that pick right through your head. You ain't a foolin' with me like 'at."

Knowing that boy grew up on top of that high mountain, I knew he meant just exactly what he said. My cousins Atlas and Archie were working that day and we kept on digging, but we looked at each other 'cause we were anxious to see if the ol' prospector from Ohio was going to get himself in some hot water. You couldn't disrespect those mountaineers, especially the ones that lived way back in there.

Yeah, we waited for it, but when that mountaineer threatened the old man, Clossman hushed up right then. He just let the man work on. I figured he'd fire him, but he didn't.

Occasionally, Clossman would have investors come in there from up north and he'd dress up real slick and talk to them, show them the operation. He had a fancy new-model car and we'd always see his big black car pass by on our roads and we'd say, "Well, there goes Clossman."

One day, he had just zoomed off to somewhere, and some investors from up north, they came to the mine looking for Clossman and they pulled up in a fancy car even nicer than Clossman's.

A well-dressed man got out and he asked some of us working there, "Excuse me, gentlemen, good afternoon! Can you tell me, what's the man's name who runs this mine? We'd like to talk with him . . ."

Some of us told him, "Clossman. Mr. Clossman. But he left outta here. He orta be back in a spell."

This ol' feller went back to his car and we heard him tell his buddies, "They said the man's name is Clossman. Of course, I'm satisfied it's *Classman*. But these hillbillies down here are saying 'Clossman'. I could barely understand them." They all laughed.

We didn't like that, boy, we didn't like that. We didn't like it, 'cause Clossman always pronounced his name like we had. Those Northerners thought we didn't know what we were talkin' about. We talked among ourselves about them calling us "hillbillies." It insulted us then, but it's funny now to think about.

Clossman never did treat us like that. If he thought of us as hillbillies, he never let on. He was all right to work for, but you couldn't do enough to satisfy him, hardly. A lot of fellers who worked for him, he'd make remarks about their performance. Atlas was one of them. Atlas was always smoking back then. He smoked a pipe, even as a young man of about fifteen.

One day Clossman came up there and Atlas had that pipe out, packing his tobacco, and ol' man Clossman said, "Well, buddy, I'll tell you something. I ran your uncle off this job because he'd rather fool around with one of those pipes than work. Smoking cost him his job. You better get rid of that tobacco or you'll go, too."

Uncle Fred Davis had worked at the mine and he smoked a pipe, and sure enough, Clossman had fired him for his smoking.

Atlas would slip around when the old man would go to town and he'd light up his pipe. Clossman never did catch him again. Clossman thought if a man smoked, he'd stand around smoking half the time and wouldn't work hard enough. He didn't want you to look up for nothin'.

He paid as much as anybody else around there for that kind of work, a dollar a day, and we had to work ten hours at ten cents an hour. When it came to payin' you, though, Clossman didn't want to keep his end of the deal. He tried to cheat Atlas and Archie out of their wages, but I made sure that Clossman kept an honest deal with me.

One Saturday, Atlas and Archie came by the house to tell me we weren't working that day. It had been raining and Clossman didn't let us work when it was raining. They said, "Do you want to go with us up there to get our checks?"

I said, "Well, just tell Clossman to send it to me and I won't have to go up there." I had something else I wanted to do.

"I heard some of 'em down at Dave's say that Clossman was just gonna pay seventy-five cents a day for the work we done," Archie said.

"If that's all he's gonna pay me, don't get my check," I told them. "I'll go and get it myself." I was going to have a dollar a day for the work I'd done.

They went up the mountain and Clossman wrote out their checks and he just gave them seventy-five cents a day. Clossman said, "Do you want Quinton's check, too?"

They said, "No. Quinton said if you weren't gonna pay him a dollar a day, he'd just come and get his check himself."

The old man, they told me, just cussed and said, "Give me those checks back. I'll tear them up and write you some more." And he paid them all a dollar a day because of what I'd said. He knew he owed it, too.

Clossman was hard to work for. Maybe he was crabby because he was losing his shirt in those mining operations. He was trying to hit it rich, but he never did find much. He found a little gold, some nice nuggets, but not enough to make the operation profitable. And the gold was too hard to find and too hard to separate from its ore to be worth his while.

There's gold in those South Tennessee hills, and everyone knew it, but they didn't have any way to locate it exactly, they all just tried to find it blind. Everybody wanted to hit it rich, or not fool with mining at all, and, of course, I can't blame them for that.

Finally, the speculator from Ohio decided he wasn't going to strike it rich, so he went out of the business. The Clossman operation was the last large-scale tunnel mining in those hills. Supposedly, there is still that "mother lode of gold" hidden somewhere near Coker Creek.

By the time I was around fourteen, I moved on to a different line of work, one more suited to a boy who'd grown up in the woods. I joined the biggest industry goin' in those hills — sawmillin'.

Logging had been done around there for a long time because Coker Creek was so densely forested. Timber bein' a "poor man's crop," just about anybody with land could get in on it. Those hills buzzed with the sounds of trees being turned into lumber. Oak and pine were the two main woods, but people would sell all different kinds.

Back then, the trees were pretty good size, I'd say an average of twenty-four inches in diameter. Some were bigger, of course, and all those trees were tall. You could cut about two sixteen-foot logs and then maybe a short one, about eight or ten feet. That's a good forty feet from one tree, and that was just the good part of the trunk. Back then they wouldn't cut very far up the trunk for lumber, they stopped where the branches started. They didn't want a lot of knots in it. They wanted only clear lumber to make furniture. Nowadays, they cut right up where the limbs are.

Drivers hauled that freshly milled lumber through the mountains down to Tellico Plains on trucks, like the ones Dave Lenderman's sons drove. They had big lumberyards by the railyard. Oh, it was a sight in the world, the lumber from all around that area. Big stacks of long, true boards, just as pretty. It was big business. The train would come in there every day with empty cars to get a trainload of fresh lumber and the drivers unloaded their trucks directly onto the boxcars.

I was still not old enough to drive yet or do heavy work, so my first job in the sawmill industry kept me right in the middle of all the sawdust—doin' something called "doodlin' dust."

At the sawmill, a lot of dust comes out of the saw and they had a chain with little cleats that scooped up the sawdust and took it out of there, but a lot of sawdust shook off of that chain. It fell down in a pit. As a dust doodler, I was hired to roll a wheelbarrow down under the saw and let it fill up, then haul it out and dump it into a pile of sawdust as big as a dwelling house.

After it rots, hardwood sawdust—not pine—is good to put on farm-land for fertilizer, and a lot of people came and got wagonloads of that damp sawdust. It was good to fill in muddy spots along our pockmarked roads, too. Nothing was ever wasted.

At a second sawmill, I did a little heavier work, what they called an "off-bearer." One of the newer inventions in that industry was the steam-powered band saw. I took all the lumber that they sawed, lifted it and rolled it onto a roller bed that rides on a track, and sent it down to a cutoff saw.

When you cut lumber, there's a slab off of it that's about all bark. It went into a pile and they had a boy cuttin' it up, and that's how they fired the boiler to power the saw. He was just a feedin' that fire all the time.

My boss told me, "I don't want to see you carryin' nothin' out, not even the slabs. I want it all cut up into wood, 'cause we've got to have that wood to fire the boiler."

After the slab, then the next cut, you get a narrow board. Then, as you go on towards the center, you get a big wide board. After that, you've got to run all the boards through an edger to take the bark off, then cut them to length, square the ends, and stack the lumber.

My cousin Atlas worked at that sawmill. His job was to cut the lumber to different lengths with the cutoff saw and square the ends. He'd get mad at me because I was having to put so many slabs on the roller for him to cut. I'd just keep 'em comin' down the line and he'd try to keep up, but they were slicing those logs quicker than he could cut them. He was working as fast as he could, his long legs and arms moving like a granddaddy spider chased by a broom.

He motioned for me to carry out the slabs, just toss them out.

I shook my head at him.

He kept on, so I walked down there. Atlas was covered with sawdust and sweat and he said, "There ain't no way I can cut all them slabs and square up that lumber and get that lumber outta here."

I said, "Well, I'm just doin' what I's told to do. He told me to put every bit of wood down there for you to cut and he didn't want to catch me carryin' nothin' out. If you can't handle it, you better talk to the boss."

Atlas wouldn't say anything to the boss. He just got mad at me. He'd throw those slabs off to the side, pile 'em up. Then, when they shut down the mill, the cutoff saw would still run and he'd cut up those slabs, grumbling about it.

Well, I had to do what my boss told me to do, 'cause in those lean times, I wanted to keep whatever job I could get. But I was eager to get out of that hot and dusty sawmill.

One of my cousins through marriage had a sawmill, too, and I got a job out logging for him when I was around fifteen or sixteen. Lloyd Dalton was good feller. He was a hardworking man and when you saw him a walkin', he just walked with his whole body. Some people will walk like what you'd call a soldier, just as straight—like Atlas did—but Lloyd'd walk bobbin' up and down. Now, I'm pretty bad to do that, too, so I've been told.

One day, I went into work and Lloyd said, "Well, I bought me a team of horses Saturday and they never have been broke to work or nothin'. I want you to take 'em to the blacksmith, get shoes put on 'em and when you come back, we'll take them horses and see if we can work 'em."

I can't think of their names anymore, but they were both an auburn color, so we called them "red" horses. One of the horses was pretty mean and he had more reddish color to his coat than the other horse.

My cousin Lloyd told me, "Now, the real red horse you can't ride—it's a wild'un—but the other'un, you can ride. Ride that'un down to the blacksmith."

Those horses were pretty skittish. I took hold of the bridles and started talking to them. "Ho! Boy, now! Settle down, settle down, now . . . Gooood. Good boy."

I patted them and stroked their coat and talked to them in a low, friendly voice. I talked to the horses just like I was talkin' to somebody. "Boys, you're gonna come with me today and we're gonna get you some shoes . . ."' Course, they didn't know what shoes were, but I kept talkin' to them and my voice kind of calmed them down.

From that sawmill, I had to go about five miles to the closest blacksmith shop—it wasn't my dad's—and I rode the one horse that was broke and I didn't have any trouble. When I got to this community blacksmith, he was a good blacksmith, but he said he didn't like to shoe horses. He got to fooling with those horses, and he found out that they were both pretty unruly and had never been trained and he dreaded it. But he said to me, "Well, all right. I'll try it."

He got the shoes on the horse I rode, though it seemed to be the meanest one.

That other horse, the redder horse, he'd been just as quiet, standin' there. The blacksmith looked over at him and said, "Well, I reckon we won't have no trouble with that other'un."

We started with that horse and it seemed to be more gentle at first, but as it turned out, that horse was really mean. The blacksmith got over close to that horse and it just made a dive at him and opened its mouth and squealed—Eeeyeeeww!—and pulled its lips back and gnashed its big ol' teeth inches from the blacksmith's shoulder. Now, a horse can bite hard, they can take a chunk out of you.

Then the blacksmith tried to get around behind the horse, and that horse would just try to kick him. A horse can kick hard. They can kill you, if they hit you in the head.

He just couldn't do a thing with that horse, that's all there was to it. He'd gotten worked up and he was as dangerous as could be. Why, it would have taken three or four people to have handled that horse right then.

The blacksmith did manage to get the front shoes on, but to get a back shoe on, he had to put a chain on that horse's leg and draw that chain across the horse's back to hoist up his back foot. He finally got that one shoe on the back foot.

The blacksmith said, "I wouldn't touch that other foot for no amount of money. You can take this'un back with three shoes on."

By the time I got back, it was late in the afternoon. My cousin Lloyd said, "Where in the world have you been all day?"

I said, "Well, we had trouble shoein' them horses. Couldn't do nothin' with 'em hardly. One of 'em don't have a shoe on it."

He didn't like that a bit, but he said, "Well, I went and got me a harness today. In the morning, let's put that harness on them horses and drive 'em around, see what they do."

When we harnessed up the horses, they didn't cause too much trouble. We drove them around a little, so it looked like it'd be a pretty easy task to get them to pull logs.

Lloyd said, "Let's drag us out some logs."

We used grabs that you drive into a log, attached to chains, and we hooked the horses to the chains to drag in the log. Then my cousin, who was trying to show me how to get the horses to work, he tried to force the horses into pulling that load.

One horse would start and then the other, back and forth, seesawing around. Lloyd got so mad at those horses—he was pullin' at 'em and yellin' at 'em, and he really got those horses upset. That was making them meaner. Those horses didn't know a thing about pullin' logs, of course. Horses don't know that, you have to train them.

When he got them started forward, the weight of that log they were pulling scared them, and they started pulling to the side, trying to break away. Lloyd started slashing at them with the whip and a hollerin' and a goin' on, making them whinny and buck around. Those horses got all tangled up in the harness and he had to straighten it out. Had a terrible time. He was bein' mean to those horses and that was no way to train anything. They were scared to death, they didn't know what was a goin' on. I felt sorry for them. Lloyd was yanking the harness, just jerkin' on their poor ol' necks.

I was watching and I couldn't say anything because I was working for him. And oh, law, it looked like he wouldn't be able to do much with those horses. I guess by that time, he figured he'd made a bad decision buying those two.

About ten o'clock, he said, "I've got to go to that sawmill, I can't stay here. You're just gonna have to drag them logs out. See if you can handle 'em."

I was just a kid, you might say, just a teenage boy, but he turned that agitated team over to me. I had a little trouble getting the horses to work together, but I was good to the horses. I wouldn't be mean to them. I petted them and talked to them, calmed them down.

"Here, boys! Come on, now. It's gonna be all right . . ." I started brushing their coat with my hand all along their shoulders and back, and I stroked their shaggy manes. I'd just pet them and pat them, gently, talking all the time. I might even have hummed a little tune. And they began to settle down. I got to where I could drag the logs out with that team of horses, once I let them know what I wanted them to do, and we were workin' fine together.

How do you get along with animals, especially when they don't know you, and they're afraid of you and shy away from you? You've got to go to talkin' to them, gentle-like, and when you get to where they'll let you touch them, then start rubbing them and petting them and keep talkin' to 'em. Animals find out that you won't bother them and then they're all right.

You've got to be real good to new horses, especially when they're wild like that. If you're even a little bit rough with them, boy, you can't hardly do a thing with 'em after that. Some people will just go to hollerin' and yellin' and jerkin' on the bridle and then you've got a battle on your hands. Animals like to be treated right, just like people do. That's the way I did and I found out that it worked every time.

I took that one real red horse home and worked with him. And he took a likin' to me. A few days later, we got that horse shoed with no trouble at all. Why, I could do just about anything with those horses. I'd go back in the woods, hook the horses to the logs and drag them to the mill, then go back in the woods for more. That was a lot easier work. The horses did all the work. I'd work them a while, drag another log, and if it was heavy, I'd stop them to rest every so often. But if I let them rest too long, the next thing you know, those horses would start pawing at the ground, 'cause they wanted to pull that load. They didn't like standing around when they had work to do. Horses are just like that. Now, a mule, he'd stand there all day if you let him.

One day, there was a big poplar tree on a tract of timber, and Lloyd told the men who were cutting it, "Now, you make that first cut at twelve foot 'cause that team can't pull a big sixteen footer."

Well, they didn't pay any attention to my cousin and when they cut the tree, they cut a big sixteen-foot log. Rather than cut it down and waste it, Lloyd said to me, "I tell you what. I'll go with you up there and we'll see if them horses can pull that big log in."

We went up there and Lloyd took over the reins. Of course, the horses weren't used to him. And there he went, a hollerin', slappin' them with the reins, and he got 'em all worked up.

They broke some of the harness and he had to fix it, and he was gettin' mad. I wasn't sayin' a thing, 'cause they were his horses.

After a while, he said "Aw, I've got to go to the sawmill and cut lumber, so you do what you have to. I don't think they can pull that log in, it's just too heavy. Reckon we'll have to cut that lumber down and waste it. See what you can do."

I didn't dare try to get that team to pull that big log until I petted the horses, talked to them, fooled with them. Then I said, "Okay, let's see what you'll do."

I told them, "Tighten up! Tighten up!" They knew what I meant, and both horses would tighten up, ready to pull.

Then I said, "GIT IT, BOYS!"

They just dug in there and here they went with that big log, a draggin' it along. And they pulled that sixteen footer through the woods, all the way to the sawmill! That liked to killed my cousin when I came draggin' that big log in. But he never did say a thing about how I handled those horses. He's bound to have thought something, but he never did say it.

Trying to be mean to animals, why, you can't do that. I'd learned that years before. My dad taught me how to handle animals. He said, "Treat 'em right and they'll do their job." But, of course, I'd learned the most by watching how he did.

By the time I had been out in the workplace a little while, I saw for myself that it was true: You got along better, went a little further, when you showed basic respect for all of God's creatures. Respect for the boss, your fellow workers, and even the work animals.

While I was working those red horses, they were just as gentle. They were both good animals, but that redder horse, as long as I worked him, let Lloyd get in reach of him, and if that horse could get loose, he'd dive at Lloyd with a big squeal and try to nip him good.

He never did try to bite me. I could fool with that horse all I wanted, because animals know when you're good to them, but if you're mean to them, they're gonna get back at you. I loved those horses and always fed them on time. Together, we kept the sawmill busy dragging in timber from the forests of Coker Creek.

I was dragging some logs off of land where a neighbor lived one day and my dad came down there and he was talking to the neighbor. I was up on the ridge, where he couldn't see me, but I heard the neighbor say, "That boy of yours can handle them horses 'bout as good as anybody I ever seen. Them horses'll do just *exactly* what he tells 'em to."

My dad said, "Well, Quinton'll do all that he can when you put him out there on a job. He really puts his heart in it."

Growing up, I always tried to do a little better job at something than my dad thought I'd do. I wasn't satisfied if I didn't do as near a perfect job as I could. That's just in me, I reckon. And my dad was always one to comment on it. I was pleased to know he had bragged about me a little bit.

By then, it was around 1940, and I'd heard that a company backed by the government called the Tennessee Valley Authority, TVA, was hiring laborers for construction projects in the area. I went to apply, but there was a long line of men and just as I got to the front of the line, the foreman came out and announced, "We're not hiring any more right now. Got all we need."

All the men started grumbling and started to leave.

But then, the foreman added, "Well, I believe we can use *one* more," and, for some reason that I'd never know, he gave the last job to me.

I went and told my cousin, "I've got a better job offer and I'm gonna quit the sawmill. I can't work for the wages I'm getting since the other company's gonna pay me a lot more." TVA paid fifty cents an hour and that just about doubled my wages from the sawmill.

"Aw," Lloyd said, "I can't let you go, how much more will you have to have?"

I said, "You can't pay what TVA pays, I know."

Lloyd begged me to stay, but I knew that my future would be better served with TVA.

Sometime later, I heard that Lloyd got out in the mountains with that team of horses, and he ran them off a steep slope, and one of those horses ended up on its back in the treetops! They said it was up in that tree, a kickin' its feet, and I don't know how they ever got that poor horse down from there, but they did.

My decision to go to work for TVA when I was eighteen years old turned out to be the start of a lifelong relationship. I traveled to job sites where TVA had building projects and I lived in camps set up for workers during the week, but I went home on weekends. I could make a lot more money and I was part of a worthy project: helping to bring electricity to the rural South.

Poverty in the Tennessee Valley region had been dire since the Great Depression, even worse than in the rest of the country. We always said, "People just didn't hardly have *nothin'*." I remember when things were so tough, two men would go hunting and if they killed a rabbit, they'd divide it, so each one got half of a rabbit for dinner. Not a whole lot of meat there.

We were all just farmers—everyone's motto was "If you ate, you farmed"—but the soil had been overfarmed in places and crop yields were down for a lot of people. Also, the biggest and best timber had already been cut from the forests and sold. It was getting harder and harder for a man to survive in rural areas back then, and we were behind the times, too. Nobody had any electricity in our part of Tennessee.

As part of the New Deal, President Franklin D. Roosevelt had created the Tennessee Valley Authority in 1933 to help manage conditions for the people of the Tennessee River Basin, which is spread out to include parts of seven states. TVA started reforestation projects, taught farmers new ways of growing, and they started controlling the flooding of the Tennessee Valley region by building dams. Those dams would also produce hydroelectrical power.

The country folk like us were still living like pioneers by fire and lamplight while a lot of the people in America's cities already had lights, refrigerators, electric ranges, and water heaters — if they could afford them. TVA aimed to change that. We'd get to have electricity, too!

Of course, we didn't know it, but the electrical power that TVA generated would one day become vital to the U.S. winning World War II. But in the late 1930s and early '40s, the only thing that really mattered to us around Coker Creek was that TVA provided jobs.

Sixteen dams were built by TVA between 1933 and 1944, and they needed construction crews by the thousands. Those dams made it possible for TVA to flood large areas of flat land — that water would back up for miles and miles — creating lakes that they raised and lowered with the dams to generate electricity at TVA's power plants.

TVA had to relocate families that lived on those lands before they could flood them and there was one story I heard about a family that didn't want to move because it would mean extinguishing their home's hearth fire, and it had been burning continuously for three generations.

I reckon TVA got them to move, because when they built those dams, there wasn't nothin' that stood in the way of their plans. Old family homes were torn down, trees were cleared, and farmlands were flooded to make huge reservoirs that changed the landscape of the Tennessee Valley.

When I got hired, TVA was building the Appalachia Dam on Hiawassee River, close to Murphy, North Carolina, just a little ways southeast of Coker Creek. My first job with TVA was common labor on a materials truck to deliver lumber for the construction of the dam and the powerhouse.

There were three or four of us young men working together. We stacked lumber when it came in and loaded it on the truck and delivered it to the different carpenter crews. Then one day, they gave me the job of carpenter's helper. There were about fifteen carpenters and about four or five helpers on that site, and we helpers carried the materials, did the dirty work.

The dams in TVA's system were created by carpenters building forms in wood and they used those forms when they poured the concrete. Those dams were built block by block. They'd raise the forms with a crane, and use them again and again. They oiled the inside of the forms and the concrete didn't stick to it. They'd lift the forms, set them up and pour concrete, let it set up, and do it all over again, layer by layer, all the way to the top. The Appalachia Dam reached a height of 307 feet. Most of my work was on the dam, but I also worked in the tunnel and the powerhouse as a carpenter's helper.

The powerhouse was about fifteen miles from the dam and they built a tunnel through the mountain to channel water down to the powerhouse. The tunnel was drilled into the mountain through solid rock. TVA had cut tunnels, kind of like the ol' gold miners used to do, only TVA had big air-powered drills that would cut circles in the rock and, of course, their tunnel was much bigger. Then they'd blast it out, and muck it out. I was glad I wasn't the one doing the mucking anymore.

I kept the carpenters supplied with wood and nails. The carpenters built forms inside the tunnel and a crew pumped the forms full of concrete to line the tunnel. By the time they were done, that tunnel was smooth concrete all the way through, a sluiceway, and TVA diverted the river to run through it.

The water ran through that tunnel, gushed out of the side of a mountain, and went down at a steep angle into the powerhouse, which gave it a lot of force to generate power. Most of the river water went through the tunnel to feed the powerhouse, but they kept some water flowing through the Hiawassee River to support fish and wildlife.

I was working at the powerhouse one day when the general foreman came by and said, "We're gonna have an apprentice program to train you boys to be journeyman carpenters, if you want to sign up for it."

Of course, that's what I wanted—advancement and a future—so I spoke up. "Well, I'll sign up for it."

The general foreman picked out only five or six apprentice carpenters and we started our training program. We had to go to school four hours during the week after work and it took 660 hours to graduate with a degree in carpentry.

The foreman told us, "Get you some carpenter tools and you can work right along with a journeyman carpenter right now. We'll have one work with you to show you what to do and help you to learn."

That sounded good.

For my first experience as an apprentice carpenter, they were building a catwalk across the Hiawassee River. My assignment was to nail it together. The foreman had paired me up with a seasoned carpenter, but he was a grumpy old man and didn't like it because the foreman had put an apprentice with him. He didn't want to have to teach and do his work, too.

I would ask him, "Now, what kind of nails do you use for this . . . or for that . . . ?"

He wouldn't tell me, wouldn't tell me a thing.

I just had to watch him and figure it out for myself. But I did it, and none of my work was any less solid than his.

I got to likin' that carpentry. I collected lots of tools and I learned how to use every one. I built a big toolbox and painted it green, like the trees in summer. That green toolbox made a good seat when the lid was closed and I'd sit on it to eat my lunch when I was on the job site. That's the only sittin' I ever did at work. When lunch was done, I wouldn't loafer around like some of 'em; I'd swing that toolbox on my shoulder—it had a rope handle that I used to carry it—and I'd go right back to work.

We'd finish one job and TVA would lay me off. They'd always say, "We can't transfer you, that's against our rules, but you be at such-and-such place Monday morning and we'll give you a job." I just stayed with them like that. They didn't do all the men that way. They liked me for some reason, I don't know why. I was just like everybody else, but they'd always offer me a job wherever their next construction project was. Well, I'd work. That's one thing I'd do, I'd really work. Some people they'd hire, they couldn't get nothin' out of them, they'd deadbeat around and I guess TVA realized that.

I was earning the best wages available in the area and I kept saving that money. Once I started working, I always had money, even when nobody on Coker Creek had any. I put the bills in a half-gallon fruit jar and hid my money down in our cellar with the canned goods.

Eventually, I saved $2,200, which was a lot for a mountain boy back in that day and I hoped to use it to start my own household. But long before that, all my hard work meant I could also buy some things that I'd always wanted, things a boy needs when he begins to grow into a man.

CHAPTER 12

A Boy's World Changes

Before I ever got my first car, I learned how to drive one. It didn't take me long. We had a neighbor who owned a Ford A-Model and he worked in underground copper mines across the mountain in Turtletown and Ducktown. He'd come home on weekends and drive his A-Model by our house on Fridays. One day he stopped in the road to call out, "Hello, Will!" to my dad, and I was standing there and I asked him, "Is these things hard to drive?" That was when I was around twelve years old.

"Why, no," he said. "They ain't no trouble. You wanna drive it?"

I said, "Well, yeah, I'll try it!"

He got out and I hopped in.

"Now, I'll tell you what to do and you do what I tell you, and you'll be all right," he said.

I didn't have a bit of trouble steering it. Maybe I had a little trouble feeding it the gas, I wasn't too smooth. Most people will mash the gas down too hard, take off too fast, then let off. That's the way I started out.

My neighbor said, "Now, when I tell you, you push in the clutch and I'll shift the gears."

I picked it up real fast like that and never did have a bit of trouble clutching when I did it myself. He let me drive to Smithfield School, and I turned around in the schoolyard and drove back to my house. Boy, I thought I'd really done something. I was tellin' everybody about driving that car. So, a couple of years later in 1936, when I got my own A-Model, I was ready to go.

I was fourteen and holdin' down my job at the sawmill and my dad and I went in together, pooled our money. I had a little bit of money saved up by then, not much, but I gave my dad all I had and we bought a used 1930 A-Model Ford for $125 from one of my cousins. That was the first car we ever owned. It was one of the first few cars there were on Coker Creek.

As far as I ever knew, they were all black back then, cars were. The A-Model I had was the car Ford Motor Company made after the T-Model, which was Ford's first successful car. The A-Model was a little better car than the T-Model, but both those cars were just a step above a buggy. They'd eliminated the horse with an engine, but the part you rode in still bounced you around on the roads we had.

The old T-Model, you had to crank it by hand to start it, but my A-Model had a battery self-starter on the engine, although it also had the crank to start the car manually if the battery died. The old T-Model had curtains to let down on the sides to keep you from freezing in the winter, but the A-Model had glass windows to roll up. That was one of the biggest improvements.

The A-Model motor wasn't much of an improvement over the T-Model, because you still had to drain the water out of it every night and put the water in every morning if it was cold out. Yeah, you had to drain your water in the wintertime; everybody I knew that had one drained them. I don't know if they had antifreeze back then, but we didn't have any on Coker Creek. It would freeze the water in the radiator if you didn't empty it at night. I think some people got to putting kerosene in the water, but that could have caused a fire. Kerosene will catch afire if it gets too hot, but it won't freeze. I never did take a chance on that. I'd usually have my mother heat me a kettle of water on the cookstove and I'd pour hot water into the radiator in the morning if it was real cold out. The car would start a lot quicker that way.

I used that A-Model Ford all the years I worked at the sawmills. My dad drove it, too, but I drove it more. I went back and forth to work and I hauled four other fellers with me and they paid me so much a day to ride, paid my expenses. I'd drive off on those Coker Creek roads and I could negotiate that A-Model through all the hairpin turns real good. Everybody had to drive slow because you still couldn't pass each other if you met. Sometimes I'd have to back up to where they'd widened out a little place so I could pull off to the side and let the other feller go by.

When it rained, there was no use getting the car out, unless you had chains to put on it. You couldn't go anywhere with the roads just being dirt, red clay, really, it was so slick you could hardly stand up on it, much less drive a car. Of course, by then, there was a better road, a gravel road, about a mile from where we lived and, if you could get there, you could travel pretty good on that.

My sister Thelma said she wanted to learn to drive my A-Model.

My dad told me, "You better not let her drive that car, she can't drive it."

I ought to have listened to him, but I didn't.

Thelma just kept begging me and one day I said, "Well, I'll let you try it."

We took off from home and we went about a mile, I guess, before we had to start up a little hill.

I said, "Now, as slow as you're a goin' you're gonna have to shift into second gear before it'll climb this hill." I took hold of the gearshift and told her, "You push the clutch in and I'll shift it in gear."

When I shifted, she let the clutch out and just poured the gas to it.

That car took off up that hill and went right off the road and all the way up the bank. When it climbed that steep bank, the car started leaning over, over, over and then it just turned over in the road on its side, like a big tree falling with a thud.

The wheels, two of 'em, were up in the air and the motor was still a runnin'. I was pinned underneath Thelma—the car turned over on the passenger side and she fell on top of me. She was a pretty husky girl and she just about crushed me. But we weren't hurt.

"Oh, law me, Quinton, what are we a gonna do now?" she said.

I turned the switch off. We crawled out of the car—first Thelma stepped on me pretty good to climb out of the driver's door and then I jumped out and surveyed the situation.

"We'll have to push that car back up on its wheels. That's all there is to it," I told her.

We got hold of the car—my sister Thelma was as strong as a man—and we started pushing with all our might. We turned it back up on its wheels and rolled it back to the edge of the road. It never hurt the car, just scratched it up a little bit.

When my dad found out, he said, "I told you not to let her drive that car; you better keep her out of that." But Thelma wanted to learn to drive so bad, she'd come and ask me again and I couldn't hardly tell her no. I thought she could learn it. I got to letting her drive it some more. My dad heard about that, but by then he didn't say any more about it, because he found out that Thelma was pretty good at driving after all.

My oldest sister, Edth, started saying, "I want to learn to drive that car, too."

She got behind the wheel and we started down the road and the car started drifting off to the side of the road and she started yelling, "Which way do I have to turn the steering wheel now, which way do I have to turn it, to get back in the road?!"

I said, "Stop this car! If you don't know that, you can't drive a car, if you don't know which way to turn the steering wheel!" At least she found the brake. Oh, we had a time. But I did finally teach her to drive, too.

Teaching both my sisters to drive were some of the last good times I spent with them before they moved away. Since they were older, they got married and started their own households before I did. Thelma married a machinist who later became a country preacher, and Edth moved to Madisonville and worked as a seamstress at a dry cleaning establishment until she married a successful grocer.

I had about grown up by then, too, and I was now working for TVA, so I wanted a little better car. I'd used the A-Model for about four years and we'd only paid $125, but I sold it back to the feller we bought it from for $160. He paid us more than he'd sold it for because he wanted that car back. It was a good car.

But the blue 1937 Chevrolet that I bought next was a *real* good car. It didn't have a lot of miles on it and I was proud of that car, yeah, boy, I was. I'd worked for it, earned it myself, and it was a beauty. It was a light-colored blue, about like a sunny sky in springtime. It was the two-door model and the interior was gray. That Chevrolet drove so much better than that A-Model, I was tickled to death with it. I drove it to TVA job sites, to the store, and I kept it tuned up, polished up, and kept gas in it. Back then, gas stayed at about eighteen cents a gallon for years.

By that time, around 1940, there was another general store on Coker Creek that sold gas, one that was a lot more welcoming to trade in than Dave Lenderman's old shoot-out store ever was. Frank and Mamie Murphy's little store had first opened in 1935 and just sold necessities: canned goods, flour, meal, salt, lard, coffee, tea. Of course, they had no refrigeration, just an icebox, for a long time. Then they got a bigger general store, which included hardware, seeds, fertilizer—Old Black Joe was a popular brand—general building supplies, and, of course, gasoline. We all referred to the place as Frank's Store.

It was run by the Murphys—Frank Murphy, born and raised on Coker Creek with moonshinin' in his blood, and his young bride, Mamie, from way down in South Texas. In the early 1930s, Frank had gone down to Texas to get away from the law for a few years because he'd nearly been caught making moonshine at an old still on Coker Creek. Down in Bay City, Texas, he'd met the oldest daughter of a Texas farmer, married her when she was just a young girl, and brought her home to Coker Creek—when things cooled off.

Frank Murphy was big and round and full of fire. No tellin' what he'd got into before he married. But when he married Mamie, he knew he'd found a good woman and, after a little while, he straightened up. Mamie was mature and sensible, even in her youth. She was like a mother hen around that store, and she was serious about the work. That store ran like a top.

The "new place to trade," Frank and Mamie Murphy's store;
Mamie Murphy on right, Maggie Murphy with ax (wife of Clarence Murphy),
and unknown customer

Theirs was a *respectable* store for trading, with no drunks hanging around the door. Frank's Store was a one-room building and had a side room that Frank and Mamie lived in. They had another side room they built for feed, for people who had milk cows. It wasn't a big store, but then I thought it was. It might have been a little bit bigger than the one Dave Lenderman had.

Frank operated that store for a little while and it came time for the U.S. Postal Service to make a change, and he put in the application to be postmaster of Coker Creek. Frank's Store got the post office.

Frank's Store had rough counters and they had something like linoleum on the counters to make them slick. They had their cash register sitting up on there. And behind that, they had to go up in a brand-new post office made of oak to get the mail and they handed out letters and packages through a little window. I guess the postal service had furnished that. It brought a lot of business to the store. When people went to get their mail, they'd usually buy something.

Of course, when they took the post office away from Dave Lenderman

Storekeeper Mamie Murphy around 1940

and gave it to Frank Murphy, Dave hated Frank from that day on. It was a sight in the world how Dave hated Frank because he got that post office. They both resented each other something awful, but they never did get into a fight over it, as far as I know.

Of course, Frank carried a gun all the time; he was expecting to have trouble with some of them fellers. And Dave still kept that gun in his store, the .45, loaded, with the hammer pulled back.

As soon as Frank and Mamie Murphy went into competition with Dave Lenderman's store, a lot of people started trading up at Frank's. We traded up there after it opened since then we had a choice and didn't have to brave the goin's-on down at ol' man Lenderman's anymore. Or have to listen to Dave bellyachin' when people ordered from Sears, "Looks like you'd learn to buy your stuff in here!" People didn't like that. They got turned against Dave and got to reporting what he was doing and I think that's why he lost that post office. I guess the mail boy knew how both establishments were run.

Dave Lenderman was always bitter about it, but there wasn't nothin' he could do. By that time—it was after he'd been tied up back in the mountains — he'd mellowed a little bit anyway.

Dave'd met a preacher man that he liked. We had a new preacher come to Coker Creek, and that preacher got acquainted with Dave and he'd go over there and talk to him and he got him to come to church. That was the only feller I ever knew that had any influence over Dave Lenderman, but Dave really liked that preacher. That preacher had been a rough character, too, before he got straightened out, and they had a lot in common like that.

So Dave did quit his drinking, but he had about the same attitude he always had.

One February, it had snowed pretty heavy and I got my Chevrolet stuck up at Frank's Store in a big snowdrift. Frank told me to leave my car there until the snow melted. Well, I didn't want to do that.

T. C. Lenderman, Dave's son, he was up there with a tractor pulling out cars that had gotten stuck in the snow. I asked him to pull my car out. After he pulled my car back on the road, I asked T.C., "What do I owe you for pullin' me out?"

He said, "Just stop down there and pay the ol' man. Pay Dave."

I stopped down at Dave's Store and saw Dave and I said, "Well, T.C. pulled me out of the snow up here, how much do I owe you?"

He said, "Where's you stuck in the snow at?"

"Up at Frank's Store."

"Hmmph!" Dave snapped. "I orta charge you five dollars for bein' in that mudhole, so maybe next time, you'll know where to buy your gas at."

It's a wonder he didn't charge me five dollars and I'd a had to pay it, but he didn't.

He said, "But I'll just charge you a quarter and maybe you'll learn where to do your business from now on."

It was worth a whole lot to him to get to tell me that, I reckon.

I kept on buying my gas down at Frank's Store. They were a lot nicer down there. You'd see good people, girls and their mothers, from all over the community. I'd drive out to Frank's Store about every day to see if there was any mail for our family and I was glad to get my packages at the new post office. Mamie Murphy and, later on, her little sister, Orangie, would be just as cheerful, handing out my mail. Why, it was a real treat.

I bought the first suit I ever owned through the mail. If I'm not mistaken, it was a blue suit. I think it was double-breasted. I'd gotten old enough to where I wanted to dress up a little bit, in case I ran into some pretty little girl at church. That's the reason I bought that first suit of clothes. I was thinking of impressing a girl, though I hadn't found her yet.

There weren't hardly any boys that wore suits back then. Archie had a suit. He ordered a suit from Sears before I did. He always dressed pretty nice. Atlas wore a suit occasionally, but he didn't dress up a whole lot. In church, only a few of the young men would wear a suit in those years, so we'd stand out a little bit. Otherwise, men usually wore a white shirt—back then you didn't see dress shirts in any colors, just white—and they'd wear dress pants and suspenders for the summertime. Of course, a lot of men would just wear overalls, their clean, Sunday overalls. So there'd be a mix in the congregation. After I got it, I always wore that blue suit. Under that, I wore suspenders like my dad always wore.

I'd drive up to the church in my shined-up blue Chevrolet with my hair freshly combed—and probably still out of place. I never could do much with it; my hair was always stickin' up or floppin' about.

Atlas and I used to sing together in the choir when we

A young man: Quinton Kelley in his Sunday best

were teenagers and on up till we were nineteen or twenty. I usually got to sing the bass parts with a few other fellers, but I don't think I really had a bass voice. Atlas did. He had a good bass voice, big and confident. Atlas always looked neat and he had well-behaved manners. He wore his hair rolled back in a pompadour. Since he was tall, he'd stand in the back row of the choir when we'd sing that gospel music, and you could always count on it to lift you up.

There were quite a few nice girls that came to church, and I'd stand around and talk and joke with them after the service. I enjoyed talking to them; they were brought up by good parents. I had several pretty girls picked out around the community that I was sweet on. There were a lot of nice-looking, nice-acting women on Coker Creek.

There was one family that had some real pretty girls, one especially was awful pretty, and they'd visit their grandparents down in Eperson, past Frank's Store. I had to go down that direction to go to work and I'd always look for them when I went out that way. If I saw one of the girls, I'd stop and talk a while, but I never did ask any one of those girls out, not from the church, nor from down at Eperson. I was too backwards to know what to say.

My cousin Archie didn't waste any time finding a sweetheart, before any of us had girlfriends or ever went into the military. He knew who he wanted: Gwendolyn Davis, one of my cousins from my mother's side of the family. Archie was, of course, related to my father's side, and naturally he'd known Gwendolyn around Coker Creek for all their years. But one day, he couldn't stand to be away from her.

I missed Archie after that. I don't think I could have had a brother that I thought any more of than him. And he thought the same about me. He wanted to be with me all the time that he could, until he got old enough to start spending time with Gwendolyn, and then I never saw him much, because he was going to see his girlfriend all the time.

Archie and Gwendolyn got married right away. Sometimes somebody would marry their cousin's cousin like that, not their own cousin—families I knew were really against that—but they'd marry their cousin's cousin from another family. So, in the case of Gwendolyn and Archie, their children would be to me what we called "double cousins," because both their mother and father were my cousins.

Gwendolyn was a real nice girl and the prettiest girl of the Davis family, and they were all pretty girls. She was kind of short and curvy, had a beautiful figure. Her face was just shaped in a beautiful way, too, and she always had a smile.

Gwendolyn had some brothers that were just as mean as could be and, one time, I saw one of them get Archie mad. I reckon Archie had done something that really got to Gwendolyn's brother.

Right after Archie and Gwendolyn married, her brother Albert was walking home from church one night and he ran up by the side of the newlyweds as they walked down the road and Albert made some slighted remark—I never did know what it was—and Archie just knocked him down. Hauled off and hit him on the jaw and knocked him to the ground.

Albert didn't fight back. I guess he figured he had his hands full with his new brother-in-law, and there was nothing he could do about it. Archie was a fine feller, but he had a little bit of a hot temper. Everyone knew he was strong as an ox.

Before we knew it, Archie and Gwendolyn had a little boy, my second cousin—my *double* second cousin—Billy Kelley, and by the time we were the age to make us eligible for the draft, Archie's little boy was already about two years old. Archie picked at him all the time. Archie would put his finger on his own nose and he'd say, "Billy, now hit me right *here*."

That little boy would just haul off and bust his nose. Of course, he didn't have much power. Archie would throw his head back and laugh out loud. He'd have that little boy doing things like that and he'd get a kick out of it.

I told him, "That's funny now, but you wait till he gets a little older and a little stronger. It won't be so funny then."

"Aw, confound it!" Archie said. "I'm a havin' fun with him now."

My cousin Atlas hadn't got a sweetheart yet but he had one girl he

Three cousins, three WWII soldiers:
Quinton Kelley, Archie Kelley, and Atlas Davis

was sweet on. Bertha Ellis carried herself well, like Atlas. Bertha was trim and neat and she wore little round glasses. She came from a fairly big family on Coker Creek, about seven children. She didn't have a lot to say to people, but she was a nice, pleasant young woman.

We were three cousins who were fit young men in the prime of life, and we had done our duty as citizens and registered for the draft. We were a lot alike in those days. We each went by our middle names—Archie, Atlas, and Quinton—and we saw each other every day nearly, went to the same post office, the same church, the same people's homes.

Some Saturday evenings, we'd go over to Atlas's house and meet up with a bunch of our cousins, and Atlas would cut hair. Atlas learned to be a barber on his own and he had some barber tools and the whole setup. He had a straight-backed chair and a robe to go around you. He'd have your hair cut in a little while. He cut my hair till we both went in the service.

I don't know whether I ever paid him anything. I think he just did it for a favor. A bunch of us boys'd go over to his house and we'd talk like boys do, like young men do—you know. Atlas'd cut up and joke with you. If you got to movin' around a little bit in his barber's chair, he'd conk you on the head with his clippers just for the fun of it.

I think we all started getting our hair cut a little more often then.

Kept ourselves neater, used our pocketknives to clean under our fingernails. I know, for me, I started getting myself a little more spiffed up when I realized there might be a sweetheart for me, right under my nose all along, though it wasn't clear at first who it might be.

★ ★ ★

There was a girl with dark, wavy hair who lived on Coker Creek, a real nice and pretty girl named Opha. She used to walk along the road a lot, going to and from work at Frank's Store, where she was a clerk. I remember one day, it was late summer and it was hot, and she was working behind the counter and she had her blouse tied up around her waist in a knot at the front, which showed her middle section. Opha was a well-built, curvy girl.

Oh, my Grandmaw Davis, she talked about that. She came in the store and when she saw how Opha was dressed, she really gave her a goin'-over. My grandmother was an outspoken person and if she saw somebody that wasn't dressed properly, she'd say something about it. Of course, my grandmother wore her clothes down to the floor.

She told Opha, "Looks to me like you'd get you some clothes on without showin' your stomach to everybody that come in here. Orta be ashamed showing your middle like that."

That was back when you hardly ever saw things like that and, boy, that upset my grandmaw. I guess it made Opha mad, but working as a clerk in the store, she couldn't say too much back to the customers.

Well, I didn't think that was anything to get in a fit over.

Opha was walking home along the road one day and I happened to be riding my bicycle and I asked her if she wanted a ride home. She hopped up on the handlebars and I drove her all the way to her homeplace. She had me to stop before we got in sight of her house.

"I can't let my daddy see you takin' me home," she said. So she walked the rest of the way down the road to her house. That's the only time I ever gave her a ride home.

It was maybe a few months later, I was walking along the road with

Two country girls, two friends:
Opha and Orangie

a group of boys, my cousins mostly, and we passed Opha walking in the other direction. Some of the boys struck up a conversation with her and we all stopped and stood around, and one of those boys asked her out on a date right then and there.

She smiled sweetly and said, "No. I'm a waitin' on Quinton to ask me."

That got me. I didn't have any idea that she liked me. I didn't say anything then, I was too bashful. I guess she was disappointed that I didn't speak up or say something later on, but by that time, I had my eye on a friend of hers, another girl who worked down at Frank and Mamie's store: Orangie Morphew, Mamie's little sister.

Mamie had invited her sister to move up from Bay City, Texas, sometime around 1940. Orangie lived with Mamie and Frank and she worked in the store from the day she arrived.

I remember when she first started working behind the counter at the store, and pumping gas out front, too. I'd never heard a name like that before—Orangie—her name reminded me of those rare Christmas fruits that we'd get in our stocking, a sweet treat to savor if you'd been good that year. I didn't get any special attention from Orangie, though. She was always polite, but I never flirted with her or anything like that when I'd see her. She treated me just like she did everybody else.

I always looked for Orangie when I went to Frank's Store, couldn't help but look—she was a pretty girl, a real pretty girl, just a little slip of a girl with a tiny waist. She waited on me many times. Orangie worked the cash register and she was the one who would always go up in the little post office and get the mail for me. She had long, light brown hair and when she worked, she wore it in pigtails, braided up, with the braids wrapped around her head like a halo. Her face was bright and

Orangie Morphew, teenager from South Texas, brings her sense of adventure to Tennessee

she smiled a lot. Her clothes were always smartly styled in happy colors, sometimes with flowers or a ruffle on them. I don't ever remember seeing her in dark clothes.

I got acquainted with her a little at a time. Because she wasn't from around there, she seemed different from the girls on Coker Creek. She had a little different way of talkin'—she talked bolder and faster than we did, for one thing—and she told me about things that seemed unusual, but were just part of her background.

Orangie had been born in a covered wagon in Oklahoma, then her family relocated to Texas when she was small, and that's where they farmed. Her mother's people had been German-speaking Swiss; her father's, Irish. Orangie had blue eyes, just like her sister Mamie, and just like the rest of us on Coker Creek.

In Texas, she'd grown up in the southwestern version of the way I did, a little better, I think, in a big old rented farmhouse. But she still survived by planting and picking crops, milking cows, churning butter, and wringing a hen's neck for dinner. It was a little different where she came from, though, in South Texas. She rode horses and herded cattle after school, while she read her homework in the saddle.

Her family had farmed some cotton and they hired black people to pick the cotton. Orangie had been the one who kept the weights and measures, and she figured the pay for the workers in her father's ledger.

"And Daddy's books better not be off by even one penny," she told me. "Did you know, it takes fifteen hundred pounds of cotton to make one bale, but one bale only weighs five hundred pounds?" She grinned.

"What happended to the rest of it?" I asked.

"Cottonseed! All that cotton went through the gin before it was baled."

At times, Orangie and her four sisters picked cotton right along with the black people in the hot Texas sun. "I always wore a big, wide-brimmed hat like the women in the rice paddies of China," Orangie said. She did have the prettiest complexion.

And Orangie had grit. She told me that she and her sisters had killed many a poison copperhead snake in the weeds by their fields. Hacked off their heads with a sharp hoe. She said, to cool off, she and her sisters would go swimming in the creek on their property—with the alligators! Her daddy killed an alligator once that was nearly as long as his car. I believe she showed me a picture. Well, he thought he'd killed it, but after he tied it to his car and drove it home, he found out it wasn't exactly dead. Had to shoot it again.

Orangie had a confident Texas air about her and some western ways that were a little exotic to a boy who'd never been out of the mountains. She was the only girl I'd ever seen who wore cowgirl boots—smooth, brown leather boots with big square heels. Women on Coker Creek never wore anything like that.

What could a Texas cowgirl ever see in a Tennessee hillbilly like me? Well, I sure didn't know. But I began to think she was the little girl that I wanted.

At some point, when I was around twenty years old, I began to notice that there was just something in the way Orangie moved around the store when I was there, she'd sort of perk up a little bit, and she was real sweet and she'd ask me questions and talk to me a little bit. I thought maybe she was kind of struck on me. I hadn't been used to her paying me attention like that, so I figured she kind of liked me or something, and I began to have the feeling that we could have a date, but I don't know, I was too backwards to ask her, I guess.

She was always working and I never did want to interrupt her with something like that. A lot of people came in the store to buy things and some of the other boys would come in there and those boys, most of the time, bought chewing gum. They had it so if they got a date, they'd have some gum to give to their girl. They'd joke with Orangie and she'd take that pretty well. She'd make a quick remark back and laugh a little.

I never did joke with her. I never approached her like that. I was just always sincere and straightforward.

Orangie was the one who handed me my draft notice down at the post office in 1942. When I saw the return address, "U.S. Army, Selective Service," I knew what it was. I was expecting to get it. It didn't excite me a bit. I had been "selected" and I figured I'd be going off to war.

By the time World War II came along, I was out working for TVA, and I knew about the war over in Europe. Of course, I'd heard about the bombing of Pearl Harbor on the radio the Sunday it happened and I thought how terrible it was that the Japanese pulled a sneak attack and bombed a whole U.S. Navy fleet in Hawaii. Sunk our best ships. I imagined all those men trapped in the hulls, drowning or burning to death in raging fires. When I heard that America was going to war, I really felt like we needed to do something, that we couldn't let the Japanese or Hitler take over the world the way they were doing. Hitler had taken over a lot of countries already.

They'd kept announcing on the news that they were going to lower the age for the draft from twenty-one to eighteen to get as many men as they wanted in the military, so I figured they'd be drafting a lot of us country boys right off. Some of the boys I knew from Coker Creek were already in service.

I knew there wasn't any way to get out of it, unless they turned me down on account of my health and I didn't have anything wrong with me that I knew of. I was willing to go and do my part for my country. I never hesitated a minute about going.

I felt I was brave enough to go off to war, but I still hadn't gotten up the nerve to ask one special girl out on a date. Luckily, Orangie offered to write to me when I was in service if I'd send her my address when I got one.

I noticed that Orangie sometimes wrote her address on the eggs at Frank's Store when some of the G.I.s would come through on furloughs. They'd buy the eggs and she'd have her name and where they could write to her on one of the shells. I reckon some of those G.I.s would write it down and send her letters.

A lot of the girls supported the G.I.s by writing to them. They'd give them encouragement in their service for their country and, I imagine, they were interested to know if any of those soldiers might be a romantic prospect for their future—if they made it back from the war alive. Maybe Orangie got her idea from the old saying "Don't put all your eggs in one basket." I don't know. But I never needed one of those eggs to tell me how to find her. I intended to write to her. Some things were just getting started.

Others were getting put on hold. I had worked hard at becoming a journeyman carpenter. I'd started my second year of training, so when I had to leave TVA and go into service, they told me, "Because you're going in the military to serve your country, when you come back, we'll give you your job back."

Archie was also working for TVA then and he had ruptured himself doing some work about the time I got drafted. He was in the hospital in Sweetwater, Tennessee, when I went off to join the service, so I didn't get to see him and say goodbye.

He didn't get drafted right away because Archie had that one child and that deferred him for a little while, and we all figured he was lucky because of that. We thought maybe the war would end before they got to him.

Atlas and I were drafted at the same time. I think we even got our draft notice on the same day. We knew we were going off to a thing called war that we'd only heard about in stories. We'd heard the tales about World War I that Uncle Napoleon told on the front porch so many times.

Uncle Pole would have a whole group gathered around listening to him talk. He'd been one of the "doughboys" in the infantry, went to fight over in Germany. On the battlefield, he got wounded in the ankle. He was tryin' to crawl across a field to safety, to the medics, and he looked up and right in front of him sat a German soldier leanin' up against a tree with his gun a layin' across his lap.

"I just fell flat down on that ground, I's so scared," Uncle Pole said. He'd lean forward in his tattered overalls, look us in the eyes. "I knowed if he saw me, that German soldier, he'd shoot me—I's so close—I just dropped down on that ground and played 'possum. In a little while, I lifted my head real slow to see if I could see what that Heine was a doin' and then I saw it—he had a bullet hole right in the middle of his forehead. And I knew he wouldn't be a causin' nobody no more trouble. Boy, I felt good when I seen that."

There were other relatives that served in World War I—a lot of them went—and we'd heard a little from them about trench warfare and dead soldiers tangled in barbed wire. I remembered that.

Every so often we'd read a newspaper article or hear a radio broadcast about the current war, descriptions of Hitler's advances through Europe or the Japanese fighting naval battles in the Pacific, but we young boys didn't really have any idea what war could be like. We couldn't even imagine.

Atlas and I appeared at the draft board in Madisonville and they explained to us that we'd have to go to the induction center at Fort Oglethorpe down in Georgia to take our physical and get prepared for the service. They directed us to be at the courthouse in Madisonville on November 13, 1942.

When that day came, we went to Madisonville in my car and, of course, my mother and father went with me. They gathered up a busload of us boys at the Monroe County Courthouse and we all rode together down into Georgia. I sat looking out the bus window as the autumn scenery passed, but I kept holding on to a vision of my parents, the way I'd seen them that morning at home before they took me to become a soldier, to prepare myself for battle in the deadliest world conflict anybody had ever heard of. My small bag was packed, sittin' by our feet, and

(Left) The Kelley family: Will and Verdie in front, with Edth, Quinton, and Thelma

(Below) The Kelleys' log cabin sits behind sisters Edth and Thelma, and Thelma's husband, Bulen Alexander

the three of us lingered in the living room as Daddy's clock ticked up on the mantel. We spent a few minutes together before we had to leave for the courthouse. I guess we were anxious, but we didn't show it. We weren't much for hugging or anything like that, so my mother and father showered me with reminders. "Keep warm . . . eat enough . . . choose who you associate with." And, of course, my father said, "Whatever job you have to do, do it the best that you can."

My father's familiar words echoed as I rode on that bus.

"And give thanks, now," he'd said. "Always give thanks."

I knew what he meant and I closed my eyes. I sure was thankful that I had parents like that, and I hoped everybody'd be all right.

CHAPTER 13

Fort Oglethorpe, Georgia

The bus took us to where the terrain flattened into rolling hills and I could see a long ways off to the horizon. The United States Army post in Chickamauga—Fort Oglethorpe—it was a real big place, spread out over hundreds of acres with hundreds of buildings and wooden barracks—thousands, I reckoned—all lined up. We saw some of the place as we drove in there and, boy, I knew that everything I was used to would be different from now on.

We got down there close to eleven o'clock in the morning with several busloads of boys. A burly sergeant took charge. He lined us all up on a big grassy slope. I don't know how many, but there were a lot of us. He had us to sit down and he explained a little bit about what we had to go through at the physical exam and if we passed it, what that would mean: induction into the United States Armed Forces.

He said to us, "You are reporting to serve your country during wartime. From this point on, you'll live by the clock and everything will be done at an exact time, on time. You will have lunch at a certain time and you will go to bed at a certain time. But we don't tell time in the U.S. military the way you are used to." He explained about the twenty-four-hour clock, which was new to me, and how we'd eat breakfast at a time called "zero seven hundred hours."

He said, "Certain things you are familiar with will have different names in the military. You're used to going to the bathroom at home—"

I guess he didn't think that for me and a lot of those boys, it was an *outhouse.*

"—but," he said, "you don't call it a *bathroom* in the army. You call it a *latrine.* And the latrine is down at the foot of the hill." He pointed to a building and he said, "If any of you need to go, get up and go right now."

Nobody made a move. The sergeant, who was a big gruff man, waited a bit, then turned on his heels and said, "OK, then, nobody needs to go, we'll go on with our training."

When he said that, everybody jumped up, every single one of those boys. They knew they didn't have a second chance. Of course, I jumped up, too. We all took off to the latrine, in a hurry, runnin' down that hill.

I didn't look back, but I imagine that sergeant must have gotten a kick out of us boys jumpin' up like that. Maybe the same thing happened to the new recruits every time, I don't know. To the military, we were just another group of green young men, this one culled from the farmlands of the South, another group to organize and prepare for the war, and they wasted no time. 'Course, it seemed like they wasted a lot of *our* time.

Right away, we were introduced to the meaning of "hurry up and wait." They had us standing in a line about the time we arrived and kept us standing in a line somewhere or other about all the time for the next three days, while they gave us our physical and psychological examinations and screened us out. There were a lot of those boys who weren't capable of going into the military—some were capable and pretended not to be, and some weren't physically or mentally capable at all of being a soldier, so the military had to weed out those people.

We stood in lines out in open fields, waiting to enter big tents. The long lines of white men ranged from scruffy and puny to tall and strong, and all those in between—that's where I fell on the scale. Most of us were pretty slim, though, 'cause we grew up poor and worked our bodies hard to make a living. It was nerve-racking, all that idle time standing around, and then I'd finally get to the door of a tent—and join another long line snaking around in there.

Inside the tents at one point, they made us strip down to nothing. We stood in line naked as the day we were born and waited for the physical. They didn't want nothin' in the way of what they had to do. It was a shock to me and, of course, to every one of us, I reckon. But we moved along and cooperated.

For the military doctors, it was down to business. They ran us through there like a Ford assembly line, checking for every disease or defect. We gave blood and urine. I found out I was five feet, seven inches, and weighed 139 pounds. The army's doctors were efficient and more intrusive than I'd ever imagined, having had no experience with doctors in my life. The army sure didn't care how you felt when they had a job to get done.

After dressing, we lined up again in front of desks to be interrogated for our psychological exam. An intimidating man asked me all kinds of questions and I answered them. He asked me about my girlfriend, if I had one.

"Well, I have my sights set on one girl in particular," I told him.

Some other boys gave the examiners all kinds of answers, crazy answers or dishonest ones. I never tried to pull the wool over anybody's eyes to get out of military duty. But some of 'em played off dumb and ignorant and everything else, crazy even, when they had good sense, but they'd try to pull things to get out of the draft. Some of those boys found out some tricks they could do that would make them sick or they'd injure their body to try to get out of going. Those boys had a hard time pulling it over on the people that examined them, though, because the military knew what a lot of those boys would do to try to get rejected from military service.

Now, that Trellis boy who got into so much trouble, Eddie Trellis, they called him in and took him to Fort Oglethorpe and he flunked the physical. I found out later, the way he did that was with soap. He took laundry soap—they used to have what they called Octagon All Purpose Soap, it was good for washing clothes and it was what most people used on Coker Creek—somebody told him to rub a lot of that soap under his arms on the day of his examination. They claimed it would cause him to have a high temperature and the military would turn him down. Now, I don't know whether that's true or not. But they turned Eddie down and sent him home. And I'm satisfied it was on account of something that he did. He probably wouldn't have been worth a nickel in there.

There were a lot of strong, healthy boys from Coker Creek and Tellico Plains, and from up on the mountain, too, that were drafted for the war, everybody, nearly, that was physically able. Many local boys had already gone into service.

There were some boys that couldn't pass the physical, though. I don't know what they gave as the reason. Some were undernourished and weak, some had bad eyesight or were lame, and some weren't mentally able. It was usually some of the boys that lived back in the remote areas of the mountains; they wouldn't have been much benefit in the service anyway.

There was one boy like that who lived near us and we always said, "He's off of his rocker." He just didn't hardly know where he was at. Dan Davis was his name. He lived closer to Tellico Plains than he did to Coker Creek—he lived at the foot of the mountain before you start to go up to Coker Creek. I'd pass along the road where he lived and he'd be out there crouched just like an animal dipping water out of the ditch line with a cup, looking wild, his hair and clothes all ruffled up. He'd look up with a glassy stare and he had real pale eyes. Everybody knew he was out of his mind. Why they ever took that boy to Fort Oglethorpe, I don't know.

Dan Davis was in the group that I went down there with. As it happened, he was right in front of me going through the mess line, and there was a little swinging door that went back to the kitchen where the cooks prepared the food. Dan went back in there and started wandering around in the kitchen and they had to lead him out of there. He didn't know what he was doing. Some of those fellers put him back in line.

Well, he sat down straight across the table from me. The first thing he did, he dropped his head down and looked all over the table, every inch, down the legs, even. He sat there and kept moving his body back and forth, from side to side, looking all around. I felt sorry for him. He saw the sugar bowl and he grabbed that sugar bowl. He poured that sugar, a lot of it, in his plate, then he took his spoon and he spread it out into a thin layer. Then he just sat back and folded up his arms. He didn't eat a thing. He acted like that all the time.

When we got ready to go back home, we had the roll call, and he was the only one that was missing. The sergeant in charge said, "Does anybody know where Dan Davis is?" Nobody had a thing to say. Nobody knew.

The sergeant said, "Not one of you will leave here until he's found, so get out there and find him!"

All of us were eager to get back on the bus to Madisonville, so we scouted that camp over. There were so many draftees that the camp was full. A lot of the boys had to sleep in tents out in open fields. I'd been lucky enough to sleep in a barracks along with some other boys I knew, including Dan Davis. Fort Oglethorpe had rows and rows of barracks and we were bound and determined to search each one until we found him, thinking he might have gone back there.

I wasn't with the group that found him, so I didn't actually see him, but I know they found Dan Davis in one of the barracks. He was just in there by himself. They said he was sitting on a bed, a rockin' back and forth and a starin' at the wall. So they got him and led him back to the field for roll call and the bus ride home.

Surely, it looks like the military would have seen that there was something wrong with that boy before we ever came down there, but evidently they didn't detect that he was out of his mind. Of course, at Fort Oglethorpe they turned him down because he was mentally off. They just sent him back home afterwards with all the men, all those rejected and all those inducted.

Atlas and I had been inducted into the United States Army. We had signed papers and taken an oath to "support and defend the Constitution of the United States" and we were issued a serial number. We were given shots against diseases and given all kinds of written tests, so they'd know pretty well where every man fit in when we left the induction center.

Our individual assignments, which were still a mystery, would be based on the military's needs. Atlas and I hoped we'd get assigned to the same company, so we could go through the war together—at least there'd be somebody we knew from home—but we figured that might not happen.

They let all the new recruits go home for a few days to get our affairs in order before we went back to Fort Oglethorpe. My time was no longer my own. It belonged to the United States Government. I was in the army now.

Atlas and I returned to Fort Oglethorpe and we were separated into different groups.

Barbers gave us haircuts that just about shaved our heads. It seemed to demoralize some of the boys but was okay with me. My hair was always like a porcupine anyway, sticking out everywhere. The army cut it so short you couldn't comb it and I didn't have to worry about it.

They issued every one of us two identification tags, dog tags, that would identify us if we were killed. They had a little notch in the metal on one end. One boy shocked some of us by telling us, "If you get killed in battle, some of 'em will take your dog tag and open your mouth and that little notch'll fit in between your teeth and hold that dog tag in place when rigor mortis sets in. So you can be identified by the troops that follow along to pick up the dead." It was a horrific image for me to imagine. My dog tags said "Kelley, James Quinton." They had a "P" for Protestant and my army serial number.

The army issued everything essential for us to have, and that's all we would have. If you asked for a Bible, they issued you one. I had one all the time I was in service. We weren't allowed to bring anything else from home.

As new recruits, our personal freedom was now gone, a sacrifice we willingly made for the purpose of preserving our country's freedom. Now our every minute would be controlled by the military, even all the clothes we wore, down to our underwear, socks, and handkerchiefs—everything. The civilian clothes we had on, we weren't allowed to wear anymore. They gave us permission to ship them home and they told us sternly, "If you come home on a furlough, you have to dress as a soldier. And you better not be caught in civilian clothes as long as you are in the military."

They issued each of us a duffel bag and our Class A uniform. What they call a Class A uniform, that's the OD uniform—olive drab—that's what we'd use for parades, ceremonies, or going to town. They issued us pants and a jacket, two sets of them. They issued us five pair of socks, five undershirts, five shorts, two pair of shoes. One pair was to take our training in and we were supposed to keep one pair polished up good to wear for parades and special occasions—those dress "brogans" that came up above the ankle. Later, they would give us boots to wear.

They gave us a hat. It wasn't exactly a hat; it was a little khaki cap that collapsed flat, and we wore it with the dress clothes. The army was particular about that cap; they never did want us to wear it straight. We had to wear it with the point facing forward, but it had to be cocked on the side of our head just above the left eyebrow.

I'd never been used to wearing a cap before, but I got used to it. It cupped my head and was comfortable. I liked that little cap all right. We'd pull it off when we entered a building and slip it up under our belt, drape it over. That's where we kept it when it wasn't on our head. Of course, the army would also issue us another type of headgear for taking our training, a steel helmet with a liner.

I'd never had very many clothes in my life, and they were just of the cheapest sort, so I noticed right away that the army's clothing was heavier and made better than what I was used to. The cotton shirts and pants were creased from newness. Mine hung on my skinny frame. Until we got things straightened out, most of the clothes fit like hand-me-downs and we all compared the sizes that were stamped on the insides in black ink and we swapped clothes, or exchanged them at the supply room.

The new dress uniforms were sharp, but they hardly made us soldiers. We were just spiffed-up country boys, awkward in those stiff clothes. The uniforms had no insignias, no stripes, no patches—they were just plain. We'd have to earn some chevrons as we grew into seasoned servicemen. The military had started us all out on equal ground, lined up in row after row, like rows of corn kernels set out at planting time.

In a few days, our whole group of neatly dressed new recruits loaded the troop train. It was an old steam engine with a long line of passenger cars. Atlas was in that group, but again we were sent in different directions, to different cars.

They had a roster, called our names and lined us up in rows. They said to our row something like "You board Car 29." We stayed in that car just about the whole time we were on the train, except for trips to the dining car.

It was a Pullman train and each car had beds that you could let down from the top. In the day, the bottom beds made a seat for four, two facing two. At night, two people could sleep on the bottom and one on top. They had us to double up because it was wartime and those were the only trains available. I'd gotten to the Pullman car before the other boys, so I took a top bunk.

I wasn't with anybody I knew, but it didn't take us long to get acquainted with each other, having to endure the same hardships. In our car and in the dining car, a group of us were best buddies for a few days. Of course, we were just a bunch of Southern boys, some from the back hills, some from cities down south.

The quick friendships started with the same question.

"Where you from?"

We compared geographic regions, stories of home. The boys I met were mostly from around Tennessee, North Carolina, Georgia, and Virginia. I don't know how far out they reached. They all seemed like good ol' boys, young, eager, and full of life.

We didn't know where we were headed, or how long the trip would be. The military wouldn't tell us, but they'd told us how to pack our duffel bag. We were told to put our heavy overcoat on the top so it was ready to go, and to put all our heavy clothing in the top of the bag.

So some of them said, "Well, that's a dead giveaway. We're going to a cold climate."

"Yep," the rest of us chimed in. "If there's one thing about it, we know we're goin' somewhere cold."

"I'll bet they're taking us way up to where them Yankees live in New Jersey and New York," one boy said.

"Oh, I dread that," another boy said. "Takin' trainin' out in a cold climate. And winter's just a startin'."

"Well, we know it can't be out in Texas or anywhere like 'at," another boy said. "You don't need no overcoat in Texas. Down there, when a snake decides to cross a road on a hot day, it gets cooked 'fore it gets to the other side."

"In December? You from Texas?" someone asked.

"Naw, I'm from Alabama. But I've lived in Texas."

"Well, we've been a headin' north for quite a spell," said a boy whose accent sounded like back home, but I didn't know him.

"Naw, you're wrong. I'm tellin' you, you're all wrong. We're goin' out west. Way out west," said a confident, cocky type of boy. I believe he said he was from Georgia. "Got a cousin in California. Said they're bringing in new troops by the trainload all the time. I bet that's where we're headed."

That Georgia boy kept needling the men in charge about our direction when they'd come through the Pullman coaches checking on us. He said, "Hey, Lieutenant, how 'bout you tell me where we're goin'?"

The lieutenant said, "I don't know. You know as much about it as I do."

In a few minutes, a sergeant came by and that boy said to him, "Sergeant, do you know where we're goin'?"

That sergeant gave him a big answer, but it was nonsense. He just made up something to satisfy us. But, right then, we believed him.

That boy said to the sergeant, "Well, Sarge, I tell you one thing. You're a lot smarter than that lieutenant. I asked him where we're goin' and he didn't know a thing!"

A little later, the lieutenant came back through our Pullman car and that Georgia boy—he was just as jolly—he piped up and said, "Hey, Lieutenant! Do you know where we're goin' yet?"

"None of us know where we're going," that lieutenant told him. "We just know we're headed in a northwest direction."

"Well, the sergeant was down here a while ago and he knew all about it. It's strange to me that a sergeant knows more than a lieutenant." That's what that Georgia boy told the lieutenant.

The lieutenant didn't say a thing. He just walked on through the car.

That boy was always picking on somebody the whole trip, especially the officers and sergeants in charge of us, and he got away with it. Of course, *then*, he'd just say anything he wanted, but when we got to the army base, he'd have to address those officers with a "yes, sir" and a "no, sir." You couldn't just act a fool with them.

There was always some joker on the train who entertained the rest of us and we all got a kick out of it. I was quiet at first, takin' it all in, but I'd do my share of laughin' at the funnies they'd tell.

That Georgia boy was a cutup, seemed to be having a big time, though it was probably how he acted when he was anxious. We all tried to have as good a time as we could, 'cause I know we dreaded what came next—an unknown fate in wartime.

All day, all night, we lived to the steady rhythm of the wheels hitting the cracks in the rails—*clickity-clack, clickity-clack*. We got used to the engine shrieking, the whistle blowing, and occasional stops. If the train was going to be stopped for a while, we'd get off and do exercise along the side of the railroad. They'd get us limbered up and let us blow off steam.

When they'd line us up by the tracks, they'd give us a little lecture. We learned what "in cadence" exercise meant. That meant for us to count "One, two, three, four!" We'd shout out each number. They did that to get our lungs strong, I guess. We learned the basic calisthenics on that train trip.

We'd go through towns and the train would stop and a lot of girls would run up and down beside the tracks. Sometimes they'd ride along in their car by the train as we came into a town, and they'd come down to the track when the train was stopped and wave at us, give us candy and different things and ask for our address. Of course, we didn't have an address then. Some of the boys would ask the girls for their address and they'd give it to them.

About all of the boys around there had already been called in service, so there was just a bunch of girls out looking at us boys, waving and cheering us on. They were excited about us going to war to protect our country. They were really nice girls. None of them conducted themselves in a sorry manner. They were supporting the war effort.

I never did talk to any of the girls along the trip, I just watched when some of those boys'd get all enthused over a stranger's smile and a scrap of paper with an address in some little ol' town. That was before the landscape started emptying up, opening into blank spaces where it looked like nobody lived for hundreds of miles.

We'd always try to figure out where we were going by the scenery. We'd try to figure out how we might still end up somewhere in the North. We passed through towns that flashed by in a glance, too quick to see hardly. Small wooden houses and a string of stores gave away no clues to our whereabouts. We'd see signs where a highway crossed the railroad and sometimes we could identify what state we were in, but we never could figure out for sure where we were headed, because they'd zigzag those troop trains to keep our itinerary a secret.

The army was afraid a train could be sabotaged if they just made a direct run. They didn't know but what there might be enemies in this country who wanted to slow down our progress, to help Germany or Japan. That's the reason they kept us wondering and took us all over the country. Part of the time, we'd be in a cold climate and were sure we were going north, but then in a day or so, it started warming up.

They had these old steam engines back then and we'd get awful dirty when we had to go through some of that mountainous country where we had to go through tunnels. The trains were enclosed, but we'd get enough smoke in there till it would smoke us up when we went through a tunnel. The windows would get dirty and we were happy when we hit some rain to wash them. It was a good thing to see the country clearly, even though the parts that the track went through maybe weren't the best parts. There was a lot of repetition to the scenes after a while.

Once in a while you'd see a cabin or some cows or horses or somebody riding a horse. But you didn't see nothin' much. Hours passed, and all that changed was the position of the sun over pastures and fields. Little ol' shacks stood along the railway, weathered and looking like what I was used to back home.

Seeing the United States for the first time was an unfolding adventure like nothing I'd ever experienced and I enjoyed it. The longest train trip I'd ever taken before that was from Tellico Plains to the Tennessee state line at Bristol, Virginia, a train trip that took hours, not days, like this trip.

I was amazed at how large the country was. I marveled at how long it took to cross the country by train, and I thought we were moving pretty fast. But it took us longer on that troop train than the five days and four nights it should have taken, because they didn't go as direct as they could have. I didn't mind it. It gave me a chance to see the great country that we soldiers represented, a land of freedom. Big, open country.

I remember it just like yesterday, though I don't know if I remember it from then or later years, but there was a lot of that flat and arid country. I remember more of that than anything, going through those Western states, seeing the kind of rocky, sandy, barren land that I'd never laid eyes on before, not even in pictures.

I remember when we began to figure out that we weren't going somewhere cold. We got pretty close to the end, way on out west, when we all figured out that our destination had to be somewhere on the West Coast. We'd talk about it a lot. All the boys said, "They done it a purpose. They tricked us. 'Cause they had us to put that big, heavy overcoat right on the top of our bag."

"Aw, boys," that Georgia boy drawled. "Why, *I* knew more than those lieutenants and them sergeants put together. I told y'all the first day that we were headin' for California. And you know what that means? We're gonna be deployed in the Pacific."

I never did see that Georgia boy again after he got off the train, never did know what outfit he went into. In fact, I didn't see any of those boys I met on that train ever again.

The troop train stopped for the last time as it was getting dark on the evening of December 7th. It was the one-year anniversary of Japan's sneak attack on Pearl Harbor.

I'd heard President Franklin D. Roosevelt's radio address a year earlier when he announced that the United States had been suddenly and deliberately attacked. I remembered him listing all sorts of places around the world that the Japanese had bombed the morning of December 7, 1941, what they called "a day that will live in infamy." Places I'd never heard of—Hong Kong, islands of the Philippines, Midway Island, and so forth, all took hits within twenty-four hours, but our own territory, Hawaii—that really shocked me. I think it woke everybody up to the fact that the world was really at war. Then we Americans knew we'd have to fight to protect our way of life and the United States officially entered the war.

Japan had declared war on the U.S. that December, and Germany and Italy had, too.

Hitler's troops were sweeping through the whole continent of Europe just about, taking one country after another, even France, a big country that even I'd heard quite a bit about. And England, our country's "motherland," they'd been fighting off Germany since 1939 and nothing was getting any better. The British were really suffering under heavy bombing attacks from the German air forces. They'd been able to hold the Germans off, but at great cost to their civilians and cities.

Over in the Pacific, the Americans had been struggling against the Japanese and we had heavy losses of men and equipment fighting in jungle terrain on little islands. World War II was by no means going to be an easy war to win. I wondered where we were bound for, what sort of land we might have to fight in.

Of course, the worst place to have to fight would be here in our own country. We'd have an advantage, naturally, but to have invasion and bloodshed on our own soil, that was something we couldn't allow. So, this night exactly one year after the Pearl Harbor attack, our government was intent on protecting our shores from another attack.

The country was on high alert against sabotage and they told us that the government had issued a blackout order for the entire West Coast of the United States. So, when we got to California, the whole West Coast was blacked out. They thought the anniversary might be the time the enemy would try to hit our mainland.

As we waited at the depot, they told us that this was the end of the line. The entire trainload of Southern boys was to be stationed at Camp Beale, in Northern California. It was a newly built camp. It had been operating for less than a month. We were some of the first troops in there.

It was already dark when we got to the camp and they had all the windows blacked out. I mean—there wasn't a light nowhere. You couldn't see a thing. You just had to feel around everywhere.

They gave us our evening meal and, of course, we couldn't eat in the dark. They had a big tent around the door of the mess hall to block out light, and inside, they had just enough light so we could see how to eat.

I remember one poor boy, he got word his mother had died when we arrived. Oh, he was so broken up about it. Just in a panic. I felt so sorry for him. He asked the sergeant if he could get leave immediately.

The sergeant said, "I wish there was something we could do to help you. But we can't do anything until tomorrow because we can't have a light. So you'll have to make it until tomorrow and we'll see what we can work out. Maybe we can make arrangements for you to go home to the funeral."

I never did know what they did. I didn't know the boy and he didn't end up in my company. We hadn't been separated into companies at that time, but right after that, sergeants divided us up into our units and got us assigned to our barracks.

We walked, in total darkness, toward our new quarters. Smoking was forbidden outside that night, and, of course, I didn't smoke and it didn't make any difference to me, but that's how dark they wanted it. Not even the light of a match could be seen. In the moonlight, I caught glimpses of shapes and shadows as we walked past rows of buildings, all the same. I could smell heavy odors, maybe like oil or machinery and fresh paint.

We had soldiers who took us to our barracks and they made sure we got to where we belonged in the dark. It was hard to find the barracks, even for them, because they were looking for small numbers painted on wood.

We felt our way up a flight of stairs to our barracks, which was the second floor of a two-story wooden building. We didn't have any lights inside the barracks, either. It was miserable, not being used to that kind of treatment. We had to just feel our way around to our bunks. To my hands, it felt like a simple setup, with the furnishings made of cold metal. The bed was low to the ground, the blanket felt like wool.

I couldn't see just how many men were bunked in there with me. Didn't recognize anybody in the group by their voices. 'Course, I was hopin' Atlas might get put in our group.

It's mysterious enough to arrive at a new place at night, in total darkness, with a bunch of strangers. But to make it worse, the military didn't tell us a thing, hardly. We didn't know what kind of outfit we were in, but we all figured we were in the infantry, most likely foot soldiers.

I didn't know what to expect of war. I expected men to line up in rows and face each other to fight. I imagined us marching up over a hill and seeing the enemy marching toward us, everyone in order until someone fired. Boy, was I livin' in the wrong century.

Strangers' voices in the dark commented to each other that soon we'd be digging foxholes, lying on our bellies, and aiming our gunsights on "those damn Japs" or "those kraut-eating Nazis."

Most drafted boys were going into the infantry, we'd heard. But we didn't really know a thing. Some of them made jokes about being "in the dark about it all" and laughter echoed in the barracks.

The hushed secrecy, the forced darkness, all added to the uneasiness of our arrival. We couldn't see where we were, and for me, I'd never been to a place in the dark that I didn't know in daylight. I knew that it wasn't anything like being in a strange part of the mountain in the dark. I was used to that. In our woods, I knew the familiar sounds of the night and

I pretty much knew all the animals or kinds of people that might be out there, and I could predict their behavior to some extent.

But out here in this United States Army camp, I heard unfamiliar accents talking all around me and I knew that there were men from all walks of life, more people on that army base than I'd ever seen before. We were from one end of the country to the other, I reckoned. Every name was new, every face. It was a cold feeling.

I settled into my new army mattress, narrow, but softer than what I was used to, and I thought about the fact that the latest machines of war were out there on the base—the guns that we'd train on—and I looked forward to gettin' my hands on them. I figured that was what you did in the infantry, and it would be my best defense in this terrible war we kept hearing about, to learn to handle all those powerful guns. I didn't really *want* to, didn't like the idea of killing people one bit. But I didn't like the idea of bein' killed even more.

Not knowing anything about the army, I couldn't imagine what training would be like. I was confident I'd make a proud U.S. soldier, but I figured I had a lot to learn if I was going to survive a war. That's what I cared about. Survivin' it. From the start, I just wanted to get back home.

PART 2

1942–1949 AND BEYOND

Private Kelley at Camp Beale, California

CHAPTER 14

Camp Beale, California

At Camp Beale, a new Armored Division was formed—the 13th Armored Division. The 13th was created for the purpose of fighting on the second front in Europe, and then for combat against the Japanese in the South Pacific. When it was activated on October 15, 1942, General John B. Wogan marked the occasion with a speech:

> *"Today, you are witnessing the birth of an armored division. Even in ordinary times, this would be a great occasion for our country. Under present conditions, it is an occasion of particular significance. It signifies America's acceptance of the challenge which has been flung in the teeth of a peace-loving and unprepared world by ruthless dictators who are leading their country and their people to certain destruction. It signifies on the part of our people, a refusal to forfeit the American way of life; it signifies, unmistakably, that our country is determined to see this war through until final victory shall be ours."*

Since late November 1942, the Division began filling out. Large numbers of recruits began arriving from reception centers to commence the task of becoming armoraiders. Contingents coming in represented a wide geographical range. The men were classified and assigned to permanent units. The most frequently asked question on the lips of the arrivals was, "When do we get a ride in a tank?"

— THE BLACK CATS: They Sharpened Their Claws in California and Texas, Then Scratched Hell Out of the Nazis. Paperback, Published by U.S. Army 1945

At first light on December 8, 1942, I saw my new home for the first time. I woke up in barracks that had two rows of bare schoolhouse windows—one facing east, one west. There were no inner walls in the place—I could see the exposed two-by-four framing that formed the structure. The only thing between us and the weather was the one layer of weatherboard that was nailed to the outside of the wooden frame. The construction was about the minimum required to call it shelter and it sure looked like the army had built it in a hurry. There wasn't much to those buildings at first, but those barracks had one big improvement over home for me, though—electric lights. Dangling overhead was a row of naked lightbulbs that we'd use from now on, since the blackout order was over.

Each barracks housed two rows of single metal frame beds that ran the length of the rectangular structure. Each bed had a metal locker at the foot, olive drab color. Everything I saw—beds, blankets, all our gear—was of the same color generally, that dark mossy color the army used for everything, whether it was metal, wood, or canvas. And if it wasn't OD, it was khaki. You sure didn't see much color in the army.

The beds, the lockers, and the hardwood floors were brand-new. We were the first boys to set foot in those barracks. There wasn't a speck of dirt anywhere.

About fifty men or so were assigned to each floor of the two-story barracks. I was up on the second floor, where the ceiling had open rafters. My bunk happened to be the second bunk from the end, down where our sergeant's quarters were.

Outside, the base was stark. There were no trees anywhere, not a one. No grass, no bushes. Just flat, gravel-covered open areas between rows and rows of identical wooden rectangles, barracks equally spaced. The rows of barracks went on for about as far as you could see and the only difference between them were the numbers stenciled over the doors.

We got a first look around, from the latrines to the mess hall, and the U.S. Army's Camp Beale looked bigger than anything I'd ever seen or imagined. Law, it was bustlin' with activity. On the streets, men marched in stiff rows and pivoted as a group around corners. Open vehicles — they referred to them as "jeeps" — carried officers all over the camp in the warm morning breezes.

Camp Beale was located in Northern California's Sacramento Valley, a sunny, pleasant place, and I marveled at how warm it was in December. Camp Beale had been named in honor of Brigadier General Edward Beale, who fought to secure the state of California from Mexico alongside Kit Carson — a familiar name from my childhood stories around the fire. That's about the only tie this place had to anything that I knew. I was two thousand miles from home, and I might as well have been ten million.

Camp Beale was a self-contained city with grids of streets and training areas, classrooms, administrative buildings, food warehouses, cold-storage plants, a bakery, mess halls, various chapels, theaters, a field house, laundry, motor repair and maintenance shops, fire stations, powerhouses, post exchanges, and a hospital. In all, including training fields, the base covered 86,000 acres and, we were told, it had all kinds of terrain — desert lands, flat lands, hills, valleys, forests, and rivers — all suited for the purpose of training an armored division.

The first time I heard "armored division," I didn't understand the term. It was on the first day, after roll call and breakfast. An officer announced to us as we lined up, "You have been assigned to the United States Army's THIRTEENTH ARMORED DIVISION," and he went on about what we could expect.

I didn't know what an armored division was. Never heard of one before. Some of those boys may have known, but I was one who didn't.

I thought it meant heavy artillery and things like that. I wasn't thinking about tanks. Well, I hadn't heard of them, either.

After formation, some of the other boys seemed pretty excited about being in a tank outfit. When they started talking about getting to drive some kind of an armored vehicle, I started looking forward to that, even though I couldn't imagine what one looked like. Long before that day, though, there would be thirteen weeks of intensive basic training—boot camp.

As new recruits, we were all lined up, straightened up, and accounted for by our last names. Tall, short, fat, skinny, light eyes and dark, pale foreheads and suntanned—we were a mixed lot of white boys brought in there from all over the country, and we were all put on equal ground from the officers' point of view.

From the moment we arrived at the training camp, we had to adapt to the way the army wanted everything. Our dress, behavior, and housekeeping had to adhere to strict military conduct at all times. We had to look like a unified force. We were taught how to stand in the same manner, snap to attention with the same motions, and how to salute just exactly the way the army wanted. We turned our heads in the same direction, and moved as a unit when we were in formation.

We were taught how to speak to officers and noncommissioned officers. You couldn't talk back to them—nothing like that. You had to address them in a very special manner, especially commissioned officers. You had to be "Yes, sir. No, sir." We learned how to speak to our officers when spoken to, and how not to draw attention to ourselves, if we could possibly help it.

Captain Richard F. Blake was the commanding officer over the outfit I was in. It may have been called something else first [3rd Battalion of the 45th Armored Regiment], but our outfit became known as the 24th Tank Battalion. The 13th Armored Division was just being put together, and a lot of their officers came over from an old cavalry outfit in Fort Meade, Maryland, I believe, and Captain Blake was one of them. In fact, a lot of the time we were in California, he wore the officers uniform of a cavalry man—not the World War II armored division uniform.

He wore riding britches that flared out above the knee, and big lace-up boots. He was a big, tall feller and he had a lot of fancy plaited braid on his shoulders that went way back to cavalry uniforms of World War I. Captain Blake was about the only one who walked around dressed like that, as far as I could see. Captain Blake wasn't very friendly with anybody except to officers. He was a rigid feller and real stern. And more than that, he was sarcastic and hateful.

He'd say, "Private! Are you standing in formation or standing there like a . . . *blankety-blank* . . . scarecrow??! Pull those arms in! Straighten those lines!"

I reckon he did that to get the attention of the soldiers. Captain Blake was pretty bad to go looking for reasons to get on you. As soon as we got dressed in the morning, we'd have to fall out for roll call and reveille. And he'd be there when we'd fall out.

Captain Blake would arrive to check every one of us to see that we had our clothes on properly, as described in our army manual. Every detail had to be just right. Certain buttons had to be buttoned or not buttoned. He'd always single out those boys who were not dressed just exactly right.

One time I had a button missing on my jacket. They had flaps on the pockets, and I had a button off on the left side. I knew it was off and I was going to put it on when I got back from breakfast, but Captain Blake caught me first. He walked down the line and when he got to me, he flipped my open pocket flap, and he stopped. I stood perfectly still.

He barked in my face, "Private! Your uniform is absent a button. Are you aware of that?"

"Yes! Sir!" I yelled out, the way they'd taught us.

"And when were you planning to do something about that?" He towered over me.

"Right away, sir!"

He said, "You *will* have that button on when you fall out for calisthenics this morning. I'm going to check you after breakfast to see if that button is on there. And it better be on there."

I had to go to the barracks and sew that button on before I got my breakfast, and then I was way back in the chow line. I thought to myself, now, he'll never check that. But, shoot, that's the first thing he did—when we fell out for exercise, he walked right over to me and checked that pocket to see if that button was on there. If I hadn't sewed it on, he'd have given me a good goin'-over—called me things I wouldn't have liked, and given me extra duty as punishment.

Captain Blake looked to see if every one of us lined up in the morning was shaved, too. I never missed a day since I started shaving, but the boy next to me one morning, he hadn't shaved.

Captain Blake yelled in his face. "Private, why are you out here without being shaved?!"

"Well, I didn't have no razor blades—sir!"

That boy was trembling just a little, I could see that out of the corner of my eye, but I didn't dare look to the side. I kept my eyes focused in the distance.

The captain said, "You'll be shaved slick in the morning if you have to find broken glass to do it."

That boy had to borrow a razor blade from somebody and shave. He didn't take a chance on it, 'cause he knew the captain would remember to check him the next day. Captain Blake was pretty bad to do things like that. He'd have the sergeant assign the boys extra duty for every little thing. Captain Blake, a lot of us called him an "old sourpuss." Some of the boys called him a whole lot worse.

The officers over us were men of discipline and that's just the way they kept the discipline in the service. With so many boys, most of them away from home for the first time, they had to be strict. If they hadn't been like that, well, the boys would have been out of control pretty soon. But they had real good discipline. We all knew we had to follow the rules and it wasn't hard to do after you made up your mind you were gonna do it, and not be contrary. You couldn't be contrary, 'cause you'd be in trouble all the time.

In our battalion, they had us separated into different companies, A, B, C, and D, and each company consisted of around a hundred and seventeen men. The companies were further broken down into platoons, and each platoon was around twenty-five men. I'd been assigned to Company C, 2nd Platoon. There were always one or two boys in the company who were in trouble all the time. They weren't living up to the training. If the captain wasn't finding fault with them, then their sergeant was always on them.

There was one in 1st Platoon, one boy from Madisonville, Tennessee. In fact, I didn't know him, but I had heard of him out there on Coker Creek before I went into the service. His reputation was widespread. He was a McDaniel. I'd been told many times that he was a hard one to deal with. He was bad to drink and people talked about how mean he was. They said, "He's got such a temper, why, he'd fight a circle saw."

When they got this boy in the army, they couldn't do a thing with him, hardly. He was always into a fight with somebody. He was used to doing whatever he wanted back home, just runnin' roughshod over everybody. Whatever his sergeant wanted him to do, he wouldn't do it if he didn't want to. And he didn't want to do nothin'. That McDaniel boy was so hard to handle, they had to really bear down on him and it was hard for him to adjust to that type of treatment. But in the army, they'll adjust you.

His sergeant, Sergeant Jarvis, was on McDaniel all the time. Sergeant Jarvis was just a young sergeant and he thought he had to be as mean as he could be to that boy, to break him down. But the harder that young sergeant rode him, the more stubborn that McDaniel boy was. So Sergeant Jarvis made McDaniel fill his field pack full of gravel, just about all he could carry, and made him carry that heavy field pack from the time he got up in the morning till he went to bed at night. Even when he had to go to the mess hall, he had to carry all those heavy rocks, sit there and eat with 'em on. Well, that didn't break him.

One day right after lunch, Sergeant Jarvis had McDaniel out there cleaning out ditch lines with a shovel, shoveling dirt. I was around there, I don't know what I was doing now. But McDaniel was down in a ditch, dripping sweat, with that pack of gravel strapped on his back. He was throwing that dirt up in the air, just as mad as sin. All of a sudden, he just threw that shovel down and jumped up out of the hole.

He said, "I'm not a carryin' this no further! I'm a goin' to talk to the captain." He went to Captain Blake's office and I don't know what he said to the captain, but I'm satisfied he talked to him about the situation. Captain Blake called Sergeant Jarvis in and talked to him. After he dismissed Sergeant Jarvis, then, directly, the captain called in my platoon's sergeant, Sergeant Hicks.

I later heard that the captain told my platoon sergeant, "I'm going to give you this boy. I believe you can straighten him out and do something with him. No one else has been able to control him. But I believe you can handle him."

And they transferred McDaniel to my platoon.

Now, the sergeant assigned to 2nd Platoon was experienced: Staff Sergeant Pearl F. Hicks. He was the sergeant we mainly saw on a daily basis. Sergeant Hicks was a tall, long-legged feller and he came out of an old cavalry outfit where they rode horses, like Captain Blake, but Sergeant Hicks wore the regular armored unit uniform. He'd had a lot of training because he'd joined the army before America got into the war. He was really an army man. Those career military men are usually pretty rough characters; they've been down the road and put up with so much stuff, they get hardened. They don't have too much sympathy for people unless somebody really treats them right.

Whatever Sergeant Hicks told you, that's the way it was and it wasn't no use of you trying to get out of it. He wouldn't back off from what he told you. Now, most of the sergeants were vulgar, and sometimes off-color in their remarks. Hicks was that way, pretty much, with some of the men. I've heard Sergeant Hicks threaten to kick some of those boys' tails if they didn't do certain things. He didn't let them push him around. The men he had to be hard on, he was. The ones that didn't give any trouble, he didn't bother. He never said anything out of the way to me. He was fair with anybody who treated him right.

When they transferred that McDaniel boy to my platoon, Sergeant Hicks didn't start off rough with him like you might expect. He started treating him nice and being friendly with him. And, boy, that made the difference in that soldier.

It was like when I took over that team of horses for my cousin after he'd been so rough on 'em. I tried to use basic respect when I dealt with those horses to get them to cooperate and pull their load. It's the same way with people. Once they understand what you want them to do, and you treat them fair, most of 'em will do pretty good like that.

When Sergeant Hicks went to treating that McDaniel boy right, he didn't have any trouble with him. That boy didn't cause any more fights or buck the system after that, and he finally became a good soldier. I guess when he went back home, his parents must've said, "Boy, they've made a man out of him!"

That other sergeant, the young one, he'd been riding McDaniel every minute, and that McDaniel boy wouldn't take that. But Sergeant Hicks knew how to handle the situation.

A thing about Sergeant Hicks that was unusual, he had a little dog that he thought the world of and she followed him around all over the base. I don't know what breed the dog was, but her name was Mitzi. She was a little spotted dog, brown and white. Pretty little dog. Sergeant Hicks had a harness for Mitzi and he put his stripes on the dog's harness and let the dog wear his sergeant stripes.

That dog stayed right with Sergeant Hicks wherever he went, didn't fool with the rest of us. Once or twice I tried to get her attention and whispered, "Hey there, Mitzi!" but that dog wouldn't even move her head. She'd just stare straight ahead, at attention. She didn't pay anybody any mind, except Sergeant Hicks. Part of the time he'd carry the dog, part of the time he'd let the little dog follow along. He'd holler for Mitzi and she'd come running from wherever she was and sit the same distance from Sergeant Hicks every time.

He was the only one that had a pet in there, I reckon. I guess it was because he'd had a lot of old-school military training and he'd come in there as part of the first troops to set up the 13th Armored Division, so the officers over him respected him enough till they didn't want to cross him up. In fact, the officers, they looked up to him, because Sergeant Hicks knew more about the military than a lot of the officers we had.

A lot of the young officers were what we called "ninety-day won-ders." They were college boys who went through an officers' training course, which was a ninety-day course, a crash course, more or less. They came out of that training as lieutenants and acted like they thought they knew a whole lot. But they didn't. Some of those lieutenants that were put in charge of us weren't very reasonable; they were sarcastic and they wanted you to know they were the boss. And we knew that, of course, but they wanted to make it a point to let us know it, when they told us to do something. They'd be hard to deal with and they were just belch-ing out orders all the time. We all called them ninety-day wonders, not to their face, though. You had to call them "Sir! Yes, sir!"

The army changed the officers around quite a bit. There were only a few of our commissioned and noncommissioned officers I remember who were with us from basic training all the way through the war.

For the enlisted men that made up our companies—each one of us starting out on the same level as "buck privates"—all the men up the ladder were our examples to follow. The sergeants, lieutenants, all the way up to the commanders, they set the tone and we recruits had to do whatever they said. We had to learn to deal with it, for better or worse. And, of course, the men over us had to follow the orders of the men who were above them, too, on up, all the way to the top.

Over the whole 13th Armored Division, which consisted of 10,500 men, was Major General John B. Wogan. General Wogan visited our camp on occasion and sometimes gave a speech. He conveyed a lot of authority and he was able to rouse us up. I got to hear him when he wel-comed the new recruits:

> *"The enemy will find the Lucky 13th to be the damnedest, fightingest, hardest-hitting, and most devastating dynamo of destruction ever turned loose on him. We are not superstitious, but we hope the enemy is. We propose to make the 13th Armored the unluckiest division in the world to the enemy—and the luckiest for the United States."*
>
> **—Major General John B. Wogan**

★ ★ ★

We had to be hammered into the kind of men that made good soldiers. We were untempered metal, like what my dad started out with in his blacksmith shop. Camp Beale was the forge where we civilian boys would become military men, under the orders of our different superiors. They'd pour the heat to us.

No two days were ever alike, but there was a strict rhythm to our daylight hours. Usually, we had to be up by 0600 hours, I believe. Of course, for me it was no problem getting out of bed that early. Some of the other boys didn't much like it, though, and they were always grumbling about how early it was.

"Off your ass and on your feet!" Sergeant Hicks crowed his crude wake-up call down the length of the barracks. Unless he was in a particularly good mood that morning, and then he might yell, "Up and at 'em, boys. Up and at 'em!" But that was rare. Usually it was "Off your ass and on your feet! Off your ass and on your feet!" He'd yell that in the morning when the other boys were waking up.

I wasn't too impressed by that kind of language. I grew up with people all being nice and polite to each other. It sure was different in the army. Some days, it seemed like, he just wanted to shock us.

When we heard him yell each morning, we hit the floor. Well, some of us did. About half the company would laze around, stay in bed till it got late and they just had to get up. If one of the boys was having a hard time waking up, some of the other boys would get together, flip the mattress, and that boy and all his bedding would tumble right in the floor. He'd jump up, rumpled and angry, ready to fight, but he couldn't fight the whole company, so he just had to take it.

I was usually the first one in the barracks to get up and get dressed. We had to mop around our bed every day. I'd go down to the latrine and get a bucket full of water every morning. Well, I was used to that. If you were first down there, you could use the latrine before it got busy, get your mop water, and come back to the barracks as the other boys were waking up. Most of the time, I got my area cleaned up first.

The floor was real smooth, tongue-and-groove pine, and, boy, you could really get it to shine. I'd have that cleaned in a minute. The feller next to me, by that time, he'd be up and he'd take the bucket and they'd pass it on down the line, until all of them had mopped their area.

There was a row of posts that supported the room and every post had a water can on it for the boys who smoked. They'd drop their cigarettes down in there. Those cans had to be emptied every day. That was the responsibility of the person whose bunk was closest. There happened to be one down at the foot of my bed, and I had to take care of that even though I didn't smoke. Every morning, I'd take that can out, empty it, and put fresh water in there. And those boys would have that can about half-full of butts by the next morning. About all the boys smoked. In the military, they gave us a pack of cigarettes every day. I traded mine for candy bars. They got the best end of the bargain, moneywise, but I got rid of the tobacco and got something I could use.

After mopping, I'd finish dressing. We wore what they called "uniform of the day." They'd tell us if we had to dress in fatigues or khakis. If it was fatigues, they'd let us wear our helmet liner around camp, without the helmet. When we went out for training, though, we had to wear the steel helmet on top.

Some days, we were required to wear dress uniform if we had a special program to go to. ODs had longer jackets and shiny brass buttons. When we wore dress uniforms, we'd wear the little caps. We learned how to feel when they were sitting just right on our heads. If you didn't get it right, Sergeant Hicks or, worse, Captain Blake would yell, "Point that cap on the left side of your head, soldier!"

Sergeant Hicks would step out of his quarters down at the end of the barracks and yell, "Fall out! Fall out!" which meant for us to get outside and get ready to line up in formation for roll call. He'd usually add, "On the double! On the double!" which meant for us to run.

"Fall in! Fall in!"

We stood outside and fell into formation. Each platoon stood in two parallel lines. My place was close to one end. We stood at attention and saluted when Sergeant Hicks yelled, "Aten hut!"

We popped our feet together and angled them out a little. You could hear all the heels snapping together at the same time. We had to stand at attention and that meant that you didn't move a muscle, and we held that salute all through the playing of reveille, until the music stopped. Then, Sergeant Hicks would release our salute and call out, "At ease."

At roll call, we each yelled, "Here!" You had to really yell it out, or the sergeant would get on you.

"Kelley, Q!"

"Here!"

They just called everybody by their last name, but to identify me from the other two Kellys in the company, they always added the letter of my middle name, because I went by Quinton. Each one had a different initial and they'd call us out like that.

After everyone was "All present and accounted for!" Sergeant Hicks would yell, "Fall out!"

Then we'd be dismissed. Some of the boys would go back to the barracks until it was chow time, but I was always eager to eat, so I went right over to the mess line so I could get in there on the first wave. When they'd holler, "Chow call!" I was usually in line with my stomach growling.

I always got up there close to the front, but I never was first. They called the ones that were up at the front "chow hounds," and they'd be at the first of the line all the time. There weren't more than ten or fifteen we'd call that. I never did think I was a chow hound, but some of the boys would drag around and by the time they came in, they'd be about out of food.

As we went into the mess hall, they had plates in a big rack and we picked up our silverware and continued down the line. We went by a counter and they'd dish out our eggs and whatever they were serving. Then we'd go by and get our coffee. For the first time in my life, I ate eggs for breakfast and started drinking coffee.

When we went to the tables, they wouldn't let us sit down anywhere we wanted. We had to take the next available seat. So we just sat with whoever happened to be in line. There were ten to a table, five on each side, and we sat on benches.

After breakfast, we had to fall out for calisthenics, which we did for half an hour. Arm exercises, deep knee bends, jumping jacks, and push-ups. As a battalion, we were taken to the camp's obstacle course, where we jumped over wooden fences, climbed knotted ropes, swung over ditches, and crawled through pipe. Part of some days was spent in class-rooms where we studied and took tests like in school, or watched movies about hygiene, health, life in the army, and the latest actions of the enemy. We broke for midday meal, then trained some more.

Everybody that went in the military started with about the same thing—how to march in formation, do close ordered drilling. We'd go to the motor pool and we'd do marching. We did a lot of those close ordered drills.

Sergeant Hicks was a good drill sergeant. They had several march orders for all the different movements we had to make. When he'd say "right flank," everybody would turn and go to the right; "left flank," to the left, and so on. All those different commands, we got familiar with. As a company, we marched all over the camp doing different maneuvers.

Sergeant Hicks would shout out, "In cadence! Count! Two, three, four. Hut, two, three, four. Right flank, march right. Column left, Halt! . . ."

All those commands, he'd run through. And, of course, "double-time"—when the sergeant made a fist and pumped his elbow downward in the air in two quick jerks—that meant to double the pace, really step it up.

They'd have us singing marching songs a lot of the time to keep in rhythm. That's the only time I sang in the service; I didn't whistle or hum little tunes then. I had to be out by myself to do that. But we'd have to sing just as loud as we could when we were marching.

I can remember the lyrics to one of those songs:
"You're in the army now
you're not behind the plow
You'll never get rich
diggin' a ditch
You're in the army now . . ."

So on and so forth. I think it had a little bit of foul language in it. We had more than that one, but that's the one that made the most impression on me, 'cause it was drilled into me so much. Certain words that we said, our right foot had to hit the ground as we said them.

I liked marching. Of course, Sergeant Hicks always said I was like a yo-yo. We used to have those toys when I was a kid on Coker Creek. I'd played with 'em and could do some pretty good tricks.

Sergeant Hicks'd say, "Kelley, quit bouncing like a yo-yo! And sling your hands three inches to the front and six to the rear."

He'd get on me like that all the time. I couldn't walk like some soldiers. Some soldiers walked just as rigid and never hardly moved a thing, only their arms and legs. But I couldn't do that. I had to really try not to bounce, 'cause I've always had a spring in my step. I'd straighten up and do a little better when Sergeant Hicks'd get on me, but it was just in me to be "a bouncin'," I reckon.

I was always in step. In step, in step, in step—I had no trouble with the rhythm. In fact, I'd get into the rhythm of the marching and I'd relax a little bit. Then I'd be bouncin' again. And I'd hear the sergeant:

"Kelley! You're bouncing like a yo-yo! I don't want a yo-yo in this platoon! Straighten up!"

Well, you know that just tickled those other boys. Later on, they'd say something about me being like a yo-yo. Oh, they'd kid me about that. I'm lucky I didn't end up getting nicknamed Yo-Yo for that.

Anything that happened, you had a group of them riding you about it, just to make you miserable if they could. Of course, I didn't pay them any attention. Some of those boys would get awful mad and almost get into fights over stuff like that. But you couldn't let that get under your skin, you had to put up with it.

When we marched, we had to carry our gas mask, canteen, and backpack just like when we went to the battlefield. Occasionally, the sergeant would give us the command for gas. When he hollered, "Gas!" we jerked out our gas mask and put it on. We'd march like that for a while.

Then he'd give us the command, and we had to get down on our knees, lean down close to the ground and pull the side of our gas mask out to where we could get some outside air to see if we could smell any gas. That was a normal procedure for checking to see if the gas was all gone. Then the sergeant'd say, "All clear." And we'd take the gas mask off and put it back in our carrying case.

Saturday morning was the time we'd take long marches. I don't know how long we'd march, but we marched a lot. Forced marches, they called it. Well, all of them were forced, of course. You couldn't get out of nothin' unless you were pretty sick.

Most of the boys, if they were willing to take the punishment, they didn't have any trouble on the marches. But some of them didn't want to take the punishment that we had to go through and they'd do things to get out of it, trying to pretend they were sick, but they still had to qualify.

Naturally, I was used to a lot of hiking, but they would really push you to the limit. We had one big twenty-five mile hike that we had to do before we qualified and we were all dreading that hike.

It was really hot that day, some kind of a heat wave came through. We'd trained all day and were already tired when we started out, about dusk. That was a real miserable hike because my legs got "galded" where they rubbed together and it created a rash. "Gall leg," they called that back home. A feller would say, "I got the gall leg." And, boy, was it painful. The tops of my legs were rubbed so raw they burned like I'd been scalded by a kettle of boiling water.

That march was pretty tough on all of us. Of course, it was at night; they picked nighttime so it wouldn't be quite so hot, but the humidity was high. We'd march fifty minutes and rest ten minutes, march fifty and rest ten, that was the procedure. It took us over ten hours to make that trip.

A lot of the boys didn't qualify. Some of them were soft, city boy types. The farm boys usually didn't have much trouble going the distance. But some of those boys who weren't used to physical punishment, even though they'd been on the fifteen-mile hikes by that time, when they started on the twenty-five-mile hike, a lot of them fell out before they got five miles. The sergeant knew that they were just falling out to keep from going. He also knew they'd finish that hike sooner or later.

I made it the first time. It was one of the things we'd been dread-ing—that twenty-five-mile hike—and in fact, they told us after we'd finished, it was actually twenty-eight miles. That was a pretty tough qualification and I was hurtin' when I got back to camp. The tops of my legs were just raw enough to bleed.

We got back about daylight in the morning. They had breakfast ready for us. Sergeant Hicks told us we had the rest of the day off. Boy, we were glad about that.

As quick as we got through breakfast, got in the barracks, and every-body laid down to rest a little bit, here come Sergeant Hicks again, "Up and at 'em. Up and at 'em! Let's go. We've got a job to do!"

He took us to where they had gasoline stored in one corner of the motor pool. Hundreds and hundreds of five-gallon cans of gas. For some reason, they wanted to move it to a different location. And the way the army had us to move it was to carry it by hand.

It took us two hours to move all that gas. Boy, we were grumbling and carrying on because the sergeant promised to give us the day off and then he came back and put us to work.

After we finished that job, Sergeant Hicks kept his word and he let us off for the rest of the day. Most of the time, we laid around and slept, since we'd missed a night's sleep.

About every Saturday, they'd gather up all those boys that didn't qualify on that twenty-five-mile hike and they'd have to do it over. They'd have to just keep doing it over until they got 'em all qualified. So those boys didn't get out of anything just by dropping out. If they'd been tough enough to have made it the first time, they wouldn't have had to march near as many miles.

After we'd qualify from one thing, they'd advance us to something else. We were given a taste of how to handle ourselves under fire. We ran a course that was similar to a real battlefield with trenches and shell cra-ters and we inched forward under barbed wire. Thirty-caliber machine gun bullets whizzed about a yard over our heads, and simulated mortar fire and hand grenades exploded around us.

We also learned the lessons of a combat swimming course and swam through oil and gasoline flames, using our shirts and trousers as flotation devices. Our basic training consisted of learning to do all the things that soldiers might need to do in order to survive on the battlefield. As a group, most of us were becoming confident as we learned all kinds of new skills.

It wasn't long before the 13th Armored Division got an official nickname. A committee of thirteen judges selected the name from entries in a contest. Everybody really played off of the superstitious "Lucky 13." The name chosen was the Black Cat Division.

A lot of those boys were superstitious. A few of 'em carried a rabbit's foot or lucky pennies, things like that. In fact, while we were required to wear that little cap on the left side of our head, some of the G.I.s got to wearin' their caps on the right side when we were off from training, to "counter the bad luck of bein' in the Thirteenth," they said. Well, I never paid any attention to that. Of course, when those boys were in town, they'd have to be careful to turn that cap back to the left side before any MPs saw them, or they'd be in trouble.

I never was superstitious. In fact, there were a lot of superstitious people back on Coker Creek, and our family thought it was strange and funny, but we tolerated it. When some of 'em came to our house to visit, they wouldn't leave through any other door than the one they came in. We couldn't get them to walk out on the back porch if they'd come in through the front door. Couldn't get them to do it. "Oh, no," they'd tell us. "That there's bad luck."

People like that, if they went somewhere, they'd always go back the same path. Some of 'em had the idea that when they entered their house, they had to go through a ritual. Maybe they'd touch a certain piece of furniture every time, or get the broom and rub it a certain way, then they felt like they were relieved of any danger. Those people lived in misery, seemed to me like. Most of the ones like that didn't have any education at all, they just thought that something bad would happen to them if they didn't do certain things every time.

Our family never was like that. In fact, we'd laugh about it, oh, we went on about it, when we were by ourselves, how some families would

just live by peculiar superstitions. And, of course, we knew the superstitions that everybody in the country knew about—like not wantin' a
black cat to cross your path.

After the 13th Armored Division was nicknamed the Black Cats,
an honorary emblem was designed by Walt Disney, since we were in
California, the movie industry state. Disney's cartoon emblem showed
a black cat arched under a ladder, standing on a broken mirror next to
a spilled saltshaker. Overhead was an open umbrella with the number
13 dangling over the cat's head. The spirit of the emblem was the 13th
Armored Division thumbing our noses at bad luck, I reckon, making
fun of superstitions that we'd all heard of, regardless of where we were
from, whether we believed in them or not.

Our official U.S. Army emblem that we wore on our sleeve was, of
course, more dignified. That patch was a three-colored triangle from the
old days of World War I, with each color representing the three compo-
nents of armored command: yellow for cavalry, red for field artillery, and
blue for infantry. Of course, now the cavalry had been replaced by
armored vehicles with a lot more horsepower. A thunderbolt cut across
the colors on the emblem to represent shock action. Underneath it was
a tank track for mobility and a cannon for firepower. It looked like other
U.S. armored division patches, except for the number 13.

Every armored division had its own nickname—Tigers, Hellcats,
Liberators, and so forth. The 13th would forever be known as the Black
Cats. We boasted, "Those Nazis don't want us Black Cats to cross their
path." Of course, we were preparing ourselves to do just that.

★ ★ ★

Black Cats are crack shots. This is shown in the proficiency
with which men of Division Trains fired the Thompson sub-
machine gun. Forty enlisted men and the two instructing offi-
cers qualified as experts. Twelve men qualified as first class
gunners, and not a man in the entire training group failed to
qualify with the Tommy gun.

— **THE BLACK CATS: They Sharpened Their**
Claws in California . . . U.S. Army 1945 (2)

We trained on a lot more guns than we'd ever use — the rifles, hand-guns, and submachine guns. We learned how to take each one apart, how to clean them, oil them, and how to adjust them. Each gun had to be adjusted a certain way before it would fire correctly. Then they progressed to teaching us about marksmanship, estimating the effective range, and we'd do target practice.

I enjoyed all that because I had fooled with guns all my life to a certain extent. Of course, I grew up with a .22 rifle. I had used shot-guns some, too, so I was familiar with their kick, but I usually hunted with rifles.

One of the guns we started out with was the M1 carbine .30 cali-ber, a short rifle. It was a self-loading shoulder weapon, but it had a shorter barrel than a regular rifle. Frontline infantry troops carried it because full-size rifles were cumbersome when they had to carry a lot of equipment.

They'd have us to fire some rounds with that carbine, standing up, but most of the time they'd have us lying on our stomachs. The prone posi-tion was the one that we could hit the best with. You're more still.

We had what they called a "shelter half," that was half of a pup tent. I carried half and another soldier carried half and if you put them together, it made one pup tent where two people could sleep if we were out overnight. On the firing range, we'd take those shelter halves and lay them down in the field and we'd lie on our stomachs and fire those carbines at targets. There'd be a long line of soldiers, and we'd be about twenty feet apart.

At first, we had an instructor who'd lie down by the side of us and tell us what to do. Then we'd do target practice in teams. One of the boys in the company would coach you and when it was his turn to fire, you'd coach him. A big group of us would fire at the same time and then pause.

It really affects you some about being on your target, having all those other guns so close when you're firing. Loud, popping noises can cause you to jump, but we had to get used to that. Most of the time, we'd put earplugs in our ears to protect our hearing, little rubber things that muffled the sound enough so it didn't bother us, though we could still hear the commotion of all those rifles firing at once.

The targets had about five circles and hung over a big ditch that was cut out in the target field. They had men at every target, down in that ditch and those men had markers to mark where the bullets hit the target. The targets were made so a man could let them down and put on a new paper target and raise it back up. After we fired, they'd bring it down to see where we hit.

If it was a bull's-eye, the man in the ditch would mark the target and he'd hold it up for us to see.

If it was a miss, it was "Maggie's drawers!" That's what they called the red flag that they held up. We saw a lot of those.

Sergeant Hicks paced up and down behind the firing line to see how we were doing. He had a pair of binoculars and he could look at the targets.

Some of those boys would hit way off center, especially at first. Some people try to get on the target going sideways, or coming from the top down and it just doesn't work as well. My dad taught me to get under the target and come up—don't hesitate, just the instant you see the target come into your sights, pull that trigger. That helped me to make a better score and it would help me if I had to use any gun in combat.

It was second nature to me to handle the type of gun that I could steady with my shoulder, but I was used to a longer barrel. I could adjust to using a shorter barrel, but that made it a little less accurate. With a short-barreled gun, if you waver just the slightest bit, you'll be way off. With that carbine, I didn't hit the bull's-eye every time, but I could usually hit pretty close to it.

When we qualified, we were rated and classified by our skill level. Classifications from lowest to highest were at that time: Marksman, Second Class Gunner, Sharpshooter, First Class Gunner, and Expert. I qualified as Sharpshooter on the carbine.

Some of the boys made good scores and some couldn't hit nothin' hardly. Five or six boys, I remember, didn't want to pass qualifications and they'd just fire off to the right or left a little bit, leave the target clean. They didn't care whether they hit anything or not. They figured if they made a good score that it meant they'd have to go to the front lines and they didn't want to have to go, so they'd just goof off. You'll have that when you have a bunch of boys, there'll be a number of goof-offs in the bunch.

I figured I was going to the front lines anyway and I wanted to do my best, so if I had to use the gun in battle, I'd be able to use it. I was learning for my own benefit, looking out for myself, as well as others. I never did have to go back a second time for any qualifications. I wanted to make as good a soldier as I could because that's the way you survive. Some good ones get killed, but more of them come out alive than the ones that just drag around.

Those boys who wouldn't try to hit the targets, they thought they'd get out of training like that. But they didn't get out of a thing. The instructors knew all about those tricks.

Some of the boys in our outfit had a hard time qualifying because they were afraid to shoot. The army rifles were high-powered and they'd kick pretty hard. The M1 Garand rifle was one of the guns we qualified on and it was a semiautomatic, so it had a pretty good kick to it. It kicks hard like a shotgun if you don't hold it tight, and some of those boys weren't used to that. It was mostly a few of the city slickers who had never fired a gun before that had the trouble. The instructors were on them all the time — they couldn't hit nothin'.

When we got that M1 — a big, heavy rifle with a long barrel — they'd told us in our classes, "*Do not* put your thumb across the top of this gun when you fire. If you do, that rifle will kick up and your thumb will mash your nose."

Well, I remembered that, but a lot of those boys didn't pay attention, or they forgot, and they'd put their thumb up on the top — it was easier to hold the gun that way.

One boy, the kind of a boy all of 'em were pickin' on a whole lot, the first time he fired the M1, that gun busted his nose. Blood came gushing out all over.

That boy said, "I'll never sight another target. They can keep me out here as long as they want, but I will not hit one single target. I'm not letting a gun do that to my face!"

After that, when that boy'd get ready to pull the trigger, he'd move his head off to the side, close his eyes, and then pull the trigger. It was a sight how the sergeants got on him, because they knew what he was doing. They were rough on him, but they never could make him look down the sights when he pulled the trigger — they couldn't *make* him do that after he got his nose mashed.

He kept saying, "No, I can't have my nose broken."

I told him, "You don't have to." I showed him how to hold the gun. "Instead of putting your thumb across the grip, you put it over here to the side and it'll miss your face when it jumps up." But he never would do it.

Of course, the rest of the boys laughed at him. That's the way they'd do, those boys in service — one of them would make a mistake or get hurt or something, and everybody would laugh at him. That made it a little worse.

This particular boy, they'd pull little pranks on him, and he'd fly off the handle, use some profanity. He could talk a blue streak of profanity. Boy, he'd curse them out and I think that just made those boys want to get him riled up even more. They liked to hear him.

That boy transferred out of our company pretty soon. He wanted to get away from the ones in our company who were riding him on everything. Didn't nobody have sympathy for you in there. You had to just be on your own.

We went through all the training with the M1 rifle and then the army got some .45 pistols, and they decided that was going to be our personal weapon. It was a .45 semiautomatic, a regular .45 pistol like the police carry, but U.S. Army issue.

We trained on that gun, how to take it apart, clean it, and reassemble it. When you put it back together, that gun was a little bit tricky. If you didn't know about lining up a little link with a little hole before you put the screw in, that gun wouldn't fire. A lot of boys missed that piece of information and had a terrible time assembling that pistol. But I could put that gun together, lickety-split, and it'd be ready to fire.

As a weapon, it was lightweight and quick to reload a seven-round magazine. The bullets were automatically fed up from the handle, and it flipped the empty shells out. I wasn't quite as comfortable with a handgun. But I did make Marksman on the .45 semiautomatic pistol.

The army took that pistol away and I was glad. Especially because they replaced it with the Thompson submachine gun, .45 caliber. That was already a famous gun. It had been around a long time. It had been the gun of gangsters in Chicago in the 1920s and the same gun that law enforcement had used to combat them.

There were several Chicago boys in our outfit and they proudly called our new gun the Chicago Piano, or Chicago Typewriter, because it had a rapid *rat-a-tat-tat* sound when you shot it. The Chicago boys probably imagined they were gangsters or Eliot Ness when they got to do target practice on the gun that everybody—even me from the back hills—had heard about as the Tommy gun.

I was real excited to see a Tommy gun. It was a good-looking gun. It had two pistol grips, one up front and one in the back. The wooden grips were curved to fit comfortably in my hands, and my fingers wrapped around the smooth tight-grained maple—that's real tough wood. Of course, the rest of the gun was steel and the barrel was quite a bit shorter than a regular rife, less accurate, good for a shorter range.

To me, when you shot it, the Thompson sounded like something burping. *BurpBurpBurpBurp*. Real quick, you couldn't count your shots, they were so fast. If you held the trigger down, it would run a whole clip out in no time. It could really spray the bullets — I think the ones we had were around 650 rounds per minute. It shot so fast, if you depressed the trigger for an instant, you'd pepper the target with bullets. And you had to really pull against that gun. If you weren't careful, you'd be shooting straight up if you kept firin' it. The Thompson really climbed a whole lot.

If we had to fire several rounds in a barrage, the barrel would get real hot, but not the pistol grip. We didn't do too much rapid firing; that was just so we could see how it would do. That's a waste of ammunition. They taught us to shoot in short bursts. If you just touched the trigger lightly, you might get off one shot, but you'd likely get more than one.

The Thompson submachine gun wasn't too accurate for long range. It was good for searching homes in enemy territory. With that short barrel, you could maneuver the gun around doorways and tight places — swing around to shoot at someone.

The Tommy gun was solidly made. It was a good weapon, had been proven reliable, and I felt confident with it. I liked that gun. It was my best. I made the top score, too. I was rated Expert on the Thompson submachine gun.

There were some of us in the company who made Expert, but not that many. None of them were from Chicago. Some of those city boys used to brag about their "Chicago Piano," like they had a special claim to it. But as far as I could see, those city boys couldn't play their Chicago Piano as well as some of us country boys.

For some reason, the army took the Tommy gun away and I was pretty disappointed about that. Especially when I saw what they issued us next. We called it the "Grease Gun." Officially, it was the U.S. Thompson submachine gun M3, .45 caliber.

Aw, it was a gun that looked like it had been thrown together. Looked a whole lot like a grease gun that you use on a car. It was all metal, no wooden stock, no wood anywhere. If you greased your own car like I always did, you used a grease gun, which has a barrel and a handle that you work up and down when you stick it down in a grease can to suck up the grease.

These guns were manufactured similar to an automotive grease gun, two pressed metal shells welded together. The barrel was held on by a simple nut and bolt. It was a cheaply made, mass-produced and stripped-down model of the heavier Tommy gun. Well, it was lighter to carry. I never did think those Grease Guns were too much of a gun, but it was better than having a pistol.

Maybe the reason the army finally settled on the Grease Gun for our personal weapon was that you could shoot it like a rifle or shoot it like a pistol. That Grease Gun had a stock on it, what you call the stock, even though this one wasn't like any stock I'd ever seen. It was a thin metal rod that curved down, and that rod telescoped into the rest of the thing. You could pull it out and put it against your shoulder and shoot that gun like a rifle. Or you could push the rod into the gun and hold the gun by the grip like a pistol. Of course, you had to hold it with both hands; it was too heavy to use with one hand. Most of the time we used that gun like a pistol, we didn't pull the stock out. But if we were really trying to hit the target, it was better to have that stock against our shoulder and shoot it like a rifle.

The Grease Gun jumped around more than the Tommy gun ever did. Best you can do, you can't hardly hold a Grease Gun when you're rapid firing. For a good weapon, the Tommy gun was much better, it was more accurate. And the Grease Gun only shot 450 rounds a minute, not near what the Tommy gun shot. It still made that *rat-a-tat-tat! Tat-tat-tat!* sound that could jar your teeth, though.

They told us, if we had to go through a village, searching houses, that gun was a lot better to have in case we ran into snipers hiding in the house. That Grease Gun only had a ten-inch barrel. We had to have something we could handle in close quarters. Also, we'd need a compact weapon so we could get in and out of a tank easily, since we'd be a tank outfit.

I did pretty well with the Grease Gun. Of course, nobody could hit too well with them. But I did as well as any of them and better than most. I liked that gun all right and I was classified Expert on it, too. By then, I knew how to carry a submachine gun in formations, field strip it, put it back together, and maintain it in combat. They even made us assemble and disassemble them blindfolded.

Sometimes we took our guns to the mess hall and practiced keeping them with us like we'd do in battle zones. On field maneuvers, we'd sleep beside them when we bivouacked so we'd be used to living with a weapon like it was part of our body. They wanted us to depend on our guns. Of course, that came natural to me.

Most of the time in training, though, we didn't carry our personal weapon. When we'd get back to camp at the end of the day, they'd collect all the guns and store them in the arms room overnight. But before they could be stored, they all had to be cleaned. The army was particular about things like that. Usually, everybody had to clean their own guns and oil them at the end of the day's training.

Most of the time, if it was a nice day, we'd get outside, lay down a piece of canvas to work on. I'd clean the barrel with little square fabric patches and a rod that has a slot in the end, to stick the patch down the barrel. When that patch comes out clean, you're ready to put some oil on it and run it back and forth through the barrel, so it won't rust. Doesn't take long to clean a gun.

It was nice to settle down and have some quiet. Even with protection, my ears'd be ringing after several hours of target practice, shooting those submachine guns. I could still feel the power of the grip in my hands as it burped rounds of ammunition. Those rhythms'd stay with you. Somebody always had a radio and if I could, I'd listen to the music they liked, just to have something to listen to.

On Saturday afternoons and in the evenings, we could do what we liked, maybe go see a movie on the post, if we didn't have other duties. Some of the other boys who stayed in camp went down to the PX to drink beer. Of course, a lot of the boys would go to town on a pass. Those little towns near the post, like Marysville, were just full of servicemen and their girlfriends and that was about all, so I didn't see any reason to go there.

Occasionally, they'd have dances at the service club on the base and hundreds of pretty girls recruited by the Marysville USO would come to dance with the G.I.s. I never went to those dances. I wasn't used to being with all those strangers, especially girls I didn't know, and what's the use of going to a dance when you don't know how to dance? Besides, all the music that filtered out of the service club onto the street was real different from the music I'd grown up on.

It was 1943, and there were trumpets in the air everywhere. Trumpets, horns, bugles—instruments I wasn't too familiar with. The big band sound was all the rage. A lot of the new tunes were lively, but I didn't much like the sound of it; I missed the old-time bluegrass music that I'd learned to love as a child. But that kind of music wasn't popular and we didn't hear much of it, the old-time fiddles, banjos, and mandolins. At least they were pleasant sounds, not trumpets blarin'.

From what I gathered, the mood of that popular music was mostly happy-go-lucky or sweetly romantic, maybe because the news from the battlefronts was so sad and worrisome. There wasn't hardly a sad song in the bunch. And a lot of that music had a positive war theme to help rouse up the people to get behind the war effort.

But the hillbilly music that I missed was about so many more different things that you find in life—faith, loss, sadness, longing, work, love, joy, hope. I thought it had more heart. It always touched mine the most.

There was one popular new song I did like, though: "Chattanooga Choo Choo." I heard that song sold a million copies when it came out in 1942, and that's when the first-ever "gold record" was created by RCA Victor for Glenn Miller, the band leader who recorded that song.

"Chattanooga Choo Choo's" cheerful sound was all over the radio. It had some happy whistling, and a catchy tune that made you remember the rhythms of a locomotive. The song was about a man making his way down home to Tennessee on the train, where his sweetheart was waiting for him at the station. And since I'd sure like to be goin' home to

Tennessee with my own sweetheart waitin' for me, it was only natural I'd like that song.

But as for all those other brassy, swingy dance tunes, like "Boogie Woogie Bugle Boy"—that's the one the Chicago boys liked—I heard 'em when I was out in California, but I'd rather listen to something else.

There were roughly two kinds of boys in our companies. Those who liked that kind of music and those who didn't. I liked the old-timey sound of a fiddle myself and so did a lot of my buddies. There were boys in our company who would have called that instrument a "violin." Of course, I reckon we all knew it was the same thing.

> *Kelley was a right-nice, good-looking young man, I would say. He and I, they called me "hillbilly" and him a "hillbilly," but I think he was raised and lived in more of a hilly country. I'm almost in flat land where I's raised.*
>
> *Everybody in the company thought a lot of Kelley. He was not a brag. He was not tellin' great tales and doin' big things and stretchin' the truth. If Tennessee's got a lot of him in it, they've got a good state.*
> **—Lonnie E. Johnson, from Smithfield, North Carolina (12)**

The boys I trained with were a mixed bag from all over the USA—Ohio, California, Pennsylvania, West Virginia, Minnesota, Louisiana, Illinois, Kentucky, to recall some of the states—but there were probably more Southern boys in there than anything else. Country boys. Most of them were just young, early twenties, although a few were older. Whatever company we were in, when we took our training, we all fell out together. So we all got acquainted, but you got most acquainted with the boys in your barracks. I was in C Company, which occupied two barracks, so I got best acquainted with about half the company.

Since everybody had to dress and groom alike, it was hard to judge the man by his appearance. You didn't know where a feller was from—some of 'em said "fellow" or "fella" and, of course, some of us would say "feller." When you get that many soldiers together, especially a lot of 'em drafted, they come in there from every walk of life, rich and poor, educated and illiterate, and everything in between.

The boys I met from all over the country asked me where I was from right away usually, because of the way I talked. And none of them knew where Coker Creek was, back there in the beautiful green mountains of Tennessee. I'd tell 'em a little bit about growing up around the homeplace and what kind of community we lived in. They got a kick out of that because it sounded countrified, and it was.

Those Northern boys from up in New Jersey and New York, and the Midwestern city boys from Chicago—it was the first time I had encountered any of them. Maybe that was true for a lot of those other country boys, too. We called the boys from up north Yankees.

They called us nicknames that were different depending on the part of the country we came from—the South or Midwest, mountains or cornfields. Country boys were sometimes called hayseeds, okies, plowboys, ridge runners, crackers, rebels, or hillbillies—all of us just "hicks" to those big-city boys.

Those city boys were a little different to the country boys. They were a lot different.

We had a lot of Chicago boys in our outfit and those Chicago boys talked about streets called boulevards and avenues. When they'd meet another boy from the Chicago area, they'd talk a blue streak and compare neighborhoods and try to see if they'd ever been to the same places back home. They'd describe big fancy movie theaters and talk about meeting their buddies in corner drugstores, like there were so many corners and so many different drugstores. They talked with pride about their big city and the streetcars that ran up and down the streets. I'd listen and try to imagine how different their life had been from mine, living in buildings taller than I'd ever seen, with noisy streets and smoky factories and steel mills and all kinds of hamburger joints.

I had a little trouble understanding the Northern boys, but I'd catch on pretty quick. I slept near several Chicago boys in the barracks and they've got an accent. They talk short, speak fast and really rattle off a lot of words. I had to get used to hearing those city boys talk.

The boys from up north made fun of the Southern boys because we had a kind of drawl. The Southern people, I guess sometimes we'd let our speech drag on, slow and long, like waitin' for the cold molasses to wind its way out of the bottom of a jar on a winter mornin'. The cadence of our speech was different, too, up and down, up and down—a little like bouncin' in a buggy on a washed-out road. And we might've used a few more words than we needed to, to say somethin'. At first, those Northerners didn't catch on to what some of us Southerners were a sayin', so I learned to straighten up my speech a little bit so they could understand me better.

The Northern boys would imitate us and really exaggerate how we talked, drag out and bend their words, if they were imitating what some of the boys from the South had said. Those Northern boys, they talked like they thought we Southern boys were ignorant a lot of the time. They looked down on us 'cause we were from the backcountry. Of course, our English maybe wasn't up to par, but they thought we didn't know a thing. I didn't care, 'cause I was proud of who I was and the good family I came from. Besides, we were all Americans.

One day, one of those cocky Northern boys was talking to some of us Southerners and he said, "Where were *you*, Kelley, when you heard the news about Pearl Harbor?" I reckoned he wanted to hear what I'd say I was doing in "them thar hills."

I dropped my head down. "Well, I'll tell you, when I heard about Pearl Harbor, that was a sad day in March . . ."

His eyebrows went up about to his hairline. "March!" He started grinning. "Took that long to reach you back in your 'hollerrrr,' did it?"

"Naw," I said, "I was just foolin'. I found out about it the day everybody else did. We's at home after church that Sunday, and one of the neighbors come a runnin' over to tell us to turn on the radio. Everybody was already a talkin' about the bombin'. Terrible. *Terrible.*"

Those Northern boys were quick to strike back. "Yeah, bet it took you hillbillies until March to find out what Hawaii was. 'Haay, Paawwww, what is that Hia-wwaaaa-heee they keep a talkin' 'bout on that thar raadio?'" And they'd just go to bending over, laughing.

Now, a lot of those city boys, they thought they were several notches ahead of the rest of us, but they weren't. They just thought that. Some of 'em were smart alecks, awful cocky and hateful. Their language was a little different, too. They used the Lord's name in vain a lot and put a curse word or two in about everything they said. Oh, they could really use raw language, whether they were angry or not. Why, where I came from, words like that, you were liable to get your head knocked off with a shotgun if you said it to the wrong man on the wrong day.

One boy like that from Chicago, Cantanacci was his name, he got on me pretty heavy one time. It wasn't my fault, but I got the blame.

It wasn't supposed to be my turn for guard duty that day, but somebody had made out the list and they failed to get one man on it, and it was time to mount guards. They rotated it around and we knew about when we'd be on guard duty. You had to be on duty twenty-four hours when it was your turn.

Sergeant Hicks came in the barracks and said, "Kelley, we've messed up on the guard list. We're short one man and your name is next on the list. You get ready, I'm gonna have to put you on guard duty."

I didn't mind.

"But," he added, "I'll give you a job so you won't have to walk guard. You'll just have to play the music."

I liked that all right. It was an easy job. They had a record player over in the headquarters building and you played music over the loudspeaker. You just had to sit over there and play it at the right time, reveille in the morning and taps at night, when we had to extinguish lights.

Then the sergeant took Cantanacci and made him walk guard because he'd given me the easy job. That made that Chicago boy so mad, because I got the better job.

Cantanacci came in the barracks and just started slinging his stuff around and he used a lot of profanity. He was raisin' Cain and he came over to me and said, "Kelley, you got me walking guard! It was my turn to play the music, not walk. What kind of hillbilly stuff did you say to the sergeant?"

I said, "Now, I didn't have nothin' to do with you walkin' guard."

He said, "I know you did."

I said, "No, I didn't. I had nothin' to do with it. I'm just doin' what I's told. You'll have to talk to the sergeant. He's the one that made them arrangements."

Cantanacci was madder than a wet hen. He just slammed his footlocker like he was mad enough to die and he cursed and went on about it. Of course, I didn't have a thing to do with it, but that boy really smarted off and I never did think too much of him for acting that way. After he got over it, he never did mention it again, and I never fooled with him either.

A lot of those Northern boys were pretty bad to do that. They were used to talking to each other in a rough way, and the Southern boys weren't used to that. We usually respected each other, but if we got to talking rough, we really meant business. But we found out that the Northern boys didn't mean much by it. It was just their style. I always got along with Cantanacci after that, though. He eventually made sergeant in there and he never did give me any trouble.

Cantanacci and those of his kind, they may have been all right once you got to know them, but you couldn't associate with them too much unless you wanted to fit in with their way of life. A lot of them drank, gambled, cursed, told filthy jokes and off-color stories, and tried to corrupt the rest of us.

They'd shoot dice over in the corner of the barracks some nights and they'd try to get me to join in. They just begged me to shoot. They said, "You've never done it before?"

I shook my head. I don't know how it was where they came from, but they acted like they couldn't believe it.

Several of them said, "Kelley, oh, you'll be lucky. If you've never shot dice, when you first start, you're always lucky."

I said, "No. I ain't gettin' into that. I might take a likin' to it, get carried away with it, and that's when the trouble starts. I ain't gonna take no part of it."

"Oh! Come on," one boy said. "Come on here and help me out. You and me can get some money out of it."

I said, "No, I won't fool with it." I never would try it.

Those boys would always say, "Oh, if you've never done this before, you'll have beginner's luck." And it's true. I've seen a lot of those boys try gambling for the first time and they'd get lucky. It had to be luck, because they threw the dice, and they'd win. I always thought to myself, it must be the Devil's trick, beginner's luck, to pull you into that gambler's lifestyle. I watched them a little bit at first, but I quickly saw how it went.

Those boys, a lot of them big-city boys, they'd sit in a smoky corner of the barracks sometimes till the wee hours, huddled around a table. A lot of times I'd hear them holler, "Come on, seven! Lucky seven! . . . Snake eyes!"

Before long, those boys would be losing their whole paycheck in a game of craps. Then they'd be calling home for money. Of course, they had to make up a big tale about why they needed it.

My dad had tried some of that gamblin' when he was growing up and he never did want me to go that way. He'd told me, "Son, that's the wrong way to travel."

While we sat around the barracks, we read our mail from home. Some of those boys would get letters from their girlfriends and they'd read them aloud to the rest of us. I was shocked to hear some of the stuff. Orangie and I didn't write real mushy letters to each other like some people did. Some of those boys would get real personal letters and read them to us and laugh about what their girlfriends said. They'd make fun of the girl, brag on, and disrespect her. The girls wouldn't have appreciated that, if they'd known about it.

A lot of times we didn't get along together, some of us didn't. A lot of boys just go on with stuff they ought to keep quiet about. I stayed clear of the type of boys I didn't want to imitate. I never had much problem. Sometimes, of course, some of the other boys would get mad and get into a fight. They'd hit each other, start scuffling around.

If it was off-duty hours, Sergeant Hicks would hear the ruckus and he'd come out of his quarters down at the end of the barracks.

"Break it up! Break it up!" he'd yell.

He'd get on them pretty stern. He kept the peace around there. The army didn't tolerate roughhousing, not even goofing around. You had to conduct yourself pretty seriously or you'd get in trouble.

I only got in trouble one time. Sometime in our training—I think it was kind of a bad weather day—they used the barracks for us to assemble in, to teach us some subject or other. We were sitting on the bunks, and the instructing officer came in and just as he came through the door, one of those boys who was sitting behind me, he grabbed me and jerked me backwards and went to wrestling with me. He was roughing me up and I was fighting back to try to get loose from him. I wasn't wanting to wrestle. This boy didn't see that officer coming in, but that officer saw both of us scuffling, first thing.

That officer said, "You two soldiers come here!"

We walked over there and he got on us real rough for wrestling in class. We were really just playing, but he thought we were fighting.

He said, "You're disrupting the whole class! Now, go out the front door and run up the street to the corner and back six times."

I believe it might have been raining. He gave us a limited amount of time, so we had to run up there and back, up there and back, as hard as we could—or we'd get more punishment.

The first time we ran by the barracks, we met some more boys from C Company coming through there, running. They had laughed at us and when that instructing officer saw them laughing, he put them out there doing laps, too. You had to really obey their rules, especially when we were supposed to be learning something that could help us win the war, or keep us alive.

That's just boys. If the boys in the barracks weren't trying to rough up each other, they'd be pulling pranks on each other. If they knew something bothered you, they'd really go out of their way to ride you about it.

Some of those boys would call out for their momma in their sleep and that would just tickle the other boys. It seems strange, grown men hollering for Momma. We'd get a kick out of listening to them call out, "Momma! Momma!" I don't know what they thought their momma could do for them. They'd just toss and turn in their sleep. We ought to have felt sorry for them, but we didn't. Some of the ones that didn't do that would laugh about it and embarrass the ones who'd talk in their sleep. "Hey, if it ain't Momma's boy!" they'd say, things like that.

At that time, there was one feller who had the bed next to me and he was an alcoholic. As soon as we were through with training in the evening, he'd go to the PX and start drinking beer and not stop until they closed. He didn't bother anybody, but he got drunk about every night, and came back to the barracks stumbling around. He'd come in right on deadline so looped up he could hardly walk and he'd just wobble over to his bed.

The barracks had little bunks for us to sleep in, narrow beds, barely big enough to turn over in. Sometimes the G.I.s would short-sheet them. They'd take the top sheet, tuck it in at the head of the bed, double it in the middle and bring the bottom end about halfway up, so it looked like a regular made bed.

Some boys short-sheeted this alcoholic boy's bunk and when that boy started to jump in his bed, he couldn't get his feet to go down, they stopped halfway. The other boys just went to laughing as loud as they could.

That boy just raised up the mattress with all the covers on it, crawled under it, and slept on the springs. He stayed there until the next morning, and he woke up and there he was! He couldn't figure out how he got that way, but he chose that himself. Slept on the springs with the mattress on top of him, so, you can imagine about how crazy drunk he was.

Most of the ones that went to the PX in the evening, they'd just stay there until it closed. The beer they had in there, they claimed it wouldn't make you drunk, but they'd consume so much that they got drunk enough till they could hardly stand up. Some of them had to be led back to the barracks. That's a terrible life. I wasn't used to that. It bothered me quite a bit, to see that rough kind of life.

You get a bunch of boys together, if they get about drunk, some of them are wild. Some of them, all they want to do is fight. Some of those same fellers are the friendliest fellers you've ever seen when they're sober. That alcohol changes their personalities altogether. After they'd drink beer just as hard as they could, they'd get a fight started with somebody. I was really fortunate that nobody ever did pick on me.

Of course, there were a lot of good boys in there that they never did pick on. They didn't pick on the boys who behaved themselves. It was just the boys who caused trouble that got picked on. They brought it on themselves. They were always having fights in camp and they'd have to call in the MPs to get them straightened out. Most of that happened around the Post Exchange where they sold beer. The PX carried most of the necessities soldiers needed, postcards, stamps, different refreshments.

I'd go to the PX to buy my razor blades and shaving cream. We had to be shaved smooth every day and it took quite a bit of that to keep you going. I'd get some ice cream, too, nearly every day. I ate a lot of ice cream out of that PX. You could buy it in pint containers and I ate every flavor they'd have. Everybody else would be in there drinking beer and I'd be down there eating ice cream. Sure, some of those boys ribbed me about it, but I didn't pay them any attention.

Back home, there was always a crowd of roughnecks in the community and my dad didn't want me to associate with them. When I'd meet them, I was friendly, I'd talk with them a little bit, but I didn't go places with them.

My dad said, "If you stay with those kind long enough, they'll get you into trouble."

When I was in the military, that influenced who I chose to associate with. I had a lot of friends in there who would try to get me to do things that I didn't want to do. They were always wanting to get me a drink of whiskey or some liquor or other.

I didn't make them mad, I just said, "No. I don't fool with that. You just as well to not ask me, 'cause I won't do it."

One feller from Alabama came in one day and he said to me, "I've got a pint of fine whiskey back here that's never been opened and I'll give every bit of it to you, if you'll drink it. Now, I wouldn't offer a drink to none of these other fellers around here, 'cause I know they'd grab it."

I said, "Well, I thank you. But I don't fool with it and I don't want it."

He wanted to see how I'd act. Usually somebody that's never been under the influence of alcohol, they can put on a pretty good show, the first time they get drunk. They don't know how to control themselves. They'll say a lot of stuff that they wouldn't say otherwise. They'll act a fool and the rest of them will get a kick out of watching.

Some of those boys would say things to officers and if the officers hadn't overlooked it because they were about half-drunk, they would have gotten in trouble. Why, even Sergeant Hicks came out of the PX one time and I saw him walk up to one of the captains and salute—he wobbled just a little—and he said, "Hello there, Smilin' Jack!" The sergeant should have gotten in trouble for calling a captain by a nickname, but he didn't.

I was always careful about how I conducted myself. I was brought up with temperance and didn't want to depart from that just because I was in the army. The boys I chose to associate with were mostly clean-cut types. Most happened to be Southerners. The Southern boys in my barracks—and there were a lot of 'em—it was easy for me to understand them. They kept their speech pretty clean, told clean jokes, like the one a Southern boy told about a man sitting in a coffee shop:

"This waitress was pourin' coffee into a customer's cup. She was tryin' to make conversation, so she looked out the window and she said, "Well, it looks like rain.""

The customer looked into his cup and he said, "Yeah, but it tastes a little bit like coffee."

He'd really call it *caaaww-fee*. The Northern boys would chuckle, they got a kick out of hearing that boy's slow drawl.

We had some boys in the barracks from my neck of the woods, relatively close.

One boy lived not too far from my home, down in Etowah. I didn't know him, but when he found out I was from Coker Creek, he came to me and asked me if I would write down his letters to his folks back home. I hated to have to do that, but he couldn't read or write. He was a real nice boy and if he hadn't told me, I wouldn't have detected that he was illiterate, just talkin' to him.

He'd tell me what to say, but he didn't know how to word a letter or anything. He'd ask about this uncle and that cousin, what they were doing, all kinds of stuff like that. He'd tell them a few things about being in the military, but not much. He was more interested in knowing how they were doing.

I'd try to write what he said, but it was a chore. Of course, I was no professional at that either. I did it because I felt sorry for him and he needed somebody and he wouldn't ask some of the other boys, especially the boys from up north—they'd have made fun of him. But I never did.

We had several boys like that in our company at first, illiterate, but in a few weeks they weeded all of them out and put them in a company all to themselves. They formed a new company and they took all the boys that couldn't read and write, put them together and used them for some purpose, I don't remember what. Most of the Southern boys in our outfit could read and write pretty well, though.

The boys I got along with best were from all over the South: Rosenberg from Kentucky; Allen from Alabama; Darnell from Georgia; two Tennesseans: Jackson from Nashville; and Knoblock from Memphis.

Lonnie Johnson was in my barracks, a real good Southerner. He was from Smithfield, North Carolina, tobacco country, farm country. He slept two bunks down from me. Some of 'em called him Brown Nose, because they thought he was always kissing up to Sergeant Hicks and the other officers. If a boy was pretty friendly with the officials, they'd call him a Brown Nose and Johnson was always pretty friendly with anybody he'd come up to, didn't matter who it was. Everybody liked him.

When we'd call him Brown Nose, he'd threaten, "I'll whup your ass!" then he'd just burst into a big, hearty laugh.

Lonnie Johnson was a big talker and jolly and we had a lot of fun together. I fractured my arm swingin' on a rafter like a monkey with him, the way I used to do in trees back on Coker Creek. It wasn't a bad break. I got over it in a few weeks and, because of Lonnie, I never did get in trouble over it.

Lonnie Johnson:

When Kelley broke his arm in the army, he was actin' up, which he loved to do. One night, they had a lot of "G.I. soup" on the floor. We was cleaning the barracks, pouring buckets of water on the floor with a lot of ol' soap suds in them. The little ol' barracks we was in didn't have a overhead ceiling in it. It had the raw two-by-fours goin' across.

Kelley jumped up and was gonna swing on one of those ceiling joists, and when he come down, the floor was slick and he fell down and broke his arm.

He said, "Oh, I'm in trouble."

I knowed he was gonna tell them the truth when they asked him how'd he break his arm, he was gonna say, "I was tryin' to skin a cat."

I said, "You just go with us. We'll do the talkin'."

Kelley said, "Well, I'll have to tell 'em that I was actin' up and actin' crazy."

So I said, "Hey, you let somebody else do the talkin' and we'll tell 'em what happened."

We took him to the medics. Seems to me like, me and Knode went with him. Knode was a kind of a slim fellow. We done the talkin' for him that time. Told 'em it was an accident, that Kelley just slipped and got hurt. And he got by with it. So then we would tell Kelley that he owes us one.

He didn't have to lie about it. And he wouldn't have. That's just the way I knew him then. Kelley just wouldn't lie to get out of trouble, even if he'd got in it by foolish acts, like he was doin', playin' and havin' a good time. (12)

Lonnie E. Johnson

Now, Lonnie did gamble a little bit, but otherwise he stayed out of trouble. But he buddied up with some boys that were really bad to play cards and gamble, and once he got started, he couldn't resist it, I don't reckon. He never could win nothin' much.

Once you get started gamblin' and you see people doin' it, you think, well, I can do better now. I'm gonna get in there and try it again. There was an awful lot of that gamblin' that went on in the army, off duty. Now, a lot of those Northern boys were the first to start up those smoky games — they'd play on into the night, and couldn't hardly get out of bed the next morning.

Lonnie Johnson:
> *You couldn't tell them nothin'. I know a lot of times when I had run-ins with Yankees, I didn't mind tellin' 'em what I thought. As a whole, they were all right after you got acquainted with 'em. But they thought they was better than a lot of people. And I don't think they were. (12)*

Of course, not all the Northern boys were like that. There was one Northern boy who was a lot like the country boys and he got along real good with me; we called him Argo. He was from Argo, Illinois, outside of Chicago, where they made the Argo starch and everybody nicknamed him Argo, so I don't remember what his real name was. He was down-to-earth and he would just do anything for me. He was a Yankee, but Argo was a good feller.

A lot of boys in the company had nicknames. We had Red, Fuzzy, Deadeye Dillard, and a boy we called Ham — his real name was Bacon. Oh, yeah, and Rubber Belly. That was me. "Rubba Belly!" A boy from LaFayette, Alabama, nicknamed me that because I put on so much weight after I got in there. His last name was Allen. The boys from Alabama, they've got a little different sound. "Rubbaaa Belly, Rubbaaa Belly!" That's what he'd call me all the time. Some of the other boys who liked to joke, Lonnie Johnson especially, started calling me Lard Butt.

That was Johnson—always having lots of fun. He was a real good soldier, though. And he looked the part. His clothes fit him real neat. He was a well-proportioned feller, wasn't real slender, wasn't heavy either. He wasn't potbellied and big-butted like I became.

I wasn't used to eating the kind of food they gave us in the army and it really put the fat on me. I was just used to good country food. Of course, I did eat ice cream about every day from the PX.

I probably needed to put on a little weight. I weighed just 139 pounds when I went in the army, but I got up to 170 pounds pretty fast. They try to put weight on you, if you're skinny. Some of them picked up a lot more weight than I did. The army also took it off the ones that were heavy; their clothes would just hang on them. A lot of us had to turn our clothes in and get new sizes.

The mess hall served good food—at least it was to me. It was something to look forward to, having plenty of different foods after growing up on Coker Creek with the same crops, livestock, and game all the time. The only problem was, a lot of times in the army, I didn't know what I was eating. I had never been exposed to some of the food that they had.

I didn't have a lot of meat back home, but in the army they gave us quite a bit of meat. Steak was new to me and I didn't like it much, but some of the other boys really went on about it. We had steak, potatoes, salad, and chocolate pudding on some occasions. I really liked the desserts, especially the big squares of chocolate cake with thick frosting. I don't guess it was too good for us, but I never did turn a thing down that they put on my plate.

Some of those boys from Chicago, New York, and New Jersey, all those places, they had a hard time eating that army food. They complained and bellyached about the taste and went on about how it smelled. They said army food wasn't any count and that the army didn't know a thing about cooking. Well, the way those Northerners put it was a little more colorful than that.

The army'd take just anybody and make a cook out of them. Everybody said, "You go into the army as a mechanic and you end up as a cook."

Once in a while I'd say to the other fellers, "What is this stuff?" Some of the other boys would tell me. Of course, there were a lot of boys in there that didn't know the difference either. I wasn't by myself on that.

The army tried to give us all something we'd like and one day, they had some Southern-style foods. One boy from up north said to me in the mess hall, "Do you think they have any more of that cake left?"

"What cake?" I said, concerned that I'd missed something.

"That cake you're eating."

"That's not cake. That's cornbread."

This boy had never even heard of cornbread before, but he found he liked it as well as any Southerner, or better. I was surprised to learn that the Northerners didn't grow up on cornbread. I thought everyone had it.

We didn't get much cornbread in the army and some of us really missed it, like my two good buddies from C Company who were Southern through and through: Darvie C. McAbee and Winfred Knode. All through training, we shared the same barracks and sat together in the mess hall when we could. Those two boys would eventually become my best buddies and we would see the war together.

Darvie C. McAbee, from South Carolina, was just "a fine'un," as we used to say back home. He was just a little feller, couldn't have been more than five foot three or so, and as jolly a feller as you've ever seen. I never saw him doing anything wrong. He was clean-cut. He didn't use foul language at all. He always treated people in a way that never did offend anybody.

Darvie C. McAbee was just a friendly country boy, and he liked to play the guitar. He'd pick his guitar, play his music for us sometimes in the barracks. The boys were always kidding him, wanting him to play. He was particular about what he played, though, he wouldn't play some of the tunes they wanted to hear, even though he knew how to do it—he could play just about anything he heard, I reckon. The Chicago boys would do their best to get him to play some songs that he didn't think were acceptable to play, like "House of the Rising Sun," because it was a song about a man who visits prostitutes.

McAbee'd shake his head and say, "No, I only play music that's worthwhile."

When McAbee started to play his guitar, oh, I was happy then. Before long, a bunch of us would crowd around his bunk. A lot of us liked that Grand Ole Opry music, the sound of Nashville—that was the sound I associated with happiness. Whether it was a rousing version of "Nine Pound Hammer," which was a prison work song, or one of the many touching bluegrass ballads, they were all a comfort.

A lot of boys from Chicago and places like that weren't used to it. By and large, the Northern boys, city boys, and the West Coast boys—I think we had one from around Hollywood, California—they all liked big band and swing, orchestras and brass.

The Southern boys all liked "that hillbilly music"—bluegrass, country, gospel. Sometimes, when it was just a bunch of us sittin' around the barracks, McAbee would play a few of the old gospel tunes that meant more to us now than they ever did, as we were preparing ourselves to go off into battle. McAbee especially liked to play old-time tunes, like "Beulah Land," and that's one I always liked. He'd sing that and different songs we all knew. Well, the Southerners, anyways. Darvie C. McAbee was the best musician in our barracks. He was a fine young man and everybody liked him.

Winfred Knode was from Virginia and was a real nice feller, too. He pronounced his name "Kenode," and not "Node," as you might expect. Some of 'em ribbed him about that, pronouncing that "K." He'd always say, "I know my own name."

Those Northern boys'd go, "You mean you K-know it."

Knode didn't like that much, but he never did say anything back. Knode carried himself like a gentleman, was a real handsome man. He was slim and stood straight as an arrow. He wasn't slouchy like some of 'em.

Knode and I got to talking and we figured out that we'd been at Camp Oglethorpe at the same time and had ridden the same troop train from Georgia to California, though we hadn't met until after we were assigned to the same barracks at Camp Beale. We became fast friends and were buddies from boot camp on. I always thought a lot of Knode. A lot of fellers didn't like him because he kept to himself and didn't associate too much with them. Knode was generally a quiet person.

Knode didn't joke with people. He was sincere most of the time. But he was comical; if he got a little bit excited, he'd get to stuttering and he couldn't say a thing, hardly. He'd stammer, "I-I-ay-ay-ee"—then he'd say the words. Some of the boys would imitate him. They'd mock his speech. Knode didn't pay them much attention, but, aw, he hated that.

One time, we had a full inspection and our company's commanding officer, Captain Blake, was coming to inspect the barracks and all our gear. Knode was getting everything ready so he would make a top grade because his wife had come to visit him and she was in town staying at a motel. He didn't want to do a thing to keep himself from getting that pass, so before the inspection, he'd taken his canteen down to the latrine and scrubbed that can and had it really shining.

We always displayed our canteens on a shelf above our bunk, with the cap open so it could get air. Knode laid his canteen up with the cap off of it, just as we'd been trained to do. The way the canteen was made, it would hold a little water on its side and he'd got water in it and didn't know it.

We had to display everything that we kept in our footlockers. Everything had its place and they told us how they wanted it. Razor here, toothbrush there. We had to have our mess kit in a certain position and our fork and knife in a certain place. We kept our steel helmet laying up on the shelf and our clothes underneath the shelf at one end, on a hanger. Our dress clothes had to be displayed. We had to display our underclothes on top of our footlocker so they could see that we knew how to fold them. Our shoes, we had to keep polished, and the boots we wore every day, we had to keep them clean. They'd issued us what they call a rawhide boot. It was rough on the outside, but we coated them with cosmoline. That would make them gloss over a little bit, and kept them from absorbing water. The army checked to see that we'd put that cosmoline on there. They checked every detail.

We were all standing by our footlockers, waiting for inspection. Captain Blake walked slowly through the barracks in a uniform as sharply creased and rigid as he was. I could hear his boots clicking on the pine floor. *Click-Click, Click-Click.* He stopped often and he had not one good thing to say, naturally.

When he got to Knode's bunk, he stopped. Captain Blake reached up and got Knode's canteen. He had to reach up pretty high to get it off the shelf. When he turned it up a little bit, it poured water down his sleeve. Boy, he didn't like that.

"Soldier, what are you doing with water in your canteen?!" He was a stern captain anyway and anything he found wrong, he wouldn't overlook it. The ol' sourpuss seemed to just enjoy getting on you about it.

Knode stammered, "Sir, I d-d-didn't know it was in there. I w-w-w-was cleaning my can-can-can-canteen and I must have a-a-a-accidentally g-g-g-got w-w-w-water in it. Sssir!"

Captain Blake got right in Knode's face. "Don't you know that an inspecting officer doesn't like that? Do you know *why* they don't like it? They don't like water poured down their sleeve!" The captain turned on his heels and said to the sergeant, "See that he gets extra duty for that! And he'll watch the next time that there's no water in his canteen."

Captain Blake moved on to inspect the next soldier, but before he did, he added, "And restrict him to the barracks this week."

Boy, you could just see ol' Knode fadin' away, because he knew he couldn't go and see his wife. I believe they hadn't been married long. Back then, we didn't have easy communications back and forth where he could call her without going to a lot of trouble.

Yeah, I felt bad for him and a lot of the boys ribbed him about being restricted. He couldn't take that kidding too well. He wouldn't say too much, but he'd get kind of mad at them for ribbing him about something he couldn't help. He was down-and-out, didn't have nothin' much to say.

Sergeant Hicks was a good feller, stern, too, but he was a real fair man. He felt sorry for Knode because he knew that his wife had traveled all the way from back East to be with him in California. After lunch on Saturday, Sergeant Hicks came to Knode and told him, "Now, I'll go ahead and let you take your pass, providing you'll just go straight to the motel and you'll not be seen on the street. If you were to happen to meet the captain on the street after he's restricted you, you know what would happen, don't you? You and me both would be in deep trouble. So, if you think you can keep hid and keep from getting caught—"

"I'll take that chance, I'll do that," Knode said.

He was tickled to death to go and be with his wife. She just had a few days to be in California. I was glad they let him go. Captain Blake didn't care if Knode or any soldier like him saw his wife or not. But it was important for his morale to go and see her, and Sergeant Hicks knew that. Luckily, nobody got in trouble over it.

The captain hadn't found anything wrong when he checked out my display. I never did fail any inspection. They usually found that a lot of the boys didn't have everything the way they wanted it, though, and the inspecting officer would tell the sergeant to give them extra duty when they should have been off from their regular training after we were dismissed in the evening.

For certain soldiers, though, it seemed like there was extra duty whether we did anything wrong or not, but in the army that's one thing you can't do anything about. If they tell you to do something, you're just as well to do it.

★ ★ ★

The farm boys were the most susceptible to that baloney of really doing the job and getting it done. Typically, you'd be assigned to do something and you'd have the whole day to do it in, and the farm boys would do it in one hour, or half an hour. That's the way they did it.

— **Cpl. Alexander Gordeuk (from New Jersey), Information and Education Officer, 13th Armored Division (9)**

I made the mistake of telling the army everything when I went in. They wanted to know where you worked, what kind of work you did, how long, all the details. So I told them I was a carpenter apprentice, learning the carpenter trade. That was the wrong thing to tell them, but I didn't know that. This is how my civilian occupation was officially listed on army papers:

Was employed by the Tennessee Valley Authority, Fadner [Farner], TN. Performed general carpentry work so as to learn the trade. Helped build houses and sheds from drawings and sketches. Did some interior and exterior trimmings. Used the usual hand tools. Was able to build concrete forms. Worked under an apprentice contract.

As quick as they got us organized when we first arrived at Camp Beale, they announced, "James Q. Kelley is going to be our company carpenter. If we have any carpenter work, we'll assign him some helpers, but he's going to be the leader."

From then on, I was the designated company carpenter. They got me a set of tools and a toolbox and they kept it in the storeroom. When they gave me a job, I had to sign a form to take out the toolbox. They had a lot of lumber left over from building the camp and I'd collect a load of lumber from a woodpile about as tall as a house and that's what I used. When I was done, I'd take the toolbox back and they'd check to see that everything was in there and give me a clear slip.

Camp Beale was so new, I had to help build some of it. I constructed no telling how many benches for soldiers to sit on when we were taking our training. My helpers and I filled a big room with those benches, made sort of like church pews.

Every time the company had something to build, they'd give that job to me. One time a lieutenant—one of those ninety-day wonders—wanted to take cold drinks out in the field when we did our training. He told me to make an icebox so big and then he said, "And after that, I want you to build another box around the icebox, a foot wide all the way around, and fill it with sawdust."

He wanted to insulate the icebox and keep the ice in the center from melting so fast. But, shoot, when you added a foot all the way around that box, that made it a big, heavy contraption. I tried to tell the lieutenant that it wouldn't work the way he'd told me to do it—it would be just too big—but he wouldn't hear of it. He told me to build it *exactly* like he'd ordered it.

When I was about finished, that lieutenant came out to the woodpile and he got all worked up. "Kelley, what in the world do you think you're building out here?!"

"I'm building exactly what you told me to build."

"No, that is *not* what I said for you to build." He argued with me a little.

So I got out a drawing I'd made of the design with the lieutenant's measurements, and when he looked at it, he said, "You're right, Kelley. That *is* what I told you to build. Tear that thing up. It won't work, it won't even fit in the truck. Just forget about it."

So I had to tear up that whole box and throw it away. It was just a waste of time, half a day. I did a lot of work that I didn't get any credit for, I just did it.

I was doing work when the other boys were out gadding about. A lot of the boys would go to town and just loafer around, and whoever they gave me as helpers, we'd be out there on the base working with saws and hammers and nails. Sometimes I'd have to work at carpentry all day, then go to class at night to make up the time that the other boys had spent in class during the day. I had a lot of extra duty because I could do things that the army needed done. I felt I got the worst end of that deal. I wasn't too fond of the situation, but I couldn't say a thing about it.

In the army, we couldn't get out of any duties that we didn't like, especially ones scheduled on a regular rotating basis, guard duty and kitchen police. KP was the chore we disliked the most. It was early, dirty, and smelly.

They usually had five boys in our company assigned for KP and you had to be there at five o'clock in the morning. The way they set it up, the first comer got the best jobs and on down, and the last one to come in, he usually got to clean the pots and pans, which was a hard job. I never had to wash the pots and pans, not even once.

I'd always make it a point to be the first one to show up for KP duty, so I'd get the best job. That job was setting the tables with coffeepots full of coffee, salt- and pepper shakers, jellies and condiments before the men came into the mess hall. After they left, we had the job of clearing the tables, picking up everything that was left and taking it up to the boys who did the dishwashing. After they ran all the dishes through three waters—wash water, rinse water, and another water to sterilize them, the forks and knives—we had so many of them—we put them in a clean mattress cover and took hold of one end, and somebody else took the other end, and we'd swing that silverware back and forth to dry it. That made a lot of clanking. Then we took the silverware and put it where the next men could pick it up.

Some of those boys who reported for KP duty dragging in late, they'd have to clean the grease traps. They had a grease trap that all the dishwater went through and it would skim the grease off and that grease would settle in the bottom of the grease trap. You'd have to drain the water off the top and scrape all that grease out by hand and put it in containers. They used that grease in making ammunition some way, so all the kitchens throughout the camp saved their fat drippings.

One morning, this boy who had a peculiar accent—I don't know where he was from—the mess sergeant gave him the job of cleaning out the grease trap. He didn't say anything to those boys who were washing the dishes up the line, and when the water got a little dirty, they opened up the valve, emptied the water out, and it came down the line and collected over the grease trap.

This boy started dipping water. He had to carry the water out somewhere, he couldn't pour it nearby. He dipped it and carried it out, back and forth, and by the time he'd get it all dipped out, they'd empty their washbasins again. That really shook the ol' boy up.

He talked real funny. "Chrriiisst! Chriiisst! Here comes the water again! CHRRISST!"

I got a big kick out of hearing him talk, 'cause I'd never heard anybody say "Christ" like that before.

The mess sergeant came by and he said, "Boy! You still foolin' with that grease trap?"

"Well," he said, "every time I get the water out, they send more water down the line and it covers the grease trap before I can clean it out."

The mess sergeant said, "Tell those boys to hold that water till you get the grease outta there! Don't just keep dippin' water, you'll be there all day!"

I don't know what kind of grease the army used, but it smelled about as bad cleaning out a chicken house and that boy just had to dip the fat out of there with his bare hands.

There were boys in our company who had never had to wash a dish in their lives, or mop a floor, or even clean up after themselves. Army life was a rugged life for a city boy or a country boy, but I think it was not as hard for the country boys who hadn't been livin' it up, and hadn't had everything handed to them. The ones who'd had it easy, they had it the worst in the army, but no matter who a feller was in civilian life, in the army, he'd better put his nose to the grindstone and do his job.

There's one thing that I noticed, though. Sergeant Hicks never would put me on KP duty, or any duty, on a Sunday, even if my name was supposed to be on the roster that they posted on the bulletin board in the mess hall. He'd wait and put me on Monday. So I didn't have to pull duty that would keep me from going to church services, because I always went. Not many of the other boys went.

A lot of the boys got to noticing that I never got any duty on Sunday and they thought the sergeant was treating me special.

I said, "Well, it ain't my fault. I just go by what they post on the board. When they put my name up there, I do what it says."

He never mentioned it, but for some reason, Sergeant Hicks would always do that, he respected me. I thought that was pretty good of him.

I was just about the only one in the whole company who went to church on a regular basis, except my buddy, McAbee, who went maybe once a month, and he'd go with me. I'd ask my buddies, "Does anybody want to come with me?" before I got ready to leave the barracks on Sunday, but nobody else ever went.

There was a Baptist chapel on the base and close by was peach orchard country. They grew a lot of peaches in California. They didn't distribute them around the camp, but groups that helped the servicemen would bring peaches to the chapel. I'd go to church and I'd bring back some of those peaches and give them to my buddies.

One of the churches in Marysville came out to Camp Beale and conducted a service on the base and I went to that. Afterwards, pretty volunteers from the local California towns handed out juice, cookies, and as many peaches as we could carry. I guess it was because we were soldiers, but those California girls were awfully nice, and they tried to do everything they could to encourage us. They just went overboard because they really appreciated the sacrifice we were making for our country. They gave me a lot of gifts and when I came back to the barracks, I had all kinds of stuff. I was weighted down with it.

Those boys said, "Where'd you get all that? I wish I'd gone to that chapel." But that wasn't the reason I went. My parents were church-goers and they lived their life like they should. That guided me along and when I was in service, I didn't depart from that.

A lot of the boys would try to get me to go along with them to drinking parties and all kinds of things, but that wasn't my lifestyle. Even though I wouldn't participate, they didn't get mad at me. A lot of the boys who were bad to drink and carry on, they'd talk me into going with them to town and they'd promise me, "If you'll go with us to town, we'll have a good time, but we won't drink alcohol and we won't do anything that you don't want to do."

They held to that when I went with them. They respected my wishes because I lived the kind of clean life, I guess, that they weren't used to, but even though they never said anything about it, I think they respected me for doin' that.

Some of the boys went into town all the time and went on drunken sprees and caused a ruckus. Some went around with loose women or visited prostitutes and some fooled their money away at gambling. I never went into town much, just when I needed to buy something and I had the money for it, which wasn't very often, sort of like the way we went to town on Coker Creek.

When I did leave the base, I got to see a little of California and it was a beautiful place. The streets were clean and neatly trimmed. There were flowers blooming all over the place, in window boxes, along the streets.

I saw trees in California that I'd never seen before, strange trees—tall, straight trunks with no limbs at all and long, floppy leaves—if you could call 'em leaves—right at the top of the trees. They'd line those palm trees up along the streets and they looked like a row of soldiers standing in formation—soldiers who hadn't had their hair cut, if their hair was as wild in the wind as mine used to be, before the army had clipped it off.

I was really thrilled with California, especially because of the climate. It was a real comfortable climate, you never had to bundle up. Of course, it would get pretty hot in the summer, but down where our base was located, it didn't get cold in the wintertime and that was new to me. I'd never really thought about places that didn't have winter snows.

Even though I really liked California, it was so different, it made me really miss home. I looked forward to hearing from home more than anything. The way they delivered our letters and packages, each of the companies had a man assigned as the mail carrier and he'd pick up the mail at the post office on the base and bring it to our barracks. The mail boy was the one person that everyone couldn't wait to see.

He brought news that all of us needed to hear, news from home, and whether it was good or bad, it was always a familiar voice that we missed. All of the letters that I got stood out to me, because I really liked to hear about people that I knew. It always cheered me up to get a letter from my mother and father. They'd just tell me everyday things, like how the old mule was doing or if they'd gotten a lot of rain, but I could read that and I knew just what it felt like to be home, sittin' down around the fireplace on a cozy evening.

I remember getting one card that I thought was unusual, a valentine from a girl that lived on Coker Creek, Elma Payne. I knew her growing up, but I never was sweet on her or anything like that, so I was surprised to get any correspondence from her.

She was one of the Payne girls, part of a big family that lived way back in the woods, up on top of the mountain. They were the poorest family on Coker Creek. They lived in a little ol' shack and didn't have nothin' to eat hardly, but they had four real nice girls, all of them slender and as pleasant as a field of daisies in summer. I always felt sorry for that whole family, they never had a thing hardly, just what people gave them.

When Elma sent me that card, it was real sweet—she was a pretty and sincere girl—but I never answered her. I looked forward to getting letters from Orangie and when I got one, I'd read it several times.

I was a little slow about answering them, because they kept us so busy. I'd get around to writing letters on the weekend and maybe not even then. I was bein' pulled away. That made me miss home all the more.

Two weeks before they would have given me my first furlough home, I got an emergency call to come home. My sister Thelma was in a serious condition. She had been expecting a child and the baby had died and Thelma was not expected to live either. I didn't have the money for the train trip and I didn't have much hope of getting a furlough, though I tried.

I walked from the motor pool back to the barracks with Captain Blake. If you were going somewhere with an officer, you had to stay in step with him or he'd call you on it. Each foot had to hit the ground at the same time. I never got out of step with him.

Captain Blake saw a soldier who wasn't dressed just exactly like he ought to be and he called out, "Soldier, get that cap on the left side of your head or I'll come over there and show you how to wear it!"

I had to tell Captain Blake that my sister was in the hospital in a serious condition.

He answered, "We still have two more weeks before we'll issue any furloughs."

"They don't think she'll live, sir," I pleaded.

"I said we will give furloughs in two weeks. We can't start before then." When Captain Blake said something, that's the way it was.

Maybe the captain thought I was lying, just telling a big tale, to get a furlough home. Some of those boys in the company, I'd noticed, would lie like a yellow dog. Back home, that's what people'd say. Yellow dogs were known to bark up trees like they'd treed a squirrel or something, when they hadn't. They'd bark and carry on just like they were chasing a rabbit, too, when they weren't. So people were always sayin', "Why, he lies jus' like an ol' yeller dawg."

Some of those boys in the company would say just about anything that suited them, I found out, so I didn't blame the captain for not believing me. But somebody must have come to him, somebody who knew me a little, and told him that I was telling him the truth.

It wasn't but about two hours later that Sergeant Hicks came to me to tell me that the captain had come through with a furlough after all. I never knew why Captain Blake changed his mind, but I sure was glad. Never did know him to change his mind about anything.

Sergeant Hicks asked me, "Do you have the means to get home?"

I said, "Well, I can get the money. If you give me a pass, I can get it from the Red Cross."

He said, "Oh, you can't go through them. They'll check out everything they can think of, and it will take them about a week to check that out before they'll give you any money. How 'bout checking with your buddies. If your buddies have got some money they'll loan you, I'll give you a pass."

So I went to the barracks and my buddies asked, "Is he gonna let you go home?"

I said, "Well, I don't have the money. The sergeant said if I could get the money, I could go. He'd give me a pass."

Those boys, they just went to gettin' out their billfolds, some of them gave me five, some of them ten, and one feller gave me a check that he got from home, for fifty dollars. He was one of the city boys from the Chicago area, Salecki was his name, and he was really nice to me when he heard that my sister was in such bad shape. He'd gotten a check in the mail that day from his parents and he just took it out, turned it over, signed it, and handed it over to me. Salecki was one of the boys from up north who didn't associate with me too much, but he turned out to be a real good friend. Of course, he knew I'd pay him back, all of them knew it.

I had the money just in a few minutes. I went over to the orderly room and told the first sergeant, "I've got the money. Can you give me furlough papers?"

He said, "Oh, yeah, we'll fix you up. You can get out of here right now."

I knew my sister was in bad shape as I rode the train clear across the country. Thelma and I were always real close, had played together as kids around the homeplace, just me and her, most of the time. Now her first child had already died before she got to the hospital, and she was about to die. They had to operate on her to take the dead child.

Of course, back then, they didn't have the techniques they have today to save people, and even if they had, we lived in such a backwoods area they wouldn't have had it. I didn't know if I'd even get home in time to see her or not, because it took five days and four nights to make it on the train.

Quick as I got home, I went to the hospital in Sweetwater to see Thelma. She'd had a turnaround and improved some, but she was still pretty weak. Every day of that leave, I drove down to Sweetwater, about an hour's drive from our cabin, and took my parents to see her. Edth was working then, but she came when she could. Oh, we were all sick about what had happened and we worried for Thelma. We'd crowd around her hospital bed and talk with her and try our best to lift her spirits up so she'd make a full recovery, and she eventually did.

Proud U.S. Army soldier, Quinton Kelley with his dad, Will Kelley, and the 1937 Chevrolet

I'd left my car at home when I went in the army, but nobody drove it except Thelma. My daddy wouldn't drive it anymore. He used to drive the car, but one day he accidentally hit the accelerator instead of the brake and knocked out the end of the garage. He built it back, but he never would drive after that. And my mother, for her, it was out of the question to think about learning to drive. She was just like that.

I loved to drive, though. I'd wind around those mountain curves in that '37 Chevrolet, and I felt sharper than ever, now that I was a U.S. soldier and I'd had some army training. Of course, I hadn't gotten to drive anything in the army—yet.

Our furloughs at that time were only twelve days and one day of grace. That day of grace was in case you didn't make it on time, they'd give you one more day that you wouldn't be absent without leave. They didn't want you to use the thirteenth day unless something happened with your transportation and you couldn't make it, but I wanted to be with the ones I loved as long as I could.

I stopped in at Frank's Store before I left to catch the train, and Orangie sold me some ice cream, and I ate it right there. She'd heard the news about Thelma and the loss of the baby and she was really kind and sympathetic, with her blue eyes all teary as we talked.

As I left, Orangie called out, "Don't forget to write me!"

I started a letter to her on the train—just figured I ought to do it while I had time, before they put me to work back at camp. I knew I'd have to wait a long time before I could get another furlough home, too, at least six months or more. We were now ready to get our promotions and start our advanced training, which would officially turn us into U.S. Army Armoraiders.

After so many weeks of being a "buck private" we were eligible for a promotion to private first class, or maybe if you were outstanding, you might be rated as a corporal. I never did get a Pfc rating. I went from a private to a corporal's rating. Then I got to wear two stripes.

You didn't get much money when you went in as a private, you only got $30 a month, a dollar a day, and you had to use about $10 of that to take care of your laundry and other little expenses, so you only had about $20 left to spend. When you went to a corporal, you got more—$45 a month and that was a big help back then. There weren't very many boys that skipped Pfc and made corporal on the first rating. I'd say, in our platoon, which was twenty-five men, there were probably four or five out of the platoon that skipped Pfc, something like that.

One boy I remember was upset that he didn't skip a class when we got promotions. He felt like he ought to have a corporal's rating. This boy had been rated Pfc, but he said to everybody, "I deserve more than that." He was really mad because he didn't get it. He complained and went on and on. Well, that was the wrong thing to do.

The other boys would slip around when he was out and sew that Pfc stripe on all that boy's clothes and they'd sew that Pfc stripe on his blanket, his socks, his underwear, just because he was so mad about getting rated as a Pfc. Everywhere that boy looked, there'd be a Pfc emblem and he'd have to cut that off to keep from getting in trouble. When they all heard how bad he wanted to get a higher rating, they just rode that boy to death about it. If he'd said nothing, they wouldn't have bothered him. Those boys were always picking on each other in the barracks. That's how they entertained themselves a lot of times.

Lonnie Johnson:

When we got through the basic training, they give us a rating. I got a corporal's rating at that time. Then they sent the Pfcs and privates that didn't make a rating, they sent them overseas. So there we were with a brand-new group of people to train again. (12)

It wasn't too long after my first furlough that the day I'd waited for finally arrived. I got to drive my first tank. It was a General Sherman M4 and it was a beauty.

I thought tanks were something wonderful when I first saw one. It amazed me that the army had built such a monster. That Sherman tank was some thirty-two tons of cast and welded steel, two inches thick in some places, with a complicated system of tracks and wheels that were waist high or taller, and the turret towered over me when I looked up to where I'd climb up to get in the hatch.

I sure was glad to be in a tank outfit then. I thought, well, a feller'd be a lot safer in that than out crawlin' around in the weeds. Since the day I first heard about tanks, I was hoping that I'd get assigned as a tank driver because I'd always liked to drive and tinker with vehicles. Of course, everybody said they wanted to drive a tank.

Before they could assign us positions, everybody in the company went out to test-drive a tank one sunny spring day. They drove us in trucks out to the field, where they had some General Sherman tanks for training purposes.

They had us go in groups of four men, with one instructor. He was a sergeant that had come in there just to train us. We got in the tanks, sat in them, and the instructor explained all sorts of different things about a tank, the mechanics and what to expect when we drove it. I was wishin' he'd just get on with the real reason we were there.

Finally, he said, "Now we're going out for a road test."

The instructor drove the tank out in the field and assigned one of the boys to drive first. He sat in the driver's seat and the instructor told him how to stop the tank and how to start it again, how to steer it, how to shift the gears and all of that. The instructor went through all the training with each soldier and he'd let him drive maybe four or five miles. He'd tell the soldier what he was doing wrong and how to do it right.

Some of the boys had a lot of trouble shifting gears and when they'd take off, they'd jerk that tank and it would just jump around and throw us against the hard metal that hemmed us in. I was glad the army had outfitted us with tanker helmets, a close-fitting, *padded* leather helmet, made like football helmets used to be.

When it was my turn, I had to wait until the instructor finished telling me what to do, even though I'd already picked it up. They made you wait in the army for every little thing.

Those Shermans had two levers in front of the driver and that's what you used to steer the tank—you pulled the left to turn left and the right to turn right—and if you pulled both levers towards you, that stopped the tank. I took those two levers in hand, pressed the gas pedal down, pushed in the clutch, and shifted the way I'd always done it back home, and that tank took off just as slick and smooth.

It roared ahead with more power than I'd ever felt. When I picked up a little speed, I shifted into the next gear, and got all the way to fifth gear, running along at a pretty good clip. When I hit a hill, I had to drop back a little, but it was no trouble driving that big tank. Why, it was a big thrill.

That instructor watched and kept score on how well each of us did as a driver. He let me drive the tank a little bit more than some of the others. When we got back to the motor pool, the officers were waiting and as we were getting out of the tank, Sergeant Hicks came around asking the instructor, "Well, what do you think? How'd you do?"

They were close by and I was listening—I heard that instructor say, "That Kelley boy can drive that tank just as good as I can. He doesn't need any training! You can't tell when that boy shifts gears."

Law me, I didn't know I was doin' that well. I thought to myself, "I've got them fooled on that!" I didn't consider myself good, I just thought I was average. But I guess it came a little more natural to me than to some of the others.

The boys who had all the trouble had never driven anything much, maybe not at all. Some of them could drive pretty well at first, but the double-clutching threw every one of them. They weren't used to it. But, even though it was the first time I ever drove a tank, it was a little familiar to me because of what I'd learned growing up. That instructor told me I drove a tank just like I'd always driven one. And really, I think that was because I'd learned a whole lot on Coker Creek about double-clutching.

I picked it up listening to those truck drivers haul wood, how they shifted to get enough power to haul their heavy loads through those steep grades and on across the mountains. The Lenderman boys used to do that double-clutching.

I practiced double-clutching on my Ford A-Model and on my '37 Chevrolet. It worked good on a car that had a straight shift, which, of course, they all did back then. I'd push the clutch in and that put it out of gear, then I let the clutch out, and I pushed the clutch back in and threw it in gear. They called that double-clutching. It was easy to do and I could do it real quick.

You didn't have to double-clutch on a car, but it was a little smoother if you did. You wouldn't rake the gears at all because they were turning and they mashed up every time. It was true, I could change gears in a car and you wouldn't even feel it.

In a Sherman tank, you had to double-clutch or you couldn't change gears on them. That tank had five positive gears. If those gears are standing still and the teeth don't happen to be matched up, you can't get the Sherman's transmission to go in gear. You have to shove the clutch in at the same time that you put the gear shifter in neutral, and you let the clutch out, and that gets those gears spinning. Then you push the clutch in again and put the tank in gear and it will just go right into gear, real smooth.

I didn't have a bit of trouble. That's the reason I got the job of tank driver, I guess, because the instructor recommended me highly. I sure was glad to be assigned as a driver.

There weren't many tank drivers in a platoon. Each platoon had five tanks, so there were only five boys in each platoon who were permanently assigned the driver position. About all the boys wanted to drive a tank; they'd rather have had that job than any of them. They were always excited about it, hoping they would get to drive. That's just in boys.

My first Sherman tank was named HYPO, and that word was painted on the side in big white print. I didn't know what it meant. I wrote home and told everybody that I'd been assigned to drive HYPO, and for some reason, my sisters got a big kick out of that word. I learned later, HYPO had been the name of the communications station at Pearl Harbor.

As a tank driver, I had to take care of HYPO and see that it was lubricated and that the oil was changed on time, that water was in the battery, that tracks were tightened to specifications. All that would be my responsibility, to see that the tank was road-worthy. Now I had something to get enthused about.

At that time, the U.S. Army had three kinds of tanks: light, medium, and heavy. The medium tanks, like the General Sherman M4 that I

One of the Sherman tanks driven by Quinton's first tank crew in training at Camp Beale: (left to right, front to back) Glosecrose, McAbee, Kelley, Foster, Knode

drove, they were the workhorse tanks, the all-purpose tanks that did the most duty. They were designed to lead the wave of attack against enemy resistance and they brought heavy firepower up close to the enemy. That Sherman tank was versatile. It could be waterproofed to drive in six feet of water or outfitted with bulldozers or flamethrowers.

They told us at that time that Shermans were well protected against our enemy's tanks, but we learned that the two-inch-thick armor, it protected the turret and the front hull only—the armor on the rest of the tank's hull was less, around an inch and a half thick. That's why those Shermans could still move pretty fast for an armored machine. They went as fast as twenty-nine miles per hour, more or less, but in training, they had governors on the tanks, so we could only go about fifteen miles per hour.

Light tanks could maneuver faster than any of the tanks, but they had less armor, so they were more vulnerable to attack. They'd cover terrain impassible for medium tanks, and they'd scout out weak points if the situation was unknown. In our tank battalion, we had one light tank company, Company D. The other three companies had medium tanks.

The heavy tanks, they had the thickest armor and the biggest guns, but they were slower and more difficult to maneuver. We were told about them, but we didn't have any at that time. That Sherman M4 was the heaviest tank used by our division and the main battle tank that America produced for the war.

The army taught us that the regular Sherman M4 could span across a trench that was over seven feet wide, ford a stream three feet deep, roll right over a straight vertical obstacle two feet high, and keep climbing a thirty-degree grade, but I believe I could get that tank to do a lot more than that. That tank would go over any kind of rough terrain, just about it. I could drive it over all kinds of obstacles — piled-up lumber,

Quinton Kelley (on right) stands on his Sherman M4

big rocks. We'd drive it up steep banks and across pretty big ditches, because when you go across a ditch, that tank would reach nearly across before the front of it dropped down. The weight of the back held it level in midair for a good distance.

That tank had heavy firepower, boy, it did. I had never seen guns that could produce a sound like thunder and make the ground quake. That General Sherman tank had a gyrostabilized 75mm gun — that cannon was its principal weapon and, of course, you could fire it while the tank was moving. It could take out big targets, but that Sherman tank wasn't

Figure 5. Medium tank.

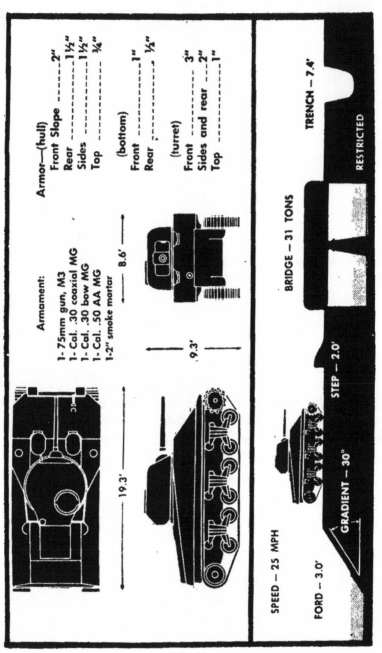

Page from 1944 U.S. War Department Field Manual FM 17-33

really designed to engage other tanks in combat. Tank destroyers with bigger guns would be called up for that.

The Sherman was fitted with two .30 caliber Browning machine guns, one ball-mounted in the bow and one mounted in the turret, and a .50 caliber antiaircraft machine gun mounted up top so we could elevate it to shoot at airplanes. Other weapons we had in the tank, like mortars, were for personnel that we encountered on the ground.

The driver and assistant driver each had our own hatches to get in and out of the tank. We rode in the front in compartments separated by the power train. We could see each other, but there wasn't enough room to trade places. We had to exit our hatches to swap drivers.

The Sherman had a three-man turret. The tank commander, the loader, and the gunner rode in there and shared two hatches up top. The men who rode in the turret were in a sort of openwork metal basket that would rotate with the cannon, and they'd rotate with it; sometimes they'd waver back and forth if they were zoning in on a target.

We were grouped with different people from time to time as we went through our training, but they finally set up a permanent five-man crew. Of course, it would have been all right to hope to be in a crew with certain people, but I don't think I ever thought about it like that. There were certain soldiers where you said, "Boy, I hope he's not in my crew." Some of those that were known to be difficult or rough, I thought that about them.

I was real pleased when I was assigned to a crew with two of my good buddies from basic training who shared my barracks — Darvie C. McAbee and Winfred Knode.

McAbee was a favorite buddy of mine, on account of his singing and guitar playing of that old-time music. He must've grown up about the same way I did and he was genuine — "gen-u-wine." He wouldn't lie for nothin'. He was easy to get along with and a good communicator. Any crew would have been happy to have him. And being just a little feller, he didn't take up much room in the tank. McAbee was assigned the position of loader and radio operator, two jobs, really. The loader was stationed in the left side of the turret. Besides loading ammunition into the main gun, the loader was responsible for assisting the tank commander with the vehicle radio, switching channels.

Knode became our gunner. He was right at the top with his scores on the range, and he was the sort of feller who would do what the sergeant asked him to do, to the letter. Since I knew he took good care of everything around his bunk, I figured he'd be a good man to have in the tank. Knode's primary job was to fire that 75mm cannon. But he also had that .30 caliber machine gun or he could use the .50 caliber antiaircraft gun. The gunner was the second-highest position in the tank; he's the one who's supposed to take over command if the tank commander should happen to get wounded or killed.

Eugene Glosecrose, it was the first time I'd met him. Glosecrose was assigned the job of assistant driver, which meant that he took up some of my driving time during training, but mostly, he operated the .30 caliber machine gun up front. Glosecrose seemed nice enough. He was from Knoxville, Tennessee, so I kind of felt right at home with the way he talked—at first. He didn't have a lot to say, though. His personality wasn't as good, I'll say, as some of 'em. He was a big chubby feller, a little sloppy, but he was dependable enough.

Our tank commander was Sergeant Glen Foster, from up in New Jersey. He was lean and lanky and some years older than the rest of us. Foster had been a policeman for several years up in New Jersey before coming into the army, so he acted quite a bit older and more settled than a lot of them. He was a good planner for the things he wanted us to do and I felt fortunate that we had a man with some experience as our immediate leader. Of course, as the tank commander, his job was to see that we did our job.

Right from the start, we all worked about well. We didn't have any uproar in the crew. Some of the crews would get a tank commander that they couldn't hardly get along with, or other crew members that would cause friction and so on, but we never had any problem.

The three medium tank companies in our tank battalion, A, B, and C, each consisted of three platoons, 1st, 2nd, and 3rd, and, of course,

M4A3 Sherman tanks of the 24th Tank Battalion, Co. C, 2nd Platoon.
Kelley's tank is second from left, above, and far left, below.

each platoon had five tanks. Coincidentally, I had been assigned to drive my tank in C Company's 2nd Platoon and assigned the position of second tank, so my position was 2/2, double twos, like my birthday. Because of that, unofficially, some of them referred to us as Tank 2/2, when we were out in training. This would be my permanent position. I liked that position and felt that maybe those numbers, my numbers, would be good luck.

After they assigned us our order, then every time we went out, we went in that order, our long, rumbling column of tanks, half-tracks, jeeps, trucks, and service vehicles rolling off to the training fields.

Darvie C. McAbee with .50 caliber
antiaircraft machine gun

Quinton Kelley with his
M3 Thompson "Grease Gun"

I had to take all the training that the gunners did. Each member of our crew was qualified to take any position in the tank. We could each drive the tank, operate all the guns, load the guns, use the radio, even act as tank commander. We understood it all so we could switch to any position if one of the crew happened to get wounded or killed. They also taught us the fastest way to maneuver wounded crew members out of their hatches to safety.

The army told us in training that our cannon would shoot through the enemy's tanks. The main heavy artillery in that tank, the 75mm cannon, had shells that were about a three-inch diameter. As heavy as that tank was, the cannon would rear that whole tank back when you fired it. That gun had tremendous recoil and when that explosion went off, it would really jar us down in there.

That cannon had sights we could use if we could see our target. A lot of times, though, we relied on our tank commander to tell us where to put the shells. He had binoculars to sight for targets in the distance when he had his head out the hatch. Of course, sometimes in battle, he'd have to stay down in the tank and just look through his periscope, a little glass window about six inches wide that gave him a view from on top of the turret.

Our tank commander, Foster, he gave directions over the intercom that was fitted into our tanker's helmets. Those headphones were attached to control boxes in the tank with a breakaway cord. In training, Foster'd communicate his commands in an ordered way, usually starting with the crew position.

Spotting a target, he might say, "Gunner! Enemy artillery, traverse right . . . A.P. . . ."

As soon as the loader heard what the target was, he went into action and loaded the right type of ordnance, in that case, armor piercing: A.P.

". . . Three o'clock," Foster'd say.

Of course, the gunner had his hand on the controls of the turret, turning right. Quick as Knode found the target, he'd say, "On it!"

Then Foster told him the range in yards, "Two Thousand. Fire!"

"On the way!" Knode'd say.

The gunner has to sight the target and do the shooting. But the tank commander calls the shots. After the first round, if he needed to make an adjustment, he'd tell the gunner, "Up, four degrees," if it was too low. Or "Left, three degrees," to zero in. We'd learned what those degrees meant on the gun barrel. We wanted to hear Foster say, "Direct hit!" and a lot of times, he did.

I really paid close attention when the tank commander instructed us on how to fire the cannon by instruments, how to set that gun sight up for so many yards, the range. When we were out training, Foster would tell me what the range was and I'd set the sights — it had a compass and little wheels on there — I could set it in a second.

A lot of times, we'd fire at targets we couldn't see. The first time we went out to fire indirectly with the cannon, we were shooting over a hill. A projectile climbs when it comes out of the barrel. You learn how far up it goes before it levels out and then it will come back down on your target.

We had an outpost, a man who was up on top of the hill and when we'd fire a round, he'd tell us where we hit, over the intercom. He'd say, "Three yards short to the left" or "Elevation fifteen feet higher," things like that. The man at the outpost was sighting us in. He was doing the job the tank commander would do in battle.

The first time I fired the cannon that way, the man at the outpost came on the radio and said, "Tank two-two, fire again. We didn't see . . . where your projectile went."

I kept the gun lined up, same as before, and fired. They called in and said, "Right on the target. You set the haystack afire. That's what we had sighted in—for you to shoot at a haystack. The target went up like the *Hindenburg*."

Some of the shells we used for target practice were high explosive and, occasionally, one of them wouldn't go off. They really cautioned us never to pick up—they called them a "dud"—never touch a dud, 'cause you never know when it might go off.

We had been out on the firing range all day, and we didn't finish. We had our tanks out there, so they left five people to guard our tanks during the night. While the rest of us had gone back to camp, these five G.I.s, for some reason—and they'd been told time and time again not to fool with the duds on the firing range—they went out to where we'd been firing, and one of them found a dud laying there and he picked it up and he said, "I wonder why they stress that so . . . not to pick up or touch one of them. Why, there ain't nothin' wrong with these things."

So he carried it back to the tank with three other boys who were with him, and he accidentally bumped that dud against the side of the tank and it went off. It killed him, and it injured the three others. I don't know whether they recovered, I guess they did, but it killed that boy who picked up the dud. And he'd been told no tellin' how many times never to do that, but he did it anyway, so he lost his life.

I really paid attention to what they told me in training. I knew it could mean the difference between life and death, though nobody had expected to see death happen before we saw combat.

As the designated company carpenter, I worked no tellin' how many days making moving targets for our company to shoot at. I framed them out of lumber in the shape of trucks or tanks, and I covered them with white canvas. The army wanted the targets to be a kind of brown color. They'd usually give me a couple of boys to help me and we didn't have any paint, so we'd dig a hole, get some water, mix up some mud, take a broom and sweep that mud on the targets. I'd put the targets on skids and the army'd pull them with a long cable and a half-track that stayed a good long ways in front of the target. We'd shoot at them with the .50 caliber machine gun.

You had to know about what the range was and you had to learn to figure out so many degrees ahead of the target when you figured out the range for a moving target. If it was one thousand yards, you had to figure out how fast it was going, and figure so many feet in front of it, and when you fired, by the time that projectile got there, you'd hit the target, if you had it figured right. You shot that .50 caliber antiaircraft gun in bursts and it'd fire maybe ten or twelve times when you mashed the trigger, then you'd let up on it. Every so many rounds there'd be a tracer, and you could watch those fiery tracers arching over to know where you were hitting.

We took special training on the .50 caliber, our antiaircraft gun. Of course, we could use it for anything we needed to destroy, but it was really mounted on top of the tank to shoot airplanes. It turned 360 degrees and we could elevate that gun almost straight up.

Sometimes, they'd have a Piper Cub pulling a target—it looked sort of like a sheet blown up in the wind. It was a good-sized target and it would be maybe two hundred feet behind the plane and we'd have to shoot at it. I know one time Knode cut the rope. He wasn't aiming at it, but his bullet hit the tow rope and down came the target.

We also trained on those .30 calibers. The two .30 caliber machine guns mounted on the tank were used for personnel. When my assistant driver, Glosecrose, got to drive, I manned the bow gun. It was mounted on a ball that swiveled around and you could easily keep on a moving target, or a fixed target, as you rolled by.

Including the tank commander who could use the .50 caliber mounted on the turret, or his personal weapon, we had three gunners on the tank, as we rolled. But if something happened to one of them, and they had to have a gunner and maybe put somebody else to driving the tank, I had to be qualified to do it.

They grouped all of our records together and I made top scores, even with the big guns on the tank. My scores were higher than the other boys in our tank crew, except for Knode, and I was glad he was our main gunner. He'd put those shells right where the tank commander told him to.

Bein' a country boy, he'd learned about guns pretty young, too. I guess it was because we were brought up that way, we were confident, knowing a whole lot about how to get on a target.

There was no way I could use a gun while I was driving a tank, of course. The driver didn't have to operate a gun, he just had to carry his personal weapon wherever he went. Every time I got out of the tank, I had to have that Grease Gun with me to defend myself.

I missed the old Thompson submachine gun, but I could see how you could get hung up trying to get in or out of that tank. I couldn't get in the driver's seat with a big long gun. I didn't have any room in there. That seat jacked up and when I got in the tank, I sat down on it, unlatched it and it dropped down. Then I pulled my hatch over my head and latched it down. Didn't have a whole lot of room to maneuver around, but it didn't bother me, didn't bother any of us, as young as we were.

As it turned out, I was a natural as a driver and a shooter. Well, I didn't know I was—I just thought I was average—but evidently, it panned out that way. I didn't let it go to my head, though, because I didn't think I was any better than anybody else.

One day, we'd been out on the firing range and we came back to the motor pool. Company C's commanding officer, Captain Blake, was talking to other officers within earshot of my buddies. They came over to me and said, "We heard the captain sayin' how he's thinkin' about doin' some swappin' and gettin' 'that Kelley boy' in his tank."

They patted me on the back. "The captain said you had the best score on the range today and he said he wanted you in his crew. Well, Kelley, looks like you're gonna be transferring into the captain's tank."

I said, "Boy, I sure hope not."

Of course, I was a driver and I guess the first thing I thought of was driving the captain's tank, but I don't know that he wanted me as a driver. I really liked being a driver because I felt like it would be a lot easier for me to drive a tank in battle than gun down men. Of course, I knew that even though the gunner did the shooting, we'd all be responsible for killing the people that our gunners shot. But it was a little different, really, pulling the trigger and seeing the feller in your sights fall. I didn't want to be a gunner or a driver for the captain, though. It meant the rest of the crew had to do everything.

The officers didn't clean or take care of things. In the commander's tank, the captain didn't help you do nothin', only just tell you to clean up the tank and do this and do that. But in other tanks, the tank commander, he had certain jobs that he did for the tank, just like the rest of us, whatever needed to be done to help maintain the tank. But the captain wouldn't have done that. I knew if I got into that top echelon, then I'd have it all to do. We'd have to keep the tank clean and he'd be inspecting it just like he did anyway. Only he was right there all the time.

You can't associate with officers like you can with the other men. Everything has got to be "Yes, sir. No, sir." Now, I've had some lieutenants that you could associate with and you could joke with. But Captain Blake was a real stern feller, he had to be in order to control the men. There can be no foolishness because the men will take advantage of somebody like that and they've got to be respected for their rank, I realized they had to be like that. But having the captain in the tank made it a little harder on the crew.

I imagine Captain Blake had the pick of the company when they

The winning display: (L to R above) Foster, Kelley, Glosecrose, Knode, and McAbee appeared in a book published by the 13th Armored Division (below)

divided them up, I guess he picked out who he wanted. I don't know how they managed that. I just went where they told me. That's the way everybody had to do, you didn't have a choice, picking out the place you were gonna serve. But I sure let everybody know I didn't want to be in the captain's tank.

I'd say, pretty loud, "Well, I'll tell you one thing—I'll never hit another target when he's around.

Boy, I'm a tellin' you, I don't want to be in the captain's tank." I was gonna disqualify myself.

I said, "Now, if he puts me in his tank as a driver, I'll break him from it. He'll be wantin' to get rid of me." I was gonna see how crazy I could drive.

And I told Sergeant Hicks, "I don't want to transfer to any other tank crew."

Most of those G.I.s would have been excited about being in the captain's tank because it was higher up. They were excited when they said, "Sounds like you're gonna get to be in the captain's tank!"

I never heard any more about that idea. Captain Blake must have changed his mind about switching personnel. Now, I never was superstitious like some of those boys—I didn't think a thing about being in the 13th—but I did like the fact that my assigned position, second tank, 2nd Platoon, matched my birth date. I thought that was a pretty good place to be and I'd rather just stay where I was.

Besides, I really liked the tank commander that I had. Sergeant Foster was a real asset to us from the start. When we had a special inspection, a full field inspection for the tanks, Foster made us really stand out.

That Sherman tank was like a rolling toolbox with all the equipment we had to have. Shovels, cables, tarps, ropes, gas cans, wrenches and sockets, first aid kit, and all our field rations were latched, hooked, and tied onto the outside of the tank as storage. Inside, every nook and cranny was filled with battle gear. They'd told us to take it all out and display it in the best manner that we knew how, and then they would select one tank crew as the winner.

We put down a tarpaulin and laid out all of our equipment. Some officers came and inspected the displays and they decided that our tank had the best inspection. Since they thought we did the best job getting everything neat like it ought to be, all the other tankers were ordered to take note of our display and see where every piece went. When we had another inspection, all the tank displays had to be laid out like ours. They took a picture of our tank crew and it was published in the 13th Armored Division's commemorative yearbook.

That was due to our tank commander, Foster. He was a real good organizer because he'd gotten a lot of training when he was on the police force up in New Jersey and he had order in the crew. We learned we could depend on him. I felt pretty settled with the crew I had at that time: Foster, Knode, McAbee, and Glosecrose.

My objection to being put into the captain's tank may have gotten me more work. I don't know if it was because of that, but shortly after that happened, whenever they had to train tank drivers, they put me on that job. They never did send anybody else.

Sergeant Hicks would say, Kelley, you take HYPO and meet so-and-so at a certain place and time.

I'd drive that tank quite a ways around the camp and report to other companies. Some of the companies didn't have tanks, like the infantry companies, and maybe some of those boys might have to be transferred to a tank during the war if a tank driver got killed and they needed somebody trained to drive that they could take from somewhere else right away.

Evidently, they must have felt that I was capable of training the newcomers. I'd take four in my tank, tell them how to shift the gears, let them drive, and rotate them around. Some of those boys couldn't shift those gears, they'd just grind and rake them. If the gears raked when you started to shift, you couldn't force the gears, you'd have to go back to neutral and start again. I had to show every one of them how to double-clutch. I'd let them drive so far, then I'd switch with another group.

I trained a company of illiterate boys, too. A lot of them weren't educated at all, and some of them could read and write to a certain extent but not enough to be considered literate. To talk to them, you might not detect that they didn't have that ability. They were nice fellers. Those boys didn't have the benefit of manuals, but as their instructor, I explained everything to them, and they got it that way. Most of those boys got to where they could drive a Sherman tank pretty well.

They were part of the 13th Armored Division, part of one of the infantry units, I believe. Of course, the rest of the 13th Armored had infantry units where the boys were educated. They take everybody in the army. It doesn't matter whether they've been to school a day in their life. There was a war on and they were drafting everybody.

I had to go out sometimes and train several platoons in a day. I got to thinking that I was getting a lot of extra duty like that. I resented it, but there's no use of you resenting things in the army. If you do, they'll just put more on you. You've got to let on like you like it.

Some of the boys would just complain and bellyache about every little thing. That gets tiresome. I never did that. Wasn't no use to complain. When they told me I had a job to do, I got to it and did it just like I was happy to do it, even if I wasn't. Maybe that's why they picked on me to do a lot of extra work, I don't know. But I was there to do a job for my country, so I was willing to do whatever they told me and I always did my best, 'cause that's how I'd been brought up.

When you drove a tank, it felt good. You felt like you were in charge of somethin'. Of course, you were. The rest of the men in the tank were expecting you to get them there and back and not cripple them up, running off of a bluff or smacking into a tree. You had a lot of responsibility in a way, when you're driving those tanks, you've got to watch where you're going and you've got to watch for everything you can see close by. You can't look a way out there in front of you. You'll run off the road or into a ditch. If you get one of those tanks off in a ditch, it takes a lot to get them out of there. Sometimes it'll take two tanks to pull one out of a mudhole.

After we'd been driving tanks for a little while, the army decided we'd take a long convoy on the highway. Oh, I was excited about it, an all-day mounted road march. This time the tanks all had rubber treads put on the tracks for when we took them on roadways. That was just for training. In actual combat, we'd just use the steel cleats that were on the tracks. Overseas, we wouldn't care about tearin' up roads.

We started out early in the morning as one big armored division, and we went on convoy, headed up into the mountains to do some maneuvers. To get there, we drove eighty-eight miles through Wheatland, Auburn, Grass Valley, and Smartsville, California. They told us that, not including motorcycles and reconnaissance elements, our column of vehicles on that march stretched for thirty-four miles.

We traveled like we might have to do when entering enemy territory. Except for the way we rode. We rode "unbuttoned," with our hatches open, so we could see the highway and all around, and I'd look out at the California countryside. In actual enemy territory, they told us, we might be "buttoned up." It was harder to see that way because we had to look through periscopes and they limited our vision.

It was pretty warm down where Camp Beale was, but we went up so high in the mountains, there was some snow at the higher elevations. While we were up there, we parked our tanks and we put on a mock battle between the companies. I guess they wanted to reward us for a lot of hard training. We divided up into two teams on a hillside for battle, but this time the only weapons we were allowed to use were . . . snowballs!

We packed that snow and were hittin' each other pretty hard. We really had a lot of fun up on that mountain, pelting our buddies with a barrage of snowballs. For a while, we were able to forget what kind of battle we'd been training for.

When we went out in the field on maneuvers, Sergeant Hicks would take his little dog, Mitzi. He'd keep that dog with him, on road marches, even in mock battles. When we were out of our tanks, he'd leave the little dog in his tank. He just took Mitzi wherever he wanted to and she never did bark.

We stayed up on that mountain for a few days, did tank maneuvers, and slept in our pup tents in the light snow. Heading back, we took off on the highway early in the morning, and we traveled all day long to make that trip.

As we were going down some mountain slopes, one boy let his tank get away from him. You had to shift down in a lower gear to hold it back on those steep grades. But you didn't want to shift gears if you were going downhill at a good speed. That tank had a lot of weight and it would get to goin' faster than the gears would go, and you couldn't get it to go back in gear. And you were out of control then.

This tank's driver tried to shift and he wasn't good at shifting. He got the tank out of gear.

They came over the intercom: "Everybody clear the road! We've got a runaway tank."

That boy had his tank just a runnin' free. He couldn't stop it with the steering levers, they wouldn't stop it. It got going too fast for that.

Just as I got us over to the side, that runaway tank came rumbling down through there and it kept on going. It went on down the road a little ways, left the highway, went over a bank, and ran down into a steep ravine. It continued on down that slope and, finally, it lodged against a big tree.

I saw that tank after it came to rest. As we moved on, we could look down and see it. Some of the outfits carried tools with them and they got a cross-cut saw and they sawed that big tree down and they took that tank on further down the mountain and they went through the woods riding the small trees down and going around the big ones. Way on down there, maybe a mile or something, where the road crossed the valley, they got that tank back onto the road. I don't reckon it hurt anybody too bad, but it was kind of exciting to the men who were in that tank. It jarred them up when it hit that tree.

On that road march, we went through a lot of little towns. We went through Grass Valley, which was a little town where it had been coming a few showers of rain. That made the roads a little slick. Now, those rubber treads that we had on the tanks so they wouldn't tear up the highway, they were slick when it was raining.

We had to make a forty-five-degree turn right in the center of town, the road came right down through the main street. I turned the corner there and I turned it a little too fast. I locked up one track and I couldn't get it released. That spun the tank plumb sideways in the road and it headed right towards a big plate-glass store window. I was really doing all I could to try to regain control of that tank, but the track stayed locked up.

That tank was sliding forward with all its weight right towards that big pane of glass. There was a sidewalk between the road and the store window. It was kind of a country town, so they didn't have wide side-walks. Well, I didn't get up on the sidewalk, but I got right to the edge of it before I got that track to release. I jerked it back the other way, and I got the tank straightened out and got it back in the street. But, boy, I came in a little bit a losin' that tank.

My tank commander knew what was going on because he was supposed to have his head out, watching, but I don't think he said a thing about it. Inside the tank at that moment, nobody didn't say a thing. I guess they all figured, well, that's part of it. Driving a tank, you're liable to do anything.

A lot of boys wrecked their tanks on that march. They spun them around in the road and turned them over because it rained on us quite a bit on the way down the mountain. If you were going pretty fast and you locked up one of the rubber tracks, that tank would spin around on you.

After that road march, I just said to myself, "Boy, I ain't a drivin' this thing no more whenever I get it back to camp." I decided that I didn't want that job, 'cause that scared me up. I thought if I'd a went into that store, I'd a been in trouble. That tank would've torn everything up, maybe hurt somebody. I decided right then that I wasn't driving a tank. Yeah, too close for comfort. I wanted a different job.

Quick as we got back to camp, my platoon sergeant was standing there in the barracks with his little dog as we were coming in, and he said, "Well, Kelley, how'd you make out?"

I said, "I didn't make it too good and you can find you another driver for that tank. I don't want no more of it."

Hicks said, "What's the matter?"

I said, "I liked to wrecked that thing. I don't want to drive that no more."

He said, "Now, let me tell you something, soldier—"

When he called you "soldier," you knew you were in trouble.

"—you're in this army to do whatever you're told to do. Whatever you're assigned to do, you're gonna do it. And," he said, "you'll be a tank driver until I tell you different."

He never did tell me different, so I had to drive a tank the rest of my time while I was in service. I thought there were so many boys wanting to drive a tank that they'd be happy for me to turn it over to them. I thought all I had to do was just tell them that I didn't want to drive it. I knew some who were standing by, just hoping they'd get to drive. But after my sergeant laid it on the line, I didn't say any more about it.

I got back in the driver's seat the next day. When I realized that there wasn't no gettin' out of it, I buckled down and put my mind to it that I was gonna be the best tank driver that I could be and I didn't mind it after a while.

In fact, when they'd have tank races for recreation, I was always out in front. They'd line us up at a starting point and we'd take off. As soon as I topped a little ridge, I'd put the tank in a higher gear just before the nose of the tank fell on the dirt. Then it would really move on down that hill.

I learned that when we'd go over a big hill, about the time I topped it, when I shifted into the next gear, all the other tanks would still be in that lower gear until they started coming down the ridge.

Not only did I shift in midair, but if we were going up a steep grade where you have to be in second gear, when that tank would top the hill, I could skip third gear and put it in fourth. I used the weight of the tank. A tank's got a lot of dead weight, and all that weight was pushing it along when it topped a hill and started down, and that made those gears go faster. When I felt the tank overbalance, I could throw it in a faster gear and that's how I could skip a gear. I had a lot more speed than the other fellers when I hit the ground. They didn't catch on to that trick. I was beating them all on it.

They'd say, "Aw, Kelley's got the best tank in the company," but it wasn't that.

I'd always say something like "No, I believe it's just the way I drive it."

As a boy, I'd listen to those Lenderman boys driving through the mountains of Coker Creek, those drunk-drivin' Lenderman boys, a haulin' pulpwood. I could hear them a long ways off. I learned from listenin', what gear they were in, how they shifted, and I'd hear them accelerate on those turns and grades that I knew like the back of my hand. They never did slow down. Quick as they'd feel that truck slowing down, they'd hit another gear. When they'd top a little hill, that truck came down with all the weight of that wood a pushin' it. They'd have it goin' so fast, they could skip a gear. That's how I learned how to get the most power out of my Sherman tank, 'cause I tried it on those tanks and it worked.

When I figured that out for myself, every hill or ridge crest became an advantage for me. So I won a lot of those tank races. I was just about top-notch on that, I guess, in our company.

I learned all the little tricks to driving that tank, tricks they didn't teach us. The other drivers never caught on, 'cause they never did beat me. I didn't tell them how I did it. You had to keep your tricks to yourself if you wanted to stay ahead.

The other boys complained: "Your tank can run off and leave us."

My crew had to put up with it. "Kelley 'bout knocked me out when he topped that hill," McAbee said. "I'm tellin' you I saw a big blue star!"

"Hey, Kelley, I broke over that hill the same time you did and I poured it on it. And you still got ahead," Lonnie Johnson said to me. Johnson was a tank driver, too, and a good one. He competed with me a lot on that. "It must be the extra weight in the front of your tank, Lard Butt," he'd say, and just laugh.

I'd smile. But I didn't tell him how I did it, how skipping gears while the tank was in midair gave it more power when it hit the ground. Every time it came down, it would really jar my crew, though, but we figured it would be like that in battle, so we'd better get used to it. I wasn't intending to drive that tank for comfort anyway.

We were being knocked around and banged up most of the time in those tanks, but I never had any training injury to amount to anything, except the time I tried to drive over a roadblock. They built big roadblocks out of logs and put them across the road. They had the crew get out of the tank, just the drivers were in there to try it the first time.

I tried to go across that thing at a pretty slow speed and the tank would get up there and stand way up in the air and just spin on the logs. I was determined to go over that roadblock, but the tank was clawing and digging, so I backed up to take a run at it. That tank had to roll down a slope first, so I got up some speed and I hit that roadblock too fast.

The tank went over the top of that roadblock as easy as you please, and when it topped it, the tank went a way out in the air before the weight of it broke down and when it came down, it hit so hard that it just knocked all the breath out of me. It just about knocked me out. I couldn't say nothin'.

They got me out of the tank and in a few minutes I could breathe all right, but they took me to the hospital. They thought maybe I'd hurt my back. They X-rayed my back and did all the testing. But I was just bruised up from being doubled up in that seat when I came down so hard. I was real sore for three or four days and I stayed in the infirmary. When I got to feeling better, they let me go back to my barracks.

I walked in and said to Sergeant Hicks, "Well, I'm back."

He said, "Kelley, I'll tell you what I'm going to do. I'm going to give you a three-day pass and you just go into town and do whatever you want to, for three whole days."

"I ain't wantin' to go to town," I said. "I'd rather just stay here and do whatever I need to do."

Hicks said, "If you stay on the base, I'll have to put you right back out to training, if you're able to do it."

I said, "Well, I think I can do it. I don't want to go to town."

"Well, then . . . okay." Sergeant Hicks didn't say anything more, but I reckon he must have had a hard time believin' a soldier would refuse a three-day pass. He assigned me back to the company and I went right out on the firing range the next day. We had to complete some firing training before they gave anybody in the company their furloughs. A lot of the boys had put in for their furlough and they were eager to get it. We stayed out on the range till it was getting almost dark, late in the evening.

One of the lieutenants came over to my tank and he said, "Kelley, you're gonna lead the convoy back and I'm gonna be your tank commander. I just want you to take us back to the motor pool as fast as you can, because those boys want to go on furlough."

So, the lieutenant got in and I just took off and I poured it on that tank.

That lieutenant was back in the turret, watching, and he told the crew, "Kelley must have a furlough coming. He's run off and left the rest of the company. They're not even in sight!"

We went around a hill and I looked back across the valley and I saw all the other tanks coming down the slope about a quarter mile behind me. I'd run plumb off and left them! I don't know how I was able to run off and leave them so far behind, but I did. And that lieutenant, he laughed about that.

I wasn't going on a furlough then, but I ran off like that because the lieutenant told me to. I was really using all my skills 'cause I liked to drive my tank fast, so naturally, I'd drive it as fast as it'd go.

I felt at home in that tank. After I found out about all the different positions I might have gotten, I said, well, I've got the best position because I won't have to shoot anybody. I've got to take the tank where other people can use the guns, but I don't have to pull the trigger or even load the chambers and I thought, that's a big relief to me because it would be hard for me to want to kill somebody, even in war. I dreaded thinking the thoughts about it.

In the 13th Armored Division, tankers made up only about 15 percent of the entire division, so I was one of the few who rode in a tank, and one of a handful who got to drive one. I was proud of that. My official qualifications said that my job was to drive a medium tank to destroy enemy personnel and equipment, and to spearhead infantry attacks against the enemy. But as one of many well-qualified young soldiers who was proud of what he'd learned and what he could do, I had to realize one thing, we all did: The military considered each of us soldiers expendable. Just how quickly any one of us could be snapped up and sent to the front lines was soon made clear.

Glosecrose, the big ol' chubby feller who was my assistant driver and bow gunner, he was all right, but I never did have much to do with him. It turned out that he was always into something and he was pretty mean and I never did take up with him, but I had to deal with him as my assistant driver. He was pretty bad to drink and carry on. There's always a bunch of rowdy boys in a company that'll cause a lot of disturbance. He was the only one in our crew like that. He was only with us a few months and he didn't get a good rating when we got promotions. The military was in need of some extra men overseas, so they took two men out of each tank in the company, but they only took one out of my tank. They took Glosecrose. They'd cull them out like that, send them overseas. Then they replaced all those crew members. They gave us another man from the replacement group and he was from Fort Worth, Texas.

He was jolly right off. When he came into the barracks, he introduced himself. He said, "Well, fellers, I'm gonna join you fellers today. My name is Ewell W. Rhodes. That's 'E-YULE.' It's not 'E-well.' It's pronounced 'E-yule.'" He really put the emphasis on that.

Some people would pronounce it E-well, the way it was spelled, but he didn't like that and he let us know it the day he came in, when he first strolled into the barracks. Well, of course, that was the wrong thing to do. As soon as those boys learned that he didn't want to be called E-well, that's all they called him. Our tank crew would call him E-well from time to time, too. He didn't like that a bit, and he'd make some remark like, "I'll answer you when you call me by my right name."

Oh, he'd tell little stories, and he'd use Texas language, but I don't remember some of the colorful things he'd say. Especially the boys from up north would get a kick out of some of the language Rhodes used. It was more like country talk, a whole lot the way we talked in Tennessee. He was pretty decent—we hardly ever heard him use bad language. Oh, he might say it was "hotter than Hell," something like that. He always had a comment to add, and he was a comical person.

Rhodes was pretty much of a cutup and everybody joked with him

Ewell W. Rhodes

and fooled with him. Comic relief, I guess. He was always kidding and picking on different ones and joking with people if he got something on them. Everybody in the company took a liking to Ewell W. Rhodes right away. He was a fine feller, a real fine feller.

Private Rhodes was our tank's permanent assistant driver and bow gunner. For a tanker, he was pretty tall and lanky. That went against him getting in and out of a tank. You don't have a lot of room, especially in that front compartment. It's hard to get down low enough to close the hatch—when he let his seat down, his head was just about touching the top of the tank. But he was a good shot with the .30 caliber and he rounded out our tank crew.

It wasn't long after our original assistant driver went overseas, till we got the message back: Glosecrose got killed. They gave us a report on all the boys they'd rounded up and sent to the battlefront, and Glosecrose was one that didn't make it long. They'd put him in another division, not in an armored division overseas. I think he went into the infantry. I never did know where he saw combat.

Word spread quickly. We usually passed the word along about the sad fate of some of those boys who'd trained with us, not by saying they'd been "killed."

We said, "Did you hear? Glosecrose went to that big PX in the sky."

"He got himself all packed up?"

The first question everyone asked was "How?"

"How'd he buy the farm?"

Seems to me like they said he stepped on a land mine. I hated to hear it. I hated to hear of anybody losing their life, but I knew he did it in honor of his country, trying to defend his country, so we looked at it as a sacrifice that he'd made, and it didn't hurt you quite as bad like that.

We all knew deep down that some of us would die in battle. That's the nature of war. The thought of dying was not something that worried me, even knowing I'd be in fight-to-the-death situations with bullets flying *at me.* I never doubted that I would come home all right. If anybody got through it, I's gonna be one that got through it. And I went along with that attitude.

Now, some of those boys talked differently. I've heard some of them say, "If I go over there and see action, I don't think I'll ever come back." I've heard a lot of them say things like that. I didn't much like to hear that kind of talk. If you go around expecting something bad to happen to you all the time, well, surely it will. I believe it makes a difference, how you look at things. I always hoped for the best.

The day was getting closer when the rest of us would be sent over, though we didn't know when. What we knew about the war was more and more disturbing, news of difficult battles taking place over in North Africa or in the Pacific, learned mostly from what we heard over the radio, or picked up from the movie newsreels that they'd show on the base.

Peace for us depends on peace for all.
— **WHY WE FIGHT, U.S. Army documentary, 1942,**
directed by Frank Capra

All the information the army gave us about the enemy was direct. They didn't soft-pedal it. We learned that Japan, Italy, and Germany started this war by aggressively conquering some of their neighboring countries. Those three conquering countries had signed a pact together and were known as the Axis powers.

The Axis powers were ruthless and savage, murdering people for being of the wrong religion or the wrong race. People in Axis-controlled countries had no trial by jury, no free speech, no free press. I learned that the people in Germany couldn't even speak out to their neighbors against what their leaders were doing if they didn't agree to it, because the Nazis would come to their homes, take them away, and they'd never be seen again. Well, I couldn't go along with that.

The army stressed all through our training how Hitler had taken over

Germany and how he had the people under his thumb, making them do all the things he wanted. They really stressed it in a way to make us hate the Germans so we'd go in there to kill them.

It was the same way with the Japanese. They didn't have to say too much about the Japanese, though, 'cause we's all bitter about the way they bombed Pearl Harbor, sneaked in there at dawn and killed our sailors. "Remember December 7th" was a popular motto with people at the time.

The military always told us that the Japanese could not be trusted—in no way, form, or fashion. If they came out acting like they were surrendering, they weren't intending to surrender, they just wanted to get the drop on you. You couldn't depend on them to do what they said.

Now, the Germans, we'd heard, were pretty honest about whatever they did. If they surrendered, they surrendered. I figured they were more like we were, and it was their leaders that had led them down the wrong road.

When the instructors or training films referred to the Germans, I was aware, of course, that my mother's side of the family was from Germany. A lot of the American soldiers were of German descent. I don't think anybody worried too much over whether any of our soldiers had divided loyalties because of their background.

All the boys I knew were so proud of the United States of America that no matter what their last name or where their family came from, there was never any question about which country they felt kinship to. There was one thing everybody agreed on: America meant freedom. Now, while there sure wasn't much freedom in the army, and even though most of us soldiers were pretty young, I think we all appreciated the fact that we lived in such a good nation. Everybody I knew was willin' to fight whoever we had to, to preserve our way of life.

We kind of felt like the army was training us for the European Theater because they stressed more of that, even though a lot of fighting was happening in the Pacific. They didn't teach us as much about the Japanese in our training as they did the Germans, and that made us feel like we were going to head for Germany.

A lot of what we understood about the war came from movies that the army showed us. They always had some new movie about Hitler and what his troops had done to different countries. When they built Camp Beale, they built a real nice theater on the base and styled it after the big movie theaters that they had in the towns around there in California.

It was a special treat to me, to go to the movies. There weren't any theaters near where I grew up, so I hadn't been used to that. I'd make sure to get my extra duties done early if I knew there was a movie that night. McAbee and I would usually sit together. Being a little feller, McAbee liked to sit pretty near the front, since most of the boys were taller than he was. I wasn't too tall either, and that suited me fine.

They showed us all kinds of movies, but a lot of the movies were about the war, those were the ones that I mostly went to. I wanted to get a look at the enemies we were facing.

I remember some of the movies showed Hitler speaking and shaking his fist before a crowd of people in an enormous rounded stadium. Hitler was a giant up on the screen, yelling in German, and it seemed like he was always jabbing his arm up in the air.

National Socialism will reshape the world!
— Adolf Hitler

The army was always telling us that Hitler wanted to take over the world and what kind of a dictator he was, how the people were bowing down to him. The people all hollered, "Heil Hitler, Heil Hitler!" every time he'd get up to speak.

I thought that was crazy that the men, women, and children would rise up and holler "Heil Hitler!" and throw their hands up in the air like he did.

In the black-and-white movies that flickered in that big theater full of soldiers, we watched Hitler's troops assemble before a stadium full of spectators. I don't remember now, but I imagine they were SS, Hitler's elite forces. Columns of German soldiers marched with the precision of clockwork and they'd really kick their legs out when they marched. They looked like they had the will to kill anyone, anywhere, to keep from being stopped.

After seeing those films, a lot of the boys would joke around and goose-step. Now, that goose-stepping, that looked like a tiresome way to march. Some of the boys would imitate Hitler's troops. They thought it was funny. They'd throw their legs out stiffly and they'd salute the air. "Heil!" And they'd sing a little song: "We are the Super Race. Sieg Heil! Sieg Heil! . . . Right in the Fuehrer's face . . . ," and so on.

One boy who did that a lot, John Kemp, he'd imitate an airplane strafing. They showed a lot of that in the movies. He'd stiffen up his hand and fly it around like an airplane, diving at somebody's head or neck, maybe poking them in the back, while he made the sound, *tat-tat-tat-tat-tat!*, machine guns shooting real fast. That boy was a cutup. He was all over the barracks strafing people.

One time Kemp came up from behind and didn't see that it was an officer he was fooling with. He just clipped him, and knocked his hat off.

The officer took a dim view of that.

"What's the matter with you!" he said to Kemp. "Soldier, there's a war on here. Men are being cut in two from Luftwaffe strafing. Is that a joke to you?"

"No, sir! I'm sorry, sir!" That boy straightened up right quick, and the officer walked on.

We'd just been learning about how Germany's leaders were spreading death and destruction on the people of other countries, and those German planes were responsible for a lot of that. Hitler's forces were sweeping across Europe, spreading terrible bloodshed, and, of course, the Allies' bombing raids to try to stop them were just bringin' Germany to ruin, too. Apparently, nobody saw this war coming. If they did, nothing was done about it till it was too late.

Back when Adolf Hitler was elected Germany's chancellor in 1933, he violated the Treaty of Versailles — the agreement which ended the Great War, the war that crippled my Uncle Pole. That treaty had restricted the German Army to 100,000 men and was supposed to prevent German development of tanks, submarines, and combat aircraft — they'd all just come into use during World War I. But ol' Hitler, they told us, he'd put his country's industry into high gear making armaments anyway.

By 1943, the newspapers were calling Hitler's Germany a "Voracious Nazi War Machine." It finally came out that the Germans had been secretly working for years to equip their armies with the latest advancements in warfare. They were now well prepared. And we were tryin' to catch up.

The U.S. Army's films showed us the firepower of German artillery, tanks, and bombs. It was our first look at some of the weapons we'd be facing. We saw the "German 88s," the long-barreled antiaircraft guns that took down Allied aircraft and put holes in tanks.

We learned that Hitler put $80 billion towards armament in preparation for war, and that was, of course, back in the 1930s. That amount of money seemed unbelievable to me.

Because of all that increased industry to fuel the war effort, unemployment in Germany had about disappeared, and I imagine that helped get the people to stand behind Hitler. They said Hitler was exalted like a god in Germany. From what I could see in the movies, the people really seemed to worship him.

We were told how Hitler lied again and again in public speeches about his intentions. He said he didn't want to conquer other nations, then, he went and invaded. The people in Germany had been hypnotized, I reckon, to think that they were members of a master race. They followed a man who believed he would control the world, and that control started with their neighbors.

In 1938, the Germans first took control of Austria and Czechoslovakia. In 1939, Germany invaded Poland. By 1940, German troops swept through Denmark, Norway, Holland, Belgium, and France, and it looked like they would keep on conquering everything in their path. England was still holding them off, but their cities really took a beating from the Luftwaffe. We all knew we had to rid the world of Germany's evil dictator and his followers. They told us that we Americans were fighting to save the Free World.

If that wasn't enough, some of the movies showed the Nazis indoctrinating children, so there'd be a new generation to carry on that evil. The little German children were up on the screen, in their classrooms, throwing their hands up in the air to salute a picture of Hitler. I couldn't go along with that.

The movies said that with Hitler in power, "Catholic and Protestant churches must vanish," and they showed us pictures of stone churches in rubble, still smoking. We saw the streets of conquered countries, destroyed by explosions. Piles of dead bodies, a horrifying sight. I saw women and children crying over their dead.

Those movies were the first look I had at the battlefield. The screen showed black smoke pouring into the sky and buildings flamin' up. I saw white snow with soldiers fallen in battle. The blood that was spilled on the snowy ground—on the screen, it looked like soot. We wouldn't see battlefields in color until we were called into action. But after seein' those movies—oh, yeah, we were ready to go.

It's us or them.
— *WHY WE FIGHT,* Frank Capra

The 13th was the only armored division in World War II that was activated in California. In honor of that, California's governor announced in a proclamation that the 13th Armored Division had been adopted as "California's Own."

> *. . . California's legislature, by joint resolution, has proposed that the State of California sponsor this splendid organization of fighting men . . . Composed of men from every state in the union, the 13th Armored Division will receive the greater part of its combat training at Camp Beale . . . and it has become the desire of the officers and men that the division be permitted to name its armored vehicles after the cities and counties of our State. (2)*

In honor of this, the division staged an official celebration on Independence Day weekend, and mayors of California towns and cities and other government officials came to tour our base and visit with the troops.

The high point was an acceptance ceremony on July 4th and a full display of our vehicles and armor. A division is a big grouping. The different units that made up the 13th Armored Division became known as:

Tank Battalions: 24th, 45th, and 46th
Armored Infantry Battalions: 16th, 59th, and 67th
Armored Field Artillery Battalions: 496th, 497th, and 498th
93rd Cavalry Reconnaissance Squadron, Mechanized
124th Armored Engineer Combat Battalion
83rd Armored Medical Battalion
513th Counter Intelligence Corps Detachment
Headquarters Company
Division Trains
135th Armored Ordnance Maintenance Battalion
153rd Armored Signal Company
Military Police Platoon
The Division Band

That day the band was really spirited and they played all kinds of patriotic music. "The Caissons Go Rolling Along" was one that I always remember. We heard that tune a lot.

> *Independence Day was truly the most memorable day in the history of the Division up to that time. The "luck of the 13th" prevailed atmospherically and otherwise. It was warm, but not torrid. More than 20,000 civilians had massed in the bleachers and parking lines bordering the review field. Christening ceremonies began promptly at noon.*
>
> *After introduction by General Wogan, Governor Warren of California gave a speech:*

*"In this our hour of crisis, our California communities are
proud to have their names inscribed on such splendid vehicles of
war as we see on review before us.... With you, as you complete
your training and move toward the actual battlefronts, will go
the thoughts, the blessings, and the hopes of each California community which you have honored." (2)*

The governor christened General Wogan's command tank, which had
been painted with the name CALIFORNIA on the side. He broke a
bottle of champagne against the armor, and everyone cheered. Two flags
flew on either side of the tank: the red-and-green flag of the Division
and the California Bear flag, because the 13th Armored Division was
now "California's Own."

*A thrilling moment came when the massed sirens of all the
tanks shrilled above the thunder of the engines in a salute to
California and a challenge to the foe. (2)*

Our outfit had gotten new Sherman M4 tanks. Three hundred and
forty-three California sponsors came down onto the field where we
were set up and they christened our tanks, smashed big bottles of liquor
against the steel hulls. Then we paraded our vehicles for the public to
see in what they called "a spectacular review of our Division's might."
During the armored review, we drove all our combat vehicles past stands
full of cheering crowds. Fighter planes and bombers flew overhead, too,
like they'd do in combat.

I drove, like the rest of the tankers, with my head proudly sticking out
of the hatch and we were lined up to show off just how many vehicles
we had. Our vehicles covered a huge field in what they called "a mighty
tide of armor."

The 13th Armored Division was set up with 263 medium tanks,
450 half-tracks, and 77 light tanks, among many, many other vehicles, like scout cars, self-propelled antitank guns, and amphibious
trucks, or "seeps." They told us, if we'd been stretched out in convoy on

the highway, our convoy would have reached from Marysville to San Francisco, around one hundred miles long.

Those new tanks we got, they'd each been freshly painted for the ceremony with the name of a county in California in big block letters. By a happy coincidence, I reckon, my new tank just happened to be named ORANGE, after Orange County, California.

Everybody had some comment about that, when they found out. I think I wrote and told Orangie as soon as they made the changes with the tanks. I really don't know what I said in my letters that I wrote to her. I didn't have enough of sense to know how to write a love letter, I don't guess. But she caught on, I think.

Oh, I probably told her that the name of my new tank didn't remind me of a sweet fruit in California, but of my sweetheart back on Coker Creek. I'd been writing to her and that's the way we got acquainted with each other. I don't know, it wasn't exactly dating, I don't guess, but we were writing to each other and, of course, all the boys asked if you had a girlfriend. Each one of them usually had a girlfriend or wife and they'd talk about her when we told stories from home.

I'd tell them that Orangie was my girlfriend, which she was. We just hadn't been out on a date yet. 'Course, I didn't tell them that.

I kept that Sherman tank the rest of the time that I was taking training. They never did change it. ORANGE was my tank.

And Orangie, by this time, was writing to me pretty often and her letters got sweeter. I sometimes took a little while to write back, though. They kept us pretty busy, and if we weren't doing work, they wanted us to entertain some of the Californians.

There were a lot of times I could have taken girls on rides in my tank. In fact, there were a lot of girls that came out to the camp, hoping to meet a serviceman, on special days when the camp was opened up to civilians to see.

When they came to see the tanks, the California girls dressed a little different to the women back home. They had tight sweaters with the arms pushed up and lace-up shoes with little white socks. Out in California, they wore their skirts a little shorter than the women did back home, although Orangie sometimes had some of those new styles, too.

The army made arrangements for us to take these California girls on tank rides. But they couldn't get me to do that at all. I was pretty shy around strangers, anyhow. I never would participate. And besides, I didn't want to meet those girls.

Lonnie Johnson:

Kelley never did enjoy life, he was too serious about it. We would tell him, "You don't even know how to have fun." But he'd always talk about Orangie. I think he was hot after her. Oh, Lordy mercy, he said he had a girlfriend named Orangie and we'd say "Well, she's off a havin' fun with another man tonight, 'cause you ain't there." We'd tell him everything. Once in a while he'd say, "Oh, pshaw! You boys don't know what you're a talkin' about!" (12)

The army selected the time for each of us to go on thirty-day furlough—they didn't give you any notice—so, of course, I don't imagine I had time to get a letter off in the mail. At least I didn't do it—I might have had time, but I didn't do it. I just decided I'd surprise them.

It took me five days and four nights to get from California back to home. I rode the train and I got off in Sweetwater, Tennessee. Then I caught a delivery truck that delivered fuel to service stations and that brought me to Tellico Plains around ten o'clock in the morning.

I ran into a neighbor from Coker Creek down at Watson's Store and he said he'd be glad to drive me on home. He had an old-model Ford, I don't remember whether it was an A-Model or T-Model, somewhere from the '30s. There wasn't much room, so I got in the backseat.

Just before we got home, about a mile from the house, we overtook my mother walking along the side of the road. We weren't expecting to see her there. As we drove up, the neighbor said to me, "Now, don't you say nothin'. Just keep quiet back there. I'm a gonna ask her to get in the front seat."

I didn't know what he was gonna do.

So he pulled to a stop and my mother got in the front seat and we rode along there and he talked with her for a little bit.

I heard her say, "Well, I's comin' back from the post office. I've been waitin' for a letter from Quinton. Haven't heard from him in a long time." She shook her head. "But I didn't get a letter. I's sure I would by now."

Then my neighbor said, "Don't you ever look 'round and see who's behind you when you're ridin' in a car?"

She looked around to see who it was. And when she saw me, it just excited her to death. Her eyes got big and wide, and she just went to smilin' from ear to ear.

She said, "I went to the post office 'cause I felt like I'd get a letter from you. But I got better'n that!"

My neighbor who was driving got a big kick out of that, because he'd been able to drive me home and get to see how excited my mother was over my being home. She kept herself under control pretty good, but you knew she was excited to see me. Yeah, oh, yeah.

When we got out of the car, I hugged her. "Momma! Boy, it sure is good to see you!"

"Sure is good to have you home! Well, it looks like you got a promotion!" she said, looking at my sleeve. "C'mon in, I'll make you a skillet of cornbread. I got us some fresh buttermilk." Momma knew I'd be hankerin' for cornbread and buttermilk after all that army food.

We spent most of those few days together, my parents and me. Of course, some cousins, aunts and uncles, and my sisters, they'd come over to visit with me.

And Orangie, I knew I wanted to see her when I got home. We had been writing for some time and I got to know her personality through her letters. I'd never had a sweetheart and it was the first time I had a desire to have one.

I came into Frank and Mamie's store about as soon as I got to Coker Creek, to buy some candy. Always had a sweet tooth. Orangie sold it to me and we talked a little while about what had been happening on

Coker Creek, but I didn't ask her out or anything like that.

I just enjoyed seeing her. She dressed real neat, had her hair pinned up. She was attractive in her clothes, the way she wore them. When she worked, she wore slacks a lot of the time, because she had to pump gas out front. It was the first time I ever remember women in slacks, around the time of World War II. That was just for work. Orangie told me that some women in Texas where she was from wore blue jeans to work in, like the rough ol' gold miners wore, but she was quick to add, "I never put on a pair of blue jeans in my life!" She was nice and ladylike — didn't get out of hand and say things that weren't proper for a lady to say, like some of them did.

I kept standing around the store, hemmin' and hawin', thinkin' of things to talk to her about, and I was about to leave.

Orangie said, "Wait just a minute," and she went in the back. When she came out, she had changed into a real nice dress and she'd let her hair down. She had real soft-looking brown waves that touched her shoulders.

She said, "Let's go for a ride."

I had been too bashful to ask for a date, but she got me around that. I guess it was a good thing she did. I might never have asked her because I was always afraid I was going to insult her. I didn't know how to ask her just right. And I figured she might say no. So, I wouldn't do it. She knew enough about me to know that I was too shy to ask her out, so she decided to move things along.

We got in my blue '37 Chevrolet and I drove her all the way down to Tellico Plains. Oh, we had a big time. We didn't sit close together, but we had a real good time. At first Orangie was a little bit quiet. But soon we were laughing together. Once she got to know me, if something was real funny, she'd laugh with her head thrown back.

I'd look over at her and she'd be smiling, all full of whatever it was she was talkin' about. Orangie was just as pretty as a flower, and as nice to see as a summer rose. She liked happy music, particularly piano music, and "Yellow Rose of Texas" was one of her favorite tunes. She sang it a little bit and I learned that she couldn't carry a tune in a bucket, but that just made my heart melt a little more.

She's the sweetest little rosebud
This soldier ever knew
Her eyes are bright as diamonds
They sparkle like the dew.
You may talk about your Clementine
And sing of Rosa Lee
But the Yellow Rose of Texas
Beats the belles of Tennessee.

We were out riding around Coker Creek coming back from Tellico Plains and we stopped along the road to walk around a little bit, and one of my neighbors came along and took our picture together, sitting on the front bumper of that '37 Chevrolet.

After that first ride, we clipped it off good. I'd go down to the store after Orangie got off work. Of course, after that, I'd ask her if she wanted to go out for a ride. I'd lost my bashfulness.

She'd say, "Let me get dressed and we'll go."

We'd go out ridin', and we'd head back in the hills on those dirt roads in my Chevrolet. I had to learn to take the twists and turns real easy, since Orangie could get a little bit sick at her stomach. Those roads were just as crooked as a snake and steep, too. Orangie said it was flat in South Texas where she'd grown up. But she never had any problem, as soon as I learned the motion bothered her. I'd take the turns real smooth and wind around back in those hollers, and we'd just be a talkin' and a laughin' and havin' a big time together. Orangie never did get carsick when I drove.

We'd pull off the road and sit out in the woods, down by a branch of Coker Creek, and watch the fireflies start comin' out just as it was gettin' dark. Have you ever watched two fireflies flirt with each other in the woods? Sometimes you'll see just two of 'em together and they'll dance with each other a little bit. They'll float on the air and circle around each other, and then they'll light up together. They'll blink that yellow glow like candlelight in perfect time with each other. You have to be still and quiet to notice those things in nature.

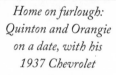

Home on furlough:
Quinton and Orangie
on a date, with his
1937 Chevrolet

We'd sit out there on a big rock and watch the fireflies twinkle like the stars above us, and listen to katydids call through the trees. We'd nuzzle like two peaches on a limb, and when Orangie'd lean up next to me, she smelled just as sweet. She said it was some perfume called Evening in Paris, and she always smelled like a bunch of pretty blossoms to me.

Sometimes we'd stay out real late at night. I'd bring her home and her older sister, Mamie, never did have anything to say about it. Mamie always liked me real well, I don't know why. She and Frank both. I'd been going to their store ever since it opened. She didn't object to Orangie going out with me. Of course, I behaved myself better than some of the boys. They'd go in the store and tell dirty jokes and go on with tall tales about some of their unfit behavior when they were standing around the store with a bunch of men. I didn't do that.

I never did ask Orangie to wait for me. She might have gone out with other servicemen, but I never did know that she did. I didn't expect her to just hang on to me, because we didn't know if I would come back from the war.

When Orangie worked at Frank's Store during the day, men sometimes gathered up and sat around with Frank and talked and they'd just go on and on, into the evening. She'd have to stay there as long as there were customers in the store, whether they were buying anything or not. One time she was wanting to get out of there to go on a drive with me, so she left the counter, went around the back of the building and started yelling, "Fire! Fire!"

When Frank and the men came running, she was just standing back there. Of course, there was no fire.

"Well, it's time to go home!" she told them.

Frank really got on her for that and it was the only time she did it, but she did get to change out of her work clothes and go ridin' around with me. We'd usually pull down a side road and sit there and talk until it was time to go home. Sometimes we'd stay together till maybe one o'clock in the morning and then I'd drop her off at her sister's.

The next morning my sister Thelma, who was at home for a little while, she'd tease me about what time I came in the night before when we sat down to breakfast. I'd enjoy joking with her and my dad, and get filled up on my mother's good country cookin', while I got filled in on all the happenings around there. We'd talk about my cousins, especially the ones in service.

A lot of my cousins had gone into the service, drafted. Very few actually enlisted. Nobody really wanted to leave their family to go fight. We all loved our country, but times were hard still, back in those hills, and families needed their men. I think most of us really felt it was our duty, though, and we were willing to go when called. That sense of duty had been instilled in us.

Now, as it happened, my cousin Atlas was assigned to the same division I was in, the 13th Armored Division, but a different company: the 498th Field Artillery, Headquarters Battery. His job had him helping to feed all the officers.

He was a truck driver for the company he was in; he drove a mess truck. They always had a mess truck with equipment to prepare food when we went out training for a few days. When Atlas was in camp, he worked around the kitchen. I heard he served officers, put food right on the plates of generals when they visited. Law, we thought he was lucky to be doing that. I imagined him preparing the plate of food with the same neatness that he'd always had. Atlas was always as particular as he could be.

I didn't see Atlas much in training. He was in one end of the camp and I was in another, about four or five miles apart. I had to walk to get there and it was the same way for him to come to see me, but I'd run into him occasionally.

My cousin Archie, whose deferment had kept him home, he'd suddenly been drafted while I was away, and they assigned him to the infantry. Archie was husky and tough and I guess that's why they put him in the infantry as a foot soldier, so he could march and dig and fight in hand-to-hand combat without givin' out.

Archie had his banjo when he was in training and the other boys would try to get him to play at dances. He told me about it. He thought playing at dances was against his religion; he'd been brought up that way. Women didn't dance on Coker Creek; people out there just thought it was sinful. Maybe some of the things women do when they were dancing and carrying on were immodest, some of the women. They wouldn't be properly dressed and they'd do a lot of things that weren't good to do before a group of people.

Archie'd play music in the barracks for the other boys, like McAbee did in our barracks. But if they wanted him to go out to where they were having a big dance, he wouldn't do that. His father, Edd Lee, was strictly against that.

When I heard that Archie had just been sent to the front, boy, was I worried. My first assistant driver, Glosecrose, was already dead and he had hardly gotten overseas when that happened, like a lot of the others the military sent over after only a few weeks of training. They'd sent Archie off to combat awful quick. Bein' a foot soldier, he didn't have armor to protect him like I'd have. I prayed for his safety. For the safety of us all.

★ ★ ★

The one thing to which we can point with greatest pride is the fact that from a group of single individuals gathered from every part of this great country, we have emerged a compact, tough, hard-hitting organization endowed with high morale and singleness of purpose.

Nothing is static in this fast-moving world. We cannot stand still. We must either progress or we degenerate. Much as we have accomplished, there is still much to be done. We know we are good, but we must become better. We know we are tough, but we must become tougher. We know we can shoot, but we must learn to shoot straighter. . . .

—**General John B. Wogan, October 15, 1943,**
Organization Day (2)

In less than one year at Camp Beale, we'd learned all the lessons of combat, sharpening our skills with firepower, hand-to-hand combat, armored employment, and heavy artillery, training first as a company, then working up to gigantic division-wide maneuvers that encompassed hundreds of miles. On an individual level, we learned to communicate clearly and work as teams 'cause we depended on each other. We changed from civilians into soldiers.

I'd found my place in the army—or had been shown it—and it was a good fit for me. I'd been fooling with wheels since I was knee-high to a June bug, so I guess that's why I was selected as a driver. I'd learned to handle tools from my dad, made wagon wheels with him in his blacksmith shop, then progressed to building my own wheeled vehicles.

I guess I'd been in training all my life. I'd had all those afternoons under the oak trees assembling axles, all those hair-raising rides down embankments as I steered one of my wagons with my feet, all that double-clutching with my A-Model. I'd taught my nervous sisters to drive, and I knew every detail of my '37 Chevrolet's engine. I was well prepared for my job as tank driver and I had been promoted to a T/5 rating, a technical rank, Technician 5th Grade. I wore two stripes with a "T." That was a higher rating than they normally rated the tank drivers while we were just in training. I reckon it made a difference that I really liked driving my tank. I liked the smells of metal and oil and gas, and always, we were movin' on.

Before we moved out of Camp Beale, we staged a dismounted review, the troops marched in order, and General Wogan addressed the men of the 13th Armored Division:

> *The success of this division in combat will be determined in a large measure by the guts of the men behind the guns and the fiber of their hearts and souls and bodies when the supreme test comes. It will also be determined by the degree of perfection with which you are trained. Therefore, while waiting for the call, which we hope will not be long in coming, carry on your training with efficiency and determination. (2)*

Now, we learned, the 13th Armored Division was going to be transported to another camp. And, naturally, that's all they told us.

CHAPTER 15

Camp Bowie, Texas

The 13th Armored Division loaded all the tanks and other vehicles onto a troop train that had platform cars. We took our same tanks with us, so ORANGE came along on the journey.

They had coaches for the crew to travel in, but the driver had to ride in his tank. I'd ride in the driver's seat with the hatch closed and when the train stopped, I'd have to get out and walk guard to see that nobody tried to sabotage us. I had my personal weapon, that stripped-down Thompson submachine gun, the Grease Gun, slung over my shoulder. The army was concerned about sympathizers in our own country who might try to aid the Japanese or the Germans in attacking us.

We had such a string of tanks, the train stalled on some of the mountains we had to come across. Evidently, they didn't know how much weight we had, for some reason the army goofed on that. We sat there half the night, waiting for another engine to arrive to get us across the mountain. All that time, I walked guard, back and forth, back and forth with the other drivers, while the rest of the boys lived it up in the coaches, playing cards and telling little jokes.

Finally, they got some railroad engine in there with enough power to pull us on across that mountain, so we went on, and that journey ended at Camp Bowie, near Brownwood, Texas.

I saw right away that Camp Bowie was about like Camp Beale, another training camp with rows and rows of wooden barracks and all the rest. They had 120,000 acres for us to use on maneuvers. This camp, too, was named after an American personality from the Wild West days: James Bowie, famous for fighting with a big knife and for dying at the Alamo with Tennessean Davy Crockett.

While we waited for the call to action, we continued our advanced training in the field. The military wanted us to get some, I guess, desert training and Texas where we were, was more of a desert country, with hot, wide-open plains.

American and British armored units hadn't been trained in desert warfare when they first entered the war. They came up against the troops of Hitler's field marshal, Rommel, in North Africa, and the sand and dust really interfered with their tank machinery. The Allies were defeated once in North Africa before they made a comeback, but by now the Allies controlled the parts of North Africa that Hitler had held, and the African campaign was already won. That gave us a lot of encouragement to hear that.

Of course, this world war raged in so many places, you didn't know what kind of terrain might be involved next. We didn't have any idea where we might be sent to fight, what kind of place, or what season. The 13th Armored Division was being trained for some special purpose, but we didn't know what.

They kept us on maneuvers most of the time. We'd pull out of the motor pool parking lot and we made a long, loud column of armor. Anybody could hear us coming miles away. The General Sherman M4, its 500-horsepower V8 engine roared with power and the wheels squeaked at a high pitch as they turned, and the metal tracks clattered. The faster you'd go, the louder that tank sounded.

In practicing for combat, sometimes we switched order—the 1st Platoon would start off leading for so many hours, then we'd switch, and the 2nd Platoon would take over the lead position for a while just to give the 1st Platoon a break on long marches.

We'd go out no telling how many miles into empty, barren scrub land, where you could see a long ways off in the distance. It was hotter out in Texas than I was used to, and you'd think that being in that big ol' steel tank, you'd get cooked. But the engine compartment is in the back of the tank and those big fans pulled air through grated metal openings in the front of the tank, especially when we were moving, and all that air came through the compartments where the assistant driver and driver sat. That helped us to stay cool.

Up in the turret where the tank commander, gunner, and loader rode—they stayed pretty cool, too, as long as we were moving. But when we stopped, it could get pretty hot in that tank. The Texas sun turned it into a kettle and it would about cook us.

In training, the drivers drove mostly unbuttoned in convoy. We'd have our head sticking out and, boy, we'd catch a lot of dust from the tracks of the tanks ahead of us like that. Sometimes, I could hardly see. Those tanks would really kick up the dust. A big yellow cloud followed our convoy and it drifted for miles and miles across that flat land.

When we stopped, if the tanks were running, the tank in front of me was always keeping dust in my face. The exhaust on those tanks was in the back and it blew up a cloud of dust, because it blew down towards the ground.

We had to have eye protection, and even then, my eyes would just water, and it would run down my nose. A lot of days, I'd take my goggles off and I'd have two big clumps of mud on both sides of my nose down to my mouth sort of like a dirt dobber's nest on each side. I'd have to get some water and wash all that off.

That dust and rough terrain caused a lot of problems; it really wore out those "bogie wheels" that turned the tracks of the tank. They had a rubber covering and that rubber would peel off so the metal wheel would be grinding directly on the metal track, and that would do damage right away if you didn't put a new rubber bogie wheel on there. As soon as you lost that rubber, you'd hear it in the tank, a metallic click-click-click sound, as the wheels ran over those tracks like a washboard. We carried extra sets of bogie wheels so we could stop and change them out.

It was quite a job to change out one of those wheels. But each tank crew had the equipment to do it. We carried a big cable and different tools. We had a maintenance crew that followed in training maneuvers, but a lot of times in real combat, they might be tied up and couldn't get to us, so we'd have to learn to do our own work. Out in Texas, it seemed like we were always breakin' down and having to change out bogie wheels.

We'd go out in the training fields, just like we were in combat, and assemble in different places. We followed all the regulations so they'd be second nature to us. We kept our radios silent at least half an hour before reaching our bivouac position, then kept them silent in bivouac, things like that.

The tank battalion operates by surprise, fire and maneuver, and concentration of effort (mass).
—Armored Force Field Manual, FM 17-33,
The Armored Battalion Light and Medium, United States
Government Printing Office, Washington, 1942.

When we were out in the field as a division, we would do maneuvers with artillery, engineers, infantry, tank destroyer units, and air units. The medical and maintenance companies were also present, just like in combat. We'd play "war games," as they called it, even though war is too serious a thing to make into a game. It was more like war practice.

We fought "Red and Blue" wars, where they divided us into a red team and a blue team and we waged mock battles at each other to simulate maneuvers on the battlefield. They'd have some of the other companies set up to attack us like they were the enemy, or they'd have us make a surprise attack on them. We'd try to track them down and we'd go across the fields after them. We'd rip through, tearin' around, runnin' cross-country and everything else. That's about what it amounted to.

The tank commander had to give the commands and tell me where to go, how fast to go, and when to stop. Foster kept our tank right where it ought to be, and on target.

We'd fire on other tanks and different real targets when Foster told our gunners to fire. Of course, we weren't firing real ammunition, just using blanks.

We followed maneuvers that the officers mapped out for us. Our orders were little fragments of the whole battle plan. We never knew what the plan was. So, I just always did as I'd been raised to do, focus on the task at hand, which was driving, and do my best.

We'd stay out in the fields of Texas usually three days at a time and set up camp all different ways to anticipate what we might find in battle situations. Where Camp Bowie was located, it had been a cattle ranch, I guess, and they had terraces cut around a slope, and there were ditches in those terraces full of water. That sure was a good breeding ground for mosquitoes, and they'd just about eat you up at night. Didn't bother you much in the daytime, but, boy, at night they'd really work on you, they'd just about carry you away. You couldn't hardly sleep, they'd just cover you up, a buzzin' 'round your head. Never did have many mosquitoes back on Coker Creek, so that was somethin' I didn't have much tolerance for.

We'd try every way in the world to get away from them — run, get in a tent, close it up, but they'd find us some way, those mosquitoes would slip in the tent. You couldn't bundle up to keep them off neither, 'cause it was too hot. So hot you couldn't sleep. Oh, we were miserable like that out in Texas.

We stayed out in the field, I believe it was three weeks one time under those conditions, that was the longest we stayed away from camp. When we knew we were going out there, we went to the PX and bought I don't know how many boxes of candy. We bought enough so each one of us would have at least a bar of candy every day, because we knew the government wasn't going to furnish us much in the way of treats. The tank commander issued them out to us. Foster would say, "Well, it's candy time." And he'd hand out the candy. That was the thing we looked forward to in the field.

The mess truck followed us and they'd prepare meals, but it wasn't like eating back at the mess hall. When it came time to eat, we'd all get our mess kits and canteens and eat whatever they were dishin' out. Never did know what some of it was.

Other times we'd eat K-rations or C-rations, food prepared to carry with us, since that was what we'd have on the battlefield. That K-ration was in a little box and we could just eat it in the tank, or wherever we were. The C-ration that we heated on our stove, it was a little better ration. It was more like a real meal. They'd tell us to eat our C-rations for dinner, what the army called dinner, the evening meal. None of the food was too good, but a feller could survive on it.

We were just out in the field when night came, and we'd set up like we were in a battle zone. We'd position our tanks to guard each other, and we'd have what you call a right guard, left guard, forward and rear guards. After we set up for the night, we'd sleep on the ground. A lot of times we didn't use tents.

We had a big tarpaulin that we carried with us. We used it to keep our tank covered when it was in the parking lot back in camp, but out in the field, we took that tarpaulin and spread it down in the grass where we had to spend the night. It was wide enough to where we could lie on one part and double the rest up over us in case it was raining. Usually, if it was raining, it would cool the atmosphere enough till we could sleep between the layers of that tarpaulin.

One of us had to be on guard. The driver always got the first turn, because he'd had to do all the work and he needed a good night's sleep. So I'd walk guard first, then wake up the next man to take over guard duty. We'd rotate all through the night.

It's a little hard if you've been used to sleeping on a pillow, just to lie flat on the ground on something like a tarpaulin. I had a little square cushion that was in the tank, the one I sat on. It had a metal base around the bottom and the middle was padded. I'd take it out of the tank and use it for a pillow. It made a pretty good pillow. I didn't have much trouble "roughin' it" out in the field like some of 'em.

A lot of crews cracked under the pressure and had trouble getting along. Some of them got to insulting each other and got into fights and somebody'd have to break it up. I was lucky that my crew got along real good together. Just one time we had a little trouble.

Winfred Knode had been walking guard duty and it was my turn again, so I relieved him and when he got back between the layers of that tarpaulin, he didn't pull the top part up enough to cover the bottom, and it started to rain. The bottom part of the tarpaulin was out in the weather so the rainwater ran down in there where we had our sleeping bags. Knode had run that water right down in there under us all.

I was out walking guard when that rain came. When I got off duty, I woke up the next man. I believe it was Rhodes. He jumped up from his sleeping bag, saying, "Jumpin' jackrabbits! Who in tarnation poured water in here?!!!"

McAbee woke up, too. "Aw, I'm all wet!"

"Somebody let the rain in here, KEE-node," Rhodes accused him.

"Who you talkin' to, E-well?" Knode said, sitting up.

"I'm talkin' to the careless scallywag who did a sorry job of protectin' us from the rain. When you got in here, you got everybody's bedroll all wet." Rhodes was direct and he had a voice as big as his native Texas.

"N-n-n-now, I didn't have n-n-nothin' to do with all that r-r-rain w-w-water," Knode said.

"I know you did. You got up to get one of those blamed smokes and you slid the tarp down, 'cause I saw you when you went to smokin' after you got off duty." Rhodes kept after him.

Knode smoked a lot, somebody or other was always getting on him for smoking. At night, he'd just about smoke us out if we were in close quarters. He'd even try to smoke between the layers of a tarpaulin in the rain.

"I d-d-d-don't have to t-t-t-take this!" Knode was getting flustered, and he started feeling around for his cigarette pack.

"Knode, you might as well own up to it and shut *him* up," McAbee said about Rhodes. "It had to be you, 'cause the rest of us were in here sleepin', except Kelley, but you were the last one to move the tarp."

Foster usually let us crew work things out ourselves, but he'd heard the commotion and he came over to put an end to the bickering.

"What's the matter? Can't handle a little rainwater?! You think the Japs are losing sleep over wet bedrolls? Go back to sleep and forget about it."

Foster'd had a lot of good training up in New Jersey before he became a policeman and that helped him, and helped us, too, because he was more settled than we were and we looked up to him. There was no foolishness about him. Foster was a good leader, a real disciplinarian.

Knode finally admitted that it must have been him that messed up, even though he hadn't noticed it. We all had to put up with a wet bedroll and we grumbled a little bit, but we got over it. Looked to me like, if that's all the problems we had with each other, we were a pretty fortunate tank crew.

We'd been out on maneuvers and on the way back to camp, one of the tank commanders lost his antenna. Some of the tanks had a type of antenna that was a big, tall antenna and it cost quite a bit of money.

I told Foster, "Did you see that antenna a layin' there in the road as we's comin' back in? Tanks ran over it and had it all bent up."

He hadn't seen it. I didn't think another thing about it. I didn't know who it was that lost it.

When we got back to camp, one of the other tank commanders got to inquiring about that antenna.

I said, "Yeah, I seen one layin' along the road and it'd been run over by a tank." I told him where it was located. Well, I just told him what I'd seen and I thought that was the end of it.

The next day, the captain sent word that he wanted me to come to his office. I went over there and met with Captain Blake.

He said, "What do you know about an antenna that you saw on maneuvers? I believe you said it had been run over by a tank?"

"Yeah, that's right," I said. "That's what I seen."

Then he said, "And you and Sergeant Hicks got in the jeep, went out there along the road and spent nearly half of an evening hunting for it, and you never did find it, is that right?"

I said, "No, I never went back out there. He might have went back to look for it, but I didn't go. I don't know anything about that."

The captain leaned back in his chair and studied me. He said, "Sergeant Hicks told me that you and he went out and spent a long time looking for the antenna, but couldn't locate it."

"No, sir," I said.

"Mm-hmm. I just wanted to find out a little more about it," he said. "You're dismissed, Kelley."

Of course, I didn't know I was gonna cause Sergeant Hicks any trouble when I told the captain all I knew.

Captain Blake called Sergeant Hicks to his office. That's one place Hicks's little dog, Mitzi, didn't go with him, when he went to see the captain.

Sergeant Hicks came to me and said, "I want you to go with me over to the captain's office. He wants to talk to us about that antenna that I lost."

I said, "Well, I didn't know that was your antenna."

He said, "It doesn't make any difference whose it was. They want me to pay for it, but I can get out of paying for it if you'll go over there and tell them that you and I did our best to find it, but that it just wasn't anywhere to be found."

I told him, "Now, I'm not gonna lie about it. I'll just tell what I know about it."

He said, "Come on."

As we were walking over there, Sergeant Hicks said, "Oh, you've really got me in trouble."

I said, "How's that?"

He said, "For telling him that you and I didn't go back out there to look for it."

I said, "Well, I just told him like it was."

So we went on to the captain's office and when we got there, the captain said, "Kelley, I want to hear your story first about the antenna."

I said, "Well, all I know about it was, we's on our way back, comin' outta those woods over there into the highway, and I seen an antenna layin' in the road and the tanks had run over it and it was all bent up. And I commented about seein' it. That's all I know about it."

Captain Blake repeated what Sergeant Hicks had told him, that we had gone out together looking for it.

He said to me, "Is that correct?"

I said, "Well, what I told you is correct. I didn't go out there with Sergeant Hicks looking for that antenna after that. I didn't know that he knew anything about the antenna." I hated to have to do that. But I wasn't gonna break down, just because the sergeant was over me.

Captain Blake looked over at Sergeant Hicks, then he looked back at me. And he said, "You're excused, Kelley. Sergeant, you stay in here."

The captain knew when I told him, he knew in his own mind that I was telling the truth. I don't know what he did to the sergeant, but I figured he'd be onto me when he came back to the barracks.

After a while Sergeant Hicks came back and he said, "Boy, I'll tell you, you got me in trouble. I'm surprised at you. I'd have lied, I'd have told a thousand lies to have got you out of something like that. And you wouldn't stand up for me over there."

I talked real nice to him, told him, "I don't lie for nobody, not even for myself."

"Nah," he said, "I've told a thousand lies, and I'll tell a thousand more, and it wouldn't have hurt you to have told the captain that me and you did what I told him we did. You really put me on the spot."

I said, "Well, I couldn't tell him that we did, 'cause we didn't. I'd already told him what the truth was."

He said, "I'll tell you, you ought to have helped me out there. I'm gonna have to pay for that antenna, I guess, unless the captain can work it out."

I said, "I'll pay for it myself, rather than to lie about it."

He said, "No, no, you can't do that."

I guess it did put him in a bad situation. I'll bet the captain gave him a going-over for making up that story. I hated that, of course. But I would have hated lying more. I wouldn't have lied, even if I'd known what Sergeant Hicks had told the captain when I first met with him,

I still wouldn't have lied. I was just brought up that way. If I'd had to go to the pen, I'd have told it like it was and taken the consequence. I'd been taught to tell the truth all my life. And I wouldn't tell a lie for nothin', for nobody. I'm always glad I kept my integrity in those kind of situations. It's hard to do sometimes, but you can do it, if you're just man enough to do it.

I never took any heat for keeping my integrity. I figured I would there, I figured the sergeant would be on me from then on. Captain Blake must have warned him. I bet the captain told him that he didn't want him jumping on me over that. He probably said something like, "You don't want to bother somebody that'll tell you the truth about anything."

Sergeant Hicks didn't do a thing to punish me. He never mentioned that incident ever again. He was just as nice to me as he'd ever been and we got along fine together. Hicks was a good feller and I always liked him.

Now, I imagine my telling the truth about that antenna seemed like a little thing. But it's little things people do that can get them in trouble. Sometimes a little thing like a casual lie can get somebody killed. Every now and then, one of the boys would get killed during training—accidents happened, of course, but it hurt you worst when you knew it could have been avoided.

We had been using an adapter to shoot .22 shells, to do some practice while we were out in the field. We were told to unload the guns before coming back to the motor pool. An officer was supposed to come around to each tank and make sure all the guns were unloaded. He was supposed to personally check, not just ask.

But that officer just asked one of the boys in a particular tank crew if he'd checked to see that their gun was unloaded.

That boy lied. He didn't think nothin' of it, I reckon, just said, "Yeah, I checked it." But he hadn't.

After the officer left, that boy got the gun out and handed it down to his buddy and it went off and killed his buddy.

Evidently, he'd assumed the gun was unloaded, and instead of telling the truth about whether he'd checked it, he just said that he had. He was careless with the truth and it seemed a little thing at the moment, I reckon, but it cost his buddy his life.

Some of those boys, I found, would lie about every breath, because it was convenient, or because they told it like they wanted it to be. It seemed foolish to me to have to sort out when to lie and when to tell the truth, when the simple, right thing was to tell the truth in every dealing. I found out I never had much to worry about in life, doin' like that.

For some reason, the army decided to do some crew switching a few months before we went overseas. They changed the tank commanders around and naturally they didn't tell us why.

I was disappointed when I heard they were taking Commander Foster out of my tank crew. I couldn't understand why they were doing that and I still don't know, unless it was because they didn't want us to get too familiar with any one tank commander.

Commander Foster was put in another tank in the same company. His new driver was a buddy of mine, Charlie Eaton, a Southerner, from Kentucky. I thought, well, Charlie's real lucky to have Foster as his tank commander.

I really hated it at the time, because I'd been happy with the crew I had and I wasn't acquainted with the new tank commander. My tank, still in the same position — second tank of the 2nd Platoon — was now commanded by Sergeant Donald E. Crouch. He would be the man to lead us through battle.

Donald Crouch made a good impression the first time he talked to me as our new tank commander. When he came over to the tank, he said, "Hi, Kelley, how ya doin'? Looks like I've been assigned to your tank. I've heard a lot of good things about you fellows."

He didn't have any accent at all really, just spoke clearly and directly. He talked to the crew a little bit and I could tell that he was a person who seemed to be real levelheaded. He had good sense and I thought, well, it's not bad after all.

Donald Crouch was what you'd call a handsome man, real good-looking, blue-eyed, I think. He was kind of tall, in fact, Crouch was the tallest man in our crew. He'd grown up on a farm where he built his muscles up, so he was big and husky, but he wasn't a heavy feller, just strong-built.

We had known Crouch some before — he took his basic training somewhere else, not Camp Beale, but he had transferred to our company in Texas, and I knew of him. He had a reputation as a real decent person. He was nice and polite to everybody. He was just a country boy from Leoti, Kansas, a little place outside of Witchita, he said. Since we were both raised on crops and hard work, he'd tell me about his home and he talked like it was a real big farming operation, where they used machinery to tend long rows of wheat.

He'd always mention his brothers, who were still back in Kansas. Donald was the youngest in his family and he had some older brothers and sisters. Sometimes he'd call them from training and talk with them. He said his brothers were taking care of the farming operation — they might have had a deferment.

Donald had enlisted after the Pearl Harbor bombing, even though his mother had tried to get him to stay on the farm. He seemed to be real proud of his family. He'd had good training at home, I could tell that by the way he treated us.

Some tank commanders weren't too good to help their crew, but Donald was good to help out with the maintenance of the tanks. He could have just given us orders, but he didn't do that. He'd fall in there and share the work, whatever came handy for him to do.

Tank Commander Donald E. Crouch

He'd give you the opportunity to express your feelings, too, if you had something to say to him. He didn't try to cut you down. He'd listen and evaluate what you had in mind. And he didn't have you doing things that weren't necessary. Donald Crouch was just that kind of a person.

His higher officials, they respected him because he was well settled. Wasn't like some kid right out of school who didn't know where they were at. Donald had been married for a little while to a real nice-looking girl and he was always wanting to hear from his wife, or go to see her when she'd take the train down to Texas.

Lonnie Johnson:

Out in Texas, Crouch and I rode together. His wife and my wife were stayin' in Texas, and he had an old car and we rode back and forth to camp in his car, and that made us be right good friends. I think Crouch and his wife done a lot of jackrabbit hunting together, on the side, back where they were from. Her name was Lillian [Lillie].

His wife would stay with my wife, Ila Mae, during the daytime sometimes. With Charles Eaton and his wife, we were a group of people that went out and ate lunch with our wives at a little ol' place called Fort's Café in Brownwood, Texas. That man fed us for ninety cents a plate.

Lillie and Donald Crouch

Because he was more our age and him bein' a country boy, Donald Crouch understood us better. It turned out he was a better tank commander than Foster. I had liked Foster—he'd taught us a lot—but it wasn't long until I just thought more of Donald. Foster was from the city and more of an order giver and he didn't get along with young boys too much. I had really respected him as my tank commander, but being a New Jersey policeman, Foster had a little different feeling towards people than Donald Crouch did.

Donald didn't demand things or belch out orders. Whatever he thought was necessary, he just talked to you like a site foreman telling you what he needed you to do, or maybe that's the way Donald worked with his brothers on the farm.

He'd approach you in a way that you didn't want to say anything back to him. He'd say, "Kelley, would you mind doing this? I know it's not your job, but we've got to have somebody to do it."

And I'd always say, "Why, no, I don't care to do it. Don't mind at all."

Donald always treated me extremely well. I reckon he just liked me. He always relied on me to do things that maybe he wouldn't ask the others to do and I was glad to help him. Once I got acquainted with him, well, I was real pleased with the change.

This postcard from the Crouch family depicts the Kansas jackrabbit drives in the mid-1930s when Donald Crouch hunted as a boy.

Of course, everybody in the tank crew took to him. We usually called him Donald, and not Crouch, for some reason, even though our crew went by our last names: McAbee, Knode, Rhodes, and Kelley. I guess if you had to yell it out in battle, "Crouch!" maybe sounded a little too much like "Kraut!"—slang for the enemy.

When we had to maneuver in mock battles and fire at targets, Donald would have us right where we needed to be. After some time, I had great confidence in him. He'd give the orders over the intercom:

"Kelley, let her eat! Top this hill without losing any speed." Donald wasn't familiar with my driving in all those tank races. I gave that tank the gas and prepared to skip a gear.

"Mac, load A.P. Knode, target at three o'clock. Kelley, pull to a stop. Cannon—lock on the target—Fire!" Donald was real clear and confident in his commands.

"Rhodes—personnel at one o'clock—knock 'em out before we get there!"

"Kelley, move out! Let's keep 'em on the run!"

We could all do our jobs in our sleep, just about, and as a tank crew, I think we were more than ready for real battle. After so long in training, we were eager to just get out there and get the job done. But still the army hadn't given us orders to move out, so while we kept our skills sharp, we marked our time and waited for passes to town or furloughs home.

One Saturday, we'd been out on the firing range and we came back to camp about noon. We'd gotten a new platoon leader, First Lieutenant Stephen Smith. He'd grown up in West Virginia and Virginia. He walked over to me and said, "Kelley, are you going on a pass this afternoon?"

I hardly ever went. I said, "No, I'm not plannin' on it."

He spoke real nice to me. "A lot of the men are planning to go on a weekend pass. They've got girlfriends and wives waiting for them and they want to get out of here. I know I could give you an order to help clean all their guns. But I don't want to do that. I'd like you to volunteer to do it, if you will. I'm not going to force you to do it, if you don't want to."

I said, "Well, yeah, I don't care to clean them guns up and let them boys go on a pass."

Lieutenant Smith smiled and said, "I appreciate that, Kelley. I know you always spend your weekends in camp. I've got another soldier who'll help you, so you'll be done in a little while." He sent over another boy who never did go anywhere either.

I thought it was good of Lieutenant Smith to ask me to volunteer instead of ordering me. That was kind of unusual. He was just a nice lieutenant. He's the only officer I ever had who was like that. I really didn't mind doing the extra duty, especially since Lieutenant Smith had asked me that way.

Now, some of those officers, like Captain Blake, or some of those arrogant ninety-day wonders, they wouldn't have given me a choice. You'd do what they said, or else. And they didn't care if you wanted to go on a pass or not. But Lieutenant Smith didn't bother us too much on anything, he seemed pretty much like we were, a regular feller, but a real professional officer.

Lieutenant Smith was a West Point graduate. He really knew the ropes. He was our best lieutenant and he had more knowledge of everything than most of the officers in there. He was reasonable and he always approached you with respect, even though you might only be a low man on the ladder.

If I hadn't volunteered to clean all those guns, those boys would have had to stay on the base longer. I wanted to be a friend to them and anyway, I liked to keep myself busy. Of course, the army kept us busy from sunup to sundown five days a week and a half day on Saturday.

Camp Bowie, Texas, was about sixty miles southwest of Fort Worth, and that was Ewell Rhodes country. My assistant driver was mighty excited about being stationed so near home. That meant weekends with family and his girl. I wished I had that. If we were going to be free on Sunday, they'd let him go home Saturday afternoon and he'd be back in there Sunday night with some big tale about someone in his family, some predicament they'd gotten into. He'd imitate them in his colorful Texas talk and go on, makin' us laugh. He was always telling me about things going on at home. Oh, he might talk about some feller he'd met and say he was "'bout as friendly as a bramblebush," something like that. Or say someone looked as "poor as a lizard-eatin' cat." He had a lot of sayings that kept everybody laughing.

Rhodes tried his best to get me to go home with him, I don't know how many times.

He said, "I've got the nicest little niece, she's just as pretty as she can be. She told me to bring a soldier home, she wanted to get acquainted with one. She told me she wanted me to bring her a *behaved* soldier. That little niece of mine, she's a firecracker and sweet, sweet as peach butter and she said to me—" Rhodes lifted his voice a little to imitate her—"Now, Ewell, I don't want one that drinks and carouses around, I'm not looking for that kind of a man. I want you to bring a *real nice* one home."

And Rhodes said to me, "Kelley, you'd be the very one she'd really like, if you'd go. I believe you'd just suit her." He just begged me to go with him.

"Nah, I don't want to go up there," I told him.

I wouldn't go for nothin', even though he pestered me to go about every weekend, I never would go. I was pretty bashful, really. I felt a little out of place, going to a strange home, but if he hadn't told me about

the girl, I might have gone with him. I wouldn't have minded meeting his parents, but I wouldn't go with him because I didn't want to meet his niece when I knew she was looking for a sweetheart. He couldn't *talk* me into going.

I already had Orangie on my mind and we wrote letters pretty often. They weren't romantic, like the letters some of the boys got. They'd still come in the barracks and read out loud what their girlfriends wrote them. I kept my letters from Orangie to myself. Our letters weren't sensational anyway—we just wrote to each other about everyday events.

I did show Orangie's pictures to some of the boys, though, and told them she was from South Texas. She'd sent me pictures of her hula dancing in a Hawaiian outfit. She'd borrowed one from somewhere and thought I might be heading for the South Pacific soon, since the war was raging there and tropical islands were always in the news. She'd be my "little hula girl, the best hula girl from Texas." She sent me another picture—the one picture I would take of her to the battlefield—Orangie her in her cowgirl boots sittin' up on the hood of her Uncle Frank's truck. Oh, she was really smiling and happy, and it gave me a warm feeling to think of her.

To answer her back, since I was in Texas, I went to town on a pass and

found a studio and had my picture taken to look like I was riding a bucking bronco. I sent it to Orangie and that's one of the little pictures she had of me while I was away in service, a jokester cowboy on a make-believe bronco.

Bein' in her home state, sometimes I'd see a Texas girl that reminded me of Orangie. There was a little girl sitting on the side of the highway as we went out on convoy one day, and when we got to where we were going, some of the boys came back to my tank and said, "I saw your girlfriend sitting up there on that car on the side of the highway. Did you see her?"

I said, "Yeah. I seen her. But it wasn't Orangie."

They said, "That girl was exactly like that picture you showed us."

I got out my picture to show them again and they looked at it and said, "Yep, that was her."

Another one said, "Bet she's here to surprise you."

I shook my head. "No, it wasn't her."

"Oh, yeah, spittin' image. Man's been away too long when he don't even recognize his own girl!" They went on, like boys do.

I just smiled.

They thought now Orangie had come home and she was out there watching us go by on the highway. I knew Orangie was tucked away back in Tennessee, but my buddies remembered that she was a Texas girl and they liked to tease me about her.

Since I was stationed in Texas, it was a lot closer to home by train—I didn't have to go clear across the country. When I got a furlough, I got a little more time to spend with those I loved—Orangie, my parents, sisters, and on one occasion, my closest cousin, who had been right on the front lines and had not fared so well in battle.

★ ★ ★

On February 12, beginning at 0400 and lasting until 0610, the enemy laid down an artillery concentration which exceeded any the [36th Infantry] Division had ever experienced. Nebelwerfer fire from the German's six-barreled rocket mortar came over in volleys of sixes, one after the other. The barrage was directed over a large front and was followed by a strong German attempt to retake Mt. Castellone. The 143rd Infantry with attached troops defended the Castellone Hill mass.

On Castellone, two battalions of enemy worked up the slope under cover of the concentration, coming in amongst our positions at daylight when the artillery lifted. A critical five-hour battle ensued, as, with hand grenades, machine guns and rifles — some of which were discovered frozen in the morning cold — men of the 1st Battalion, 142nd , drove off the German bid.

Had Mt. Castellone fallen, the entire Allied defensive line in the hills across the Rapido would have been seriously threatened. . . .

—A Pictorial History of the 36th Division,
U.S. Army, Austin, Texas, 1945

Sometimes I'd get to make a surprise visit home. If it was a short-notice furlough, I never did let anybody know that I was coming home. That was exciting. I was just tickled to death gettin' off that train. I was always anticipating some happy times with my family, but this one time I was a little bit worried, 'cause I'd gotten some upsetting news. It was springtime of '44, and I'd found out that my cousin Archie was in the hospital in Memphis after being wounded in combat.

Archie's deferment because he was married with a family had seemed like a good thing, but as it turned out, when the army suddenly needed additional

Archie Kelley

troops, they took whoever they needed, and this time, those boys didn't get the extensive training that I had. They only had a few weeks of training before they were sent off to the front lines.

Archie had been drafted in '43 and went overseas the same year, fighting with the 36th Infantry Division. First he'd gone to North Africa to prepare and then to Italy for combat. Now he was almost home.

I had to change trains in Memphis, so I thought I'd stop at the hospital and surprise Archie. Figured he could use some cheerin' up. I had a layover early that morning and the next train home wasn't till six o'clock that evening, so I caught the city bus over to the Veteran's Hospital, a brick rectangle with rows of white windows. Archie'd written that he could see a grassy slope from his window and, boy, he said, it was peaceful down at the Veteran's Hospital back in good ol' Tennessee, and it was.

I went up to the headquarters to ask where Archie Kelley's barracks was located. They had a gate and they were supposed to have a security guard. There wasn't anyone manning the post and I waited for a while. I thought evidently they don't have a guard on duty, so I went on down the corridors, lookin' around — saw a lot of wounded G.I.s as I passed by — and I found Archie.

"Confound it!" he said when I walked through the doorway into his room. "Quinton! Never in a coon's age did I 'spect to see you here!"

He rubbed his eyes with one hand, he was so surprised.

I was, too. They had his other hand in a medical contraption and it was all bandaged up. Other than that, he looked all right. Boy, was he glad to see me.

It was pretty early in the morning and he'd just gotten back from eating breakfast. We joked about hospital food and army food. Naturally, the first thing I wanted to know was what had got him.

"Shrapnel from artillery shellin'. I was down in a foxhole — it was way before dawn — but I's just a fixin' to take out a little ol' ration. Next thing I knowed, a bunch of shrapnel was a whizzin' by me — them Jerries started up, artillery attack. Well, I stayed low and that stuff was explodin' over us, in the dirt in front of me, everywhere. After a while, one of them things come in my foxhole and tore out a big chunk of my arm. Boy, I knew I's in trouble then."

Archie's arm was all strapped up to his elbow with hospital dressings.

"Some of the boys got it worse in that attack, though," he added. "Several of my buddies got killed right off. Boy to my left, cut his artery and he was just a spurtin' blood and his life was a drainin' away. He was prayin' to the Lord when he died. He was a real good feller, always had a funny thing to say—except then."

It was the first I detected the shock of battle. Archie said it all pretty calm as if he's readin' it in the newspaper, but he had an unfamiliar look in his blue eyes that I would understand eventually.

"And there was another good buddy, a feller who loaned me some money one time, well, after a while he was a layin' out there with machine gun fire a whizzin' over him, and he was a twistin' and a callin' out for his momma. Then, it got quiet where he's a layin'. Some of 'em die slow when bullets and stuff are a flyin' and nobody can get to 'em to help 'em." Archie fell silent.

Archie was as close to me as a brother and what he'd experienced, I could imagine. That about sent a chill through me.

"Biggest thing to me was, I knew we just had to leave 'em there and we moved on. You don't bury nobody on the battlefield. You just leave 'em for somebody later on." Archie shifted around in the hospital bed, restless. He always had a lot of energy, he never stopped movin'.

"Them shells and shrapnels and all them bullets don't stop for nothin'. They keep lookin' for you day and night. You figure one of 'em's gonna get you and you jus' keep prayin' it won't."

"Well, I sure prayed a lot that you'd be back," I said.

"I just thank the good Lord," Archie added.

Well, we got off that subject and started catchin' up on news at home. We had lots of cousins and kin that we liked "to hear tell of." Different ones got married or took ill or built a house while we'd been away.

It wasn't long, though, till I came back around to the action he'd seen. I guess I wanted to hear more about what I was facing. I asked him, "What did you do when you's over there?"

Archie'd talk a little about the fighting in Italy, but not much. Then he'd go to tellin' me more about how he got wounded. Other than that, he never did want to tell me much about his service.

Archie fought with one of the waves of troops that was right on the front lines in Italy. He was right in the thick of all that ground fighting.

For the U.S., the first ground fighting we did in mainland Europe was in Italy. The Italian people had been under their dictator Mussolini's thumb when he sided with Hitler. The Italians first thought they were fighting for the right cause to support their leader, but they weren't. They soon found that out, though, and changed their minds.

When the Allies were about to invade their country—we'd already taken back North Africa and Sicily from the Nazis—that was enough to get the Italian people on their feet out in the streets with uprisings, and finally the Italian government officially surrendered to the Allies on September 8, 1943. Italy was the first Axis power to fall.

That surrender didn't change a thing for the Allied troops about to invade, though, because German soldiers still occupied Italy. It was just one day later when the first Allied troop landing on European soil was made at Salerno, Italy. Archie's outfit, the 36th Infantry Division, was part of that, but Archie joined them after the initial assault.

Archie arrived in Europe for combat in December, when the 36th Infantry fell back from fierce fighting in the months after the landing at Salerno. They had to get replacements for all those killed and wounded. That was where Archie came in. Private William Archie Kelley fought in the 143rd Infantry Regiment, Company D.

Being a foot soldier, "a dough foot," as they called them after World War I, Archie was on his feet, lived on the ground, in trenches, most of the time. He had whatever he could carry with him, a backpack, bedroll, rations, canteen, grenades, and rifle. When he got in combat, he'd crawl around, get behind bushes to hide and find barriers to protect himself.

He joined the battles as the Allies were moving north and had already taken the important port city of Naples. The main goal was Italy's capital. But before the Allies could get to Rome, there was one natural obstacle, a barrier of mountain ridges that included Monte Castellone. There, the Germans locked Archie's division in a stalemate at the beginning of 1944 and Archie was right in the middle of it.

"Found out, at one point, the 36th lost two thousand men in just two days," Archie said. "It's a wonder we didn't all get killed over there. When it come time to run, I's a movin' faster than a fox with ol' Buck on his tail!"

I thought about the fox hunts back in the hollers of Coker Creek. Archie and I always went, but now those traditions were fallin' by the wayside since the war had come along.

"They had minefields over in Italy that were thick like a potato patch with Jumping Betsys," Archie said. "When somebody trips one, they jump up before they explode and hit you right here!" Archie tapped on his chest with his good arm.

"Them Germans was strong fighters, too, and they didn't show any sign of givin' up. They's well equipped, well positioned. Bullets was a hittin' all around me, but I was still a fightin'. I made it through all that. I stayed low, and you know I's always a good shot. I could still show you up at target practice."

I smiled. "I'd take you up on that, but I'd hate to take advantage of a crippled-up soldier."

"Aw, when you got as much practice as I got with them Nazis, ain't no trouble bein' crippled up a little. I'm as good a shot as I ever was."

"Never was good enough to outdo me," I joked him.

"If that's what you'd like to believe," he shot back.

One of the slopes that Archie was guarding, a real old Catholic monastery was located up above it, on the mountaintop they called Monte Cassino. The battles of Monte Cassino had made the newspapers, in fact, they were a little bit controversial, because of a famous religious building up there. Archie said it had been the talk of the troops when word spread that the Germans had seized that monastery as a lookout point so they could direct artillery attacks from up there.

The Allies really hated to bomb the place because it was historic, nearly as old as the gospels, but they finally did bomb it, to try to stop the German soldiers from using their artillery on the men who were coming up the mountainsides, men like Archie.

"Now, I never much believed you should bomb a church, or nothin' like that," Archie said. "But we figured them Jerries took it over and they's a usin' it to sight in artillery. And nobody could get up there to get 'em outta there. That's when I got hit. We's workin' our way up one of them slopes."

It was in the coldest part of winter, and the 36th Infantry was fighting to maintain control of the mountains where all the Allied supplies traveled through. Mule trains were the only source of supply—couldn't get vehicles up there to bring in supplies or evacuate the wounded. I think Archie said it took about seventy-five mules to supply one battalion each day.

"We had to advance along the side of the mountain in some pretty rough terrain. In Italy, they had mountains," he said, "but not like we know mountains. Them I-talian mountains are bare of trees mostly, just scrubby stuff and rocks."

Because that terrain was open, the melting snows made it muddy, and Archie told me how that mud would just stick to their boots, cake on it, and get all over everything. Of course, that helped them to blend into the hillsides.

"We's havin' it all—rain, snow, and sleet, and the hardest thing was to keep my feet warm and dry. My boots'd just wear out on them sharp rocks as I's workin my way up there, it just ate that shoe leather up," Archie said. "Sometimes I's knee-deep in mud, and if you could dig 'em, them foxholes would just fill up when it rained."

As a foot soldier, Archie'd have to dig in to keep from gettin' killed. Of course, a lot of the infantry boys would get killed in their foxholes; they were there one minute and gone the next. But those foxholes would give them some protection, just before they'd come out and attack. They'd get organized and get up close to the front lines and they'd all come out of there and charge the enemy, and, of course, the enemy was waiting for them.

The Germans had the advantage, defending a country where they were already set up. They used the slopes to hide barbed wire and thousands of antipersonnel mines and they had machine gun nests all over those mountains. The Germans were holed up in there, so they had good protection when the Allies charged them from below. They'd mow down a lot of boys and they repelled several Allied assaults, but the troops kept pushing forward and I thought Archie was the bravest man I knew, to fight all that way, under such terrifying conditions.

Archie shook his head and I never saw such a look on his face. Before I could study him, he jumped out of the bed and went to the window. "Them Krauts was always ready and a waitin' for us. We kept tryin' to advance, but our men was a dyin' all over the place. Some companies lost all their officers. They'd send us replacements, and we'd mount an attack. Then those confounded Nazis drove us back . . ."

I listened. I'd never seen Archie like this before. He'd seen war.

"That artillery was trained on us day and night, and we's runnin' low on ammo 'cause them Krauts got our supply lines cut off, and they got us pinned down on them hillsides, trying to work our way up to the top. I never did get up there."

The 36th Infantry Division stayed in the line for a month, more, and they dug into those cold Italian slopes. They'd advance a yard a day, sometimes five, that was about it, Archie said, and they paid with their blood every time they made some progress, but they were advancing.

"See, when I got hit, we was a guardin' this hill, part of the Monte Castellone ridge. We'd been workin' our way up that hillside for I don't know how many days and nights. When the Germans'd shoot that artillery from a distance, there'd be an explosion and big scraps of metal come a flyin' everywhere. A big scrap of metal caught my left arm just below my elbow and it tore out the meat along here. I looked down and my arm was just a spurtin' blood, and I don't know, I just couldn't do nothin'. I's covered in blood and I's so cold I's a shakin' like the last leaf of autumn."

Archie's buddy got to him and helped him out of that foxhole, but he didn't remember much about that.

Now, when Archie got wounded, the ground he'd gained, making it nearly to the top of that ridge, that became a hindrance to him. He was bleeding badly and the aid station was down at the bottom of the mountain. I guess they dressed the arm some way to slow the bleeding and when they could get a break in the shelling, Archie and his buddy started on the long journey back down the mountain to the aid station. I believe he had to walk part of the way and then they put him on a mule.

If it hadn't been for his buddy that was with him, Archie wouldn't have made it. He told me that. He was losin' so much blood, he went to gettin' sleepy and he wanted to lie down and sleep. But his buddy knew not to let him do that. He just kept encouraging him, kept him awake. If Archie'd been there by himself, he never would have made it, because he was gettin' to the point where the life was just drainin' out of him. If he'd gone to sleep, he'd a never woke up. His buddy, whose name I don't remember, he made sure Archie got to the medics and they took care of him after that. They had to give Archie a blood transfusion to save him.

Archie had only lasted in combat a few months. But it was better to be wounded and come home than to be one of the other possible casualties—to be captured and made prisoner, missing in action, or killed in action. Archie would be home with his beloved Gwendolyn and little Billy soon. I hadn't even gone into battle yet.

Archie sure seemed happy that he'd made it back. He'd seen so much death, he said, he didn't want to dwell on that. He was lookin' forward to some happier days with his growing family.

I tried to imagine what and all my cousin went through, seein' your buddy get killed right next to you, and knowin' that it coulda been you, but it wasn't. I couldn't begin to imagine how that felt. I'd had a lot of mock battle training, a lot more than Archie, but I knew that without the real fear, it wasn't anything like battle. How would I act, when I was faced with mortal fear? I'd find out, but I wasn't givin' it too much thought then.

In the hospital there in Memphis, the doctors had doubled Archie's hand all the way back to his wrist nearly, taped it down, and as he was getting better, they'd straighten it up so many degrees, a little at a time and rebandage it.

"I was lookin' to get a new banjo after the war," Archie said, looking at his arm. It was his left arm, the one he made the notes with.

"Aw, it'll heal," I told him, knowing it would. But I wondered if he'd be able to use that arm much. That metal had just eaten out a big hunk of his muscles.

Archie said, "Let's go into town. They'll give me a pass. Let's just go to Memphis and we'll ride the bus and look the town over."

When we got to the gate, the guard was there and he asked me for my pass. I didn't have one.

The guard said, "You mean you got in here without a pass?"

"Yes, sir. I didn't know I had to get one. Nobody was here and I stayed around a while and nobody came. I decided they must not be manning this office, so I went on in to look for my cousin."

The guard said, "There's supposed to be a man here around the clock. I just came on the shift. I don't know what happened, but now I'm supposed to call the head officials and report you." He looked us over. "I'm liable to get in trouble over this," he said, "but I guess I'll just let you go on."

We went to town and spent the rest of the day. We rode the bus all over Memphis for a little of nothin'. You just had to pay one fee and you could keep riding all you wanted. We looked the place over from one corner to the next. Memphis was a pretty good sized place when you ride from one end to the other.

We'd go looking for these "penny arcades" where they had pinball and all kinds of little ol' games. We had a whole lot of fun playing those games, though Archie had to play with one hand. We passed a few music shops where they had banjos and guitars on those Memphis streets. We looked a little bit, but we didn't go in. Then we'd get back on a bus and ride around. We talked as the scenery passed or until we spotted another penny arcade. I sure enjoyed that day. I stayed with Archie as long as I could, and he went with me to the train station. I caught the train and he caught a bus back to the Veteran's Hospital.

From Memphis, I took the *Tennessean* which was a fast train for those days, and it stopped at all the main towns on its route up north. I got off at Sweetwater, some forty miles from where I lived. I arrived there way in the middle of the night, it was about two o'clock in the morning. At that time of night, there wasn't any way to catch a train out to Tellico Plains, the next closest town towards home.

I started walking along the highway. A soldier back in that day, all he had to do, 'bout it, was get out on the highway going in the direction where he lived, and somebody would pick him up and help him get home. Wouldn't hardly nobody pass up a soldier. I hadn't walked but a little ways and a car pulled over, and the man driving it wanted to know where I was going.

"Out to Coker Creek."

He said, "Well, I'm a goin' as far as Tellico Plains. You can ride with me over there and then you can catch you a ride on out."

When I got to Tellico Plains, I knew of a man who lived there that ran a taxi service. I went to the taxi driver's home. I got up pretty close to the front door—I didn't get up on the porch—but I hollered, "Hello! Hello!" several times.

Directly, a light came on and I knew I woke somebody up. A man came to the door in his undershirt and he said, "What can I do for you? Who are you?"

I told him who I was and where I needed to go, and he said, "I don't believe I know you. What's your daddy's name?"

I told him my daddy's name and he said, "Well, yeah, I know your dad." It was the best way to know who you were dealing with, to know who a man's father was. A lot of people knew Will Kelley.

The taxi driver said right away, "Give me time to get my pants on and I'll take you out there."

He didn't take me all the way home, though. He didn't want to go up into Coker Creek—people that didn't live there were a little bit afraid to be out there at night. With its local reputation, a feller could understand that, I reckon, but I never felt a bit uneasy.

We got to the road that goes up to our house. He said, "Do you mind if I let you out here? Could you walk the rest of the way?"

It was about a mile and a half from home, and I said, "No, I don't mind at all."

He turned around and went back home and I went on, walking on the dirt road in the moonlight, carrying my duffel, and probably whistling some little tune to myself. When I got home to that little cabin that I'd missed so much, I walked up to the gate. I didn't open it, I just stood outside the paling fence.

Of course, at night, you couldn't see very well in the dark, through those tall palings. My little black dog I'd had for years, I'd been gone so long, that dog didn't recognize me, I don't reckon, and he was just having a fit, boy, he was in behind that fence and he was just barking and carrying on something awful. I didn't call his name, though.

I changed my voice a little bit and I hollered, "Hello!" I kept hollering, "Hello!" in a real deep voice.

It was customary in those rural areas not to approach the house and knock, but to stay far back, outside the gate if there was one, and holler, "Hello!" to rouse somebody out. You didn't venture up and knock on the door unless you were in a community where you knew everybody well, 'cause you didn't know whether they would receive you or not.

It wasn't long till my dad came out on the porch and he hollered, "Hello!" back to me from the shadows.

I reared back and deepened my voice, "Would you let an old man that's tired and give out spend the rest of the night with you?"

My dad hadn't caught on. He said, "Well, it depends on who it is. Identify yourself."

I said, "It don't make no difference who I am. I need a place to sleep." I talked pretty independent, with a big, growly voice.

He said, "It does make a difference. You've got to tell me who you are."

I said, "I don't see no use a that."

He said, "Well, if you come in here, you'll have to identify yourself!"

Of course, everybody back in there was a little bit jubrous of strangers comin' to their home in the middle of the night. I would have kept on with it, but then I just went to laughin' and he recognized me at once. Oh, it just tickled him to death, and he laughed about me pullin' that on him. We just about doubled over with joy.

I went on in the house, and my mother got up out of bed and gave me a big hug. My dad didn't hug me or anything, we weren't much for that, I don't know why. I'd put my arm around my mother, but my dad didn't do that, he kind of resented it when people went to hug him. His upbringing was different. He was really happy that I was home, though. I know he thought about me many a time.

My parents were proud of me being in the service, you just don't know how proud they were. People back then were a little closer than they are today. Families really had deep caring for each other because they lived closer together and depended on each other more when they were growing up. My parents showed their caring in every move that they made. They let me know that they thought a lot of me. And, of course, I was the same way about them. Our family was just like that, we were real close to each other.

Of course, at that time in my life, my thoughts included a future family of my own, and Orangie was at the center of my hopes and intentions. We might not have been the most romantic pair in public, but I guess it was my upbringing. The people around Coker Creek, they didn't do anything in public where people would know they were sweethearts. They were real strict about appearances. They didn't act in a way that people would talk about them.

I'd go down to Frank and Mamie's store, pick Orangie up, and we'd get out and ride around. That '37 Chevrolet still ran like a top. We'd ride all the way up to Bald River Falls, which is in the direction of Tellico, but out a ways, along the river. There's an old logging road out to the falls, rutted out, bumpy, and dusty, but it was worth the drive.

Near where the Bald River meets the Tellico River, a tall waterfall cascades down about a hundred feet, and the water rushes over the rocks so fast, it's just solid white most of the time. Everybody knew about those falls as bein' the biggest in all East Tennessee back then, when the rains really fed those mountain rivers.

*Traveling carnival
pictures (above)*

*Orangie and Quinton at
Smithfield School (right)*

Orangie and I would
get out of the car and
walk around, watch the
water and feel the cool
spray from the falls. We'd
sit on the rocks or wade
around in the shallows
and we had a big time
talking together. That was
a special place.

Sometimes my cousin
Atlas would be home on furlough at the same time, and his girlfriend,
Bertha Ellis, would go with us on double dates. We'd go on picnics up
at Bald River Falls and take baskets of food.

Bertha was always a nice person. Most people said she kept to herself,
but she was friendly with me. I guess when she got struck on my cousin
Atlas, she figured I'd help her out. Bertha was real good company to be
out with when you got to know her. I'd gotten acquainted with a lot of
people in the army and I knew a lot of funny little jokes. I'd tell a few

Quinton, Orangie, and Atlas at Bald River Falls

funnies and she'd giggle if you got her tickled. Of course, in the army you hear all kinds of stuff, but I never did tell anything ugly.

Atlas had his own jokes that he'd heard in the mess kitchens and he kept us laughing, too. We all just had a good clean time when we went out to Bald River Falls. Orangie and I were always glad to be together and we spent quite a lot of time out there when I was home on furlough.

Orangie was a hardworking girl—she was always working at some job or chore—and besides working at Frank and Mamie's store, she did some other work, too, while I was away, some that involved supplying the war effort. For a little while, she had stayed in a boardinghouse with some women down in Lupton City, and they all worked in a thread factory, manning machines that were just automated spinning wheels, spinning cotton into thread. Before the war it had been a man's job.

She and other women had rows of machines to tend to, she said, and she'd walk back and forth, wearin' those wide pants that women started wearing then, and she'd keep the cotton fibers from clogging the machines. I imagine that thread went into cloth for G.I. uniforms, something like that.

Orangie had been doing her part. A lot of women started working for the first time in this country during that war. Orangie already liked to get out and work for herself, so she was real glad to try different jobs that opened up because the times were changing.

Americans were really pitchin' in, too, rallying together and helping the war effort by conserving. A lot of materials were scarce because they were needed for the war. Because of that, women weren't wearing stockings, and Orangie said some of the women down at Lupton City drew a line down the back of their legs with an eyebrow pencil to look like the seam in real silk stockings.

Some women were still sewing their dresses out of feed sacks that used to come in colors and patterns — and that saved cloth. People saved rubber, scrap metal, tinfoil, and their used cooking grease and they'd take that to collection sites for the government. People bought war bonds to help finance armament. Gasoline, sugar, meat, milk, and coffee were all rationed and the government issued stamps that allowed every person to buy only so much per week. Mamie would take the coupons down at the store and sell the rationed amounts of essentials. You never did hear people grumbling about that. Everybody seemed to have a spirit of helpfulness. The whole country was willing to sacrifice to win the war and bring our soldiers home.

Sometime before I shipped out to the war zone, Orangie had gotten a job on the site of a new industrial complex about seventy miles north of Coker Creek, at a place known locally as Black Oak Ridge. At that time, there wasn't anything going on for miles and miles around, then hidden down in a valley between two parallel mountain ridges, the hustle and bustle was like a beehive.

I'd heard that a big factory complex was being built for the war effort sometime before that, somewhere up above the other side of Madisonville. All we knew about it back then was that in the fall of '42, the U.S. government went into little farming communities in the Tennessee hills and sent the inhabitants a letter saying the government was buying up land in that area and the families had to move within six weeks and leave their homes and their farms for the good of the country.

I don't think the government paid them all that much for their land, but they paid 'em. Then they cleared out the land right away and started building an industrial complex—and an entire city to support it.

Orangie went to work up there at a cafeteria built to serve the people employed on a big top secret project. Her badge, which she had to wear at all times, had two names: J. A. Jones Construction Company, Charlotte, N.C., and a facility mysteriously called Clinton Engineer Works. That's all it said.

Orangie commented, "Everybody up at Oak Ridge says, 'You go to work and you don't know nothin'. You go home and you don't know nothin'!'"

Nobody knew what they were working on, or manufacturing, if that's what it was. All anybody knew was, it was for the war. That's all that mattered. Of course, everybody wanted to "bring the boys home." And back then, you were just glad to have a job and be making a little money, so you didn't question anything.

They'd built a big train and bus depot to serve the facilities at Oak Ridge, and it was so jammed with people, Orangie said, that they'd just shove and crowd you out when you had to get on the only transportation allowed in and out of there. That was unusual behavior for our region.

Orangie lived on the site and she came home on weekends, but other workers who didn't live on site, the government bused them in to work each morning, and they'd bus them home at the end of the day. Orangie said that place was running at least three shifts, seven days a week.

"Whatever they're working on, they're not losing any time," she told me.

★ ★ ★

It was late in 1944 when we got word that we were about to be deployed in the European Theater of Operations. Before I shipped out for combat, the army let us go home on furlough one last time. It was a worrisome time, but the whole family came in and we were happy to be together for dinner at the homeplace. The familiar spicy scent of Momma's apple stack cake filled the kitchen, and because it was around Christmastime, we also had coconut cake and fresh oranges to eat. We ate Sunday fried chicken when it wasn't even Sunday. What I remember most, though, is we just sat around that kitchen table and talked with each other every minute that we could.

From the start, it was harder on my parents than it was for me, when I went away to service. They were used to my being at home a lot of the time, and when it was the first time I was far away from home, they always worried about what kind of people I associated with and what kind of corruption I was exposed to. Growin' up, they always wanted to know what I was doing, why I was going someplace, who was with me. I was used to them picking out the people that I went with, but when I was in the army, they didn't need to worry. 'Cause I wasn't getting out into the world like a roughneck, like some of them did. I was always loyal to my family. I'd write them pretty often. I told them about my tank crew, of course, what fine fellers they all were, and about other buddies I associated with.

They knew I was the only one that went to church in my barracks. Oh, maybe once in a while McAbee went with me, but I usually went alone. I noticed, though, that all my buddies expected me to go to church every Sunday. They'd mention it, and they were respectful. They might ask if it had been a good service that day, and I might tell them a little bit about it. But that was all. Whether they agreed with my thinking or not, they all were good fellers to me. They always expected me to be the kind of feller that I was, and I always lived up to that.

I heard one boy tell some of the others, "The only hopes I've got of making it through this war is because of Kelley. I know the Almighty's gonna look out for him, sure enough, and I'll be close by, so maybe some of that'll rub off."

Now, that boy wasn't from my tank crew, but he was in my company, a tank driver. He'd gamble a little bit, but he was a good buddy of mine. I never did know why he said that, but he did say it, and I guess he looked up to me a little bit.

Sometimes in a group like that, someone who sticks to his convictions is ridiculed by some of the meaner kind, but I never did have even one problem with anybody myself. Everybody treated me just as nice all the time.

On the eve of battle, you might say, my parents had more serious worries than my moral character. My dad said he'd always listen to that ol' radio I bought from Sears, to hear news broadcasts about different battles in the war. Now, more than ever, my parents worried about the consequences of war. I know that just sent a chill right through them. Nothing could protect me, if it was my time.

When it was time to leave for the train, my mother hugged me with all the strength and tenderness that were in her little hardworking arms and she hesitated to let go of her only son. She always showed so much love, so quietly.

I'll always remember my father's direct blue eyes and what he said to me before we walked out the front door. He put his hand on my shoulder and he looked squarely at me. He said, "Son, don't forget to pray." And that's all he said to me.

He realized that if I made it back, it'd be through prayer.

I took his advice. Yeah, I sure did.

CHAPTER 16

New York City

"On the double! On the double!"

I heard Sergeant Hicks barking all through the barracks. The day had come for us to move out of Camp Bowie and word was, we were headed for battle. No more delays. Sergeant Hicks told us it was time to clear out and we'd better be ready to go before dark. We loaded the tanks up, ready for transport. Everything was "Get a move on! Double-time!"

We got all our luggage and transported it to a big warehouse-sized train depot and we thought we were in a hurry to get on the train when we got there. Then we had to wait for that train all night at the depot and didn't have anywhere to sleep, only a concrete floor, and we were fussin' about that. We'd lie down and use some of our baggage to make a pillow. It was late the next morning before that train ever came to pick us up and we were really worn out. That was just the way the army did things, there wasn't no use to complain.

The 13th Armored Division left Camp Bowie, Texas, and we rolled into Camp Kilmer, New Jersey, on January 8, 1945. That first evening, they were showing a movie on the base. I wish I could remember that movie, it was a real good movie that we'd been wanting to see, so a bunch of us went to see it. It was so cold that night, it felt like the wind was comin' off a block of ice—that's something I still remember. We had to walk about a mile to the theater, and when we got back to our barracks, the furnace had gone out and we didn't have a bit of heat.

We had a cold night, one of the coldest I'd ever had, and we bundled up with our gear, even though we didn't have enough stuff to keep us warm. I reckoned they were toughening us up, getting us ready for the conditions we'd have on the battlefront.

Before we shipped out, the army issued us all three-day passes to New York City.

Oh, you never saw such a group of boys so eager to get somewhere and live it up in all your life. All the servicemen on the train to New York that bright morning had big ideas and big plans. Some of them had arranged to meet their wives at a hotel and take them on tours of the city. Some of them said they were gonna find 'em a girl in New York—they called it "chippy chasing" or "going on skirt patrol"—and they planned to dance with them to that big band music. And some of 'em were lookin' to get into trouble and find every liquor establishment in that city, I reckon. It was a big thrill for every G.I. no matter where he was from or what he liked to do, to get to visit New York City.

McAbee and I buddied up and hit the town. Both of us had never been around a large city like that and we decided to stick together. We just wanted to see the look of the place, maybe find a few penny arcades. As soon as we got in the city, we located us a hotel room. Quite a few of us from the company stayed in that hotel. It wasn't in a real tall building, maybe three or four stories up, but it was the tallest building I'd ever been in.

McAbee and I ventured out onto the streets and got tourist information and a map, and we started out with the idea that we would cover that city from one end to the other.

The Big Apple was what you heard people call it a lot. That got started back in the Great Depression when people needed money so bad they were selling apples on street corners. Now, on street corners, I saw newspaper boys with the latest news of the war and pushcarts selling different kinds of food that I wasn't familiar with. We started out right in the heart of the busiest district, I reckon, where every building and every person was just crowded together like a field of corn that had never been thinned out.

Men who were too old for military service hurried to work in wool overcoats and brimmed hats. Yeah, you didn't see a head without a hat on it. We noticed the women walking on the sidewalks, too, going to work, and how nice they were dressed. Of course, everybody was bundled up, but the ladies in New York wore all kinds of stylish hats and scarves and they looked real smart.

I think the skies were clear on that first day, but I don't know for sure. I don't know if it was very cold, but it probably was. I don't remember 'cause I was too excited about seeing the famous city that our country had built as its greatest civic achievement. That was really a treat for a country boy. I'd heard a lot about New York City and I knew it was the largest city we had in the U.S. and that its vertical buildings were something fantastic. In fact, they were at that time the tallest buildings in the world. So I liked the thoughts of being in America's largest city and the world's tallest city. Naturally, I expected to be impressed. Right away, New York exceeded my expectations.

It was amazing to see skyscrapers for the first time. You'd just about have to lie down to see the top of them from the streets. Of course, I knew what skyscrapers looked like, 'cause I'd read about them and seen pictures of them in magazines over the years. In person, it was overwhelming to see structures that humongous, and to know how they had been built, with those steel beams all riveted together, one level after another, by men balancing themselves on those beams, building up into the sky.

That didn't amaze me quite as much as the subways, though. I thought to myself, what about that!—underground trains! I'd never even heard of subways growin' up. The trains had steel rivets around the doors and windows, and the windows were big, so I could see some of the tunnels we traveled through. All of that network underneath the city was amazing to me. We could just go anywhere we wanted, and it didn't hardly cost us a thing, get off wherever we wanted and come up on the street and fool around. Go back on the subway, ride another stretch, and go somewhere else.

There weren't too many cars up on the streets in New York, because gas was rationed and that slowed everything down. But the subways were crowded. There were always a lot of people, shoulder to shoulder. You just had to stand up and people rode hanging onto straps so they wouldn't fall into their neighbor. They'd just cram in there. You barely had room to get in those electric doors before they closed on you. And they don't give you much time, neither; you've got to get in there 'cause they don't wait on nobody. I found that out myself. They'll just take off when you're trying to get on them.

McAbee and I kept on the move. We could cover any territory we wanted, go see somethin' we'd heard about, right quick. We really rode those subways. We must have ridden every one. That's the way we traveled and we covered that city from top to bottom, one end to the other.

I was amazed when we'd run up the stairs to the street and we'd be right close to whatever it was we wanted to see. I remember coming up to the street in Times Square. I can't describe it a bit more than nothin'. I just remember that we went to Times Square and I saw giant advertising signs as big as the buildings. If you're not expecting to have to tell what you see, you don't try to really absorb it, like you would if you went there for that purpose. But I didn't see a thing that I didn't like the looks of. Oh, I thought New York was a fine city.

I thought it bein' a big city and all, it'd be hard to find your way around. I was afraid we'd get lost, but we didn't have a bit of trouble. We found that New York City was one of the easiest places to find your way around, with streets and avenues neatly arranged in numbered grids.

Of course, we went down to the old part of New York, where they had cobblestone streets with names, not numbers. The buildings were of red and brown brick, and a lot smaller than the skyscrapers. They had all the things you'd expect on a main street in any town — grocery stores, drugstores, coffee shops. It was a sight in the world how many there were, though. Street after street of businesses. And, of course, we saw the apartment buildings where people lived pent-up on top of each other.

We found the people to be helpful and friendly. People in that city kind of reached out to us, 'cause they figured we had a job to do and they depended on us to get it done. They said, "Hello!" to us on the streets, and they offered to take us out for lunch and different things. Aw, we wouldn't go with them, but they'd ask us. Most of the time, we just took care of ourselves 'cause the army had cautioned us about not getting too familiar with people. There were people out there who would pick you for information that the enemy would like to get. So the army really cautioned us not to mix and mingle with people that were too friendly. But I think most of the G.I.s violated our government rules a lot on that.

McAbee and I looked in the doorways of some places where servicemen went in and out, where we could hear the brassy sounds of that big band music on the street. I never did stay in a place like that, though. Everybody was always drinking and I kept myself out of trouble. But as we passed, the music made me turn my head, and some places, we stopped in just to see what it was like. Being a musician, McAbee liked to hear what kinds of music they had up in New York, too.

Dolled-up ladies with fancy hairdos leaned into microphones and sang all those jazzy tunes that were popular. I noticed those singers liked to close their eyes when they belted out their songs. It seemed to make them sound better, when they reared back and closed their eyes to sing. It wasn't our kind of music, but McAbee and I couldn't help tapping a foot to the rhythm. They were singing a lot of songs from Glenn Miller at the time.

Some of 'em said that Glenn Miller, the famous big band leader, practically created the big band sound. He led the Glenn Miller Army Air Force Band and entertained the troops with songs like "Moonlight Serenade" and, the one I always liked, "Chattanooga Choo Choo." But just about three weeks before I got to New York, Glenn Miller had been in U.S. Army aircraft that crashed over the English Channel and the newspapers reported that he was missing in action. So we heard a lot of his tunes, especially at that time, as everybody was remembering his music.

We'd stay up till about midnight before we ever turned into our hotel. A lot of things were open late into the night. Now, some girl, in one place I remember, she tried to get us to join a party. It was a pretty fancy kind of a place.

She stepped out of a doorway and onto the street, smiled at us and said, "Hi, boys. Some girlfriends of mine are having a party and I don't have a date. How about coming with me in here and keep me company?" She motioned to the half-open doorway, where smoke, music—and liquor, I reckoned—were mixed.

I just said, "No, ma'am, we're not lookin' for a party."

That girl followed us a little ways down the street, tryin' her best to get us to come back. I ignored her.

McAbee called to her, "There's another group of G.I.s a comin'. You'll find you some company there."

We were just goin' up and down those streets to see what there was. We went to some of these places where they had—I don't know, something like a penny arcade—where they had all kinds of little ol' games to play. Most of the time they had a bunch of girls that operated them, 'cause I guess most of the boys were in service. One place, they had a girl in there and that girl tried her best to get me to go in the back room with her.

She said, "Come back here. I want to show you something," and she motioned with painted fingernails to someplace behind a curtain.

I wouldn't go with her, I didn't know what she was up to. She reached out and took my arm. She was trying to get me to go back in a room at the end of the hallway.

She said, "Come on. I want to show you something that I think you'll like." I don't know whether she was up to some mischief or not. She was being a little too friendly to suit me, now. Me bein' an ol' country boy, I hadn't been used to nothin' like that. Of course, I didn't tell her that I was just a country boy, but I guess she detected it and that was the reason she kept on. She could tell it was embarrassing me, and she thought she'd really play it up. But I wouldn't go with her. I didn't take any chances on that. I reckoned she was being so friendly because I was in service.

Being in the military was probably the only way I would have ever gotten to see New York. We met a lot of people who'd talk to us because we were servicemen. They'd just go out of their way to try to entertain us and they treated us extremely well. We were a little bit like celebrities.

People would offer to pay for our meals or give us tickets to a show, just because we were dressed as an American soldier.

"Southerners are supposed to be known for hospitality," McAbee told someone we met, "but y'all New Yorkers have us 'bout beat on that. We sure do thank you, but we can't accept."

McAbee was quick to make a good-natured remark, and the New Yorkers that we encountered seemed to appreciate it. McAbee was the best-natured feller you ever knew. He was a little-bitty feller, not too much meat on him. He had thick eyebrows and looked serious, like he was eyein' you up, but really, he was a jolly little feller.

We were at a city bus stop and noticed that somebody had dropped quite a bit of change under the street. There was a metal grating and under it was an opening that went several feet down and we could see all kinds of coins down there. McAbee and I were joking about how we could get them.

A feller standing near the bus stop told us, "You see those men with long sticks? They make their living by picking up coins when people drop them. They put chewing gum on the end of a stick, reach it down between the gratings and pick up the coins." He cautioned us, "You better not get caught trying to get their coins, or you'll be in trouble. They guard their turf." We thought that was unusual, and we moved on.

McAbee and I wandered into a big department store, pretty sure it was Macy's. We weren't lookin' to buy nothin', but how come us to wander in there, we were walking down the street, and right by the door this feller introduced himself. He talked to us a little bit and he said, "I'd like to take both of you through this department store and show you around, give you a full tour."

Since we were servicemen, he wanted to do something to entertain us. I was a little bit leery of him at first. He was a little older than we were, but not much, dressed as a civilian, and he told us that he had a disability discharge from the U.S. Army. He'd been in the military, so we thought it'd be okay to go with him.

In that big department store, the people in there everywhere seemed to know him. He'd just say, "I'm showing these boys around."

And they'd say, "Why, certainly, go ahead," and they'd call him by name, but, of course, I've forgotten what it was. He took both of us through all the different departments and introduced us to all kinds of people. Some of them wanted to know where we were from, and they seemed to get a kick out of hearing that we were from South Carolina and Tennessee. Reckon some of 'em hadn't met too many Southerners.

That feller took us all through that big department store and told us it covered the entire city block between two avenues. If that wasn't big enough, it was, oh, several levels. There was an elevator to travel up and down through the store. That store had enough stuff to make a Sears and Roebuck catalog look like a little ol' pamphlet. Oh, it amazed me, 'cause I never had seen anything like that. I didn't look at the merchandise too much, 'cause I didn't have money to buy stuff. I just liked to look around and see how the place was laid out.

After we'd covered that store from top to bottom, that feller said, "I grew up here and I'd like to show you both around the city, if you'd like to go."

Now, of course, the army had told us to beware of people who tried to befriend you, but we didn't pay a bit of attention to that. We took him up on it and he took us to a lot of the New York attractions.

He said, "I'd like to show you Madison Square Garden. Have you ever heard of it?"

"Oh, yeah!" McAbee said.

"I grew up listenin' to all them fights they had there," I told him.

I'd first heard about Madison Square Garden sitting on the floor of my neighbor's cabin, hearing the radio on Saturday nights. I liked to listen to the big prizefights and I'd imagine what the ring and the audience looked like by listening to the echoes of the bell and the roar of the crowd. The way the announcers called the fight, you could imagine what was going on just like you were seein' it. I was mighty excited to see where all those famous prizefights took place.

When we got to the gate, that New York feller said to the security guard, "I'd like to take these boys in here and show them around."

The guard said, "Why, certainly! Take them right on. Just show them around good." I saw that the guard was acquainted with that feller and that gave me a feeling that he was all right. They were charging other people. They had to pay a fee to get in there. But we just walked in like we owned the place, free of charge for us.

There wasn't a show going on at that time. What we got to see was behind-the-scenes. That New York feller knew all about the building, how they managed to change from a regular show, like the circus, to an ice show. That's one thing that I remember more than anything. We went down to where their cooling system was located, and he showed us how, when they wanted to have an ice show, they turned it on and froze ice on the floor so they could have ice hockey games and ice-skating reviews.

He pointed out that in the bleachers there at Madison Square Garden, one of the handrails was bent way back. He said they'd had a rodeo where they were roping bulls and one of those bulls had butted that handrail right where people were sitting and really bent it back. Those bulls just about go crazy when they get them in a ring and lasso them. It makes them mean. There was a woman in a red dress sitting in the first row, that feller said, and that bull just went wild after her. When the bull bent that handrail, they never did straighten it out. He said, "That's been here for years."

That New York feller told us stories like that about the place. He said this was the third Madison Square Garden that they'd built. Well, it wasn't square at all and it had nothing to do with a garden. It was just a huge rectangle with tiers of seats, and from the outside it had a lot of glass and a big lighted sign. He said the first one was built near a place called Madison Square back in the 1800s, but they'd moved the location since then. Over the years, those New York businessmen kept building those arenas bigger and better, like most of the things they built in New York.

Everywhere we went, people knew that New York feller who was showing us around. Law, he must have been like a celebrity around there, but I don't know who he was. All he had to do was tell the manager he wanted to take us through someplace, and they always said, "Go right ahead!" So he was well known. He stayed with us for a long time that day. We were lucky to get a tour like that.

He wanted to take us to lunch that afternoon and McAbee and I felt it would be all right to go with him. I was glad we did, 'cause it was a

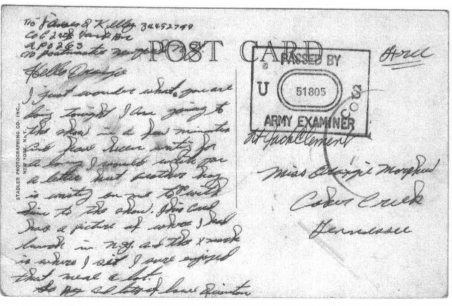

fancy place down on Park Avenue, some kind of private club for businessmen called the Advertising Club, and the food they served was some of the best I'd ever eaten. When we left, he told us to be sure and see the Chrysler Building and we thanked him and set off in that direction.

It's not as tall as the Empire State Building, but it's nearly that tall. The Chrysler Building's elevators took us up about as high as we could go, I guess, and a lot quicker than I expected. I was surprised it made my ears pop.

The Chrysler Building had a public observation area at that time. It was where the top of the building narrows, so the walls slanted in. They had them decorated with stars and planets. Of course, up that high, the only thing you wanted to do was look outside.

The windows were shaped like the letter "A." You could walk up to them and look down over the rooftops and see how many buildings there were. Oh, it was just block after block of towers, all crowded together down below. I could just pick out all of the beautiful buildings. It seemed like the way the city was laid out was real sensible, without a bit of waste.

I could hardly believe I was standing that high above the ground. I could see over the city and everything, even the water that circled the island. And being up there in the sky, why on some days, I bet you were standing in the clouds. The day I was up there, it was clear, and that sky was just as blue. That view made a real pretty picture, for a city.

There was a guide up there talking to the groups of people who were touring and he told us how the Chrysler Building came to be built around the time I was just a floppy-haired kid on Coker Creek. Up in New York, the big businessmen were competing with each other to see who could build the tallest building in the world. There was a race on and a lot of buildings started going up, but two of 'em were neck and neck to win the title of world's tallest skyscraper—the Manhattan Bank Building and the Chrysler Building. When the Chrysler's builders learned that the Manhattan Bank was going to be built two feet higher than their building, they pulled a trick at the last minute.

The Chrysler's builders designed a metal spire—it looked to me sort of like a church steeple—and they kept it a secret as they pieced it together inside the top floors of the Chrysler Building. When it was too late for the Manhattan Bank to change their plans, the Chrysler's builders hoisted up the entire point of their building and riveted it into place. It was so tall that they topped out their competition by over a hundred feet.

The guide told us that gleaming spire up top was covered with a new material that wouldn't rust, a type of stainless steel made by a German steel manufacturer, Krupp Steel—who now manufactured arms for the Nazis.

When it was completed back in 1930, the Chrysler was the tallest building in the world. But that same year, the Empire State Building started going up. It quickly took the title of the world's tallest building and in 1945, it still was. I could see the Empire State Building from the windows of the Chrysler. It was pretty close, and I could tell it was taller, but I didn't have a desire to go up in it. I really liked what I saw of the city's second-tallest building.

On that tour, they showed us some of the first television sets that had been made. They were just developing television technology at that time and they demonstrated it. There were quite a few servicemen and they picked out one G.I. and had him go into another room where they had a television camera set up and they had him to say a few words to us.

The rest of our group watched a television set. It wasn't hardly clear, it was a little bleary, but it was clear enough till you could tell it was the same boy they took in there. I was really amazed.

WCBS-TV had a transmission tower at the top of the Chrysler Building and they were able to broadcast pictures from there. Of course, television wasn't really on the market then. It was a new technology that they were trying to perfect and the broadcasts were mostly experimental. Up till then, I'd never even imagined that anything other than sound could be transmitted into people's homes, and the radio still seemed miraculous to me.

They told us that by the time the war was over, we might be able to buy a television set, as soon as there were some made. That was a coming thing, and they were sure that televisions would be plentiful one day.

I didn't hardly know what to think, 'cause I didn't know what it took to do that. But it was amazing to know that one day we would see people clear across the country, and they'd look like they were talking to you in your living room. And really they were, you could pick them up and pull them in.

Before we left New York, some of us bought tickets to see a show at Radio City Music Hall. That's the first time I ever got to see anything like that, and McAbee, too. It was a big treat for us.

We went with some servicemen, but there were a lot of civilian people there, mothers with children. I looked up from the crowd, and the building just about took my breath away. The lobby was decked out with glittering mirrors, hanging lights, and a wide, curved staircase. Oh, it was a beautiful theater. The ceiling arched over a big stage and row after row of seats went right up to the roof. It seated over six thousand people—the largest auditorium in the world at that time.

The thing that amazed me the most was the stage. It was really something to see, the way it was fixed. That was the first time I'd ever seen a choir come up out of the floor, raised from beneath the stage. When the singers finished their song, they'd lower them down. There was some sort of cover; they did other things over the top of it, singing and dancing in costumes. It was more than likely some kind of music pertaining to the military and the war, but I don't remember exactly what they sang, just music to rouse people up in support of our troops and our country.

Songs like "God Bless America" were popular. A lot of radio broadcasts ended with "The Star-Spangled Banner." It was a patriotic time.

On the streets of New York, I saw lots of American flags flapping in the winter wind and stars up in people's windows showing that a family had sons in the war. It was a heartening sight to see. It was real heartwarming, too, all the generosity and appreciation from those New

Yorkers because they saw that we were about to ship out for our tour of duty. They just bent over backwards to see that we had a wonderful time before we went off to fight.

Being in New York made me feel swelled with pride to be an American. I felt as tall as the great skyscrapers, about a thousand feet high. That American Spirit—to be the best, to reach the top, to *win*—that feeling was all around me, everywhere I looked. The competitive spire of the Chrysler Building, the well-dressed men and women riding those clean underground trains, from top to bottom, I saw some of the best that this country had to show.

In 1945, America led the world in architecture, industry, and all kinds of technology. The freedoms we'd had made it possible for people to succeed in many ways, and this fine city was just one result. Oh, that Big Apple, I really liked that city. New York had a way of makin' you feel small and tall at the same time.

By now, I'd seen quite a bit of the country—California, Texas, and now, New York—and, boy, I felt the USA was a great place to live, a great land to call home. I was glad to do my part to protect it. I felt like I really wanted to do my best for my country by the time I left New York.

CHAPTER 17

Liberated France

We carried our duffels up the gangplank of the transport ship and some of those boys who'd been drunk for about the last three days, they could hardly walk that straight line. I think some of 'em were seasick before they ever got on a ship.

We had to walk what seemed like a mile through a maze of steel hatches, down hallways, up and down ladders, all painted the color of an old gray mare. Everybody was bumping their heads and grumbling about it. When we got to our quarters, they had us packed in there like chickens in a coop, bunks stacked three high.

When we went to bed, we hadn't moved out of the dock. The next morning, we woke up and some of the fellers said, "Well, we're still sittin' here in New York. We ain't never moved off the dock."

The ship was just as still, seemed like.

A few of the boys got up, got their clothes on, and went up on deck.

They came back all excited, saying, "You can't see land nowhere. We're already way out at sea!"

The next night, we hit a pretty rough storm. Those waves made that ship just rock and roll. That ship would dip into the ocean and the front of it would go down so deep, the water would come up over the bow and come way back on the deck.

Down in the bunks, some of those boys would call out for Momma! in their sleep. It was really getting to them. I guess their mothers had babied them around. I never did hear one call for their father, though. Always calling for mother.

About the time we had to get up, everybody that jumped out of their bunks, nearly, got sick, about the time they hit the floor. They'd start to get their clothes on and just as soon as they did, one right after another, they'd have to vomit. I hadn't got out of my bunk yet, but they'd told us when we bedded down the night before to hang our steel helmet right by our bed because if we got sick, we'd need something to vomit in. I was laughing at some of those boys who were grabbing their helmets, bending over, and filling them up. I thought I was doing just fine.

When I got up on my feet and went to tryin' to get my clothes on, everything just started going 'round and 'round. Yeah, they'd told us, "Have your steel helmet handy. You'll need it." And, boy, I did.

I'd have to go and empty it, wash it out, when I got to where I was able, so I just stayed in the head most of the time during the day. That was rough. That seasickness is a terrible feeling, about the awfulest feeling ever.

It helped a little, I reckon, to get fresh air. A few days into the journey, there'd be several of us fellers a layin' up on deck, so sick we could hardly move. It was bitter cold and the spray from the North Atlantic felt like ice. It was the first time I'd ever been on the ocean. When I looked out across that dark water, it looked like it could swallow up that big ship in one mighty wave and, of course, it could. That horizon kept sliding up and down like a seesaw.

I was just as sick as I could be, a layin' out there on that deck, head hangin' over the side of the ship, a vomitin'—again.

Sergeant Hicks came by and he said to me, "Soldier! You better get back here. You'll fall off the ship."

I said, "I'd be better off if I did, sick as I am."

He just walked on.

It took us eleven days to cross the Atlantic and I was sick all the way and didn't eat hardly nothin'. That ship had a big mess hall and good cooks, or that's what some of 'em said. A lot of the boys weren't bothered by the rocking of the ship and they'd go through the chow line twice. But the smell of that food trapped down in that ship made me sick all over again. The only thing I could eat were some little ol' cheese crackers that I bought. I was so weak when we got to Le Havre, France — that's where we unloaded — we had our duffel bags to carry and I could hardly carry mine.

It was January 29, 1945, early in the morning, when we got our first sight of liberated France. We came into a harbor there and the weather was foggy and snow covered the ground. Le Havre was a big harbor where you could land equipment. Germany, I know, hated to give that up because that gave us a good chance to bring our equipment in closer to the battle zone.

Our ship tied up along the docks. Through the fog, I could see that some of the piers were splintered and the buildings on the waterfront had big holes — if they were even standing at all. There at Le Havre, they'd really had some battles. I could see a lot of destruction from when the Allies took that port from the Germans. The British had done saturation bombings. There was just rubble and stuff, buildings blown apart, torn down, or maybe just one wall of a building blown out.

There were some French people at the dock in ragged clothes, and they looked like they'd had it pretty hard. They looked up to us and called out some things that I didn't understand. Some of the boys tossed down cigarettes, oranges, and chocolate bars from the deck, and the French people scrambled around to catch the presents, yelling, "*Merci! Amis!* Americans! Yanks!" and they waved at us, glad to see us. I reckoned they were so happy 'cause they were out from under Hitler's rule.

The Allies had been striking hard at the occupying Nazis, restoring freedom to people. They'd been forcing Hitler's troops to retreat across France, back towards the German border. The goal as the Allies moved inland was to push into the heart of Hitler's "Fatherland," but Allied ground troops hadn't been able to invade Germany yet.

Even though the battles ahead of us would be deadly, I was sure thankful that I hadn't been part of the bloody battles that had come before us, from what I heard.

We all heard stories about the storming of Normandy beaches in June 1944. They had young boys in there, our own American boys that hadn't had but a few weeks' training. They didn't know what to do, hardly. They put them on that Normandy beachhead and the Germans just mowed them down, killed them by the thousands, and that's if they even reached the beach before they died. They said the water along the beach turned red, more blood than water. They sent those boys in there, wave after wave. They must have sent the less experienced boys in because they knew they were gonna get mowed down. Evidently, the army didn't want the well-trained soldiers, like we were, to get killed right off. That's what we figured.

Of course, there at Normandy beach wasn't a good place to have launched an entire armored division. We had to use armored equipment in terrain that we could travel over, and just coming off of a beach wouldn't be a very good place until after you got back from the beach quite a ways. Our military used a lot of artillery and brought in vehicles, but as far as tanks, they didn't use a lot of tanks when they first invaded.

The Germans had a lot of machine guns set up and tunnels dug—they were well fortified. The Allies had to overcome that. And we did, just by having more people to die on our side than on the German side, 'cause they had more protection. The American soldiers didn't have much protection going in there, but we had to do something, we had to make a turning point in the war and that was the turning point, overcoming that Normandy beachhead. Then the Americans fought their way inland and kept pushing the Germans out of France.

By late August of '44, the city of Paris was liberated from German occupation. By autumn, much of France was in Allied hands. Now, the Allies included the Soviets—they didn't fall to Hitler's armies over in Russia—and together, the Allies had already freed much of Eastern Europe. Parts of Poland, Czechoslovakia, Romania, Bulgaria, and Yugoslavia were under Allied control by this time in the war.

When we got to France, they'd just had what everybody called the Battle of the Bulge, over in Belgium. We just missed that. There was a whole lot of talk about that Battle of the Bulge. We'd get our information from military briefings when they informed us about what we were facing, and the *Stars and Stripes*, a newspaper put out for servicemen. Of course, stories passed through the troops, when we learned just how terrible the situation had been for our fellow G.I.s.

Germany had lost that Battle of the Bulge, but they sure did kill a lot of our men. It was really the big battle that happened in the wintertime of '44 and '45. The Germans were more adapted to the winter weather and that gave them an advantage. They had white uniforms that made them nearly invisible in the deep snow, and our side just had olive drab—didn't even get winter uniforms. I knew from winters on Coker Creek, when snow lays on the ground in the woods, you can really see a target movin' a long ways off.

In that Battle of the Bulge, the Germans took our troops completely by surprise in a forested region of Belgium, the Ardennes. They attacked during a heavy snowstorm that grounded all Allied planes, so there was no help from the air, not even air reconnaissance. Back then, of course, aircraft relied on visuals and if it was cloudy, that pretty much grounded them.

Three German armies surged into the Ardennes region where the Americans were heavily outnumbered. That's where the Germans penetrated the Allied front line and drove part of our troops back. That's why they called it the Battle of the Bulge, because of that bulge of Allied troops that got trapped by the Germans. They were completely surrounded in the town of Bastogne, under siege, and they got cut off and had to wait until reinforcements and supplies could reach them. I heard a lot of them got frostbite waiting for help. Of course, frostbite was a minor thing, when they were being slaughtered. The Germans tried to get the Americans to agree to a surrender, but they refused.

Of course, as it happened, the weather finally cleared and the Allies airdropped supplies. Bombing attacks began on German tank units. And troops like Patton's Third Army that were racing to get to the trapped soldiers, they arrived and then the Americans were able to put up a good fight and drive the Germans back. The Germans started retreating when they saw that the Allied troops were overrunning them.

That was the only battle that really went against us, for a time, that Battle of the Bulge. The Germans liked to have pushed us back. They really killed a lot of soldiers there. The Americans alone had over 80,000 casualties. A lot more than at Normandy beach. That was the last big stand for the Germans that really counted for them, and after we defeated them there, they had their back broke then. They never could make a comeback, but they sure tried.

Winning that Battle of the Bulge gave us control of more roadways into Nazi Germany. Now, a mass invasion of Germany was about to happen. We all knew the Germans meant to defend their country to the last shell, the last bullet, the last man. They would be setting up defenses to try to keep us out. That's when the 13th Armored Division arrived in the European Theater of War.

The Germans hadn't been gone long from where we were in France, near Le Havre, because there were dead soldiers layin' along the banks of the road when the army transported us from the ship to our assembly area. We stood in the backs of open trucks for about fifty miles in freezing weather with the wind whippin' us. Every once in a while somebody would point out a body, where a German soldier had gotten killed and nobody had picked up the body. Of course, the Germans didn't have a chance to pick up their dead. And the Frenchmen, they didn't fool with doing it, 'cause I guess they were mad at the Germans for getting into war with them. The bodies of the German soldiers, they'd just be a layin' there, where they fell, on either side of the road, twisted and lifeless like a dead rattlesnake. I believe they were usually facedown, and you knew right away that they were German soldiers from their gray uniforms. I just remember seeing them as we passed and we commented about it.

"There lays another Kraut. Won't bother nobody else," somebody'd say and flick his cigarette butt toward the crumpled body in the ditch.

It didn't have much effect on me, 'cause I expected to see all of that and maybe a lot worse. I knew why we were there.

We arrived at our assembly area in the interior of Normandy. Headquarters battalion set up in the nicest building, a mansion of some type. Other troops, like the infantry, stayed in humble homes or barns or just about any kind of outbuilding that was available.

Our crew was a little luckier than that. They took the 24th Tank Battalion to an abandoned schoolhouse, a brick building that was three or four stories tall, in a place called Totes, France. That's where our company stayed until we got organized and ready for our first combat.

That schoolhouse was just a shell of a building. Not a stick of furniture in the place. No running water. Not far behind the school and down a little bank, there was a creek and it ran pretty and clear. Some of us would get our water out of that creek and we'd use purification tablets that we had. I was used to getting my water from a creek anyhow.

They had a big cistern at the corner of the school building, and it bein' a lot closer, I think some of the boys got their water out of there. But I just couldn't bear the thoughts of drinking the water that came out of that cistern, because I didn't know what those Germans might have thrown down in there. They might have thrown dead animals and everything else down there, and you wouldn't know it, so I tried not to use that water.

The schoolhouse had been abandoned by the Nazis shortly before we got there. They'd lived in those same rooms. We slept where they'd put down their Lugers and Mausers. The walls were damaged plaster and there were several floors of rooms. Our company was in the upstairs. My tank crew bedded down in one little room, four of us, except Donald. The tank commanders got a little nicer room where they slept, 'cause that's the way it was in the army.

We had to sleep on the floor in our sleeping bags. The Germans had put straw in there and we just put our sleeping bags on the straw. I was really worried about that, because Knode was almost a chain smoker, and when he saw it was getting time to head for Germany, he'd wake up all through the night and have to light up a cigarette. I was afraid he'd go to sleep and set that straw afire. I'd caution him about it. "Knode, you're gonna fool around and burn us up in here. You'll nod off to sleep with one of them lit cigarettes."

He said, "Oh, there ain't no danger there. I never go to sleep smokin' a cigarette." Now, I didn't know whether he would or not, and he didn't know either. But he'd argue that there wasn't a bit of danger. We all tried, but we couldn't talk him out of his cigarettes.

Naturally, Knode was on edge thinking about what was to come. We'd hear about so many troops getting killed in places that were a lot closer to us now, it began to seem a little more real. We didn't know exactly what to expect, but, of course, it was good that we were young and rarin' to go. That was a big help.

Weapons, ammunition, fuel, and vehicles began to arrive. The army shipped new vehicles over there. All the drivers—truck drivers, tank drivers, or anyone who drove—we went to work picking up those vehicles.

They took us on a truck to the port of Le Havre every morning. We'd get whatever they unloaded off the ship—trucks, half-tracks, or tanks, and we'd bring them back in a convoy to a little town where the army distributed all the equipment. Other companies would meet us there and pick up their vehicles.

The army never did know exactly when the ship would arrive at the port. We'd have to just wait around in the town of Le Havre and it would be late in the evening when we'd leave and we wouldn't get back to camp till midnight or later. Then they'd get us up early the next morning and send us back down after another bunch of tanks or trucks. It took a lot of time to assemble all the equipment an armored division needs.

One night, we went to Le Havre to pick up equipment and I got to drive a half-track. I never had driven one before. That's a vehicle with truck tires on the front and tank tracks on the back half. We had more men than equipment that night, so Lonnie Johnson, who was also a tank driver, he got to ride back with me.

As it happened, Johnson and I were on the tail end of the convoy. Now, I never did like bringing up the rear. It was the first time I'd gotten a position like that.

I had been excited about driving the half-track—until I realized that I couldn't keep up. The vehicles in front of me were headin' off pretty fast, getting smaller and smaller.

"Lordy mercy!" Johnson said. "Kelley, you better floor this thing. They'll be out of sight in no time."

I was flooring it, but that half-track wouldn't go any faster. The army had governors on all the vehicles when we were in training to keep them from burning too much fuel, but when we got over in France, they gave us permission to open the governors up, if they weren't set for maximum speed, 'cause they figured we'd need all the power we could get.

On this half-track, they had the governor on it set too low and it couldn't get enough fuel to keep up. I hadn't been trained on half-tracks, and neither had Johnson, so we didn't know where the governor on it was. So I just kept that pedal on the floor.

After a little while, the column went out of sight and Johnson and I were just out there drivin' in the night. I didn't know what might happen to us, just out there by ourselves. We were a little bit leery about being picked off by a sniper in that open vehicle, but we made it in okay.

Over in France, you didn't know if all those people were your friends. Of course, they'd been overrun by our people and didn't have much choice but to be friends to us. The French were usually pretty friendly, but you didn't know if they were telling you the truth. And you didn't know if one of them might get off a shot at you along a dark roadway, maybe try to steal something off of you, 'cause they were desperate. Hitler had taken just about everything they had—food, clothes, fuel.

While we were getting ready to move into Germany, we got a shipment of gas that came in five-gallon cans. It was no telling how many five-gallon cans of gas we had. Took a pretty good-sized tract of land to sit it on, and they put guards out there.

I pulled guard duty one night and I was walking around all that gas and I heard a little bit of noise. I was going in the direction of the noise, and I hurried it up, pretty fast. When I got out there about where I thought the noise was, I started shinin' my flashlight around. I don't know if it had been an old creek or roadbed or what, but all along the perimeter of that land a ditch ran down by the side of the stacked gas cans, and I saw two cans of gas sittin' up on the bank of that ditch.

I said to myself, now, somebody's carried that off and heard me a comin' and they set it down. I just kept quiet, turned my flashlight off. I thought, well, maybe I'll see somebody move. The moon was shinin' a little bit.

I stood there waiting a long, long time. I thought maybe a man was down in that ditch. I thought he might come out if he thought I walked around the back side of all that gas. So I walked on until I was out of sight and I thought, now he'll come out of that ditch directly, and I doubled back.

In a little bit, sure enough, I saw a motion way down there and I could tell it was a man. He'd come up out of that ditch, but he was a long ways from me. He'd been watchin' me, 'cause he waited till I'd walked out of sight and then I saw him hurry away through a bunch of trees. I don't know whether it was apples—they had a lot of apple orchards in France. He went through the orchard and was out of sight just in a few seconds. I said, well, that was the feller that was gonna get the gas and carry it off. I was just guessing, it might not have been. But I scared him off.

I didn't know who it was, a Frenchman, or it may have been some of our own troops, because some of them were pretty bad to steal stuff like that. They could sell it to the Frenchmen and get money out of them, or get whatever it was they wanted, maybe get liquor from them. It was a shame, but we had to guard against some of our own people, to keep them from selling our supplies to the French.

You had to report anything that happened, so I reported it the next morning to my officer of the guard and he reported it to the lieutenant in charge. When we had our formation the next morning at roll call, the lieutenant announced, "Last night, we had a man who almost got away with our gas and this man was neither shot at nor killed."

This lieutenant was pretty put out. He paced back and forth and said, "And we have a man in this company who let that thief get away." Of course, he told them who it was. "Kelley was on guard last night and he decided that he knows better than his superiors. He knows better than the United States Army about when to shoot . . ." He went on with a bunch of stuff, giving me down the road, and I just had to stand at attention and take it.

He said, "Kelley! After this formation, I want to see you in my quarters."

The officers had a little office set up in the old schoolhouse. So I kept thinking about it and I said, boy, that lieutenant's gonna give me a real goin'-over, now.

I'd really had no chance to shoot at the man. I could have shot down in that ditch, shot down towards whoever might be in there, but I had no clear sight to hit anybody. And I didn't even know who it was; might have been somebody that wasn't even up there to get that gas supply, since those cans were a sittin' on the bank when I first saw 'em.

In his office, the lieutenant asked me, "Why didn't you shoot at him?"

I said, "Well, I didn't know who it was, sir. I didn't know whether it was one of our soldiers 'cause I could just barely see him in the moonlight. I don't know whether he's the one that carried that gas out to the edge of the ditch or not. I figured it might be, but I didn't shoot at him 'cause I didn't know for sure."

Aw, he didn't like that. He said, "You should've shot at him and if you'd killed him, it would have been all right."

Then the lieutenant never did say any more about it. He said, "You're dismissed, Kelley."

I saluted him and left.

I had been reluctant to shoot. I might have shot down there and killed one of my buddies slinking around in the middle of the night. That would have been terrible. I don't believe any of my best buddies would have done that, but we had some in our company that wouldn't have cared to sneak around and steal stuff and sell it to the Frenchmen. So I didn't think I ought to shoot just whoever was movin' around in the moonlight.

'Course, if I'd just shot up in the air, that would have gotten me off the hook. I wouldn't have told the lieutenant I was shooting in the air, but if I'd told him I took a couple of shots, he'd have been satisfied. But

I thought I did the right thing. You have to make some judgements on your own.

We had a lot of Southern boys in our outfit and the first reaction in seeing the countryside of Europe, our G.I.s couldn't get over the fact that despite the war the French homes and villages that were still intact were neat, there was no debris around, stuff was picked up. . . . When these boys saw France with their neat homes and barns, whitewashed walls, flowers, flower boxes, their reaction was, "What are we doing helping the French? They live better than we do." The poorest French person was living in a nicer environment than the average Southern boy that was in the army.

—**Cpl. Alexander Gordeuk (from New Jersey), Information and Education Officer, 13th Armored Division (9)**

One night, we had a convoy of tanks from Le Havre. We stopped in a little town and we pulled right up close to this curb built up out of cobblestone. The French, instead of concrete curbs, they used stones placed on end. Their sidewalks were up about five or six inches higher than the street.

I don't remember why we stopped, but when we left, we'd parked so close to the curb that as we pulled out, the back part of our tracks caught that cobblestone curb and tore the stones out, one after another. About everywhere a tank was parked, it would tear out a bunch of cobblestones and just about the whole sidewalk collapsed into the street.

We hadn't hardly gotten started out of town till the lieutenant stopped us. That lieutenant said, "We've got to go back and fix the street, we've torn up the street back there."

This little French town was neat and everything, but not too far away, the Germans had blown down some buildings and they were just in a rubble. It didn't matter. We had to get out and line up all those cobblestones before we could go on.

It was about two o'clock in the morning. We never were so mad. It really upset us, 'cause we were worn out and tired and hungry and we had been kept out so late anyway.

Some of those boys just bellyached. "Those Frenchmen must have been watchin' and they've raised a ruckus. Ought to be glad to clean up after their liberators."

I heard some of those boys say that Frenchmen weren't worth much as soldiers, that they weren't any good on the front lines, but I never did know a thing about it, that's just what I heard.

I saw that France was a beautiful country and the army really wanted us to have respect for that country and its inhabitants while we were there, even despite the fact that a lot of places were all bombed out and shot up. Out in the country, though, there wasn't too much destruction. The surroundings were a whole lot like it was in America. They had little villages and they had fields where they farmed and raised livestock.

In France, they weren't as modernized as I thought they'd be. All the farmers that we saw were still farming with horses. Of course, in the U.S. they'd gone to tractors, most of the farmers. Over there in Normandy, they hooked up three horses side by side when they were pulling heavy farm equipment in the fields. They did have some beautiful horses. And they were well cared for, seemed like, because the French people had to depend on them to make their living. Some of those horses had a stall right next to the kitchen in the dwelling homes.

In the countryside of Normandy, the French farmers tilled the soil about like what I was used to back home. But when I saw how some of them lived, I wasn't too impressed with that. Sergeant Hicks would send some of us into the village with food to hand out to the French people and we'd go into their homes. We liked that detail. It was a little like bein' Santa Claus.

On the little ol' farms that I saw, the French kept everything in close quarters. You just went from your living room right into the stall to milk your cow. I never saw anything like that before and I didn't much like the idea.

The French were not the cleanest people in the world. They'd clean out those livestock stalls and they'd just shovel the litter out the door and onto the sidewalk, piles of that manure. If you were walking up a sidewalk and you came to a big pile of manure, you just had to walk around it. I guess the farmers picked it up later and took it out in the field.

The French people I saw weren't as clean with their food as some people, either. Most of them in that Normandy region had apple orchards around their house and they made a lot of cider. We'd buy that apple cider, oh, I thought it was good—until I saw them making some, and I never would drink it after that.

They had their apples in a cellar to keep all winter, maybe longer, and they had their mill in another building where they pressed the juice. They'd just take a wheelbarrow and shovel up those apples, big piles of apples, and bring them over to the mill. There'd be a lot of rotten apples and they'd just run the rotten ones into the press along with the good ones. Didn't wash them or cull them or nothin'. When I saw that, I said, well, they're too filthy to suit me. I didn't want no more of that French apple cider, no sir.

We all saw the French differently. Some of those boys were pretty taken with the place and liked to associate with the local people. They weren't supposed to do that, but they did. They were the ones who went into town and found themselves some apple brandy, *calvados*, they called it, and they'd smoke and carouse around with women who liked to get the Lux soap that our army issued the servicemen. Some of the G.I.s would give their chocolate bars to the women, too.

Some of the boys liked helping the French people when they found out our American army rations of cigarettes, chocolate, and soap were in high demand. Some of them'd trade our goods with the French people for different foods, like cheese or wine. My tank crew would always swap them for eggs.

We'd buy eggs from the French, and boiled them ourselves, 'cause we were having to live off of field rations when we transported vehicles. We didn't usually take dinner rations with us and if we got held up for a long time, we just had to be on our own, find us something to eat. We'd buy food from the Frenchmen at their homes, if we had a few francs. The army transferred some of our money into francs and they'd taught us a few words in French. We'd try to put things together. We could say enough French that they could understand us. It was aggravating, though.

Rhodes'd say, "Go on, Kelley. Tell that pretty Frenchie over there what we got a hankerin' for."

"Aw, shoot," I'd say. "My French's no better than yours. She might bring us a horse."

"Hey, they eat horses over here, did ya know that?" Rhodes said.

If they roped me into it, I'd talk French in my hillbilly way, I guess. I still remember some of the phrases the army taught us. One of them is when you ask for eggs.

"J'av U drayz OOFSsss?" I said to a French girl.

She giggled 'cause she couldn't understand me, I reckoned.

Then I tried again. "I mean, *Avez-vous . . . des OEUFS?*"

Of course, I never could understand what anybody said back. But it didn't matter because they'd usually disappear and come back with a few eggs. We bought eggs or anything that they might have to offer us. If they didn't have eggs, they might bring us bacon or milk or some bread with a crust so hard you could hardly tear it off with your teeth. All their bread was stale, I reckon. I never did see anything like good, crumbly cornbread over in France.

Of course, we had a mess truck that would cook familiar foods back where we were living at the schoolhouse, something like what my cousin Atlas drove, over in the 498th Artillery. I didn't see him when I was in France, I just knew he was in our division over there.

Where we'd set up camp, they had light sockets in that schoolhouse, but when the Germans left out of there, they hadn't left us even a lightbulb in that whole building. I figured the Germans must have taken 'em 'cause they didn't want us to have the benefit of lights.

We went into a little town and found a store to buy lightbulbs. We'd just about have to put on a show to explain what we wanted. The French people would catch on pretty quick and you could kind of illustrate a lightbulb, but I imagine how silly we looked with all the motions we'd go through just to make them understand us. All the French people I met were real helpful, and we usually ended up laughing together.

In France, they just seemed like happy-go-lucky people, because the Germans had been driven out of there. They'd just cheer us when we were going down the streets, if we were moving about as a convoy. The French people were pretty friendly, but they were expecting us to give them something all the time. Of course, they were about on starvation. Hitler had taken about everything they had and they were usually looking for a handout from the American G.I.s.

The army gave us a pack of cigarettes a day over there. If they missed a few days, you'd get three packs. I traded mine for candy, one pack of cigarettes for a bar of chocolate.

I'd share my candy with the children. Usually, there'd be three or four children together, girls and boys, and they'd come up to us on the street when we stopped and we'd hand out candy and talk with them a little bit. Some of the children could speak English pretty well. Oh, that just tickled us, giving those kids something that Hitler had taken away from them.

France was a pretty nice country overall and I liked the people, even though the French people weren't clean enough to suit me. I think we all enjoyed getting to see France while we waited for orders to move out. Most of us could trace our roots to somewhere in Europe anyway, like France, Ireland, Poland, or Italy. Of course, quite a few, like me, had some German in them. I think Donald Crouch came from German people. Some of the boys in our outfit could even speak German, and that helped us in the war.

Even though most of us felt kinship to wherever our families had come from, we were one team, from one homeland, Americans. That spirit made me really appreciate our whole country and made me proud to represent it overseas. I think that's the reason why we won the war — everybody felt that way, and we all went to the battlefields for the purpose of winning.

Of course, we didn't know the outcome at that time, but I don't think any of us ever doubted that we would win. We had a lot of confidence in our leaders to make the right decisions. We had a lot of confidence in our countrymen — and women — back home to manufacture the supplies we needed and get them to us. What we didn't know was how long the war would last, what battles we'd fight, and what the cost would be in lives lost and men crippled.

There were soldiers who were always out in town, finding themselves apple brandy or champagne. Oh, that "French Champagne" — those kind were always talking about that, looking for it, and for loose women, so they could live it up in case they died.

Most of us in the company, though, kept focused on preparing for battle. Our battle cry was "Home *alive* in '45." It was now the end of February 1945.

Every tank crew had a lot of work to do to get ready for battle. My crew was a pretty serious bunch when it came to the jobs we had to do. When we got our new tank, it was a regular Sherman M4, with a 75mm cannon, like we were used to, even though some of the Shermans coming in had been upgraded to 76mm guns. The biggest difference was that these tanks had steel plates welded on the sides. Those Sherman tanks needed extra armor. Evidently, the army knew that the German guns were more powerful than they'd first told us.

The tanks arrived pretty well prepared, but we had to mount the 75mm cannon. Had to mount the .30 caliber machine guns, too, and get them ready to go, so, of course, the main gunner was responsible for a lot of that work.

Knode had to maintain the 75mm cannon, the .50 caliber antiaircraft gun, the .30 caliber antipersonnel gun, plus his personal weapon. Even though he was particularly neat about his hygiene and appearance, Knode often smelled a little of cosmoline or varsol because he was always cleaning guns and fooling with them. But he was about the best marksman with any weapon we had and I was glad of that.

Donald usually helped Knode with the guns. For a tank commander, he was good to do that. He was used to having brothers with him on the farm and he related to us a whole lot like that. Coming from that big-time farming family, Donald was used to being up early, staying busy all the time. He was always looking for something he could do to help us out.

McAbee, our loader and radio operator, he always had to see that the radio was in working order. He'd have to switch to different channels during battle. And as the cannon's loader, he was responsible for checking the ammunition bays, keeping track of how many rounds we had, and keeping the ready racks loaded. Being a little feller, he didn't take up much room in the turret, and he was quick as a cat.

I kept my focus on the road, so I never did know what went on much back in the turret. But Donald said that in training, McAbee never missed a beat and he'd get the shells in the chamber so fast that Knode never missed a beat, either. I figured we were covered there.

Rhodes, or "E-well"—as we said when we kidded him—he was our assistant driver, and that really meant he was our full-time bow gunner, 'cause I always drove. Rhodes made good scores in all his training on the .30 caliber machine gun. He kept that gun in top shape. Other than that, he didn't have a lot to do. Oh, he'd help me fuel the tank and things like that, but a lot of the time, Rhodes'd keep the rest of us entertained with his colorful Texas talk.

The assistant driver position was what the army termed the "least important position" in the tank. We all knew that tank crews were subject to having their assistant drivers pulled out to replace other tanks' drivers if the going got rough and they started getting injured or killed. I'd sure hate to lose the team I had now. Any of 'em.

I had about the biggest load, as the driver, when it came to the maintenance of the tank. I was entirely responsible for the engine. The driver also checks and maintains the fluids, keeps oil in the crank case. The biggest job was keeping the tracks running smoothly. The tracks had bearings where the bogie wheels ran on the tracks. If we drove very much at all, especially in dusty conditions, I'd have to regrease the tank, go clear around it, greasing those fittings. We carried a grease gun in each tank—not just our awkward version of that Thompson submachine gun—but a real automotive grease gun. I'd use mine about every day—unlike my firearm, I hoped.

Some of the companies painted names on their new tanks over there. Our crew didn't fool with that. Best I remember, all my battle tank had was the big white stars that marked American tanks.

That Sherman tank was radiator-cooled and that always worked well, not like the air-cooled light tanks that our D Company had. Those smaller tanks went up to fifty miles per hour, but they were always giving engine trouble. There were a few heavy tanks that the army had over there, too, they had more armor, but they weren't good for much, 'cause you couldn't maneuver around in them very fast. As the war developed, speed turned out to be more important than armor. I was glad I was in the Sherman. It turned out to be the best all-purpose tank in that war—even though by now, we knew that the Germans had plenty of guns that could shoot right through them.

When we started getting our own tanks ready to go, we knew we were subject to movin' out at any time. On the last few nights in that French schoolhouse, everybody was making sure their personal weapon was in top shape. Everybody had that stamped-out Grease Gun, except Donald. Well, he had his, too, but he also had a .45 caliber semi-automatic handgun.

The tank commanders were allowed to carry a pistol, if they wanted one. Donald had mentioned to us that he'd like to have a pistol to carry overseas because that Grease Gun, it was unhandy to carry all the time. The barrel got in the way, gettin' in and out of a tank. When we first got to France, he had asked about getting a pistol and they told him they couldn't issue him one but said, "If you can get a pistol sent over here, you can use it instead of your submachine gun."

So he'd written his wife and she found him a U.S. Army .45 semi-automatic, just like the officers wore. I don't know where she got it, but she sent it to him over there in France and he'd just received the package from home with that .45 pistol in it. I don't remember now what make it was. It was covered in cosmoline, a substance they put on guns to ship them across the ocean so salt air won't rust them. It's a mess when you get one.

Donald started cleaning that pistol in the schoolhouse one evening. They had some rooms with tables and chairs and we'd do little tasks in there. He got some varsol, and he took that gun all apart and he cleaned that cosmoline off and he started putting it back together, and he couldn't get it to work. He just worked and he worked and he kept fooling with that pistol. He wouldn't ask anybody anything about it.

I was sitting in a room off to the side, with a few of the men. I don't know what we were doing now. I knew just exactly what Donald was doing wrong, but I didn't want to say anything to him unless he asked me. I could have put that gun back together just in a minute.

Donald kept working with that pistol, getting frustrated with it, and he finally said out loud, "I don't know what I'm gonna do. I'm doing something wrong, I know that. I can't get this gun together so it will work." He had it apart again in his hands, fooling with it. He asked, "Does anybody know anything about putting one of these together?"

"Yeah," I said, "I know how to put them together. 'Cause we took training on them at one time." Donald hadn't taken all his training with us and evidently he'd missed instruction on that gun.

He said, "Okay, Quinton, you show me how."

I said to him, "Well, that gun's a little bit tricky. If you don't know about it, you might not figure it out."

There was a little yoke in there and it had a hole where a pin had to go through it, and you had to line it up with the screw hole, stick the pin through the yoke and screw it in there.

When Donald was taking the gun apart he didn't realize that the yoke would pivot—it was loose. You had to tilt the gun to line up the holes. But if you didn't know that detail, you'd be there till doomsday tryin' to put that gun back together so it would work.

After I showed Donald the way it went together, he got that pistol assembled lickety-split. He said, "I sure am proud of that." He just thanked me.

"Well, glad to show you," I said.

Donald seemed real proud that his wife had sent him that gun. He told me, "Lillie really came through for me."

He said his wife was staying with his mother back in Kansas on the farm. Donald often talked about his family's home, where they must have had a pretty big-sized farm, the way he talked. Wheat and corn, I think. I'm not even sure what and all they raised, but it must have been a real professional operation, helping to feed the country.

Out in Kansas, it's a lot of that flat country. The little place he was from was surrounded by fields, with miles and miles of straight rows of crops, and, growing up, he only had a wide spot in the road to call a town. Donald grew up about as far from big cities as I did.

Donald came up like I did, too, around the family table. He wasn't a rough character like a lot of boys that I met in the army. He was clean-talking. He didn't use profanity and off-color stuff like some of them. A few times he went with some of the roughnecks into town, but he wouldn't get drunk, he'd maybe have a drink to associate with them. I don't know whether he had a faith in God. He might have. He never made it known. But Donald Crouch was a fine feller.

Donald and I were sitting around in that French schoolhouse talking together as the room emptied out, and he took out some little pictures of his wife and baby and he showed them to me.

He said, "You know, I left New York mad at my wife because she didn't bring the baby up there. I wanted to see my little girl."

As soon as we knew we were going to New York, Donald had called his wife and told her he had a three-day pass and to come to New York to see him before he shipped out. I guess there was some miscommunication and I reckon it was a lot of problems for her, traveling on the train with a baby and all. But Donald was really upset about it.

"I thought all the time she'd bring the baby. I was looking for them at the train station. I saw lots of mothers with babies. And then I saw Lillie." Donald shook his head. "There she was, standing on the platform, just Lillie and her suitcase. I wanted to see my little girl more than I did my wife."

He said, "I was plumb mad at her. I never will get over that, I don't guess." Donald never sounded angry with us, ever. He always had a good even-tempered way. But when he talked about the last time he'd seen his wife, he said, "I'm mad at her for that. It really got to me and I let her know it. After that, I didn't enjoy her visit one bit. You know how women are."

I nodded, even though I'd never had any problems like that myself.

I had met Donald's wife in New York before we got on the ship. She was a real nice-looking girl. They were saying goodbye to each other before Donald walked up the gangplank. I hadn't detected it then, but they were upset with each other.

I hated to think of Donald and his wife struggling to have a nice time together before he shipped out. I hated to think of him missing out on his baby's inno- cent smile, so he could carry that thought into battle. He didn't get to say goodbye to his little girl. That was the worst thing about having to go overseas, Donald said, not getting to see his little girl before he shipped out. When he told me that, I really felt sorry for him having to go away with that on his

Lillie and Donald Crouch with their daughter

mind, and I guess his wife knew it, too, and she was probably upset back in Kansas. Donald Crouch was the only one in our crew who had a child back home.

Donald didn't seem too happy about the way things had gone in New York, but there wasn't much he could do about it. I could see it really hurt him, but if he hadn't told me the story, I never would have known. He was the strong-minded professional leader that he'd always been, and a good buddy. Donald would talk to me a little more than some of the others. When we were over in France, he mentioned about getting so mad at his wife, but then after that, he never did say any more about it. I guess they made up after that when he'd write her letters.

Hearing from home was about the best thing anybody could hope for on any given day — besides hearing that the war was over, of course. They delivered mail to us regularly while we were in France and we stayed in Normandy for nearly two months waiting until they wanted us to enter the war. I got quite a few letters from Orangie. Once in a while I'd have a chance and I'd write to her. I knew that when we got into Germany, we wouldn't have much time for that.

The only surviving letter from our correspondence, dated February 19, 1945, from "*Somewhere in France*," is about everyday events, like the tank crew biding our time, but it was full of terms of endearment. Orangie was in Texas, on a visit with her family. I wrote:

> ... *Darling, I wish I was back in Texas now, maybe I would have a chance to see you. One of my buddys is from Texas, Ewell W. Rhodes, and he is all the time telling me something to write you, but I am a little bit afraid to write what he says, for you might get mad. But I can say if all Texas boys is like him, there isn't any use of me looking for you when I get back. Ha.*
>
> *Honey, about that picture you was asking for. I wish I had a good one to send, but don't have one now and don't think I will be able to have any made, for there isn't any place where they make pictures or at least I haven't saw anyplace.*
>
> *Darling, I am sending you ten Francs as a souvenir, it equals to*

twenty cents. I would send more but can't send but a small amount. . . .

Honey, I bet you haven't got a letter from me in so long, you are thinking I have forgotten you. But don't ever think that, just think we are a long way apart as far as mail is concerned, but close together in thoughts. . . .

I always signed, "*Love, Quinton.*" It was about as romantic as I got, but she got the message. I sure hoped she'd be there waiting for me whenever I came back. I didn't have any assurance about that. I didn't hardly think it right to ask her to wait for me, since I was subject to getting killed or maimed and ruining her life when she was just starting it.

Some of the boys had recently gotten "Dear John" letters while we were over there in France. Some of them would get so torn up, hearing that their girlfriend or wife had decided to leave them for another man, they'd really go off on a big drunk. Sometimes women back home didn't want to wait for servicemen, or take a chance on the soldier getting killed or seriously injured. Or they just plain found somebody else to love. And there wasn't nothin' those poor boys could do about it over there, about to go into battle. I felt so sorry for those boys and I always thought those girls should have had more sense than that. They ought to have realized that a man going off to war doesn't need those problems on his mind.

All the different battalions that made up the 13th Armored Division traveled together, so we experienced a lot of the same things. Each battalion had a man who wrote up a summary of the big events that happened, with all the dates and places. 'Course us being in the 24th Tank Battalion, we didn't usually know what the other battalions of the 13th were doing when we were over in Europe. It wasn't until after the war that we read about what we all did, in the individual Unit Histories of the 13th Armored Division that the U.S. Army published:

24th Tank Battalion:

By March 17, 1945, our vehicles and equipment were ready to go; we mounted up and rolled to Soissons, then on through Vitry to billets near Avricourt, March 19. (1)

45th Tank Battalion:

Two nights were spent in Soissons and Vitry as we passed the World War I battlefields of Compiegne and Chateau Thierry. The last day of the 300 mile march took us through historic Nancy and then to Bourdonnay, a ghost town in the heart of nowhere of Eastern France. German and American tanks rusting amid scattered minefields gave evidence of the major engagements fought in the surrounding fields.

During our brief stay in France, the Allies had recovered from the Battle of the Bulge, had pushed through portions of the vaunted Siegfried Line, and had taken the famous Remagen Bridgehead across the Rhine and were now striking toward the heart of Germany. (10)

Orders came to move out. All of a sudden, in a big whirlwind of activity, the whole 13th Armored Division—all the battalions—rolled out of our field base in Normandy in one long convoy on our march through France. From then on, we were on the go pretty much until the end of the war. Never did slow down, except for a time or two.

We headed in an easterly direction—the general direction of Germany's capital.

"They won't say where we're headed, but looks like we're headed towards Berlin," Donald told us over the intercom. He'd met with the tank commanders and they'd gotten their orders for the day. "All the capitals Hitler held, he's givin' 'em back, one by one." Donald's voice was strong. "Bet we'll have to take Berlin."

"If we have to, we'll do it!" Knode said. He was always at the ready, and the rest of us, too.

"Hey, Quinton!" McAbee broke in—he usually called me Kelley. "I saw a road sign when we stopped back there, there's a town north of us called Saint Quentin. You think you's named after that?"

"Nah . . ." I said. "More likely San Quentin Penitentiary."

"Didn't you know, Kelley's from a family of outlaws." Rhodes put his two cents in. "Parents named him after that prison 'cause he's got moonshinin' and bootleggin' in his blood. They figured he'd wind up there."

"Well, I ain't yet. That's why I can drive this tank so fast," I said. "All that runnin' whiskey, I reckon." I liked to joke with them.

I heard Donald laugh. "Kelley, just keep her rollin' like you're goin' down one of those Tennessee hills. We've got a long ways to go."

We always got along real well, even after many hours together in that cramped tank. When we were moving, most of the time we were not doing any talking, except maybe the tank commander. "Okay, let's can the small talk and keep the line open," Donald'd say to us. We generally practiced keeping silent on our radios in convoy, unless important information needed to be given.

We never really knew where we were going and it didn't matter. We were just looking out for our survival. So I never did know the names of a lot of the places we passed through or fought in. We'd pass some road signs and they pointed to historic towns with fancy names that I never could pronounce anyway.

We rode unbuttoned when we were driving through France. I could jack the seat up—it was spring-loaded—just unlatch it and it would spring up. A driver can see a whole lot better with his head out the hatch, rather than looking through the periscope, 'cause having to look through that little window was like a horse wearing blinders.

The tank commander could ride unbuttoned, too, at least for now. Once we got into enemy territory, though, we'd be glad to button up, even if we did have reduced vision.

The French towns were mostly quiet; people kept off the streets when we rolled through. We just went rumbling through villages, day and night, engines roaring and tracks slopping over puddles and wet cobblestone on our way to what we figured was the German front.

Half-tracks—the M3 half-track personnel carriers—allowed the infantry to keep up with the tanks. Tanks and infantry are dependent on each other. Most of the time, tanks tackle enemy armor or take out big targets with their firepower. Tanks give cover to the infantry, and the infantry follows through, takes the ground, fighting house to house to secure the towns and villages.

Our big guns, the artillery pieces, they could attack the enemy from the most distance, so their role in battle would be to clear a path for the tanks and infantry first, so we could rush in with the second wave of attack. Of course, there were other battalions that would go out in front, too, like the engineering battalions, when they had to build bridges ahead of us so we could cross rivers.

The one company of light tanks, which each tank battalion in the 13th Armored Division had, Company D, their job was to race out in front as quiet, quick reconnaissance to locate the enemy or spot obstacles and report back. Sometimes they'd locate areas that were mined.

In France, the Germans planted a lot of mines and when they had to retreat out of France, they'd left the fields just full of mines. A lot of those farmers would get out to plowing in the field and every once in a while, you'd hear a big explosion, where they'd run into a German mine.

Those were antipersonnel mines, those "Jumping Betsys." When they'd go off, they'd jump up about chest high and explode, so they'd be sure to kill you if you were standing up. The Germans didn't want to just maim you, they wanted to kill you.

What we had been trained to do, if we hit any of those mines, was just to fall flat on the ground when the mine popped up out of the dirt. Chances are, it would bounce up and go off over you, but if you were standing up, it would get you when it detonated. We were trained for it, but we didn't usually run into that situation, being tank crews. Now, some of our infantry I'm sure did. They had foot soldiers that detonated mines—they had detectors that could find metal, which most of the German mines had. I saw our infantry clearing some places along our route.

When we got away from the towns, the French countryside itself was a beautiful landscape, but it was nothin' like home. To me, what I saw of France looked like a lot of big, open fields dotted with little farming villages, real nice, but not like the cozy wooded hollers of Coker Creek, where I'd felt safe and carefree.

Each of us probably held on to a picture of home in his mind, being so far away, about to go into battle. I knew my crew well and I'd heard enough from each of them to know how they pictured home. I knew that Knode loved the pleasant well-tended countryside of Virginia, with its horse pastures and white fences. It must've looked a lot like some of these French farms, except that over here they used thick hedgerows instead of fences to divide pastures.

McAbee was used to it being warm down there in South Carolina where they had palm trees, he said, so the frosty mornings as we mounted up to drive deeper into the continent of Europe really nipped his nose. He said there was nothin' like the warm Carolina sunshine.

Rhodes's native Texas—dusty, scrubby country, as far as I'd seen—it was hardly much to compare with this rolling countryside, where grass was just coming to life after winter. But when I thought of that hot and mosquito-infested Texas, it still seemed better than any place at the edge of a war zone, so I know Rhodes missed Texas something terrible.

And Donald, on his Kansas farm, there were cornfields for hundreds of acres, he said when he described it, and he'd look off to the horizon. Rows and rows as far as the eye could see from the seat of a tractor, tall green stalks standing like soldiers, like armies. I don't know if there were any big cornfields like that in France. I didn't see any evidence of it if there were.

We did drive by rows and rows of little white crosses that stood lined up in fields to the horizon, as far as you could see. We passed by the enormous United States military cemeteries where the World War I veterans were buried. It was sad to see all the men that gave their lives in World War I—and, of course, that was just part of them, buried there. They were American soldiers and people who were fighting with our side, our allies. But, law me, all those white crosses—just no tellin' how many thousand there were. It was hard for me to comprehend how many when I kept on driving and I could still see that cemetery stretching along the road for a long ways. Not one of the soldiers buried there wanted to have to give their life, I know. It reminded me of what war with the Germans could do, and I had to wonder how many more crosses our company might add to that number. So, I thought about that as we drove past all those well-kept graves. I'm satisfied we all did, though no one in the tank said a word.

CHAPTER 18

Entering Nazi Germany

This is the history of the 13th Armored Division . . . a story written not in the bone-dry dust of the historian, but rather with the sweat and blood and honest fear of the infantryman, the tanker, the cannoneer. These men worked together, lived together, and some of them died together — died in the filth and rubble of the war-ravaged Ruhr or in the rivers and forests of Bavaria. But most of the men lived — and killed Germans — and helped win the war. (2)

Over in the European Theater of Operations, the 13th Armored Division was assigned to different U.S. armies, depending on the job that needed to be done. Our missions were part of well-planned teamwork that came from the top down, though, of course, we tankers never knew anything about the strategy or where we fit in the scheme of things. We only knew what was happening within our company most of the time, and sometimes not even that.

The tank commanders would be called into a huddle with the officers over them, and they'd all get out and gather somewhere behind a little building, and that's where they were told what type of area we were going into. We had good reconnaissance over there. They knew pretty well what type of resistance we were going to run into. Donald would come back and explain to us what the officers had told him. He was real good about keeping us informed.

"We're heading for what they call the Dragon's Teeth," Donald said over the intercom one March morning. "It's a lot of concrete antitank barriers. We're expecting artillery. They say this is the last place along the Siegfried Line to fall."

"We'll get 'em to fall—like rotten apples on a bull's scratchin' tree!" Rhodes always had a thing or two to say.

"Yeah, we'll make some Nazi apple cider," Knode piped in.

That two years of training had made our entire outfit into a finely tuned unit and we were all proud of our skills. There was an assurance in that, even though you went into battle knowing it was just the luck of where the shells were hittin', a lot of times, that determined your fate.

I tried not to let negative thoughts distract me. I remembered to keep focused on the task at hand—driving, usually. And waiting, staying alert. I think we were all just a waitin' for that first shot from the enemy. Of course, as soldiers, we were always expecting the first rounds of enemy fire at any time along the way.

THE KITTEN, Ruhr Battle Extra:

The Division stopped temporarily in the Mosel Region, close to Alsace-Lorraine, and on MARCH 19 the Division's Artillery saw battle action for the first time. The armored artillery-men took part in the Seventh Army's offensive through the Siegfried Line. Along with other units, they poured a concentrated barrage into Siegfried Line defenses. (6)

497th Armored Field Artillery Battalion:

We had a long way to go before we could get to shoot our guns—from California to the French-German border. Last leg was on March 19 when we proceeded . . . to firing positions near Spicheren, which was about 2,000 yards from the enemy lines in Saarbrucken. The rest of the Division was not in this action — the Division Artillery did the first fighting for the 13th.

At 1700 on that day "A" Battery fired the first shot of the Division at the enemy on a target in Saarbrucken. Our long months of diligent training paid dividends, the first round was "Effect on the Target!" The other batteries joined in, and we were embarked on our combat career. (13)

498th Armored Field Artillery Battalion:

. . . The battalion fired harassing and interdiction fire all night, and by noon of the 20th fire slacked off as the infantry moved into the ruined city. (14)

496th Armored Field Artillery Battalion:

. . . We moved onto German soil at Ommersheim, Germany. We registered but the enemy was retreating so rapidly that within two hours they were beyond the range of our guns. (7)

Our artillery battalions moved forward and supported offensives that cleaned up the last of the Siegfried Line. The rest of us were held back in little French villages near the border of Germany. From where we were, we could hear the thundering booms of artillery off in the distance when our forces bombarded the towns. At night, I could see fiery flashes light up the clouds, when the artillery exploded, like lightning from a far-off electrical storm.

The weather had been rainy and blustery and our tanks were covered with mud. Those tracks would just sling that mud off everywhere. The tank crews weren't much cleaner. We'd accumulated grease, gasoline, and road dust from our different stops. It had been a long haul across France at top speed, some three hundred miles, and, of course, when we stopped in a little village, everybody went to find some water and wash. The drivers, though, had to do all the tank maintenance first thing before they could wash. That was the job I had to do every time we stopped—get that tank ready to roll out again at a moment's notice, rain or shine.

The tanks needed constant maintenance to keep them in top form. Whenever we had a layover, I'd check the oil and keep it topped off, grease the fittings, check the hydraulics, and keep the right amount of pressure on those bogie wheels, stuff like that. If you always took good care of your tank, you didn't have any trouble with it. So, when I stopped driving, I went to work. I kept my General Sherman in first-class condition all the time.

A lot of the drivers wouldn't take good care of their tanks. Their tank commander had to be after them to check this and check that. Nobody ever had to tell me to do a thing to that tank. I kept up on it myself.

I didn't know what other men in the 13th Armored were doing, but for us tankers, we spent about a week test firing and tuning up our equipment. Then we received orders for another move, the one we all expected: we were headed across the border into Nazi Germany.

24th Tank Battalion:
We got under way again on March 25, crossing the German border as the sun was climbing up off the horizon. It wasn't but a day later, and we were in sight of the Siegfried line at Pirmasens. (1)

I could see the signs of battles along the road and out in the fields. All we knew was, the regular battles had moved on, and we moved on behind them.

We started seeing roadblocks that had been set up and blown through. It gave me a start to see German tanks and some long-nosed artillery guns set up along the road, in position to fire, but we rolled on past. They'd been abandoned long before we got there. They'd been "knocked out"—that's when some of the Allied troops were able to knock off a track and immobilize the German tank or the towed gun, so our artillery could go to work on it. We saw big Panther tanks that had been knocked out, some were upside down, and the hatches were blown off.

Allied artillery forces had blasted holes right into them. It had to be our artillery, 'cause our American tanks' guns couldn't penetrate the German armor like that.

The Germans had good equipment. Their biggest tanks, like the newer Tiger tanks, they were really something to fear. They were fitted with an 88mm gun that could penetrate any of our tank's armor at over two thousand yards. As tankers, we were outmatched with that. We all hated that our 75mm cannon couldn't even penetrate our enemy's tanks. Didn't have a bit of a chance with most of 'em, unless we happened to be right close to the tank and aimed for the turret, where we could do the most damage, maybe take out the tank commander. We went into battle knowin' we could just probably knock out the Germans' tanks with our tank's guns — knock off a track, damage the wheels, something like that, so they couldn't go.

If the Germans couldn't go, they'd have to bail out of the tank. If they came out shootin', well, they'd get killed with our automatic gunfire. If they came out with their hands up, we'd take 'em prisoner. We had troops that followed for that and they dealt with the ones that surrendered.

Even though our cannon was not nearly as powerful as the German 88s, we did have the advantage of our gyrostabilizer, a hydraulic thing that floated the guns and kept them on target when we were moving. The Germans, they said, had to stop their tanks if they wanted to be accurate with their big guns. I heard they had to use a hand crank to turn their turrets. Our Shermans had a turret that you could rotate 360 degrees with an electrical control switch. So we could be quick with our first shot and knock 'em out.

When we did that, our artillery battalions had all kinds of antiaircraft guns, 105s, and the M7, a self-propelled howitzer gun, our big gun, backing us up. We had good firepower supporting us out there and we felt well prepared for battle. We were fresh and well equipped with all our American-made gear. The Americans had lots of fast tanks, good fuel supply lines, and plenty of ammunition — unlike the Germans at this point in the war.

"Lieutenant says we're already in Germany," Donald told us when he came back from a huddle with the officers. We had to stop occasionally on convoy, to refuel, things like that.

"Sure not what I expected," he said, looking out at the quiet meadows. We'd crossed the French-German border in the morning, although we never knew exactly where it was.

Shortly after we crossed into Germany, we drove through a big town where just about every building was a pile of rubble. The buildings on some streets were all bombed out, walls blown down, with maybe just one corner of a building left standing. Roofs torn off, just hanging down on one side of a house, bricks tumbled in heaps along the road, wooden beams snapped in half—that was a sad sight to see, people's homes destroyed by war. Allied bombings and the13th's artillery battalions had really laid the place to waste so our column could advance into Germany.

Forces ahead of us had cleaned up the area and infantry had swarmed through and rooted out entrenched German soldiers that might have given us trouble. The drivers and tank commanders were still riding unbuttoned and I had my head out—I could see all that destruction pretty well. You couldn't look too long, though. You had to keep your mind on your driving.

The Nazis were on the run and they'd pulled back further inland. The Germans were being more cautious than we were, because it was their own country. They knew how to use the landscape for defense and particular towns to their advantage to fight us off. People fight better in their own country. We were taking over their country. But we knew we had a job to do—we couldn't let ol' Hitler take over the world like he'd been doing, and the sooner we got the job done, the better it would be for everybody, so we went after it.

We rolled on through countryside heading closer to that big landmark, the "Dragon's Teeth," and I saw more German tanks torn up out in the countryside, big monstrous tanks that had burnt up, but not as many as ours. A lot of the tanks I saw were Sherman tanks turned over on their side, with that white star. Alongside the roads, some sat blasted out and blackened from the raging fires that erupted when the Sherman got hit just right. If it did, the ammunition was likely to explode. The Shermans would burn pretty easily anyways because they used gasoline, not like other tanks I'd heard about, like Russian ones that used diesel and were safer in that respect. Sherman tankers could get trapped in an inferno of hot metal, what the enemy called a "Tommy Cooker." I just remember seeing another Sherman like mine, on its side, where a big shell had turned it over, a layin' out there in a field. There was a big hole blasted right through it. I said to myself, law me, if I get us in the path of one artillery piece, it'll take us all out.

We got our first sight of the Siegfried Line. I'd heard a lot about it before we went over there, how hard an obstacle it would be to get through and I didn't realize what it would be till I saw it.

That Siegfried Line, boy, the Germans had spent the money and labor making that barrier. They'd built just thousands of concrete cones with sloping sides, set in rows, several rows deep, zigzagging and winding all along the meadows, just big concrete piers sunk into the countryside. That barrier ran for nearly four hundred miles. We could have walked through there, but we couldn't drive through. It would have been impossible for us to ever get equipment through unless we blasted out enough of those concrete "teeth." But that's what they did; some of the American troops blasted out a throughway in the Siegfried Line with heavy artillery shortly before we got there. That Siegfried Line, the Germans didn't intend for us to cross it. All it did, though, was just slow us down so they could try to pick us off. We were lucky that it wasn't us leading the first wave through there.

By the time our column of tanks rolled through, the officers told us that they didn't expect for us to encounter any resistance, unless there were some stragglers still hiding out. Sure enough, when 1st Platoon got up there, some of 'em near the front found there were still a few German troops hiding in the pillboxes, lying in wait.

Lonnie Johnson, 24th Tank Battalion, C Company:
The Siegfried Line. Lordy mercy, that was a time. They had these embedded guns and they was superior in their firepower

than we were because we were a moving troops. They was sta-
tionary. And they had the pillboxes close enough that they could
shoot you with big guns anywhere between the two guns. You
couldn't hurt the things they's a bombin' us from, 'cause they were
concrete, some of 'em was three foot thick. And they had small
guns for troops on the ground.

Finally, we got an infantryman—I really don't know what
outfit he was with—but he took a flamethrower and put it on
his back and slid on his belly up to it, and threw the fire in one
of the holes and then threw grenades in there. Once we captured
the pillboxes on each side of the road, the big tanks made a rush
for it, and run right on in. (12)

Whatever delays we had as we crossed that Siegfried Line, I reckon
the troops at the front of the column took care of it. In convoy, the best
position was the middle, like my position, 2nd Platoon, second tank. A
lot of times, there was one full platoon in front of me and one behind.

The Germans were known to have their tricks for the tank companies, the army warned us. Sometimes they'd let the first several tanks roll
past and then they'd block off the road, so the tanks in front wouldn't
have any backup, and they'd attack those tanks after they were cut off.
If you were in the middle of a column, your chances were a little better, I figured.

'Course, the platoons didn't always keep their assigned order. Sometimes they wanted the 2nd Platoon, or the 3rd, out in front. They called
the platoon at the head of the column the spearhead. It just depends on
who the commanders wanted to spearhead the column that day. The
officers rotated it around. They were fair about it. They didn't make just
one platoon do all of it because that was a lot of pressure all the time.
But even if our platoon was chosen to spearhead, I'd still be the second
tank. There was always a tank ahead of me, so at no time would I ever be
out in front, or left behind.

Most of the time, the tank out in front would be the one that was in
the most danger. The officer that was commanding us would be in that

first tank, he was usually a lieutenant, and he passed the orders down over the intercom system to the rest of the tank commanders.

The tank that we had, we could transmit to other tanks. They didn't all have a transmitter. There were only two in our platoon, I believe, that could transmit and ours happened to be the other one besides the lead tank that had a transmitter in it. As the second tank in our platoon, we were equipped to take the lead if the first tank happened to get knocked out. So, Donald could talk to other tank commanders, back and forth, in the tanks that had transmitters. Most of the other tanks just had to listen, they couldn't talk back. I could hear all the conversations on the headphones, as McAbee switched channels back in the turret.

Up to this point, we had been allowed to ride unbuttoned if we wanted, so we could get some air. Of course, it gave the drivers and tank commanders a chance to survey the landscape. Evidently, though, the army didn't believe they'd gotten every last German soldier out of the area. For that reason, they announced to us that we would be driving buttoned up until further notice since we were well into Hitler's Fatherland. The drivers didn't much like that for long periods, but it was better than having your head shot at.

With a squeak and a heavy metal thud, the hatches closed us in. Up front, the compartments we sat in were tight, not even enough room to turn around in. The driver and assistant driver were strapped in our seats to keep from being slung around on rough terrain. Of course, we had padding. The hatch cover was thick with padding, so if we hit hard after topping a hill or some obstacle, we wouldn't knock ourselves out.

We were all glad to be in our cramped spaces behind armor. As tankers, we were aware that we were a big target, something the German tanks and artillery really looked for, but we also knew that small arms and shrapnel couldn't get us if we stayed down in that tank. So we felt we had it a little better than the infantry did at least.

We knew we wouldn't be surprising any Germans. Anybody could hear those armored columns comin' for miles. When we got moving, those Sherman tanks were loud. Oh, yeah. Loud on the outside—with the engines roaring, the wheels squeaking and tracks clattering on the streets. Inside, you had to have earmuffs. You couldn't hardly stay in there without them. Of course, your headphones were connected to your ear muffs, so you could hear your orders and all that went on.

With the hatches closed, it was dark inside the tank except for the little instrument lights that were powered by our Homelite generator. Everything was painted white in the tank, and that helped us to see in there. But you couldn't see all that well inside — or outside. Now that we were buttoned up, our vision was limited by the tank's little glass periscopes and they were always gettin' dirty and fuzzy.

Up in the turret, the tank commander's periscope lifted up out of the top of the tank and gave Donald a slit of vision, which he could turn 360 degrees. But he could only see a little slice of the pie at a time.

I depended on Donald to guide me if I had to turn around, or go in reverse, things like that. And, of course, Knode would depend on him to sight the targets for the cannon.

Naturally, my periscope didn't turn 360 degrees. I could turn it from side to side a little bit. I had to turn my head to do that and it would turn the scope. As the driver, I generally had to look straight ahead. I'd lean my face against the rubber casing, look through the periscope's glass eyepiece, and I'd watch all the two-story barns, horse pastures, and roadside villages goin' by in that little window, hour after hour, as I drove into Nazi Germany.

I don't know just how far inland we were, but we were entering this little village. It was a nice little village. They had a lot of them in Germany and I couldn't tell you one from another. I could see the cobblestone street in the center of my periscope and the little whitewashed houses with open shutters creepin' by. We were going pretty slow through town.

That's where I saw my first living German soldier. Our tank was less than a hundred yards away. He came down a flight of stairs to my left. He had his hands up high above his head, waving them in the sunshine. It was about springtime, or gettin' close, so it wasn't too cold that day. He had on a real nice uniform, regular army, I think it was, and it looked like it had just been pressed, all neat and clean. I figured he'd made up his mind to surrender because it looked like he'd gotten himself ready to be taken prisoner. Evidently, he was living upstairs.

He had a pistol in a holster. I knew he wasn't gonna try to use it, because he didn't have a chance against all those tanks anyway. I don't remember if he had a white flag. Some of them did, but I don't think he did. He just kept his hands up and he stepped down onto the sidewalk. That German soldier was expecting somebody to take him prisoner.

We never bothered him, we were just gonna drive on by.

And just before our tank got to him—I saw him bend over and he started to sink down to his knees and he went to tryin' to get his pistol, he reached for it, tryin' to pull it out. But it was too late for him.

He'd been hit. It was just one shot. I couldn't see where the bullet hit him, but it was a fatal shot. Quick as it hit him, the German soldier doubled in two and he just sunk on down. The gunfire came from a tank behind me. That really hurt me 'cause he was trying to surrender.

By that time in the war, we'd heard some of the Germans were beginning to give up on Hitler's cause when they began to see that the Allies were just overrunning them and that the end of the war was coming. So the first German soldier that I saw—a nice-looking young man—he was giving himself up when he got shot.

We just went right on by him in the tank.

"Oh," I thought, "whoever did that, he did the wrong thing."

When we got to where we assembled for the night, there was a boy out in camp bragging about it. I knew him real well. He was from up north and right now, I can't remember his name. But I remember how he looked, struttin' like a rooster.

He said to a group of them, "Did you see that Nazi Kraut with his hands up? One shot! I got a kill on the first shot . . ."

Of course, I didn't know who'd killed that German soldier till I heard that boy start telling his story and then I knew, I knew who'd pulled the trigger then. He kept tellin' it just like it happened.

". . . He tried to grab his pistol and take his last shot, but he dropped dead in a split second from my .45."

That boy reared back against the hull of his tank and laughed. "I always said if I had to come over here, I'd kill the first Kraut I saw, 'cause he's the reason, Germany's the reason I had to go fight. Yeah, the night I left home I made a vow. I vowed if I had to fight these . . . Krauts, I'd kill the first . . . one that I laid eyes on. And I got to do that today!"

Of course, he used some ugly profanity in *his* tellin'.

He told us all that night, "I fulfilled my . . . vow."

Aw, I didn't think much of that boy, after he told that story. I just didn't think that was the attitude he ought to have had. But nothing that went on in war seemed fair and square. Everybody was out for themselves.

I had my head hung low and said to some of my tank crew, "Well, I never would have thought anybody would have killed somebody and them with their hands up, a tryin' to surrender. I thought it was a dirty trick when I seen it, and I thought it when that boy was a tellin' it, too. It was a real dirty trick of him."

"He had no business doin' that," Knode agreed.

"Ain't right." Rhodes shook his head.

None of my crew or the good buddies I associated with would have shot a man trying to surrender, and I sure was glad. But some people were so bitter because they had to go fight, they just wanted to do as much damage as they could as soon as they got into Germany, and probably more than one of them made a vow like that.

Now, of course, we didn't know it at that time, but as it would turn out, the boy who shot that surrendering German soldier, he would have some pretty bad luck a comin'. Sometime after that—when we got into combat—a big shell came along and hit his tank. It might have been an 88 from a German tank, I don't know, but it was one of the bigger guns that got him.

He was a gunner and the shell hit his cannon and it just drove the gun into his head. He was looking through his periscope, sighting a target, and it shoved all that metal into his skull. Just about crushed his head, but he did live. They said he probably wouldn't ever know a thing. He had so much brain damage, I heard he'd be a vegetable for the rest of his life.

I've always thought about that. I said to myself, well, he took the first feller he saw and I guess that's his payday, for doing it when he didn't have to. If you *have* to kill someone, it's different than just volunteering to do it, especially a man who was surrendering. He wasn't going to bother anybody. That young soldier wanted to live just as bad as we did, and he was trying to give himself up to our side. He saw he was outnumbered and he knew he was going to be killed if he didn't surrender, but then, of course, he got killed anyway.

The army had really taught us about taking prisoners of war. We were told not to kill or mistreat any prisoners. What we really wanted was for the enemy to surrender. We wanted to end the bloodshed. If we started killing the ones who surrendered, well, pretty soon, they wouldn't want to take a chance on surrendering to us, if they thought we were gonna kill 'em in cold blood.

59th Infantry Battalion:

On March 26, the 59th Infantry Battalion marched to Zweibrucken, Germany and 59th soldiers caught their first glimpse of the "Super Race." The mission was to police the area and support Military Government. (8)

496th Armored Field Artillery Battalion:

For three days at Ommersheim we first became familiar with the problems of Military Government, prisoner handling, burial of the dead and occupation of a German town . . . and for the next two weeks we were engrossed in the problems which beset occupational troops both in the vicinity of Zweibrucken and later in the town of Hermeskiel near Trier. We occupied towns, guarded bridges and regulated traffic. (7)

The Division:

So then we were occupation troops, policing the towns of the Saar and searching German houses and frisking Kraut civilians

for hidden weapons. Servile, they were, with their "Nicht Nazi"
and "Hitler kaput." You couldn't find a self-admitted Nazi from
Zweibrucken and Waldmohr to Trier or Merzig. But the CIC
had a list of Nazis marked for automatic arrest and they scoured
the countryside with their teams of German-Speaking Black
Cats. (2)

On our march, sometimes we'd get held up in places for some reason that we never even knew about, stay in one little town or another.
Most of the time, about two or three nights was the most we'd stay in
a village, and then we'd take over another one pretty soon, making our
way forward.

The German soldiers had already moved out of the area, so it was
quiet as far as firefights went, even though sometimes we'd hear German
planes overhead. It made us a little nervous, I guess.

Our company was always ordered to take over one of the villages
that didn't have much damage, to set up quarters in the people's homes.
I found the German houses to be pretty much like what we had in
America. There were some brick houses, but the biggest part of them
were lumber with rows of windows and shutters, sometimes built pretty
close together on little streets. One-family dwellings, most of them.

The infantry would pull into the town and they'd dismount from
their half-tracks and go through the houses, clean out all the people, get
them together and take them outside. They wouldn't hurt the German
people, but they took them out of their homes. They'd round up everybody that lived in that village — it was mostly older people and women
and children. All the able men were soldiers, away somewhere. You
didn't find one of them, unless they were just hid in there for the purpose of tryin' to kill you.

They'd assign maybe one street for so many men to search the houses,
and so many houses for each crew. They'd use the tank crews if they
needed more men. A few times, my tank crew would have to go through
those German houses, searching for soldiers. They'd give Donald the
orders, tell him what to do, and he'd go through the houses with us. You

didn't know whether you'd get killed or not when you went in.

It was a fast maneuver. We'd file through the house and each one of us would take a room, go through it, clear it out. We looked in all the closets and under the beds and everywhere that there was anyplace for a soldier to hide. Of course, we had our Grease Gun strapped across and in hand, ready to peek around the next doorway.

You had to have your gun ready in case you ran into a lone straggler hiding out in one of those civilians' homes. There were some in that town. If a soldier was in there, expecting you to come in, he'd a good chance to kill you before you knew where he was hid. You had to have that in your mind all the time, that maybe there was a gun pointin' right at you, ready to fire. You always had that feelin'. But I never did find any German soldiers hiding in a house when we went through.

We'd find civilians who lived in the house and we'd always make them leave. The civilian people cooperated, but it was sad, to me, to see. A lot of the places, the women would cry and beg us to let them stay in their homes. Oh, they'd just cry and beg.

Sometimes the civilians didn't know that we were gonna do them that way, I guess, and they'd come out on the streets to see what was going on and our soldiers would just round them up, and they'd want to go back in the house to get something they needed, or maybe hide their valuables, but the guards wouldn't let them go back in there.

After we'd collect the people in the streets, then the infantry took over. They'd just take hundreds of them, thousands, I guess, in some towns, and they'd walk them out to a big field outside the main town and make them stay there. They'd circle the civilians with guards so they couldn't leave.

After we searched the village, if it was during the daytime, they'd let the people go back inside their homes, but if it was late in the evening, we'd sleep in their houses and they'd make the German people sleep out in the field. It was early spring and it wasn't very cold, but it was pretty cool in the mornings. I don't know if our military provided the civilians with blankets. A lot of them had coats on. Of course, there'd be so many of them, they just bundled up together and that kept them warm, I guess.

When we occupied a town, the army put guards at each road that came into the village. They'd guard the entrance to the village to keep people from slipping in. Our outfit set up a telephone that went to the headquarters. If somebody came along and had a good excuse to go in the village, the guard would have to call our command post and tell them that somebody wanted to enter the village and what their business was. If the officers wanted them to come on, they'd say, "You instruct them where to go and we'll watch for them." Any German civilians entering the area had to report to a certain building so they wouldn't trick us.

I know one time I was on guard duty and they had a German feller who worked for the fire department and he needed to go through the village to get to a fire somewhere else. I called in ahead for him. He was riding a motorcycle and they told me to send him on up to headquarters. They checked him out and he seemed to be all right and they let him go on through the village to the highway that he needed to travel. Usually if it was reasonable, they'd let them do it. Most of the time it was men who came up to the guards and wanted to go into the village for different reasons. Women, I guess they were a little afraid to risk doing that.

Occasionally, though, one of the women would come over to a guard, wanting to get back in their house, just a beggin' to get back in there, but we wouldn't take a chance on 'em. We weren't allowed to let them go back in their homes until we were finished with the town. That was kind of sad, havin' to turn them away, seein' some of the women in distress.

The army'd keep control like that until we got ready to move out, and then they'd tell the townspeople that they could go back to their homes. When they did, they found everything in a mess. Yeah, the German people sure found out that a lot of the G.I.s didn't have any regard for their property—especially if they found any swastikas in the house.

In one of the first houses we occupied, some of the boys were wanting to see a little picture on the wall—I heard one of them say he was gonna take it with him. My assistant driver, Rhodes, was looking for a souvenir 'cause, he said, "We're kickin' Hitler's ass all the way to Texas, and I want something for havin' to come over here and do it."

Now, overall, the boys in my tank crew were pretty good about leaving the German's personal things alone. McAbee was a real nice person and didn't bother anything in people's houses. Knode and Donald usually minded their own business, but they kind of got a kick out of watching the other boys look around.

So, when Rhodes took that picture down off the wall, there was a big black-and-red swastika hanging behind it. We were all surprised at that. The people that lived in there, I guess, had hung that picture over the swastika because they didn't want to take it down, but they didn't want us to know about it, if we happened to come into their house. They had evidently been sympathizers, probably. Well, the German people, they had to go by the orders of Hitler, 'cause if they hadn't, he would've had them killed. You'd think the civilians thought a lot of him by all their displays of Nazi symbols, but when the war began to end, it was a different story.

After we found out that's what the Germans were doin', every house we'd go in, we'd check to see how many swastikas we could find. I don't know, we just got to doin' that. Did we find a lot? Oh, yeah, in a lot of places, they'd have those swastikas hanging behind every picture, behind clocks, in the back of cupboards. I guess, before it got so near to the end of the war, they had Hitler's symbols displayed all the time, but when I was in Germany, they began to hide them.

It didn't bother a one of us to be in somebody's house and go through their private stuff, 'cause we's over there in a war. When we were in France, we had to be careful about not tearing up things, but in Germany we didn't worry about it. Of course, when the battles were going on, the more stuff we could tear up, the better it would be for us. But in areas where the Allies had taken over, some of the boys didn't care how much damage they did in civilian people's homes, 'cause they were mad, mad as the devil that they had to go over there to fight a war.

I didn't feel like that, because I felt like the civilian people we saw didn't have a thing to do with it. They hated to be in a war, I guess, just as bad as we did, but they were just forced by their leaders to be in a war. I never did tear up a thing, and none of the boys in my tank crew did either, but a lot of crews just took pride in seeing how much stuff they could tear up when they went through the houses, they were so bitter against the Germans.

One of the things that the Germans did which caused a lot of unnecessary damage was to lock their pianos. Nearly all of the nice homes had pianos in them and every household locked the cover over the keyboard. Of course, the boys, they'd tear them open—once they found out that's where the Germans stored their valuables, under that keyboard cover. They'd find gold watches and jewelry in there. They took a lot of German watches. The German people didn't have any idea that we'd do that, I don't reckon.

Some boys would just bust that cover off those keys with anything they could find. Take an ax to it, if they had to. I could hear the sounds of wrecked piano keys and springing piano wire and cracking wood, when some of them splintered up pianos to get the covers open. If the Germans had just left their pianos so you could raise the lid, probably most of our boys would have just gotten the souvenirs out of there that they wanted and spared the pianos.

But some of the boys were mean anyway, and they'd use any excuse just to take it out on the people and their homes. I didn't feel like there was any advantage to that. Some of the boys were like me and felt sorry for the civilians, especially the women and children who got caught up in the middle of this war.

As far as I know, the American soldiers respected the German women real well. Some of the German girls were mighty pretty. A lot of the girls would take after the American soldiers. They'd just take up with them. It was a sight how friendly the German girls were. I guess they'd been tied down under Hitler's power and they wanted freedom. They were real happy that we were there to end the war for them. A lot of the boys would—well, some of them, I understand, went back after the war and got married to the girls they'd met during the war.

Of course, there was strict army policy—unenforced as far as I saw—that soldiers didn't have any social contact with the German civilians. "No fraternizing," they'd told us. One boy in our outfit met a

German girl in one of those towns, and he just fell for her, and she was so taken with him, she started following him along our route and she met up with him in several little towns around there where we took over. I don't know how she found him, but she did. None of us in my tank ever got involved with local girls on our way through Germany, but you saw all kinds of things that went on with our troops.

We all enjoyed sleeping in the Germans' houses. They had some nice beds and we'd take a room and sleep in them. If there weren't enough beds, we'd lie on the floor and then we needed something a little softer, our bedroll.

A lot of times, I slept in their beds if I got in there first and claimed one. We always found the German bedding to be clean. I noticed right away that the people in Germany were really neat and clean about everything. I'd look things over before I'd bed down. I looked to see what kind of mattresses they had. The Germans had three-piece mattresses, different to what we had in the U.S. They had three little strips that went across the frame, crossways, and it made a good comfortable bed. We sure needed a soft place to sleep. That sleeping wherever you find yourself is hard on a feller.

The German people kept their kitchens and pantries neat and clean, too. We'd get into their cupboards and canned goods, looking for something to eat. On the move, I was gettin' mighty tired of those powdered army eggs. Even the poorest German homes had sauerkraut. That reminded me of home a little bit, 'cause my mother used to make her sauerkraut from an old German recipe. It was good to have something different to eat once in a while.

That was taking a chance, I felt, because the Germans could have put some poison in the food that they left there when they saw that we were taking their neighbors out of their houses. I thought a lot of times that it was a good way for the Germans to make us sick if they were Nazi sympathizers, put poison in some nice-looking food they left out, but I never did know of anybody getting sick eating the stuff they got out of the German kitchens.

Well, some of the boys, they found their own poison. Some of them were wild. There were a lot of 'em that got over in Germany and they just did about anything they wanted—usually they'd find some whiskey and go on a big drunk. They dreaded going into battle and said it eased their nerves. But they didn't know what they did half the time. The homes in Germany had a lot of alcohol and the boys that fooled with that stuff, they'd find liquor in houses where we took over. Some of the tanks had crews that would discard their ammunition to make room in the racks for the bottles of liquor that they'd collect. I thought that was just downright foolish.

> *Death must not be feared. Death in time comes to all of us, and every man is scared in his first action. If he says he's not, he's a *!%$?#! liar. Some men are cowards, yes, but they fight just the same, or get the hell slammed out of them. The real hero is the man who fights even though he's scared. Some get over their fright in a minute, under fire. Others take an hour. For some it takes days.*
>
> *But a real man will never let the fear of death overpower his honor, his sense of duty to his country and to his manhood. A man must be alert all the time if he expects to stay alive.*
>
> **— General George S. Patton,**
> **Commander of the U.S. Third Army**

24th Tank Battalion:

Our next move was a 75-mile march to Birkenfield to join the U.S. Third Army commanded by two-star General George S. Patton, on April 2. (1)

45th Tank Battalion:

The First and Ninth Armies had carved out a pocket in the Ruhr and the 4th Armored Division was deep in Germany when we received our next movement order. We moved to join the Third Army at Alsfeld, Germany, near Kassel, at that time, the scene of heavy fighting . . . the report spread that we were immediately to relieve the famed 4th Armored on the drive into the heart of Germany. (10)

Word traveled fast through the ranks. We'd been with the Seventh Army mopping up in the Saar, but now we were assigned to General George S. Patton's Third Army. We all thought we were heading toward Berlin, to take over the German capital, and we *were* headed in that direction.

The push was on for the Allies to take Germany's capital and end the war in Europe as soon as possible. We all knew that Berlin would be the big prize and there was a lot of talk about who would actually spearhead the offensive into the city. Everybody knew General Patton was known for spearheading attacks, so we figured he might be the one to lead the charge. 'Course, down there in those tanks, you didn't know very much.

We knew the name Patton, though. As tankers, we'd learned about him in our classes back in training. He was known for pioneering a lot of our armored tactics, and as a general, he had a hit-'em-hard, hit-'em-fast, style of fighting. Under his command, we wasted no time.

It was raining the night the whole division rumbled out of Trier. Our immediate mission was to relieve the 4th Armored Division at the front—or so we thought.

The Division:

On April 5, 1945, the vehicles of the Division moved out of the occupational area and proceeded across the Rhine River by way of the pontoon bridge at St. Goar, Germany. (2)

THE KITTEN, Ruhr Battle Extra

. . . The Cats took off for a long ride across the Rhine. The historic river, for all the castles along its banks, turned out to be less spectacular than expected and one Pfc. from Division Trains was even led to remark that it "had nothing on the good old East River." (6)

We made our approach to the Rhine River. The Rhine was the last natural barrier to the German heartland. It had been an obstacle to the Allies' ground forces invading from the west, but we knew we were not the first Americans to cross it now.

It was the first week of April, and Allied troops had crossed the Rhine a few weeks earlier at places like Remagen, where the first German bridge was captured almost intact and crossed by the U.S. First Army. After that, the Allies started crossing the Rhine in droves, at different places, using our bridges that we'd brought with us, 'cause the Germans always blew out their own bridges, if they could, to slow us down as they retreated.

"Our engineers have the bridge ready. And Jerry's cleared out," Donald's voice came over the intercom. "Word is, Patton doesn't want us to lose a minute."

The 13th Armored Division crossed the Rhine at a real old town called St. Goar. I can remember going down to that river. Our convoy traveled through some low mountain country, and we came down, down, down into a valley, where that really wide river was, the beautiful Rhine. We were on a winding road—it was hilly country around there—and they had grape vineyards to the left, all along the hills. The Germans had put their grapevines on posts with a cross arm on top, like a crucifix. I saw whole vineyards of them, spread out and spaced sort of like that cemetery in France. They had the crosses every so far apart and the grapevines would hang down where you could walk under them to pick the fruit. I thought that was a pretty good idea to fix grapevines like that. I don't know why I remember that, but I can just see that as we were driving down the road—those grapevines attached to all those crosses.

We came down from the hills to a town of half-timbered houses, and I could see the big, wide river everyone was talking about. The Rhine River at St. Goar had high terraced banks that were steep and up in them sat some stone castles and a round tower built into the hill.

We always had the stuff to get across those rivers, and there were a lot of them in Germany. The engineers that traveled with us brought truckloads of bridging and metal tracks. They would get to the rivers first and build bridges with sections of inflatable pontoons. They put those pontoons out there in the water and connected them across. The pontoons floated a couple of feet apart, sometimes less. Across that line of pontoons, the engineers would lay the track and then they fastened the track together. They built it little by little, all the way across, under cover from our artillery. When the bridge finally reached across that river, those metal tracks that they'd connected to the pontoons made a floating roadway for us to drive on.

It took a pretty good while for the whole convoy to cross that river because you had to have a big space between vehicles. We had to cross that thing with thirty-four-ton battle tanks, and that wasn't even the heaviest of our equipment. I don't remember how many, but we had to be several feet apart, because you couldn't get too many tanks on that pontoon bridge at the same time. We'd line up on the road and have to wait. We were backed up through that village a pretty good while, creepin' along through the streets.

"Well, Patton wouldn't be too happy if he knew this. Burning fuel and not getting anywhere." Donald liked to keep moving, too. "Knode, you think you could put those smokes out till we get across the river?"

Knode was just sittin' back in there with nothin' to do and he kept a cloud of smoke around him 'bout all the time. The engine was idling when we waited to cross the river and the way that tank was built, it could get pretty hot and smoky back in the turret, even if they opened the hatches.

I reckon Knode put his cigarette out.

Donald was always good to tell us things to pass the time. He went on. "Across the river, there's supposed to be a huge slate rock that's famous, part of an old German legend. One of the officers was telling us about it—his grandmother's German. Legend's about a girl named Lorelei and for some reason, the story goes, her lover broke her heart, so she jumped off the high rocks over there and drowned. They say her spirit sits on that rock and she sings to hypnotize sailors. She lures them off course and wrecks their ships. The local people claim they can hear her echoes."

"Let 'em hear the echoes of our thunder," Knode said. "That'll give 'em something to talk about."

"Sounds like one of those trouble-making Nazi *fraulines* to me," Rhodes said. "Let's blast that rock of hers to pieces—and shut her up!"

"Get the lieutenant to let us, and we'll use that rock for target practice." Knode was rarin' to go. Of course, that was out of the question. Gunners were always thinking about targets.

"Maybe we can spot that rock up there, when we get a little closer to the river. Except you, Kelley, you keep your eyes straight ahead," Donald said. "We don't want that siren to lure *you* off course."

"Will do." I couldn't be looking up and around anyway, and I wasn't interested in sights. But the other men, the gunners especially, they didn't have anything much else to do—yet.

"Keep 'er in the middle," Donald reminded me about our training as we crawled forward onto the floating tracks and they bobbed down in the water. Where we crossed, the Rhine narrowed quite a bit—even though it was still a wide river—Donald said it was real deep here. That made its current swift and turbulent. Those pontoon bridges did their fair share of bobbin' about.

"Nobody start gettin' seasick in here, now," Rhodes joked.

"If anyone gets seasick, Kelley'll be the first," Donald said. They all remembered how sick I was on that ship comin' over and got a chuckle out of it.

I had my face pressed against the periscope window, both hands gripping the steering levers in front of me as I drove across that pontoon bridge. Everybody was a little bit nervous, I guess, the first time we had to cross a big river like that and they depended on me to stick right to my training.

The pontoons held the bridging up enough to keep us afloat, but they would go way down in the water when you drove that tank on them. I could see the tank in front of me floating, so I knew where to drive, but right where the tank was up ahead, the whole bridge would mash down and disappear, the tanks were so heavy.

If you got too close to the next tank, you'd both just sink down from the combined weight, and go under. You really had to be careful, you had to stay right where you were supposed to, and you couldn't get over to the edge, the pontoons would maybe flip out from under you. Law me, imagine being trapped in a steel tank at the bottom of a river!

That was a nerve-racking thing, to drive that tank across the Rhine River on a pontoon bridge. It took the whole company a pretty good while to finish the crossing, but the individual tanks traveled across that river pretty fast. Oh, we'd travel at a speed of about two miles an hour, about like you'd be walking. Once we got on the bridge, we'd be across it in a few minutes.

Headquarters, Division Artillery:

Patton had the 13th now. Everyone hung onto his hat as we took off for the front lines, crossed the Rhine at St. Goar and, despite a shortage of replacements for shredded bogie wheels, continued to assembly areas. (16)

The Division:

The 13th was ordered to the vicinity of Homberg, near Kassel. For the first time the men saw the famed Autobahns that were to play such a vital role in the defeat of Germany. The convoys rolled day and night . . . Overhead the ever-welcome P-51s and P38s rode herd over the earthbound vehicles. (2)

We had a monstrous column of vehicles traveling through Germany — all those muddy trucks, half-tracks, and, of course, the Sherman tanks, all growling like big beasts in a long line that stretched way on out of sight. It was smooth riding when we got on their superhighways. We could really pick up speed then. They had some nice highways, *Autobahns*, they called them.

The Germans had some of their main roadways poured in a continuous ribbon of concrete. I'd never seen anything like that before and it made a good surface to drive on. The Germans cut a groove across the concrete every so many feet apart, so the roadway could expand and not crack. I thought that was a good way to engineer a road. I could see the grooves disappear under my tank as we got goin'. Our convoy kept on the move. The dirty vehicles drove evenly spaced and all the drivers were a pourin' on the gas in a hurry to get to our first battle—wherever we found it.

★ ★ ★

The Division:

The Division closed into Homberg on April 7 and girded for combat. But we didn't fight there either. We turned around again and lit out for the Ruhr back over the same Autobahn. (2)

Headquarters, Division Artillery:

Last minute plans to head toward Leipzig and meet the Russians were formed and reformed; Division patches put on and taken off again; vehicles loaded and radios tuned up—nothing could stop us now. So, with a 150-mile about face we returned to Horhausen, just south of the Ruhr pocket, where we joined the XVIII Corps (Airborne) as part of the First Army. (16)

Donald came back to the tank and told us, "We're about halfway to Berlin right now, but there's been a change of plans. The First Army needs us more in the Ruhr Valley. They've surrounded a big pocket of German soldiers up there—they say it's not more than a hundred thousand of 'em—but the Germans've probably got a lot of firepower hidden up there. We're goin' in to get 'em. So, we're turning around, goin' back the way we came."

Well, I don't know about any of the others, but I thought fighting a trapped pocket of German soldiers sounded better than invading the German capital. So, before we did any fighting with Patton's army, they switched us around and for this mission, the 13th Armored Division was being attached to General Courtney H. Hodges' First Army.

General Hodges wasn't as famous as General Patton. I heard that

Hodges was a Southerner and what impressed me was that even though he'd flunked out of West Point, he went back and started out in the army in the ranks of common enlisted men—and he worked his way up to being Commander of the First Army. Under Hodges, the First Army had been the first to cross into Germany and breach the Siegfried Line, and the first to reach the banks of the Rhine River.

That First Army had just completed a link-up with the Ninth Army about a week earlier, on April 1, 1945. Those two armies met up in what everybody was calling a "pincer movement" that encircled a big pocket of German soldiers backed up in the Ruhr Valley, so it was being called the Ruhr Pocket, or some of 'em called it the Rose Pocket. The First Army needed additional troops to spearhead a drive into that pocket of Nazi soldiers. That was us—we were goin' right into the middle of that beehive.

Our reconnaissance told us that those German soldiers were reorganizing, getting more soldiers together and setting up defenses in the Ruhr Valley—a spread-out region of cities, villages, farmland, and factories. The German soldiers would have plenty of places to cluster up and defend what resources they had left. I reckon those German factories were still churning out supplies for the war, despite all the British bombings that had been going on since 1940.

The Ruhr was over a hundred miles away, and, of course, everything was "on the double, on the double!" Usually the tank'd go around twenty-five miles per hour, sustained speed. We had the governors open on them as far as they would go, so they might've gone as fast as thirty miles per hour if it was on good smooth terrain, which the Autobahn was. That seems real fast in a tank. If you were driving in a car, you'd think you were just foolin' along, but in a tank, they're pretty bouncy and it seemed like we were really movin' on.

The driver had to be careful—you could turn a Sherman tank over at that speed. Of course, if you locked up a track, that tank would spin around with you. And if you ran them so much that you got your brakes hot, they'd get away from you.

In that Sherman, since the steering levers did the job of both steering and braking the tank, if a brake got hot on a Sherman, it could lock up.

Then you were in trouble—you couldn't steer that tank.

Now, when we doubled back, we just made a U-turn right in the road where we were when we got the orders. We traveled facing the rest of our division on the same stretch of highway before everybody could get turned around and all going in one line in the same direction. There was such a monstrous column of vehicles that we met each other for a long, long time.

Even though those German roads were wide, we had to leave quite a bit of room between the opposing columns and I had to run my right track off on the shoulder of the road, in the dirt. It was softer than the road, and that caused me to have to pull on the left brake all the time to compensate. I kept the brake on to keep the tank from going off the road. After a while, that one brake got so hot, it just quit. Locked up.

I came to a little curve in the road, and I saw right away that I couldn't make the curve, I couldn't steer it. I just went straight off the road and down the bank and Donald called out, "What are you goin' down here for?!"

I said, "Them brakes got hot and I can't steer it! I've got to steer around through here and I'll get back on the road when I can."

I was wrestling with that tank. I came down the slope and I just happened to go into an open field. I drove a little ways in that countryside and I got some control over that tank and steered it through a little ravine and back up onto the highway down the line, and I got back in the convoy. The brakes cooled down pretty fast with all that air rushing over them. I was all right then.

"Kelley, when you pulled outta line, I thought you'd flown your coop," Donald said.

"Nah, figured I'd just wake us up in here," I said. "Turned out to be a good little shortcut."

Now, that scared me up, knowin' that tank was out of control in real enemy territory. We were lucky that it wasn't a minefield. Boy, I was real careful after that.

Several of the drivers had problems on that long march. Anytime, really, those tanks were subject to having problems, brakes locking up, bogie wheels breaking down, things like that. That was happening to somebody pretty often.

497th Armored Field Artillery Battalion:

By this time we had begun to get into serious trouble with our bogie wheels on the M-7's. Replacements were few, and the tremendous amount of traveling was blowing them out right and left. It was not unusual to arrive in a new location with only three or four of our eighteen M-7's with us, the rest trailing in from then on for about twelve hours or so. The problem was never quite cured. (13)

24th Tank Battalion:

April 8, we set out for Schonberg to join the First Army for a Ruhr Valley cleanup. We arrived there with only a few road-weary tanks, the rest of them were strung out over the 159 mile route with blown bogie wheels. Combat loomed the next day. (1)

Word came down the line that we were headed into battle within the next twenty-four hours. We'd traveled a long ways with our tanks as fast as we could go and the wheels on the tank that turn the tracks—the bogie wheels—they were about shot on a lot of the tanks. Those bogies've got a rubber coating around them that runs on a steel track and if that rubber peels off, it's metal to metal, and that'll just grind things up. You have to put another bogie wheel on there right away.

That day the company had so many bogie wheels that went bad, we had plumb run out of 'em and we'd used up all the spares. I had one blown bogie on my tank. Several other tanks in the company were the same way, with just one or two bogies blown. We were all held up somewhere in the German countryside.

We heard that the officers decided to set one good tank aside from our platoon and take all of the good bogie wheels off of that one tank. They'd put one wheel on one tank, put one on another. Like that, they'd get three or four tanks to where they could go.

One of the lieutenants came by and said, "Your wheels are in pretty good shape, Kelley. We'll take the rest of your good bogies to distribute to the company. Pull out of line."

Well, I didn't much like that.

But just a few minutes later, Donald came back to the tank and he said, "I just saw the lieutenant. He said Captain Blake changed the plan. We're goin' on. They're giving us a new bogie wheel and we'll be on our way to the front."

"Let's get 'er fixed and keep 'er rollin'!" Rhodes said.

Donald continued. "Captain said to let the tanks that're easiest to fix go on ahead. They've got three other tanks that need some work, so they're taking the rest of their good wheels to give out to the company."

The tanks they selected to stay behind needed so much other work anyway, they figured they'd get the rest of us going, and have the maintenance crews that followed get all their problems fixed. So they took off what good wheels they had, and gave two to our tank, so we'd replace our bad wheel and have a spare. Then we took off.

I was glad. We could go on our journey, because the next day, we were supposed to be on the battlefront in the Ruhr. I'd rather be with the rest of the battalion than out isolated. Of course, you were liable to run into trouble no matter which way you went.

My first tank commander from training in California, Foster, his tank was one that was selected to stay behind. The driver he'd got in Texas, Charlie Eaton, was with him, a real jolly feller. They took all kinds of parts off of Foster's tank to put on other tanks and they left that tank back behind the lines, with a couple more tanks from our company, all waiting for maintenance to get to them. I think those tank crews were glad to be pulled out of the convoy.

Lonnie Johnson, 24th Tank Battalion, C Company:

They told us to take the rollers off of Charles Eaton's tank and put on our tank, that needed a roller. That just about stripped his down and he was tickled to death. He said, "Boy, I got it made.

It's liable to be a week or two before they get up here with any rollers to fix mine." And he said, "I'm gonna fix you boys some supper." We had a little ol' heater thing. You just strike a match to it and you could fry an egg on it or whatever you had. Mostly, what we had was just canned food and he pretended to be fixing a meal for us and heated up some of the canned stuff. We was carryin' on, and he was talkin' about how lucky he was. (12)

I remember Foster's driver, Charlie Eaton—he was from Kentucky—he told us when we got ready to pull out, "I'll be thinking about you boys when you're up there on the front lines and us just a layin' back here eatin' good, warm meals and everything." He was sitting up on the front of the tank, and he just rubbed his belly and laughed. "I'll be thinkin' 'bout y'all up there!" He was always kind of a joking feller.

We left those tanks behind and we traveled on. The villages we drove through looked similar to what some of our country villages are in the States, most of time out in the farming land, just little farming villages. It reminded me some of Tennessee, the German countryside, only the houses were a little different style.

As we neared the battle zone, we passed through towns and countryside where troops before us had pushed the Germans back and we could see evidence of the German's retreat. They'd left their artillery set up along the highways.

I remember that we came to a sawmill set up along the highway, and they had one of those 88s sitting in there. That big, long barrel was just sticking out through some brush and stuff. Nobody was manning it. If they had been, they could have picked us off. But the German soldiers had retreated. They'd found out that the Americans were overrunning them, so that saved us. Saved a lot of lives, right there.

Sometimes the Germans had to leave their big guns behind, they didn't have any way of moving them fast when they retreated. A lot of those guns had to be towed. We started to see a lot of artillery set up in the field, whether they were the antitank guns or the bigger antiaircraft guns, they had them dug in to where I just saw the end of those big barrels sticking out, ready to knock us out. They'd be sittin' there silent, with no sign of life anywhere around, so I knew the enemy soldiers had moved out. I could spot an 88's muzzle pretty quick in my side vision. The biggest of them were the antiaircraft 88s and they had a long, tapered barrel. As we drove in front of them, I could never forget that they had the power to shoot right through my tank.

That evening, we came into a little village to spend the night. We'd come through some pretty good-sized towns that day. We didn't usually stay in a big town, or in cities. If you stayed in a larger town, well, you didn't have much control. There were so many people there, you couldn't handle all of them. That's why we stayed most of the time in villages, so we could get the people out and have protection. We'd get our tanks in behind buildings, where it would be hard for the Germans to knock them out with artillery because there was a lot of stuff in the way. Once in a while we'd have to stay out in an open field. But we were always subject to bein' a target out there.

We were setting up camp when we got word that one of the tanks in the convoy broke down on the last leg of the march. They were just sitting out in the country, alone. If you got broke down out there, well, you were in trouble. If the German soldiers were anywhere around, they were pretty apt to kill you or capture you. All alone, there wasn't much way you could protect yourself while you had to wait for help. You could shoot off some shells or small arms fire if the Germans came, but if you couldn't go, they were bound to get you if you stayed in the tank, and likely to get you if you bailed out.

One of the lieutenants came around and told Donald, "We've got a tank stranded a few miles back down the highway, stopped right on the railroad track. I'd like you to take your tank and get everybody back here. And get all the equipment out of their tank."

We didn't just volunteer.

Donald told us, "Gear up. We're gonna go pick up those boys. And let's double-time it. We've got to beat the Jerries to 'em."

It was just one tank with the crew out there, and one tank sent to bring 'em back. It was the first time we'd had a solo mission. Something had happened to their engine and it left them a sitting duck, when all the others went on and left them, and now it was dark. Of course, them bein' stuck right on the railroad tracks, they didn't know if the Germans would try to use the railroads. We didn't know a thing out there.

When we went off, the lieutenant warned us, "Now, you're in enemy territory. You may be in trouble if they spot you. Stay blacked out."

We couldn't drive with lights on. We didn't want the enemy to detect us. The lieutenant had cautioned us that the German's air force, the Luftwaffe, were known to be in the area.

Those Sherman tanks had what they called "cat eyes," that's how we could drive in the dark. Those cat eyes were little slits that shined down towards the ground. It was kind of a little beam of light along the edge of the road. You could see to stay in the road with them, but you couldn't see to drive very fast hardly at all. With those cat eyes, you can only see just straight in front of you, and only a very little. An airplane wasn't supposed to be able to pick up those lights from the air.

It was really the first time I tried to drive by the light of cat eyes in Germany. Even in my training, it was really hard for me to do. Of course, it was good they made me, 'cause when you're over in the combat zone, if you have to drive that way, you already know what to expect. Didn't make it any easier to do it, though. I had to just force myself.

We were quiet on that drive out into the darkness alone. Knode was always smoking a cigarette if he could, and he smoked more when he got nervous. He could smoke in the tank as much as he wanted because we hadn't hit resistance yet. We all knew we were bound to, though.

If I turned, I could see his feet and legs back in the turret. The basket they rode in was made out of heavy metal, but it wasn't solid. It had holes punched in the metal, and I could see through them a little bit back in the turret, but not much. They had the ammunition back there to load the guns, so they had to have enough light to do that, and it threw some shadows into the front of the tank where Rhodes and I sat.

Up front, the driver and assistant driver had little lights and the instruments were lit, too, but the light wasn't bright enough to be seen from an open hatch at night. In the turret, the lighting was a little brighter, maybe it could be seen from the air. All of us could see what we needed to when we were riding buttoned up, but you sort of felt like you were underground most of the time. In hostile zones, all the drivers kept buttoned up, because we were down low where they could really pick us off from a little hill or a second-story window, 'cause we were driving by. I don't know of any who ever raised the hatch to drive. Except at night.

I was having to drive pretty slow, 'cause I couldn't see much through that little periscope. It was evidently a cloudy night. Like back home, Germany'd had some April showers and it was dark enough that it was a real strain on my eyes to see the road, especially after looking through that periscope all day, traveling at top speed.

"Reckon I could drive with the hatch open?" I asked Donald. "I can't hardly see a thing through that periscope with just them little cat eyes."

"If you feel it's safer, all right, but keep your head down." Donald knew I had to see pretty well to do my job.

I peeked out above the hatch opening — and kept my head as low as I could get it, about halfway out of the hatch.

A lot of the German roadways were lined by rows of trees that had a white ring painted around the trunks. That made it easier to see them at night, otherwise, on a dark night, those tree trunks would just disappear.

I was headed out to the railroad crossing and I was making a sharp turn. I could see the broad outline of a big oak tree on my right. I thought I was missing that tree, but my right track hit that tree — hit it hard. I hit it so hard, it just about stopped the tank.

The jolt propelled me forward, threw me against the hatch, and I hit my face against the edge and, boy, I really laid my top lip open, just split it wide open from one end to the other, right under my nose. Of course, every part of that hatch was solid metal and it cut me pretty good when I hit that tree.

I hated that because I'd seen the tree and I thought I was gonna miss it. It was a tight turn and I evidently misjudged where my right track would hit.

I had blood running down my lip, but I had to drive. I held my handkerchief with one hand and grabbed the steering levers in front of me with the other hand. It took a while to stop the bleeding and my uniform got messed up. My lip was not cut deep enough for any medical attention beyond our field kit, I reckoned. It would leave a pretty good scabbed-up place there for a few weeks. A big long slash right above my top lip.

Down the road, I saw the broken-down tank sitting right where the lieutenant said it would be, where the roadway crossed the railroad tracks. When we got close, those boys came out of that tank like ants out of an anthill. They were glad to see us, oh, yeah. They were scared to death 'cause they figured they'd be captured and maybe killed and they didn't know what could happen.

They were a crew from our forces, but I'd never met them.

Their tank commander told us, "The rest of the column went on out of hearing. We listened to it fade away. We didn't have a bit of power. I told everybody, 'Looks like we'll be spending the night out here.' None of us had a good feeling about bein' out here alone. But as soon as we heard the sound of your tank coming back this way, we knew we were saved."

In the still of the evening, you could hear a lone Sherman rumblin' from a long ways off.

They were all real happy to see us, but we wanted to get out of there as fast as we could, so we got to work, helped them get their equipment into and onto our tank in the dark.

The other tank's driver noticed my lip and the blood on my shirt.

"You meet some resistance comin' up here?" he asked.

"No, but it looks like I'm helpin' the Germans a little bit, 'cause I done it myself," I said.

"Kelley bounced us off a tree." Donald flashed us his bright smile. "That's what they do in the backwoods where he's from."

"Aw, them cat eyes don't do a bit good lightin' up the road," I said. "Couldn't see a bit more than a goose through that periscope. And drivin' with my head out the hatch, I still couldn't see much better. But this broke me of that habit."

"Maybe it's a warning to stay buttoned up," the other tank driver said.

We just left that broken-down tank on the railroad tracks. I don't know whether maintenance ever came along and fixed it or whatever happened to it. But we got the guns and all the ammunition out of it, the radios and stuff that we didn't want to fall into the hands of the Germans. The men rode on the outside of our tank. That was kind of dangerous, but it wasn't as dangerous as staying out there all night by themselves.

As it happened, we didn't have any trouble. We didn't encounter any resistance that night. We brought the men back to the company and they spent the night there and went on their way the next morning with us, I guess, in another tank. The army had to replace tanks right away when they got 'em broke down.

The next morning, the division moved out and we started reaching places where 88 and mortar shells began to hit in our battalion area. The Germans were just sending them over, hoping to hit something, but I don't believe they had our range. Down in that tank, we could faintly hear the rumbles of them hittin' the ground over the growling of the Sherman's motor, underneath our muffled headphones.

We pulled all the tanks into a pine thicket for cover. There was a big pine grove right at the edge of a river, and we were a fixin' to cross that river. It was just about daylight, and those Germans started shelling us with artillery and they hit some of the pine trees behind us. They kept shelling us, off and on, knocking out the tops of those trees.

They knew we were there, but they didn't happen to knock out any of the tanks that I know of. They'd hit real close, but the Germans couldn't reach us. They had their range wrong. They couldn't see us and we were lucky they never did figure it out while we were there, assembling. But the thunder of artillery wasn't off in the distance anymore.

Our intelligence had information about where the German stronghold was and where we could expect to run into the first battle zone. We'd been told this was it: The Germans were waiting for us on the other side of the river. We were expecting to have to go into heavy combat somewhere after we crossed it. We just didn't know exactly where.

We'd already gotten up to the banks of that river and were lining up, preparing to cross it. About that time, one of the tanks that had been left behind the day before with the blown bogie wheels caught up to us. We heard the news and it spread like wildfire: Commander Foster and the other tanks that stayed behind, they'd run into trouble. Some of the men had been killed, several were wounded. A few had been captured.

The Germans didn't capture all of the survivors. The ones that got away joined up with us and they told us what had happened.

The night before, when we'd left those three broken-down tanks behind, the maintenance crew caught up with those tanks, pretty quick. They brought up parts, got the tanks repaired and outfitted them with new bogie wheels so they could come on and join us before we entered battle.

Those tanks traveled way into the night, hurrying to catch up to us, and they got lost. They were getting pretty close to us—well, they thought they were getting pretty close to where we were, but they'd got off on the wrong road. When they tried to find us, they pulled in right close to an airport. The Germans were still occupying it. They guarded their airports more closely than they did other places.

I guess the sound of those tanks alerted the enemy. And it was in the still of the morning. It was before daylight. One blaze of fire streaked the sky first, they said; it came out of nowhere, like lightning. Then the Germans filled the sky with a rain of fire, and those few tanks out there on their own, they got hit in the barrage. The Germans really opened up on them with heavy artillery. Those men had nobody to protect them, no other flanking to shoot back and take out the German guns.

The tank commander who'd been my tank commander all through training in California, Glen Foster, his tank got hit. That knocked Foster's tank out right away. It started burning and they had to bail out. Foster didn't happen to get killed himself, but he got wounded.

That first shell penetrated the tank right where the driver sat. I thought, boy, it's a good thing I wasn't Foster's driver then.

Foster's driver, Charlie Eaton, he was a coal miner when he worked at home in Kentucky. When the Germans opened up on them and that

88 shell went right through the tank where Charlie sat, it cut off one of his legs. Just went right through it.

I guess they left that one leg in the tank, I don't know, but they got him out of that burning tank as fast as they could, and they laid him on the ground. I think they may have put a tourniquet on his leg. They said Charlie was tryin' to get up off the ground with that one good leg, like he didn't know the other one was gone. Oh, law, I could hardly bear to hear that about my good buddy, Charlie.

Then there were some German medics that came out. I don't know how they signaled, how they knew about him bein' injured, but after the shelling stopped, the German medics came up there with white flags to assist them. They were pretty good to help us like that. The Germans were the only Allied enemies who would do that, I heard, whose medics would come out and help our wounded when the firefights ended.

They started to take Charlie to an aid station, somewhere close to the airport. The two German medics got on each side of Charlie to hold him up. He was a pretty husky feller. At first, Charlie was tryin' to hop on one leg, they said. They might've got him to a stretcher after that, I don't know. Charlie'd lost so much blood, though, that when they tried to take him to that first aid station, he died before he got there. He'd lost too much blood and he died.

Yeah, the men reported back about how they'd tried to save him. If he hadn't lost so much blood during all that time, well, we wondered about it. It took a little time to get him out of the tank with all the shelling and commotion. I don't really know what happened in Charlie Eaton's last minutes, 'cause I wasn't there, but a lot of them were talkin' about him. Anyway, the report we got, I believe they said he was callin' out for his momma; that was about the last thing they heard from him.

The other people in Eaton's tank didn't get killed. I think most of them got wounded, but they all made it. Some of them got away and they ran. But poor ol' Charlie Eaton, he got killed and there was also a tank driver in another tank who died. The Germans killed two of our tank drivers that night.

Lonnie Johnson, 24th Tank Battalion, C Company:

The Germans had a shell that would penetrate a tank and by Charles Eaton bein' out of place, when it got light, they had zeroed in on his tank and they just tore it up. Shells went right in on him.

Donnie Knight went berserk. He got out of his tank and went down in front of his tank with his little ol' Thompson submachine gun, which wouldn't hit nothin' hardly. He went down the road a firin' his gun and a cussin' the Germans. He just lost it and said, "I'm gonna kill 'em all," and went down the road a shootin' his gun and they just mowed him down with a machine gun. The Germans, they just cut him near about half in two, with bullets right there. He'd lost his nerves, he just went berserk. He couldn't stand it. It was the strain of expectin' to get killed, was what it was. Knight was high-tempered. He just couldn't take it. (12)

That other tank driver who got killed was a feller from up in Pennsylvania, Donnie Knight, and he was the meanest little booger. Knight never said a word without using a curse word some way or somehow and he got shot up real bad.

They'd knocked his tank out, too, and when the crew bailed out, the Germans opened up on them with a machine gun. Knight, they said, he didn't take cover like the rest of 'em. I remember them telling me that he just went berserk. They said he stood out in the open, laid on the trigger of his Grease Gun, and yelled, "No! I'll kill 'em all. I'll kill those—." Well, he said a lot that wasn't fit to say, let alone remember.

Some of those boys told me that the Germans just filled Donnie Knight full of bullets and he suffered terrible. Knight lived for a few minutes and they said he cursed just as long as he had breath and just as hard as he could. That was sad to hear. I wished they hadn't told me that.

Now, Donnie Knight was one who had profanity on his lips all the time, from training right on into the war. He must have grown up around rough characters, because he used foul language about every other word he said, whoever he was talkin' to, about whatever it was, even if he was just talking to you about the weather. Unless he was talking to an officer and they wouldn't allow it. But he was just like that.

"He was spittin' and chokin' on his own blood and he was cursin' every Kraut and takin' the Lord's name in vain somethin' awful," one of the boys told me. "Yellin' every curse word I ever heard as he went out of this world. His last word was a curse word."

You'd think that when a man's that near death, he'd think of somethin' besides that. But Knight didn't. He was really bitter—of course, the Germans shot him up, killed him. But he didn't change his way of life at all, even at the last moment. I hated to hear that. I thought, well, that's sad to know that he went out of this world a talkin' like that, but, of course, he was mad at the Nazis for cuttin' him down. He wanted to live as bad as anybody. Like all of us, he'd had big plans for his life when he got home. I thought about Donnie Knight. He died just as mad as the devil, and he died knowin' that he was one of the first men in our outfit to get killed in combat.

Knight wasn't in my platoon, he was in another platoon in our company. I wasn't as well acquainted with him as Charlie Eaton, who'd been in my barracks since basic training. I thought about what happened to Charlie more, I guess, because Charlie was a good-natured feller and I liked him, and it was especially sad because I knew that he'd just had his heart broken.

During the war, soldiers were all the time getting a Dear John letter, where their wife or girlfriend took up with somebody else and they'd write them a letter saying goodbye. Charlie always said, "That's one thing I don't have to worry about." He said, "My wife'll never do me that way. I know it and I don't have to worry 'bout it."

So, not long before Charlie Eaton got killed, he got a letter from her and she said she had found her another lover and she no longer loved him. That liked to worry Charlie to death and he worried about that till he died.

Lonnie Johnson, 24th Tank Battalion, C Company:

Charles Eaton's wife was named Sylvia. Right pretty girl. He had two children, he had a beautiful wife. But the thing about that, we was in Texas before we went overseas. We'd done been told to send our wives home, that we had to leave to go overseas, and Charlie sent Sylvia home so she wouldn't be out there when we was gettin' ready to go. He didn't know he was gonna get a furlough home after that.

Then he got home two days before she did. And he knew.

I'd got on the same train she did, and I know she was layin' in another man's arms before we got a hundred miles down the railroad tracks. It was a kind of a mess. It affected Charlie Eaton. I know it did.

There was a lot of boys that would drink everything they could find. Most of those Germans had champagne, and their beer was a lot stronger than ours. They'd fill up the tank with champagne and stuff like that. I was not a drinking man, Kelley wasn't, either. Knode didn't drink. But there were a few that did, especially if they got bad news from home. (12)

One of my buddies, might've been Johnson, he told me that back in the States he got on the same train Charlie Eaton's wife did, and he said, "We hadn't much more got out of the railroad station and Charlie's wife was all armed up with another soldier. But I never would tell Charlie, 'cause I know it would just break his heart. He thinks she's really true to him. But I can tell you right now, she ain't."

Now, Charlie brought some of that on himself, 'cause he told me about his behavior back home. He wasn't bad to drink when he was in service, not much, but he'd go home on a furlough and he said he'd get out there with a bunch of boys and he'd go on a big drunk. Charlie said he didn't hardly, half of the time when he was home, didn't see his wife. He was out livin' it up and drunk, so I'd say he brought a lot of that on himself. She figured he didn't care much for her by doing that, and a drunk man is liable to do anything. That's the reason why people ought to lay off of that stuff that causes them to do all the things that they wouldn't do otherwise.

Some of them said Charlie kept pretty drunk after his wife left him, but I never did know it. He was still pretty jolly after he got the news, except for when he told me, "I used to say Sylvia'd never do me that way. And I never thought she would."

Well, he was wrong about that.

The thing I thought more about, though, was what Charlie said to us when they took the bogie wheels off of his tank and put them on the others, including mine.

Charlie was grinnin' from ear to ear as he said, "I'll be thinkin' 'bout you boys up there on the front lines . . . Yeah, I'll be thinkin' 'bout y'all!" I could still hear him calling out to us as we left. That's the last thing he said to us. He thought he had it made. He thought it was safe, but it was more dangerous for him to travel with just two or three tanks than if he'd been with the whole company.

I geared up for my first battle feeling real sad to hear about Eaton and Knight's last moments on this earth. That really got me. What got me, too, though, was knowing that my tank had first been selected to stay behind that day, and I guess I would have if the captain hadn't changed the plan and gotten my one bad bogie wheel fixed. Yeah, what about that. I thought about that a lot. Things in life, you wonder why things work like they do. Sometimes it works to your favor.

But in war, you never knew at any moment if you were gonna take a turn and maybe die. That made me a little bit jubrous. But that's just the way war is. I wasn't worried about it. You couldn't go into battle worried about things like that. Despite what'd just happened to Charlie Eaton, overall, I felt like there weren't too many men that got wounded in tanks, and I intended to stay in mine most of the time. It took a pretty big gun to get you in a tank, unless you stuck your head out.

The Division:

Battle plans called for the 13th, now part of the XVIII Airborne Corps of the First Army, to strike north from the town of Hennef, cross the Sieg River, and pass through Siegburg toward the center of the Ruhr pocket. The enemy was known to have heavy concentrations of 88mm and 20mm anti-aircraft guns in this area for the protection of the vital war industries. These guns could—and did—do double duty as anti-tank and anti-personnel weapons. (2)

CHAPTER 19

Fight for the Ruhr

The American First and Ninth Armies lay coiled around the Ruhr like a giant octopus, probing its tentacles ever deeper into this richest of all German industrial areas. Without the Ruhr with its steel and coal, the German war effort was doomed. It was into this all-important battle that the 13th was committed to battle for the first time. (2)

We were in the Ruhr Valley and this is where a lot of our action took place, many battles. We stayed buttoned up and crossed a small river—Germany had a lot of little rivers. We knew that the Germans were dug in somewhere on the other side, waitin' for us to come along.

The only way I knew anything was just what I heard, what our tank commander told us, what villages we were going through and so forth. I don't remember the names of those places. Nobody was a bit interested in the names of the cities or the rivers that we crossed, we were all just interested in living, really.

We knew our job as a division was to spearhead the attack through the center of the Ruhr Pocket and to "mop up." That meant to round up or eliminate all the remaining German soldiers, get 'em out of there one way or the other.

The regular German Army had already been slowed down, cut up and disorganized by the troops that fought them before we got in there.

In spite of that, we heard that Hitler got on the radio and broadcast to the Germans, "Stand and fight to the last breath."

I couldn't believe any of 'em would still follow Hitler's orders, 'cause we were now invading in such force that it should've made all the Germans surrender—but, of course, they didn't. Some of 'em were just determined to fight to the very end. That can be one of the most dangerous times for soldiers. You're not expecting it all the time. You don't know where they're set up for you.

Our intelligence told us that some of the Germans' best troops, some of the infamous Nazi SS, Hitler's elite, were regrouping. They were gonna put up heavy resistance, so we'd have to fight our way through, take every town where they started firing on us. And the Ruhr Valley was what the U.S. Army was calling "Germany's last arsenal."

The Ruhr was where the Germans did a lot of mining and they had all kinds of factories to churn out war materials. Companies like Krupp Steel, the one I'd heard about in the Chrysler Building, they'd made a lot of the weapons we were facing—ammunition, tanks, and artillery. Their big factories, like most of the resources the Nazis had left, were further north in the Ruhr, and we were headed up that way. We had to stop Germany from manufacturing and transporting war materials. Of course, they were gonna do all they could to try to disrupt our supply lines, too.

The Germans had been well qualified to prepare for war, but by now, they were about beaten down. The British had been pounding the factories of the Ruhr with air raids for about five years, and had bombed some places completely to rubble. And just before we got there, the U.S. First and Ninth Armies' airborne units had canvassed the Ruhr with air raids. We rolled down their highways and I remember seeing a lot of that destruction through my periscope.

Some of those German factories had been big, long buildings. They had some that had been five or six stories high, I guess, just demolished—bombed out, and just part of the outer walls were left standing. They weren't still smoking, or anything like that, not where we were then. We'd pass by some places and we'd see where all the windows had been shattered or where the walls and roofs of whole buildings were shot up and had tumbled down. I saw dwelling houses with big holes in the tile roofs where they'd been strafed or shelled.

The civilian people who lived around there, they must have suffered something terrible. The Nazis were determined to keep their factories going to supply the war, so they defended those Ruhr towns and that just heaped more suffering on the civilian people. Sometimes, on roads that didn't have too much destruction, I'd see civilians pull back a curtain and peek out at us rollin' through. Our column of armor was so long, it must have looked endless to the German people.

I stayed a distance from the tank in front, and the one behind me did the same. We had to stay about fifty yards apart, no closer than that. If you got any closer than that, you were getting in danger. They'd taught us that two tanks, too close together, make an attractive target and would be sure to draw fire if any Germans were set up as we passed by.

At first, I'd see where the German soldiers had moved out. Along the highway, I saw their slit trenches—empty—but I could see that they'd been there. They'd leave their cigarette butts behind, and I could see where they littered the dirt. The German soldiers had been set up for a while, judging by the number of cigarette butts scattered in one place. I reckoned those soldiers must have been pretty nervous waiting for the Americans to show up. There weren't any dead Germans there, so we knew they'd retreated. We never knew why they'd moved out, or when. We just drove through there lookin' for signs of the enemy.

In the Ruhr, the 13th Armored Division was divided up so we could do different maneuvers to flank our troops. Each battalion was part of a battle group called a combat command. We had three combat commands and each one was about a third of the Division's strength. We had an A team (CCA), B team (CCB) and R, or Reserve team (CCR).

My outfit, the 24th Tank Battalion, fought as part of Combat Command B (CCB). Each combat command had all the battle elements—tank, infantry, artillery, and engineer battalions. We were usually grouped with part of the 124th Engineers—they dealt with the bridges; the 59th Armored Infantry Battalion—the "Fighting 59th"; and the 496th Armored Field Artillery Battalion. Their slogan was "Fire and Move!"

Each of the three combat commands splintered off to complete different missions, sometimes as part of task forces, then we'd all meet up again to take off together as a division. That's how we functioned in the field. It was all part of a big plan coordinated with other divisions, though we soldiers didn't know a thing about that and it wouldn't have mattered anyways. A whole lot was goin' on all around us and most of it we never did know.

The Division:

CCA and CCB crossed the Sieg on April 10 and the 13th was a maiden no longer. CCB bypassed Troisdorf, later mopped up by CCR, and fought through Wahnersheide and Urbach to Dunnwald on the next day. CCA advanced along the Autobahn to take Lohmar and then attacked Breidt. Thus began the Battle of Germany for the 13th Armored Division. (2)

46th Tank Battalion (CCA):

In the middle of the night, after two days and nights without sleep, and after a fatiguing march, orders were received to cross the Sieg River at Hennef. . . . Task Force Delnore with Task Force Sheffey in the lead spear-headed the Division in a northward attack on 10 April 1945. Soon our radios announced contact with the enemy. Near the rolling river country of Diessem we received our baptism of fire from concealed 88 and 20-mm AA-AT guns. The casualty toll of several tanks damaged, two men killed and twenty-five wounded was indicative of the fierce fighting of that first engagement. (17)

Combat Command A (CCA):

Enemy resistance was strong ahead, and it was learned that German 88-mm gun positions were strong and numerous in the area. . . . The weather turned bad, and a steady drizzle set in. Reports were received that the total enemy strength in the Ruhr pocket was greatly in excess of the previously estimated figures. These reports were verified by subsequent operations. (18)

59th Armored Infantry Battalion (CCB):

The 59th AIB entered combat on the afternoon of April 10, when Task Force Malone was to secure a crossing of the Agger River. A blown overpass blocked the advance temporarily, but a bypass was established and here Company A suffered the first casualties. Advancing northeast the task force arrived at the Agger River. The bridges had been destroyed, and the river was found to be unfordable. At 2000 the First Platoon of Company A established a bridgehead under intense mortar, artillery and flak fire from the vicinity of Troisdorf. (8)

124th Armored Engineer Battalion (CCA & CCB):

On the 10th and 11th of April, after jumping off in the attack at Siegburg, Company C built a 228-foot treadway bridge over the Agger River, in the vicinity of Siegburg. Company B erected an 82-foot treadway bridge over the Agger River, at Lohmar. Company A, during this period, constructed a 72-foot treadway bridge over the Wupper River at Burrig. Captain Karrick and Company A, craftily sought to deceive the enemy by performing the operation during darkness, but all their plans were to no avail as Company B succeeded in placing a trailer loaded with 1,500 pounds of TNT directly in the path of a German mortar shell. The resulting boom and flash left no doubt in the enemy's mind that something was cooking. (15)

24th Tank Battalion (CCB):

Night found us coiled in Siegburg. The next morning saw us crossing the Agger, another river, to swing west toward the Rhine. . . . The battalion first came under fire at 10:00 just

west of the bridge over the Agger. Our first casualty came from
antiaircraft gun fire. Sniper fire commenced; then artillery fire
dropped in while Company D mangled two 88 guns at Spitze.
B moved in to smash antiaircraft guns and the war was on! (1)

In our column, we really didn't know we's gonna hit that resistance till we began to see soldiers poppin' their heads up out of slit trenches along the road. We began to see that they were trying to slow us down, trying to knock out a tank. I don't know if I remember the first one. I remember some that we hit that first morning.

Our tank was up high on the road and I could see down in those trenches a little bit. The German soldiers were dug in all along the highway in zigzag slit trenches — cut back and forth so airplanes flying in a straight line overhead didn't have a good chance to kill a lot of soldiers. If they'd been in a straight trench, well, a plane could have lined up and strafed them, just a sight in the world.

I saw the curved brim of those German helmets and I could see the soldiers' backs just a stickin' up. And Knode was shootin' them with the machine gun. Of course, the tank commander gave him the command. Knode didn't shoot unless he was told by the tank commander.

Donald told him, "Pick those Krauts off!"

I saw them raked with gunfire from both our gunners, Rhodes and Knode, hittin' German soldiers with .30 caliber bullets and a killin' 'em there.

I could see them jump, I could see when those bullets was a hittin' them in the back, they were layin' prone in those stone-gray uniforms. When those bullets went into them, they'd just jerk and go limp. I can see them, just as plain today. And you know, it hurts you to see that happenin' to somebody. But you have to get used to that and not let it worry you none.

Well, in a way, I was glad. Of course, they'd been a waitin' till we could get up there to where they could knock us out with one of their bazookas. We just happened to get the upper hand on 'em. I hated to see anybody killed, but I was glad we beat them to the draw, so to speak. I thought that was the thing to do, 'cause if we hadn't done it, they might have knocked the tank out. You had to do those things, there wasn't no other way out. You were in there and you had to fight your way out, or they'd kill you, or capture you, one or the other.

The Germans, they'd have bazookas sittin' in about every one of those holes. That's what we called 'em, 'cause they were a lot like our bazookas. The Germans called it a Panzerfaust—"armored fist"—an antitank weapon that a man could fire from his shoulder through a hollow tube and it would stop one of our tanks dead, if he hit it right. A Panzerfaust could punch a hole in a tank about as big as a man's fist—it'd glow cherry red—maybe even get the tank to burn. It might not always go through the armor, but it could still immobilize the tank so the crew was stuck there, knock off a track or something. Then the Germans would really go to work on the tank with bigger guns. We had that in our mind all the time, on the lookout for a soldier with a bazooka, hidin' like a snake on the backside of a log, just waitin' for us to come along.

Eighty-eight fire rang out when we approached some turns in the road and black smoke started risin' up from those German cannons in the distance. We knew we were on the outskirts of a hot battle zone and we headed right into it.

We went into a hostile town with our guns just a blazin' on every side. And they didn't have much chance. We really poured the ammunition to 'em. Yeah, we'd just pin 'em down, run 'em out, kill 'em or whatever.

I'd follow the tank up ahead, and there'd be one behind me, and, of course, we'd try to keep about the same distance apart, if we could. But the tank in front of me would just jump when the cannon recoiled. The recoil on that gun would jolt the tank so much, it'd interrupt a Sherman's forward motion. Of course, our tank'd buck around, too, when Knode fired the 75mm cannon.

A lot of times, I had to drive around piles of bricks and twisted rebar, over broken-up concrete and snapped beams where large buildings had been blown up and tumbled into the streets. The tank was a bouncin' and a jerkin' and I had to drive right over the top of that rubble while Knode was a firin' that cannon. Of course, the 75 had that gyrostabilizer, so that helped the gun to stay on target.

The Germans would shoot back at anything they thought they could knock out. Of course, that's one advantage you had with tanks, small arms fire didn't have no effect on 'em—those bullets'd just ping off that steel hull—but the Ruhr was full of Germans who used antiaircraft and antitank guns on us. Looking through that periscope, sometimes I'd see where a German shell whizzed by and missed one of our tanks, but most of the time I'd just see machine gun tracers and smoke and dust.

If the Germans were using machine gun fire, they had tracers—that helped them to know where they were hitting—and those tracers helped us to zero in on them. I don't know how the Germans had their guns set up, but our machine gun belts, every fifth round, I believe, that came out of the barrel would shine a light as it streaked across the sky.

You don't really know all that's going on around you when you're penned up in something like a tank, you just have to imagine what was taking place a lot of times. What I saw of the battles was just whatever happened right in front of me in that little glass periscope, and it passed out of my vision as more came into view. I kept my eyes on the road and the tank in front of me, and tried not to let anything I might see, get to me.

We found a lot of resistance here and there, but it wasn't just all the time. When we'd run into resistance, if it was foot soldiers we were lookin' for, the infantry would move up and take care of 'em. Our infantry had to get off the half-tracks, get on the ground and run, shoot, duck into buildings. Their fight was more up close and a lot of them got killed taking over the streets. The Germans were set up where they could pick them off pretty easy. They'd be down in trenches with a rifle; sometimes they'd pretend to be dead and they'd pick off our foot soldiers. I saw that happen through my periscope, our infantry gettin' shot.

16th Armored Infantry Battalion (CCR):

We captured the towns—Troisdorf, Urbach, Spitze. A lot of us will never forget that Spitze. Not much of a town. Just a cross-road with a few houses. But the Jerries had plenty there—105's, 88's, machine guns and riflemen. It was a strong point all right. And we were new. It was a rugged twenty-four hours, but we took Spitze and a lot of "good" Germans were left lying around, testimony that training paid dividends. (19)

I could see tracers crisscrossing in the air, but I couldn't hear it in the tank, you couldn't hear the guns unless you were awful close to them, unless they were right on you. The loud rumblin' sound of the tank drowned out nearly everything else. We had the headphones on and we could just pick up all the tankers a talkin' back and forth to each other. The headphones were noisy when the battles started gettin' heavy.

"There's a lot of Jerries dug in along the road. They're popping their heads up and I'm gettin' them with my pistol!" Donald came in loud over our private line. He kept us informed of what he saw as it happened. He'd raise the hatch and just peep out. He could see a little better that way. The tank commander was the only one who would look out the hatch in battle. When we were in the middle of a hot battle zone, it was safer for the tank commanders to keep the hatch closed and sight targets through their periscope, but a lot of them would look out the hatch anyway to see better. Donald would pop his head out, take a couple of shots at the German soldiers, then duck back down. He got the first two or three pretty quick. They could have fired their bazookas at us, just barely missed us, and as a driver, I wouldn't have known a thing about it.

Of course, if there were any big guns anywhere around, Donald was more interested in taking care of them, 'cause the bigger guns were always looking for us. We had a lot of firepower that the Germans'd like to take out. Our tank commander's the one that had to be on the alert and make all the decisions. He'd tell the gunner what he'd be shooting and where to aim. McAbee would hear him and know what to load. As soon as he put the shell in, Knode already had his sights on the target.

Every time Knode fired the cannon, McAbee had to put a shell in there. He'd have those shells already out of the rack, and he'd shove them in the chamber, close the breech, and the gun was ready to fire. Mac had a lot of rhythm from all his guitar playin' and he stayed right in step with Knode. They kept that cannon a bangin' and they took out a lot of targets, but I don't know what and all they were. That only happened for short periods, though. Then things would quiet down again, and sometimes that was just as bad, waitin' for the next round.

"Personnel, one o'clock!" Donald called out. Then we knew we were running into troops, not another tank company or something, and he'd say, "H.E.!" for high explosives. They had some high-explosive shells; if they saw a group of soldiers fixin' to fire on us, they could shoot high explosives from the cannon, and when they hit, they splatter out. You might kill ten or twelve soldiers if you shot with that. But if it was a truck or armored vehicle, Donald'd say, "A.P."—for armor piercing—and Mac'd load that.

Now, it takes a pretty good gunner to hit distant targets with the cannon while the tank's moving, even with that gyrostabilizer.

"Stop the tank. We're gonna bombard an 88 position up over the hill," Donald said.

If I stopped the tank, that made it a lot easier.

Most of the time, though, Knode fired that cannon on the fly at targets he could see through his sights because it was safer to keep moving. Knode was a real good gunner. Real good. He'd take out German transport trucks, things like that—hardly ever did miss, they said, usually got 'em in the first shot.

"AA gun at three o'clock, seven-fifty!" Donald called out the target position, and the distance in yards.

Mac and Knode did the rest.

I felt the tank shudder.

"Hit!" Donald said for the rest of us to hear. "That's one ack-ack gun won't spit out any more shells!"

I could feel it every time the cannon fired, 'cause it just about stopped the tank. Knode got to firin' that cannon and kept it so hot, it seemed like we's just barely gettin' anywhere. But we kept movin' on, since a moving target is a lot harder to hit. In an all-out firefight, you had to keep those tanks on the move, if you could. Donald always let me pour on the gas and I'd sure pour it on it.

"Kelley, let 'er eat!" Donald said when we crossed an intersection where we thought the Germans might be set up for us.

I'd feed that tank the gas and we speeded on through. I was glad to be in the driver's seat. When I went through hostile towns in Germany, I'd always try to go as fast as I could go. Sometimes I couldn't, though; there'd be other tanks in front of me.

We'd leave one little town or village and come to another, and we'd find places where the Germans were dug in on each side of the road. They had artillery set up trying to stop us and they hit some of our tanks.

That one boy in our company who'd killed the first German soldier who tried to surrender to us, that was when he got his head crushed in, on that first day of fighting in the Ruhr.

"Eighty-eights! —both sides of the road," the lieutenant came in over the radio. "We'll take out the left. Tank two-two, take the right."

"Behind that barn!" Donald spotted the targets real quick.

"On 'em!" Knode was firm, didn't stutter.

Our training kicked in and we didn't have to think twice about what we were doin'. Flames were blazing in some buildings as we drove by.

★ ★ ★

THE KITTEN, *Ruhr Battle Extra*
13th Tankers Learn to Respect 88s

"Say, when we left France, I was still skeptical about ever getting into action," commented Sgt. Alfred Middlestadt, the driver. "You know the Division kicked around for so long. But when those 88 shells gave two of our tanks the business, I decided we must be in this thing pretty deep all right." (6)

Lonnie Johnson, 24th Tank Battalion, C Company (CCB):

The Ruhr Pocket they called it, that was one of the first battles we's in. And we were told that they didn't have no big guns left and that's where we lost most of our command 'bout the first day. They had everything they told us they didn't have. Their firepower would be greater than we could stand and we would retreat and regroup and go back again. (12)

496th Armored Field Artillery Battalion:

We gave close support to CCB, eliminating strong enemy resistance . . . Our guns were firing in four different directions simultaneously. Battery A firing two missions, Battery B being displaced forward with the advanced guard, while Battery C was firing directly to the rear on a combat target in Elsdorf. (7)

We'd go as far as we could go in one day, and we might not get far. The German soldiers had their guns set up where they could put artillery on us. Those shells'd streak by us. Donald would sight targets and have Knode sending shells over and our tank was buckin' like a bronco. There'd be some pretty good battles like that.

A lot of times, though, some of the battles, you wouldn't see 'cause they'd be so far off. The German soldiers could be back two or three miles with that artillery and be zeroed in on us. That's where they'd do their damage. They'd take out some of our tanks. Then, directly, somebody else might take them out, and the shelling would stop. You never knew why.

We'd move on to another place where the German soldiers were set up. You wouldn't see them at first. You wouldn't see nobody. If we approached a town and we didn't see lights, if we didn't see anything move, we knew we were in for a fight. All of the civilians had left town or were in dugouts or hid out or something; they didn't come out. That was a pretty good indicator that we's gonna have a lot of resistance. So we knew when we's in trouble like that, and we'd just go into those towns with guns a blazin' and just overrun the Germans before they knew what was happening, really.

We knew the German soldiers were hid somewhere lookin' to surprise us. But we also knew that, all around us, behind us, every major street was occupied by our forces. We mighta felt like it, but we were never alone.

When we prepared to enter a town, the company commander, Captain Blake, he'd round up his lieutenants and his tank commanders and tell them what our immediate plan was during a huddle, over behind a building somewhere, and he'd hand down the orders he'd gotten from higher up. Of course, they couldn't do that over the radio, in case the Germans picked up on it, so they'd get out and find a safe place to meet.

They'd tell us the marching order of the different companies and they'd brief us on what roads we were going to take. They'd say who was gonna be on the advance guard—that was the first one in. We always had an advance guard, rear guard, right and left flanks, even though they might be a mile or two apart. You wouldn't see them usually, but they kept communications with you most of the time, and you knew where they were.

The Germans had the best roads I'd ever seen. They had them branched everywhere. A lot of the cities and towns in the region pretty much had roads coming into them from every side, like spokes in a wheel. Every road that went into a town, we'd have convoys on those roads and they'd all focus into one point and we'd just take over a town like that. Those were the tactics, so we'd be well protected. When we ran into battle, we had people on each side of us, people behind us, where we could spread out and form a line real easy like that.

Our troops ahead of us had overrun a section and there were still a lot of German soldiers that they'd passed up, where they'd been really dug in. They couldn't get every one and the ones left behind were ours to deal with. We rooted all them out that got by on the first wave.

Rhodes, our full-time machine gunner, our bow gunner, he had to keep his gun hot a lot of the time in the Ruhr. He'd have to strafe those trenches. Those machine gun bullets are on a belt and Rhodes'd just start that belt through there and empty it in short bursts, and he'd load up another. Boy, those machine guns really ate up the bullets. Rhodes carried the ammunition for his gun up front and he had those belts crammed in 'bout everywhere.

If we had a lot of personnel targets in some spots, Knode would operate his .30 caliber machine gun from back in the turret. He had to put his head in a brace that fit around his forehead so he could turn the periscope with his head as he fired.

If we were in a heated battle, those machine guns, they'd get so hot, they'd automatically fire themselves. That was the danger about one of those .30 caliber barrels, it was mounted right over the driver's hatch. Knode could turn that gun's barrel, if he turned the turret, but if that gun was pointed over my hatch, it was really dangerous gettin' out of the tank when we'd been firin' it a lot. You had to let those machine guns cool down before they'd quit firing. Anytime you got in front of those .30 calibers, if they were real hot, they could pop off a shot or several of 'em.

So, I was always real careful about crossing in front of one of our machine guns. You'd have to get out of the tank sometimes, to get something off the back of the tank. You'd wait just as long as you could, get out, do what you had to, and slip back down the hatch quick as a rabbit down a hole. 'Cause if it wasn't your own guns a misfirin', a Nazi sniper might have his sights on you.

When our gunners were runnin' low on ammunition, they'd have to turn the turret to where they could get to our ammunition stowage. In the turret, Knode, McAbee, and Crouch rode in that steel basketlike compartment that could turn around 360 degrees and it was punched with holes—some of them were big enough to reach through. The tank had compartments where we stored ammunition like the 75mm shells—that tank could store ninety-seven of 'em—and they're about as long as your arm. McAbee could reach in those compartments and get shells out to fill the ready racks, but to get to 'em, Knode'd have to turn the turret to where the openings in the metal basket lined up with compartments, and some of them were down under the floor. When we got a little slack during battle, they'd get more ammunition out, so they wouldn't have to get it while we were in combat.

This one time, Knode didn't know it, I don't reckon, but he had his foot stuck through one of those metal openings into a compartment and Donald sighted a target approaching.

"Personnel, six o'clock! With bazookas!"

Knode traversed the turret around, and when he did, that metal basket caught his foot—liked to cut his foot off, too. That caused a little bit of excitement in the tank—Knode started yelling and stuttering and making a big commotion and we didn't know what was wrong. But he knew right away what had happened, and he turned the turret back the other way. I guess somebody else took out the target, I don't remember now.

If Knode hadn't been the one controlling the turret, it would have just crushed his foot. If it had been the tank commander, it would've been too bad. That was the first time Knode had ever done anything like that. It crippled him up for a few days. He had to limp around, but he'd spend most of his time sitting in his seat to operate the guns.

Sometimes we'd get pinned down. Our column hit a roadblock. They had a lot of them in the Ruhr, all different kinds. We were going around a winding road at the foot of a hill and the Germans had put a big roadblock across there out of logs. They had a lot of their roadblocks made to where they could drop big logs down in a row and stop up the street.

We couldn't get through that roadblock and we couldn't go around it, so we called the infantry to advance up and clear everything around us to protect the men who cleared out the roadblocks. That slowed us down, of course. And we were sitting ducks.

The men in the trucks and the half-tracks were a lot more vulnerable than we were, but they didn't venture up until we called for help and then they'd go down in the fields and check foxholes. I could sit up in that tank and see our infantry on each side of us covering those fields.

The road was usually up a little higher, because the Germans built the roads up pretty high above the fields over there. The Germans had foxholes all up and down those highways, just about everywhere you went. And they'd have bazookas a settin' in there so if they had to retreat, they had some guns set up to slow us down. I didn't see any of our infantry get killed when they went up to help clear that area, but they did take out some German soldiers who'd been a firin' on us.

We had what they call tank destroyers—tanks outfitted with bigger guns than ours—and they followed us. They had a big gun on there just for close range, a short-barreled gun with high-powered explosives, and they'd go up front. They could blow out a roadblock that we couldn't tear out with a Sherman tank. They'd open up the way for us, then we'd go on through.

We were held up I guess maybe an hour before the tank destroyers could get to us that time. The motor in that Sherman tank heats up fast. If you're pinned down somewhere in a village, slowly fighting your way through, or just sittin' held up at a roadblock like we were, it gets pretty warm in that tank even in cool weather. The heat from those engines really makes it miserable, especially cramped up in the front of that tank.

Rhodes'd talk in his Texas way, "It's hot as Hell in here!"

We wore heavy boots and thick two-piece OD uniforms—they smelled of grease and mud and sweat—and after a while Rhodes and I'd get pretty smothered up. The three men back in the turret had it a little better, but not much. When it idled, that whole tank got pretty smoky anyways, and then, Knode'd light up. We had to sit there and we didn't know if the Germans would shoot artillery at us, but I reckon they were kept busy by our forces.

The tank destroyers finally got there and got up to the front of the column to blow that roadblock out. There was a side road that came into the main road, right below the roadblock, and I was watching an old man riding his bicycle through there. Just as he went behind that roadblock, they blew it out. And he went flyin' through the air.

When we rolled on through there, well, that old man was just a layin' over there on the ground, him and his bicycle a few feet away. That back wheel was just slowly turnin' in the air.

Some of us in the tank saw it happen and I said, "Well, he ought to knowed not to done that—he seen all them tanks over there. He ought to not took no chance as that. But he mighta been wantin' to get killed."

"Coulda lost his whole family, you don't never know," McAbee said.

"Yeah, or he just lost his mind," Knode said.

Sometimes people went berserk with the stress of war. We heard about things like that. This part of Germany had seen a lot of Allied air raids, so the civilian people had been through a lot of nerve-racking conditions already. Now the American armored units were taking over.

About that time, over in this field to our right, there were some German soldiers. Donald could see them in his binoculars and he told the gunner, "Zero in on those boys over there. We might knock 'em out."

So Knode fired into them. And I don't know, he probably didn't kill 'em, 'cause there was a woman—there was a house just a little ways out there—and this woman came running out of that house and she knelt down over the three—I believe it was three soldiers. She knelt down over them, then she ran back into the house and she came out with what looked like a bucket of water. By that time, we were ready to go on, and I don't know what happened to them, whether they were just wounded or whether they got killed, or what. But I know the tank commander gave our gunner orders to shoot 'em. And Knode did hit them. They were way over in a field, a pretty good ways off. I could see them with my natural eye through the periscope, but I couldn't tell whether it was soldiers or what, hardly, when I saw them fall. I could twist that periscope around, and see side to side pretty good.

The rest of what I knew was what I heard the tank commander and the others say over the intercom. Donald'd talk to us and you could pick up anybody in the tank—that's the only way you could hear each other in that tank, but you could hear everybody real clear through those headphones. Donald talked to us all the time during battle, telling us what he was observing and what was up ahead and, if we weren't observing radio silence, he kept in contact with the higher officials.

When Donald would peep out, a lot of times he'd use his own gun. He had that .45 caliber pistol that his wife had sent him. Of course, he had his Grease Gun in the tank, but his pistol was a little handier. He'd kill the enemy soldiers if they poked their head up out of a foxhole. If he seen 'em, he'd try to pop 'em. For every one he got, he said he was gonna file a notch on the handle of that gun when we got to where we could stop for the night.

I never wanted to kill nobody myself. If I'd a had to, I would. Of course, I had to drive the tank, and I've seen the gunners on our tank kill a lot of soldiers. I didn't even like to see that. But that's the way war is. You don't want to see that happen to people, but when they bring it on themselves, then you have to do something about it. And it didn't worry me none, I mean I could sleep if I got a chance to. I didn't let it keep me awake. Of course, I got so tired during the day, by the time I got a chance to sleep, I could sleep about anywhere, even sittin' up in that steel tank. In the evening, we usually found someplace to circle around, post guards, and get a little rest.

Combat Command B (CCB):

The next morning, the trains of the 59th Armored Infantry Battalion were ambushed in Urbach. A task team from Headquarters Company, CCB and other parts of CCB reserve was rushed to the rescue and after a stiff fight, killed 50 Germans and captured 250 to save the Combat Command's supply line from being cut. (21)

59th Armored Infantry Battalion (CCB):

On the morning of the 12th, with C Company as the point of the force, the column was ambushed at a small village where civilians were waving white flags. Resistance was eliminated and the task force moved rapidly toward Dunnwald. At the outskirts of Dunnwald the column was delayed by a defended road block. As the First Platoon of Company C attempted to reduce it, the enemy counterattacked down two parallel streets. C company "Doughs" fought valiantly and repulsed the attack only after bitter fighting in which they lost four men killed and five wounded. (8)

497th Armored Field Artillery Battalion (CCR):

On the 12th, in direct support of CCR, we took off in a rapid advance up through the pocket which was halted by strong enemy resistance shortly beyond Berg-Gladbach, and the battalion went into position . . . Few of us who heard it will forget the first salvo fired from that position in the center of town. It was just after dark, and the guns sounded like the crack of doom as they echoed back from the houses. . . . Glass fell out of the windows of the houses for blocks around, and the streets, which had been full of civilians a few seconds before, were cleared like magic. (13)

496th Armored Field Artillery Battalion (CCB):

On the 12th of April, we moved into . . . the "hottest" position we were to occupy in combat. Almost every combat mission fired was counter-battery on German 88 batteries on which we were able to get observation only by the diligence of our liaison pilots and observers. As a result of the assistance of our "grasshoppers" and that of some displaced Russians who pinpricked German gun positions on our maps, we took a heavy toll of 88 batteries. (7)

If we were approaching a town the German soldiers occupied, a lot of times, they'd have blockades built on the streets leading into the town, and we couldn't get through them. We'd have to blow them out or go around. They'd built some of them years before we got there, maybe before the war began, they'd built big structures that could lower steel beams across the road. So, when we found a place that the Germans could blockade off that way, we figured we's gonna run into trouble.

Usually, you found if the Germans put up a roadblock, they'd heavily guard it, 'cause if they got you stopped and all grouped up pretty close together, they could knock out more vehicles. When they tried to trap tanks like that, they'd use heavy artillery. That was what we were on the lookout for all the time.

Well, we got around this one particular roadblock, went on a little ways, and the Germans were dug in, in slit trenches and foxholes along the road trying to knock out our tanks, and we were firin' on sight.

I'd see a German about to fire on us with a bazooka and one of our gunners'd get him first. He'd slump down in his foxhole. I've seen a lot of 'em. Sometimes I didn't know whether we killed them or whether they just ducked down in their foxhole.

What we didn't knock out, the tanks behind us would probably get. We had a lot of force. Of course, when you were going down the highway, you felt a little bit like you were by yourself because of that interval between you and the other tanks. If they surprised you, the German soldiers could pick off a tank right quick, immobilize it for artillery to go to work on it.

Using heavy artillery, like an 88 gun, it's hard to hit a moving vehicle, especially if we were a little distance away. We took a lot of training on that and it takes somebody that's got a lot of practice, to be able to figure out the speed of a vehicle and set the artillery to fire so far ahead of it and allow for the wind and so forth. The Germans were sending shells over, and they'd streak by now and then and explode somewhere.

Most of that action was just a blur from the driver's seat. A lot of those battles in the Ruhr looked about alike. The more battle we were engaged in, the less I have to say about it 'cause it was all calamity in my tank's periscope: tracers in the air, bursts of flame, horses galloping in the streets, bricks and concrete tumblin' to the ground, clouds of dust and smoke from buildings up in flames. And soldiers—some wore gray, some black, ours had OD—I'd see 'em runnin' down cobblestone streets, or fallin' to the ground in the countryside. We took out as much of the resistance as we could, and lost some good men, too.

We just kept on goin' to the next little village or town. Our plan was to cut the German soldiers down, overrun 'em and a lot of them would surrender. There'd be other mop-up crews comin' in to take care of the ones that we didn't get. We just kept wave after wave coming in, cleaning everything out, and we just kept moving forward like that, looking for resistance here and there.

We rolled through all kinds of farmland in between the towns. I remember that Ruhr Valley, it was pretty land with horses in pasture. Where the Germans were dug in to surprise us, we'd go to shootin' and a bangin', and those horses would go wild, just runnin' every which way, scared to death. I've seen some of those horses get hit, too, when the guns were goin' off, and they'd go down just a thrashin'.

The Germans used the horses to pull ammunition and we saw a lot of them. Our tanks encountered wagons with teams of horses and some of those horses got killed. I saw one team that had one horse down, it got killed, and the other one was just a stompin' and a prancin' around tryin' to go, but it was harnessed up and couldn't go. That was rough on those horses.

I don't guess our boys were trying to kill the horses, and then, they might have been. Some of the boys might have been trying to kill them to keep them from delivering their loads. The Germans used horses and carts to move the ammunition because they'd got down to where they were running out of gas to run trucks.

★ ★ ★

The Germans were great gun collectors. We destroyed the finest gun collections you ever saw, they went down the drain, we just ran tanks over them. That's a shame, there were probably guns that were worth millions of dollars that we just demolished. They weren't useful, they were from 1878 or whatever, handmade, beautiful guns, hunting guns.
— **Cpl. Alexander Gordeuk, from New Jersey; Information and Education Officer, 13th Armored Division. (9)**

We captured a whole regiment of German soldiers and we destroyed their guns and equipment and they didn't put up no fight. Boy, was I glad when I saw that happen. Yeah, we were beatin' ol' Hitler back.

If Hitler had known his men were surrendering, he would've had 'em killed, he wouldn't have gone for that. But now, the German soldiers could tell the war was coming to an end and a lot of times there'd be several of 'em surrender at one time, maybe a whole company.

This time there must have been five hundred German soldiers, regular army, who surrendered to us one evening. If they had decided to put up a fight we'd a had to deal with that. But we's just advancing through the countryside, cleaning out whatever pockets were left, and our column just happened onto a big barn and discovered these German soldiers holed up in there. They had their rifles and everything. They came outside with their hands up over their heads, so we didn't bother them. We had interpreters who talked to them, told them what to do after that.

Usually the infantry dealt with the prisoners. They searched them, rounded them up, and marched them to the rear. But in some places, the infantry had more German soldiers surrender at one time than they could handle and the tankers were brought in to help handle prisoners.

Our tank crew was given a whole bunch of soldiers to search, but we didn't find any personal weapons on them. If they were surrendering as a group, German soldiers always laid down their weapons. They didn't want to be caught with a gun, they were afraid that would cause us to kill them.

We had those German soldiers hold their hands up and we patted them down and went through their pockets. They cooperated with us real good. They let us search them thoroughly. Of course, we couldn't communicate with them directly, 'cause we couldn't understand them and they couldn't understand us, but we showed them with gestures what we wanted them to do.

We took everything off of them that they could use for a weapon. Even took their forks. Their mess kit was made out of metal, we took that, and we took their knife, of course, but we left them a spoon because we figured they couldn't use a spoon as a weapon and we knew we'd have to feed them. We took everything else off of them, if they had a pocket-knife or anything. I had some pocketknives I got from German soldiers.

I kept them and used them and don't know what I ever did with them, wore them out, I guess.

The infantry took over and they always made the German prisoners march down the road with their hands folded over the top of their heads. Long columns of German soldiers, a lot of 'em dressed in long coats, they marched down the road back the way we came in, to the rear of the line. The army had camps set up, different places, to put the prisoners in and they left them under guard.

After that whole regiment of soldiers surrendered, they gave our tank crew the task of destroying the rifles. A lot of times, if our boys were searching prisoners and the German soldiers had a nice sidearm that they'd laid down, one of them would get it and take it in the tank with him to take home as a souvenir. This particular regiment of soldiers was outfitted with just rifles and there wasn't no use tryin' to bring a rifle into a tank.

Every one of them had a rifle, all different kinds, they had at least five hundred rifles. McAbee said to me, "Do you reckon they have all the guns in there loaded?"

I said, "Well, I guess they's loaded. Let's see."

We went in the barn and McAbee just stuck one up in the air, pulled the trigger. It opened up a big hole in the roof. All of them, I guess, were loaded.

We carried the rifles out and laid them down in the road, just big ricks of rifles like firewood, and we ran over them with the tank. We could destroy them faster that way. As the tracks went over the rifles, it just mashed them up. We's afraid things might go wrong, and another group of Germans might come in there and get those guns and cause us a lot of trouble.

While we were there, one of our men came whizzing down the road in a jeep and he got out and informed us that President Franklin D. Roosevelt had died and that Vice President Truman had taken over. He died on April 12. I don't know when we learned it, but that's where we's at when we heard the president died. I remember that. It was a real shock.

President Roosevelt must have known that the war in Europe was about won, even though he didn't live to see the end of it. Once the Allies got across that Rhine River and just kept on a comin', a lot of the German soldiers began to realize it was over for them. Those German soldiers, some of 'em were eager to surrender, when they saw the amount of armor that the Americans poured into their country under the leadership of our late president. I reckon a lot of Germans figured, better to be a living prisoner of the winning side than a dead soldier for the losing side. That's the only way a lot of them survived. They waved those white flags. But at this time in the war, there was a lot of confusion for the Germans. Some of 'em saw that they were beaten and gave up, but others kept right on fighting, right on to the end.

THE KITTEN, Ruhr Battle Extra

... The 24th Tankers and the 59th dough boys had reached the Division's first objective—points north of Lunnewald [Dunnwald], 25 miles from the starting position. Other elements of the Division were delayed, held up by strong 88 fire, but they were able to arrive the next day. (6)

That night we were runnin' low on gas. We had enough fuel to run a little bit, but we were 'bout out of fuel this time—what was in the tanks and what we carried with us. We were somewhere outside of a little town. Our tanks were stopped in the road and a lot of the infantry came up to where we were. We were waitin' for orders about what to do and the Germans opened fire on us with artillery. Our infantrymen ran down off the bank and got into abandoned German foxholes by the road because they didn't have any other protection. Of course, we stayed in the tank.

Outside of this town, there was a big, open field where the Germans had been dug in before us. They'd taken a bulldozer and scooped out a low place where they'd put their 88 guns down to where just the barrel was above the ground, so we couldn't knock them out as easy. But at this particular place, they had pulled out and they'd taken their guns with them.

We pulled our tank down in one of those depressions with some other tanks from the company. The big part of our tank was down in it, but the turret was up above ground level. The rest of the tanks had to circle up on flat ground.

Pretty soon things settled down, but we were stuck there. It was late at night. They came around and told us, "They can't get the fuel trucks up here to us. The Germans cut them off back there. They're held up."

Those tanks burnt a lot of gas, especially when you got down in low speeds and low gears. I'd have to get out and top them off whenever we got a break in combat. We'd refill all the tanks when we circled for the night, too, but this time we got ahead of our supply lines. We learned right away that the Germans had stopped our supply vehicles from gettin' through to us. They had *us* in a pocket then. We couldn't do a thing without gasoline. Well, we could defend ourselves where we's at with our guns, but we couldn't travel.

Donald told us, "We'll be here till our troops can break through."

Most of the time, to get the fuel to us, they had to fly it in, if they could. They'd clear an airport or a landing strip, they had a lot of them in Germany. The Germans had them prepared for their own use, but when the Allies cleared one, our planes would be in there in a little while. Then they'd haul the gasoline out to us in a big convoy of trucks that were driven by black men.

Sometimes they got held up, but they always made it through to us. Our superiors told us, "If it takes five gallons to get one gallon of fuel to you, you'll get it." Yeah, you'd hear that repeated quite a bit. Some of 'em said that Patton said it. "If it takes five gallons to get you one, we'll see that you have fuel." They wanted us to know that our military was committed to supporting us out there.

So we stayed in that big field that night and, of course, I had to walk guard first shift. Drivers had to do the first hitch because they had been driving all day and after they walked guard, they needed to get a pretty good night's sleep. I had to walk between two tanks with that Grease Gun for two hours at a time.

Our tanks were set up in a semicircle down in that depression. Each of the three platoons in our company would put out a guard and we'd walk from one tank to another, back and forth, spread out around the semicircle. When you walked guard, you just had to keep alert and see that the Germans didn't slip into camp.

The Germans thought they knew where we were that night. They started firin' those big artillery shells and they'd just come flyin' over there where we were parked. Shells'd come whistling right over my head in the dark. Just go *Whhooeesshomp!* They were so close, they'd just pick up my hair. I mean, they'd feel like they were gonna pull my hair out!

They'd hit way past me over in the field, blow out a big crater in the dirt. When they were using armor-piercing shells, it would just be a big thud. Like a clap of thunder. It wouldn't be an explosion. But it was pretty loud. Out there in the open, the sound of those shells would 'bout make your teeth rattle.

They just kept shellin' us and those shells were just goin' over— *Wwwhheewwmp!* They'd hit way on past us. Just in a few minutes, here would come another. I'd have to keep walking back and forth, not break my step, and every few minutes, a shell'd come whistlin' right over one of our turrets. I said to myself, "Boy! They'll find our range directly. If they do, we'll be out of luck." Any minute, I was expecting the Germans to locate right where we were, but they were overshooting us a little bit down in that dugout.

They were so far away, they couldn't see us. Artillery can be quite a ways away and shoot at a target they can't see. You can shoot artillery over hills like that. When a shell comes out of a barrel, that's it's fastest speed and it'll climb till it reaches its maximum, then it goes to declining, coming down. It'll arch over and that's the way they use it. If the Germans had the range just right, that shell would hit exactly where they wanted it to. They may have been accurate with their aim, but not their information. They didn't know exactly where we were, but they knew we were close by.

It was hard to walk back and forth with them shootin' right over my head. I didn't know but what they might lower their gun a little bit, and then they'd get me. But these were things we had to do. I just thought,

"Well, I'm ready to go if they hit me." I had my peace made with my Lord and I just trusted in Him. I didn't know whether I would make it or not, but I knew if I didn't make it, I had a better place to go. Of course, nobody wants to leave this world till they have to. It puts you under stress, in a strain.

We didn't know where the Germans were located. I'm sure we had other forces following us that must have stopped them because they quit firing on us. So something happened, I don't know what.

A lot of times when you were in battle, the firing would stop and you never knew why. It was because we had other forces on every side of us, following us — artillery and air cover and different troops. I supposed they pinned them down to where they couldn't fire on us or knocked out their guns, or took them prisoner. Something happened that we didn't know about.

My time walking guard was up and I woke up the next man and put him out there. A lot of times in the Ruhr we all slept in the tank. I sat up in my seat and I could lay over against the side and sleep pretty good — a young person can sleep about anywhere.

The next morning, it was just as quiet as it could be. Donald called the Germans "kraut eaters" and Donald said, "Well, looks like those kraut eaters moved out last night."

We wasn't hearing no sign or nothin'.

If everything was clear, we'd usually get out of the tank and get our little gas stove out there and heat water for coffee and heat up some of the food we had to eat. Some of those army rations you could heat up, and that made them a little better, but not much. So we all got out and I got our little gas stove off the back deck of the tank, put gas in it, and lit it. By that time, the whole company was out there heating some coffee water, getting ready to eat breakfast.

The Germans must have found out where we were, 'cause right then, they opened up on us and this time, they had our range. They started firing their big guns right into that field. Dirt was just bursting up in the air when those shells'd hit the ground. Shrapnel was flyin' right into our camp.

I mean, you talk about gettin' in that tank! We all just made a dive for it. In the turret, there was one hatch for the tank commander and one hatch shared by the gunner and loader. Crouch, Knode, and McAbee all slipped down in the tank.

Up front, I dropped down in my hatch.

Rhodes, my assistant driver, he got scared and he dived in his hatch headfirst and that was a no-no, 'cause you didn't have room — you didn't think you did. You can't hardly get in a Sherman tank headfirst. But he went in that way.

Ewell W. Rhodes, yeah, he was in his seat with his head down against the seat and the bottoms of his feet were sticking out of that hatch and he was just a kickin' in the air. He was gonna protect his body, and if he got his leg shot off, okay, I guess. Bein' a pretty tall, lanky feller, he couldn't get down in that tank and the Germans were a shellin' us and he was just a goin' on, "Krauts ain't gettin' *me* like this! They ain't gettin' me 'fore I've had my dang coffee!"

Rhodes was stuck there for a little bit, trying to get down inside. He doubled up enough till he got himself down in the tank and he got turned around and I don't know how he did it. It was pretty close quarters and he was a squirmin' around every which way before he finally got squared away in his seat.

We laughed at him and he said, "Just laugh all you want to. I got in here, didn't I?" Rhodes talked with that Texas twang. "You fellers can laugh at me, but I was gettin' my vital parts down in here."

He liked to never got straightened out, and we thought that was the funniest thing in the world. Can you imagine us a laughin' at a time like that? But we got a kick out of that, while the shells were explodin' around us.

They shelled us hard there that morning and they hit some of the tanks and crippled some of the men. It didn't happen to kill any that I knew, but it wounded some of them. Those were the men who dived under their tank. A shell hit right down on the track of this one tank, on one of the bogie wheels, and when it did, some of the shrapnel flew off and hit the men who'd taken cover between the tracks instead of getting inside the tank. If they'd got inside that armor, they might've been all right. But they were too scared, afraid they'd get killed climbing up on the tank to get to their hatches. So some of our troops did get wounded there.

The Germans didn't happen to hit our tank. Of course, as it happened, we had pulled down in that dugout so just the turret was all that was stickin' up and that made it a lot safer for us. A lot of the tanks and vehicles in the company were sitting up on flat land, where the Germans had a better shot at them.

The Germans let up after a while. We figured they might start up again. But after everything settled down, we went back out and took a chance. That cookstove was still outside, so we lit it, heated our coffee. Then we got back in the tank as quick as we could.

We were just holed up and pinned down in our tanks there, waiting on the rest of our troops to get to us. It was gettin' on up pretty late in the morning, and the gas truck never had got there. We kept a waitin' and a waitin' and then it was about lunchtime.

When it wasn't safe to get outside, we'd take care of meals inside the tank. We'd eat rations—little ol' crackers and spread and canned rations that the army'd prepared for us. They had them packed and labeled, C-rations, K-rations—one for breakfast, one for lunch, one for the evening meal. Of course, we didn't have room to keep much stuff in the tank. We had a box on the back slope of the tank where we carried our food. One of us would have to get out and get our rations off of the back deck of the tank every time we ate.

Donald said, "I've been going out there and getting the food the last couple of times. Whose turn is it to get out and get it this time?"

Nobody was shootin' at us right then, but we didn't know what might happen. Everybody knew if you got out of that tank, you were liable to get killed. Some of the other boys had gone out before and gotten stuff off of the tank and we usually tried to take time about, especially getting the food.

I said, "Well, I guess it's about my turn. I've not been out there yet, so I'll get it." I got out of the tank and went back there.

I suppose one of the things I thought about was bein' cautious every time I had to get out of that tank. Oh, I hated that, because I always felt a little more protected inside the armor. When I was out, I always tried to keep the tank between me and where I thought the enemy was, if I could. But I didn't know where the enemy was most of the time.

Growin' up in the deep woods, my dad always taught me to be cautious. "It pays you to be alert," he'd say. He told me to stay away from a lot of dead timber, 'cause a big limb can fall on you at any time. Occasionally, it would be just as calm and we'd hear a tree fall somewhere in the woods. If you don't teach children about the dangers around them, they won't know it as they grow up. And if you grew up like I did, you had to be taught about danger, right quick. Growin' up on Coker Creek made me more aware of danger in general. I think that helped me in combat.

Of course, you don't know what might happen to you on the battlefield. You have to be on the lookout for the worst, so it doesn't happen to you, if you can help it. Sometimes you can't. Why, anything is liable to get you at any time and you wouldn't ever know where it came from.

I was up on the back deck of the tank. I got the rations out, closed the box up, and just as I turned to step down—I hadn't moved, I bet I hadn't moved one step—a big shell just went right over the top of that box. It came whizzin' over the back of the engine right where I'd been a standin' and just buried into the bank of the dugout. Oh, that shell missed the tank by maybe a foot.

When that shell drove into the bank, it knocked a big, deep hole in the dirt right behind me. It was probably from an 88 and it was an armor-piercing shell and didn't explode. It wasn't a high explosive or it would've gotten me anyway, 'cause a high-explosive shell when it hits, it just bursts all to pieces and catches anything that's around it. But they don't usually shoot high explosives at armor, 'cause it will just splatter and not penetrate the hull. The Germans used a lot of armor-piercing shells and if they'd hit our turret with that one, that shell would've gone through it.

I said to myself, "Shoot! In one more second, I'd a been gone."

Oh, it made a big noise when it hit in the bank. Everybody knew that, even in the tank. If the Germans were that close on us, oh, yeah, you could hear the boom and feel the thunder inside that tank. Of course, the crew didn't know whether I'd gotten killed or not.

It scared me so bad, I hopped back in the tank right quick and said, "Boy, that liked to got me!" I suppose that's what I said. I wanted them to know that I wasn't injured. 'Cause they didn't know for sure till I told them something. I said, "A shell just come right over the back of our tank right where I'd been a standin'! Aw, it was just almost a split second between missin' me and killin' me. It would've blowed me all to pieces. They know where we're at now!"

We expected another round any minute, but when something like that happened and nobody got hurt, we didn't think too much about it, 'cause we knew we's subject to that happening anytime. And it didn't bother me after the initial shock.

I'd held on to our rations, so we tore into our meals. Of course, when you're young that way, you don't let stuff bother you much. Most people don't. Some will worry themselves sick. Most of the boys didn't let it bother them much, though. That's just the youth. That's the reason they like to get young boys in there. They don't know what danger is, really. Older people's different. They begin to wise up as they get older. I wouldn't want to be in that situation now. I'd starve a long time before I'd go out to get something to eat when I expected a shell or a bullet to go through me. But that's the difference in youth and old age.

We didn't know where the Germans were, but we were expecting them to open up on us again. But they only hit that close to our tank that one time. I thought, "What about that? Just as I went out there!" Boy, was I thankful they'd missed us, missed me.

It wasn't but a little later and we heard the news on our radio. "The fuel trucks are on the way up here with some fuel." Evidently, our forces had fought their way through.

Sometimes they'd call in air cover if we needed it. The Allies had taken over an airport nearby to bring in our fuel, and they flew overhead and held the Germans off so we could get out of our tanks to meet the fuel trucks.

Those fuel trucks would drive up alongside the column and distribute that gas. Every time I saw truckers deliverin' fuel, they were black men. The army used black soldiers for truck drivers mostly, as far as I knew, to deliver goods, ammunition, gas and stuff. They worked out good like that, 'cause people back then were always sayin' that black men were not very good as foot soldiers. People thought they were more of a nervous-type soldier. It's different now, but then, that's what people said about them. They claimed they weren't any good on the battlefield, but they were good at driving trucks. The army tried to match the man to the job. We thought they did that pretty well. But back then, blacks were just beginning to integrate with white people.

That black company that delivered fuel, they liked to drive those trucks, it seemed like. They were fast. Oh, boy, they didn't waste any time. Their trucks'd be loaded with five-gallon containers. They'd come by and they'd yell out, "How much you need?!"

I'd usually say, "Set me off ten tanks." Ten or twelve tanks, that was about the usual number. I could look at the gas gauge and I could tell about how many gallons it would take to fill it up right to the top.

The truck driver would jump out and set off so many gallons of fuel for every vehicle and then race off to the next tanks down the line. This time, they had to unload a lot more than usual, though. I needed about thirty five-gallon cans just for my tank. That Sherman tank would hold 172 gallons, I believe it was, and we didn't always run them near empty. But this time we were really low on fuel, and I had to put in around 150 gallons, five gallons at a time. It usually took around twenty or thirty minutes to do the job if you didn't get interrupted, depending on how far we'd come without refueling. That's a long time if Germans are a firin' at you.

That was the hardest thing about my particular job, the responsibility of fueling the tank in combat. Those Shermans had two gas tanks, one on each side, and I stood up on the back deck of the tank and poured fuel in there, so I was a good target to anybody that could see me. I never knew if a sniper was watchin' or if artillery would break while I was out there.

Of course, the rest of the crew would help out when there was a lot of refueling. The bow gunner or radio operator usually helped me. One of us would get up on the tank and pour gas in, and the other one would be down on the ground, opening the cans and handing them up.

You couldn't pour that gas in as fast as you wanted to. The Americans' gas cans had a pretty good opening, but the thing of it was, ours, if you turned it up too far, it'd just guggle, guggle, guggle and it couldn't get air.

Now, the Germans had their gas cans made to where you could just turn 'em up and pour it in there just as fast as water would pour out of a pitcher. The German can had a strap across it and when you pulled the lid up, that opened the spout and it gave it air somewhere so it didn't get air locked. You could empty one of them in half the time that you could one of ours.

We'd talk about that and say, "Looks to me like the United States could come up with a better method than what they've got. These Germans have got a good gas can."

So we got to swapping. We'd gather the German cans up and throw ours away, and use the German gas cans when we stored extra gas on the back of the tank. We carried several gallons. Those German cans saved us a lot of time and danger in combat.

I think we got three or four cans of gas put in the tank and those Germans opened up on us and we jumped back in the tank. When I heard guns a firin', I didn't know if I'd be the next one they zeroed in on. Of course, all of us out there were having to do that, it wasn't just me.

When things settled down, I got out and poured in the rest of the fuel. It still came down to the tank driver to see that the gas was put in there. When I was by myself, I'd turn up a can in each gas tank, empty it, pitch it, and go on to the next can. I'd have all the others lined up on the ground. While the first two were emptying, I'd jump down and be opening the cap of the next one.

If the Germans had opened fire on us and hit all that gasoline lined up there, yeah, it woulda been too bad for me. But that didn't scare me much, though. To a young boy like that, there's something different about bein' in that situation than for an older person. I didn't think much about it.

After we fueled up, Donald relayed to us, "We're gonna move out, and go as far as we can go before dark."

So we took off and I don't know how far we went, but we went on our way to another little village that had been cleared by some infantry. We got in there about dark and we assembled for the night. We felt pretty safe from German artillery there, 'cause the Germans didn't generally use heavy artillery on their own towns trying to get us since their buildings were in the way, but now, snipers were taking crack shots at us every once in a while.

Combat Command B (CCB):

. . . A new attack was mounted on April 13. The Germans fought bitterly to hold back our armored thrusts and our CP came under heavy artillery attack. (21)

59th Armored Infantry Battalion (CCB):

The task force next received orders to attack to the northeast, departing on Friday afternoon, April 13th. The full significance of the date was to be revealed by nightfall. As the leading elements entered Kemper, a half-track was smashed by two enemy bazooka shells and simultaneously, large numbers of automatic weapons opened up from the houses, forcing the men to dismount and deploy. A fierce struggle ensued as Black Cats clawed their way slowly into the town. By dusk, the 59th AIB had lost eight men killed and nineteen wounded. (8)

67th Armored Infantry Battalion (CCA):

Meanwhile, Company C was driving to Rath where they captured a German stalag and freed approximately 1,000 Allied POW's. (20)

The Germans had captured some of our Allied soldiers in earlier battles, and they'd put them in a camp and now they'd left just young boys to guard them. Sometimes we'd roll through a place and surround those camps and those boy guards didn't have any choice but to surrender to us or die, and those young boys would just go all to pieces. They didn't have enough of manhood about them to know what to do and that made it a little different. They'd start cryin'.

I didn't really run into a lot of the children, but a lot of our infantry troops ran into groups of them that were just young boys when they'd liberate some of the prisoners. The Germans had got down to using their youngest soldiers to guard prisoners because they'd run out of older men, and I think those kids wanted to be rescued 'bout as bad as the prisoners they were guarding.

The younger boys, they didn't give no trouble, they were glad to surrender, 'cause they didn't know what to do. You didn't have to worry too much when you captured them. Of course, one of those kids with a gun could kill you, if he got a chance to. You had to always be alert and take care of yourself.

At this point in the war, the enemy came in a lot of different ages, all different levels of training, with all different kinds of uniforms that they could scrape together. They didn't all dress exactly alike. Some were in black uniforms, some were gray or other colors, but we learned to recognize a lot of the German fighters from the flared brim of their helmets.

Lonnie Johnson, 24th Tank Battalion, C Company (CCB):

We knew who the enemy was. The war we was in, anybody that didn't have on a uniform like ours, he was the enemy. The regular German soldiers had a different color uniform and they stayed well dressed all the time. We looked like a bunch of tramps most of the time. Fatigue britches on with side pockets about halfway down your leg. We didn't change clothes too often. I stayed in my tank without gettin' out for several days. I'm sure Kelley did, too. I slept in the tank, settin' in the seat that you drove it in. I'd open up a can of rations, C-rations, in a tin can and eat on it two days, hopin' it would make me sick, and it didn't even hurt me. (12)

One of the worst problems was, if you were in battle, and you had to use the bathroom, you didn't have no bathroom in those tanks. You had to get out of that tank to relieve yourself once in a while. You didn't know whether you'd get killed before you got back in there or not. And when you had to go, you had to go. There wasn't no other way out.

Even when it was dangerous, our crew never used the tank for that purpose. We'd always get out and get by the side of it or get under cover somewhere. Some of the fellers stayed in those tanks as much as eighteen hours, more, before gettin' out. I don't know how they managed. They may have carried something inside the tank with them. But the tank crew I was in, we didn't carry anything for that purpose, 'cause you didn't have no room for nothin' when you got your tank loaded with ammunition and all of the things you carried in the tank for battle. So, when nature called, we just took a chance, got out of the tank and ran for cover. Of course, we tried to wait until we had a break in the action.

When I got out, a lot of times, I could hear bursts of machine gun fire off somewhere. It sounded like the woodpeckers around the ol' home-place on Coker Creek. *Tat-tat-tat-tat-tat! Tat-tat-tat-tat-tat!* Only, there was no happy rhythm from that, 'cause I knew those were the sounds of somebody probably gettin' killed.

When Donald met with the officers to get his instructions, he'd come back to the tank and tell us what we's facing. Sometimes, he'd say, "Well, boys, it looks pretty bad. We're gonna try to advance ten miles towards this little village and we've got to be on the lookout for nests of artillery. We know they've moved 'em somewhere. We've got to stay sharp, especially at intersections."

Other times he'd have a good story to tell us, like we were entering territory that had been cleared out by another unit. But not today. Now that we were in the heart of the Ruhr, most of the news was the kind we dreaded to hear.

"They say the Krauts are gathered up, the further north we go," he told us.

I hated to hear that.

Donald would tell us what highway we were gonna travel and where we were gonna go, as far as we could go, that is, until we hit resistance. If we hit too much resistance, we might not make it all the way.

We were probably in the first wave on a lot of those towns where the Germans had retreated to wait for us. In some places, they gathered up, made ready to fire their weapons, and aimed their sights on the roads that we traveled. Intersections in some of those towns were set up with 88s aimed at the lead tanks. They'd be hid down the side street, so when we'd come to an intersection, we'd speed up as fast as we could, 'cause we knew what the Germans might do.

To be a good tank driver, you had to be willing to do whatever your tank commander told you, regardless of what it was. Be willing to do whatever he said, just drive right into a firefight if he told you to. Of course, you could have gone against his orders, but you would have had to suffer the consequences. I found it to be the best thing to do, to follow Donald's instructions to the letter, 'cause he was the one that had been selected to be a tank commander and he was a little higher educated than the rest of us.

Donald never did tell me a thing that I objected to doing. He talked to me just like he was talking to an everyday friend, not like he was giving me commands. He'd say, "Slow down a little," if he wanted me to slow the tank down, and he stayed calm in the heat of battle. Even when we were about to get fired on, he gave orders without any trace of panic. He was always real sure of himself and kept his crew calm. Donald was just a real nice feller and looked after his tank crew to the best of his ability and he had a good ability.

If we weren't observing radio silence, the commanders of some of the other tanks would talk to him over the intercom. They'd be up in front and hit resistance here and there. When it looked like we's gonna be slowed up, they kept us informed, as much as they knew, except when somebody in the company got killed, they didn't just automatically announce that. No, they didn't tell you nothin' like that in battle. You just heard about it later. You figured that so many of 'em was gonna get killed.

A lot of casualties happened in the mop-up, 'cause we had a lot of resistance. The Germans, they fought till the very last, till they knew they couldn't make it, before they'd give up. They were really dedicated to Hitler, the biggest majority of them were—the regular army, the Wehrmacht, and Hitler's elite Waffen-SS troops. But a lot of the soldiers we came in contact with had been conscripted near the last of the war to fight. That was a lot of just young boys and old men. A lot of them didn't want to fight for Hitler's cause. They just did what their leaders forced them to do. It always hurt me to see one of the Germans get killed just as much as some of our own boys. I hated to hear of anybody losing their life. I wasn't one of them that wanted to kill people. I hated the thought of killing anybody. Of course, a tank driver doesn't have much of a chance to fire a gun. But I had my personal weapon when I was out of the tank, and if I encountered the enemy, I'd have to use it.

When Donald collected notches on the handle of his .45 pistol, he seemed pretty proud that he'd saved American lives by taking out a German soldier before he'd had a chance to fire on our column. In combat, he'd always announce it when he got one.

He'd come over the intercom, "Got another notch for my gun—that makes four. Black uniform—looked like SS!"

I imagine Donald knew the circumstances of each one of those notches that he was collecting and those moments were only known to him.

Rhodes was pickin' soldiers off, too, and I could watch—I was driving and I could see those .30 caliber bullets just a cuttin' the dirt, right above those foxholes where the German soldiers were. Those flared helmets would just bob up as they'd look to see whether they could get a shot. Of course, when one bobbed up, Rhodes'd just cut the dirt off the trench with those bullets.

I've seen Knode pickin' 'em off, too, his machine gun bullets just a poppin' a lot of them in the head when they'd stick their head up out of a foxhole. I could see all that a goin' on. We were just movin' down the highway and that was just along the sidelines. But I couldn't really see a lot from that tank's periscope and I guess it was a good thing that I didn't.

Knode and Rhodes were good at their job. It wasn't that they liked to kill—they didn't want to have to do it, but they did whatever they were ordered to do by the tank commander. That's the way it is in war. You may not want to kill nobody, but if you're in a position that you've got to do that, you've got to do it, or just let them kill you. That's all there is to it.

I was really glad that I was a tank driver and I didn't have to fire a gun. But see, I had a hand in killing. In a court of law, if I'd a been tried, I'd a been guilty, 'cause I had a hand in it. But I didn't feel that guilt like I would have if I'd a been pullin' the trigger.

We had to protect ourselves and our country. We had to stop the Nazis. Hitler'd taken over and ruined a lot of countries and he was determined to take us over and he would have, if we hadn't put up a fight. If we'd just let him, well, no tellin' what would have happened to our country, and the world, if he'd a took over and got in charge in America. He'd a probably had us executed and just had his own people taking over. He was a wicked, really a wicked leader. So you don't know what you'll have to do in life. That was one of the things that I didn't want to do, but I had to do it.

★ ★ ★

Well, that particular day, our platoon lieutenant, the tank he had, his transmitter went out and he couldn't transmit to the rest of the tanks. Of course, my tank was the only other tank in our platoon that had a transmitter that could transmit to other tanks.

The lieutenant came back and he told Donald, "I have to swap places with you. You command my tank and I'll take your tank and get out in front to lead the way."

So he traded places with Donald, and I drove us up to the front of the line 'cause the lieutenant's tank always went first. I hated to lose my tank commander on that deal. And I didn't much like bein' up front, the lead tank, but that's the way it is in battle.

We were going through this town and we came to a cross street. Now, of course, the army had taught us in our training to go as fast across an intersection as we could, in case the Germans had a gun set up on the side street to get you in the side as you came through there.

So every time I'd come to a cross street, I'd just pour the gas to that tank. And this lieutenant got on to me, he said, "Kelley! Slow down, don't go so fast."

I just said to myself, I'm gonna do what I was taught to do in training. I think it's the right thing to do. We were in a place where we were apt to be fired on. I'd just slow down till I came to another cross street, and then I'd take off. I'd do it every time I came to a cross street.

The lieutenant got on to me again. "Kelley! I said slow down! You're running off and leaving the rest of them."

I wouldn't say nothin'. I'd slow down then, so the other tanks could catch up a little bit. And then when I came to another intersection, I'd really fly across there.

The lieutenant never did call me down after a couple of times. I guess he decided that I was gonna do what I'd been trained to do.

I thought, my life's on the line as well as the rest of 'em, so I'm gonna do what I was taught to do. The other tanks should have been doin' that, too, speeding up at the cross streets, but evidently, they weren't doing it behind me. But I drove to protect myself and the tank I was in.

The Germans may have been ready to fire on my tank from some of those cross streets, maybe they couldn't get a good shot at me, I don't know. I never did know what was up those side streets, 'cause I could only see pretty much about a thirty-degree angle through that periscope. I couldn't see unless I turned the periscope and I couldn't turn it too much, 'cause I had to watch where I was goin'.

It just seemed like you were driving down the highway and expecting something to happen to you every minute. You didn't know whether it would or not. What I dreaded more than anything was one of the big guns hitting our tank, just knocking it plumb out.

But we got through that little town without any trouble and we rolled to a stop. We had a break in the action there and they got the lieutenant's radio fixed right away. The lieutenant went back to his tank and he took the lead. I sure was glad to get Donald back. Our tank dropped back in place and rolled on through some pasture and farmland to the next spot of resistance.

The 13th Armored Division:

The initial objective of the Division was Berg-Gladbach, and the drive north continued along the Rhine. German towns fell by the score and prisoners surrendered by the thousands. The fighting was marked by the sharp clash for each locality and then the dash to the next . . . A kraut with a burp gun could hold a dough boy up for just so long, and there was the tanker to ease the kraut out of the picture. Or that other one with the Panzerfaust could slow up the tank, but the Infantryman was there to knock him out with an M1. And behind them both was their long-armed buddy in an M-7 ready to reach out with his 105 and smash the enemy. It was the teamwork that did the trick—and General Wogan who called the plays. Only we lost the general in the Ruhr when he was struck by Nazi rifle fire. Seriously wounded, he was evacuated by the 83rd Medics and later shipped stateside. General Millikin took over from there. (2)

THE BLACK CAT Newspaper

General Wogan was wounded when a German sniper shot him through the neck while he was personally reconnoitering the positions of CC "A" troops in the Ruhr Pocket action. The same bullet wounded Lt. Col. Victor E. Delnore, 46th Tank Battalion commander, and Capt. Jackson, also of the 46th. General Wogan was given emergency treatment in a front line foxhole, then was removed to a drug store in a

Ruhr town which was set up as an aid station. There it was determined that the bullet had gone through the left shoulder and injured the nerves controlling the left arm. General Wogan sent a note to General Millikin, who would take over the 13th. It ended with: "Don't let the krauts get you, but give them hell for me." (4)

24th Tank Battalion (CCB):

Further advance in Wiehagen on [April] 14th was thwarted by blown bridges and boggy ground. We returned to Dunnwald and struck out for Opladen, blasting roadblocks with tank destroyers through Sand and up to a big steel roadblock south of Opladen which had to be bypassed, while the infantry swirled through the town and held crossings against night counterattacks on the northern edge of the town. (1)

Our column stayed out of the big cities and traveled the outskirts. Most small towns and villages had escaped total destruction. It was mostly the bigger cities that were bombed out and shot up.

The houses and business buildings in some of the little towns had several floors of windows. The roofs were steeply pitched with dormer windows looking out from the attic. That's where a lot of those snipers liked to hide, so they could shoot down on you. They might use a bazooka if they wanted to knock us out to start with, or they might be a sightin' through a rifle, lookin' for infantry, or for a tank commander if he popped his head out of the hatch. A lot of times, the Germans used towns and villages to their advantage because they had more cover. We expected that when we'd come into a village.

We could always tell whether we were gonna have resistance or not. Some places, you'd go into a village and you wouldn't see nobody. Not a soul. Then we knew the Germans were hidin' out, dug in and a waitin' for us.

We were entering this pretty good-sized town after we got past one big roadblock. We figured we'd run into some fierce opposition in that town, but when we got in there, the civilian people came running out of their homes and told us, "Nazis kaput!" and they waved their arms and pointed down the road, all excited. They could give us sign language and we knew what they were talking about. They told us that the German soldiers had already pulled out before we got in there.

While we were doing all the things necessary to get our column around that roadblock, the Germans were gettin' out of town. They had put that roadblock up to slow us down to give them a chance to mobilize before we could overtake them. Yeah, I felt like we were nippin' at their heels then.

The Germans had a lot of stuff set up to slow us down, steel roadblocks and all kinds of things, and if they couldn't trap us and go to work on us, then they used the roadblocks so they could move all their equipment out and set up somewhere else down the road where they thought they had a better chance. I really don't know what and all those German soldiers were doing, of course, but I imagine they were scurrying around like a bunch of rats in a barn fire, 'cause we just overran them.

The advance of the Allied armies on all sides was really disrupting the Nazi troops — what was left of them — they were scattered and becoming isolated. I could tell we were making progress when we'd run into spots where they didn't raise the steel beams of some of their roadblocks. Their communication systems probably broke down till they didn't know when to raise the beams to catch us in between places. Or maybe they'd just abandoned their positions. We never knew why a roadblock was left open.

'Course, we always remembered that open roadblocks could be dangerous. The Germans'd keep a roadblock open and let as many tanks as they thought they could handle get through there, then they'd block off all the roads. If they could get you trapped in town, then they had a better chance to kill the ones that had already gotten inside the town. They could really work on you, 'cause you couldn't get out and your other troops couldn't get in until they blasted through those roadblocks. It was a big problem. That was just one of the German tactics we dealt with.

★ ★ ★

A lot of the German trestles and bridges were loaded heavy with explosives, so if we tried to use them for any reason, they'd blow them up. Especially bridges, if they didn't want us crossing a river or a creek, they'd have 'em loaded. We figured we were in trouble when we run into somethin' like that. We knew they's there and they's a waitin' for us.

We approached one of those traps in a place where a railroad crossed the road overhead on a trestle. We had to go under that railroad and they had that trestle really packed full of explosives, so if we started under there, they could blow that thing up and it would come down on the street and block the street. I could see that overpass in my periscope as the column came to a halt. The Germans evidently thought we wouldn't see the explosives. I was thinking that the Germans were intending to let a number of us get by that trestle, get inside the city and blow that trestle out so we couldn't go back out the way we came in, then they'd really open up on us, really work us over. One of our sergeants, a tank commander, took it upon himself, risked himself, to prevent that.

We had one sergeant that everybody kind of made light of in our training. I wish I could remember his name. He was from one of the western states. He was in our company since basic training and a lot of the boys didn't like him. I didn't have any problem with him, he was a decent feller. He didn't have nothing much to say to people, though, and he was an odd kind of a feller. He usually kept his nose in a book. The boys used to tease him because he didn't joke and carry on. A bunch of boys, they'll pick on somebody like that. But he didn't pay them much attention.

That sergeant evidently suited the higher officials who selected the tank commanders. He was the commander of one of the tanks in front of me and that day, his tank happened to be the one that was going under the railroad trestle when we discovered those explosives. This tank commander didn't radio for anybody to come up there to defuse the explosives. He just crawled out of his tank, got up on top of it — the trestle was close enough that he could climb up on top of the turret and reach where they'd tied a lot of dynamite to the overpass. He must have been pretty sure he knew what to do, but he really took a chance. He cut the wires and got back in his tank. He had enough of nerve to do that himself.

Nobody had liked that sergeant much back in the States, but after that day, well, they went to changing their opinions about him. From then on, everybody respected him. I heard some of the boys talk about that a lot. They said they doubted if anybody else had the guts to do that. That sergeant proved out to be a good soldier when he got to where he was needed. Because of him, that roadblock didn't hardly slow us down and none of our tanks got cut off there.

I remember one particular place in the Ruhr—it was sunny, but the roads and fields were muddy, 'cause it had rained on us the night before. We'd been speeding through some open country where two-story farmhouses sat along the way and big shade trees lined the road.

Along that road, German engineers had wired explosives to about thirty poplar trees and they blew them just as we arrived. They were mature trees and they fell across the road and blocked our advance. The German soldiers were manning that roadblock with 88s camouflaged by branches and brush.

We took off in a field to go around that roadblock and we's taking a chance to do that, 'cause a lot of times they had mines in the fields. If you ran over a mine it would knock a track off of your tank. We didn't have time to call up the infantry. The German artillery started coming at us and we had to make a run for it.

We had to run those tanks over some soft ground and they could get bogged down in the mud and leave us stuck out there with the Germans a firin' at us. Some of the tanks might've gotten stuck in that mud, but our tank got through that trap and we returned fire.

I don't know what kind of resistance the infantry who followed us found, how they had to handle it, 'cause we were pretty well protected.

We just kind of overran that situation and we went on. But we sure did know that there were soldiers dug in there and they were tryin' to get a shot at us. When we could see German soldiers dug in along the road, more than likely they'd have a lot of forces nearby, and if they got our column stopped, they could really knock off a lot of tanks.

We were startin' to run into places where they didn't have an easy place to set up a roadblock, so the Germans would slow us down by felling trees. The Germans had lots of trees spaced along their roadways, quite a few maple trees, hickory trees, and poplar. I knew what type of trees they were by the shape of their branches and the look of their bark. Some of the roads, they'd been beautiful because of the German's orderly spaced trees.

The Germans knew they were gonna have to do something to slow us down and they were willing to give up big healthy shade trees that had taken many decades to grow, they were willing to sacrifice them. They were getting down to using everything they could think of to hold us off.

The German soldiers had cut a notch in each tree next to the road and they'd sawed a cut in the back with a charge of dynamite or some explosive that they could detonate. They'd blow a lot of trees down in our path just before we'd get somewhere. They'd be layin' across the road. We'd have to find some way to get around them.

If it was a lightly wooded area, we'd take off and tear down a path. You didn't have to worry about running over much of anything in a Sherman tank, they'd run over just about anything that got in your way. Small trees and bushes, you could go through the woods a layin' 'em down right in front of the tank.

We had to be careful about how we pushed down young trees, saplings, in our way. Once in a while some of the drivers would try to run over too big a tree and climb up on it until the tank couldn't go any further and couldn't back up, and they'd get stuck like that. If you happened to get stuck, they'd have another tank from behind to hook on and pull you back and get you going again. That happened to some of the tanks.

One time is the only time I ever got on a tree that I couldn't back off of and I had to get pulled off of it. We didn't get in wooded areas too much. We were traveling roads through open country, fields and places like that.

If it was open country and we encountered any type of roadblock, we were usually afraid to pull off and try to go around the highway because we knew the Germans would put land mines out there for us, if it was a big empty field near the road. The Germans thought that's what we'd do—go around—but most of the time if we thought they'd laid mines, we'd just run over those treetops with the tank. We'd tear them up, running over the tops of 'em.

It was spring, so there were hardly any leaves on the trees, maybe just some tender buds. The limbs were bare and those young branches are pretty flexible and we'd roll right over them with the tracks, one tank after another. Of course, a tank will go over a pretty good log, and if you get up there towards the top of the tree, you can go over them without much trouble. Those tank tracks would just grind up the treetops and that would make those tree trunks just jerk and shake.

Along those roads in the Ruhr, I've seen their big trees where they had them wired ready to fall, but for some reason they never did get a chance to detonate them. I drove past one long row of shade trees, and each one was ready to blow, but not one was detonated. I wondered what had happened before us, why the Germans didn't get to blow even one of those trees across that road. Well, the Germans were being overrun. For a long time in the war, back when we were taking our training, it was the other way around, but the Allies finally gained the upper hand on Hitler's forces. And we kept getting enough equipment, supplies, and soldiers sent in there to keep them on the run.

★ ★ ★

The Division:
Well, we fought north all right, through every roadblock the Heinies could throw up, and every artillery barrage they could throw at us. It took us just 6 days to blast our way across four

rivers and the valleys between — the Sieg, the Agger, the Duhn, and the Wupper. (2)

59th Armored Infantry Battalion (CCB):

At this time, the Combat Command was ordered to change direction and attack to the north, with Mettman as the objective. On the following morning the attack across the Wupper soon became a rout and the task force moved swiftly to Haan. Masses of dejected prisoners heading to the rear gave us an indication that the Battle of the Ruhr was nearing its close. (8)

24th Tank Battalion (CCB):

Racing recklessly north through Haan, one Company C and two Company B tanks fell to antitank guns short of Gruiten; by 1730 we reached Mettman and were welcomed by wildly cheering liberated factory workers before they began surging through plate glass store windows on a shopping tour. (1)

Our pace quickened. At first when we got into the Ruhr, we might fight all day and not move a hundred yards because we had to just keep movin' back and forth—they'd have us pinned down with artillery. Then after that, it got to bein' what some of 'em called a "rat race," when we sped through ten or twelve miles a day, and there wasn't resistance all the time.

We had to cross some little rivers. We never went over any German bridges, they'd all been blown out. I can remember the big rivers, but smaller rivers I don't remember. It wasn't any big deal to go across the smaller rivers, our engineers went ahead of us and they had the bridges in by the time we got there. So we just went right on across those pontoon bridges. It was so quick, we hardly even knew we left the ground.

We'd go into several small villages that had all their lights on and the streets were full of civilian people. It was more women and children than anything, 'cause the Nazis had all their men in the armed forces. Even had a lot of twelve-year-old boys in there. They'd got down to where they were having to use everything they had, so the towns were mostly populated with women, and there were lots of children, that's what I remember most.

We could tell that the people were really happy that the war was coming to an end because they'd just come out of their houses and they'd line up in the streets and they'd be wavin' flags and different things as we crept by. I guess it must have been a freedom flag. It wasn't a swastika. It wasn't an American flag. But they had some kind of flags and I don't know what they represented. They were just cheering us on as we rolled by, and we knew we had it made. Seemed like they were just tickled to death to see us a comin'. That war, boy, they were gettin' tired of that war.

We'd unbutton in places like that, where we felt safe, so I drove with my head out the hatch. Women would run up to the tanks, they'd throw flowers at us, and oh, their faces were smiling from ear to ear and they'd holler up at us. Of course, everything they said was in German and I couldn't understand them, but they were excited. Children were jumping up and down in the streets, squealing with delight, it looked like. The German people tried to do everything they could to cheer us on, and when you see that, you don't need to understand the language. They were glad we'd come to liberate them.

I never really expected to see that goin' in, never even thought about it. It was a nice surprise. It made me feel like we were doing a real good thing for the people of Germany when I saw that. Some of them really gave us a hero's welcome. And I guess to them, that's what we were—heroes. But to us, we were just American soldiers doin' our duty.

It was heartwarming when we got to some towns in Germany and the people were glad to see us. Yeah, it sure was. They'd been under all that pressure for many years under Hitler and they didn't have freedom, or nothin' much, and, of course, they wanted freedom. They just seemed like they were thrilled to death when the Nazis pulled out of there and the Americans arrived.

I guess they knew enough about America to know that we's gonna treat them right. They didn't seem to fear us at all when they got a chance to express themselves to us. As far as I know, there were very few American soldiers that ever mistreated anybody over there. They always seemed to treat civilians nice, wherever they were. Of course, we may have had some, you'll probably have that anywhere.

So we didn't have any trouble when we ran into those kinds of villages, but when we didn't see a soul, that's when we knew we were in trouble. There were still straggling groups of German soldiers who believed in following Hitler to the end. They'd take over German towns to try to hold us off—even though I heard that some of the German civilians at that time were just begging the German Army to leave their towns, 'cause they knew the Americans would really lay 'em to waste.

497th Armored Field Artillery Battalion (CCR):

During these days, the German will to fight was very spotty. They were surrendering by thousands in some places—in others they fought as long as they thought they could get away with it. Snipers caused a good many casualties throughout the Combat Command. From Mettman we fired a few rounds into Dusseldorf, but that city surrendered without putting up much resistance. (13)

496th Armored Field Artillery Battalion (CCB):

On the morning of April 17, we moved from Gruiten to Steinkoffen and Mettman, crossing a ridge en route later dubbed "88 Alley" by the battalion. The entire column was subjected to direct fire from German artillery firing at right angles to the line of advance. The fact that we suffered no casualties testifies to the poor marksmanship of the enemy for we were "sitting ducks" for one-half hour.

The battalion then rolled into Duisburg, the Division objective, and the job of the Black Cats in the Ruhr campaign was completed. (7)

46th Tank Battalion (CCA):

A highlight of the Ruhr Campaign was the capture of the German Headquarters at Mudlinghoven. On 17 April the 46th Tank Battalion's reconnaissance platoon of eleven men, under the personal command of Lieutenant Colonel Delnore, captured two major generals, Rantzau and Sommerfeld, with their staffs, and forced the surrender of 600 Germans. (17)

The Division:

CCA sped into Muddlinghausen with hopes of capturing Field Marshal Model and his staff. Though Model had fled, the bag of prisoners included two major generals. With the fall of the German general staff in that area, organized resistance ceased. (2)

THE KITTEN, Ruhr Battle Extra:

Enemy units in the pocket were by now completely cut up and disorganized and thousands of Nazis streamed out to get thumped back toward PW collection points. Over 8,000 prisoners were collected on April 16 and 17. (6)

Lonnie Johnson, 24th Tank Battalion, C Company (CCB):

The Germans were losin' 'cause their gas gave out. They had plenty of ammunition, but no gas. The Germans just hooked trucks to trucks and tried to pull them goin' down the road away from us, until they all gave out of gas. Right at the end, you'd see somebody hold up a white flag down the road, half a mile, it looked like sometimes. They'd put a bedsheet on a pole and they waved it back and forth. If you didn't shoot 'em, there'd often be a thousand men behind it, marchin' down the road, and they just kept on marchin' all the time. They'd surrender in long lines. (12)

16th Armored Infantry Battalion (CCR):

At the time, what was most important, each Kraut had a Luger or a P-38, if you could find it. (19)

The Germans had called themselves "supermen," but the German soldiers we saw now, prisoners of the 13th Armored Division, they looked pretty puny to me. They were ragged, tired, and downtrodden as they marched. Some of 'em were wounded from earlier battles. A lot of their uniforms didn't fit 'em, 'cause the Germans were just running out of everything. The lines of enemy soldiers grew longer and longer and they marched to the rear where our infantry led them into PW cages, as they called them, big fenced areas somewhere—I never did see one.

I've seen plenty of German prisoners, though. We always made them interlock their fingers on top of their head and march to the rear of the column. Sometimes there were so many, we sent them back without guards. Before the Battle of the Ruhr wound up, hundreds of thousands of Germans laid down their arms.

Now, a lot of them, when they would surrender, if they had a sidearm or pistol—they knew we liked to collect them—they'd come out with their gun held up over their head, and they'd give us their pistols. That's how we'd get their guns. That's how I got my Luger. When I first went overseas, I told some of the boys, "I'm hoping I can get me one of them German Lugers to bring home."

There were three soldiers in a house we came to one time—they came out with their hands up, holding their weapons overhead as we approached. We stopped the tank and we motioned for them to come over to the tank.

I could see their pistol holsters on them, and I thought, now, if they've got a German Luger, I'm gonna get that. It had a long, slender barrel. Everybody talked about that gun. It was the German's special gun.

I said to Donald, "That looks like a German Luger that feller's got. If it is, I want it, 'cause I've been a lookin' for one of them." I believe Donald had already collected a Luger for himself.

Donald said, "You go ahead, Kelley. Its yours."

The boys in the tank agreed. "If there's a German Luger, yeah, Kelley, you get it."

So, when the German soldiers got to our tank, each one of them had a pistol, and, sure enough, one of them was a German Luger. The one in charge, I guess he was an officer, he had the Luger. The others had a smaller pistol, something like a .32 caliber pistol. Some of the boys in the tank got the other two pistols.

I got the Luger and it had a belt, holster, and an extra clip—it was a real nice one. Since my tank crew all knew I was looking for one, they were real glad for me to get it.

Oh, I was proud of that Luger. Everybody seemed to want one of them. And I got one. I just kept it in the tank with me, didn't fire it or anything. It just looked like a new one. And we didn't have to shoot nobody to get it. So I felt pretty good about that. If I'd a had to kill somebody to get one, that would have been on my conscience. But I didn't have to do that.

★ ★ ★

THE KITTEN, *Ruhr Battle Extra:*
Cat Tankers Murdered by Captors

Three Black Cat tankers were lined up in a drainage ditch near Hilden, Germany, and murdered by a German officer after they had surrendered to a Nazi anti-tank squad on April 16, an investigation by Division officers revealed today.

The tankers were members of F. Troop 93rd Cavalry Reconnaissance Squadron. The murder was witnessed by three newly-liberated Russian slave laborers and a German youth.

The action occurred during the final stages of the battle in the "Ruhr Pocket" at a time when German resistance was collapsing under the pressure of U.S. First and Ninth Army drives.

The 93rd tank was advancing up from a railroad underpass northwest of Hilden in an area defended by the 503rd German Army Flak Group when it was hit by an AT shell. Two crew members were killed and the tank caught fire. The rest of the Black Cat crew—consisting of one lieutenant and two sergeants—jumped out unhurt and raised their hands in surrender when they saw the German squad had them covered.

A Nazi lieutenant came up and took charge. He ordered the Americans to march to the drainage ditch and the three Russians and German boy, who were watching from the road, heard him yell, "Verdammte amerikane schweine!" (Damned American Swine!) and saw him open up with an automatic gun. The bodies were found later lying in the ditch.

It is believed that the Nazi officer and the entire squad were later captured by other soldiers of this Division. (6)

I don't know how all our boys treated German prisoners, but some of them treated them good. I also know that some of our troops were pretty mean to prisoners of war, especially if those prisoners were Hitler's SS.

The Waffen-SS troops were Hitler's prime soldiers, really highly trained and, boy, if you got captured by one of them, you's just out of luck. Those SS soldiers, I'd heard, were gonna take your life or give their life, but they didn't back down, no, not one bit. They must have been brainwashed into that.

Sometimes SS troops would get surrounded to where they'd have to surrender. A tank driver from our forces was telling me about capturing, I forget how many, about fifteen German SS and they were searching them to see if they had any weapons or anything and the SS prisoners weren't cooperating. They stood there staring straight ahead and they weren't responding, so one of the boys from the infantry who was searching them — he walked up to one of the tank drivers and he said to this tank driver, "Give me that Tommy gun!"

The tank driver handed it to him and he just took that Thompson and he mowed every one of those SS soldiers down.

He said the German soldiers didn't bat their eye, didn't move a muscle. When one fell, the next one in line just looked right in the eyes of that boy holdin' the trigger as he just mowed 'em all down.

So that was one of the things that soldiers would do sometimes. Our commanders wouldn't have gone for that, but they didn't do a thing about it because it was war. And the Germans might have done us the same way if we'd rebelled against them; more than likely they would, if they captured us. I heard about things like that a happenin', too. Hitler's SS were known to be the worst. I heard that they'd always been known to gather up people—men, women, children, it didn't matter—and take them out in a field and just shoot them.

Division Headquarters:

German opposition started to collapse all around us as our armored columns broke through the Nazi defense lines. German soldiers, by the hundreds and the thousands, straggled by us looking for PW cages and we sneered a little and said, "Humph, Supermen, eh?"

Then the Germans were Kaput in the Ruhr and there were civilians all around us and begging to shine our shoes and insisting again and again that they were "Nichts Nazis." These were the same people who'd thrown out their arms heiling Adolph Hitler a short time back and so we got disgusted and decided to leave them. (22)

THE KITTEN, Ruhr Battle Extra:

Ruhr Valley, April 18 (Delayed) - Out of ditches and cellars and from behind bushes and one-family homes they come—by the hundreds and hundreds and all they want is a nice spot in a Black Cat PW cage. They're all washed up on the war they helped old Adolf Hitler to begin. . . .

Some of your Black Cat buddies got killed in the Ruhr and if you'll just keep remembering that they could have been home and happy if the German people hadn't started a war, you won't have to worry about having the wrong attitude toward conquered peoples.

Sure, some of them may be nice, and some of them never wanted Hitler in the first place. But which ones? The guy who protests the very loudest that he hates the Nazis with all his guts? He's the same guy who's got a chest-full of swastikas hidden down in his cellar. The woman who claims she's been waiting for months for American soldiers to liberate her? She's the female who swooned when her Fuehrer rode by and then swore her everlasting soul to the ideals of the Nazi Party. (6)

A lot of the men had anger in their hearts toward the German people—soldiers, civilians, it didn't matter. But I never thought that was the right way to be.

As a tanker, I didn't really have many dealings with civilians during the war. Most of the Germans we saw were soldiers, the ones we took as prisoners, they were regular soldiers like we were, or even just folk who weren't fit to serve, not SS or any of the really dedicated Nazis. I realized that the ones I saw were required to do a job for their country, whether they liked it or not. So I felt we should show them basic human respect, on account of what their evil leaders forced them into. They were good soldiers, the ones that were trained, were well trained. In fact, most of the regular German soldiers, I imagine, had better training than some of our own Allied troops. We just out-materialed 'em and outdone 'em.

Now that the German resistance in the Ruhr had just about fallen, we were able to clear out a little village to take shelter in some of the houses. Just about every time when we'd take over a village like that, it was late in the evening. When our infantry cleared all the civilian people out, they'd come out of their homes and cheer us on, and, oh, they just seemed tickled to death that we took over. Then you'd go into their houses and see all the swastikas that they'd hid when they saw us coming. Yeah, nearly everywhere in the house, if they had a picture hanging on the wall, you could take it down and there'd be a swastika behind it.

I guess Hitler really put the pressure on the people to have those symbols of his regime out where they could be seen, but when the people knew the Americans were going to take over, they'd all hide them. Didn't destroy them.

The civilian people were looking out to survive, I realized that, so they supported their leaders because I understand they could have been killed if they didn't. I can't go along with government like that. I don't think the German people really wanted a war, it was just put on them — they had to fight and we had to fight.

Germany, to me, was a good country, one of the best countries over there, I guess. I felt, in a way, that we were fighting the wrong people. The Germans were some of the most intelligent, advanced people in the world, but Hitler had a lot of them brainwashed. I don't know how he did it. The German people didn't get wise, or they didn't get wise fast enough.

Somebody was already wrecking a piano to find something valuable in there when I went in one house where we were gonna bed down for the night. We went upstairs and some of the other boys had beat us getting to the beds, so we just put our sleeping bags down on the floor where they had a big picture window. I was layin' there and just got to sleep when the Germans opened up on us with artillery, and they busted out that window and glass flew all over us on the floor.

I don't know where that shell hit, but the projectile didn't come inside the house. When it knocked that window out, boy, I'm tellin' you, we jumped up, got out of there, ran down the stairs, and bedded down in the basement. Ought to have been in the basement all along, but we didn't think about that.

The Germans shelled the town, just shelled it everywhere. They came very close to gettin' us there. It scared us when it happened, 'cause we's expecting another round just any second. We thought we had them all cleared out. But we didn't. Their artillery was back far enough to where we didn't know about them. I don't guess the Germans knew that they'd come that near to gettin' us, or they would've kept shellin' our position.

Could have reduced that house to rubble with us in it.

After we got in the basement, we went right back to sleep. We slept the rest of the night down in that basement. Seems like it would have caused a person to stay awake, expecting another attack, but we didn't have much trouble going back to sleep.

A lot of the men felt like the military was doing something to us to make us where we could just lie down and go to sleep. They'd talk about that. A lot of us wondered if they put something in certain rations to keep us from being so afraid. We'd get stories like that—and they may have done that. I don't know whether they did or not. If I ever got anything like that, I didn't know it. But I thought it was strange that I could just lie down if I got a chance to and go to sleep and sleep all night in a war zone with artillery goin' off and it didn't bother me.

Of course, we were young then. When you get older, it's hard for you to go to sleep bein' that near death all the time. I just always figured, well, if my time comes, I'll just have to go like the rest of 'em that's gettin' killed.

When your country calls for your help, and if you've got a country like we've got, you want to do all you can to preserve it. So I think most of us felt that way, 'cause I didn't hear none of them grumbling about what we had to do. All of our soldiers, seemed like, were willing to lay their life on the line.

But some of them talked like they thought their time would come when they were in service over there. Some of 'em were worried about that, about dying.

I always thought I'd make it. I didn't ever think I'd get nipped or nothin'. I said, "I believe I'll be back home." And that was the way it was. 'Course, I liked to not got back.

Before I went to Germany, I had figured it would shake me up when we got in battle. I didn't know how I would react. I thought I might even fall apart, but I got along fine. It didn't seem to shake me up one bit. I remembered that some people came back after the First War "gunshocked" and I didn't happen to get that way from fighting through the Ruhr, as far as I could tell. But some of them did.

Some of those boys in the army were big, strong fellers all right, but they'd just go all to pieces. The ones that had been babied their whole life and hadn't had to take care of themselves, they were the first to crack. I grew up back in that rough hill country. I was used to dangerous things happening around me. I think that helped me.

The thoughts that somebody could shoot you at any time, those weigh heavier as time goes on. If you thought that somebody was gonna pull the trigger on you all the time, it's a lot of pressure. Some of the boys would do pretty good, but a lot of them really got shook up bad after a while. If the guns got to following us around, they'd run for cover every time they were out of their tank, and that really got to them. They were just in a panic. The army would have to replace them because they weren't worth much as soldiers. Some of them didn't know how to take care of themselves.

We'd be in places where we just had to crawl to get behind things when we were out, so they wouldn't kill us, and some of those boys got so scared, they just didn't care what they did. They'd want to run out in the open and holler and do all kinds of crazy things. A few times, I talked to some of them to help calm them down.

I said something like, "Look, now, we've got to lay low. It's dangerous for the rest of us if you draw attention like that. We're gonna make it through, but we've got to get out of here first. . . ."

I don't know, maybe one of those boys who made it back, maybe he made it because of what I said to him at a certain time. But then, some of 'em didn't pay no attention to that, and it'd really hurt you when you'd see 'em get shot. In battle, you can't make too many mistakes. You've got to do the right thing all the time, and do it carefully.

Lonnie Johnson, 24th Tank Battalion, C Company (CCB):
There's no way you can imagine the feeling that you have. Dead cows, dead horses, mules, hogs, chickens. Dead men settin' beside the road, like they just got shot to death. Some of 'em layin' down, some of 'em in a ditch sittin' up like they's alive,

right on and on. You don't want to see that in your mind. It's terrible. It smelled terrible. They had shells that would scream like a woman, and they would fire 'em at night to keep you from restin', so you'd be tired in the daytime.

And when you can hear shells a hittin' your tank for about two or three hours, you can believe one thing—you're ready to go to a screamin'. My gunner in my tank had a nervous breakdown, and we had to just about hold him at night to keep him from jumpin' up and runnin' out and hollerin'. His nerves come all to pieces. (12)

★ ★ ★

THE KITTEN, Ruhr Battle Extra

At 0930 on the morning of April 18, CCB's armored Cats cleaned out the last corner of the Ruhr Pocket north of Dusseldorf and 97th Infantrymen cleared Dusseldorf itself. The battle of the Ruhr ended that day.

Almost 350,000 PWs (more than the Americans captured in all of World War I) had been taken and the German Army's hold on Europe's No. 1 industrial prize had been completely broken in nine days of combat. (6)

Ruhr Battle Big Success, Ike Asserts

The Ruhr Battle was crowned with a "complete success," General Eisenhower reported in an order of the day to Yank armies in Europe issued after German resistance in the rich industrial area had been completely liquidated.

According to the Supreme Commander, twenty-one enemy divisions were eliminated and approximately 320,000 prisoners of war were taken. He called the Ruhr victory a fitting prelude to the final battle to crush the ragged remnants of Hitler's armies of the west "now tottering on the threshold of defeat." (6)

59th Armored Infantry Battalion (CCB):

With the Ruhr Campaign past history, maintenance, resupply and the resting of weary troops took priority. Preparations were made for a march to the southeast to join the Third Army. (8)

We were in a little village we'd made it to that day. It was in an area that'd had a lot of action, but by the time we took over that village, we thought we had every German soldier rooted out. Evidently we missed one.

Darkness was overtaking us just about the time we got set up. It might have been a cloudy day, but it was gettin' late anyway, so I had just enough light to see how to do my job before we bedded down. The other boys had gone off for different reasons, to wash up or look for the letter carrier. The mail would catch up to us and they'd get their letters from home and go off to read them.

They'd just always leave the driver with the tank to do the necessary tune-ups, and to guard it. I had to check the bogie wheels, grease the fittings, change the oil and so forth. I didn't try to do that during combat. I had to do that when we were out of danger.

I always had to be out there working all around that tank, on both sides, up on the back deck, to keep it ready to go and topped off with gas. Sometimes we'd get to places where the bullets had just been a flyin'—and I always dreaded havin' to open that hatch and get out.

I never did worry a whole lot about it, though. Of course, when you know someone's shootin' at you and gettin' close to you, it's something that's kind of a shock—and you don't always do what you think you would do.

I had just finished my work, changing the oil. I wiped my hands on a rag that I kept in my back pocket. I climbed up on the tank, dropped my legs down in the hatch and I had my right hand on the cannon—I always put my hand up there to hold my weight as I slipped down the hatch. But before I could get down in there, a sniper fired on me.

That bullet came across from my left side and I felt my clothes flutter—my shirt just flopped against my chest—and I thought, "Whew! I believe he's hit me!" It startled me. I wondered if the bullet went through my chest and I hadn't felt it, 'cause some of 'em said you didn't always feel the pain when a bullet went through you. But I sure felt it fan my clothes and I saw some blood. And, boy, I *mean*—I got under cover quick then.

I don't know why I did a foolish thing—I jumped up out of that hatch and crawled under the tank. That was the wrong thing for me to do. That bullet scared me enough to make me not think straight for a minute. 'Cause I know that gettin' inside the tank would have been protection against small arms. I should've just dropped down in my hatch. But I didn't think of that for some reason. I thought about gettin' under cover the first thing, 'cause they train you to do that, to take cover. Then you have time to evaluate the situation. But I just came up out of that hatch when I was already halfway down in it, jumped off the tank, and crawled in between the tracks.

Well, I knew I was hit. I thought that bullet went right through my body and maybe it had numbed me. When I got down under the tank, I got to patting and feeling around and I began to realize I wasn't hurt much. The bullet had cut across the back of my right hand. That was the only place that bullet hit me. I was really proud that there wasn't nothin' else. It didn't even put a hole in my clothes. But it sure cut a groove across my hand. It wasn't cut very deep, just almost like you'd laid a red-hot iron against the back of my hand.

Boy, that was a close call. I liked to got picked off. A Nazi had me in his sights. It gives you a scary feeling when you almost get killed, yeah, it gives you a scary feeling for a little while.

That German soldier knew where I was at and I didn't want to let him get a second shot. So I stayed under the tank, and I thought, now, why did I do that? I waited a while and, oh, I didn't stay under there but for a few minutes.

I came out of there, got the first aid kit off the back of the tank, got in the tank, and doctored my hand. I had to take a chance. But everything you do in war, you have to take a chance. You don't know when you step out of a building but what there's two or three a fixin' to cut you down. You don't never know. 'Cause the German snipers done a good job of concealin' themselves. Had to, to keep us from killin' 'em. A lot of times there'd be snipers left in a town when we took over. We didn't find 'em all.

The German snipers were real clever people. They knew the duties of war. Hitler had those snipers highly trained, and they usually didn't miss on that first shot. I felt lucky that sniper didn't get me. Boy, he came close, though, to gettin' me. I'm satisfied he was hid in an upstairs apartment somewhere. I just happened to be the target, 'cause I was the easiest for him to get.

I guess some of our boys rounded up that sniper. I never did know what happened, but he only fired one shot. That gave his position away. He never did get another chance at me, but he liked to have ended my story right there.

Yeah, I won't never forget that day. 'Cause that one liked to have got me.

I told the rest of the crew about it when they came back to the tank. It had gotten dark by then. I don't know where they were right at the time it happened, but I showed them where that sniper's bullet cut across my hand.

They were all amazed, but we had to laugh a little.

"Leave you alone for two minutes, Kelley, and you go and get shot!" Donald joked me.

"Yeah, what about that?!" I said.

Rhodes called me One Lucky Something or Other, and Knode and McAbee agreed that the Almighty was watchin' over me that time. Then we just went on with our duties.

I never did make a report of it. I thought, well, I'm not hurt bad enough to bother with anything. 'Course, I reckon I should have gotten a Purple Heart out of that.

When that bullet grazed me, it did shake me up, but not for too long. I began to snap out of it in a little while, and I started doin' the things I needed to do. So, I don't know, it was just one of them things that happened to people over there. You expected it to happen, but I was gettin' scraped and raked pretty close.

You can't get killed if the Lord don't want you dead.
—Lonnie E. Johnson

CHAPTER 20

Bavaria — Battle to the Inn

24th Tank Battalion (CCB):

Catching our breath, we began retracing our way south April 20 through Bamberg, Altenkirchen, Schnaittach to Berazthausen for another mission in Bavaria. (1)

496th Armored Field Artillery Battalion (CCB):

Following the Ruhr campaign, the Division was re-assigned to the Third Army. Another road march carried us from Duisberg to Schwaig, a suburb of Nuremburg [Nuremberg]. (7)

Donald had just come back from a huddle and he told us, "We're headin' for the lion's den, Berchtesgaden. We're goin' in to get ol' Hitler himself."

We'd all heard that name, Berchtesgaden, from the movies and newspapers—we called it "Burgess Garden"—and we knew it was where Hitler's hideout was located. It was supposed to be up high in the mountains of Austria and very protected.

"Well, that's what we're here for," Knode said, "to finish ol' Hitler off."

We geared up with new enthusiasm for the mission. We didn't really know what was goin' on, though. We all thought Hitler was holed up in his home country of Austria at that time.

"Move out! Move out!" The order came down and we started a long march into a beautiful region of mountains and valleys — Bavaria.

Donald kept us informed, even though most of the time, it didn't really matter to us where we were goin', so long as the shells and bullets weren't flyin' there. 'Course, they would be eventually, 'cause we'd been told we were headed for another battle.

On our way, we drove right by the big stadium where Hitler made his speeches. They'd shown us movies back in camp of Hitler's rallies at a stadium that held many thousands of people and I guessed right away that this was the one: Nuremberg Stadium.

The way that stadium was made, we could see through the gates into the heart of it as we drove along the highway. It was laid out like a garden and at one end it was closed in with a stage and a podium. That big podium was where Adolf Hitler spoke to the people when he gathered them in. We could see where Hitler stood and chopped his hand in the air to make his points and where the German people had cheered him on in the stands. They had really cheered him on. Boy, they did. The Fuehrer, they called him. "Heil Hitler! Heil Hitler!" the men and women and children used to call out to him, throwing their right arm into the air. I could almost hear the chants and cheers of the people who didn't have any idea, back then, that such destruction would come of it.

"Looks like the Nazis had a poor turnout for their latest rally," Donald came in over the intercom.

The stadium was so deserted, I guess you could have heard a pin drop, if it wasn't for the loud rumble of armor rolling by. Boy, I wondered, what did the German people think of Hitler now? What misery he'd caused to be heaped upon his Fatherland that we kept hearin' about.

"Well, I see Kilroy showed up," Knode said about the mysterious drawings of a big-nosed man peeking over a wall, a cartoon we saw scrawled on walls from one end of Germany to the other. Somebody always made sure they drew that and wrote "Kilroy was here," in as many places as they could. I never did know what it meant.

Being the driver, I didn't talk much on the intercom. I kept my attention focused on the road ahead. But as we rolled by, I did turn the periscope to take a good long look at that stadium so I could one day tell my children and grandchildren about it.

That Nuremberg Stadium, I can still see it. It hadn't been damaged at all, it was still a nice, big stadium. They had flagpoles clear around the top of that stadium, high poles with great big red flags that had a white circle and black swastika in the center. They still had those Nazi flags up — they hadn't been taken down yet. There were so many flags circling the top of that stadium, when the wind was a blowin', they'd just almost touch each other.

The people really went for those swastikas over there. I never saw any one symbol used so much. We'd take over towns and every little timber house that we went in, we hardly ever saw a swastika, not a one in sight — but, of course, we knew where to find them.

Now we were with the Third Army again and General Patton didn't want us foolin' along, so we didn't stay in any little village more than a night or two. When we were out of range for a few nights like that, we'd get to line up for chow and get a hot meal, and we'd just hunker down and really eat it up. Then we'd hear the stories about what had happened to our buddies, the close calls, and the shock of losing some of them. A buddy would get wounded or killed and the army'd replace him right away with somebody from another outfit, so there were new faces now.

We'd wash up as good as we could when we were at a place where we could do that. When we were into a hot battle zone, we stayed buttoned up and we just went around dirty most of the time. We'd go without washing and I really don't know how long, but we'd go quite a while. Maybe at least four days, probably.

Now we could use a washcloth, soap, and water. We'd put water in our steel helmet. The helmet we wore had a fiberglass liner and the steel helmet went on top of it. We were supposed to wear that steel helmet when we were out of the tank in case a sniper took a crack pot at us — but we'd take that helmet off anyway and heat water in it.

Most of the time in the field, we used our steel helmet to shave. We had a little gas stove and a tripod that held the helmet up off of the fire. The fuel was in a container, it was just like jelly, and you could light it to heat water.

I still had a pretty good scabbed-up place over my upper lip to shave around from the night I drove into that oak tree. That seemed like a long time ago. Now my right hand was bandaged up, too, but I wasn't complainin' 'bout anything after all I'd seen.

The only thing I might ever have complained about was water. One of the worst things I had to contend with over there was gettin' good water. You had to have water to drink and you had to fill your canteen just wherever you could. In those towns where we saw a lot of swastikas, I was always scared that the water wasn't fit to drink. I felt like the Germans could have put something in the water before they left that would harm us. The army gave us tablets to put in the water and they said if there was any kind of poison in it, it would kill it, but I was leery of that anyhow.

We'd assemble in small villages where we had facilities and we'd wash our clothes and get our uniforms in order as much as we could in the field. We did try to change our clothes in battle — you had to change your underclothes pretty often. But you could get by with your other clothes for a while. We'd always wash our undershirts and shorts in containers that we carried on the tank. I guess it was ten-quart buckets, something like that, and we'd put our underclothes in them, put water and soap in there and wash them. Once in a while, we'd have time, between times we'd be in combat.

When we got in Germany, we wore our OD uniforms, our dress uniforms. The army wanted us to wear them in battle. They didn't inspect us while we were in battle, but the army wanted them kept clean, they wanted creases in the legs of the pants, that's the way they wanted them to be.

Well, that OD stuff, you couldn't wash it in water without ruining it. Water would just make those uniforms be wrinkly. Now, gasoline wouldn't take the press out of them. The only way we had to clean our uniforms in the field and get them to dry right away was to use gasoline. So we'd just take us a big bucket of gasoline, wash our uniforms in it, and hang them up to dry. That gas would evaporate from the clothes in a little while. Of course, there'd be a little odor to them.

I don't know what anybody else did, but I always saved any extra gas that we had left from washin' and stored it on the tank, 'cause the way I was raised, we didn't waste nothin'.

> *Patton needed gasoline urgently, and GIs in the back would be using gasoline for cleaning fluid. They'd take a five gallon can of gasoline and clean their GIs because they always would get pretty dirty and greasy . . . They'd just take a five gallon can of gasoline, Patton's dying for it, and dump it in a big bucket of some sort and they'd wash one set of GI pants and shirts out and then dump the gasoline. If Patton had seen that, he'd have killed them.*
>
> **—Cpl. Alexander Gordeuk, Information and Education Officer, 13th Armored Division (9)**

★ ★ ★

59th Armored Infantry Battalion (CCB):

On April 24th, General George S. Patton, Jr., Commander of the Third Army, addressed officers and non-commissioned officers of the Division. He spoke highly of the Division's work in the Ruhr and also stressed the importance of the final push against the Nazis. (8)

496th Armored Field Artillery Battalion (CCB):

We were addressed by the Third Army Commander, General George S. Patton, and were informed that the mission of the 13th Armored Division was to spearhead the attack of the XX Corps in their final major drive of the European war. (7)

497th Armored Field Artillery Battalion (CCR):

His address measured up to expectations. The new operation was designed to sweep southeastward through Bavaria, to meet the Russians who were driving northwest from Vienna, and keep the Germans from massing their forces in the so-called "Redoubt Area"—the Austrian and Bavarian Alps—for a last stand. (13)

In case of doubt, attack.
—**General George S. Patton**

We'd traveled quite a ways and we stopped to spend three days in some little ol' village to get our equipment ready. I was lookin' forward to gettin' some rest. We were going into another battle soon, and General Patton, he met with our division and talked to us.

But the thing of it was, I didn't get to see him, and none of my tank crew did, either, because we had trouble with the tank. Those Shermans had a little gasoline engine called a Homelite that generated the power to run some things in the tank, like the automatically traversing turret. You could manually traverse the turret, if you had to, but you couldn't hardly turn it as fast that way. Our speed with the guns depended on that little generator, and ours had quit running.

The army had set up a service shop quite a few miles from where we were gonna spend the night, maybe fifteen, might have been twenty miles, I don't know, but it seems like it took us a long time to get there.

They checked out some of the companies to see if any other vehicles needed repairing. When they did, they found a half-track that wouldn't run, so they hooked it behind my tank for me to tow. The driver had to be in the half-track to steer it and we towed it with a cable.

We had a lieutenant who led the way in a jeep and he said he knew where to take us. It was getting nearly dark when we left the company and we hadn't gone very far till it was dark. We just kept a goin' down the road into the night.

We had to drive blackout. They'd told us, "Don't turn a light on, 'cause those planes'll be watchin' for you." So I was looking through that periscope, doin' my best to drive by the light of the little cat eyes that shined down on the road.

The lieutenant was supposed to know the way, but he didn't know the way. He took us down a road he shouldn't have, and we got down that road a ways, and there were guns a firin' everywhere. It was a real dark night and I could see those red-orange tracers arching over just as plain. You can see them from a pretty good ways off.

I didn't know where the fighting was exactly, but I reckoned that we got right down on the front lines of some battle that night—the bullets were a flyin' so. We were still out of range from what I could tell, but we were headed right towards the source of the firing. That lieutenant in the jeep just kept goin' and goin' on, and I knew something was wrong. I figured that if we went on, we were gonna be in trouble and I didn't know how we were gonna get by that. Now, that gave me a scare, just us out there alone.

The lieutenant didn't tell us we were lost till he went to seein' a lot of those tracer bullets and he began to realize that he was on the wrong road. In a few minutes, he stopped. We stopped in behind him and he walked back to the tank—we couldn't use our radios out there 'cause the Germans might hear us. Donald and I opened our hatches, popped our heads out.

That lieutenant said, "We made a wrong turn back there. Now we're into a battle zone."

I didn't much like the sound of that, especially us out there on our own, two vehicles, with one in tow, driving through Nazi Germany at night. I don't imagine any of us in the tank could forget what'd happened to Charlie Eaton and Donnie Knight, when they got on the wrong road like we were now.

The lieutenant said, "We'll have to go back and find the right road, but first we'll have to go ahead to a place where you can turn around."

It takes a pretty good space to turn a Sherman tank around, and I was towing that half-track, too. So we had to continue a little ways towards where they were firing those guns and the tracers were crisscrossing and gettin' closer.

We came to an intersection in the road. The lieutenant stopped, came back and asked me, "Do you think you could make a U-turn here with that half-track behind you without having to unhook it?"

I said, "Yeah, I believe I can."

He turned the jeep around, and he went on ahead of us. I made the U-turn all right, didn't have any trouble. We got turned around, and I felt pretty good then. I knew we were going the opposite direction to where the firefight was.

So we kept going. And Donald, for some reason, he hadn't looked back after we made the turn I don't reckon, because he came on the intercom and he said, "We've lost that half-track back there. We don't have it with us."

I said, "Well, what do you want me to do?"

He said, "We can't turn on the lights. See if you can catch the lieutenant."

So I took off. The faster I'd go and the closer I'd get to that lieutenant, the faster he'd go. I couldn't catch up with that jeep, because when he saw I was getting close to him, he'd just speed up to keep safe distance and, of course, a tank is no match for runnin' a race with a jeep. There wasn't no way for me to stop him.

Donald said, "Kelley, what are we gonna do now?"

I told him, "Well, would you give me permission just to flash on my headlights—just on and off—one time? We're gonna have to take a chance. Let me just jerk the headlights on and off, right quick, and he'll know somethin's wrong." That was a big risk.

Donald said, "Well, he may not see it, but we'll have to take a chance, I guess, that's the only way we can stop him. There may be some German planes overhead watching us."

So I just jerked the tank's lights on and off and when I did, the lieutenant stopped the jeep and we pulled up behind him. He came back and we told him that we lost the half-track and the man that was driving it, of course, he was in the half-track.

That lieutenant said, "Aw, we'll have to go ahead and find a place where you can get turned around again and you'll have to go back and get him. Hope you didn't alert any Jerries." The lieutenant didn't seem too pleased with the way things had been goin' that night. He stayed by the side of the road with his jeep and waited for us.

The road was pretty narrow and lined by big trees. We had to go on a little ways till we found a place where we could turn the tank around. Then we went back down the road lookin' for that half-track. When we got to the place where we'd first turned around, that half-track was sitting right in that intersection.

The driver, he was up on top of that half-track, sittin' on the steel cab with his rifle a layin' across his lap.

He said, "I was gonna sit up here where I could see. I wasn't gonna let a Jerry sneak up on me . . ." He talked a mile a minute as we got his half-track hooked up to the tank.

He said, "When you turned around, I made the turn all right and then in a few seconds I saw your tank getting smaller and smaller. I thought for sure you'd stop in a little while. But you didn't. I was sitting here and I said to myself, now I'm stuck. I don't know what I can do by myself. They kept firing guns down the road and I was afraid they'd heard us. I thought, they'll send somebody out and they'll find me. I got up on the cab—thought I might be able to pick off some Krauts. Then I heard your tank coming and I knew I was saved. What took you so long?"

"Aw, I don't know. It's so dark out here tonight, we couldn't see you wasn't behind us," I told him. "Then we had to go a ways to get turned around."

We didn't waste any more time—we took off towing that half-track, joined up with the lieutenant, and got on the right road. We got to the repair shop sometime in the middle of the night. They worked on my tank and by the next evening, we drove back to the company. Never did get any sleep.

When we got back, everybody was all excited and came up to us with something big to tell us. Some of the tank commanders said, "You just missed General George S. Patton. He was here and he talked to us and he told us a lot of stuff. He said, 'The Germans are dug in right over the top of those ridges, waiting for you.'"

Our whole division was camped at the foot of a bunch of ridges, kind of mountainlike, wasn't high ridges, but it was ridges.

Patton had everybody all riled up and rarin' to go. They went on. "Patton said that in the morning, we're gonna top those ridges at daylight. And he said, 'Every gun you've got better be talking—or you won't last a minute, 'cause they're waitin' on us up there.'"

All of 'em were talkin' about Patton's speech. Though I wasn't there when he made it, I remember what some of my buddies told me Patton said: *"When you get to the top of those ridges, you'd better have all your guns talking."*

The army would always tell us when we were going to go into combat. We'd be up close to the front lines and they'd say, "Now, tomorrow, we'll be facing the Germans and you better be prepared for them, or you won't live. You can't go up there and just wait around and shoot whenever you think you see somebody. You've got to pin them down and overrun them."

That was Patton's theory and he had a good theory. He believed, hit 'em hard and overrun 'em, and you've got 'em. When you do that, you get them all disorganized and they'll surrender. They know they're gonna have to surrender or die and most of the German soldiers would rather surrender than to die. Those were Patton's tactics and he was a winner.

We were getting right up close to the front line, a fixin' to go into battle when General Patton met with our division. That was just before we went across the mountains where he said we'd hit that resistance. So we were prepared when we topped those ridges to have all our guns a blazin'. Naturally, we were pretty tense driving through those hills at the break of dawn. As it happened, it wasn't good daylight.

Well, we didn't see no Germans. We got to the top of the hill, and evidently, the Germans had decided they'd better back off. They'd pulled back to set up more of a defense line, 'cause I guess when they saw all of the armor that we had, coming in there over the top of those hills, they figured they didn't have a chance. And they backed off to a better position. We did encounter the German soldiers later, but we didn't encounter them right where we'd expected.

We'd traveled all day without any resistance and we took over some little ol' village. They were all about alike. When the army decided we'd spend the night in a village, we pulled in there and lined up our tanks, making a motor pool. Usually we'd try to get them in a big circle or semicircle, depending on how the village was laid out, so we'd have protection all the way around us, about it, if we could get it that way. A lot of the infantry and other companies would move in, too.

They told us to check all of our equipment, we were sure to hit some resistance the next day. So everybody was checking their guns and getting ready to move out, 'cause they'd already given us our orders.

I was getting something off of the back of my tank and another tank's .30 caliber went off and it fired one shot right by the side of me, right into the tank. I didn't even know where it was coming from. I thought it was a plane overhead, strafing us. The bullet bounced out, but it made a big dent where it hit. It was just .30 caliber, but it penetrated into that metal, drilled a hole maybe a half-inch deep. Oh, it would have drilled a hole in me. Boy, that time I got over there, jumped down in the tank!

I found out, this boy and his tank commander were in the turret of their tank working on the machine gun. They were having trouble with it malfunctioning. They got to fooling with it and it started firing. Those .30 caliber machine guns would do that sometimes.

Now, they oughta had it turned some other way, but they had it turned right straight into our tank. A lot of those boys drafted in there, some of 'em were replacements for the ones we'd had injured or killed, and maybe they weren't used to being around guns from way on back. They had good army training, but still, sometimes, they'd forget and point their guns in a direction they shouldn't. My dad always cautioned me, "You don't ever want to point your gun at anything you don't aim to kill." I kept that in mind.

I almost got hit by one of our own guns that time. If that gun had shot more than once, it mighta got me. And that was another really close call.

The next morning, we were ready to pull out, I remember 'cause I was already in my tank with the hatch closed and I was looking ahead through the periscope, and I saw a boy get killed—he was the tank commander for one of the tanks in front of me. He was up on the back deck getting something out of a container. I was watching him.

I saw a roof beyond him with clay shingles and I saw bullets knocking the shingles off of that house. Those clay shingles were just a flyin' everywhere. I thought it was a German fighter plane coming down, strafing us. I saw that boy standing up on the back deck of his tank and he just went to turning around and around real slow and he fell off of the tank. I thought the Germans had killed him.

We found out later that it was one of our own guns that malfunctioned, that same gun that'd almost got me. They'd loaded their .30 caliber and it went off and went to shooting just like a sewing machine. They couldn't get it stopped quick enough. They had to twist the belt to get it to stop. That's what you had to do, take that ammunition belt and twist it good and jam the gun if it started firing on its own. You've got so many people fooling with guns and some of them are not careful enough and even if they are careful, those automatic guns can malfunction. They'll run a whole belt through if you don't know how to stop them.

They'd had the gun elevated, but evidently when they lowered it, that boy happened to be standing right in the path of those bullets. That was a sad moment when we found that out. That tank commander had made it all through the Battle of the Ruhr, and then to die because of an accident seemed senseless. I thought it was even more sad, too, 'cause the evening before, that tank commander had found a little German motorbike there in that village and he got that thing out, and it would run, so he put gas in it, and he rode around through the streets. He just had a big time riding that motor scooter all over the place. I got a kick out of watching him. I thought about him a lot after he got killed. I thought about what a good time he was having, zippin' around, ridin' that thing, and then he got killed the next day.

Lonnie Johnson, 24th Tank Battalion, C Company (CCB):

We got back in our tanks, or I did, and there was a .30 caliber machine gun right over my head and I slid down in my tank and when I slid down in my tank, that .30 caliber gun went off. My assistant gunner had got in there to see if it was loaded and it went off and killed a tank commander in front of us. He was up on the tank in front of us, where we's parked. He got about five rounds before we could stop it. If I'd a been a second later, it would have hit me. The Lord wasn't ready for me and I'm glad he wasn't. (12)

Our tank companies were a real close-knit group of people, sort of like a big family. It didn't matter what kind of background somebody was from, everybody depended on the other feller to help him any way he could. We all stood by each other. Whenever we heard news about one of the boys in our outfit getting killed or seriously wounded, it always made a real sad feeling in your heart. I know it did in mine and I'm satisfied the other boys felt the same way.

Some of those boys would find themselves whiskey, brandy, or champagne in those German homes and they'd take it and drink it. Seemed to dull the pain, I reckon. Some of them fought the war about half-drunk all the time. But the most of them during combat were really concerned about surviving. They were really concerned about it and they tried to do everything that they'd been trained to do to be able to survive and stay alert to the enemy.

★ ★ ★

The Division:

After a march of approximately 300 miles through Remscheid and Limburg, Bad Nauheim and Hanau, the 13th reached the Danube River at Regensburg and was once more thrown into battle.

Now an integral part of the XX Corps of the 3rd Army, the Division crossed the Danube on bridges provided by the 65th and 71st Infantry Divisions. CCB hurdled the Danube at 1830 on the 27th of April, using the 71st Infantry bridge. They were closely followed by the tanks and tracks of CCR. CCA crossed on the 65th bridge but concentrations of enemy artillery and mired roads hindered their advance. (2)

"The Germans are dug in somewhere across the river, if we can get across there," Donald's voice crackled a little over the intercom, as we prepared to cross the Danube River on a pontoon bridge.

Some of the boys said they expected this river to be bluer than other rivers. Why, it was famous for being blue, McAbee said. "As blue as the blue Danube," and he hummed a little tune that I never had heard.

The river was a wide one, but it wasn't blue, not even clean. It was muddy and swollen 'cause we'd been having some springtime rains. That river was surrounded by low boggy ground. And that made those roads leading up to the pontoon bridges almost impassible.

Down in the lowland where several of the Bavarian rivers were, that ground got pretty thick with mud and that caused us a lot of delays. The combat weight of those Sherman tanks was something like thirty-four tons, and some of the tanks would get bogged down. Those tracks would just sink down in that heavy, sticky mud till they couldn't go. The engineers had to put treadways down for us to drive on.

The engineers always had a lot of work to do before they could get us across those rivers. When we approached the Danube River, they had to run a different type of bridging out to support our tanks until we got to where we could get on the pontoon bridges. The engineers had to lay "corduroy," they called it, crossties over that muddy ground. They laid those crossties close together so they looked a little like corduroy fabric. They had sheets of metal that came in big rolls and they'd unroll it over those supports and that gave us a cushion to drive on when we were driving along the edges of rivers. While we were fighting one place, the engineers would be on up ahead building bridges. I don't know how they managed to do all that work to get those bridges in there with the Germans shootin' at 'em, but they were able. We never did know much of what went on before we got somewhere.

Each of our armored columns had their own route and some were lined with German soldiers and some were not. The bridge we crossed the big Danube River on, it was no problem for us. So we went across that pontoon bridge without a shot being fired.

We got over there and traveled on, I guess about a mile or two. We stopped, got out, and got to lookin' around. We got to talkin' and said, "Why, those kraut eaters left out of here."

They had foxholes everywhere, and, of course, we saw their cigarette stubs where they'd been smokin'. And it looked like they'd just left out that day. They figured that our tank force, I guess, was too much to stop. Yeah, we never knew what to expect of the enemy. So far that morning, our tank hadn't had any combat. We thought the Germans were waiting on us when we crossed the river, but they'd moved somewhere else. We didn't know where we might encounter them.

After we got in Germany, we were in enemy territory all the time until the war ended. There wasn't no time that you felt safe. A lot of times we'd travel a long time without any resistance and that was tough, almost like holdin' your breath, waitin' for that next shot. Some of the boys said they figured the Germans were all but give out by this time, and maybe we wouldn't see any more fightin' at all. Of course, we hoped that was true.

We'd crossed that Danube River late in the day and had to wait on the rest of the division, so that night we slept in our tanks the best we could — the army wanted blackout conditions — and we waited for dawn, when we had orders to move out again, in a hurry.

★ ★ ★

THE BLACK CAT Newspaper

'. . . The attack proceeded at daylight the next morning with rapid progress. A light tank company moving on the left flank of axis liberated 125 British Prisoners of War, who had been imprisoned for five years, northwest of Straubing. (4)

24th Tank Battalion:

Bound for Berchtesgaden, we launched our forces across the Danube near Regensberg, and on the morning of the 28th smashed on through Ram, Rinkham, Straubing and Salching. (1)

The Division:

Held in a close formation by the [Danube] crossing, the Division hit the south bank and fanned out like water through a broken dam in their forceful rush to the Isar River. The attack was in three columns echeloned to the right. CCB with the 59th Infantry and the 24th Tanks rolled along the left flank through Rain, Rinkham and then into Straubing, where a bull dozer reduced a road block that had been holding up the column. (2)

It was right along before dawn. I hadn't slept too well cramped up in that driver's seat, and Donald could see I was a little slow gettin' goin' that morning.

"Kelley's been driving this tank the whole time," Donald said. "I think it's time for him to get a break from all the driving. Rhodes, how 'bout you start out for a couple of hours."

As our tank commander, Donald was really concerned about us doing our best on the job, especially at this time in the war. We could see it was winding down. In case we ran into a battle, he really wanted us to be well prepared, 'cause we all wanted to get home.

I had been driving a lot, all the way through France and Germany. I'd just driven that repair mission without gettin' hardly any sleep, and I was still a drivin'. Of course, Patton didn't have us slow down for a minute. I hadn't been having any problem, so I just kept on doing the driving. My assistant driver, Rhodes, he'd stayed the bow gunner the whole time, and I was glad, 'cause he'd been doin' his job like a professional.

Rhodes asked me, "Do you want me to drive some? You have been drivin' an awful lot."

I said "Yeah, Rhodes, I think maybe you're gonna have to drive this tank a little while. I'm just give out. Yeah, I'd like for you to drive for a little while anyways." I figured I could sit in the assistant driver's seat and catch a wink or two.

The thing of it was, my assistant driver, he hadn't drove none since I don't know when. It had been way back when we were in training in California, last time he drove.

Rhodes got over there to driving just as the sun was coming up. We were going through some countryside before we got into a little village. We hadn't gone very far when we ran into the Germans. They'd set up a defense line and, boy, they started a firin' on us. The Germans were after us there. They were dug in all along the road and they had the road blocked and they opened up on us without warning. They's in foxholes with bazookas. When we got close, I could see them stickin' their heads up. When our tanks got up by the side of them, if we hadn't seen them, they were going to knock our tank out. But they didn't get the chance.

The tank commander told the gunner to kill them. I was watching them to my left. And Knode was shootin' at 'em. He shot all of 'em, the whole row. One right after the other. He kept shootin' as we went up through there and he mowed down every one.

I sat in the assistant driver's seat — the bow gunner's seat — and I guess I would have been usin' that .30 caliber like we'd all been trained to do, 'cause that's what my tank commander would have ordered me to do. I'm satisfied I was a firin' on targets as we rode through there, but I don't know why I can't remember much about that.

Sometimes in a situation like that, you couldn't tell if you hit anyone. The bullets were a flyin' from everywhere, 'cause we weren't the only tank a firin' on 'em. It was more like bein' part of a firin' squad, 'cause you didn't know what you hit, hardly. I remember seein' those German soldiers go limp. But it's strange that I can't remember any more about that.

When our tank got up to where the Germans had set up the resistance, they'd cut a bunch of trees across the highway, so we had to leave the highway and go down off of a bank, down through a field and all around, to get around that roadblock. To get back onto the highway, we had to go up a pretty steep bank.

Havin' to drive under all that intense fire, that got my assistant driver nervous. Rhodes started up that bank without shifting the tank down into a lower gear and the engine started stalling on him. That got him all excited and he drove up there a little ways and then let the tank run backwards down the bank—he was gonna get up some speed. And Donald hollered at him in the headphones, "Get this thing up there on the road, they'll sure get us here!"

Rhodes got so scared that he was trying to shift gears in that tank, and he got it out of gear and he couldn't get it to go back in gear.

"Get this thing to rollin'! You're gonna get us all killed!" I could hear Donald blasting over the intercom.

Oh, you ought to have seen Rhodes, he was just a fightin' and a grabbin' hold of everything in there and he got so tore up, he didn't know what he was a doin'. We couldn't switch seats, the way the tank was made. You'd have to get out of the tank to switch drivers and it was a hot battle zone. Boy, that was a killin' me. I just sat there thinking that I should have been the one a drivin'.

Rhodes got the tank up that bank again and just as we were about to get in the road, he stalled the engine—again, he didn't have it in a low enough gear—and Donald said, "Get us down from here! You've got the bottom turned up and that's the thin part of this tank!"

He was afraid a shell would come right through the bottom of our tank when it bobbed up to get back in the road, 'cause that turned the belly of it up before it broke over. There wasn't much armor underneath.

Boy, Rhodes was so tore up, he just about went all to pieces, but he let the tank roll back down the bank and he tried it again, and he finally got the tank up over that hill and onto the road. And the Germans were a shootin' right near us, but none of them happened to hit us.

We got through that battle and the first time we stopped, Rhodes said, "I'll never drive that tank another foot! I don't care what they do to me. They can just shoot me down. They can kill me. I don't care."

I'd never seen Rhodes so tore up. He said to me, "I'm too nervous to drive it. You're gonna have to drive, even if you are tired."

I said, "Well, okay."

We knew we couldn't get him to drive after he got all shook up. Of course, he was refusing orders to do what his position required, officially, but we were in combat so he could get away with it.

Donald really got on him. He said, "You almost got us killed!"

I'd never had any trouble, never did get flustered when I was driving and we got into a battle like that. It just didn't bother me. I knew all the time what I had to do and I could perform just about as good under pressure—and it was tremendous pressure, now that I think about it. They gave me enough training until it was second nature to me.

Rhodes was trained to be a driver, of course. He could drive good back in the States when we were taking training. But he hadn't had near as much experience as I had driving. They ought to have given him more practice.

The first time Rhodes drove the tank over there was the last time he drove it. I had to drive from then on. It might have been better that I did anyhow. The tank commander didn't want Rhodes driving after that either, 'cause he got excited and that caused us to be in danger. So Rhodes never drove again. Never did.

That morning they'd told us, "There's gonna be some fierce resistance up ahead. We're expecting every trick the Nazis've got. More mines, all kinds of 'em, roadblocks, antitank guns. This is where the SS is backed up to. They're determined to keep us out of Austria."

We felt that the war was winding down, so it was disheartening to hear that we'd have to fight some of the most determined Nazi soldiers before we were through. It was something the Allies feared called the National Redoubt.

The Allies were afraid Hitler's most devoted followers would make a last stand where the Nazis began, in the mountains of Austria, where maybe they had a lot of weapons stored up. So, for all we knew there in the field, we might still have to fight for a long time, even though everybody said the war in Europe was surely about over, 'cause the damage the Allies had done was so devastating, and German soldiers were already surrendering by the thousands.

That morning, it was still early—but by now, it was just getting light enough to see good—and I remember when we moved out and crossed some little hilly country, we went down a long slope and as we went down there, we were in combat. Our column was shooting at buildings and at everything that moved. I could see people running here and there through the smoke from the burning buildings.

The town had a cross street where I saw a horse hooked on an empty two-wheeled cart and that cart was bouncin' over those loose cobblestones, and that horse was just a runnin' around the rubble that fell down as we blew out the side of buildings. That horse was runnin' fast as it could go, scared to death, and it came down that street and ran right in front of my tank, just a flyin'. I had to pull on both my brakes as tight as I could to keep from runnin' over that horse.

There was a big picture window in a store, and that horse went across the street, up on a sidewalk, and right through that plate-glass window into that store, him and that cart. I'd done and gone on by then, so I don't know what happened, whether that horse killed itself or what happened after that.

Our tank was bucking like a bronco again, shooting that cannon at targets way out there that I couldn't see. Knode shot at big stuff in that battle. You had to keep all the guns hot in a battle like that. You had to keep those Nazi soldiers pinned down. We were spreading destruction in all directions. Buildings around there were a blazin' up and clouds of smoke made it hard to see the Germans in some places. They were startin' to slip up on some of the tanks.

We went on there a ways, down this long hill into a village, and there was a whole bunch of German soldiers in that village—we could see them, they's running every which way. They had mines that they were putting in the roads.

When the Germans laid mine belts, that would slow us down a little bit. The Germans had antitank mines that would cripple the heaviest tank, but they wouldn't go off when a foot soldier walked over them. It takes quite a bit of weight to set them off, so they'll have a better chance of doing damage when that mine gets under a tank. A mine couldn't penetrate the tank's armor, but if it knocked off a track, then the tank was just a sitting duck for bigger guns and the crew would have to bail out and abandon the tank.

If we ran into a mine belt, they'd call and bring up a tank that was equipped with a "snake." It was a big, long thing you hooked on the front of a special tank. It was loaded with explosives and they'd slide it out about fifty feet and then they'd detonate it.

The driver was the one who pushed the snake out there and the gunner detonated it. The snake had a target on the end and the gunner would shoot that target and that would detonate the charge and it would just blow out a big path. Then we could move up another fifty feet. I could see the puffs of smoke up ahead, while they cleared the way for our column to continue.

We got to shootin' into that village and one of our shells set a house afire. The whole house was in blazes and the flames were shootin' up through the roof, burning the shakes, and you could see the crisscrossed lathing as the roof burned away.

And here come a German soldier out of that house with a bucket and he went around the house and filled that bucket with water and started to go back in the house to try to put that big fire out. As he started back in the house, somebody shot him. He just fell in the doorway. I can just see him now — he fell in the doorway with that bucket of water in his hand.

I said, "Boy, he was foolish for doin' that, comin' out there and tryin' to put a fire out and us comin' right down on him." I guess it was his home and he didn't want it to burn up. It seemed strange that he thought he could fight that fire one bucket of water at a time, but, of course, he didn't get that chance.

He could have surrendered and maybe nothing would have happened to him, but he didn't do that. He wanted to put out his fire. I guess he figured we wouldn't kill him, but somebody did anyhow. If you didn't put up your hands, you were just out of luck. Of course, by that time, from what I'd seen, I knew that some of the ones that surrendered did get killed. There were some of our boys that would have killed 'em even if they'd been down on their knees a beggin'.

I never wanted to harm anybody, especially one man singled out like that. Of course, when I was out of the tank with my submachine gun, now, if a German soldier had showed up—and he didn't have his hands up—I'd a had to kill him to save my own life. And I'd a done it. But some of those boys were just eager to do it, that was just in them. That was just bad blood. They would have killed Americans, I guess, if they'd give 'em a reason. That's the kind of people we had in the army, every walk of life. We saw it all.

Some towns we'd go to, right at the end of the war, we'd give them a chance to surrender to spare them from further destruction. We'd come into a town where we hadn't hit any resistance before we got there, and we'd stop on the outskirts. We'd send an interpreter into the town. We had a few boys of German descent who could speak good German. They usually kept them close to headquarters so they could get the messages from the Germans if they had to talk to them. They helped as interpreters and they would always go with the officers and talk for them with the German officials.

There'd be three men—a lieutenant, a captain, and one interpreter, and the three of them would walk into town to see if the town would surrender. Each one of them carried a white flag. The Germans wouldn't bother them as long as they walked down those streets with that white flag, showing that they wouldn't do any damage.

They would talk to the German people to find out where the military was, and the town officials. Then they'd ask the town officials through our German-speaking Black Cats, were they gonna surrender to us, or did they want to put up a fight? They'd give them a chance to surrender to save their buildings and civilians, because we were going to take over the town if we had to fight 'em.

Our interpreters would get their answer, and the Germans let them leave and come back to us. They could have killed them and there would have been nothing we could have done about it, only just waged war with them. But they always let them come back. There they'd come walkin' back, carrying those white flags. The Germans would honor that white flag. We were supposed to honor a white flag, if they came out with one.

Now, we kept hearing that the Japanese were a different type of people. You couldn't bargain with them like that from what I had been told. Of course, I'd never had any contact with the Japanese. But from what I saw of the Germans, they were pretty sensible in that respect, it seemed like.

If we didn't see nobody, nobody nowhere — not even peeking out a window — then we knew the Germans were set up there a waitin' for us. I remember one town we went into, the officers and interpreter came back and said, "Well, we're gonna have to take this town. The German officers refused to surrender."

We had to go into battle. We went through that town a bangin' our big guns and I don't know what and all we done. The Sherman tanks would just go down every street, a shootin' and a bangin'. The infantry followed us, cleaning up all of the ones that we didn't see. But we got that town. A lot of needless damage happened because the German military didn't want to surrender.

Now, it was also in that area where there was some other little town that our interpreters went to and they came back and said, "Well, we're gonna have to take this town, too."

But when we went into that town, we had very little resistance, just a little mortar fire. We felt like after our officers left the meeting with the German officials, the German soldiers made up their minds to leave instead of putting up a fight. We figured we'd have a lot of resistance, but we didn't have enough to be worried too much about.

We'd find it to be like that. Sometimes when you thought you were really gonna have a big battle, you didn't have much and when you wasn't expectin' it, that was when you's surprised.

The Germans had the road blocked in front of us and we couldn't go on into the next little town until our forces got that roadblock destroyed and cleaned out. It was dangerous having to sit there and wait, especially because the road was built up higher than the terrain around it.

Our infantry came up to keep German foot soldiers from crawling up on us. There was a field that went down over a bank, a big flat field out there. I remember the infantry going down in that field by the road and Donald looked down there and he said over the intercom, "I want you to look over by that fence."

It was a German soldier, lying facedown in the field.

"There lays a kraut eater that'll never bother anybody else," he said. "Yeah, he won't give us any trouble."

In a few minutes, the infantry got up there and they spread out in those fields and when they got to that feller, they ran up to him and poked him, and he was alive. He just got up. There wasn't a thing wrong with him, he was just playin' dead.

They had a lot of foxholes dug down through that field and I guess he was trying to get in one when we rolled in there and he dropped down on the ground before he could get to his foxhole. That saved his life. If he'd been trying to run across that field, somebody would have picked him off. But he was smart enough to lie down and play dead until they came along and captured him. He could have shot someone, but he'd have got killed sure enough if he'd shot somebody.

The infantry put him with some more that they captured and they sent that group of German prisoners walking back down the road with their hands on top of their heads.

Our forces finally got that roadblock cleared out and we got through there and got into a town, and the infantry rounded up a lot of people in that town and took them out in a field to get them out of the way. It was mostly women and children—we didn't want them to get killed. We didn't know how much resistance we had there.

I watched the infantry as they cleared the town. While they were rounding up civilians, I was looking out the periscope and I saw one of our men get shot. I think it killed him, best I remember. He wasn't in our company, he was infantry that had come up there.

Our troops heard where the shot came from. It was from an upstairs apartment. So some of them got the German sniper, he was regular German army. They didn't kill him. They captured him and brought him out of that house with his fingers interlaced over his head and sent him to a PW cage.

★ ★ ★

We went on and we were runnin' low on fuel. Those Germans had the airport held up, but our forces got in there. Of course, they sent the infantry in there to clear the airport out, and they told us, "As soon as they get it cleared out, there'll be planes landing in there with your fuel."

When we needed fuel, if we's up on the front line, they'd have to bring in fuel, didn't matter where we were. They'd load it on trucks and bring it out to us. We were preparing to move out when the fuel trucks came by.

The black drivers would always drive up by the side of our tanks, ask us how many five-gallon cans we wanted. We depended on them to deliver our fuel all through combat, so we got pretty used to dealing with them.

Several of the men in our company said, "Oh, them fellers are really nice. Why, black men aren't much different to what we are. They're just as nice. I wasn't expecting them to be that nice to us." For some of the men, like me, the army's fuel deliverymen were the only black men we'd ever had a chance to deal with.

The boys in our outfit always treated the black men good; some of them joked with them while they were setting off the gas cans. They always came back with a pretty quick answer and they didn't seem to get mad at anything. They talked real jolly a lot of the time. When I talked with our black drivers, I never thought nothin' about it, but I never did joke with them myself 'cause I was afraid I might offend them in some way. I thought they were just as good as I was and I knew they'd had a harder time comin' up in the world than I'd had.

While we were refueling, German artillery located us and started firing on us. People back then used to say that black men were no good under fire. That was just tales they told on 'em 'cause the Germans were a firin' on us a lot of the time and the black soldiers that delivered gas did a real good job of gettin' it delivered quick. They'd set those cans off and they'd drive on, movin' on down the line like wildfire.

If there was a lot of shooting and banging around and I didn't know when they'd maybe pick me off, I'd have to jump in the tank or under it. Sometimes you could get under it quicker. I'd have to hide till they quit firing. Then I'd have to get out and pour some more gas in that Sherman.

They kept opening up on us with artillery. They sent a lot of shells over there, but they didn't happen to hit right close to my tank. I figured they would maybe the next time. We didn't know where they were getting their signal from. They kept shellin' us and one of our lieutenants finally figured out that some German civilians must be helpin' the Nazis right under our nose.

There was a farmhouse down the road a little ways from where we were refueling. Our officers decided that the Germans must have a radio in there and that there was somebody in the farmhouse calling in to the artillery, telling them where we were located, 'cause they's right on target.

So they sent some foot soldiers down there to check that building out. They found three men in there dressed as civilians—one old man and two younger men—and one old lady. And they found a transmitter in there. They were transmitting back and forth to the German artillery people. They were telling them where their shells were hitting.

Our soldiers tore that transmitter up and got the men out of there, took them as prisoners. They didn't bother the old woman, but they put her out of the house and she came running through a field. It was a big field of clover and it had a wove-wire fence at the far side. She was running across that field and she was pretty old—her skirts were long and she couldn't run fast. But you could tell, the way she was going, she was scared to death.

I sat there in my tank and watched her. Nobody tried to kill her or shoot at her 'cause she was a woman. As far as I know, our men never did bother the women, unless they just accidentally killed them. But naturally, it scared them to death, because they didn't know—she didn't know but what we might kill her. She ran back and forth along that fence, trying to find a way to get through it, and she finally found some-place where she could get down and crawl under the wire. She crawled under that fence and got up, and then I saw her go on out of sight behind the hill.

That day—and it was the longest one—we'd run into resistance here and there, but not a whole lot. We came to a ravine, a sort of big ditch at the edge of a town—there wasn't any water down there, but there was a bridge. It was a concrete bridge and it had a sidewalk and handrails.

I was approaching that bridge and as soon as the tank ahead of me got off it, I was going on. Of course, it's a rule on these short bridges that not more than one vehicle gets on it at a time, because if they knock out the tank in front of you, then they've got two vehicles on a bridge, and, well, it ain't no trouble for them to pick off the second tank, too.

We's a followin' the lieutenant's tank, and it was out about the mid-dle of the bridge and the Germans knocked that tank out. Somehow, I missed seein' them get hit, but evidently something hit them to stop their tank. Of course, you wouldn't hear nothin' like that hardly with the racket of the tank's engine. But we knew something happened when that tank stopped on the bridge, 'cause that was definitely a place you wouldn't stop.

Quick as he saw the tank stopped, Donald knew it wouldn't do for us to get out on that bridge. He said, "Back up, back up quick!"

I was just a fixin' to go onto that bridge, but I stopped the tank and put it in reverse.

"They're turning the cannon on us!" Donald said. "Get behind that barn or they'll pick us off, too!" There was a big barn on the right, close to the end of the bridge. Donald guided me back there, 'cause I couldn't see behind me in that tank.

I was moving it in reverse just as quick as that tank'd go. A tank won't go very fast in reverse 'cause they're slow-speeded in the low gears, they go real slow. I had that engine wide open, but it seemed like we were just a creepin' back. I was expecting a shell to come through our tank any second.

Just as soon as I pulled behind that barn, a big armor-piercing shell came through there and knocked the whole end off of that barn. It was a brick barn and those bricks came tumbling down and piled up right by the side of us. Well, I sure knew they were after us then! Boy, they come in a hair of gettin' our whole tank there.

I thought maybe they'd take another shot at us. We were all expecting it, I don't know why they didn't—I guess 'cause we were blocked by the rest of that barn. We sat there for a few minutes. And right then, I couldn't have moved that tank another foot.

I was really shaken—*I mean,* that *really* got me shook up. 'Cause I remember when I pushed the clutch in to stop the tank, I couldn't hardly push it in. It took a little bit of strength to push that clutch in and my foot was just a jerkin' so, I couldn't control it. I couldn't hardly control the tank, I was a shakin' so. Yeah, I was pretty scared at that moment.

I'll tell you what I thought.

Over in Germany, a few times I'd thought about home, but most of the time I had to concentrate on what was happening at the present time. Well, just after they knocked out that tank in front of me on the bridge and I thought we were next—that is when I *really* thought about home.

As soon as our tank came to a stop and my foot was a shakin' over that clutch, I started prayin' to the Lord to spare my life so I could see my mother and father one more time. That was my greatest desire right then. 'Cause I knew they were lookin' forward to seein' me, and I hated for them to get the message that I'd been killed. I could just imagine them a gettin' one of them letters. It was the one time that I got the most scared in all my life.

While we were sitting there waiting, I closed my eyes. I did a lot of praying in that tank all along, to myself. I found it helped me to get over my fears.

So, really, that day the Lord answered that prayer and, in a little while, that fear left me and I was ready to go again. I never was scared after that, I don't know what it was, but a calm came over me and from then on—no matter what happened—I found I could face it and I wasn't afraid.

We pulled the tank up a little hill where we were shielded, but we could watch what happened to the men in that first tank on the bridge. In a Sherman tank, there's an escape hatch in the floor that you can unlatch and it will drop down on the roadway. That escape hatch opened and I saw the tank crew start coming out from under the tank. That shell had knocked out the tracks, but it didn't happen to kill any of the boys in the tank. They crawled out of the tank, one by one through that floor hatch.

There was a sidewalk along the bridge and it had a curb built up, maybe six or eight inches above the bridge. The tank crew laid in behind that curb where they could get under cover. The Germans shot at them. They'd just knock the concrete off that curb with automatic gunfire, but it stuck up high enough to shield those boys and the Germans couldn't hit them from where they were.

The tank crew laid there for a while and the Germans quit firing, so they crawled on across that bridge. That's where the enemy was, across that bridge. They were all excited and didn't know what they were doing and they went right into the enemy territory. I knew they were just shook up. We were watching them from the tank and I said, "Oh, they've done the wrong thing now."

Those boys got down off the bridge and headed for a patch of woods at the edge of a little village where there were some houses down there. One of them got shot—we saw him get hit. The other four members of that tank crew, they got captured. One of them was the lieutenant.

We were having to sit there in the tank and wait till the infantry got things squared away. I was watching that bridge and, in a few minutes, along came another boy from our company—I believe he was from Chicago—he was pretty bad to drink during combat. He'd got hold of something and he was pretty drunk, so he got out there in the open, and he just wandered over to that tank sitting knocked out on the bridge. The Germans opened fire on him and he dropped down and laid behind that sidewalk and they didn't happen to hit him. He laid there for a while behind the curb and then he just got up and walked back to our company. Just walked like he was out for a Sunday stroll. I was looking for them to kill him. But he got back to his tank. I never did know why he took a notion to walk out on that bridge, but I reckon he just did that 'cause he was drinkin'.

I guess it helped him have enough nerve to do his job. I guess it made him a little braver. But if soldiers do that and they get in tight places, they don't really know what they're doing and they'll take a lot of chances. Sometimes they'll get by. I don't know how.

We sat there in the tank and just talked to each other about what we could see. Across the street, there was a hedgerow. We saw a lot of German soldiers crawl up along that hedgerow. We could see them. And we didn't shoot at them. I don't know why we didn't. But we saw them through that hedgerow a little bit. They were down on the ground a crawlin' along. Our gunner didn't try to take them out. That was up to the tank commander, what he wanted to do. They never did attack us. So, finally, they must have retreated. We quit seeing them.

While we were waiting for our orders to move out, I saw two German medics walking towards us, they had a white flag, and they were leading one of our men back to the company. He was the driver of the lieutenant's tank that they knocked out on the bridge, he was the one who'd been hit. He was Sergeant Parent, and the Germans had shot him right straight through the neck.

Some of the German medics had got to Sergeant Parent and they led him up the road, one on each side, and they brought him past our tank. He was able to walk with no problem. They took him on back to the medics who followed us, and they turned him over to our forces for medical care.

Sergeant Parent had been with us a long time and he was in the army long before we were. To us, he was a senior citizen, but he was still young enough to be in the military. And while I'm talking about that, Sergeant Parent did eventually recover from that gunshot wound and he came back to our company after the war was over, before we left Germany for the States. That's when he showed me the bullet hole in his neck and where it came out. It went in just below his ear and it came out just above the shoulder blade on the other side. That bullet made a big scar where it came out, just made a little one where it went in.

He said the doctors in the hospital told him, "We don't know how you survived that. We can't understand how that bullet went through your neck in that spot without killing you. You couldn't stick a broom straw through there without killing a man, where that bullet went. We just don't understand it."

So nobody understood why, but Sergeant Parent got shot straight through the neck and he was all right, didn't seem to bother him. Must have been a Higher Power took care of him.

Of course, we didn't know all that when we were sittin' in the tank, overlooking that little bridge. The army got the bridge cleared up — hooked that knocked-out tank onto a heavy vehicle and pulled it on across the bridge so we could advance across it.

We stopped in the little town on the other side, and by then, the infantry'd cleared it of Germans.

It wasn't very long after that tank crew got captured that the lieutenant escaped and he found us in the little town, made it back to the company. He told us where the Germans were guarding the three other members of that tank crew in a one-story house, just down the hill from where we were.

When the Germans had captured that tank crew, they took them to a two- or three-room dwelling house and put them under just some kids for guards, something like twelve-year-old boys, and they left them there. Those young boys carried guns and they were trying to be soldiers, but they didn't know what to do. They were scared to death, and liable to shoot you just out of nervousness.

The lieutenant told us that he'd outsmarted those boy guards once the regular German Army left. This lieutenant spoke a little German and he got his guard to go in another room. I think he tricked him into going in there to get him a book, and while that boy was in the other room, the lieutenant slipped out the door. But the other three men from our company, they were still in the house, under the armed boy guards.

The lieutenant told the company, "The guards aren't even trained, they were conscripted a few weeks ago. Let's overrun them and bring our men back to the company!"

Some of our outfit went down there and surrounded that house and when those young guards saw all our firepower aimed at them, those boys just gave up. They got scared and came out with their hands up, their guns held above their heads, and I heard that one of those boy guards wet his pants. Then our infantry took them prisoner.

As it turned out, nobody got killed in all that. Our men that got captured weren't injured or nothin' and they got back to the company in time to move out with us. And the only man to get wounded, Sergeant Parent, his close call was just a miracle for some reason. That was something to be thankful for.

We went on our journey and kept runnin' into spots of resistance that afternoon. Yeah, we were on high alert.

24th Tank Battalion:

. . . Avoiding our first minefield in Aiterhofen about noon, we pushed on to Strasskirchen, barged through smoke from burning buildings into a minebelt which wrecked four tanks of the leading platoon. (1)

THE BLACK CAT Newspaper

. . . The attack continued through the early afternoon to Strasskirchen, where tanks met brief, but determined resistance. Four tanks were temporarily impaired when Germans added smokepots to the smoke from already burning buildings to conceal mines laid hastily across the street. (4)

Lonnie Johnson, 24th Tank Battalion, C Company (CCB):

I had been leading the column in battle 'bout all day. I was in the 1st Platoon. I think Kelley was probably 2nd Platoon, which put him back from the front of our column. Anywhere except right on the front line, you had a good chance to survive.

Once in a while, now, when we was fixin' to go into a little town — most of them was little villages — the company would stop. Every tank would pull up beside a building or behind a building, and all the soldiers, we would just gather up. And the commanders would get orders of what they thought would be the best way to take that place. You would get new instructions on where you'd be and what your job would be. So we had a little ol' rally there at the edge of that small town in a little building along the side of the road.

My company commander, Captain Blake, he told Donald Crouch to take the number one position, so that was Kelley's tank. They told him to take the lead.

I had been leading. They put me to fifth or sixth tank back or something. They would shift you around. That's the way it worked. They did that to relieve me of the pressure and expectation of bein' killed. It'll get on your nerves.

When I got further back, I was pretty safe. Kelley's tank was taking my place. Well, we hadn't gone two hundred yards, I don't reckon, when I got the call to take the lead again. (12)

That afternoon, Donald came back from a huddle and said to us, "Captain Blake told us, 'If you feel safer for yourself and your crew by opening the hatch so you can see better, you've got permission to do that. Or you can keep using your periscope.'"

Captain Blake had been requiring the tank commanders to have all the tanks buttoned up since we'd gotten into such a hot battle zone, shortly after we'd crossed the Danube River, but some of the tank commanders had been complaining that they couldn't see through the periscope as good as they needed to.

The Germans had been running up to the tanks and knocking them out. They'd been using some magnetic mines that would stick to the side of the tank and they'd go off after so many seconds. They'd try to blow a track off of them. With all the smoke we had to drive through, a German with a mine like that could put it on the tank and the tank commander might not know it, if it wasn't for the other tanks around us to spot him and knock him off.

Of course, the best way for a tank commander to view the battlefield was to ride with his head out of the hatch, but our outfit didn't usually do that during battle. Donald stood up to see out if he was riding unbuttoned, but most of the time he'd sit and look out through the periscope to call the shots. It was in a sort of helmet and it turned with him, but he had to look out through that peephole and it was quite a strain to keep looking through that thing and keep an eye on all the action that was 360 degrees around the tank. The worst problem was, though, Donald couldn't see anything close up around the tank.

I remember Donald had said several times while we were in Germany, "I feel like it would be a lot safer for me and the whole crew if I could see better. I can't see a whole lot through that little periscope. I've got to keep turning it back and forth, and a German could slip up on us."

So, because the tank commanders had that problem, our officers changed their policy.

When he came back to the tank that day, Donald said to us, "For the sake of you fellows and myself, too, I've decided I'm going to ride with the hatch open. I feel like it's a lot safer. I'll be ready to pick off any Kraut I see comin'."

Donald had his .45 pistol that his wife sent him. He'd been collecting notches throughout Germany, and he showed us where he'd filed several notches into the handle of that gun already.

"I'll just bob up and look around, then duck back down," he said.

With all the different tanks gettin' knocked out, people gettin' killed or injured, they switched the tanks around pretty often and this time our tank was given orders to move up to the first position in the column to relieve the spearhead tank for a while. So we took our place at the front of the line and we ran into some strong resistance.

That was a pretty severe battle there and we couldn't advance very far. They kept us pinned down with artillery fire. The Germans were doing their best to stop us from advancing and they were trying to use everything they had to stop us, but I don't know what and all they done. I just know there were a lot of explosions and flames and smoke.

We just mostly heard the tank commander's voice over the intercom.

"... Nine o'clock!"

Knode fired the cannon.

The tank shuddered.

"Keep 'em comin'!" Donald called out. "Rhodes! Personnel — two o'clock!"

We saw German soldiers here and there and the bow gunner took a pop at them. There were some lying in a ditch along the highway, ready to stop us with bazookas and mortars, and Donald gave both our gunners orders to shoot them with the .30 calibers, so I was watching those dark gray figures down in that trench as I drove. I could see where the tracers were hitting. I could see those fellers just jump when the bullets hit them. That's about all they ever did.

The resistance, it didn't last a long time, we just kept moving through there and they didn't knock us out, so we passed through it.

I heard Donald come in over the intercom. "Well, I can put another notch on my pistol when I get a chance to. That's seven."

And then, the gunner went to hollering. Knode was just goin' on makin' a lot of noise and trying to talk to me without going through the intercom and I couldn't hear him.

I hollered back there and told him, "Knode! Get on the intercom. I can't understand nothin' you're sayin'!" I was trying to drive and I just kept hollering at him to get on the intercom.

Knode would stutter pretty bad when he was excited, and he was scared to death. He was a nervous type of boy anyhow and he was so excited, I couldn't understand what he was yelling. I wasn't doing what he was wantin' me to do, 'cause I didn't know what he was wantin' me to do. The only thing I could finally make out was "S-S-STOP!"

I stopped the tank, but I knew we shouldn't be a sittin' still. I knew somethin' was wrong. I just kept hollerin' at him, "Knode, use the headphones!"

I turned to look in the turret and I could see through the mesh of the metal basket that my tank commander was down, but I couldn't tell much else. Knode was sitting in his gunner's seat, and Donald had fallen on him, had him pinned down. And law me, Knode just went all to pieces and he was a yellin' and goin' on somethin' awful, flinging his arms around, and McAbee was tryin' to help him get on the headphones.

He got on the intercom, but Knode was still just a hollerin' and a goin' on over that intercom and I couldn't understand nothin'. He was just hysterical.

I said into my headset, "Knode. Calm down so you can talk till I can understand you. I don't know what you're a sayin'."

I finally did understand one thing. He said, "D-D-Donald's been hit!"

That was when I realized that my tank commander got hit. It really was a shock to me the moment I understood it. Even though I could kind of see Donald down back in there, I didn't really know that he'd got hit with gunfire until the gunner finally said it over the headphones.

I didn't hear a thing from McAbee. Up front, Rhodes didn't know what was goin' on any more than I did. But even though I was scared bad, it didn't affect me physically. I was pretty calm. The rest of us were pretty calm.

Knode, he just about went berserk.

"Calm down, Winfred, calm down and tell me what you want us to do." He was supposed to command the tank if the tank commander couldn't. He finally calmed down enough to tell me.

"B-b-b-back up! See if we can get him to the m-m-medics. We got to g-g-get him out of the t-t-tank. B-b-back up!"

So then I understood what he was saying. I said, "Well, you'll have to guide me back."

I put the tank in reverse and started backing up. He had to guide me, right and left. He was able to tell me which way to go so I could stay in the road, but he was still pretty excited.

We backed about a few hundred feet, I guess, and Knode had me to stop the tank by a little cabin, right by the side of the road. Of course, we had communication between the tanks, and the other tankers heard what was going on, and somebody called for the medics to come up and meet us by a little building.

Knode said, "Kelley, you'll have to g-g-get out and help us."

I know there'd been a lot of fighting goin' on just before that, because Knode had been firing that .30 caliber machine gun and that gun had gotten so hot, it was firing all by itself. Of course, when they got hot, they'd keep firing whether there was a finger on the trigger or not. And that gun was still a poppin' off on its own, but not in a rhythm. The barrel was pointing right over my hatch, just above my head. It just happened to be turned like that when Donald got hit, so I couldn't get out of the tank. Knode could have turned the barrel away from me, but he didn't.

I told him, "Knode, turn the turret! You've got to move the machine gun. It's right over my hatch. I can't come outta here."

That .30 caliber fired. As it cools, it gets a little further in between those stray bullets.

"Winfred! Move the turret. The machine gun's right over my hatch. If I'm gonna help you, I have to get out. I can't get out."

Nothing happened. Knode was so torn up, he wouldn't do it. He never would turn the turret. The gun stayed right over my hatch.

"Winfred! Twist the belt. Twist the belt." At least if he wasn't gonna move the gun, he could stop it from firing. It spit out another bullet.

Knode just lost all sense. That's all there was to it. I never did know what McAbee was doin' back there.

"Well, I'll have to wait till that gun cools off," I said. "My case'll be, when I start out of here, it'll fire."

The only time in combat that I had to come out of that tank in front of a hot gun was to help get my tank commander out of the tank. I said, "Well, I'm gonna take a chance."

The gun popped and I jumped up out of the hatch.

I was being as careful as I could not to get my clothes hung up while I was in front of that gun. I climbed up on the top of the tank so I could help them lift Donald out. I thought he might be injured.

But, yeah, when I seen him, I knowed it was different. As quick as we were gettin' him out of there, I seen that he was dead.

That bullet had just knocked the whole back of his head out, about it. And it really messed the tank up in there. It had just splattered his brains on the inside of the tank, I could see it. And, of course, his blood was all down in the floor of the tank there and everywhere. So I knew there wasn't no hopes of him breathing no more. I knew that he was gone.

Donald was a pretty big, strong man, 'bout a two-hundred-pound soldier. It was hard to get him out of that tank, 'cause there wasn't nowhere for us to get. We couldn't pick him up like we could if he was a layin' on the ground. It took all of us to get him up out of the hatch.

Rhodes and I stood on top of the tank, we had to lift him out, and McAbee and Knode were down in the turret—they pushed to get him up. It was a hard task for us. That was a sad job.

I could see where the bullet went in. A sniper had hit him just above his left eye. Donald had bobbed up to peep out of the hatch, when he got shot. He'd had his steel helmet on, but the bullet went right through it. The bullet came out lower on the back of his head.

A tank's up pretty high, so the sniper who hit him must have been up in a building somewhere. We weren't in a town there, we's just out in a battlefield, but there must have been some houses close by, 'cause I know the sniper had to be up above our level or that bullet wouldn't have traveled down like that. If it had hit Donald from the ground level, the bullet would have gone up instead of down. But it came out closer to his shoulder. Yeah, when the bullet hit him, he just dropped down in the turret—he didn't know what hit him.

We really took a chance getting his body out of there. Of course, we were targets the whole time. If we hadn't traveled a little ways after Donald got hit, the sniper might have picked us off as we got up on the tank to lift him out of there. But Knode had me back the tank up and that was a good decision. Even though he went berserk and I couldn't make out what he was sayin', he knew enough to have us back the tank up and stop behind a little building and it was down in a little low place. I think that's what saved us. The Germans couldn't see us to pick us off.

We put Donald Crouch in a little building by the side of the road, his body. It was a cabin about the size of a chicken house. I don't know what the Germans used it for. We put him in there and we had to leave him.

The medics already knew it was our tank commander that got hit and they came up there. They thought they'd maybe help him, but, of course, when they got there, there was nothing for them to do. I don't know what they did with his body. It was the last we saw of him.

Nobody had nothin' to say to each other. We's really down-hearted there.

When Crouch got hit, Knode was second in command until the army could put another tank commander in there. The way it worked, the gunner was in line for the command next, and they usually moved the loader up to the gunner position, and moved the assistant driver up to load the ammunition. He could do that position easily. It was just a matter of loading a gun. It was easiest to find someone else to man the bow gun. But it didn't work that way in our tank.

Knode was supposed to take command of the tank, but he went plumb crazy and couldn't command nothin'. Of course, it bothered all of us, but he really just went into pieces there, 'cause he'd been sitting down, using the gun, and Donald was standing up with his feet right behind Knode and he just fell down on top of Knode, dead weight, and pinned him in his seat. Naturally, that affected Knode more than it did the rest of us in the tank.

It wasn't but about fifteen minutes, and they had another tank commander in there. They gave us a new man, never had met him before and we had to take orders from him. So we just went on our way and we drove on a bangin' and a shootin' 'cause we had a battle a goin' on.

Knode was all right after we went on. He manned his gun and he calmed down. From then on, he was able to handle it, but he didn't have much control over himself when the war came right inside our tank that day.

We were still in that combat zone and we had to fight our way through it. The new tank commander was with us the rest of the war. Yeah, and I don't even remember him now. I don't remember his name, didn't get acquainted with him. He wasn't even from our company, I don't think. I can't remember what he looked like or nothin'. But he did a good job. I've thought about that a lot of times and wondered who he was.

I sure remember Sergeant Donald E. Crouch, though. He was a real nice feller and I hated when he got killed. He was trying to protect all of us in the tank and that's what cost him his life.

"I'll just bob up and look around," he'd said. Well, he bobbed up at the wrong time, that's all there was to it. That sniper got him.

That's the only time they told him he could drive during the day, in heavy combat, with the hatch open and his head out. They thought it might save the whole tank crew. Yeah, they thought it was good advice, but for him it was bad. It might have been good for us. That last German soldier Donald picked off, it might have saved us, you don't ever know.

Well, I knew that was the last of Donald. I knew that was war. We expected that. Everybody expected that to happen to somebody every day. It was just a common thing during the war. We just didn't know who it was gonna happen to. And, of course, the war had something to do with keeping your mind off of your problems. You had to keep your mind on doing the right thing to keep from gettin' killed yourself. You had to keep your mind working, you couldn't just be wondering about everything else. You had to be prepared to face everything that came along, best you could. And that helps you to survive. Otherwise, I might not have survived, if I hadn't kept my mind on my business. So, it being at that time, it didn't bother me like it would have if we'd been back at camp; if something like that had happened, I'd have worried about it a lot more. But in battle, everything around me demanded my attention. We had to continue in combat.

Lonnie Johnson was drivin' his tank somewhere behind me when Donald Crouch got killed. That stopped our tank for a little while and Lonnie's tank came up and took our place.

Lonnie Johnson, 24th Tank Battalion, C Company (CCB):

Donald, a sniper had got him. Then I had to come around and take the lead again and I passed Kelley's tank, and I didn't go another hundred yards before they blowed the track off of my tank, and then one shell come in the assistant driver's side and tore up my assistant driver. Fixed him up pretty bad and I got a couple of little ol' pieces in me, not big enough to go to the medics. I got 'em out myself.

Anyhow, when I got my wounded man back to the medics — which was two hundred yards at the most — he had to go to the hospital. I'd crawled on my stomach with him, I put him on my back and I drug him back to safety where the medics could get him.

I didn't know who he was, didn't never ask him his name. I'd got him in there out of the air forces. We was losin' so many men that they'd taken my assistant driver, put him in another tank, and gave me somebody from the air force that didn't know nothin' about tank outfits. He didn't ever get to fire a gun.

My tank commander and gunner was helpin' me with him and we finally got him back to safety in a little shack. And Donald was already layin' there. The bullet went right through the brim of his helmet, above his eye. They'd got Donald Crouch out of the tank and put him back there where we had made the little rally. That's where I saw him, found out how he got killed and everything about it.

It's a dread, you're expectin' to get killed every minute. It didn't ever happen to me, but when you go back and see somebody that you knowed all the time you's in service, layin' there dead, you knowed your time's got to be next, or somethin' like that.

My tank was disabled. Kelley got to go on with his tank. It was a couple of days before I saw Kelley. The rest of the tanks went on and the rest of it was a rat race down for another thirty-five or forty miles and then it ended. That was the closing out, the last of the war.

Well, the day Donald Crouch got killed, I had been the lead tank about all day. We had stopped to get orders of what was comin' up and they told Crouch to take the lead, and he looked at me and he said, "Johnson," I believe he called me. I called him Crouch. He said, "This is it for me. I'm not gonna make it."

The front tank was the most dangerous one, of course, because they was gonna hit it if they could. I don't know, he just had that feeling, I think. It had to be.

I said, "Aw, bull. We ain't got but twenty minutes to fight and then we'll be done fightin' for the day. You make it a few more minutes, and then we'll have all night to be together."

And he didn't make it, he didn't make it ten minutes after he said that. He had his head out the top of the tank and a sniper got him in a little ol' place, kind of behind a building, and everything flew apart before we got two hundred yards from where we's at.

Yeah, I still remember Donald Crouch clear as yesterday, when they told him to take my place on the front line, he said, "This is it for me." (12)

THE BLACK CAT Newspaper

The Division's advance to the Isar river was made with three combat commands moving abreast. CC "B" reached the river first to find that the enemy had blown all the bridges . . . (4)

24th Tank Battalion:

A race to capture intact the bridge across the Isar at Plattling ended when the bridge erupted skyward as leading forces reached it. The battalion waited in the town under a hot exchange of artillery, dueling for control of the bridge site a scant thousand yards away. (1)

We traveled the rest of that day with the new tank commander before we got a chance to wash the tank out. Just about night we got to this river and right before we got there, the Germans blew out the bridge. This river was the Isar River, I believe. We had to wait for our engineers to get a pontoon bridge across it.

I think they had running water where we stayed—we stayed in a little village that night, right on the banks of the river. We got buckets of water and soap and we washed the tank out where Donald's blood and stuff was all over the tank. It was a mess in there. There was a lot of blood in the tank. By that time, it had dried up enough to where it was kind of hard to wash off of stuff.

The crew all helped, the four of us. That was a hard task to do, to mop up his blood. I probably did shed some tears. I was just heartbroken, 'cause I liked him, he was like a brother to me, and there I was having to wipe up his blood and now he was gone. Boy, that's a shock, now. You wouldn't know that unless you had to go through something like that, how that affects you. It really gets to you.

Of course, that was heartbreaking to all of us, to have to wash up the blood of our tank commander, somebody that we thought a lot of, one of our best friends. It was hard to do, but you had to do them things. There wasn't no way out. None of us really talked about it. Never said much about it at all.

I saw his helmet. It fell down in the tank when he got shot, and we got it and passed it from hand to hand. We all saw where the bullet had hit just above his left ear, where the brim and crown of the helmet comes together.

Havin' one of your buddies get killed right there in your tank, there's no way I can explain how down you feel. I knew that things like that were liable to happen. I was prepared, I thought, to cope with it. But I didn't cope with it as good as I thought I would.

I saw his pistol a layin' down in the tank. That gun his wife had sent him, he'd had it in his hand, and it fell down in the tank when he got killed. Donald had filed a notch on that pistol for every German soldier he killed. Right before he lost his life, he said, "Well, I can put a seventh notch on it when I get the chance."

I said to myself, "Well, he never did get to make that seventh notch."

He had shown us that gun before where he'd taken a file and filed little marks on it. Several times, he'd come over the intercom in our tank to announce, "I just picked off another kraut eater." Something like that. He'd make a remark.

He was watchin' for 'em and he'd peep out, and maybe that's the reason he got killed. Of course, if you've got your head a stickin' out, naturally that's what they're gonna shoot at.

Now, I got that .45 automatic pistol out of the tank, cleaned it off, and I was gonna bring it back and send it to his folks in Kansas. I had it in my hand and that was what I'd made up my mind to do.

One of our sergeants found out I had it and he came over to me and said, "How 'bout letting me have that gun. I'm gonna go see Donald's folks when I get back. I'm gonna go visit them. I'll take it to them."

He put up a story that I thought maybe was reasonable and I let him have it. But I wish I hadn't. I could have brought it back. I would have sent it to the family. The sergeant who got Donald's .45 with his notches on it, I hope he really did go and give it to the family and tell them what happened that day, but I never knew if anyone did.

Yeah, everybody in the company knew Donald and liked Donald, and they were down-and-out. One boy, he found some cognac, I believe, some type of alcohol drink, and he took a few drinks of it. His name was Salecki, from up around Chicago area. He's the one who'd loaned me money to get home way back when we were in training in California.

Salecki was a good tank driver and a good friend of mine, and he came over to the tank, walked up to me, and he said, "Now, Kelley, I know you don't ever drink. But," he said, "how about taking a drink in honor of Donald Crouch?" Salecki offered his bottle to me.

I had my head down low and I shook it.

"C'mon, take a drink with me, in his honor." He tried to offer it because he was a wantin' to kill the pain — and he could see it was hurtin' me. You know, some people in times like that, if they get under the influence of alcohol, they can get along a little better, bear it a little better. I guess that was the reason he was drinkin', he was hurt over what had happened to Donald. Salecki was the type of boy that would take a few drinks, but I never did see him get drunk before that day.

It sure did hurt me that Donald got killed, especially 'cause we knew the war in Germany was just about over. Salecki was holdin' that bottle right in front of me. He was from one of the tanks that I usually followed.

I looked up at him and said, "Well, I'll tell you. It wouldn't help Donald one bit, wouldn't help him a bit, and it'd maybe be a downfall to me. I never have took no alcohol and I don't know what it might cause me to do. I might get a little intoxicated, and I might go to wantin' it, maybe not could get off of it."

He didn't see it that way, and I could see that.

I said, "I appreciate you offering it to me, and I sure want to honor Donald with you, but that's not the way I want to honor a good friend like he was. He'd expect me to stick to what I am."

Salecki didn't get mad at me. He said, "Well, okay, I just wanted to offer it to you."

I said, "Well, I thank you, but I'm not gonna partake."

Salecki knew me pretty well, so he walked on. He was a real good friend to me, before that, and after, too.

I would have really felt bad about that. I wouldn't have thought that was much of a send-off. In a time like that, I didn't want to be startin' any behavior that I wouldn't do otherwise. I was gonna stay true to my upbringin'. Pretty much everybody around me knew that, too. I was just genuine what-I-was.

Donald Crouch, he was a real good feller and I didn't think it would reflect too good for me to go against my principles to honor a man that I thought a lot of. Oh, he was just a farm boy from Kansas, but he was a good person to deal with, he treated you right. He was really my boss as tank commander, he was like a boss. You could always go to him about your problems. He was real good to talk to.

Donald was really a good tank commander, did a real good job. He always took care of us, really looked out for us. That's the reason why he got killed. The biggest heroic thing to me was, when we went into the battle that he got killed in, the commanding officers told the tank commanders, "If you feel safer for yourself and your crew by looking out the hatch, you've got permission to do that." It was his choice. And, of course, that was a mistake. I guess a lot of the tank commanders traveled that way that day, but he was the only one in our company who got killed like that.

I soon had to dismiss those things from my mind. I said, "I can't dwell on stuff like that." 'Cause things like that, when you go to war, they're gonna happen, so you can't dwell on it and just let it drive you crazy, you've got to get over it.

I'd get so tired going through battles all day long, when I'd get a chance to go to sleep, things like that usually didn't bother me about sleeping, especially 'cause there wasn't a thing we could have done to prevent that. We were doing all we could do. If we'd been goofing off in some way, and then Donald got killed, it would have bothered us about sleeping. But doing all you can do, and something happens, it's just one of them things.

That night, we bedded down on the front porch of a dwelling house. It was a big porch with white railings and a whole bunch of us laid our bedrolls all in a row and we hadn't hardly got laid down when the Germans opened up on us with artillery. We all jumped up and ran, and after that, we spent the night somewhere around there, stayed in the tanks, of course, 'cause the place was crawlin' with Germans.

★ ★ ★

THE BLACK CAT Newspaper

The two-day struggle to get over the Isar was perhaps the highlight of the campaign. The Isar is a minor German river, and no one had ever heard of it before. Even with all the tricks the engineers had to get us over the mud, the approaches to this river mired the columns...

On the outskirts of Plattling, the 496th Armored Field Artillery Battalion fired 2,500 rounds on enemy installations across the Isar. Capt. Robert Peters, Able Battery Commander, called for 200 rounds of artillery in one mission, aiding the dough boys of the 59th and the 24th Tankers in Task Force McRae to form a bridgehead....

On April 29, all combat commands were lined up along the Isar and 16th Infantrymen of CC "R" established a second Division bridgehead across the river. This bridgehead was formed in the face of stubborn enemy fire. The Germans held high ground on the east bank and their accurate artillery fire proved a tough nut for Black Cat soldiers to crack.

124th Armored Engineers were detailed to construct a pontoon bridge that would enable heavy armor to get across the river. While 496th, 497th, and 498th artillery guns pounded German units on the east bank, the engineers braved harassing Nazi fire to complete the bridge. (4)

The Division:

If the Heinies hadn't blown up most of their bridges from one end of Germany to the other, the 124th Engineers wouldn't have been kept so busy. When we hit the Isar, the Krauts touched them off right in our faces and there we were with no way of getting our vehicles across till the engineers came up to put up a treadway bridge for us. But that didn't stop the dough boys from getting over. The main push was at Plattling and the boys of the

59th forced the river on a railway bridge, wading waist deep through the swift current. (2)

16th Armored Infantry Battalion (CCR):

Remember how the bridge over the Isar was blown and the only way you could get across was to climb over on the girders? And remember how tense you were, and that empty place in the pit of your stomach as you scraped your knees on the steel and tried not to see the water rushing by a mile a minute right under you? And once you were across and into Mamming, how surprised you were that the enemy would counterattack, not just once, but three times? How about that Jerry that put an MG-42 into action under your window? You polished him off with your Garand, and two more who tried to take his place. Or the one who crawled up close enough to knock out your machine gun with a panzerfaust. It was comforting to have the assault guns and mortars of Headquarters Company giving you plenty of support that night. And it was good to know that Service Company was keeping the ammunition rolling up there. You didn't have an inch that night, and when the 80th Infantry, with their red scarves, came over the next day to relieve you, there were plenty of dead krauts, and you still held that bridgehead. (19)

Our engineers worked to get bridges across that river, with Nazi artillery goin' off in a counterattack. For a while, those skies were lit up like the Fourth of July over that water. They'd have to stop working and wait it out if the firing got too heavy, then they'd get back out and get that bridge together.

That was when they told some of us tankers that we'd have to go across the river on a detail to help get the bridge in. So they took a whole bunch of us from C Company to help carry supplies.

It was soft, muddy ground along that river because it had been raining pretty heavy. They needed for us to lay crossties — the corduroy — on the other side of the river for all our heavy vehicles to run on so they could get to solid ground when they came off the pontoon bridge.

There was a railroad trestle that went across that river and the Germans had blown out that trestle and it was down. It was just a mess of twisted steel that was up out of the water in some places and the rest of the bridge span had just fallen down in the water. We could walk across that rubble, but sometimes you'd have to wade the water about knee-deep a ways. We'd have to hang on to whatever we could grab — steel that had been bent by a terrible force — and we could go across the river like that, carrying supplies on our shoulder. We went back and forth over that fallen bridge, just up and down, in and out of the water, carrying cross-ties to the far side of the river to lay along the bank.

All along the muddy bank of that river, oh, there were bullet holes just about as close as your fingers, where our troops'd been shootin' small arms fire across there. There were a lot of German soldiers killed along that river. They were a layin' all over the place, where they'd stuck their heads up and got killed.

There was one German soldier in a little bombed-out building near the river and he was on fire. We had to walk right by him carryin' those timbers. His body was just a burnin' up in that building, 'cause it was just a blazin' up, and it really put out a terrible odor, the awfulest odor I ever smelled. I'd just have to hold my nose.

★ ★ ★

59th Armored Infantry Battalion (CCB):

By nightfall of the 30th of April a bridge had been constructed and the task force crossed the Isar under complete blackout conditions, behind the Reconnaissance Platoon of Headquarters Company. (8)

24th Tank Battalion (CCB):

Finally on the 30th, infantry pushed across, engineers built a bridge and our armor poured across in the darkness, fighting on through the night while buildings flamed in our wake. (1)

We waited a day for them to get that bridge in, so it was late in the evening by the time we were ready to cross. We crossed the Isar River in the dark. Had to keep our lights off, so we just had those little cat eyes to see by and the tank in front, in the moonlight, mashing those pontoons down in the water.

We figured that it would be the best chance for them to knock us off—while we's on the bridge. But evidently, the Germans couldn't get to us. Seems like we got on across that little river in the blink of an eye, nearly.

Of course, we had so much cover over there, the Germans had a hard time doing what they did. We had a lot of stuff over there, airplanes and artillery and all sorts of troops that I didn't even know about. The Germans couldn't do what they'd like to have done, I'm sure. They had airplanes, but didn't have enough gas to fly them and didn't have enough pilots. They'd had a lot of good equipment, a lot of it better than ours, but the Allies had just exhausted them.

Usually, we'd travel in the day and we'd stop at night, travel in the day and stop at night. But this one time, the night we crossed the Isar River, the whole outfit traveled all night with those little cat eyes. We were doing the run in the dark to make a surprise approach to the Inn River at the border of Germany and Austria.

Blackout driving in those tanks, you can't see but about eight or ten feet in front of you, and you hardly know if you're in the road or not. We couldn't see through that periscope at night well enough to drive, so that night, they decided that we had to drive with the hatch open, with our head stickin' out. I drove looking out to the slits of light where the cat eyes shined down on the road. We were on high alert going through those valleys in Bavaria and that's the way we had to travel. I had to have my head sticking out because they felt it was safer for the drivers to have better vision. Of course, you can imagine what I thought about that.

Some of the tank drivers got killed that night. Not in our battalion, but I heard about it happening. The Germans would shine a flashlight on the drivers and shoot them in the head because they had their head sticking out, trying to drive. We thought, it bein' dark, it'd be okay, drivin' like that, but it wasn't. Oh, I dreaded that drive, but I made it.

★ ★ ★

THE BLACK CAT Newspaper

The overnight advance of the 13th towards the Inn completely surprised the enemy. Bewildered by the speed of the Black Cat drive, the Germans were unable to form an organized defense line and surrendered by the thousands.

... During the surprise night move from the Isar to the Inn River the column passed through the city of Osterhofen near midnight. Civilians removed road blocks and guided the column through the well-lighted city, whose streets were lined with cheering civvies.

At Jagendorf the convoy surprised 150 sleeping German soldiers, who were promptly rounded up ... Their anti-tank guns and small arms were mangled in the streets of the town by the crushing effect of the tanks of A-24.

By dawn, the head of the column reached Malgersdorf and the enemy. The lead tank was hit and destroyed by direct 88 fire. The entire column immediately opened fire on the 88s, the town, and surrounding woods — destroying four 88s, flushing machine gun positions from the woods, and firing the town. (4)

The Division:

That the German Army was now collapsing like a paper bag was a certainty as the Division broke through the defenses of the Isar and dashed to the Inn. The end of the war was in sight as the 13th rolled through Bavarian towns like Pfarrkirchen, Tann and Eggenfelden. (2)

24th Tank Battalion:

The objective was now Salzburg; Eggenfelden was taken, and Company D branched off to race for another vital bridge over the Inn River. . . Meanwhile B, leading the main body, reached the bridge at Neu Otting only to have it sent crashing into the swift river a scant 30 yards from the leading vehicle. (1)

THE BLACK CAT Newspaper
24th Tanks Hit 60 Mile-A-Day Speed
Armored Dash at Night
Climaxed Race to Inn

Racing across rivers and through towns, Combat Command "B's" 24th Tank Battalion reached the Inn river early on May 1 after an advance of 142 miles in five days. Leading elements of a medium tank company, commanded by Captain Lester G. Hansen of San Fernando, California, reached the west bank of the river just as the bridge leading into Neu-Oetting was blown by the enemy.

The run which totaled 60 miles in less than 24 hours during one phase, 30 of which were clicked off during the hours of darkness, met only sporadic resistance. Two 88 antitank guns challenged the head-long advance of a medium tank platoon commanded by Lt. Noah I. Krall of New Haven, Conn., with one round each from a range of about 700 yards. Both missed. Two tank turrets traversed left in unison to bellow a reply with two 75 shells. Neither missed, and the tanks roared on through Falkenberg. (4)

The Division:

The Division mop-up of the area between the Isar and the Inn was accomplished by the three combat commands moving abreast through light resistance to the Austrian border. CCA rolled behind Task Force Smith to the left and entered Simbach on the Inn to find the bridge down. CCR found the Marktl bridge a mass of twisted girders but seized a civilian ferry at Kohlburg to transport the 16th Infantry over the Inn. Once across the river, the three companies of the 16th marched afoot to Burghausen on the Salzach River and Hohenwarth on the Alz, capturing a Nazi prison camp and freeing 11,000 prisoners of war — 4,100 of them Americans. CCB veered to the right and hit the Inn opposite Neu Otting, crossing the river in assault boats manned by the 124th Engineers and seizing the town. (2)

67th Armored Infantry Battalion (CCA):

Company C seized the Ering Dam intact and then A and B companies prepared for an assault on Adolf Hitler's famous birthplace city of Braunau, Austria. Braunau lay just across the Inn River from Simbach but the Germans had blown the bridges across the water just before our forces were able to reach it. The German garrison at Braunau at first defied our surrender order but capitulated just before we were scheduled to pound the city with our artillery. (20)

The Division:

We were sitting on the banks of the Inn right across from Braunau, that medieval Austrian city whose only claim to fame was that Hitler had been whelped there . . . So, we sent the mayor of Simbach rowing across the river with an ultimatum to the defending garrison of Braunau. "Surrender or have the city destroyed . . ."

Division Artillery made ready to bombard the town at noon, but at three minutes to the hour, the garrison surrendered. So ended the Battle of Central Europe for the 13th Armored Division. (2)

"Hitler kaput!" the civilian people called to us as we rolled by. It seemed like to me that most of the civilians wanted to give up the war. We'd go into these towns and if all the lights were on, you could see it right away and we knew what that meant. The people'd come out on the streets, cheering us on and then we knew we had it made.

We came down a shady lane from a little village and we saw the bridge over a river — that was the Inn River. If you crossed it, you were over into Austria. The Germans blew the bridge out right in front of us just before the front of our column got up there. Concrete flew into the air and the center span fell down. Had we been just a little earlier, some of us might have been crossing the bridge when they blew it out. Our column came right up to the banks of the Inn River and we stopped.

We assembled in a little village right by the river to wait for our engineers to get a bridge across there. We all knew Hitler's hideout lay just a few miles beyond and we thought we were gonna march on "Burgess Garden." But while we waited there in that little village, the war in Europe ended.

The bridge over the Inn River that was blown out as the 24th Tank Battalion approached.

(Below) Quinton Kelley poses atop the rubble.

CHAPTER 21

Victory in Europe

124th Armored Engineer Battalion:

On 1 May the companies were set up, in a light snow, along the northern side of the Inn River, between Braunau and Neu Otting. (15)

497th Armored Field Artillery Battalion:

Rest and maintenance operations immediately went into effect, while rumors flew around that this was the end of the war, that it wasn't, that we were to leave on another mission, etc., etc. (13)

THE BLACK CAT'S KITTEN EXTRA

Vol. 1, No. 66, Bavaria, Germany, Tuesday, 6 May 1945

VICTORY IN EUROPE

The war is Europe is over. The official end will come at one minute after midnight tonight, after three days during which the announcement had been expected momentarily.

The unconditional surrender of the once-mighty German armies to the forces of the United Nations was made yesterday afternoon in General Eisenhower's headquarters, a schoolhouse in Reims. (11)

We'd had rumors of it through the troops in the last days. German soldiers were surrendering in droves. They were just cloggin' the highways. You'd see long lines of 'em marching with their hands on top of their heads. So everybody knew it was about over. They did eventually assemble us all together to tell us that the war in Europe was over, but we'd already got the message from person to person, from tank to tank and so on. We's so glad it was over with, we sure spread the news. It was May 7, 1945, when we finally put Nazi Germany down.

Well, it was exciting. It was real exciting when they announced it to us. Everybody around camp was really livin' it up and enjoying themselves. Some of 'em had champagne they'd found in people's homes and they'd shake it up and spray it on each other, drink from the bottle, pass it around. I just rejoiced with them. I didn't do nothing in particular, or do anything different from what I usually done. I was just glad to know it was over. My thoughts turned back to "When will I get to go home? I want to go home." I think everybody, that's what they wanted.

We were out there walking around the tanks, pattin' each other on the back and all that, and up in the sky we saw a German plane comin' toward us. We didn't know if he knew that the war had ended. In just a moment, somebody shot that plane down.

The pilot bailed out. I saw his parachute open up and as he came down, they shot him. He was floating on down, just a hangin' there in his harness, and I watched him come down, down, down, just as limp, and he went behind some buildings, out of sight.

They announced it to us there, that a German man had been killed after the war ended. I don't know who killed him. We found out later that the German plane was flying from Italy into Germany and they knew that the war had ended, so I reckon the pilot thought it was safe. He wasn't flying very high and he came right over a battle zone after all the hostilities had just ended and somebody got trigger-happy and shot him down.

★ ★ ★

V-E DAY IN GERMANY. TWO 13TH ARMORED DIVISION SOLDIERS VIEW A PICTURESQUE
BAVARIAN TOWN WHICH THEY HELPED CAPTURE.

The 13th Armored Division's newsletters, *The Black Cat* and *The Kitten*, summed up all the news of the day and the news was big—boy, I'll tell you, it was. It was the first time we'd heard any news about Adolf Hitler. We all thought he was alive and hiding in Austria, while we were fighting and racing to get there.

THE BLACK CAT'S KITTEN EXTRA
HITLER WAS WAR CASUALTY

Adolf Hitler, the master criminal who embroiled the peoples of the world in their greatest war since the birth of mankind, was reported to have died only eight days before his armies of aggression were finally crushed.

If his purposes had not been so sinister and his applications of them so horrible, Hitler's climb from obscurity to power might almost be called an accomplishment without parallel in history. At the high water mark of his conquest all of Europe lay within his grasp, but the forces of

BLACK CAT SOLDIERS AT HITLER'S BIRTHPLACE IN BRAUNAU, AUSTRIA, WHICH
WAS CAPTURED BY THE 13TH ARMORED DIVISION.

freedom were organized in the nick of time and finally the German Army was beaten to its knees and the whole Reich was occupied.

The German Fuehrer was born in Braun-au-am-Inn, an Austrian town across the German border which was later destined to be captured by the Third Army's 13th Armored Division in one of the final operations in World War II. (11)

THE BLACK CAT, May 15, 1945
Adolf's Midwife is 'Glad He's Dead'

BRAUNAU, AUSTRIA, May 7 (Delayed) - Stooped, wrinkled, 83 year old Rosa Horl, the Midwife who prodded Adolf Hitler into mortal existence here 56 years ago, said today that although she "knew nothing about politics," she was glad to hear of the Fuehrer's death because he "had led Germany and Austria into ruin."

The Hitler family moved out of Braunau when the child who was later to gamble for a world empire was only three years old. 67th armored dough boys who took the town intact one day after the Fuehrer's death was announced, were prowling through the birth-home yesterday looking for photo souvenirs and snapping pictures of the building site. On the second floor, a huge notice had been posted which reads: "All is kaput in Hitler-town - 13th Armored (Black Cat) Division." Underneath was scrawled the words: "Jim De Marco, Division Artillery, New Castle, Pa."

Austrian passersby, asked for their opinions about the late dictator, almost unanimously disagreed with Frau Horl's assertion that "Braunau thought Hitler a very good man until the Prussians turned his head." All of them had derisive stories to tell about the Fuehrer and they said these anecdotes had been common gossip in Braunau for years.

"Only 36 people in Braunau liked him. The other 6,000 always hated him," said Gottlieb Auzinger.

"He was a thief, dumb in school, and he used to steal the butcher's meat," said Frau Genoverr Filznisser.

"His father told him that he was a robber, a good-for-nothing, and a murderer and no good would ever come from him," said Jacob Mussack. (4)

Most of the G.I.s were always looking out for souvenirs of the Nazi Party and they'd go through houses over there and they'd take all kinds of things. At a little place, not far from where we came to rest on the banks of the Inn, there was a big mansion of some type. Some of the infantry that we traveled with, they went over there and found a collection of pictures made by Heinrich Hoffmann, a Nazi photographer. They took the photographs as souvenirs. They showed Hitler dressed in all his glory, surrounded by high Nazi officials. In those pictures, he looked like he should have been a great man, with all the honor people were showing him. But the truth was, he made nothing better of himself than what his father had called him, according to the papers that we read. Adolf Hitler was just a cold-blooded murderer.

I heard that elements of the 13th Armored Division marched into the town where Hitler's old homeplace had been and set up our command post right in the very house where Hitler had been born. Everybody was proud of that.

Our engineers did bridge the Inn River, but we were never ordered to go across with our tanks and equipment. We stayed in camp and I was glad. Some of the boys went across to Austria and they came back with reports of what they saw and they collected different souvenirs. One of them claimed to have found Hitler's top hat.

A lot of the boys volunteered to go over to see what kind of hideout Hitler had in the high Alps. Berchtesgaden was the most popular spot for sightseeing. Whole groups of our soldiers went across the river on ferryboats, just to go up in the mountains and visit where Hitler's big hideout was—the "Eagle's Nest."

I never did go. I had every opportunity to cross that river and tour Hitler's hideout but I didn't have a bit of interest in seeing where a monster like that had ever lived. About half the company went over to see it and the other half was like me, wouldn't waste another minute on that sorry ol' scudder or anything that had belonged to him. But the ones who went, they came back to the company pretty excited and they were all talkin' about what they'd seen. The Allies had bombed most of that hideout to rubble, but I heard there was one building up there that was still just the way Hitler'd left it.

Lonnie Johnson, 24th Tank Battalion, C Company:

I don't remember how it was I wound up in Berchtesgaden, where Hitler's hideout was. Sometimes you could volunteer to go out on a big truck and see what was out there and come back and report the damage or what was left beside the road or somethin'. Just go ride several hours and that's why we got to go up there. We was about two hours on an army truck.

I know when we came into that town, it was in a little

mountain cove, and you couldn't get out no way but that same highway you come in, and then you could go around the mountain.

We went up there on a detail and they announced the official end of the war on the radio that we had with us while we was in Berchtesgaden. I was settin' in Hitler's chair and eatin' a can of C-rations, or whatever it was. Might have been a sandwich that the mess hall fixed me. But I was settin' in Hitler's chair in his house, when they officially declared the war over.

There's no way hardly to tell you everything, but you could sit in his chair, he had a swivel chair in the middle of his house. I'd never seen one like that. We didn't have 'em here that I knowed of. He could turn around in that chair and see in his bedroom, his living room, his den, kitchen. See the girls a takin' baths in a glass bathroom on one side of the house.

He had a big deck out in the front, way up high, and it had coil springs on it. The train track come right up to his door. He could step off of his porch onto the train and leave. It was on the side of a mountain. You could look over the whole town down in the valley. A beautiful little ol' town. You could see snow from his house on the top of the next mountain. I was up there in May. You could see snow, and it was warm enough to be in shirtsleeves where we were at. (12)

T/4 Rodgers, Medical Section Headquarters Company, 45th Tank Battalion:

At 2:00 p.m. on May 22, 1945, we mounted in trucks and started for the Hell-hole of Ibensee . . . The town of Ibensee is an innocent looking little mountain village. Little children waved to us and adults smiled and called out to us as we passed through the town into the gates of Stalag No. 6 . . . Our vehicles halted just inside the gates of the labor camp. . . .

While we waited for the officer in charge to arrange for a guide we were approached by a group of the more healthy inmates, a group of five Hungarian boys of Jewish ancestry ranging in age from 9 to 15 years and so thin that we were afraid that the slight breeze which was blowing might at any moment whisk them away. They spoke German well and one of our boys who speaks German began to question them. We learned that these boys had been brought to the camp 15 months ago with a group of 1500 of their friends and neighbors. Of the original group of 1500, only 185 remained alive and the boys we were talking to said that they were the only ones of the group that could still walk. Their eyes gleamed with hope and a semi-worship as they told us of the tanks which appeared along the brow of the hill two weeks previously and brought an end to the hell in which they had been living.

They stated that they had overheard plans for the extermination of the whole remaining 4000 which remained in the camp, plans which were blasted by the appearance of the American tanks. They had overheard SS Troopers planning to run the whole lot of them into one of the subterranean factories on which they had been working and to bury them alive by blasting the entrance. Some of the braver members of our group slipped over to one of the buildings close by and peeked in the window. A peek was enough for them as they turned away quickly, faces reflecting the horror which they had observed. Remnants of what had once been men, writhing in the last struggle for the life which had been slowly taken from them by starvation and overwork.

Our officer in charge and the guide approached . . . The guide told us at this point that we were about to view what had been the worst of the Nazi labor camps, Stalag No. 6, more commonly known by the name of the Austrian town of Ibensee. The capacity of the camp in narrow three decker beds was about 6000 and for the past several months had been accommodating in its monstrous way about 22,000 with a turnover of about 300 daily. By turnover it is meant that 300 fresh prisoners were brought in to replace those which died or were killed during the twenty-four hour period. The crematory of the camp had a capacity of burning only 100 bodies a day so the other 200 each day were collected in piles for about five days while a large hole was dug by the living at the side of the growing pile of flesh and bones. Then a bulldozer would push the entire 1000 into the hole and cover them. The enormous death rate of course was the result of starvation, maltreatment, and disease, either individually or collectively. The prisoners of the camp were worked under armed guard from 7:00 a.m. to 10:00 p.m. digging mammoth excavations into the mountainsides of solid rock. When they worked well they were given one pint of soup made from the peelings of the potatoes which the SS Guards ate and one-third of a bun of bread per man per day. When they were no longer able to work they were either taken to the hospital or left in their quarters and cut to one half the rations they received while working.

During the last few months before the camp was liberated there was so much disease among the starving men that the death rate reached its peak of 300 per day. The hospitals were incapable of taking care of the great influx and the men were left to lay four and five to a narrow bunk and die in their own excrement. When the Americans took over they found several buildings adjacent to the hospital buildings with hundreds of dead and dying men lying 4 or 5 to the narrow bunk, the living ones too weak to shove the dead ones off of them.

We were led through a series of living quarters and although they had been scrubbed the stench was still so strong that it was sickening. In spite of the hopeless condition of most of the men in these quarters, there were placards in all including the worst of the hospital wards printed in English, "Welcome to our Liberators."

A number of the inmates were Germans. In this situation and similar situations all Germans that have thought about anything other than Nazism and the inhuman tendencies of that party have suffered right along with the people they refused to abuse.

In the hospitals we were greeted by WACs and women of the Nurse's Corps who have been enlisted to work with the emaciated bodies and souls of the liberated prisoners and they informed us that in two weeks time the death rate had been cut from 300 per day to 12 per day and that they had hopes of reducing it still further.

On leaving the area of the camp we were taken to see one of the enormous excavations which the prisoners had been forced to dig . . . . This particular excavation was fully equipped as a factory for airplane motors and would have been in operation within a few days if the Americans hadn't taken over . . . . The airplane factory . . . was started in November 1943, and at an estimated cost of 28,500 lives in the building, was ready to send forth messengers of death.

A greatly impressed bunch of G.I.s were loaded into their trucks again to ride into the beauties of God's natural cover for the Devil's Workshop. Although no man alive can see what we saw and ever forget, we tried for our own good to slip back into the reality of our lives as American Soldiers. (23)

16th Armored Infantry Battalion:

And can you ever forget those three days in Burghausen? How we freed those 2,000 slave laborers, and how they swarmed all over you trying to kiss you or shake your hand? And those gaunt American PWs, 4,000 of them, who roamed the town and countryside rounding up more prisoners of war for us? (19)

Yeah, our division had freed a lot of prisoners of war as we'd moved from town to town. There was one Nazi camp up in the mountains where our troops freed the prisoners, and then took their own prisoners — Nazi guards from that camp. They brought them down and we had to search every one to see that they didn't have any weapons. We spent about half a day doin' that.

They lined them up and we just walked through there. We'd stop at each one and check them. Of course, we couldn't understand anything they said. And they couldn't understand English, either, or if they did, they didn't let us know it. They had a mess kit, and we went through one after another and took out all the knives and forks. We just left them a spoon so they could eat.

We used those German prisoners to clean up our garbage around camp. They arrived in a truck and they'd come around and work every day. We had Americans guarding them. The guard would stay on the truck where he could watch them while they picked up stuff. Of course, we didn't have to worry too much about the German prisoners causing any trouble. They'd already gone through the war and it was over.

When the German prisoners came around and picked up garbage from the mess area, the thing I noticed, they would find gallon cans where we'd opened peaches or whatever, and they'd punch two holes in the can where they could tie a string through it and they'd carry it around their neck. They'd find food scraps that we threw away and they'd collect it and put it in their tin cans. I guess the army gave them some food, but we didn't give them as much as they wanted. And we threw away a lot of food when we were out like that. So those German prisoners would collect our garbage and carry it with them in that tin can until they were allowed time to eat and that's what they'd eat out of.

24th Tank Battalion:

Settling down to garrison life in the picturesque town of Neu Otting, the battalion cleaned up, rested, played ball, decorated its heroes with 4 silver stars, 69 bronze stars, and 100 purple hearts. A few lucky ones drew passes to Paris, the Riviera, and other resort centers while awaiting news about going home. Four battle-tested sergeants, Jarvis, Pyatt, Turnbull and Myers turned in their stripes for new second lieutenant bars. (1)

One of our lieutenants, First Lieutenant Stephen H. Smith, he was the West Point graduate, he'd been outside his tank when the Germans shelled us and a big piece of shrapnel hit his steel helmet. It hit right above the brim and it cut a big place on his head. But the medics, they patched him up and he went on that day.

That shrapnel cut a big hole in his helmet. If he hadn't had it on, it would have killed him. So he kept that damaged helmet in the tank, and he said he'd bring it home with him from overseas. He said, "I'm keeping that."

And if he's still a livin', I guess he's got that hanging on his wall. First Lieutenant Smith was one of the best officers we had. He did a lot of brave things during the war, though I don't know what and all they were, but he was awarded the Silver Star for Gallantry in Action.

My platoon sergeant, Sergeant Hicks—Pearl F. Hicks—he was promoted to first sergeant during the war. Battlefield commission. He might a been a tough'un, but he was fair and good to his men and he did well on the battlefield. He'd really had a big hand in making us into good soldiers, kind of like a father figure to us.

Sergeant Jarvis, the young sergeant who'd had all that trouble back at Camp Beale makin' that McDaniel boy do what he wanted him to do, well, Sergeant Jarvis had learned a lot about handling people since then and he did real well in battle, too. He made second lieutenant. And that McDaniel boy from Madisonville, Tennessee, he was still in my platoon. He made it through the war. Turned out to be a real good soldier.

Company C's commanding officer, Captain Richard F. Blake, the ol' sourpuss, he was awarded a Bronze Star. My own tank commander and good friend, Sergeant Donald E. Crouch, was also awarded a Bronze Star. 'Course, he didn't know it. I know his family sure felt the great cost of that medal, when they got the sad news.

Lonnie Johnson, 24th Tank Battalion, Company C:

Casualties, we had two boys named Ford—one was a tank commander and he got killed on the back of a tank from accidental fire, and the other one, the last time I heard, he was in a coma with his wounds.

Knight got killed. Charles Eaton got killed. Sergeant Hicks got a shell close to his elbow, and it messed up his elbow. A boy named Stroud from Texas, he lost one arm. Donald Crouch died. And as a whole, we lost a big part of our command.

Charles Eaton was the first one in our outfit hit and killed and the last one killed was Donald Crouch. If he'd made it that day, he wouldn't a got killed. That was the last battle that we was in. It was downhill from there on in. (12)

There were several boys close to me that got killed, but it didn't bother me like it did when Donald Crouch got killed. The thing that got to me the most was when I thought about what he said to me in that French schoolhouse, when he told me about the time he called his wife from Texas and told her that he had a three-day pass and he wanted her to come to New York. He thought she would bring their little girl and she didn't.

I don't reckon anybody'll ever know what Donald and his wife said to each other, or how they left off in New York. That last look at each other, those last words, only they knew. I couldn't forget that he'd said to me, "I didn't enjoy her visit one bit."

I thought about that. That really got to me when he got killed. I hated so much that Donald had been mad at his wife the last time he saw her.

Aw, people will do things. Now, his wife thought she was doing the right thing, I reckon, 'cause it would have been a lot of trouble to her, I realize, to have traveled on the train with the baby. She probably thought, "Well, I'll only get to be up there and see him a short time and there's no need to go through all of that." Of course, she thought she was doing the best thing at the time.

She didn't realize how that was gonna affect him, though. She just didn't know how important seeing his daughter was to him. For some reason, he told me that he wouldn't have minded so bad coming overseas to fight in a war, if he'd gotten to see his little girl before he left. He made some remarks like that. When he got killed, I bet it sure caused his wife a lot of tears.

Donald had time to write letters before he got killed, and I hope he apologized to his wife for leaving mad at her. Of course, I'd like to think they made up in their letters, when the mail would catch up to us in Germany. I never did know. I do know he felt sorry about what had happened. And I know he really wanted to get back home and make things right with his wife and see his little daughter. He wanted everything to go just right in the tank, and he was trying to protect us when he got killed.

So it was all sad then, after Donald died. Now, of course, I wouldn't have thought much about it if he had survived, it wouldn't have meant a thing. It would have been just one of those little upsets along the way between a husband and wife. But with him not surviving, it's what I thought about most. I bet that was hard on his wife.

I reckon I'm the only one he ever told. And it hurt me something awful to think about him wanting so much to see his little girl, but he didn't get to.

'Course, the little girl wasn't old enough to remember him. All she'll remember about him is what they tell her. And she'll think she knows a lot about him, but she'll never know what a hero he was, really, for his country. 'Cause she didn't see him in battle, like I did.

What hurt me most was how close he came to seein' her. If he'd just made it through that day, he'd have been all right. But it wasn't meant to be that way.

★ ★ ★

Considering that kind of thing, I didn't have much heart to put in for the two Purple Hearts I could have got, one for when I hit that tree and busted my lip, and one for the sniper's bullet that cut across my hand. I didn't even go to the medics. I just doctored myself with the first aid kit.

I was a combat-wounded veteran, but I never put it on record. The only people who know it are me and the people around me at the time. There were probably a lot of us who didn't bother to put in for Purple Hearts.

Sure, I realized that they had a point system. You got so many points for different things, so many points when you got wounded, and you could get a discharge after the war was over, on points. The ones that had the most points got out first. I could have gotten two Purple Hearts and got out of the service sooner.

But you had to keep up with it yourself and turn the information in to the medics, they kept a record of it. I never thought a thing about that. All I thought about was just livin'. I never thought too much about gaining anything else. I was willing to stay in the service till they let me out. That was my attitude.

The right attitude, in my opinion, is to do the very best you can, and be the best soldier you possibly can be. And that's about all you can be. Just do as much as you know how to do and do it with the attitude of winning. Of course, we wanted to win the war and we were there for that purpose. And in order to win, it took doing the things that we had to do, things we maybe didn't want to do. A lot of those things, if you had just been asked to volunteer, you wouldn't do that. But we were forced, in one sense, and it wasn't our own people that forced us, it was our enemy that forced us to do these things. It was just forced on us to take lives and property in order to put evil down.

So I don't feel that we were held responsible for doing some things that we couldn't help. It was war. I think that we need to stand up for what we believe's right, even if it takes going to another country and overrunning it, to liberate people who are suffering like they were in Germany at that time.

While we were occupying Germany, Winfred Knode got a big map that the U.S. Army produced showing the entire route that we'd traveled from the time we landed at Le Havre all the way through France and Germany to the border of Austria. The official count said that our tank odometers had clicked off 1,608 miles, but mine was more, on account of some of that extra driving I always got to do.

A lot of my buddies gathered around and signed that map, even though some of the boys were off on passes that day.

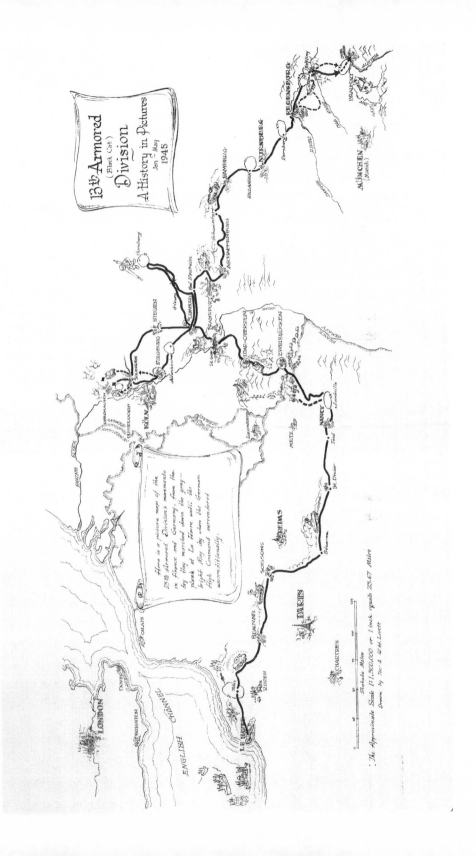

13th Armored
(Black Cat)
Division
A History in Pictures
Jan-May
1945

Here is a picture map of the
13th Armored Division's movements
in France and Germany, from the
day they marched down the gangplank at Le Havre until the
bright day by when the German
High Command surrendered
unconditionally.

The Approximate Scale 1:1,500,000 or 1 inch equals 225.67 Miles
Drawn by Tec-4 W.H. Lovett

Just a few who proudly made their mark:

Sgt. Harry P. Bacon, "Ham," Chesterfield, Missouri

T/4 C. A. Puckett, "Red," Portland, Oregon

Sgt. L. M. Frost, "Frosty," Elmira, New York

T/5 Edmond Pressler, Livingston, New Jersey

T/5 Harold V. Markl, Pipestone, Minnesota

T/5 Edward Salecki, Summit, Illinois

Pfc. John Kemp, Charlotte, North Carolina

Sgt. Charles Ford, Cleveland, Ohio

Sgt. John V. Brown, "Brownie," Mobile, Alabama

Sgt. Gillis L. Knoblock, Memphis, Tennessee

Pvt. Frank K. Young, Mott Street, New York City

Pvt. Alteo Casevecchia, Ridgefield, Connecticut

Cpl. Valentine Messer, Yakima, Washington

Sgt. Glenn Smith, Los Angeles, California

Pfc. Ernest M. Carr, "Hillbilly No.1," Perry, Iowa

Pfc. Sol B. Rosenberg, Louisville, Kentucky

T/5 Ralph W. Rogerson, Elizabeth City, North Carolina

Sgt. Vernon Parent, Oregon (He survived that gunshot wound right through his neck.)

Cpl. Thomas E. Allen, LaFayette, Alabama (He's the one who used to call me "Rubba Belly!")

Pvt. Ewell W. Rhodes, "Rocky," Dallas, Texas (We never called him Rocky. He was "E-well.")

First Sergeant, Pearl F. Hicks, Durham, Missouri

There was a big blank space where I looked first, so I signed just exactly smack in the middle of that big map:

T/5 James Q. Kelley
Coker Creek, Tennessee.

It was the last time I'd write *T/5*. The army promoted me to T/4 after that. Usually, the one that drove the commander's tank and the platoon

Quinton Kelley poses with his Grease Gun in a Bavarian town.

leader's tanks, they were rated as T/4s. All the other drivers, the highest rating they normally gave them was a T/5. But for some reason, they gave me a T/4 rating after the war—that was equal in pay to a sergeant—and I didn't drive the commander's tank or the lieutenant's tank or anything like that. After that, I wore three stripes with a "T."

As soon as the war was over, they started having those early-morning inspections. We'd have to fall out and Captain Blake came by and checked each one of us to see if we's slick-shaved and he checked our uniforms to see if we had every button buttoned and all of that. They went through that procedure just like they did when we were taking our basic training.

But because the war was over, we just left our tanks in a motor pool where we camped. We parked them and left them behind. I didn't want no more of that tank anyhow.

★ ★ ★

The numbers that I remember are the three close calls that I got personally, and that one really close call for the tank that I knew of.'Course, we were under fire a lot of the time, but when you didn't know how close you came to bein' hit, you never thought about it.

The other boys in my tank crew, as far as I know, they didn't happen to personally get any close calls over there. Knode, McAbee, and Rhodes might have been shook up, but they made it.

Overall, as a division, the 13th was lucky. We didn't lose a lot of men. We lost some, though. The 13th Armored Division reported that we had:

Killed in Action — 214
Wounded in Action — 912
Died of Their Wounds — 39
Missing — 22

The whole armored division had a little over 10,000 people. That's not many killed, compared to the number of men that we had. I'm satisfied we took out a lot more German soldiers than they did us.

I'm glad they kept us in the States for two years and gave us all that training, getting us ready. We always were told from the very beginning that we might go to Japan or to Germany, one of those two places, when we completed our training. But we never did know till right at the last, where we were going.

They told us they were training us for a special job. We all thought we were slated to take over Berlin, but when we doubled back to the Ruhr to support the First Army, then we thought that the Russians had beat us to it. Later on, I learned the Allies had let the Russians take Berlin on account of the destruction that the Germans had caused them in Russia. The Russians took over Berlin and eventually put up that Berlin Wall.

The 13th Armored Division ended the war as part of General Patton's Third Army, whose code name, I learned, had been Lucky. Now, of course, I wasn't part of the Third Army the whole time and they did a lot more fighting before I joined them than they did after. But I was a part of that, and General Patton's Final General Orders pertained to us all and it made me proud:

All men and women of the six corps and thirty-nine divi-
sions that have at different times been members of this Army
have done their duty. Each deserves credit . . . In proudly con-
templating our achievements, let us never forget our heroic dead
whose graves mark the course of our victorious advances, nor
our wounded whose sacrifices aided so much in our success. . . .

During the course of this war I have received promotions
and decorations far above and beyond my individual merit. You
won them; I as your representative wear them. The one honor
which is mine and mine alone is that of having commanded such
an incomparable group of Americans, the record of whose for-
titude, audacity, and valor will endure as long as history lasts.

—General George S. Patton, Jr., Headquarters, Third United
States Army GENERAL ORDERS 9 May 1945, Number 98

The Stars and Stripes, Southern Germany Edition
War Cost Over 6 Million Lives
46 Allies Fought: Rhine Offensive Broke Foe's Back

The European phase of World War II—which Adolf Hitler had hoped would fulfill Germany's dream of world conquest—has come to an end with the collapse of the Reich that the former Wehrmacht corporal promised would endure 1,000 years.

The ground, sea and air forces of the United Nations joined to defeat the Axis—Germany and Italy. Now only Japan remains to be finished off.

The war that engulfed 46 nations and three continents opened Sept. 1, 1939, with a razzle-dazzle of propaganda, secret weapons, armored spearheads, bombing armadas, parachute troops, fifth columnists and political sleight of hand.

It was the second great war of the century and was estimated to have cost close to one trillion dollars and the lives of more than 6,000,000 men. (5)

THE BLACK CAT Newspaper
Nation's Press Gives Division a Solid Plug

... The Division's drive through Bavaria and into Austria was described by leading metropolitan newspapers as "smashing," "brilliant" and "rip-roaring." The Washington (D.C.) Post ran a banner headline "13th Armored Division Captures Hitler's Birthplace" over its front-page story describing the seizure of Braunau.

The New York Times, widely regarded as the outstanding American newspaper, devoted a full account to Division operations in the Ruhr and Redoubt.

In Brownwood, Texas, the "Bulletin" paid tribute to "Camp Bowie's Own" with frontpage streamers devoted to the 13th and with an editorial saluting "the men we have taken to our hearts." (4)

The 13th Armored Division had fought Nazis, captured towns, liberated prisoners, and helped win the war in Europe. We all liked to read the newspaper stories about what we'd been a part of and what great effort it took to put down Adolf Hitler and his followers.

Boy, ol' Hitler, he must have been planning and scheming and making deals and manufacturing for years before it came to war. I don't know why our government didn't know what was going on. Maybe they did, but they didn't do anything about it. Hitler had really prepared for that war. Germany'd been preparing for that ever since World War I. It was a sight in the world the stuff that they had for war — superior tanks, airplanes, powerful guns of all kinds, and a lot of highly trained soldiers, too. Hitler thought he was going to take over the whole world, I reckon. He was just that kind of a nut. And he got a good start at it, for a while, but it finally backfired on him.

Germany thought they's gonna win, 'cause Hitler thought he had everything going his way, but his country is nothing like the United States. He should have been smart enough to know that he couldn't out-material us. That's what defeated him. We kept up a lot of manufacturing in America to help win that war.

After the Americans joined the battle, it began to go our way after a while. We kept the Germans on the run so they couldn't manufacture enough to supply themselves. Then they ran out of materials, fuel, and even soldiers.

The cost of all that aggression and defense was just utter ruin. I drove right by a lot of that destruction from one end of Germany to the other. It seemed like everything in Germany was just demolished, except for the little villages out in the country.

The village where we stayed on the banks of the Inn didn't really have damage except for the bridge. There wasn't much there but a railroad station and a few buildings that serviced the stop, just a couple of masonry buildings that had windows dressed with shutters.

We camped near a building that had been a cafeteria, a place where they served food, but it wasn't in operation then. It was a pretty good-sized building and after we took it over, part of us in the company slept in there.

After the war, we didn't have much to do all of a sudden. Sometimes we'd sit around in the evening and read our mail. We'd sit outside in chairs up against the wall of that cafeteria and the sun would be low and it was shady. We'd pass a ball back and forth to each other, up and down through there.

The cafeteria building was right on the highway, before you got to the Inn River, and sometimes the German townspeople would come across the river in a boat and walk up the highway, and some of our boys were as mean as could be. When the German people had their backs turned, they'd throw that ball as hard as they could and purposely hit them in the back. Act like they were throwing the ball to their partner.

The Germans wouldn't say a thing to them out of the way. I think they were so glad the war was over, they didn't want to stir up anything else. But I felt sorry for the civilian people myself. I hated to see some of our soldiers conduct themselves in a sorry manner.

There was a German family that lived behind that cafeteria, they had living quarters in the back, and I guess the whole family probably ran it

May 1945, Neuoetting, Germany. The 24th Tank Battalion passes time outside the restaurant near the Inn River where they billeted. Quinton Kelley, above left.

Ferryboat crossing the Inn River. The photos of Germany were taken by Winfred Knode with a camera he acquired during the war.

as a restaurant before the war. They would come out and talk to us and they could speak a little English, enough to communicate with us. They were just as friendly and nice. The German people I met were real pleasant to the G.I.s who'd liberated them. It had been a long siege for the population of Germany. They were tired of that war.

The children didn't have much to do with us when the war was still going on, but after the war ended, the children that lived around that village, they were really friendly and we'd give them our candy. A few of them could speak English. They were just tickled to death that the war had ended.

The German people, I liked them better than any of the other foreign nationalities that we were around. The few I met were just country village people. We lived there with them until we loaded the train to go back to France.

They were gonna ship us out in boxcars, just empty railroad cars. Me bein' a carpenter's apprentice when I went in the service — and, of course, I had to put that on my records, everything on there — they still had me appointed as the company carpenter. So they put me to building bunks in the boxcars.

There was a lumberyard close by where the Germans had a sawmill and we got some lumber. I worked up there two or three days just by myself fixing those bunks in the boxcars for the boys to lay their bedrolls on. They finally did give me some boys to help me, and we built all the bunks for the train ride.

I got wove wire, something like chicken wire, and made frames and stretched that wire over them. I made three bunks, one right over the top of the other and filled the whole boxcar, but left a walkway down the middle.

I found a piece of real strong canvas, and I said, "Well, I'm having to do this job so I'm gonna fix me a softer bed." I put that big piece of canvas on my bunk. I thought I was doing the right thing.

When we started out of there, we hit a pretty good rainstorm. Those boxcars were rusty and old, and that boxcar started leaking right on my bunk. The rain was just a pourin' down in there and the water was ponding up in that canvas. I knew I was going to have to get out of my bunk if I didn't get rid of the water. I got my pocketknife and punched a hole in that canvas. That feller down below, talk about raisin' Cain!

He didn't know it was my fault. He just knew it was leaking in there. He thought it was coming through the roof. That was a little bit of a mean trick, but I had to get rid of that water somewhere.

Lonnie Johnson, 24th Tank Battalion, C Company:

When we got ready to leave from over there, they had us to build us some things in a boxcar to sleep in, but the old train track was so rough, we tore those out and throwed 'em away about the first hour.

'Course, I got lucky; they come and got me to drive a jeep for the advance party, so I rode all the way back through Germany and France on a jeep. (12)

Quinton washes at Camp Atlanta.

24th Tank Battalion:

June 25, boarded German train for Camp Atlanta, France, near Mailly, arriving June 27. Here we crated and packed for the ocean voyage home, took short trips to Paris and Reims and finally entrained July 9 for the staging area in Camp Old Gold. (1)

When we got back to France, they had some camps set up—they had them named after cigarettes—Old Gold, Lucky Strike.

When we first got there, they said, "Now, we've got a big boiler room set up with hot showers." All the men cheered.

The first thing they had us do was go to that boiler room and take a hot shower. They had big, long rooms of showers, one right after another, and they'd just take the whole company down there and we'd all go through there. That's the first time we'd got a good hot shower since we'd been overseas.

We stayed at Camp Lucky Strike, I believe, about three days and it was like bein' in a big city, just a beehive. They had it set up to handle a lot of people, because they were going to ship out soldiers from there until they got all the soldiers out of Germany and France.

They had a church service one Sunday, and I remember they encouraged all of us to attend that service and I went. And I never was so surprised when I ran into my cousin, Atlas Davis, standing right outside of that big old church!

That was a happy reunion. Oh, yeah, it was. We didn't know, of course, but what the other had got killed or injured. But there he stood, as tall and straight as always. Yeah, both of us had made it through the war in Europe and we's ready to come back home.

I hadn't gotten to see Atlas at all in Europe, there were so many of us over there, just swarms of U.S. soldiers. It was amazing that I ran into him at all.

Atlas told me that he'd put food on General Patton's plate several times during the war and that the famous general could be pretty moody, either he was real friendly or as sour as a green persimmon.

The biggest thing Atlas had to tell me: He'd been just a few feet away when the 13th Armored's top man, Major General John B. Wogan, got shot. Atlas just happened to be standing nearby as General Wogan's jeep drove up. The unit was pinned down in a little town because a bridge was out, and the general came up to personally see what was holding them up. The thing of it was, his car had a general's flag flying on it, with big white stars, easy to see. Atlas told me that the car came to a stop and the general got out and an officer ran up to the jeep and snapped "Get those flags off that car!"

Sniper fire rang out, pierced General Wogan's throat and he stumbled over beside his jeep. Other officers were wounded in that same attack. The general would eventually recover, but he never commanded the 13th Armored Division again.

"Why, the general oughta knowed better than to get out with insignias, 'cause them snipers all wanted high brass," Atlas said.

Atlas and I went on into the church and it was packed with servicemen. They may have had a choir, they may have had an organ—I don't know anymore. But I do know that I had a lot to be thankful for that morning. Boy, I sure did. The war in Europe was over and I had come through it with two little ol' scars, both of 'em only skin deep.

I was thankful that morning, oh, I sure was. And everybody else was, too, that was there. Of course, there were a lot of the boys that didn't go to church and didn't know a thing about church. They didn't go. But the ones that had ever come up in church, they were there that day. The chaplain always had a good word of encouragement for everybody and he helped us to realize how there had been a blessing in some way, and that helped us to make it through all that.

I prayed for the families of Donald Crouch, Charlie Eaton, Donnie Knight, and so many others, whose names, I'm sorry to say, I've forgotten. Time does that. I've never forgotten their faces or their sacrifices, though.

A lot of them got killed 'cause they didn't know how to take care of themselves. But, of course, a lot of them died because it was war and a certain number will get killed, no matter how careful they are. I was almost in the wrong place at the wrong time on several occasions. The good Lord was just with me, I reckon. As it would turn out, God had other plans for me. He meant for me to have a long life.

★ ★ ★

THE BLACK CAT'S KITTEN EXTRA
EDEN CALLS FOR DRIVE ON JAPAN

Anthony Eden, British Foreign Secretary, said today that all energies of the United Nations must now be devoted to winning a victory over Japan.

"This is a majestic and triumphant hour," he said. "We must now summon all our strength for final overthrow of the other enemy, Japan." (11)

I know I survived, so I couldn't have made too many mistakes, but I don't know how well I did in battle. I did as well as the rest of 'em, I reckon. I never heard any complaints. Anyway, I made it, that was the main thing. I felt pretty lucky.

I'm sure that all of us who made it felt fortunate to have lived through the big battles of the Ruhr and Bavaria. We'd had it pretty hard, we thought, but we were all glad of one thing: We hadn't been chosen to be out in front, leading the wave of a big attack, like those soldiers that stormed Normandy beachhead. But some of the boys I fought with, they started sayin' that our luck was about to change.

The army had always told us that the 13th Armored Division was being trained for some special purpose and they announced it to us: We were to lead the charge in the final phase of World War II—the invasion of Japan. That was the most heavily guarded place, of course, the Japanese homeland. It was expected to be much like the invasion on Normandy beachhead—it was going to be a bloodbath, that's all there was to it. And worse, the Japanese fought differently than the Germans, we'd heard. They didn't usually surrender.

The army didn't tell us too many details at that point in the war, but we knew we were going to invade Japan and we figured that's what was in store for us. And we's all a dreadin' that. We got orders that the army wanted us back in the U.S. just as soon as we could get back. Some of the American troops had to stay over in Europe for a while, but we got shipped out early, because we were headed for our next mission. They wanted us to take a little specialized training before we invaded Japan.

They first said that we might go through the Panama Canal and head for the Pacific, and not take that extra training, and, oh, we really worried that we might go right out to the Pacific and not get to go home. But at the last minute, they decided that we needed to take that training back in California. I was glad of that decision. They told us that just before we left Europe.

★ ★ ★

Our "Collectors" were just as active as any other out-fits—And who blames them? Of course, some of us just about made the gangplank, but, think of the tall tales we can tell our grandchildren about those guns.

—The Thirteenth Armored Division, A History of the Black Cats from Texas to France, Germany and Austria and Back to California. 1946, U.S. Army.

When they found out we were gonna get to come back home, a lot of the boys would collect up as much stuff as they could to bring back. They got jewelry, cameras, paintings, guns, liquor, violins and harmonicas, just all kinds of souvenirs when we were overseas.

But before we got on that ship and headed back for the States, we prepared for a major inspection.

The army told us, "We'll go through everything you've got with a fine-tooth comb. And if we find anything that you're trying to carry out of this country, it will be taken away from you. We will leave you over here in the occupational force. You'll have to stay here a year or two. So, if you don't want to have to stay over here, you'd better not get caught with anything trying to get on the ship."

They announced it so firmly that you knew you definitely better not get caught takin' nothin' back with you, so I took their word for it. I said, "Well, I don't want to stay over here." And I took out my Luger. It was a nice one—it had an extra clip to go with it and a real nice leather holster.

So one of the boys came over to me—don't know who he was now—and he said, "I'll tell you what I'll do. I'll take a chance on taking that German Luger home if you'll trade it to me for this watch." He had some kind of German-made wristwatch. It was a good watch.

I said to myself, I'm not gonna let wantin' that gun stand in the way of my goin' home. So I told him, "Well, I can't take a chance on having to stay over here, so I reckon I'll just trade with you. I believe I can get that watch back to the States."

I handed him that Luger. He was gonna take a chance, but I wasn't that big of a chance taker. I was gonna bring it back, but I got afraid that I'd get caught with it, so I traded it off for that gold watch. I don't even know what that watch looked like now.

We used to get our tooth powders in a kind of funnel-shaped container. It was big at the bottom and it tapered up towards the top. I took out some of the tooth powders, and I took the bottom out of the container. I made a false bottom and I put that German watch up in there, packed some paper around it and I put the bottom back in it. I still had tooth powder in the top part of it. I said, "Now, I don't believe they'll go so far as to tear that apart just looking for something."

Well, they didn't bother a thing. No, they didn't search a one of us when we got on the ship. I could have brought that Luger home, carrying it on my side, I guess, and they wouldn't have said a word to me. They told us they'd go through everything we had. They just told us that to scare us out of it. We could have brought anything back. Why, one boy in the division brought back two German boxer puppies in his field bag! And the soldier that got my Luger, he got it home.

I'm glad that *I* got back, but I wish I'd brought that gun with me. I didn't take that chance, and I soon regretted that. Yeah, I hated that, 'cause I'd always wanted a German Luger, even before we ever went overseas. But I's wantin' to come home more.

Boy, was I glad to get that Luger when I took it off of that Nazi officer who surrendered to us in the Ruhr, and then I didn't have enough of nerve to bring it home and I let that feller talk me out of it! So that's how I lost my German Luger.

At the time, though, I quickly got over that. I was just as glad to leave all those guns and stuff behind me. I was glad that I never did have to fire my Grease Gun in combat. I was sorry, though, that I never even tried to fire my German Luger before I went and gave it up.

★ ★ ★

24th Tank Battalion:

On July 14 we moved by truck to Le Havre, double-loaded on the USS General McRae and steamed for the States. Hampton Roads, Virginia on July 23 and Camp Patrick Henry for a special dinner—steaks, vegetables, milk, fresh fruits and ice cream. By July 25 we were on the way to reception stations for 30 days home. (1)

A big brass band played on the deck of the ship as we boarded for our voyage home and we heard some mighty spirited music. Flags hung across that ship like clothes on a clothesline. Our big banner with the 13th Armored Division's "unlucky" black cat was proudly raised. And, of course, many beautiful red, white, and blue American flags flew along the deck of the ship, waving in the sunshine.

I only got seasick one time on that voyage, just a little bit, and it didn't bother me too bad. It was smooth sailing from then on, and I think all of us had a real good time on our way back home.

Lonnie Johnson, 24th Tank Battalion, C Company:

When we first went overseas to France, Kelley was sick on his stomach and I was, too. Man, I thought sure I'd rather been in the bottom of the ocean almost.

Comin' back, Kelley said, "I'll give you five dollars if you bring me one Co-Cola a day. I'm gonna lay down on the floor and just lay there, 'cause I don't want to get that sick no more."

This time we got on a big ol' ship, a luxury liner, and it was just like ridin' down a highway in a car. There wasn't a wave on the sea nowhere and nobody got sick. We could enjoy it the best.

I loved to gamble a little bit and I knew Kelley didn't. I'd shoot dice and play cards and everything we hadn't ought to have done. So I give Kelley some of my money. We got paid and oh, we was rich. We had a couple of hundred dollars or more.

I think I give Kelley a hundred dollars and I told him, "Don't let me have it now, no matter what I say, don't let me have it." Because I would gamble a little bit, and I knew if I spent that money, I wouldn't have nothin' to start off with when I got home. I said, "Now, I mean it, don't give it to me." I knew I might lose it if I had another hundred.

And sure enough, we hadn't been sailing but a few hours before I needed some of that money so bad. I looked at Kelley and he said, "No need to ask. You ain't a gettin' it."

I would've took it away from him if I'd a thought I could.

Kelley said, "You neen' to come toward me. You ain't a gonna get it."

He kept it, too, until we landed and come back to Virginia. And he gave it back to me. That was what I wanted him to do. I had some money when I come home. If it hadn't been for that, I wouldn't a had any when I come home. (12)

CHAPTER 22

Home

Well, you don't really know how free you are till you go to a country like that and come out of a war and come back home and set your foot on American soil. It's a great country, my country. I know our form of government is the best in the world and I'm thankful for it. Glad to be an American. Sometimes that gets me all choked up. Yeah, it's somethin' that really gets to you.

The war made me really appreciate the United States, because I saw a lot of things that we didn't have to put up with in the U.S. and I said, "Well, I wouldn't trade my country for no other place that I ever seen, or heard of, 'cause I love America." Of course, it's got its bad points as well as good, but I wouldn't trade it, because, here, we believe that every person has the same rights, and we are free to say our piece, and I think that's a good way to live.

I've heard people say that "Freedom is not free." I have some thoughts about that.

Freedom is really a privilege, and in one sense of thinking about it, you have to do something to earn it. It just don't come free in this country or any other country. We get more freedom here than anywhere, but you've got to earn your freedom by doing the right thing. You just can't do anything you want and expect to have the freedom. You've got to stand up for your government, if they're right. And, of course, we feel like we've got the right form of government, because the people have a say in it. Some governments, some countries, people have no say, only the men in charge have a say, and people just have to knuckle down to whatever they decree.

I really believe that everybody should have a desire to be free and be able to state their own feelings publicly. It gives you a sense of loving your country more, I think, if you can express your feelings about your country. And you want to feel you have a say in its direction. That's the way of the U.S.—it was founded by our forefathers to be that type of country, to give everybody an opportunity to make a speech if they wanted to say a speech.

So I really love my country and if I was able to go to a battle today, I'd go, if it would save the country. I wouldn't hesitate. I didn't hesitate then, and I still wouldn't. Of course, I know they wouldn't use me at my age today, but I might be worth something to them, if it came down to that. Germany had to use a lot of their senior citizens and young boys. Of course, they were fighting for the wrong cause and they didn't win.

Hitler planned for his empire to last a thousand years, but it lasted about twelve. Maybe that's because what he was trying to do wasn't anything a man could be proud of doin'. Mistreating people is no way to build up a nation, no way to lead. Hitler and men who think like that are always dead wrong. You've got to have respect for your fellow man, that's all there is to it.

I know people need to be liberated sometimes, but they'll put up a pretty good fight just to continue the way they've been living because they don't know any other life if they've never had our kind of freedom. If they had a taste of the life that we have in this country—the life I've known in the years of my lifetime—there wouldn't be too much problem. I think that we need to stand up for what we believe's right, even if it takes going to another country to liberate people who are suffering because they've had to live under the sword, you might say. If they got out of line, they'd be killed, or their family was killed, even their children. Or they were rounded up and taken to concentration camps. I can't go along with that kind of government. And a lot of men and women in America couldn't go along with it either during

World War II, so they were proud, when duty called, to join in and serve their country for the cause of Freedom.

Well, let me add to that, a lot of Americans didn't have the opportunity to serve like I did. Maybe they weren't at the age to go in service during the war, or they would have gone. A lot of people didn't have the opportunity to stand up for their country like the men that were of age. We had the opportunity to go and stand up for our country, and I was proud of that. But a lot of people would have been willing to go, and their health wouldn't permit it, or they were too young or too old to go, and they probably thought just as much of America as I do. I know my father would have fought for his country, had his country called on him.

After the 13th Armored Division made it back to the States, they let us go on furloughs home. One of my friends on Coker Creek, he came home with us from church that first Sunday I was back, had Sunday dinner with us, and he said, "I come over here 'cause I want you to tell me about the war—what and all happened and what you went through over there."

So we sat on the front porch of the cabin and I told him a little bit about it, but I didn't tell him very much. I told him about what happened to some of my buddies who didn't make it. And that sort of satisfied him. I didn't know how to tell him a story like that and really explain it, and I realized I didn't like thinking about it. I'd had enough of that death. So I didn't want to talk about the war when I came home. No, I wanted to get it off of my mind, and it was pretty easy to forget— I didn't exactly forget it—but it didn't just haunt me. I had other things to think about—bein' with my family while I was home on leave, and spending some of those warm days with my sweetheart, Orangie, 'cause for all I knew, I was a fixin' to ship out for the Pacific Theater.

★ ★ ★

I'd just been home a few days on furlough and I went down to Frank Murphy's store, where Orangie was working again, and she had the *Knoxville Journal* there on the store counter. There was a big rush to come into the store and get a look at that paper.

I'd never seen such big letters in a newspaper. About half the front page was taken up with the words "WAR ENDS!"

Japan had surrendered unconditionally. I knew what that meant for me: There would be no invasion of the Japanese homeland.

Everybody was all happy when the end of World War II was declared. Every family was really, really relieved. And my family was just as happy as anybody, knowin' that I was stayin' in my home country, where we were safe and free.

I was as shocked as the rest of the world to learn how we got the Japanese to surrender. The United States created and dropped the first atomic bomb, a uranium bomb, on the city of Hiroshima on August 6. When the Japanese didn't surrender, President Truman decided to drop a second atomic bomb, a plutonium bomb, on Nagasaki three days later.

I could hardly fathom the destruction. It must have been a sight that made you think of the hellfire and brimstone that the country preachers preached about, that cloud of fire over those Japanese cities.

I didn't realize how powerful that blast was until sometime later one of my friends told me what he'd seen over there. Another Coker Creek boy, he was serving over in the Pacific when they dropped the atomic bombs and his unit went in there around Hiroshima to help clean up the mess. He said that the solid metal railroad tracks in that city, the atomic bomb melted them and spread them out on the ground into a flat sheet of metal about twelve inches wide. I thought a lot about something that could do that in just a flash, how hot it must have been.

Even with such destruction, Japan's emperor took a few days to surrender. But by August 15, 1945, Japan's unconditional surrender was official.

That A-bomb, as they called it, it was a weapon that none of the public could have imagined, and when I learned that a lot of the material to make it was manufactured only about seventy miles from Coker Creek, Tennessee, that was a big shock to me. Especially since Orangie had worked right there and she didn't know it either.

Naturally, she told me a little about what she had been doing, but she didn't know much. The civilians who worked in and around the industrial site, they were instructed to keep a tight lip on everything they saw, heard, or did at work.

"J. A. Jones Construction Co." was what Orangie's badge had said, and that was the North Carolina contractor that had built the facilities. Orangie's job was in a brand-new cafeteria that served food to just about everybody who worked in Oak Ridge at one time or another, even a lot of top-level scientists. She'd worked back in the kitchen, where the pots were so huge, she said, you couldn't reach your arms around one. All she knew was that she was preparing salads and vegetables to feed people who worked at the site. She didn't deal with the people much, like some of the other women did, but she was struck by how much secrecy was stressed.

"They drilled it into us all the time," Orangie said. "If anybody comes in here and asks you any questions, any questions *at all*, even something as simple as 'What time does it get busy for lunch?' you tell them, 'I'm new here. I don't know.'"

Everybody there worked among signs and posters that warned workers not to talk about anything at all:

"What you see here
What you do here
What you hear here
When you leave here
Let it stay here."

Because the camps to house the workers were put up in a rush, there wasn't time to build roads, so all the roads around there were dirt, and then mud after the winter thaws. You couldn't hardly walk anywhere, Orangie said. Everybody was gettin' stuck in the thick, deep mud.

They needed workers so bad, they didn't have room for all of 'em and Orangie had to share a hutment with three other women, like a lot of the workers did. The four women each had a cot that centered around a potbellied woodstove for heat. Each woman had one suitcase that she lived out of and that was all.

Orangie didn't work at Oak Ridge too long. It was cold and wet when she was up there and she took the measles and had to go back to

Coker Creek to recuperate, and she never did go back to Oak Ridge. That's all I knew about it then.

What I didn't know then, and not until years later, was that those Tennessee hills had been the site of the largest industrial project in the history of the world up to that point. And nobody, hardly, knew a thing about it until afterwards, when it came out what was goin' on back in there.

Late in 1942, the U.S. government began their secret engineering project along the Clinch River to manufacture nuclear materials for a new type of weapon. It was what they called Top Secret and part of the Manhattan Project, the program that produced the first atomic bomb. The project included sites in other states, but the largest facility was at Oak Ridge, Tennessee, where one U-shaped factory was a mile long when you walked from one end to the other. Back then, it was the largest industrial plant ever built.

This was needed to support and run a uranium-235 enrichment facility to make the raw material for the first nuclear weapon. The U.S. and Nazi Germany were in a race, really. Our government knew that some of Germany's top scientists were working on an atomic bomb, too, and we had to be the first to create a weapon so powerful it might just decide the war.

In the amount of time that I was in service, an entire industrial complex got built in East Tennessee, and around it, a "secret city" of homes, schools, churches, stores, a movie theater, train station, bus station, and a hospital for all the employees and their families who had to live on site for security reasons. Within two and a half years, the sleepy little farming area known as Black Oak Ridge became Tennessee's fifth-largest city. But it was a secret city because Oak Ridge, as it came to be called, never appeared on any maps until after the war was over.

The U.S. government chose their remote location in the Tennessee foothills because mountain ridges surrounded the site, and this was supposed to keep the activity isolated — and maybe protect the people who lived on the other side of the ridges, if there was ever a nuclear accident.

The Tennessee Valley Authority—TVA—my old employer, that was also a big part of why the U.S. government chose East Tennessee for the uranium-enrichment facility. TVA had been busy since the 1930s building a system of dams and power plants in the region to control water flow and generate electricity. TVA provided thousands of jobs for us "hillbillies" back in "them thar hills." I'd been out a little bit and that's what I'd heard people say of us descendants of the pioneers who lived down in the South, in the mountain country. But we did our part to build this country. Every group of us here can claim somethin' we did to help build up America, I'd hope.

Working for TVA, we'd constructed the dams that generated electricity that fed the manufacturing plants that allowed us to win the war. By the end of the war, the United States was really a bona fide world power and TVA had become the nation's largest electricity supplier. TVA supplied power customers that were vital to the war effort, like an A-31 bomber factory in Nashville. The aluminum used to build bombs and airplanes came from the Aluminum Company of America, ALCOA. They had a factory south of Knoxville—at that time, it was the largest aluminum plant in the world. TVA's electricity served ALCOA, and by '43, TVA was powering the uranium enrichment operations at Oak Ridge. They said that during the war, Oak Ridge used one-sixth of the nation's electricity in their process of enriching uranium, the raw material that would detonate as the first atomic weapon ever used on an enemy.

The citizens of Hiroshima and Nagasaki, many of them women and children, they paid a terrible price for their country starting a war. I don't like to see that happen to anybody. But they followed their leader like he was a god and he led them into bloodshed, trying to conquer other nations. It cost a lot of lives when we dropped those two atomic bombs, but that's the way war is. If the war had gone on the way it was, half a million, maybe even a million more Allied soldiers would have died fighting the Japanese on their soil to end that war. Our military estimated that twice that amount would have died fighting on the Japanese side.

The important thing was that Japan surrendered and World War II ended, and that ended the bloodshed on both sides, finally. Using the atomic bomb cost a terrible price, but it ended the war and I believe it saved more lives than it cost in that war.

You go into a war to win it as quick as you can. You go into a war to end it.

Some Thought on the Black Cat Division, by T/Sgt. Tracy E. Goodwin:

The 13th Armored Division would have been a part of the Coronet Invasion which was slated for March 1, 1946. The 13th Armored and 20th Armored Divisions plus six infantry divisions would have been responsible for an invasion on the Tokyo Plains and their assignment was to sweep around the city of Tokyo and form a giant pincer movement — which would have permitted them to isolate Tokyo. . . .

On D-Day, three Infantry Divisions would establish a bridge head south of Tokyo. On D-Day plus 3, the 13th Armored Division was to push through the bridge head and drive up the Tokyo plain toward Tokyo.

The Army estimated that the defenses would be so savage that the 13th would have to be replaced on D-plus 6 with 80% casualties. The 20th Armored would then relieve the 13th and drive on to Tokyo.

History of the 13th Armored Division,
50th Anniversary Edition (3)

I figured they'd saved a lot of men's lives in the 13th Armored Division alone, by dropping those two atomic bombs. That's what saved us. Yeah, I'm tellin' you, we were happy that it turned out like that. We were dreadin' that invasion of the Japanese homeland.

When I went over to Europe, I always felt like I'd come back. I might not have felt that way if I'd had to go to Japan to fight. But that didn't have to happen. Yeah, those two atomic bombs might have saved my life.

But with the dropping of that first A-bomb, the old ways of war started changing, just as they'd changed when airplanes and tanks were introduced during World War I. A new weapon had been invented and used in war.

It was one of many changes that World War II brought to us. I can see now some of the things that changed on the homefront, too. Women increased their opportunities in the country, holding down jobs, even men's jobs, during the war. That opened the door for them. Orangie learned a lot about people and business working at different places, and that's somethin' that helped her in life.

By the end of the war, black men were beginning to be given more of an opportunity in the military, and at home, too. Even on ol' Coker Creek, I heard about some changes that were a long time in comin' when I first got back from the war.

Orangie was back living with her sister, Mamie, and working down at the store after she left Oak Ridge, and I don't remember all the little details, but this one story she told me stands out. I don't even remember who the man was, or the name of his son, but he had been known for being against black people. Everybody knew that about him. Well, his son got killed overseas and the army always sends a soldier with the body to take it wherever it has to go. That soldier happened to be black. I remember Orangie telling me about the black soldier who was sent to escort the body home.

He was coming out to Coker Creek, but when he got to Tellico Plains, that's where he stopped. I reckon he saw the ol' sign.

He had to get in touch with the father of the boy who had died. The funeral director would have done that from Tellico. Frank Murphy had a phone down at his store by then. Everybody used his phone. The funeral director called the store and someone got in touch with the family.

They had to check with the family to see if there would be any problem. They wanted to know if the father would agree for this black man to escort his son, or not. It would have been terrible if they'd turned him back.

When they were able to get word to the father, they asked him, "Do we bring the black man out to Coker Creek or do we stop in Tellico and leave the body for you to come and get?"

As I heard it, the old man said, "You tell that black soldier, if he served for this country and he come out here with my son, you tell him, bring my boy on home. He's welcome up here."

When Orangie told me the story, her blue eyes filled with tears.

The sheriff came along with the black soldier out to Coker Creek. The sheriff was gonna come with him anyway, because he was travelin' in that county and there might've still been a few crazy kind of people out there, even then. They were isolated and slow to change their ways.

I guess that black soldier felt a little like bein' in enemy territory, havin' to have a police escort just to bring a body home for burial. But everybody up in Coker Creek was nice and polite and nothing went wrong. And when that old man who'd been known for bein' against black people met the black soldier who'd come all that way to bring his son's body home, well, I heard, he shook that soldier's hand.

A lot of attitudes were a changin'. Sometime after that, the old sign along the road, the one that said *Black Man—Don't Let the Sun Go Down on You Here*, it disappeared for good.

★ ★ ★

After the war ended with Japan, the U.S. Army contacted every one of us at home on furlough and they told us we'd be getting discharged as soon as they could process us, so they extended our furloughs a good, long time.

My cousin Atlas was home on furlough at the same time. He'd been writing to Bertha all through the war, and like me, he was spending a lot of time with his sweetheart. By now, the leaves around Coker Creek had turned gold and were a fallin'. Well, Atlas and Bertha were determined to get married before Atlas's furlough ended.

About everybody in that area back when the war was on, they went to a place called Blue Ridge, Georgia, to get married. In Tennessee, it took quite a few days to get your license and all, but over the state line, a couple could get married right away. During the war years, things happened fast.

Bertha wouldn't go to Blue Ridge to get married unless somebody else went with them. Bertha said to Atlas, "I won't go, just me and you."

Her family was really strict on the girls. They wouldn't have agreed to let her go across the mountain with Atlas alone, but if they were with another couple, four of us, they didn't object to it.

So Atlas asked me if Orangie and I'd go up there with them the next day so they could get married and to be witnesses at their wedding. He said they weren't going to go unless we did.

I wasn't intending to marry as long as I was still in service, but now the war had ended and Orangie and I had talked about getting married someday. We'd talk about it. I didn't propose exactly. I'd just say, "Well, when are *we* a gonna get married?" We were planning to get married, but we weren't planning on it that particular day. But because of Atlas and Bertha, we were going across the state line anyway and we'd be in front of an official who could marry us.

That evening before we went across the mountain, Orangie and I sat in my car and decided that it would be a good time for us to get married, too.

Neither of us wanted a fuss, and there wasn't much to plan, so when we got up the next morning, which was a Sunday, everybody dressed for church. Orangie was wearing a pretty blue suit when I picked her up in front of Frank's Store, real early. Of course, I was spiffed up in my OD uniform.

Instead of goin' to church, though, we met up along the road with Atlas and Bertha. The tires on Atlas's car were bad. I had good tires on my car and we took that. I drove that blue Chevrolet up the mountain, headin' for Blue Ridge, Georgia.

I'd kept that 1937 Chevrolet all through the war. I had it when I went in the service and it was just like I left it when I came back. It was a good car, but somewhere along the way it quit on us, just quit running. We were way up on the mountain, not too far from Blue Ridge, and the engine died on me, so I steered it over to the side of the road just as it coasted to a stop. I got out of the car and raised the hood.

It was an unusually cold day in early November, bright and sunny. There wasn't a cloud in the sky nowhere. North wind was really a blowin', it would just cut you. The pant legs of my uniform were a flappin' against my legs. The sound of a woodpecker drilling into a tree gave me a start. For just a moment, I got that feelin' that I should watch my back. It had been nearly six months since I'd heard automatic gunfire. The scar from that sniper on my right hand was still easy to see. I reached into the engine and started checking on things.

I had to get that car fixed. Law, the four of us couldn't get stranded up on the mountain in the cold, but I wasn't worried. I'd made up my mind that I was gonna get married to my sweetheart and I had to get us to the justice of the peace. I couldn't let a little thing like a car breaking down mess up the most important day in two couples' lives.

Back then, I liked to fool with cars so much, I'd learned a lot about them. I was really up on the engines that they had and I figured I could fix it. I think it was something wrong with either wiring that had come loose, or something about the firing order with the spark plugs. I had it fixed in a few minutes.

"Atlas, start the car!" The spark caught and the engine started right up. I had it a goin'!

"Tank boy!" Atlas saluted with a big grin.

The girls laughed and everyone was in a glad-hearted mood. We were able to drive on to Blue Ridge.

We got down there looking for the justice of the peace. We drove up, found his house. We didn't know if there was anybody at home, so we started hollering, "Hello! Hello!" You didn't just venture up and go to knocking on the door.

His name was Judge Stiles. Yeah, the Honorable Judge Stiles of Blue Ridge, Georgia. The old judge was really nice. We called him out on a Sunday, which wasn't customary. I don't remember why Atlas and Bertha decided to get married on a Sunday, but they made the arrangements.

We asked the judge to marry us, a double wedding.

He lived pretty close to the office he worked out of. He told us to go down to his office and he'd meet us there in a few minutes.

When he came down to his office, he took Atlas and me aside and he said to us in a real serious way, "I'm gonna tell you somethin' that I don't like to do. I don't like to perform marriage ceremonies on servicemen, because as long as they're in the army, you never know what's goin' to happen to them." He looked us straight in the eye and went on. "Now, boys, I'll tell you, I don't like to marry servicemen because a lot of times, they're away from home and they don't really know what they want to do. And the marriage doesn't usually last too long. They get dissatisfied because they weren't thoroughly convinced that it was the thing to do. I don't like to do that. I'd feel a lot better if both of you were out of the service."

I remember what he said, oh, yeah. I thought we were gonna have to find somebody else to marry us. He said, "I'd feel a lot better if you didn't ask me to do it."

But we insisted on it. We had driven that far and we were determined. We reminded him that we'd be discharged soon and we wanted to get started with our lives.

"Well, that might be true," he said. "But it's a very serious decision you're making about two lives when you get married. It's not to be entered into lightly."

I don't know what we told that judge, exactly, but Atlas and I must have told him that we had gotten to know our brides-to-be over several years and we convinced him that we loved them and we knew we wanted to spend the rest of our lives with them.

"Well," he said, "if you insist on it, I will do it."

I said, "Well, we come a long ways to get that done. We want it done."

"Who's first?" the judge said.

Bertha nudged Orangie. "You go first."

"Yeah," Atlas joined in, "Quinton, you an' Orangie get hitched first."

I was eager. I looked over at Orangie, and for a moment, she looked like she might have to think it over. Then she smiled. She said, "Let's get married!" So, after we'd got the justice of the peace to agree to marry us, we got married first.

A lot of people back then during the war got married quick. They didn't go in for parties and fancy ceremonies and all that. They'd take a

Wedding Day 1945: Quinton and Orangie in Blue Ridge, Georgia

notion to get married and they'd go and ask some preacher or judge to marry them and it was done.

So that's how it was that Orangie and I were married in a double wedding along with Atlas and Bertha Davis on November 4, 1945. I married Orangie because she was just on my mind, I reckon. I decided I wasn't going to look for anybody else. I thought about her a lot of times before I went overseas, and in Europe, too. We got to know each other writing letters during the war. I knew she was a good woman. And she was just as pretty as a picture. She had a real tiny waist—I could circle my hands around her waist, press in, and get my fingers to touch.

I might not have been the only soldier who wrote to her and hoped she'd be their sweetheart, but she was mine. I don't know what she saw in me, an ol' Tennessee mountain boy, but I got the little girl I wanted. My South Texas cowgirl.

Orangie didn't tell anybody that she was gonna get married. When she told Mamie she was married, Mamie told Orangie, "I believe you picked a good one." Mamie Murphy always was real nice to me. I always liked her.

I didn't tell my family the night before either, the idea came up so quick. They didn't know I'd gotten married until we got back. They knew there wasn't no use to say nothin', after we'd already tied the knot. My dad wished us a happy life together and made a few comments like that, and my mother, too. I believe my dad might have said, "Son, I want you to be good to your wife." But that was something he didn't have to tell me.

The army went to making preparations to discharge us, since they didn't need us any longer. Of course, they offered you the opportunity to sign up to be there regular if you wanted to. But I'd had enough of that army life forever.

I had to go all the way back to California to get discharged. Orangie went with me. We rode the train together.

I didn't return to Camp Beale where I'd learned to be a tank driver. In fact, I was no longer a part of the 13th Armored Division which I was so proud of. Created for World War II, the 13th Armored Division was inactivated November 15, 1945. Now it was peacetime, and its purpose had been served. The 13th Armored Division, "California's Own," was also World War II's own and it was associated with just one theater of action: Nazi Germany at the closing months of the war. Our casualties in those battles were tragic, but they were a lot less than they could have been because of when and where we saw action. Lucky 13th, I reckon.

I was not officially discharged yet, so the army transferred me to another outfit at Camp Cooke and they kept us out there for a couple of months. They couldn't discharge everybody at the same time, the separation centers were so crowded.

Around camp, they just let us do what we wanted, about it. They'd give us calisthenics in the morning and they had us doing duties around camp to keep us busy. Of course, we did have guard duty at night, just like we did during the war.

I'd found a hotel that was reasonable and it looked after servicemen's wives. Orangie stayed there. I'd go home to that hotel at night.

When I pulled guard duty the first time, one of the boys in there said something about it, said, "You gonna have to walk guard tonight, ain't you?"

I said, "Yeah."

He said, "No, you ain't. I'll take your guard duty for you. You go on home."

I said, "Well, if you make it right with the sergeant of the guard, I'll be glad for you to do it."

He said, "I'll take care of that."

Several of the boys were really nice to me when they found out I had my wife with me out there. They just came to me and said, "I'd like to take your guard duty, so you can go into town and be with your wife."

I thought that was awful nice of them. They just volunteered. I never asked them. I didn't have to walk guard no more.

Yeah, we thought a lot of each other. It was just more or less, got to bein' like a big family. You just felt about as close to those boys as you did your own family. The majority of them were really nice. We'd been through a lot together. Some of them would really bend over backwards for you.

Wherever we'd been inducted into the army, they sent us back to that region to get discharged. I was discharged from the U.S. Army on February 12, 1946, at the separation center at Fort McPherson, Georgia, and I went back home to Tennessee with Orangie by my side.

The year 1946 was looking like a year of freedom and possibilities as high as the sky. I could breathe free, stretch out and get a move on. Really kick up my heels, so to say. It was like that long-awaited first warm day of the year when I was just a boy out on Coker Creek, and I'd take my shoes off and see how fast I could run. Now I was free of that army life, I was a newlywed and ready to start my own family. Of course,

I needed a job. I was fresh out of the military and you don't hardly have nothin' when you're in there.

Before we were discharged, the army gave us a talk and they'd told us about getting back into civilian life. "Plastic, that's the wave of the future," they said. "Go into the plastics industry."

Well, I'd never heard anything about plastic before and I couldn't imagine what that would lead to. So I dusted off my green wooden tool-box and prepared to finish my training to become a journeyman carpenter, where I could work with my hands. TVA'd told me, "You'll have a job when you come back."

I went to the main TVA office in Knoxville and they told me, "We're sorry, we're not hiring now."

Some men that I knew went up to the TVA Fontana dam site in North Carolina and got hired as temporary labor. So I took my tool-box and went up there. I got hired for a few weeks, and Orangie and I moved up there near the site in a little travel trailer.

One day, the carpenter foreman came along and said to me, "Get in the truck with me. Come with me to the personnel office." I didn't know what he wanted.

He said, "I don't know why they haven't hired you back."

We went down there and he told them, "This boy was a carpenter's apprentice when he went into the military. I want him to have his job back so he can continue his trade."

And TVA hired me permanently. Put me back on the carpenter apprentice program and I continued my education to be a journeyman carpenter. At the same time, I worked on the Fontana dam site. At 480 feet high, that dam was the highest dam in the TVA system, and the highest concrete dam east of the Rocky Mountains. I did all sorts of carpentry on facilities around that beautiful Fontana dam site. I took pride in doing the best job I could, 'cause I've always been that way.

It was now April 1946, and I hadn't been back from the war even a year. We were livin' up at Fontana, and Orangie and I had been married about six months and we were already expecting our first child, when one day that April, I got the shock of my life.

Archie and two of my other cousins came out all that way to see me, up in the North Carolina mountains. They'd hitched a ride part of the way, and walked the rest. They came walking up to the trailer late in the day. I thought that was unusual.

I said, "Well! What are you fellers a doin' up here?!"

"Oh, we just come up to visit with you a little bit. We're just lookin' around . . ."

I could tell something was different, three of my cousins showin' up there in the evening, but I couldn't tell what it was.

They just talked to me a little bit about the weather, seemed to have something on their minds.

Then Archie said, "Quinton, I've got some real bad news for you. Uncle Willie has died." That's what he called my dad.

Boy, that hurt me somethin' awful. Just like bein' punched in the stomach. I couldn't hardly believe it. I just went into spasms, crying, and they just about had to hold me up.

Archie told me, "He had one of them spells again and had to lie down, and your mother sent for the doctor down in Tellico. The doctor came out and he gave him a shot right in his heart. And he died nearly before the doctor even got outta sight of the house. Your mother's takin' it real hard."

Orangie and I got our stuff together and we all piled into my car and I drove us to Coker Creek.

My dad had a heart attack, we reckoned. He'd had different spells before when I was growin' up, where he'd start sweating, and maybe vomit and have to lie down. He'd lie down on the front porch, and he'd be all red and wet with sweat, and we children used to worry ourselves to death runnin' back and forth carryin' water from the spring and we'd throw buckets of water all around the porch to try to cool off the air, to cool him down. We didn't know what else to do.

If we called for the doctor to come up from Tellico Plains, the doctor would always tell him it was "acute indigestion." My dad wouldn't be able to work for a day or two and then he'd get to feeling better. We never did think much about it back then.

Of course, we didn't know what we know today about diet and all that. My dad favored gravies and lard and bacon. He'd have my mother pour a little more hot grease from the pan onto his food. But he wasn't a heavy man, because he worked it off. He'd work in the field a long, long day. He'd seemed in pretty good health when he died. He died way too soon — age fifty-six. I never was so broken up in all my life.

My Uncle Edd Lee got out there in the field looking around after my dad died and he said he'd figured out what probably brought on that heart attack. He told us that he saw where my dad had been plowing with his new horse.

My dad had traded ol' Joe-Boy — that red mule had gone gray, he was gettin' pretty old by that time, and my dad liked him so much, he didn't want to watch him get feeble and have to put him down. So my dad traded him off for a young horse that was spirited.

The man who sold him that young horse told him it had been broke to work, and it had. But not as well as ol' Joe-Boy. That new horse wanted to race along. My uncle said that before my dad fell to his knees in the dirt, he had been taking strides more than three feet long, to keep up with that young horse. It was too much for him. He didn't know he had a bad heart, but it gave out on him. Yeah, they said he "had a bad heart," but we never knew for sure, of course. What I did know for sure was that my dad had the biggest, gladdest heart of anybody I ever knew.

Now, the thing of it was, when he had that last sick spell, it scared my mother and she called for the doctor down in Tellico Plains to come up to the homeplace, but they didn't send the usual one. They had a new, young doctor down there, and they sent the new one. We hadn't heard of him before — or since. I've always thought that doctor did the wrong thing by giving my dad a shot in the heart, 'cause my mother said he was dead about as soon as that doctor was out of sight of the house. Now, I don't know if that shot had anything to do with my dad dyin' like he did, but I've always thought it did.

Orangie and I stayed at the old homeplace out on Coker Creek for the funeral. The church was swelled to burstin' with people from all over Coker Creek and Tellico Plains who knew my dad.

That was one of my last visits to the homeplace while it was still standing. My little black dog was there, too, and I think he knew Will Kelley wasn't coming back. He laid around a lot and looked up at us with sad eyes. We gave him to Edd Lee after that. I couldn't take him with me where I was living, and besides, he belonged on Coker Creek. I've had some other dogs from time to time, but they didn't take the place of that little black dog. He was just special to me. That dog lived a long, long time, got to be a real old dog.

Oh, I liked to remember my dad playin' with that dog every evenin', in the twilight, sittin' out on the front porch. He'd have that dog on his lap in a minute. That dog would just look up at him and turn his head.

Dad'd say, "Come on up here!" and he'd slap his leg and that dog would just jump up and lie down in his lap, and he'd keep that dog there for an hour or two. He'd pinch the dog's toes, and that dog would jerk his feet back and my dad would just fool with him like that.

My dad was a tenderhearted man and he always liked to pick up puppies or kittens. And he'd always ask to hold the babies that women brought to church. He'd carry them around, talk to 'em. Children just loved him.

As a child, I would always look forward to snow 'cause my dad would always go out there in the yard with us kids and we'd have us a snowball fight, three against one. My sisters and I would pelt him with snowballs till he'd say, "All right, now, you're gonna have to quit." We'd be squealin' with delight, a hittin' him with that snow. And he'd say, "All right, you better quit it, now . . . All right, quit, that's enough." He'd just have to make us stop.

We'd all go home a laughin', out of breath. Oh, my father was full of love, a real giving man. But he was simple, really an old mountaineer. He would have been like a fish out of water in the city. He knew that, too, and wouldn't take a trip anywhere. He never traveled out of Tennessee his whole life.

He never had the opportunity to get much of an education. But he was clever and smart. He'd figure out all kinds of carpentry and construction, and people would come to him from all over the countryside to have him figure out how to build different buildings. He was just self-taught, but he did about the best work around the Coker Creek community, and he'd done work for nearly everybody in those hills.

A lot of people have used that term "hillbilly" to refer to some of the fellers of Scottish or Irish descent—the Williams, Wills, and Bills and all their kin—who immigrated to this country and moved back in the rural areas, especially in the South. William Marion Kelley was what you'd call a hillbilly all right—poorly educated and isolated up in the Tennessee hills—but he was a big hero to his family and the Coker Creek community in general, because of how he chose to conduct himself, because of his character as a man, and what he stood for.

To me, the real hero isn't always the brave man on the battlefield. My cousins, and all the boys I knew who served in the war, we didn't feel like heroes at all—we were just soldiers who'd had jobs to do. I know the word "hero" is used a lot and I wouldn't want to diminish all the war heroes who gave their limbs or their lives in sacrifice for their country, no sir. But to me, for all those years growin' up, I only knew one hero—my daddy. I think the very first idea of a hero that a boy has is his daddy. And how a man lives his life day to day is what sets him apart as someone worth lookin' up to.

Everyone in the community liked Will Kelley. No one ever had a negative thing to say about him, I don't reckon. He took good care of his family. He was strong, but about as gentle as a man could be, too. And he was honest in every dealing.

"Quinton," he used to say, "tell the truth even if it hurts you."

I was always proud of my father. Will Kelley was known all over the community as upright and dependable. He was just the same from one day to the next, and with every person that he'd meet. If he told you something, that's the way it was. He was really a "good'un," as we used to say.

Of course, my cousins like Archie and Atlas, they were proud of their fathers, too—Edd Lee Kelley and Jim (James) Davis—my uncles. My uncles were fine men, brought up like my father was, and those cousins, well, they were 'bout like me. I never did know of them getting into trouble.

In our families, our fathers built the foundations of everything, from our dwelling houses to our character. They taught us the way we should go, and when we were old enough to leave home and go serve our country, we didn't depart from that. We made good soldiers and good citizens because our fathers taught us to be good men. They showed us by their deeds what kind of men to be. And we listened to their attitudes without even realizin' it, and that guided us.

Shoot, lookin' back, I learned more from my father than I did from anything else in life. I tried my best at livin' up to what he taught me, too, starting with the attitude I had when I did service for my country in World War II, and with my own family, carryin' on my father's example as much as I could through life in general. I believe it was the best way to honor his memory. And, law, I miss him. I tell you, I'd give anything to talk to him just one more time.

I have heard people say they had a hard time sleepin' for months and years after they came back from World War II. It never did bother me, though. I soon forgot all that, when I got back. In fact, I hardly ever thought about the war unless someone asked me about it. But, of course, I never did anything that went against my integrity over there. No, if I'd done a lot of mean things, like some of them did, I guess it would have bothered me.

But the thrill of comin' back home after the war, gettin' married, makin' a home, startin' a job and a family, that took up my attention pretty fast. My first daughter was born four months after my father died and the wheel of life revolved another turn. Life is just like that. Someone passes on and someone else comes along to fill the space. With all that goin' on, oh, yeah, pretty soon the blasts and bullets of wartime Germany kind of drifted away.

But sometimes when I have a fever, I dream. It's the only time I ever have nightmares. The only time that it ever bothers me, the things that went on over there, was if I was to get sick and run a temperature — then I'd dream all night about combat. For some reason, it causes the war to come back to me maybe even more horrible than it was and it was pretty horrific. That seems strange; no matter how old I get, it just seems like I am right over there back into it.

It's nerve-racking and hard on you and dangerous and everything else and you don't seem to gain very much and then it's all over, said, and done. Of course, we did put ol' Hitler down. That was one good thing. But just think what it took to do that. All those lives and homes wrecked in so many places. And besides the dead, a lot of crippled boys — some of them were invalids the rest of their life. That's the way war is. Of course, every one of them is a little worse than the one before. If we were to have another big one, they might use nuclear power and it'd be a lot worse. I don't want to see anybody go through war and all that stuff. It's something that stays in your mind, you can't get it out. But thankfully, when I do dream those bad dreams, I wake up from it and then it could be years and it won't bother me any other time. I'll never even think of it.

I never talked about the war after I came back. Never did tell anybody much about what went on over there, unless somebody asked me a question and I tried to answer it. I'm just telling the story now because my youngest daughter asked me about it, and it's part of history, so it needs to be told.

There are things an old soldier can tell a young one. From the beginning of my service, I always thought, "I'll make it back." I always figured I'd be back home and never worried a bit about not making it. Even on the darkest days of battle, I never had the slightest doubt. I always thought I was gonna make it.

Back then, I talked to a lot of other boys who got drafted and they'd say things like, "Well, there's one thing about it, if I ever go overseas, I'll never make it, myself. I've just felt that way all the time — I'll never make it back home."

Most of the time, the ones that talked that way, they didn't make it. That's strange. But that's the way that I found it to be. It pretty well worked out the way they had it pictured.

If they didn't have no hopes of ever makin' it, most of the time something would happen to them. Maybe they didn't protect themselves enough or something, I don't know. It may have been just something instilled in them, that told them they wouldn't make it. 'Cause you know a lot of them have to give their lives in a war, 'cause if nobody gave their life, it never would end a war, would it? So that's just the way it is. Sad. We sacrifice in one generation to ensure peace for the next generations — hopefully.

Now, while I always felt like I'd make it, of course, I realize you don't ever know what's going to happen to you in a war. But I felt that way then, and I've felt that way whatever I've done down through life. I've always just had that kind of faith. I think it's due to my parents. My parents were real good people. They brought me up to go to church. And the teaching that I got from the Bible, it gives me great confidence that whatever happens is supposed to be that way and that I'm gonna make it, whatever the situation is. And sometimes the situation has been pretty tough. But if you just go around thinking you're gonna get killed the next day, well, something's liable to happen to you. So you don't want to let those negative thoughts get you down. I always try to look above that part of life.

About fifteen to twenty young men related to me — first cousins and distant cousins — they went to serve in World War II and about all of them made it back. Most of the boys from Coker Creek that served in the war did pretty well over there.

I think it was our upbringing that helped us most. In my way of thinking, we all grew up in such rugged conditions that we had better protection for ourselves than the boys who grew up in the civilized areas. I believe that had a lot to do with it. We were brought up rough and learned from the earliest age to take care of ourselves pretty well. You have to take care of yourself first. It's okay to look out for other people, but your instinct has to be to look out for your own survival.

Of my cousins who served, I believe the only one to get wounded was the cousin who was like a twin to me, Archie Kelley. He had to live the rest of his life with a handicap. He'd stayed in that hospital in Memphis for a long time, and when they bandaged up Archie's hand, they kept changing the angle a little at a time until they got it almost straight, but Archie was always crippled pretty bad in that left hand.

He was right-handed. He could work, but after that, he wasn't very good at the banjo anymore. He could still play a little bit, but he didn't want people to hear him. He just couldn't make his fingers work like they used to. It was hard for him, and at first, he tried to get back to his old playin' style, but after a while he realized, I reckon, that he was gonna be crippled forever in the hand he made the notes with, and he never did play the banjo as much after that.

But Archie turned out to have a real good life—for quite a few years. He and his wife, Gwendolyn, lived out there on Coker Creek and they were just crazy for each other. They eventually had fourteen children. Some years later, though, when he was still fairly young, Archie was in a tractor accident.

Archie had been working in timber, had his tractor out dragging logs with several fellers. At end of the day, Archie took his tractor and drove it up the mountain. He didn't say anything to the fellers he worked with about it. He just took off and that was unusual.

Up there on that mountain road, somebody came along later and found him pinned under his overturned tractor. Whoever found him said that Archie had a little toolbox with saws and files and tools for cutting logs, and they found that toolbox sitting up on the bank along the road. People figured he'd gotten off the tractor for some reason, left it idling, and set that toolbox down. Then the tractor must have started rolling and Archie ran to stop it and the tractor got on uneven ground and just turned over on him. I think it crushed his head.

Why he would have driven up to that high ridge, where he had no business a bein', gotten off the tractor and set his toolbox off on a bank by the side of the road, is a mystery that baffled people on Coker Creek. Because of that, some of the superstitious people said they felt like

Archie was just drawn to his fate, that it was "meant to be." I don't know about that, but that's what people on Coker Creek said and they must've talked about that for years.

Boy, when I got the news that Archie was dead, it hurt me more than anybody will ever know. I never did get over it. Archie was a wonderful friend. We grew up together and he was just like a brother to me.

My cousin from my mother's side, Atlas Davis, he was one of those lucky ones that got through the war real well, and life, too, I reckon. He never changed, stayed just as slim and carried himself well, like always. He and his wife, Bertha, had one daughter. Bertha never liked her husband bein' called Atlas, for some reason. After they were married, she had everybody to call him by his first name, Herbert. But he'll always be Atlas to me.

Atlas always said, "I'd never live no place but Coker Creek, Tennessee." He and Bertha still live on Coker Creek to this day, on a real pretty spread they call the Peacock Ranch. Atlas has peafowls around their house, and they'll shake those bright blue-and-green tail feathers and they'll squall, oh, it's a sight how they'll squall.

Atlas has always been the one to look after the local cemeteries, to keep the graves trimmed neat, especially the veterans. I try to go out there for Decoration Day—that's a holiday when everybody comes from all over the country to put flowers on the graves. The people of Coker Creek usually dedicate a Sunday in June for honoring the kin that have passed on. That's an old tradition that's been going on for years and years, way back before my time and my grandparents' time, probably. People always recognized their kin and they'd go out there to see that their graves were cleaned off and that flowers were put on them. Oh, it's a sight, all the colors of the flowers—just bunches of 'em, crowded all the way up the slope of the cemetery.

Atlas probably never did miss a Decoration Day, I don't reckon. He comes to talk with people and still gets a gleam in his eyes when he tells stories of his service during World War II. We can still laugh together about life in the army.

I always had a good, jolly time whoever I was with in the army. I'd joke with them, and they'd joke with me and we just had a good time together. The boys I served with, they just seemed like family to me, too, as much as Archie or Atlas. I really hated to see the day that I was separated from my army buddies, 'cause I knew how life was. I said to myself, "Well, I'll never see them no more."

The first one that comes to my mind is my tank commander, of course. But of the ones who survived the war that were real close friends, I figured I wouldn't get to see them any more in this life either. They were from different parts of the country, each one of them, and they had stories to tell about their families, so I felt like I knew their families, but I didn't meet their families. Sure enough, there've been a very few of my army buddies that I have seen since we got discharged.

One boy from our company, Darvie C. McAbee—our tank's loader and radio operator and my sidekick in New York City—he came out to Coker Creek to try to find me after the war, but he never got to see me.

He asked my sister-in-law, Mamie, down at the store, if she knew where to find me. Mamie told him, "He doesn't live here anymore. He's working up at Fontana, in North Carolina."

Orangie and I went down to the town in South Carolina that McAbee was from, but I never could find him listed in the telephone directory. He never could find where I was and I didn't know how to find him. I hated that I never did get to see him again.

By incredible coincidence, I ran into Winfred Knode, our tank's gunner, just a few years after the war, on Main Street in Elizabethton, Tennessee. We never were so happy to see each other. He was married to a real nice girl from there and I'd just built my first home in nearby Bluff City, 'cause I was working for TVA on Watagua Dam by then. Knode and I found ourselves living in the same area of Tennessee for a little while. We kept in touch for many years at Christmastime, but ol' Winfred, he kept on smokin' those cigarettes like a chimney, and eventually he lost a battle with lung cancer.

★ ★ ★

Lonnie Johnson:

The greatest regret I've got out of the whole thing was Donald Crouch's wife wrote me a letter to ask me how he got killed. That was way back a year or two after the war, and I never have been able to find her address or get with her anymore. At that time, I figured it might be better if she didn't know. And I never did answer her letter and tell her exactly what happened. I've been through life and tried my best to do the best I could, but a lot of times you don't do the right thing. You don't at the time, when it don't seem like you ought to do it. The Lord'll forgive us for that, I hope. (12)

Now, ol' Lonnie Johnson, tank driver, and the big cutup of our organization, he's one who kept up with me a little bit over the years. Early in 1949, Lonnie got in touch with me. He said he had started going by his middle name, Edward, after the war. "I'm just plain ol' Ed Johnson now," he said.

Johnson used to like to gamble a lot in the army, I remember that, but that's the only thing out of the way about him. Well, when he contacted me, he said he'd gotten his life straightened out and he had a wonderful wife and a happy family and he was really blessed. He said he'd joined a local church where he lived in North Carolina and he invited me to come to his church for a special service.

Johnson said, "This church I joined, we're gonna have a foot washin' service, would you go with me? You don't have to participate, but it'd sure mean a lot to me if you'd come to the service."

I did. I didn't participate, but I saw that night that Lonnie—Ed Johnson—had changed and I was glad he'd invited me to see his commitment to a new way of life.

"I never did like mule-faced religion," he told me. "You know, worshiping with a long-drawn chin. But, Quinton, I saw from you that it doesn't have to be that way. You can have a good time and still be an upright person." And he told me that seeing the way I lived really affected him. I never imagined that he'd think about it like that, but he did. And that really surprised me, but that's what he said. I reckon if you do the right thing, sometimes it'll actually rub off on other people.

I didn't hear from Ed Johnson again for decades. I never joined any veterans' groups. I got so tired of that army, that war, I was glad to get away from it. We were all so glad to get away from that stuff. We wanted to forget it all. Nobody, I don't think, was too interested in keeping up with army buddies then. In later years, though, that changed.

Ed Johnson:

Kelley and I slept within a bed or two of one another all the time we was in the army. Three years, and we's just like brothers. I would say that Kelley influenced my life, sure enough. He was a Christian when he was young and I was a sinner. And by him bein' a friend, and not takin' part in drinkin' a can of beer, or cursin' or swearin' or carryin' on, I have thought about him. He was a great influence on my life. And I appreciate that greatly. I joined a church in 1949 and I've tried to live a life like I thought he was a livin'.

Kelley influenced me more than anybody else. 'Cause I found out through him that you could live a good life and be honest and truthful with everybody. I've thought about him a many a time. And tell him not to change either.

A lot of people tell me I don't look like I'm eighty-eight. But you know, beauty fades fast, ugly stays with you.

— **Lonnie Edward Johnson, Selma, North Carolina;**
interviewed by S. L. Kelley 2/28/2008 (12)

It was also in 1949—December—that Coker Creek finally got to have lights. TVA brought electricity out there four years after I'd moved away. I heard about it, of course, and saw the changes when I went to visit, but I never did live on Coker Creek again.

By then, I had finished TVA's apprentice program, took four years to finish it. When I completed it, I was a journeyman carpenter.

During my training, I'd worked on different dams and power facilities for TVA, including Appalachia Dam, my first; Fontana Dam over in North Carolina; Watagua Dam at Elizabethton; and facilities at South Holston.

At that time, Orangie and I had two children, a daughter and son, and we were living in a big old two-story farmhouse in Rogersville, Tennessee. I worked as a carpenter in the maintenance department of TVA's John Sevier Steam Plant in Rogersville on hourly.

They announced one day that they were hiring a carpenter for a permanent maintenance position. I went to apply, and didn't think I had a chance when I heard the boss say, "I think every man who's worked here at this plant has applied for that position. We've had at least two hundred carpenters who've worked here who want it." But he put my name down. He told me, "When the time comes, we'll go over the list and decide."

One day they called me and asked if I was still interested, and said, "We've decided you're the man we want." I took the position and stayed with TVA for the rest of my employed years.

I worked with some fine men out there at the steam plant. I always chose who I associated with pretty carefully. One of the men I worked with invited me to join the Freemasons, an outstanding organization, and I eventually became a 32nd Degree Mason.

The Freemasons are an ancient organization. They teach you how to treat your fellow man, how to be upright in all your dealings. It's things people ought to know naturally, but they don't. If a real Freemason tells you something, well, you can bank on it bein' just the way he said. Freemasonry is about honor, charitable deeds, and quiet good works. It's a place for honest men. The better man you are, the better Mason you'll be. If you're not honest, you've got no place in the Freemasons. Every now and then, somebody will get in there who's not honest; the others will find that out pretty soon and then that feller's just out in the cold. You couldn't go in there with ten million dollars and buy your way in, your character's what gets you in. I'll be a Freemason until I die, and every day I continue to follow their teachings.

★ ★ ★

In 1962, I built a custom home in a small town in East Tennessee, and Orangie and I have lived there ever since. We eventually had three children, and later on came their children and *their* children.

TVA finally moved me up to the powerhouse at John Sevier Steam Plant, which was the best place to work, and I did all the maintenance around there for a long time. Over the years, one by one, TVA had let the carpenters go as our building projects were finished and they needed carpenters less and less. They never did let me go, or ask me to retire. In fact, in the last few years out there, I was the last carpenter—just me and my helper. By then, I 'bout ran out of little jobs to do, everything was working so well, so one day I just said, "Well, I guess I'll retire."

My boss talked like it just about broke his heart and he tried to talk me out of it. Well, some people just do a job to be done with it. But I think TVA liked to keep me around because I always did everything as near perfect as I knew how.

After I left, TVA locked up my shop and they did away with my position and they said, "Everybody'll have to do their own maintenance work from now on." TVA gave me a little card saying forty-two years of service, counting my time served during World War II, which was thirty-nine months.

Like my dad, I always liked to work for myself, too. As a journeyman carpenter, I did a lot of woodworking over the years. I really enjoyed crafting fine furniture out of walnut, mahogany, oak, and cherry, smoothing and varnishing their finishes. I used to build custom furniture for people—cabinets, tables, bookcases—in my own workshop, a red brick building that houses all my woodworking tools, kind of like my father's blacksmith shop.

Like my dad, I built some houses. I built two for myself. I built a children's day care center for my wife, which she ran as a successful business for many years. After I retired, my friends wanted me to build some houses for them, and I built several houses for the first four or five years,

Quinton and Orangie, in their mid-eighties, revisit the site of their courtship, Bald River Falls, Tellico Plains, Tennessee.

did finish carpentry. Then I decided, if I'm really gonna retire, I'll have to quit that.

I kept my love of driving down through the years. Orangie and I traveled the highways of America, and over the decades, we explored mountains, deserts, plains, and seashores. I drove Chevrolets, Fords, and Chryslers and, in later years, I pulled an Airstream RV. Sometimes we'd go in a caravan, a big long line of silver trailers, just like a military convoy, only we were heading down the highway to enjoy someplace beautiful.

In all, Orangie calculated that I've driven over 400,000 miles on vacations, traversing the countryside from Maine to Florida, from Washington State to Southern California, and through nearly all of the states in between, in this big, free country that I love to call home.

This was a new kind of life for me, one a lot easier than my childhood, but it echoed what I grew up with—hard work and commitment to faith and family. I'd had ponies for my daughters, flew kites with my children, and read them bedtime stories. I kept up the tradition of building and driving go-carts with my son and we did some squirrel hunting together when he was a boy.

I always tried to be a good husband to Orangie, the way my dad, Will, had been to his beloved Verdie. I'm glad I met Orangie while I was living on Coker Creek, and got to know her, really, when I was away in service, through her letters. We got along real good together. I knew I'd met a wonderful person, and I loved her then and I love her today. We've been together all these years and I hope to spend many more together.

I always tried to give my family the love that I had seen and felt as a boy, though not particularly thinking about it in that sense, but I tried to do the right thing, like my parents before me, and evidently it must have helped because today I've got a wonderful family and, boy, I'm thankful for that.

Epilogue

I'm an old man now, well into my eighties, and when I got older in life, I realized I was glad that I'd stuck to what I'd been taught growin' up. It served me well, clean livin', and it was good for my family. I've been really blessed because our home and family life has always been a great source of comfort and pride to me. I'm proud of all my children, of course, but I'm especially proud that my son is a U.S. veteran, too. He served his country in the U.S. Air Force in the Vietnam War. He also retired from a lifelong career with TVA, like his father.

Of course, like most people looking back, I do have a few regrets. I wish I could have spent more time with my young family when I was starting out and having to earn a living, but I tried to spend as much time with them as I could. And I wish I'd used the G.I. Bill to advance my education after the war.

As for the war, I have no regrets about my actions; thankfully, I still sleep well at night. Sure, I wish I'd crossed the Inn River to see Hitler's hideout so I could tell my grandchildren about it. And I still think about givin' up that German Luger, too—my Luger, with the holster and the extra clip—oh, can't tell you how many times I've thought about that. But those things don't matter.

I do have one real regret from the war, though. I've always wished that I had visited or at least called my tank commander's family after I came home from the war to tell them how their fine son, brother, and husband died a hero.

I've thought about it a lot of times. I would have told them who I was and I would have said, "I've got firsthand information if you want it . . ."

And I'd a told them just what happened, how Donald died aiming to protect all of us in his tank crew. I've said many, many times in my life that I wished I had called the family 'cause I thought a lot of Donald and I knew he had family that lived in Kansas, and he had a wife and he had a little girl. But I never could bring myself to contact them. Every time I thought about it, I'd think, "Well, I'll just be bringin' them information that'll cause them to be upset all over again." And I hated to do that. But now that I'm older, I can see that it would have been a help to them. Every time I'd see some military men somewhere down through the years, I'd think about Donald Crouch. I didn't do what I should've done, and that always bothered me. I wondered if his family ever received that .45 pistol with his notches on it.

Donald Crouch didn't get the chance to be a good father to his little girl. It was his supreme sacrifice and her great loss. I know he really wished he could have seen his daughter that last chance he had, he told me that. I've long wished I could tell her just how much he thought of her. She may be out there somewhere today, I don't know, but she never knew her daddy. I doubt she ever knew how he died, rolling through the exploding Bavarian countryside, choosing to risk himself to keep his crew safe and losing his life in the last battle that we had.

Over the decades, I hardly ever thought about the war, and never talked much about it until recently. But, as you get older, you get more tenderhearted, and things like that get to you when you get to thinking about them. And you do get to thinkin' about 'em.

I drove a tank through firefights in the streets of Nazi Germany, and I can still see the jerks and quivers of a shot and dying soldier so clear that it could be right outside my window, in the street. It's just like yesterday when I get to thinkin' about it. I can hear those shells a whizzin' by, just as plain. For some reason, you don't forget somethin' like that. I'll forget somebody's name or where they're from, but I sure don't forget that war. It made an impression. Knowing that death was whistling over my head. It seemed like death was right close by.

I try not to dwell on any of it. No matter how it came out for me, a lot of men—some of them my real good buddies—lost their lives in

World War II. Over 400,000 American soldiers never came home to their mothers and fathers and families after that war.

I was one of the lucky ones. It seemed I had been lucky in everything during that war. Chosen to drive a tank instead of running around on foot with a gun. Assigned to mop up after major battles instead of leading the charge. Getting that two years of training instead of the few weeks some other boys had. And those shells and bullets that ruffled my hair and grazed my skin—miraculous timing, for which I thank a Higher Power.

I believe my faith in God and my positive attitude helped get me through the war with the fewest scars. I believe that the way a person chooses to live life makes a difference. And this philosophy has served me well ever since.

There are times in life, though, when that's still not enough. Sometimes things turn sour in unexpected ways, and all the faith and strength you can muster up doesn't seem to help and then you need one thing more. One thing that only someone else can give you.

In 2001, I had minor outpatient surgery. The surgery date fell on the 22nd—two-two, numbers which had always favored me. But instead of the expected quick recovery, there were complications. I contracted not one but *three* infections that left me fighting for my life, on morphine and unconscious, in the intensive care unit of a large hospital. I had to undergo repeated surgeries as the infection spread and it was resisting the antibiotics.

I remember nothing of the early part of this ordeal—thankfully—though my family has explained every detail to me since, and it is clear that I probably should not have survived. When this happened, I was seventy-nine years old.

My family later told me that when I came to, I had said from my hospital bed—probably half out of my mind on drugs—"Why don't you just let me die?"

My devoted wife and children were determined not to let that happen. They were just sick about what had happened to me and they did everything they could to help me. Throughout the slow months of my recovery, they rotated in shifts and stayed with me around the clock, holding my hand, reading and singing to me, praying, questioning the doctors, doing their own research, feeding me all sorts of health drinks, and generally keeping my spirits up when they lagged.

Once I got well enough to know what was going on, I never did worry. I never doubted that everything would turn out all right, and it did. It was a long road before I got back in good health, but all along, my family looked out for me and their love and support helped me to pull through to a successful recovery. Sometimes, you can only do so much by yourself, and in the end it is love that makes all the difference.

Love of family, love of God, love of country—these fill my heart. Though today I live comfortably but modestly, I feel that I have always been a rich man—richly blessed with the love of my family and friends. I am grateful, too, that I was raised in a home with an abundance of love and that feeling has never left me, even though not much else exists from my childhood on Coker Creek.

After my recovery, I made a visit back to the site of my old homeplace and I hardly recognized it. Of course, the ol' homeplace is gone now. Gone, just like that pioneer way of life I enjoyed so much.

Where the land was once cleared, I peeped through underbrush and tried to figure out where things had been. Gone was the little shack that was my daddy's ol' blacksmith shop where I'd spent many a busy hour. Gone, too, were the old barns, the chicken coop, the springhouse, the corncrib, and any other sign that we ever lived there. Even the old corn and cane fields were grown up in tall timber now.

I had a hard time locating the site of our log cabin, until I spotted the two oaks that had once flanked our front porch. They had grown twice as tall as I remembered, but they were still there! Those two towering oak trees were all that remained of the days when we used to sit out on the front porch in the summertime, tellin' little stories and watchin' fireflies twinkle, while we shelled beans into a dishpan. I could almost hear my mother encouraging us to "keep on shellin'." I knew the next day, she'd fill the house with the comforting smells of buttery cornbread and slow-simmered beans. Oh, I spent many a happy hour around the homeplace, hours that were sweet as honey, long days that seemed like they would never come to an end.

The old log cabin didn't make it long after my father died in the spring of '46. My mother moved in with Thelma and she rented the house, but the tenant put up a moonshine still right along our creek. My Uncle Edd Lee found it. He told my mother, "You're gonna have to put that feller out. He's makin' whiskey right below your house."

That made her mad. She said, "I'm not gonna put up with bootleggers operatin' out of my old homeplace, and not out of Will Kelley's, surely not!"

So she just had the house bulldozed and buried, let the grass grow over it. I wish she hadn't torn it down. I know it wasn't much of a home, but it was to me.

No one knows what happened to any of our family possessions we'd stored in the attic, whether the moonshiners sold 'em or what—things like my Uncle Chester's sad, silent banjo, daddy's chiming clock, mother's worn hand-pieced quilts, my first harmonica, even Orangie's wartime letters, all lost. All that survived time were my dad's anvil, vice, and hammers 'cause they were out in his blacksmith shop. Now they're my sole keepsakes from those happy years.

My mother lived to a ripe old age, but she never got over losing my dad. It took the joy out of her. They had loved each other so much, but she had to spend more years without him than she did with him. In her later years, she suffered memory loss, and eventually she didn't know where she was at. She remembered nothing but her youthful years, when my dad was alive and us kids were still runnin' around the ol' homeplace. It was surely a kinder place to be, reliving her memories of family life on old Coker Creek, not so far from Heaven.

On that first visit back to the ol' homeplace in a long, long time, it was springtime and the air was cool and quiet, except for the occasional woodpecker tappin' out a rhythm. I could just about hear the familiar sounds of my daddy's hammer and anvil, a pingin' and a ringin' in the holler, and Archie's ol' banjo a singin' off in the distance, his fine pickin' driftin' through those misty hills, playin' a little tune from long ago and far away that's still always with me.

I walked among the hills where I'd run as a boy. I could see myself runnin' barefooted just as hard as I could go, my eyes just as blue as the sky and my hair as wild as the wind. That was a long time ago. Now I've only got, oh, two or three hairs to keep combed, and I can only run like that in dreams.

And I do dream of Coker Creek. The reason I liked growin' up on Coker Creek so much was on account of all that freedom. I could go as far as I wanted through the woods, do what I wanted, just have a big ol' time. If I wanted to make me somethin', I'd just cut down a tree and build it.

The community of Coker Creek has changed now, like everything else, though it's still rural. The roads are blacktopped and wide enough for two lanes. Even the dirt trail I used to travel to the old gold mines is now a gravel road and there are driveways to brand-new fancy vacation homes along the way. Retirees movin' in, they say.

The old store where I met Orangie, Frank Murphy's store, it was torn down a long time ago, and the one that they built after that, it burned

Dave Lenderman's store as it looked in 2003

down. Ol' Dave Lenderman's store, the site of so many lawless shootin' scrapes, it was still standin'—empty, weather-beaten, and boarded up. It sits right at the edge of the highway that twists through Coker Creek, not far from new arts and crafts galleries. I expect somebody to come along and tear down that ol' shack any day.

The old-time mountain folk are 'bout gone, too. That hard way of life, with no electricity, no plumbing, and havin' to raise your own dinner, that's just about dried up now. Just got a few left who remember how it was. As they'd say, "Them old ways is a dyin' out and a fadin' away."

Even the water's changed out there. We had a pretty good little creek on our property, but my dad always talked about how much bigger the streams were when he was a boy. He said those mountains just gushed water. When I was a boy, he used to tell me that the streams had dried up a whole lot and I thought they were pretty good-sized back then. And now, I can see they've gone down a lot more. Our little spring was nearly dry. A lot of springs have dried up in those mountains. The creek where we made our swimmin' hole, you couldn't even tell where it had been.

It was sad to see Coker Creek changed so much, but time does that, and we needn't expect things to stay the same. What does stay the same are the precious memories of times gone by, of that simpler way of life that is no more. I believe the good values that we shared in those days of hardship and togetherness can still live on, handed down. Some of those values can be traced back to the pioneers who settled this country and they're what the United States of America was built on.

As long as there are families that gather together and children to be raised, I know that what I learned growin' up on Coker Creek, that's somethin' that will remain timeless. It's knowledge I've found helpful from the battlefields of World War II to my everyday life in small-town America. I was not highly educated, but I was taught well. My parents led by example. All those things, I remember.

I can still hear my father's voice saying to me—when he only had a dime in his pocket and no way that day to make a wage—"Now, son, don't let it worry you none. We'll be all right. There'll be better days ahead."

And there were.

I'm thankful that from that day to this, regardless of life's ups and downs, I've been able to whistle a little tune and keep a glad heart. Lookin' back, my dad's lasting legacy was his attitude. I carry that with me, 'cause I will always be my daddy's son.

THE END

Honor thy father and thy mother:
that thy days may be long upon the land
which the LORD thy God giveth thee.
— Exodus 20:12 KJV

Train up a child in the way he should go:
and when he is old, he will not depart from it.
— Proverbs 22:6 KJV

Afterword

S. L. Kelley

While he could still appreciate it, I tried to help close the circle on the unresolved regret from World War II that bothered my father all those years. I made numerous cold-call attempts from Kansas phone books starting back in 2006, and occasionally thereafter, looking for any relatives of his tank commander, but with no success. Then in 2011, on Memorial Day, I tried again. "Hello, I'm trying to reach any known relatives of a Sergeant Donald E. Crouch, who died in World War II . . ."

And this time, someone knew who it was! That random phone call put me in touch with the cousin of "Crouch's little girl," as my dad had referred to her. And soon I was talking with her.

I learned that Sergeant Donald Crouch's daughter was named Donna, and she was a social worker and a married mother of two. Coincidentally, her son was a tank commander in the U.S. Army.

Most surprising to all was a twist that no one in the story saw coming back in 1945. After the war, it turned out that at least one man did go out to see Sergeant Crouch's widow—Sergeant Pearl F. Hicks.

Sergeant Hicks eventually married Lillie Crouch, and he raised Sergeant Crouch's daughter. Sadly, both Pearl and Lillie Hicks had already passed away by the time I found Donna.

As a child, Donna was told about her hero father, her "Daddy-Don," who died in the war. She was overjoyed to hear news about him and, later, to read my father's recollections of her father and his words from a conversation that took place in that French schoolhouse, words that haunted my father most of his years and now amounted to a love letter from a daddy to his little girl, delivered some sixty-six years after they were spoken.

"We were a family created by death," Donna told me of her post-war family. Her stepfather was good to her, her mother, and her new little brother. In Donna's words, "Tell your father not to worry. Everything turned out all right."

I told my father these events while he still lived at home, and he nodded, absorbing the information. He could hardly believe that Sergeant Hicks was the man who had married Donald Crouch's widow. "Is that right? I sure wouldn't have imagined that!" he said.

Lonnie Johnson expressed similar astonishment at the very late breaking news.

After my father learned the update to his story of the war, he seemed to let it all go. Hearing Donna's message satisfied something in him. He no longer talked about the war or wondered aloud what happened to the boys he knew back then, and he didn't talk about his tank commander anymore. He was at peace with it. And his mind was failing him. After recovering from the infection at age seventy-nine, he'd had some good years, but later on, he'd had to bounce back after two hip surgeries, a few mini strokes, and an incident with a woodstove where he accidentally set his leg on fire and needed a skin graft. My father was a tough'un, as he'd have said. Always, he remained cheerful and enjoyed life.

When the day came that he had to go live in an elder-care facility, we never let him feel forgotten. One of us from the family was with him at most meals, every day. My mom brought him protein drinks and home cooking. My older sister played ball with him and rolled his wheelchair outside in the sunshine, to collect wildflowers together. My brother brought him hamburgers and milkshakes. I brought him family pictures, spinning whirligigs outside his window, and bluegrass music on his own iPod Shuffle. And I sang to him—karaoke and a capella—country, big band, hymns, gospel, "America the Beautiful."

And for a long, long time, he still played his harmonica to the delight of his great-grandchildren and a lot of strangers, too, but he played just one song: "Cripple Creek."

I could always just imagine him running barefoot as a kid, running down to the creek to have some fun.

★ ★ ★

"Daddy, we're on the road driving to get to you, we're passing Chattanooga, so you know how far away we are. I'm comin', Daddy, I'm comin' to see you, so stay with us . . ." It was my last phone call to him. I know he could hear me on the other end, but he never made a sound.

We did arrive before he died, twelve hours or so before, as it turned out, and I had time to tell him the confessions of gratitude and promises that are bestowed from loved ones to loved ones on deathbeds — if they are fortunate.

Our family has been thankful that dad never suffered, except for the difficulties that come from the decline in memory and abilities as he aged, which had happened gradually over some years, so gradually it was as if he was an old-fashioned radio and the volume knob was slowly being turned down, down, down. When my father "passed from this world to the next," as he would've said, it was so peaceful, it went unnoticed.

My mother had left the room for a few minutes, and I was at his bedside holding his hand and I remarked to him, "It's just you and me in here right now, Daddy, just us two. They say you have bad circulation, but your hands are toasty warm all the way to your fingertips!"

I talked to him for a few minutes and he managed to raise an eyebrow, once. Then I sang five verses of "Amazing Grace" as close to perfect as I could.

"Now I'll let your hand go, so these nice ladies can come in here and help you, okay, Daddy?"

When one of the health care workers bent over him, she stood up suddenly. "Honey, I don't think he's breathing."

I never knew when he stopped.

My mother returned, heard what happened, clasped her hands in front of her chest, and declared, "You sang him right into Heaven!"

Daddy made it to ninety-two. In fact, he'd lived through nearly all of his ninety-second year—his next birthday was less than a week away.

James Quinton Kelley was laid to rest during a beautiful tribute that included a Masonic ceremony with representatives from two lodges, a Baptist church service, and a graveside military funeral with two buglers and a twenty-one-gun salute. It was a cold January day, but the predicted snow never came. Instead, it was sunny, though the wind kicked up a couple of times. When the U.S. flag billowed high like a sail, then gently settled on the casket, almost like a sigh, perfectly in time with the last note of taps, several of us whispered, "Look at that!"

We agreed, "He's at peace."

TAPS

Day is done, gone the sun,
From the hills, from the lake,
From the sky.
All is well, safely rest,
God is nigh.
Thanks and praise, for our days,
'Neath the sun,
'neath the stars,
'Neath the sky,
As we go, this we know,
God is nigh.

Traveling On To Mansions
Excerpt from Original Song by Edd Lee Kelley

I hope to stand at God's right hand when called from Earth away
To meet the deeds that I have done while living here below.
I hope to hear Him say "Well done" thou faithful trusting child
and be at rest forever more in that bright heavenly home.

Chorus

We're traveling on to mansions bright and fair
We soon shall reach that land where none shall roam
Where all is peace and joy beyond compare.
We'll greet each other by and by in that bright heavenly home. . . .

ACKNOWLEDGMENTS

I owe the genesis of this book to Michael Mancusi, who was the first person to realize that my father had lived an extraordinary life. My deepest appreciation for showing me where to look, for artistic enthusiasm and inspiration, and for unwavering creative support all along the way.

Thank you to Donna Benton for the family photos.

Again, I will always be grateful for the contributions from Ed Johnson, Herbert Davis, and Richard Knode.

Thank you to all my early readers who gave valuable feedback on rough drafts and helped to make this book better. My gratitude also to my circle of professional colleagues, friends, and family who are invaluable when I need them. *You know who you are.*

And especially to Mom, my heartfelt thank-you for your encouragement and insight, and for having the good sense to choose Daddy!

IN GRATEFUL AND LOVING MEMORY

James Quinton Kelley

2/2/1922 – 1/28/2015

Citation Sources

The Thirteenth Armored Division, A History of the Black Cats from Texas to France, Germany and Austria and Back to California. 1946, Division Headquarters, 13th Armored Division, U.S. Army. Army and Navy Publishing Company Building, 234 Main Street, Baton Rouge, LA. The book was written and compiled directly after WWII. Each unit in the 13th Armored Division submitted a brief written account of their activities from the birth of the Division to the end of the war. The following citations are unit reports from this book: 1, 7, 8, 10, and 13–22.

1. *History of the 24th Tank Battalion.*

2. THE BLACK CATS: They Sharpened Their Claws in California and Texas, Then Scratched Hell Out of the Nazis. Paperback, published by U.S. Army 1945.

3. *Some Thought on the Black Cat Division* by T/Sgt. Tracy E. Goodwin, in History of the 13th Armored Division, 50th Anniversary Edition, edited by Elmer Bowington; Turner Publishing Company, Paducah, KY 1992.

4. *THE BLACK CAT* Newspaper, May 15, 1945, editor Sgt. Joseph Lepo; published by Public Relations, 13th Armored Division.

5. *The Stars and Stripes,* Wednesday May 9, 1945, Southern Germany Edition; published at the auxiliary plant of the Nurnberg 8 Uhr-Blatt, Altdof, Bavaria, Germany for the U.S. Armed Forces under the auspices of the Information and Education Division.

6. *The Kitten,* **Ruhr Battle Extra,** 13th Armored (Black Cat) Division; editor Sgt. Joseph Lepo; published by P.R.O. and I. and E., G-3 at a printing plant deep inside Germany, April 25, 1945.

7. *History of the 496th Armored Field Artillery Battalion.*

8. *History of the 59th Armored Infantry Battalion (AIB).*

9. Alexander Gordeuk Papers and Interviews, Rutgers University Libraries, Special Collections and University Archives, Rutgers Oral History Archives of WWII. Born and raised in rural New Jersey as a farm boy, Gordeuk was a graduate of Rutgers University College of Agriculture. During his varied service with the army in WWII, he served the 13th Armored Division as information and education officer (noncommissioned). The quotes used are from an interview taken April 1, 1996, and they illustrate some of the attitudes present in the 13th Armored Division.

10. *A History of the 45th Tank Battalion.* Also published in *45th Tank Battalion* by Cpl. Russell Beckwith, Company Clerk (45th Tank Battalion), **History of the 13th Armored Division, 50th Anniversary Edition;** updated by tank crew members; Turner Publishing Company, Paducah, KY 1992.

11. *THE BLACK CAT'S KITTEN* **EXTRA,** Vol 1, No. 66, Bavaria, Germany, Tuesday, 6 May 1945.

12. Lonnie Edward Johnson, Tank Driver, 13th Armored Division, 24th Tank Battalion, C Company. Quotes taken from original audio tapes of interviews between S. L. Kelley and Lonnie Edward Johnson, recorded on July 23, 2006, and February 28, 2008, via phone to Selma, North Carolina (recorded and used with permission).

13. *History of the 497th Armored Field Artillery Battalion.*

14. *History of the 498th Armored Field Artillery Battalion.*

15. *History of the 124th Armored Engineer Battalion.*

16. *A History of Headquarters, Division Artillery.*

17. *A History of the 46th Tank Battalion.*

18. *A History of Combat Command A.*

19. *16th Armored Infantry Battalion.*

20. *History of the 67th Armored Infantry Battalion.*

21. *History of Combat Command B.*

22. *Division Headquarters.*

23. *The Devils Workshop in Heaven's Basement* by T/4 Rodgers Med. Sec. Hq. Co., 45th Tank Battalion. From the City of Gmunden, Austria; in **History of the 13th Armored Division, 50th Anniversary Edition;** Turner Publishing Company, Paducah, KY 1992.

Author's Note: The U.S. Army unit histories and newspapers quoted in this book often contain spelling inaccuracies of German place names as the information was gathered on the battlefield and directly after the war, and in the interest of history, should be noted. But in the interest of the reader's visual ease, most of the quotes remain as originally written, without note. The corrected place names followed by their misspellings are listed below:

Page 416: Hermeskeil – Hermeskiel

Page 423: Birkenfeld – Birkenfield

Page 432: Schoeneberg (Altenkirchen) – Schonberg

Page 450: Wahner Heide – Wahnersheide

Page 470: Dunnwald – Lunnewald

Page 497: Mydlinghoven – Mudlinghoven; Muddlinghausen

Page 511: Duisburg – Duisberg

Page 511: Nuremberg – Nuremburg

Page 526: Regensburg – Regensberg

Page 526: Rain – Ram

Page 526: Rinkam – Rinkham

Page 562: Neuoetting – Neu Otting; Neu-Oetting

Page 563: Neuoetting – Neu Otting

Page 566: Neuoetting – Neu Otting

Page 576: Neuoetting – Neu Otting

Page 569: Braunau am Inn – Braun-au-am-Inn

Obscure Selected Resources

13th Armored Division, paperback; publisher Pat Shannon, U.S. Army, 13th Armored Division at Camp Beale, CA, 1943.

COKER CREEK: Crossroads to History by Fred Brown, copyright 1991, Coker Creek Ruritan Club.

A History of Tellico Plains, TN, 10,000 B.C.–2,001 A.D. by Charles Hall, copyright 2001 by Tellico Publications, Tellico Plains, TN; printed by Russell Printing Options, Knoxville, TN.

The Complete History of World War II by Francis Trevelyan Miller, Litt.D., LL.D., with a Board of Historical Military Authorities; copyright 1945, 1948, Ann Woodward Miller. Reader's Service Bureau, Chicago, IL.

About the Author

Adventurer, explorer, journalist, and documentarian, **S. L. Kelley** is also a multi award-winning video producer and writer. Her assignments and research have taken her to some of the most remote and extreme places around the world. She's documented treasure hunting high in the Andes Mountains, explored a lost city with archaeologists in the Arabian Desert, and searched for shrunken heads in the Amazon Jungle. Her recent work has focused on her home country and includes video interviews with some of America's remaining World War II veterans.